Spanish American Literature

A Collection of Essays

Series Editors

David William Foster
Arizona State University

Daniel Altamiranda
Universidad de Buenos Aires

A GARLAND SERIES

Contents of the Series

Twentieth-Century Spanish American Literature since 1960

Edited with introductions by

David William Foster
Arizona State University

Daniel Altamiranda
Universidad de Buenos Aires

GARLAND PUBLISHING, INC.
A MEMBER OF THE TAYLOR & FRANCIS GROUP
New York & London
1997

Library of Congress Cataloging-in-Publication Data

Twentieth-century Spanish American literature since 1960 / edited
    with introductions by David William Foster and Daniel Altamiranda.
        v.   cm. — (Spanish American literature : a collection of essays ; 5)
        English and Spanish
        Includes bibliographical references.
        ISBN 0-8153-2677-7 (set : alk. paper). — ISBN 0-8153-2681-5
        (v. 5 : alk. paper)
        1. Spanish American literature—20th century—History and
    criticism. I. Foster, David William. II. Altamiranda, Daniel.
    III. Title: 20th-century Spanish American literature since 1960.
    IV. Series: Spanish American literature ; 5.
    PQ7081.A1T84 1997
    860.9'98'09045—DC21   97-202999
                                                            CIP

860.9
T971f

Printed on acid-free, 250-year-life paper
Manufactured in the United States of America

Contents

Isabel Allende (1942–   )

Reinaldo Arenas (1943–1990)

Rigoberta Menchú (1960?–   )

Series Introduction

Many and varied are the factors that underlie the growing interest in recent decades in the literary production of Latin American writers, such as, for instance, the international recognition of several Latin American writers such as the Argentine Jorge Luis Borges, the Colombian Gabriel García Márquez, the Mexican Carlos Fuentes, and the Chilean Pablo Neruda, to name only a few of the most renowned figures. Out of these writers, two are Nobel Prize Literature winners: García Márquez and Neruda. Another factor that has fueled this interest is their commercial success and the accompanying cultural diffusion of the so-called Boom of Latin American fiction. And last but not least, is the new and vigorous feminist body of writing, quite unique in Hispanic letters for the richness and variety of its innovations.[1]

Despite the fact that the task of translating some authors into English, such as the Cuban Alejo Carpentier, had begun a little before the crucial decade of the 1960s, it is only beginning in this latter period that there arises an explosion of publishing activity oriented toward making Latin American texts known among English-speaking readers. Furthermore, the creation of Latin American studies programs in numerous North American universities resulted in the institution of a specific field of research that comes to be considered a natural adjunct of Spanish literature. It is evident that all of the interest is not an exclusive result of the internal development of literary history, as though such a thing could occur in the abstract, but rather it presupposes a concrete response to the sociopolitical circumstances of the period: the triumph of the Castro Revolution in 1959, which turned Cuba into a center of enormous political and cultural consequences and whose influence began to be felt early on in the farthest reaches of Latin America.

The factors mentioned above provided the context for the development of extensive research programs whose goals included the elaboration and periodic examination of the literary canon, the analysis of specific texts, authors, periods, and problems. All of this activity has resulted in innumerable dissertations, theses, and books published by academic and trade presses, as well as articles that appeared in journals traditionally devoted to literary history and philology, along with the flourishing of new specialized journals and the organization of national and international congresses on specific themes.

In the face of such an enormous proliferation of commentary and study, it is necessary to offer students undertaking the study of Latin American literature a body of basic texts to assist them in providing an initial orientation in the diverse research areas that have emerged. Consequently, we have chosen to include essays and articles that have appeared in periodical publications, some of which are difficult to obtain by the Anglo-American student. These articles are not limited to philological minutiae or the discussion of highly specific aspects. Rather, they address major texts and problems from an interpretive and critical point of view. Although principally directed toward neophyte students, the present selection will undoubtedly be useful to advanced students and researchers who find themselves in need of a quick source of reference or who wish to consult newer issues and approaches to Spanish American literary studies.

Notes

[1] Although the term "Latin America" will be used throughout as a synonym of "Spanish American," it should be noted that, in its most precise usage, the former includes the other non-Spanish but Romance language-speaking areas to the south of the United States and in the Caribbean. This collection has not sought to include a representation of Portuguese and French-speaking authors on the assumption that it will be used principally in nonresearch institutions where Brazilian and Francophone Caribbean literature is not customarily taught.

Volume Introduction

Latin American literature of the second half of the twentieth century gives evidence of a complex, heterogeneous development in permanent expansion. Critics have proposed various labels, such as "new novel" and "new new novel," boom and post-boom, women's literature, testimonial, postmodern literature, and the like in order to account for the variegated manifestations of more recent Latin American literature. Given the fact that none of these designations is entirely satisfactory for fully charting the complex map of literary phenomena, we have opted for an arrangement based on the birth date of the authors represented. However, a difficulty that could not be easily overcome was that of providing a balanced representation of the most representative literary production of the trends in force at the end of the twentieth century. In fact, we have omitted almost any representation of dramatic texts and drastically reduced that dealing with poetry. Moreover, we have adhered to a selection criteria that favors names that have transcended the boundaries of national literatures and achieved a certain international notoriety, which implies that many figures of interest whose production will, undoubtedly, come to be recognized in the future have been for the moment relegated to the sidelines.

María Cecilia Graña develops a detail analysis of the city image in *Sobre héroes y tumbas* (1962) by the Argentine novelist and active defender of human rights, Ernesto Sábato. After recognizing the presence of a set of dualism that generates the image of the city in the novel, Graña concludes that the terms "tradition" and "abnormality," even though they are not antithetic by definition, constitute a matrix that reiterates and reproduces itself throughout the text.

Gustavo Pellón examines the connection between madness and homo-sexuality in *Paradiso* (1966) by the Cuban José Lezama Lima. The critic situates this relationship in the context of Lezama's philosophical system, where ethics and aesthetics are two inseparable constituents. Pellón's rendering of the question contributes to overcome the polemics elicited among Lezama's critics.

Haider Ali Khan considers the poetry of Octavio Paz to anticipate the questioning the deconstruction and contemporary poststructuralist philosophy have performed with respect to orthodox critical thought. Via a panoramic revision that recovers the three distinct stages of Paz's poetic production, Khan identifies the central thematic complex of the poet, whose texts are characterized by their dense subversive force that is at the same time poetic and political. Both Emil Volek and Anthony Stanton concentrate on what has been called the third phase in Paz's literary evolution. Volek focuses on Paz's poetry after *La estación violenta* (1958), that is, when Paz extends the horizon of his surrealism and embarks on a program of even more experimental and innovative poetic creation that will bring him to create works like *Blanco* (1967), *Topoemas* (1968) and *Discos visuales* (1968). Stanton analyzes Paz's essayistic work in order to detect the fundamental elements of his poetics. According to the critic, Paz's poetry in the end is only one part of his cultural criticism: it is inseparable from the rest of the artistic manifestations, as well as those on history, politics, morals, and eroticism.

The publication of *Rayuela* (1963) confirmed for its author, the Argentine Julio Cortázar, a privileged place among writers of the second half of the twentieth century, in particular among those writers associated with the phenomenon of international proportions that has come to be called the Latin American literary boom. Ana María Barrenechea provides an explanation of the complex game of doubles that takes place in the novel beginning with the correlation between the novelistic text proper and the "Cuaderno de bitácora" in which the author noted observations toward a registry of the process of construction of the novel. However, Cortázar's recognition is not only based on his novelistic work; it includes more commonly his numerous short stories through which he summarizes all of the narrative possibilities offered to him by his predecessors. Maurice J. Bennett studies "Axolotl," one of Cortázar's most anthologized stories, as representing the fantastic mode of which the author is a modern master. Bennett's reading shows how the story recreates the classic topic of the monster in the labyrinth, while establishing an interplay of recognition and obliteration of absolute distinctions between the universe of the quotidian and that of the extraordinary.

Paul W. Borgeson attempts to identify the ways in which Juan Rulfo's short stories achieve their particularly unsettling effect through the use of different devices associated with the stream of conciousness narrative. The critic established the connection between these experimental techniques and the fictional world that the writer depicts, a world where chaos and order are in a constantly unstable balance.

Josefina Ludmer provides a lucid introduction to the narrative production of the Paraguayan Augusto Roa Bastos, taking as a point of departure the description of the heroes his stories present. According to Ludmer, Roa's heros run the gamut from the oral to the written, and they are basically differentiated on the basis of whether they tell or are told about, whether they write or are written about. Particular reference is made to *Yo el Supremo* (1974), which is one of the high points of contemporary postmodern Latin American fiction.

The novelist José Donoso has been one of the contemporary Chilean writers who attracted immediate international attention. William Rowe undertakes the analysis of Donoso's novel *El obsceno pájaro de la noche* (1970) through an examination of the extensive bibliography that has attempted to read the work in terms of various psychoanalytic approaches, and he proposes that the concept that most allows for an account of the structures of consciousness it represents is Freudian narcissism. Narcissism describes the behavior of the main character and, at the same time, instead of concentrating the interpretation of the plane of the purely individual, it allows for the exploration of the relationships between the social and the psychological.

The Mexican Rosario Castellanos was probably one of the first Latin American women writers to construct a vast literary work centered on the unmistakably feminist exploration of the problem of woman's expression. Naomi Lindstrom studies the novel *Oficio de tinieblas* (1962) and puts in practice an idea by Castellanos that she herself had anticipated: the narrative techniques that women writers employ—especially voice, understood in a broad sense, and point of view—to illuminate the expressive concerns of women that, as a consequence, should be interpreted as implicit postulations regarding the difficulties they confront when they wish to express themselves verbally. Barbara Bockus Aponte concentrates on the play, *El eterno femenino* (1975) and on the use of dramatic techniques drawn from the patriarchal literary tradition that Castellanos alters in order to transmit a feminist message. The prominent elements are the use of Brechtian distancing techniques, the staging of figures drawn of Mexican cultural history (for example, La Malinche, Sor Juana, Carlota), although reconfigured in a critically imaginative fashion, and satire as a mechanism of subversion of the stereotypic roles society assigns to women.

Alicia Borinsky presents a discussion of the different figures of reading that appear in various works of the Colombian Gabriel García Márquez: *Cien años de soledad* (1967), *El otoño del patriarca* (1975), and *Crónica de una muerte anunciada* (1981). Her analysis makes clear the need to distinguish between readings and readers as they are represented in each one of these works of fiction and as they appear as plot elements and critical readings and readers in the basic sense of these words. In the interplay of differences implied by the three works examined, an analytical process takes place that, without requiring the reader to engage in a complex use of technical terminology, facilitates an appreciation of the lucidity that is provided by fictions that analyze other fictions. Debra A. Castillo focuses on one of García Márquez's most celebrated stories, "Funerales de la Mamá Grande," a tale that is constructed in polemical opposition to official history. Toward this end, the author makes use of a figure of the narrator who conceives of himself as a storyteller who explicitly rejects history as scientific knowledge and the work of historians even though, paradoxically, one has no choice except to imitate their norms, methods, and style.

V. Emilio Castañeda undertakes an interpretation of *La muerte de Artemio Cruz* (1962), the novel that confirmed the importance of the Mexican Carlos Fuentes as one of the most interesting experimental novelists of the 1960s. According to Castañeda, the textual complexity of the novel, the result of the use of varied narrative techniques, does not prevent the author's central message from expressing itself with total clarity: the Mexican Revolution must be understood as a historical failure to the extent that it abandoned its initial ideals—the reformation of the country in favor of the dispossessed—allowing the country to fall into the hands of opportunists and the corrupt. But this phenomenon should not be understood as absolute, but rather as representative of the cyclical history of Mexico that, in the view of the author, has repeated over and over again these failed revolutionary endeavors. Jonathan Tittler provides a comparative study of Fuentes's novel *Gringo viejo* (1985) in its English version as *The Old Gringo*, on whose preparation Fuentes participated. After pointing out the difference to be found between the two versions, which are so extensive such as to reject the notion of a translation as a way of accounting for the relationships between both texts, Tittler analyzes the ways in which history and fiction intersect and lead to the formulation of questions having to do with the literary genre chosen by the author, the historical novel.

Juan Goytisolo proposes a so-called Cervantine reading of the novel *Tres tristes tigres* (1964) by the Cuban Guillermo Cabrera Infante. Toward this end, he offers a judicious exposition on the literary theory that is implicit in *Don Quixote*, the masterpiece that grounds a textual tradition that, rather than subjecting the reading to the rules of a well-known game, creates its own rules as it goes along. Cabrera Infante's novel belongs to this tradition, which brings with it an intricate network of connotations and references not only to elements of popular culture, as numerous critics have correctly pointed out, but also to the vast world of books, such that a permanent intertextual dialogue is established. In this sense, *Tres tristes tigres* presents itself as a complex and elaborate literary discourse that defines itself and becomes meaningful by means of its tight-knit relations to various contemporary forms of fiction.

Lucille Kerr examines *Boquitas pintadas* (1971) by the Argentine Manuel Puig, a novel that is as much the chronicle of provincial life as it is the story of a romantic intrigue modeled along the lines of true romance magazines. In this essay, the work takes on a particular sense when it refers to other texts and puts into play traditional distinctions between "high" and "low" culture. According to Kerr, the novel is constructed as a sort of play between formal, discursive, and thematic paradoxes that question textual authority as much as the cultural traditions that underlie the texts.

Cynthia Steele offers a detailed reading of *Hasta no verte Jesús mío* (1969) by the Mexican Elena Poniatowska. If it is true that the text is the result of a cooperative enterprise between a real informant, Josefina Bórquez, who appears textualized with the name of Jesusa Palancares, and Poniatowska, Steele concentrates on the tensions that accompanied the process of writing as they have been registered in a series of transcribed interviews and various rough drafts of the testimony.

In "Self-Destructing Heroines," Jean Franco offers a feminist reading of several contemporary writings. According to her, "the Latin American novel came into being as a national endeavor programmed by masculine phalansteries and feminine marginality." To confirm the continuity of this condition, she appeals to examples taken from the last decades, finding in the novel *La casa verde* (1963) and the play *La señorita de Tacna* (1981), both by the Peruvian Mario Vargas Llosa, two vigorous forms of female silencing, which is one of the many manifestations of a patriarchal order. Then Franco points out several cases of women writers—Griselda Gambaro, Rosario Ferré, Luisa Valenzuela, and Marta Traba—who faced strong preconceived ideas about literary creativity and made an effort to overcome them.

Carlos J. Alonso provides a reading of *La guaracha del Macho Camacho* (1976) by the Puerto Rican Luis Rafael Sánchez, who takes into account the fact that the text proposes to free itself definitively from the conception of literary discourse as a vehicle of cultural self-definition as much as the fact that the novel does not renounce in any complete way its condition as an instrument of knowledge. In these terms, Sánchez's text seeks to recreate the heterogenous cultural reality of contemporary Puerto Rico, while at the same time dismantling the academic and solemn conceptions regarding the problem of cultural specificity that had come to constitute the center of concern for Puerto Rican intellectuals.

René Prieto studies two narrative texts by the Cuban Severo Sarduy, *Cobra* (1973) and *Maitreya*. He underscores how violence, castration, and death function as decorative mannerisms or rhetorical figures in the narrative scheme. The unlimited proliferation of the "I" in Sarduy's fiction, in accordance with which being is presented as a permanent becoming, marks the beginning of all of the transformations that abound in both novels.

According to Cynthia Tompkins, the novel *Como en la guerra* (1977), by the Argentine Luisa Valenzuela, is a self-deconstructing artifact since it deals with the problem of self-knowledge and the definition of national identity, but leaving aside the Western concept of a unified subject. This distinguishes the text as a postmodern experiment, as a feast of becoming, to use Ihab Hassan's expression, where the process of search is as important as the development of the protagonist.

Janice A. Jaffe develops the metaphor of translation-as-prostitution in order to account for the relationship between two of Rosario Ferré's texts, *Maldito amor* (1986) and Ferré's own translation into English as *Sweet Diamond Dust* (1988). At first glance, it could seem that the author embraces a distinct cultural identity for each one of the languages used. Thus, when she writes in Spanish, she criticizes the discrimination her compatriots suffer as Hispanics in the United States. English, on the other hand, would seem to lead her to an assimilationist position in which the native language is marginalized, as well as the nontechnological worldview Spanish represents for her. According to Jaffe, in the process of switching between languages, Ferré begins to articulate the future image of a positive Puerto Rican identity beyond colonialism.

Robert Antoni describes the particular relationship that exists between the Chilean Isabel Allende's *La casa de los espíritus* (1982) and the novel that is, by all evidence, its immediate literary antecedent, as well as its source of inspiration: Gabriel García Márquez's *Cien años de soledad*. Although *La casa* can be read initially as a sort of noncorrosive parody of the Colombian's novel, it is quite evident that Allende employs— at least as the point of departure for the construction of her own—the language of the paradigmatic Latin American writer. The result is that, more than merely a rewriting of the earlier work, Allende's novel is constructed in terms of an internal displacement that moves from magical realism to a political writing based on testimonial and denunciation.

Beginning with the analysis of the circumstances of reading and writing that the imagination of Jorge Luis Borges postulates in his celebrated story "Pierre Menard, autor del Quijote," Alicia Borinsky establishes the bases for interpretation of *El mundo alucinante* (1969), a novel by the Cuban Reinaldo Arenas, presented as an instance of rewriting of the works of the Mexican Fray Servando Teresa de Mier (1763–1827).

Since its publication in 1985, *Me llamo Rigoberta Menchú y así me nació la conciencia*, the testimony of the Guatemalan Indian Rigoberta Menchú, has become the focus of attention of many critics and researchers in the social sciences. David E. Whisnant endeavors to develop, through a detailed reading of the text, a typology of how traditional culture functions in the social change processes. In general, it is accepted that traditional cultures take shape in a way that does not leave any room for social change. Thanks to *Me llamo Rigoberta Menchú*, Whisnant manages to identify several elements in the Quiché culture—cultural continuity but oriented toward the future, clear notions of community and solidarity, pragmatism, syncretism, a politics of self-trascendency—that favor a general awareness in the population and, in consequence, could become a viable way to social revolution.

REVISTA DE CRITICA LITERARIA LATINOAMERICANA
Año XXII, Nº 43-44. Lima-Berkeley, 1996; pp. 247-265.

TRADICION E INNOVACION
EN LA IMAGEN URBANA DE ERNESTO SABATO:
SOBRE HEROES Y TUMBAS.
LA CIUDAD COMO CUERPO Y COMO TEXTO

María Cecilia Graña
Universitá degli Studi di Verona-Italia

1. La imagen urbana de *SHT,* recoge los dualismos existentes en el *corpus* literario de los proscriptos de 1838, que volvieron a recurrir a la tradicional imagen femenina, objeto de seducción y menosprecio[1]. De 1850, período de la tiranía de Rosas, a 1950 bajo el discutido gobierno de Perón, los cambios ocurridos en Buenos Aires fueron enormes y, a pesar de ello, las antítesis románticas subsisten en la "imago mundi" de *SHT;* los hechos del siglo XIX sirven para desdoblar o bien para contraponerse a los del XX. Así la Buenos Aires bajo el gobierno peronista recuerda a Sábato la de un siglo antes, y por eso no es casual que la narración mítico poemática de los últimos días de Lavalle[2] se alterne con los sucesos narrados en la historia principal. Cabe preguntarse, por lo tanto, de qué modo particular la "imago mundi" de *SHT* retoma y renueva la imaginería urbana decimonónica.

Es sabido que en la literatura posterior a 1950, la ambigüedad y la polisemia corroen la imagen denotativa de la urbe, tanto como su alegoría o personificación, al punto que en algunos autores esta irradiación de significaciones transforma el objeto concreto −es decir Buenos Aires−, en un elemento versátil, engañoso, casi ausente[3]. De esta forma la referencia local se vuelve imaginaria como en Borges, o está representada no por lugares precisos, sino por una atmósfera recreada por medio del habla de los personajes como en *Rayuela* de Cortázar.

Sábato, en cambio, retoma las polarizaciones del siglo pasado y las carga de un nuevo simbolismo (la ciudad visible y la subterránea implícitas en el título, por ejemplo) donde se alternan los aspectos infernales y los utópicos en una continua oscilación; pero las antítesis que estructuran la novela, son asimismo paralelas a intentos de unión y a símbolos de absoluto (como el incesto, una visión 'idealista' de la

1

lucha de clases, la solidaridad y la utopía del viaje al sur). La ambigüedad de esta alternancia no quita que Buenos Aires pueda ser recorrida con precisión por el lector, siguiendo el deambular de algunos personajes desesperados por encontrar una verdad, o bien indiferentes morales (los "hombres sin fe", que tan bien había definido Onetti), o "desterrados" como los de los cuentos de Quiroga –pero esta vez en una jungla de cemento.

1.1. *Tradición-Anormalidad.*

Algunos de los tantos dualismos de *SHT* aparecen representados en un motivo espacial, la casa de los Vidal Olmos. Situada en la calle Río Cuarto e Isabel la Católica, dentro de la novela es el sitio que contiene una mayor carga de "tradición", como si fuese un palimpsesto de historia argentina y literaria. No podemos olvidar que todas la referencias familiares de Alejandra tienen que ver con la época rosista, con la lucha entre federales y unitarios; y el barrio de Barracas, donde está situada la casa, remite directamente a *Amalia* de Mármol, aunque en 1950 aparezca degradado y, de señorial, se haya convertido en una zona industrial, proletaria, de conventillos ("¿No ves donde vivimos? Decime. ¿Sabés de alguien que tenga apellido en este país y que viva en Barracas entre conventillos y fábricas?" p. 43)[4], de la misma forma que la historia de los Vidal Olmos fue transformándose en subversión (y elijo el término pensando en Fernando), en una "novela mala" de lo que antes fueron.

La casa está constituída por dos partes: la planta baja y el Mirador[5]. El Mirador, bastante común en residencias veraniegas o de fin de semana, constituye la parte superior de las mismas y, en el caso de la de los Olmos, está sobre un objeto arqueológico ("La casa era viejísima. Sus ventanas daban a la galería y aún conservaban sus rejas coloniales: las grandes baldosas eran seguramente de aquel tiempo, pues se sentían hundidas, gastadas y rotas" p.50), no sólo desde un punto de vista físico, sino también en cuanto a los valores que defiende, pues allí el abuelo de Alejandra vive "añorando las antiguas virtudes aniquiladas por los duros días de nuestro tiempo" (p.467). Por esto me parece acertada la homologación que hizo Matamoro entre la casa y la "tumba de los héroes" del título[6].

Evidentemente la palabra "mirador" se pone en relación con el imaginario sabatiano (la fobia hacia los ciegos) y con el léxico de la mirada en toda la novela. El vocablo no solo indica "desde donde se mira" sino que también sugiere "el que mira", pues el lugar después del incendio aparece como una calavera: "cuando anochecía, sobre las paredes apenas iluminadas por el foco de la esquina se abrían los huecos de la puerta y de la ventana [del Mirador] como cuencas de una calavera calcinada" (p.525). Y justamente por medio del motivo del fuego, podemos establecer ulteriores correspondencias entre la ciudad y la parte alta de la casa de los Vidal Olmos. Así como hay un incendio en el Mirador, donde muere Alejandra en una especie de autoinmolación, también aparece el hecho histórico de la quema de las iglesias de la ciudad bajo el gobierno peronista, hecho que recuerda las apocalípticas profecías de Natalicio Barragán anunciando el castigo de Buenos Aires por el fuego.

La palabra Mirador, connotando el ojo y la vista, condensa ciertos signos adjudicados a Buenos Aires, sobre todo a partir del siglo XIX: se sabe que el ojo es símbolo del Cosmos[7]; y Cosmos o Civilización era lo que significaba Buenos Aires para la generación de 1838, con el fin de oponerla al caos de la barbarie del interior. Y siempre en este orden de paralelismos se puede asociar la disposición especial del Mirador con la concepción que la generación del ochenta tenía de Buenos Aires: ese lugar "por encima" del resto de Latinoamérica y desde el cual se miraba a Europa. Y además, como la procedencia referencial del Mirador es distinta de la del resto de la casa de los Vidal Olmos, nos hace pensar en la *city* (el centro) de la Buenos Aires del 80 que, arquitectónicamente, fue una transposición de la París de Haussman.

Pero ese estar "por encima" y las acciones que ocurren en el Mirador, vinculan también el lugar con Fernando Vidal Olmos, el cual –según Bruno– "se consideraba por encima de la sociedad y de la ley" (p.495). Todo lo que ocurre en el Mirador excede la norma: No sólo es el sitio de perversas relaciones (allí tendrá lugar, así como en el subsuelo de la Iglesia de la Inmaculada Concepción, el posible incesto entre Alejandra y Fernando) sino que allí había vivido, con la cabeza de su padre degollado por la Mazorca y sin salir nunca –desde 1852 hasta su muerte en 1932–, la "niña Escolástica".

El sitio había sido durante ochenta años espacio de la locura: En el Mirador nos encontramos con un cuerpo sin cabeza (Escolástica está loca) y con una cabeza sin cuerpo (la cabeza degollada)[8]. Alejandra misma subraya ese estar "fuera de la norma": "Comprenderás que con la cabeza no podía pasar nada normal, aparte de que nada de lo que pase con una cabeza sin el cuerpo correspondiente puede ser normal" (p.55)[9].

Sin embargo, al mismo tiempo que actúa en forma anormal, Escolástica –y subrayo el nombre– utiliza un lenguaje que conserva los rasgos lingüísticos del siglo XIX: "su vida y hasta su lenguaje se habían detenido en 1852" (p.55). Lo singular es que anormalidad y conservación serán también los rasgos que caractericen ese texto dentro del texto: el *Informe*.

La casa de los Vidal Olmos resulta, pues, un motivo desarticulado; dentro de los espacios urbanos es el que contiene una mayor carga de tradición y, al mismo tiempo de anormalidad. Esto implica la idea de una paradójica Buenos Aires como consecuencia de su desarticulación con el resto del país; desfase manifiesto en otros niveles y en otros pasajes del texto como las digresiones de Bruno: "porque acá (decía) no somos ni Europa ni América, sino una región fracturada, un inestable, trágico, turbio lugar de fractura y desgarramiento" (p.273).

1.2. Sin embargo, la casa de los Vidal Olmos con su paradójica combinación de tradición y anormalidad no es un resumen de todos los componentes sociales y culturales de la Buenos Aires de 1950; es más bien, un lugar representativo elegido por la enunciación al conjugar los Olmos (una oligarquía venida a menos y cuyos miembros "padecen una suerte de irrealismo", dando "la impresión de constituir el final de una antigua familia en medio del furioso caos de una ciudad cosmopolita y mercantilizada, dura e implacable" (p.484), y los Vidal, tenebrosos y violentos.

El vínculo anormal de la oligarquía con su momento histórico, parece haberse originado hacia 1880 cuando Buenos Aires empezó a mirar sobre todo a Europa y olvidó las añejas tradiciones criollas, tema que en la literatura apareció de inmediato; por ejemplo, en *La gran aldea* con la problemática representada por don Benito frente al europeizado Mirafiori o, en *Libro extraño* de Sicardi, con la nostalgia por el pasado del patricio abuelo Del Río. *SHT* recoge esa tradición literaria cuando dice que los "Olmos mantenían desde luego sin advertirlo, las viejas virtudes criollas que las otras familias habían arrojado como un lastre para no hundirse: eran hospitalarios, generosos, sencillamente patriarcales, modestamente aristocráticos" (p.484), mientras que sus parientes lejanos y ricos, "no habían sabido guardar esas virtudes y habían entrado en el proceso de mercantilización y de materialismo que el país empezó a sufrir desde fines de siglo" (p.484).

Fernando, aunque haya vivido en casa de los Olmos, no condivide la actitud de ese patriciado cuya época de oro fue el gobierno de Mitre; por el contrario, sus acciones son análogas a las de la clase adinerada de la época de Roca (viajes por todo el mundo, participación en los negociados de la tierra, jugar grandes sumas de dinero a la ruleta). Y al amar a Alejandra, busca, como los arribistas de *La gran aldea,* la unión con la vieja clase criolla, pues su hija tenía rasgos de Georgina y sabemos que ésta era "la quintaesencia de la familia Olmos".

Según el *Informe,* después del incesto Fernando se vuelve "ciego" –como Edipo cuya transgresión fue castigada con las tinieblas–, y "sordo" como los Olmos, "que ni sentían, ni oían, ni comprendían, lo que curiosa y hasta cómicamente les daba de pronto la ventaja paradójica de atravesar el durísimo muro de la realidad como si no existiera" (p.467). En cuanto la sordera implica la interdicción del diálogo, la repetición de lo mismo (es decir la ecolalia), puede llegar a simbolizar la homogeneización malograda de la ciudad llena de inmigrantes de diversa procedencia[10], así como la negación de la babélica metrópolis, pues, si el diálogo implica pluralidad e intercambio, la ecolalia da lugar a la negación del otro. Esta interpretación simbólica creo que evoca la actitud predominante de la oligarquía porteña finisecular, en la que el rechazo por el otro será un motivo habitual, ya se refiera a los inmigrantes, ya a nuevos sectores hegemónicos, pues la unión con el igual constituyó su único modo de relación. Un ejemplo son *Las causeries* de

Mansilla, o la actitud de Andrés en *Sin rumbo*, el día de la fiesta del 25 de mayo, cuando el centro de la ciudad está repleto de italianos recién llegados; o bien la actitud del narrador de *La gran aldea* frente a la formación de un nuevo patriciado durante la época de Roca.

Así pues, la relación entre la anormalidad y la tradición representada por Fernando será un vínculo privilegiado por la enunciación al volverse representativo de un territorio, una nación, un modelo cultural, el de Buenos Aires, gran metrópolis del ochenta, pero actual "tierra de nadie", que ya Onetti había anticipado con su narrativa. De hecho, dice Bruno:

> los locos como los genios, se levantan a menudo catastróficamente, sobre las limitaciones de su patria o de su tiempo, entrando en esa *tierra de nadie*, disparatada y mágica, delirante y tumultuosa que los *buenos ciudadanos* contemplan con sentimientos cambiantes, desde el miedo hasta el odio, desde el aparente menosprecio hasta una especie de pavorosa admiración (pp.465-466, el énfasis es mío)

1.3. Frente a esos individuos, "fuera de la norma", "excepcionales", que conservan "muchos de los atributos de la tierra en que nacieron y de los hombres que hasta ayer fueron sus semejantes", se encuentran los "buenos ciudadanos", "los mediocres pecadores" aquéllos que no injurian, no maldicen, no transgreden y siguen atados a las convenciones. En definitiva los componentes de la pequeña burguesía, aquella que Sicardi en *Libro extraño* había propuesto como símbolo del país futuro. El problema literario que se le plantea a la enunciación de *SHT*, es que la Buenos Aires de 1950 aparece constituida sobre todo por pequeños burgueses desarraigados, y sin embargo, el *aurea mediocritas* de la pequeña burguesía, la aspiración a una modesta felicidad, no resulta representativa, si no véase el destino que tuvo la recepción de *Libro extraño*, jamás reeditada.

Una forma de dar solución novelesca a este dilema será el recuperar a la pequeña burguesía por medio de su versión anormal, arltiana, en ese actante "mixto" que es Fernando, el cual, en 1950 es un desclasado. Expulsado de la mansión de los Olmos, se une con la burguesía hebrea adinerada por medio de un matrimonio. Luego de dilapidar el dinero así conseguido, termina en un departamento de Villa Devoto desde donde, a través de la escritura hará de contrapunto con la enunciación de toda la novela, para finalmente, volver a unirse a los Olmos en su relación incestuosa.

Como decíamos, Fernando, en su vida anterior a 1950 había actuado como un arribista del ochenta, y luego buscará vínculos simbólicos con la aristocracia tradicional; no obstante esto, en el personaje aparecen, asimismo, algunas peculiaridades psicológicas de los personajes de la obra de Roberto Arlt, como el gusto por "el delineamiento de los defectos de la moral burguesa"[11] y "el privilegio del crimen, el abandono de la desdicha y el quebrantamiento de las leyes del sentido común"[12]. Pero en él no se evidencia la típica humillación arltiana de pertenecer a la clase media; Fernando no es un 'humillado' como los personajes arltianos; por el contrario es un soberbio con manías de omnipotencia y delirios persecutorios. A través de la "ejemplaridad" de sus acciones no se nos muestran las contradicciones de aquella clase; se las evidencia, más bien, desde una perspectiva externa. Fernando es un "salido", pero de la oligarquía que, por eso mismo, siente un placer especial en iluminar la hipocresía de las convenciones pequeño burguesas, haciéndolo con un movimiento que va desde arriba hacia abajo:

> por ahí abajo, en obsceno y pestilente tumulto, corrían mezclados las menstruaciones de aquellas amadas románticas, los excrementos de las vaporosas jóvenes vestidas de gasa, los preservativos usados por correctos gerentes, los destrozados fetos de miles de abortos, los restos de comidas de millones de casas y restaurantes, la inmensa, la innumerable Basura de Buenos Aires (pp.424-25).

O bien hablando desde la más extrema posición de abajo:

> Imaginaba arriba, en salones brillantes, a mujeres hermosas y delicadísimas, a gerentes de banco correctos y ponderados, a maestros de escuela diciendo que no se deben escribir malas palabras sobre las paredes; imaginaba guardapolvos blancos y almidonados, vestidos de noche con tules y gasas vaporosas, frases poéticas a la amada, discursos conmovedores sobre las virtudes patricias (p.424).

Queda claro, pues, que Fernando siendo un gran perverso, nunca está en una posición "media":

> Alguna vez le oí decir, justamente, que en el infierno como en el cielo hay muchas jerarquías, desde los pobres y mediocres pecadores (los pequeños burgueses del infierno decía), hasta los grandes perversos desesperados, los negros monstruos que tenían derecho a sentarse a la derecha de Satanás (p.465).

1.4. Si se considera al incesto como una *hybris,* un exceso, una maldición de los personajes que lo cometen, se puede decir que el tema, sugerido en modo velado en el *Informe,* configura a éste como una injuria. Pero no obstante Fernando narre su experiencia del subsuelo maldiciendo, lo hace "diciéndolo bien"; Fernando, personaje arltiano en algunos aspectos, no lo es en su escritura: las novelas de Arlt, con sus personajes pequeño burgueses y una escritura "mala" como en el mismo *SHT* se afirma[13], han sido vistas por la crítica como un idiolecto creado para contrastar la voluntad de "escribir bien" de los intelectuales de las primeras décadas del siglo XX, y de los cuales Borges —con sus mitos nostálgicos de un pasado heroico criollo reinvindicado también por la vieja oligarquía— será el principal heredero y el mejor representante[14].

Leyendo el *Informe* vemos que en el mismo se respeta una organización tradicional del relato con su introducción, nudo y desenlace. Las secuencias lineales aparentan la cronología y respetan la causalidad (aunque las causas y los efectos sean delirantes)[15], y esto en contraste con el enunciado total de la novela que no sigue las pautas de la narrativa realista tradicional, pues la relación entre trama y fábula no presenta correspondencias inmediatas.

La dialéctica entre la versión y la subversión de la ciudad, la Buenos Aires cotidiana y la ciudad de las cloacas que Fernando presenta en su *Informe*, aparece también en la novela, pero siempre en relación invertida con ese núcleo matriz que es el texto de Fernando[16]. La relación se establece a nivel de significado entre el exponer una serie de valores pertenecientes a la pequeña burguesía de la Buenos Aires de ese período y la subversión de los mismos en el interior del *Informe;* y, a nivel del significante entre innovación en toda la novela y tradición en el *Informe sobre ciegos.*

El *Informe* pues, es un maldecir por medio de un estilo cuidado y ominoso como el de Borges, más que un "decir mal" de la propia clase social, como fue el caso arltiano. De allí que, a mi modo de ver, sigue respondiendo a esa mezcla de tradición y anormalidad de la que hablábamos: aunque su forma sea lineal y escolástica, su mímesis es aparente pues la realidad que describe resulta, a la postre, delirante.

Esta larga introducción ha tenido por objetivo establecer los términos de ciertos dualismos que tienen carácter generador para configurar la imagen urbana en *SHT*. Los términos "tradición" y "anormalidad", por ejemplo, aunque no son antitéticos ni vinculables por definición, por su contenido semántico y su función dentro de la novela, se contraponen: Hacia 1950, la tradición aparece encarnada por el viejo patriciado originalmente mitrista, como la familia Olmos, cuyo espacio es la planta baja de la vieja mansión de Barracas; la anormalidad está representada por esa nueva oligarquía que nace hacia 1880, y cuya versión en la época peronista es una clase corrupta y prostituída que trata de ser favorecida por el momento político; clase que Fernando, con sus acciones de oligarca del ochenta más su anormalidad arltiana, había anticipado y cuyo espacio simbólico es el Mirador, incendiado como las iglesias de toda la ciudad.

Es a partir de esta pareja de vocablos que se puede realizar una lectura del texto que pretenda reconocer los elementos constitutivos de la imagen ciudadana y explicar, a la vez, la interacción existente entre ellos desde un punto de vista axiológico y escriturario: el *Informe*, por ejemplo, será el significante de esa relación: una unión de la escritura de Borges con los contenidos de Arlt y Lautréamont.

Considerando que las polarizaciones se iteran a lo largo de *SHT*, la forma elegida para realizar esta lectura es la que provee el concepto de *carré semiotique* de Greimas, pues permite entrever, a partir de los dualismos, cómo ha sido estructurada la significación en la imagen urbana de la novela.

Un cuadrado semiótico se genera, pues, a partir de la oposición existente entre "tradición" y "anormalidad":

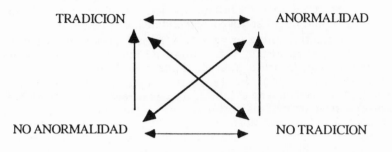

Y éste es paralelo a otro que surge a partir de la relación entre el "decir bien" y el "maldecir":

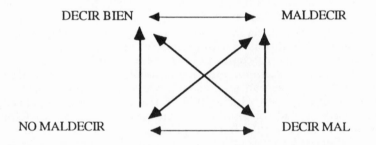

2. Anormalidad-No tradición.

La casa de los Vidal Olmos aparece como el símbolo de una serie de tradiciones ciudadanas que se remontan a un siglo antes de los hechos narrados en la novela, tradiciones que llegaron a configurarse con mayor precisión cuando la oligarquía comercial porteña se vuelve hegemónica allá por el año 1870, poco antes de la llegada masiva de la inmigración europea.

El elegir la quema de las iglesias (un signo ecuménico de la ciudad) por las fuerzas peronistas, pone en evidencia una representación urbana en el momento en el que se fractura la congregación de los seres humanos bajo una misma creencia. Es decir, cuando la violencia y la inversión carnavalesca voltean los símbolos de la fe en ciertos valores que unen a un pueblo. La irreverente manifestación aparece como un símbolo de barbarie, de anormalidad que termina por cancelar la memoria colectiva ("Ahora se levantaban grandes llamaradas de la curia: ardían los papeles, los registros" (276)), efecto que no se limita a ese episodio aislado, sino que se extiende al parecer, a todo el período peronista. De hecho, Alejandra comenta amargamente cómo van desapareciendo los signos urbanos que remiten a las viejas tradiciones oligárquicas: "papeles, nombres de calles. Es lo único que nos va quedando". Sus palabras recuerdan algunos versos de Borges (el escritor del polo de la tradición en el cuadrado semiótico) que ella misma cita y en los que el deíctico de lugar parece querer volver a un tiempo anterior al de los signos, en donde las cosas eran más verdaderas:

> Ahí está Buenos Aires. El tiempo que a los hombres
> trae el amor o el oro, a mí apenas me deja
> esta rosa apagada, esta vana madeja
> de calles que repiten los pretéritos nombres
> de mi sangre: Laprida, Cabrera, Soler, Suárez...
> Nombres en que retumban (ya secretas) las dianas,
> las repúblicas, los caballos y las mañanas,
> las felices victorias, las muertes militares[17].

Pero los sujetos representativos de esa sociedad metropolitana bajo el peronismo no serán sólo los exaltados cabecitas negras que unen el maldecir de la violencia ("¿Por qué no se irá a la puta madre que la parió?) con el "decir mal" de los sectores pauperizados ("La murga de Chanta Cuatro/ se vamo a retirar..." p.279). En realidad aparecen otros que se ven focalizados desde arriba por Alejandra, o desde abajo por Martín, y que tienen algo de híbrido −como lo era esa "sociedad híbrida, incolora" de la época de Roca en *La gran aldea*[18]−, lo cual termina por darles características monstruosas. Molinari, por ejemplo −que cuando joven fue socialista y más tarde se transformó en un defensor acérrimo de la libre empresa; integrado dentro del peronismo pero con el lema de "ni dictaduras ni utopías sociales" (p.165)− aparece definido por Alejandra "como una especie de animal mitológico", "como si un chancho dirigiese una sociedad anónima (p.57), "un Pilar de la Nación (...) un perfecto cerdo, un notable hijo de puta" (p.169). Y, Janos, el marido de Wanda, aparece definido como "un pegajoso monstruo".

En realidad, Molinari, Janos, Wanda, Bordenave, Quique son todas manifestaciones de una burguesía que, como la que nace durante el período de Roca en el siglo pasado, no cree en nada, salvo en el propio provecho y, al carecer de cualquier tipo de tensión metafísica, cae fácilmente en la corrupción, en la prostitución, destruyendo los símbolos del pasado por afán de dinero.

De hecho, no tiene prejuicios ni rémoras en cambiar el aspecto urbano de Buenos Aires; pero si en el ochenta se habían demolido calles y casas de estampa española para reemplazarlas por avenidas y mansiones en el estilo de la París de Haussman, ahora los viejos edificios caen dando lugar a modelos arquitectónicos norteamericanos: "Es un café muy cerrado, pero me gusta. No va a durar mucho, piense en los millones que vale la esquina. Es fatal: lo echarán abajo y levantarán rascacielos, y abajo uno de esos bares interplanetarios llenos de colorinches y ruidos que han inventado los norteamericanos".

(p.174). De este modo la ciudad al perder sus puntos de referencia espaciales, al no ser "ni Europa ni América", acaba por ser sólo un lugar de fractura.

El carácter híbrido y monstruoso de este sector social se refleja refleja también en el lenguaje, tal como lo hace en el *corpus* narrativo de la generación de escritores del ochenta. El lenguaje de esta burguesía adinerada de la época peronista (y el mejor ejemplo es el habla de Quique, asiduo visitante de la boutique de Wanda) parece una réplica de la del nuevo patriciado porteño de fines del siglo pasado, que incluía –para demostrar su europeísmo, su estar al día, y para ser aceptado más rápidamente en los círculos que contaban– más palabras extranjeras que castellanas (recuérdense, por ejemplo, los parlamentos de Montifiori en *La gran aldea*).

Otro aspecto vincula también a este sector social con el representado literariamente a partir del ochenta y sobre todo una década después: si bien la oficina de Molinari es descrita –a través de los pensamientos de Martín– por medio de imágenes alegóricas explícitamente tomadas de Chéjov, este espacio de la Gran Burguesía que hace Negociados se concretiza, asimismo, por medio de sintagmas que parecen salir de algunas descripciones de la Bolsa en *Quilito* de Ocantos y en la novela de Martel[19]: es un "recinto sagrado" (p.157), "lleno de acontecimientos financieros importantes", cuyo mecanismo "parecía de pronto volverse loco" (p.160). Esa oficina, en la que Molinari hablará de trabajo y prostitución, resulta el símbolo espacial de una época anormal en la que a un sector de la sociedad sólo lo mueve el dinero y, con este afán, destruye las tradiciones y los símbolos comunitarios, de la misma forma que los "cabecitas negras" queman las iglesias.

La falta de una tensión metafísica, el no creer en nada han transformado a la burguesía porteña en "un aventurero sin escrúpulos" como Bordenave, quien se ha vuelto representativo de todo un país, ya que Alejandra lo define como "un argentino". De la misma forma está caracterizado, supuestamente, Perón, "un cínico que no cree en nada, ni en el pueblo, ni en el peronismo siquiera, porque es un cobarde y un hombre sin grandeza" (p.173). Y esta falta de fe se extiende a la capital argentina en la que todos parecen moverse "como en un caos, sin que nadie supiese donde estaba la verdad, sin que nadie creyese firmemente en nada" (p.218).

Así pues, la representación urbana que implica la anormalidad con la no tradición remite, no sólo al período posterior a la capitalización de Buenos Aires, sino que sugiere, al aparecer controlada por sectores populares como en la época de Rosas, que la ciudad junto al Plata es un caos, y la barbarie y la confusión la caracterizan, tal como sucedía en el *corpus* de la generación del 38. Sin embargo, la enunciación de la novela parece rescatar a las clases marginadas y a la pequeña burguesía en la medida en que defienden ciertos valores comunitarios. Como el incesto en la relación "tradición-anormalidad" había sido un modo de conciliación simbólica de elementos contradictorios, la enunciación intenta ahora anular el caos y el interés individual resultante de la implicación "anormalidad-no tradición", tratando de conciliar las clases altas con las bajas por medio de un breve encuentro entre los cabecitas negras que se piensan "verdaderos peronistas" y una mujer del Barrio Norte, representativa de la relación "tradición-anormalidad". Esta, aunque "feroz", "decidida", "enloquecida" (p.278), es capaz de dejar su paraguas con mango de oro para recuperar un símbolo de unión comunitaria, la Virgen de los Desaparecidos; y el joven peronista, con el mismo fin, es capaz de enfrentarse con compañeros más fanáticos.

No obstante, en la contraposición "anormalidad-no tradición", prevalece la negatividad de Buenos Aires, cuya topología simbólica (la cloacal y subterránea del delirio de Fernando) se repite para referirse a la ciudad visible. De hecho, la joven Vidal Olmos define Buenos Aires como "esta ciudad inmunda" y cuando Martín se entera de que Alejandra irá a trabajar a la boutique de Wanda –un antro de aquella burguesía sin escrúpulos–, su alegría desaparece, "como agua cristalina en un resumidero, donde uno sabe que se mezclará con repugnantes desechos" (p.155). Además, si los laberintos de la ciudad subterránea pueden asociarse –desde un punto de vista antropológico– con una imagen de acogimiento, maternal[20], sugestivamente, la verdadera madre de Martín definida por el joven como Madre-cloaca sólo logra expresar el sentido opuesto, el deseo de expulsar al hijo de sus entrañas, cosa que se repetirá con Alejandra con la cual para Martín "había sido como buscar refugio en un caverna de cuyo fondo de pronto habían irrumpido fieras devoradoras". La significación antropológica positiva de la ciudad invisible resulta, entonces, anulada por los sentidos homólogos, pero negativos, que aparecen en la ciudad visible.

3. No tradición-No anormalidad.

La serie de elementos que remiten a lo híbrido de la cultura ciudadana (los personajes, por ejemplo, se encuentran en bares, restaurantes u hospedajes de nombres "Moscovia", "Helvética", "Ukrania", "The Criterion", "London", "Warsavia") denotan la difícil condición de una sociedad metropolitana de inmigrantes cuya homogeneización ha fallado y donde las tentativas de homofonía (Elmtree-Olmos) no han dado grandes resultados –como que el padre de Tito D'Arcángelo sigue hablando cocoliche.

La nueva y abigarrada realidad en la que conviven y se desviven los personajes es, ahora, una cosmópolis masificada con una fuerte presencia extranjera bajo un gobierno en el ápice de sus contradicciones. De allí que Bruno se pregunte:

¿Cómo representar aquella realidad innumerable en cien páginas, en mil, en un millón de páginas? (...). Seis millones de argentinos, españoles,

italianos, vascos, alemanes, húngaros, rusos, polacos yugoslavos, sirios, libaneses, lituanos, griegos, ucranianos.
Oh Babilonia.
La ciudad gallega más grande del mundo. La ciudad italiana más grande del mundo. Etcétera. Más pizzerías que en Roma y en Nápoles juntos. 'Lo nacional'. ¡Dios mío! ¿Qué era lo nacional?
Oh Babilonia. (pp.179-180)

Y el referente se refleja en la misma enunciación de *SHT* que, si por una parte intenta representar Buenos Aires por medio de símbolos de unión o de conciliación, por otra, está caracterizada por lo heterogéneo, la dispersión y la polifonía[21].

Las relaciones "No anormalidad-No tradición" se mueven dentro de sectores sociales que comprenden la pequeña burguesía, los lumpen y los trabajadores peronistas. Pero es sobre todo la presencia inmigratoria la que se evidencia en estas implicaciones del cuadrado semiótico, y aparece definida sobre todo por una carencia, la de las propias tradiciones. Como señala Martín, vivir en el extranjero, "era tan triste como habitar en un hotel anónimo e indiferente, sin recuerdos, sin árboles familiares, sin infancia, sin fantasmas" (p.273).

Para estos inmigrantes la tradición está en "otro lugar", no en el mundo en el que viven; de allí que sólo puedan recuperarla por medio de la interiorización y de la memoria, y acaben soñando "con otra realidad, una realidad fantástica y remota" (p.218).

Y para estos inmigrates como para sus hijos, la nostalgia es un componente fundamental de la existencia: "A veces me pongo a pensar, pibe" –dice Tito D'Arcángelo– "que a este país todo ya pasó, todo lo bueno se fue para no volver como dice el tango, que el fóbal, que el carnaval, que el corso, ma qué sé yo" (p.119). Como afirma Bruno, "pocos países debía de haber en el mundo en que ese sentimiento fuese tan reiterado" (p.219), pues todos sus habitantes en mayor o menor medida han perdido algo (el gaucho, el indio, el inmigrante, el viejo patriciado).

El tema, al aparecer en *SHT* vinculado con los inmigrantes, contrasta dos formas de existencia en la está implícito el deseo de regresar a la de procedencia, como sucede con el viejo D'Arcángelo, sabiendo que es imposible. Pero además se desarrolla otra versión de la nostalgia que resulta análoga a la que expresaban los sectores medios de finales del siglo pasado en el *corpus* de la Bolsa: sectores que no se sintieron involucrados en la transformación de Buenos Aires y quedaron signados por los contrastes entre un tiempo añejo en el que todo era más cercano, más simple y más nacional, y una época moderna, extranjerizante, caótica e indiferente. Pensemos en don Pablo Vargas en *Quilito* o en el narrador de varias de las viñetas de Fray Mocho de *Cuentos y salero criollos.*

Tito D'Arcángelo expresa cómo se ha perdido una memoria colectiva reemplazada por otra superficial ("la nueva generación no sabe ya nada de tango. Meta fostró y todo ese merengue de bolero, de rumba, toda esa payasada" p.119), y cómo el progreso ha ido arruinando el ahora pintoresco y entonces honrado trabajo de su padre, conductor de coche de plaza ("Mi viejo é una de la tanta víctima en ara del progreso de la urbe" p.117).

Pero esta nostalgia por un pasado donde las cosas tenían un valor y un sentido, se ve anulada en Tito –que constituye "el riguroso negativo de la filosofía que predicaba"– por una actitud derrotista que termina igualando el pasado (la memoria histórica) con el presente en una suerte de *qualunquismo*:

> Aquí todo es cuestión de coima. Y te alvierto que yo no estoy hablando de Perón. Porque cuando yo era así de chiquito, (...) ¿ quiénes manejaban l'estofao? Lo conserva: coima y robo. Cuando yo era así (...) radicale: coima y robo. Después el Justo ese: coima y robo. ¿Recuerdan el negocio de la Corporación? Después ese chicato Ortiz: coima y robo. Después la revolución del 45. Siempre eso milico dice que vienen a limpiar, pero a la final coima y robo (p.114).

Tito es un tragicómico personaje discepoliano al igual que su padre ("caricaturesco y cómico símbolo del tiempo y la Frustración" (p.219), que no consigue percibir la realidad que lo rodea para interactuar con ella, y al que le gustaría creer pero no lo logra, pues está convencido que los que creen terminan crucificados:

> Vo estudiá, hacete un Edison, inventá el telégrafo o curá cristiano, andate en el Africa como ese viejo alemán de bigote grande, sacrificate por la humanidá, sudá la gota gorda y va a ver cómo te crucifican y cómo lo otro se enllenan de guita (p.114).

Su reiterada mirada hacia la calle Pinzón, era una "mirada abstracta y en cierto modo completamente simbólica que en ningún caso condescendería a la real visión de hechos externos" (p.111). Así, enajenado, oscilando entre el escepticismo y la ternura, incapaz de adoptar una actitud cínica que lo vuelva concordante con su tiempo, expresa sus frustraciones frente a un país que le ha dado muy poco y una ciudad que no le ha permitido irse a vivir fuera del conventillo.

Pero aunque resentido, desesperanzado, nervioso, inquieto, a diferencia del delirante Fernando o de la anormalidad del cinismo de la rica burguesía, Tito es solo "medio loco" (p.118), gracias a su generosidad y a su ansiosa y permanente espera de algo" (p.219). Y en este sentido se vuelve representativo de los argentinos, "un pueblo de gente atormentada", todo lo contrario del cínico, "que se aviene a todo y nada le importa". El argentino, como Tito, "está descontento con todo y consigo mismo, es rencoroso, está lleno de resentimientos, es dramático y violento" (p.219).

Este personaje aparece descrito en manera tópica, pues su aspecto físico, como el elenco de sus acciones, y el espacio que lo circunda (la pizzería 'Chichín' en la Boca, el conventillo) dan la impresión de ser una "indicación" teatral –"como quien dice 'señas particulares' ya que únicamente un burdo mistificador podía pretender ser Humberto D'Arcángelo sin el escarbadientes y la *Crítica* arrollada en su mano derecha". Su habla incorrecta, como la de los personajes del teatro discepoliano, resulta una mezcla de vulgarismos, lunfardo y cocoliche, que se conjugan para expresar los temas reiterados de su conversación (fútbol, tango y política).

Por todo esto podemos decir que la enunciación recoge la tradición del grotesco criollo para representar un tipo de argentino que muestra siempre la 'misma cara'. Hecho singular si lo comparamos con el misterioso Fernando, cuyo rostro era múltiple y cambiante, o con el de Quique que siempre adopta una máscara distinta para ocultar su propia soledad.

Y esta función que adquiere la configuración del personaje de Tito, es análoga al rostro de Hortensia Paz –la cual, con su actitud solidaria, y su entusiasmo vital ("Hay tantas cosas lindas en la vida", "Nada hay tan hermoso como la música, eso sí"), parece lo contrario de la 'anormalidad'. De hecho, a diferencia del rostro "borrado" de Borges, o del inexistente del sacerdote en el sueño de Alejandra, "los sufrimientos y el trabajo, la pobreza y la desgracia no habían podido borrar del rostro de aquella mujer una expresión dulce y maternal" (p.544).

Este motivo del rostro, de la máscara, reiterado a lo largo de la novela, sugiere una respuesta a la búsqueda de Martín en la configuración tópica del personaje de Tito. No en vano, con alivio, Martín encuentra en él, así como en Hortensia o en Bucich, unos camaradas de camino: "Como había dicho Bruno una vez. La guerra podía ser absurda o equivocada, pero el pelotón al que uno pertenecía era algo absoluto. Estaba D'Arcángelo. Estaba la misma Hortensia" (p.546). Pero sobre todo esta Bucich, un gigante inocente, que habla mal ("Si yo sería gobierno" p.551), pero que no maldice. Que cree ("Qué grande es nuestro país, pibe..." p.557), como Hortensia y a diferencia de Tito. Uno al cual no le interesan las ganancias a expensas del prójimo ("-Tengo ochenta y tres pesos- dijo Martín. [para pagar el viaje al sur] "-Dejate de macana- dijo Bucich"p.39) como Molinari o Bordenave. Un personaje cuyas características resumen las palabras claves de la existencia de Martín (frío, soledad, limpieza, nieve, Patagonia) y que concilia –al ser "candoroso y fuerte"– aquéllo que representa el sur o la frontera para el joven: "una suma blancura y una extrema dureza como símbolos de algo puro y honrado" (p.39).

En este sentido, si Hortensia y Tito connotan la solidaridad en el lado "No anormalidad-No tradición" (en un caso por medio de la esperanza entusiasta, en el otro a través de un pesimismo esperanzado), y se unen en un lado del cuadrado semiótico, Bucich, en el polo de la no anormalidad, parece proyectarse como "una silueta gigantesca" hacia un no lugar y, al mismo tiempo hacia un lugar feliz que Martín busca denodadamente.

14

4. No anormalidad-Tradición

Martín es el actante que se mueve por todo el cuadrado semiótico y se relaciona con los sujetos que representan los distintos polos en manera diversa. Hay una neta división entre Martín y el lado de la "anormalidad-no tradición", en la medida en que sus elementos y actantes son vistos en términos de rivalidad (Fernando), o rechazo (la burguesía adinerada y corrupta; la violencia de los cabecitas negras). Sin embargo, no se puede negar que el joven resulta influenciado por la "anormalidad" pues, como dice Bruno, al referirse a su búsqueda de detalles sobre su pasada relación con Alejandra: eran detalles "maniáticos y minuciosos *no porque Martín fuese un anormal o una especie de loco*, sino porque la maraña alucinatoria en que se había movido siempre el espíritu de Alejandra lo forzaba a ese análisis casi paranoico" (p. 457; el énfasis es mío).

Martín establece relaciones con el polo "No tradición" sólo cuando éste aparece implicado con la "no anormalidad"; como cuando ayuda al cabecita negra que quiere salvar las imágenes religiosas, es decir, cuando la violencia se transforma en conciliación; o bien cuando recibe ayuda y solidaridad de parte de Tito D'Arcángelo. Sábato, al rescatar moralmente la pequeña burguesía así como un sector obrero que puede constituir –dentro de una tonalidad sicardiana[22]– la salvación del país, los propone como el polo de la "no anormalidad" y en esto se diferencia de la narrativa de R. Arlt.

Así pues, si bien la representación urbana de Buenos Aires aparece mostrada por medio de los diversos antagonismos sociales y sus contradicciones histórico-culturales, la enunciación procura resolver (o mejor compensar) los conflictos por medio de figuras de unión y conciliación. Este aspecto "bienintencionado" de la enunciación de la novela (en oposición dialéctica, como es evidente, a la búsqueda del Mal, manifiesto en la enunciación interna, la del *Informe*) se reflejará también en la trama de la obra, pues el final esperanzado y utópico, la partida hacia el sur de Martín, no corresponde cronológicamente con la conclusión de la fábula, ya que el adolescente volverá de su viaje para seguir buscando, en una enrarecida repetición, el recuerdo de Alejandra.

La construcción de la trama al final de la novela, sugiere además una conjunción entre la "no anormalidad" y la "tradición" pues el proyecto de irse al sur se encarna en dos personajes como Bucich y Martín y el tema del viaje aparece retomado paralelísticamente en la heroica huída de la legión de Lavalle hacia Bolivia, legión en la que se halla otro adolescente, Celedonio Olmos, tatarabuelo de Alejandra. En efecto, simétrico y especular es el viaje de los dos jóvenes en dos siglos diversos hacia los extremos opuestos de la Argentina y uno, el de Martín, en su ansia de salvación, parece repetir anacrónicamente el del joven Elmtree. Pero esa conjunción es secreta, no dicha, pues lo que sucede en el sur no aparece contado en la novela, aunque Martín vuelva a Buenos Aires y se encuentre con Bruno para continuar hablando sobre la misteriosa muerte de Alejandra.

La elección del sur como meta del viaje de Martín, conjuga un intento de unir la pureza y la solidez (encarnadas en su compañero de viaje y en los adjetivos adjudicados a la Patagonia) con las añejas y heroicas tradiciones argentinas. Pero esto no se realiza sólo por medio de la organización alternada del tejido textual del final de *SHT*. Hay también una serie de asociaciones que se generan a nivel connotativo, al haber elegido el escritor la palabra "sur" en lugar de "este" u "oeste" o el mismo "norte". El vocablo "sur" en la Argentina del siglo XIX significaba "frontera" y en cuanto tal, connotaba peligro y, al mismo tiempo significaba territorio para poblar, proyección, utopía. Por otra parte, desde un punto de vista literario, "el sur" es también el título de uno de los mejores cuentos de Borges, cuento que, como sabemos, pone en una relación de carácter fantástico, el pasado y las tradiciones de su protagonista con su vida presente, y que no sólo trata el tema de la argentinidad como mezcla de culturas, sino que retoma las gestas heroicas contra los indios o las luchas civiles del siglo XIX como la esencia del criollismo. El sur que "empieza del otro lado de Rivadavia"[23], zona en la que está situada la casa de los Vidal Olmos[24], resume según el cuento de Borges, "un mundo más antiguo, más firme"[25]. Resulta entonces signo de ese pasado que en la Buenos Aires de 1955 de *SHT* parece haber desaparecido y que la inmigración pauperizada no pudo hacer otra cosa que ignorar. Pero en *SHT*, ese lugar firme y antiguo que se busca, para oponerlo a la conjunción "anormalidad-no tradición" del período peronista, es un *no lugar* en ese momento histórico, una utopía (como lo había sido la "ciudad virtual" de la generación del 38) en la representación urbana de la novela.

5. Martín, de vuelta del sur, continúa su búsqueda intentando descifrar el enigma de su amada, y para ello recorre nuevamente las calles y lugares de Buenos Aires compartidos con Alejandra, "como esos familiares enloquecidos que se empeñan en juntar los mutilados destrozos de un cuerpo (...) pero no enseguida, sino mucho después, cuando esos restos no sólo están mutilados, sino descompuestos" (p.154). Su intento se vuelve, así, análogo al de Isis, tratando de recuperar el putrefacto cuerpo de Osiris. Por otra parte, si ponemos en relación el Mirador de los Vidal Olmos, que connota la altura y la vista (opuesto al mundo subterráneo y de la ceguera del *Informe*), con la búsqueda llevada a cabo tanto por Martín como por Bruno y que consiste en recuperar una verdad, un modo de expresión, recuerdos, palabras como si fueran pedazos de un cuerpo, volvemos a entrever la figura de Isis, la "pupila del mundo", "la diosa de los signos", el "ojo de la razón"[26].

Cuando finalmente Martín logra reconstruir la figura de la muchacha a través de recuerdos heterogéneos ("Era Louis Armstrong tocando su trompeta en el Mirador, cielos y nubes de Buenos Aires, las modestas estatuas del Parque Lezama en el atardecer, un desconocido tocando una cítara, una noche en el restaurante *Zur Post*, una noche de lluvia, refugiados debajo de una marquesina (riéndose), calles del barrio sur, techos de Buenos Aires vistos desde el bar del piso veinte del Comega" (pp.175-76)), la ciudad se representa como un cuerpo constituido por miles de partes, un cuerpo polimorfo diferente del de la ciudad subterránea del *Informe*, misterioso laberinto como el cuerpo de la madre en el que todos los personajes desearían penetrar en un ilusorio deseo de homogeneidad.

El intento novelístico de recuperar, a través de los signos representativos de la urbe, la unidad de un cuerpo dividido en miles de partes y resucitar simbólicamente el pasado y sus muertos, se vincula con el universalismo, corriente harto frecuentada en la literatura argentina. La búsqueda de un cosmos, de un orden a través de los signos, se vuelve –nos dice Bruno– "una especie de reconciliación con el universo, de esa raza de frágiles, inquietas y anhelantes criaturas que son los seres humanos" (p.521). De esta manera, el intento del novelista es análogo al del ciudadano de la Buenos Aires moderna y al de cualquier habitante de una gran metrópolis, y Fernando, el emisor del *Informe*, es como el Hombre, que contínuamente vive "su gran desgarramiento" pues al constituir ese universo de signos que es la cultura, ha dejado de ser un animal "pero no habrá llegado a ser el dios que su espíritu le sugiera" (p.521), y ambos habrán encontrado en la ciudad "la última etapa de su loca carrera, la expresión máxima de su orgullo y la máxima forma de su alienación" (p.522).

NOTAS

1. Buenos Aires es una ciudad circundada de agua y barro que eleva sus ojos al cielo en "El matadero" de Echeverría, o es una figura femenina recostada sobre la pampa en *Amalia* I, 8. Y al mismo tiempo, al ser la sede de la dictadura de Rosas, resulta objeto de menosprecio y de terror.
2. Véase a propósito de J. Alazraki. *Significación de Juan Lavalle en 'Sobre héroes y tumbas'*, en J. M.López de Abiada y A. López Bernasocchi, *De los romances-villancico a la poesía de Claudio Rodríguez. 22 ensayos sobre las literaturas española e hispanoamericana en homenaje a G. Siebenmann*, Madrid: J. Esteban, 1984, pp. 33-48.
3. Cfr. de M. L. Bastos. *Relecturas, Estudios de textos hispanoamericanos*, Buenos Aires: Hachette, 1989, pp. 139-140.
4. En el texto cito de la siguiente edición: E. Sábato. *Sobre héroes y tumbas*, Barcelona: Seix Barral, 1981.
5. La casa ficticia se constituyó con dos referentes de procedencia diversa: la casa "está en la calle Río Cuarto, tal como en mi obra pero no tiene Mirador. El Mirador lo tomé de otra antigua mansión en ruinas que está en H. Yrigoyen casi Boedo" (*El escritor y sus fantasmas*, Madrid: Aguilar, 1964, p.17.
6. B. Matamoro. "En la tumba de los héroes", *Cuadernos Hispanoamericanos*, ns. 391-393 (1983), p. 487.
7. J. E. Cirlot. *Diccionario de símbolos tradicionales*, Barcelona: Labor, 1969.
8. Dentro del motivo –que se reitera en otros niveles de la narración (en los épico-líricos, la legión huye con la cabeza de Lavalle, por ejemplo)–, está

implícito el reiterado tema sabatiano de la escisión entre la Razón y el Instinto.

9. El tema de las conflictivas relaciones entre Buenos Aires y el interior y el motivo de la cabeza degollada que aparecen en el libro sugieren un vínculo intertextual: en su ensayo *La cabeza de Goliat*, Martínez Estrada habla de "la decapitación de Buenos Aires con respecto a todo lo nacional interno", y agrega "a este sueño metropolitano, sin remordimientos ni sobresaltos, lo he comparado otra vez al sueño de una cabeza decapitada". Buenos Aires: CEAL, 1968, pp. 11 y 15.

10. E. Romano señala que "la relación incestuosa entre Fernando y su hija debía estar, como otras del *corpus* (se refiere a la serie de novelas que se publican entre 1955 y 1965) vinculada con una aspiración homogeneizadora" en "*Sobre héroes y tumbas* en sus contextos", *Cuadernos Hispanoamericanos, loc.cit.*, p. 390. Pero si Romano ve el tema del incesto como una "contrafigura imaginaria" de procesos de lucha aludidos en el texto (unitarios vs. federales; peronistas vs. antiperonistas) no se refiere al proceso de integración de gentes de diversa procedencia que, en otros países como los Estados Unidos, tuvo un resultado diverso.

11. Ibid., p. 22.

12. Mirta Arlt. *Prólogo* a R. Arlt, *Novelas completas y cuentos*, Tomo I, Buenos Aires: Fabril editora, 1963, p. 13. Fernando, como los personajes de Arlt, "Sufría alucinaciones, tenía sueños enloquecedores y de pronto perdía la conciencia" (p.495); de joven tenía el gusto por los delitos gratuitos y sorprendentes y había dirigido una banda de asaltantes, pues para él, asaltar un Banco era atacar "el templo del espíritu burgués" (p.477); participó también en el movimiento anárquico a la vez que consideraba que "la ley está hecha para los pobres diablos". Su vena arltiana se evidencia asimismo en su pasión por la alquimia y la magia, y en el ver en el dinero "algo mágico y demoníaco" (p.495).

13. "*Los siete locos* está plagado de defectos. No digo de defectos estilísticos o gramaticales que no tendría importancia. Digo que está lleno de literatura entre comillas, de personajes pretenciosos o apócrifos, como el Astrólogo" (p.213).

14. Dice Bruno: "su prosa es la más notable que hoy se escribe en castellano" (p.211).

15. Ver los desfasajes cronológicos del *Informe* en M. Gálvez Acero. "Sábato y la libertad", *Antrophos. Extraordinario 8. E. Sábato*, nos. 55-56 (1985), pp. 92-93.

16. Recordemos además que en el *Informe* la ciudad a la cual se acerca Fernando tiene forma de polígono con un perímetro igual al de Buenos Aires, sin embargo sus torres están invertidas: "Y cuando más cerca estaba de las torres, mayor era su majestad y su misterio. Eran veintiuna, dispuestas sobre un polígono que debía tener un perímetro tan grande como el de Buenos Aires" (p.436).

17. De "La noche cíclica", citado en *SHT* en p. 128.

18. En el libro de López, el narrador habla de una "sociedad híbrida e incolora" (p.151) y, al referirse al salón del Club del Progreso así lo define "El salón, híbrido, y en el cual el gusto refinado de un *clubman* de raza tendría mucho que rayar" (p. 147-148). *La gran aldea*, Buenos Aires: Biblioteca de la Nación, 1908.

19. Cfr. la descripción de la Bolsa en *Quilito*. Buenos Aires: Eudeba, 1964, pp. 99-100, y algunas escenas de *La Bolsa* de Martel (Buenos Aires: Huemul, s/f), p. 40.

20. Cfr. M. Eliade. *Myths, Dreams and Mysteries*, New York: Harper and Row, 1967, p. 171.

21. En el sentido que recurre a géneros diversos (prosa, poesía, digresión, informe, investigación detectivesca, historia, mito, novela familiar, relato de amor, noticias periodísticas, canciones populares, etc); utiliza hablas, tonos y tiempos diversos, explicita vínculos intertextuales y se fundamenta en la constante interacción de voces.

22. Los honestos trabajadores de Sábato, pueden ser equiparables a los "libres trabajadores" de Sicardi, pues no son violentos como los anarquistas, ni son fanáticos como los obreros católicos, ni tampoco son corruptos como las clases pudientes de *Libro extraño*.

23. J. L. Borges. *El sur* en *Ficciones*, Buenos Aires: Emecé, 1970, p. 190.

24. Mansión que, dijimos, resume una determinada representación de Buenos Aires, así como, en el cuento de Borges, "la ciudad, a las siete de la mañana, no había perdido ese aire de casa vieja que le infunde la noche, las calles eran como largos zaguanes, las plazas como patios" Ibid., p. 189.

25. Ibid., p. 191.

26. Cfr. las definiciones que se dan de Isis en el tratado de sabiduría y de alquimia hermética titulado *Koré Kosmou* en *Corpus Hermeticum*, T. IV, Texte établi et traduit par A. J. Festugière. Paris: Les Belles Letres, 1954, fragmento XXV-XXIX.

19

The Loss of Reason and the Sin *Contra Natura* in Lezama's *Paradiso*

SEXUAL DEVIATIONS IN JOSÉ LEZAMA LIMA'S novel *Paradiso* are represented as dead ends from which it is impossible to issue to the golden region of poetry, the space of Gnosis, where creation, death and resurrection can occur. The concept of the golden region is explained in Chapter IX as follows: "La compenetración entre la fijeza estelar y las incesantes mutaciones de las profundidades marinas contribuyen a formar una región dorada para un hombre que resiste todas las posibilidades del azar con una inmensa sabiduría."[1] Reaching this golden region is both an ethic and aesthetic goal for Cemí, since in Lezama's view ethics and aesthetics are inseparable. Homosexuality with madness and suicide (the three are associated throughout *Paradiso*) are seen as the most dangerous detours faced by Cemí in his years of poetic apprenticeship.

Since the publication of *Paradiso* in 1966, the significance of homosexuality in the novel has elicited polemics where both extraliterary and critical concerns have been addressed.[2] However, the curious connection made in the novel between madness and homosexuality has yet to be examined in the context of Lezama's philosophical system in *Paradiso*. This is the problem I will attempt to elucidate.

Enrique Lihn's "*Paradiso*, novela y homosexualidad" argues convincingly for the ambivalent horror and fascination that the sin *contra natura* exerts on the "casto e inocuo voyeur, Cemí" and Lezama himself.[3] Ambivalence notwithstanding, Lihn correctly assigns a negative value to homosexuality in the novel: "el *discurso valorativo* de *Paradiso*, ...y la historia (el destino de Foción entre otros) condenan y castigan a la homosexualidad, intentan quizá exorcizarla, le contraponen 'una categoría superior al sexo', la androginia perfecta y creadora de Cemí,"[4] and sees the hesychastic rhythm achieved in the realm of androgyny by the young artist at the conclusion of the novel as an antidote to homosexuality.[5]

It is now generally accepted that Cemí, Fronesis and Foción, besides being metaphors that became characters (as Lezama has explained)[6] are indeed aspects of one personality.[7] Thus in this triad of friendship, Fronesis, whose name in Greek, *phronesis,* meaning "prudence" aludes to the prime virtue of the Stoics,[8] represents order, a life guided by a *telos,* heterosexual intercourse, and an expansive or diastaltic style. Foción embodies chaos, a life without a *telos,* homosexual intercourse and a contracting or systaltic style. Cemí, as we have already seen, incorporates the essential aspects of Foción and Fronesis, chaos and order in a life guided by hypertelia, androgyny and characterized by an appeasing or hesychastic style.[9]

I believe that the three friends are also echoed by the three objects Foción always describes when someone visits his room: the bronze statuette of Narcissus (Foción), the flute player on a Greek vase (Fronesis), and a statuette of Lao-tse, "el viejo sabio niño" riding a buffalo (Cemí). Foción defines or characterizes each one of the three objects in the following manner:

> Señalaba el Narciso y decía: "La imagen de la imagen, la nada."
> Señalaba el aprendizaje del adolescente griego, y decía: "El deseo que conoce, el conocimiento por el hilo continuo del sonido de los infiernos." Parecía después que le daba una pequeña palmada en las ancas del búfalo montado por Lao-tse y decía: "El huevo empolla en el espacio vacío." (pp. 410-411)

Significantly only Lao-tse, who symbolizes Cemí, survives the fury of the red-haired boy: "Dentro del cuarto de Foción, el búfalo, tripulado por el maestro del vacío del cielo silencioso, se sintió de nuevo dueño de la montaña y del lago y del oeste impulsado por el sonido de las colgadas placas de nefrita, la piedra sonora" (p. 415). The sound of the nephrite chimes seems to be an allusion to the hesychastic rhythm, the rhythm of androgyny and poetic self-sufficiency.[10]

The leading paradigm of madness in *Paradiso* is Foción, who loses his reason (his *logos*) because of his deviant *eros*, and particularly because of his frustrated desire for Fronesis. Cemí encounters Foción at the very moment of his mental crisis which is precipitated by the realization that the mother of the red-haired boy has been encouraging Foción's homosexual relationship with her son in order to avert a greater evil, her son's incestuous advances. Foción remarks: "Me rogó que buscara a su hijo, ...Le parecía normal que su hijo se abandonase al Eros de los griegos, con tal de que no fuera monstruosamente incestuoso," and adds with bitterness: "Lo único que hace siempre el homosexualismo, ...es evitar un mal mayor, ...no me he suicidado, pero creo que me he vuelto loco" (p. 495).[11] When Cemí next sees his friend, Foción is in the ward for mental patients at the same hospital where Augusta, Cemí's grandmother, is dying:

> Al lado del álamo, en el jardín del pabellón de los desrazonados, vio un hombre joven con su uniforme blanco, describiendo incesantes círculos alrededor del álamo agrandado por una raíz cuidada. Era Foción. Volvía en sus círculos una y otra vez como si el álamo fuera su Dios y su destino. (p. 518)

Cemí has no difficulty interpreting Foción's inexorable circling of the tree. The poplar is Fronesis, who is both Foción's God (*Logos*) and destination (*telos*): "Cemí supo de súbito que el árbol para Foción, regado por sus incesantes y enloquecidos paseos circulares, era Fronesis" (p. 519).[12] Cemí's grandmother dies the next day, having opened her eyes for the last time the previous night during an electric storm. During that storm the poplar is struck by lightning, and Cemí discovers after his grandmother expires that Foción is gone:

"El rayo que había destruido el árbol había liberado a Foción
de la adoración de su eternidad circular" (p. 520).

The revelation of Foción's fate and liberation acquires the
nature of a warning for Cemí, particularly in the context of
his last conversation with Augusta. This conversation re-enacts
the famous scene of Chapter IX where Cemí's mother con-
secrates him to the poetic search that will earn him salvation
and differentiates between the danger undertaken by the sick,
a danger without epiphany and the necessary danger that will
lead to transfiguration (pp. 320-322). On her deathbed, Augusta approvingly marks Cemí's progress, and contrasts his
gift for observing "ese ritmo que hace el cumplimiento, el
cumplimiento de lo que desconocemos, pero que, ...nos ha
sido dictado como el signo principal de nuestro vivir" (p. 518),
with the sterility of persons who disrupt, "favorecen el vacío"
(p. 517), persons like Foción.

The association of madness with sexual deviance and ceaseless circular movement drawn by Foción's fate is both prefigured and repeated in other episodes of *Paradiso*, but nowhere with the richness of symbolism found in the story of
Godofredo el Diablo told by Fronesis to Cemí at the end of
Chapter VIII.[13] As in the case of the passage that we have
just examined, the story itself gains in significance from the
context in which it is told, Cemí's first private conversation
with Fronesis. The story of Godofredo's loss of reason comes
to complete the triad, filling the future place of Foción, whom
Cemí has not yet met. Godofredo's beauty is immediately
described as being dominated by a fury similar to that of the
Tibetan bear, also known as the Chinese demon, "que describe incesantes círculos, como si se fuera a morder a sí mismo"
(p. 302). This fury already foreshadows Foción's circling of
the poplar.

Godofredo's sexual deviance (voyeurism) and his madness
in turn reflect those of Father Eufrasio whose study of con-
cupiscence in St. Paul, "la cópula sin placer, le había tomado
todo el tuétano, doblegándole la razón" (p. 305). The priest's
sexual obsession, "Cómo lograr en el encuentro amoroso la
lejanía del otro cuerpo y cómo extraer el salto de la energía
suprema del gemido del dolor más que de toda inefabilidad

placentera, le daban vueltas como un torniquete que se anillase en el espacio, rodeado de grandes vultúridos" (p. 305), is also described by a circular movement, the turning of the tourniquet which is both the symbol of his madness and the prosaic instrument of his deviant eroticism.

Godofredo secretly observes Father Eufrasio exercising his mania with Fileba, and causes her husband's suicide by making him witness the act. While fleeing from the dreadful results of his voyeuristic intrigues, Godofredo is blinded in one eye by one of the snake-like vines, "se curvaban como serpientes verticalizadas," which we are told, "le hizo justicia mayor, retrocedió, tomó impulso y le grabó una cruz en el ojo derecho, en el ojo del canon" (p. 309). It is then that the red-haired Godofredo also loses his reason: "Sus caminatas describen inmensos círculos indetenibles, cuyos radios zigzaguean como la descarga de un rayo" (p. 309).

This story of punished voyeurism, which seems to be a warning directed at the innocuous voyeur, Cemí, contains all the *topoi* which Lezama links to sexual deviance in *Paradiso*. The deviant eroticism of Godofredo and Father Eufrasio is linked to their madness and to the suicide of Fileba's husband. Godofredo's circular walks, the image of the thunderbolt, and Godofredo's red hair, which foreshadows that of the incestuous red-haired boy, all forecast the episode of Foción's madness. The three alternatives Foción outlines in the café: suicide, homosexuality and madness are already present in the story of Godofredo, although dispersed among several characters.

Upon closer examination the allusion to the canonical eye in the story of Godofredo, which on the surface appears to be an impertinent digression, reveals another important nexus. The significance of the "ojo del canon" is partially explained in the story itself:

> El ojo de nublo era el derecho, el que los teólogos llaman el ojo del canon, pues al que le faltaba no podía leer los libros sagrados en el sacrificio. El que no tuviese ese ojo jamás podría ser sacerdote. Parecía como si inconscientemente Godofredo supiese el valor intrínseco que los cánones le dan a ese ojo, pues se contentaba con ser Godofredo el Diablo. (p. 302)

Beyond the fact that the loss of his eye makes him an outcast and leads him to opt for evil, there is an additional sexual significance to Godofredo's blinding. Since he is a voyeur, his eye can be considered to be his sexual organ and his blinding may be seen as a symbolic castration. The sexual meaning of the loss of the canonical eye is reinforced when we recall that canon law traditionally proscribed a man who "caret aliqua membrorum" from holy orders.[14]

In *Paradiso*, as we shall see, homosexuality is associated with castration (p. 344), blindness (p. 492) and with exclusion from the "priesthood" which leads to poetry and salvation. This exclusion of homosexuals and eunuchs from Paradise and/or Resurrection, based on St. Thomas Aquinas's characterization of homosexuality as a sin of bestiality rather than lust, is discussed by Cemí in his answer to Foción's defense of homosexuality in Chapter IX (pp. 376-378). Godofredo's tale incorporates all the major potential dangers which Cemí must overcome in order to achieve the hesychastic rhythm.

The endless circling of Foción, Godofredo el Diablo, and Father Eufrasio, and the snake-like vine that pierces Godofredo's eye recall one of Lezama's favorite *topoi*, the *ouroboros*, the snake that swallows its own tail. In fact the first description of Godofredo is an allusion to the *ouroboros*: "como si se fuera a morder a sí mismo" (p. 302). In the context of Lezama's novel, the *ouroboros* signifies both the sin *contra natura* and its punishment. Foción's etymological games with the name of Anubis (the jackal-headed god who conducts the dead in the Egyptian underworld) shortly before losing his reason, reveal both the meaning of Godofredo's blind eye and the new meaning Lezama attaches to the *ouroboros*. Foción describes the anus as the eye of Anubis by playing on the pun: *ano/Anobis*. He then characterizes it as a blind eye, and sodomy as "la anía [pun on *ano* and *manía*] del dios Anubis, que quiere guiar donde no hay caminos, que ofrece lo alto del cuerpo inferior, el ano, el anillo de Saturno, en el valle de los muertos" (p. 492). Sodomy, then, recreates the symbolic gesture of the *ouroboros*; "el serpentín intestinal" (p. 343) described in the Leregas — Baena Albornoz episode of Chapter IX swallows "la serpiente fálica" (p. 493) of the gods who accompany Anubis in Chapter XI.

In order to transcend the merely physical analogy between the sin *contra natura* and the *ouroboros* and understand the new philosophical significance that Lezama attaches to this ancient symbol, we must first note two relevant stages in its genealogy: its meaning in Gnostic systems and in Alchemy. In the Gnostic systems, the snake had the opposite symbolism that it has in the Judeo-Christian system:

> Gnostic snake worshippers, the Ophites...radically reinterpreted Genesis. In their view the snake was divine because he wanted to enlighten mankind with the knowledge of good and evil and give them eternal life, while God...wished to keep men earth-bound and ignorant.[15]

From this snake of the Ophites, giver of eternal life and knowledge, we go to the *ouroboros* as interpreted by the Alchemists. The tail-eating serpent "has no beginning and no end; it devours itself and renews itself. Life and death, creation and destruction, are an unending circular process; out of the one comes the other."[16] In their imagery, the alchemists, unlike the Ophites, dwell both on the positive and negative aspects of serpents: "Serpents (or toads and dragons, which have the same associations) represent base matter, which must be 'killed.' They are 'venomous' and 'evil', but at the same time carry the Philosopher's stone within."[17] The goal of all alchemists is to find the Philosopher's stone and extract it from base matter. Thus for the alchemists the *ouroboros* is a symbol of the eternal cycle of life and death.

In Michael Maier's *Atalanta Fugiens* published in 1618 we find an alchemical variation of the *ouroboros*.[18] In this case the cycle of life and death is represented by a woman nursing a poisonous toad. She then sickens and dies so that the toad, who is seen as her son, may live. This emblem leads us back to *Paradiso* where Foción enlists a similar scenario in order to urge the acceptance of homosexuality:

> Cuando Electra creyó que había parido un dragón, vio que el monstruo lloraba porque quería ser lactado; sin vacilaciones le da

su pecho, saliendo después la leche mezclada con la sangre. Aunque
había parido un monstruo, cosa que tendría que desconcertarla,
sabía que su respuesta tenía que ser no dejarlo morir de hambre,
pues la grandeza del hombre consiste en que puede asimilar lo
que le es desconocido. (p. 348)

Foción's literary allusion (or Lezama's) has been radically
altered both in content and interpretation to suit the needs
of the moment. It is Clytemnestra who in Aeschylus's "The
Libation Bearers" dreams that she gives birth to a snake, suck-
les it and is horrified when it draws blood with the milk. Ores-
tes, told about the dream, interprets it as a prophecy:

> But I pray to the earth and to my father's grave that this dream
> is for me and that I will succeed. See, I divine it, and it coheres all
> in one piece. If this snake came out of the same place whence I
> came, if she wrapped it in robes, as she wrapped me, and if its jaws
> gaped wide around the breast that suckled me, and if it stained
> the intimate milk with an outburst of blood, so that for fright and
> pain she cried aloud, it follows then, that as she nursed this hideous
> thing of prophecy, she must be cruelly murdered. I turn snake to
> kill her. This is what the dream portends.[19]

For Aeschylus the nursing snake is a symbol of the horror
of matricide, whereas for Foción the nursing dragon signifies
the greatness of the human race, its ability to assimilate the
unknown. The symbolism attached by Foción to the dragon
is diametrically opposed to the role played by the dragon in
Cemí's (and Lezama's) conception of artistic creation as it
is suggested in the description of Rialta's fibroma at the end
of Chapter X, where the dangerous proliferation of the cells
becomes an emblem of Lezama's own style in *Paradiso*.[20]
Foción associates the dragon with homosexuality, but for
Lezama all sex *contra natura* falls under the aegis of the *ouroboros*.

Within Lezama's system of imagery, therefore, the tail-
eating snake is not seen as the ultimate symbol of the creative
process, since the eternal cycle of life and destruction posited
by the *ouroboros* (a concept borrowed by the alchemists from
the Stoic doctrine of the conflagration)[21] is essentially inimical

to Lezama's fundamental, if heterodox, Christianity. The progress of the poet in life must, like Christian history, have a moment of rupture like the *Parousia*, it must reach a stage of transfiguration. This is why for Cemí and Lezama, the *ouroboros* which is *atelic* (goal-less) is also *atelos* (incomplete, imperfect), and must be destroyed, not so that it can return in the same form, but rather in order to precipitate a necessary metamorphosis. The snake must be transfigured into a hybrid, the dragon which here becomes the symbol of hypertelia, of resurrection:

> en los cuerpos que logra la imaginación, hay que destruir el elemento serpiente para dar paso al elemento dragón, un organismo que está hecho para devorarse en el círculo, tiene que destruirse para que irrumpa una nueva bestia, surgiendo del lago sulfúrico, pidiéndole prestadas sus garras a los grandes vultúridos y su cráneo al can tricéfalo que cuida las moradas subterráneas. (p. 453)

To the contracting or systaltic rhythm of homosexuality, the *ouroboros,* Lezama opposes the tranquility of the hesychastic rhythm of androgyny, the dragon. This all-encompassing rhythm is the goal of Cemí's poetic apprenticeship, and in the often quoted end of Chapter XIII, Oppiano Licario verifies Cemí's achievement: "Veo...que ha pasado del estilo sistáltico, o de las pasiones tumultuosas, al estilo hesicástico, o del equilibrio anímico, en muy breve tiempo... Entonces, podemos ya empezar" (p. 589). These very words close and, at the same time, open the conclusion of *Paradiso,* "ritmo hesicástico, podemos empezar" (p. 645).

As we have seen, for Lezama in *Paradiso,* madness, the loss of reason (the *logos*) is equated with the loss or waste of the *logos spermatikos* (seminal reason) in homosexuality. Lezama repeatedly associates homosexuality with the waste of the seed, sterility and castration. Probably, the clearest example is his description of Leregas's sexual preference, "su Eros de gratuidad," as "el fuego del nacimiento malo, de la esperma derramada sobre el azufre incandescente" (p. 342), and although we know from his exhibitionistic adventures in Chapter VIII that Leregas is a "coloso fálico" (p. 278), after his intercourse with Baena he is described as an "eunuco poseedor" (p. 344).

For Lezama the sterile circularity of the *ouroboros* reflects the waste of the seed in all sex *contra natura*. Those who lose their *logos* are condemned to wander incessantly in Luciferine circles like Godofredo el Diablo, Foción, and even Fronesis' real mother who likewise suffers from a sexual psychosis, "en forma de dromomanía mitomaníaca, caminaba, caminaba y bailaba por las noches de Viena, en seguimiento de dólmenes viriles" (p. 399).[22]

To this endless and destructive wandering Lezama opposes Fronesis' *telos* and order. The configuration of the opposition between Fronesis and Foción represents the equilibrium which will permit Cemí to reach the all-encompassing state of androgyny. Though he is stricken like Foción by the fear of the "vulva dentada," Fronesis utilizes the *ouroboros* in the form of a circle of cloth cut from his undershirt as an antidote to overcome his fear of Lucía's "delicioso enemigo."[23] When he throws the undershirt into the sea Fronesis rejects the *ouroboros*: "La camiseta...se fue circulizando como una serpiente a la que alguien ha transmitido la inmortalidad" (p. 417).

Heterosexual coitus is seen in this passage as a loss of immortality, but that very loss is the source of creativity: "era necesario crear al perder precisamente la inmortalidad. Así el hombre fue mortal, pero creador, y la serpiente fálica se convirtió en un fragmento que debe resurgir" (p. 417), once more that fragment is the dragon of hypertelia. Coitus between man and woman ends the paradise of childhood and re-enacts the fall of Adam and Eve in Eden, but the *felix culpa* must be repeated. Paradoxically mortality must (as in Christianity) be embraced in order for creation and a true hypertelia of immortality (resurrection) to be possible.

In Chapter IX of *Paradiso* we are given two rival interpretations of the term "la hipertelia de la inmortalidad." Foción, who actually coins the phrase, identifies it with homosexuality:

Todo lo que hoy nos parece desvío sexual, surge en una reminiscencia, o en algo que yo me atrevería a llamar...una hipertelia de la inmortalidad, o sea una busca de la creación, de la sucesión de

> la criatura, más allá de toda causalidad de la sangre y aun del es-
> píritu, la creación de algo hecho por el hombre, totalmente des-
> conocido aun por la especie. (p. 351)

But Cemí corrects him, bringing the discussion to the privileged ground of Christian theology. He redefines the hypertelia of immortality as "la resurrección de los cuerpos" (p.
378),[24] and characterizes homosexuality as "una falsa inocencia" (p. 372).

Like the snake of the Gnostic Ophites, homosexuality and
other sexual deviations offer Cemí the knowledge of good
and evil and a form of immortality which is understood as an
eternal cycle of destruction and creation.[25] Cemí sees this type
of immortality as a false *telos* whose true nature is revealed
in the *dromomanía,* the ceaseless wandering of all the sexual
psychotics in the novel. The immortality Foción preaches is
precisely the type of danger without epiphany exposed by
Rialta to her son Cemí. Foción's way is well represented by
the circle of the *ouroboros* and by the statuette of Narcissus
which he describes as: "La imagen de la imagen, la nada" (p.
410).

By means of his triple protagonist, Lezama gives not one
but three portraits of the artist as a young man. The goal-
less Foción is the portrait of a failed artist, overcome by darkness. In Fronesis Lezama depicts the opposite: a young man
who will perhaps not go beyond an earthly *telos* because of
an excess of light. Cemí is Lezama's attempt to surpass this
dichotomy and to resolve it in an equilibrium which will put
an end to all passion and all striving. This is why Cemí is guided
not by a *telos* but an *hypertelos*. He rejects the goal of immortality but by accepting death he hopes to achieve a form of it
through resurrection. Cemí will not wrest immortality through
Luciferine pride or through the light of reason, but will yield
to the "fijeza" of the hesychastic rhythm and the self-sufficient
immobility of androgyny. In this sense José Cemí in *Paradiso*[26] is as much a repository of José Lezama's dreams as a
self-portrait.

University of Virginia
Charlottesville

NOTES

1. José Lezama Lima, *Obras completas*, II (Mexico: Aguilar, 1975), p. 329. All further references to Lezama's works appear in the text. The quotations from *Paradiso* come from *Obras completas*, I.

2. For these polemics see Emir Rodríguez Monegal, *Narradores de esta América*, II (Buenos Aires: Editorial Alfa Argentina, 1974), pp. 133-135. He rejects the view that *Paradiso* is an apology of homosexuality (in the manner of Gide's *Corydon*) disguised as a novel. See also the discussion of this issue in the open letters by Vargas Llosa and Rodríguez Monegal, pp. 141-155. Although Rodríguez Monegal correctly stresses the basic formal and ideological differences between *Paradiso* and *Corydon*, the dialogues on homosexuality in Chapter IX of *Paradiso* owe much to Gide's tract. As in *Corydon*, the discussion is motivated by a scandal, and zoological, philosophical, historical and moral arguments are employed.

3. Enrique Lihn, "Paradiso, novela y homosexualidad," *Hispamérica*, VIII, No. 22, 1979, p. 14. For a more positive view of Foción see Raymond D. Souza, *Major Cuban Novelists* (Columbia: Univ. of Missouri Press, 1976), p. 63.

4. Lihn, pp. 16-17.

5. For a different view see Gustavo Pérez Firmat, "Descent into *Paradiso:* A Study of Heaven and Homosexuality," *Hispania*, 59, No. 2, 1976, where he makes a case for Cemí's homosexuality and argues that "throughout the novel homosexuality and androgyny are identified." p. 254.

6. Centro de Investigaciones Literarias de la Casa de las Américas, *Interrogando a Lezama Lima* (Barcelona: Editorial Anagrama, 1971), p. 29.

7. See Margarita Junco Fazzolari, *Paradiso y el sistema poético de Lezama Lima* (Buenos Aires: Fernando García Cambeiro, 1979), pp. 75-76, "Los tres son parte de la misma personalidad, las divisiones que ocasionó la caída. Son las tres partes del alma según los místicos alemanes: los instintos, la razón y la chispa divina." See also Lihn, p. 6.

8. For a discussion of the concept of *phronesis* in Stoic philosophy see: Eleuterio Elorduy, S.J., *El estoicismo* (Madrid: Gredos, 1972), II, p. 146 and p. 410; Emile Brehier, *Chrysippe et l'ancien Stoicisme* (Paris: Gordon and Breach, 1971), p. 236; and Edward V. Arnold, *Roman Stoicism* (1911; rpt. New York: Arno Press, 1971), p. 306. Although many critics of *Paradiso* identify the character Fronesis with wisdom, I feel that it is necessary to stress the Stoic definition of the word *phronesis* as "prudence," since Lezama himself emphasizes Fronesis' Stoic characteristics from his first appearance in the novel: "Fronesis mostraba siempre, junto con una alegría que brotaba de su salud espiritual, una dignidad estoica, que parecía alejarse de las cosas para obtener, paradojalmente, su inefable simpatía" p. 303. The relationship between Cemí and Fronesis is thus ruled by the

Stoic concept of *sympathos*, whereas for Foción Cemí clearly experiences the opposite: "Las leyes del *apathos* de los estoicos funcionaron de inmediato, no, no le cayó nada bien Foción a Cemí" p. 319. The Stoic definition also permits a distinction between *phronesis* and *sophia* which is important in distinguishing the roles of Fronesis and Cemí. *Sophia* (wisdom) will be the province of "el viejo sabio niño," Cemí; *phronesis* (practical wisdom, according to Aristotle) that of his friend.

9. The diastaltic, systaltic and hesychastic styles are the three keys of ancient Greek harmony. *The Oxford English Dictionary* gives the following definitions: *diastaltic,* "Applied to a style of melody fitted to expand or exalt the mind;" *systaltic,* "Applied to a style of melody having the effect of 'contracting' or depressing the mind;" *hesychastic,* "Applied to a style of melody which tends to appease the mind." In *Paradiso* Lezama never mentions the *diastaltic* style but his characterization of Fronesis fully warrants the association I suggest.

Roberto González Echevarría has underscored the importance of the concept of *hypertelia* in Lezama. See the essay "Apetitos de Góngora y Lezama" in *Relecturas: estudios de la literatura cubana* (Caracas: Monte Avila, n.d.), p. 113, "Lezama aspira en su obra al milagro — a la encarnación del verbo... Esa resurrección no refleja únicamente el notorio catolicismo de Lezama, sino que representa lo más radical de su estética. La resurrección es el mundo de la poesía 'substanciada', de la *hipertelia* (más allá del fin) a que se refieren los personajes en varias de sus discusiones, la superfluidad a que hemos aludido." González Echevarría stresses here the significance of hypertelia in Lezama's aesthetic system. In the present article I am primarily interested in the ethical dimension of hypertelia in *Paradiso* where both Foción and Cemí propose rival definitions of the concept.

10. For a discussion of Taoist symbols in *Paradiso* see Pérez Firmat, p. 255.

11. The meeting of Foción and Cemí in the café at this crucial moment suggests a confrontation of ideologies. Suicide, homosexuality and madness, the three alternatives which Foción perceives as his lot in life are opposed to the heterodox Catholicism of Cemí who sees poetic epiphany as the means to salvation and resurrection. The series of alternatives presented or implied in this episode recall the three choices which according to André Gide are available to modern man: suicide, homosexuality or Catholicism. Lezama not only fuses his concept of Catholicism with poetic revelation, but following Dante associates homosexuality with violence done to art. The essay "Plenitud relacionable," a Lezamean *salto mortale*, which characteristically attempts to metaphorize the essential philosophical stance of Dante, Gide and Claudel, explictly makes this link between homosexuality and violence towards art:

> El más paseador y sombrío de los gibelinos [Dante] pareció pre-
> figurar arduas relaciones contemporáneas. En el séptimo círculo,
> recinto tercero, puesto a la moda por ciertas indiscreciones de
> Gide, [*Corydon*] los violentos contra la naturaleza aparecen nive-
> lados con los violentos contra el arte. *Obras completas,* II, p. 475.

The essay is ultimately an attack on what Lezama calls the contemporary
"self-destructive fervor" which he sees as frivolous and superfluous. Addressing Mallarmé, Valéry and Gide, he rejects the concept of randomness,
and siding with Claudel concludes: "el cátolico sabe que ninguno de sus
actos es inconsecuente, tiene gratuidad, sino que aun en la revelación tiene
composición" p. 479. This *gratuitousness* rejected by Lezama is also that
of Gide's Corydon, who uses his characterization of sexuality as "luxe"
and "gratuité" to refute the view that homosexuality is "contre nature."
See André Gide *Oeuvres completes,* IX (n.p.: N.R.F., 1932), pp. 226-227.

12. Souza interprets the passage as follows: "The tree is a dual image.
On the one hand it represents Foción's obsession with Fronesis, and, on
the other, it could represent the tree of life that embodies all the positive
and negative aspects of existence. Foción's incessant circling of the tree
reveals his attempts to control the chaos of his life and...to resolve the enigma of existence... The bolt of lightning that releases Foción indicates the
sudden gaining of an illumination and insight that frees him from his obsessive anguish" p. 64. The only objection I find to Souza's interpretation
concerns the lightning. If it signifies illumination, it is Cemí who benefits
truly, and Foción's enlightenment would seem to be merely transitory.

13. Carmen Ruiz Barrionuevo, *El "Paradiso" de Lezama Lima* (Madrid:
Insula, 1980), p. 66, sees this story which closes "la apertura al eros del
capítulo VIII" as a warning to Cemí spoken by the voice of wisdom, Fronesis.

14. For a complete discussion of the history of the irregularities which
bar men from the priesthood see "Irrégularités," *Dictionnaire de Théolo-
gie Catholique,* (Paris: Librairie Letouzey et Ané, 1927). The major scrip-
tural source cited by popes and councils of the Church is Leviticus 21, 16-20:
"None of your descendants, in any generation, must come forward to offer
the food of his God if he has any infirmity — no man must come near if
he has an infirmity such as blindness or lameness, if he is disfigured or deformed, if he has an injured foot or arm, if he is a hunchback or a dwarf,
if he has a disease of the eyes or of the skin, if he has a running sore, or if
he is a eunuch." *Jerusalem Bible,* (Garden City, N.Y.: Doubleday, 1966).
Another source is Deuteronomy 23,2. According to *The New Bible Commentary Revised,* eds. Guthrie et al. (Grand Rapids, Michigan: Wm. B.
Eerdman, 1970), p. 223, "The exclusion of emasculated persons was a protest against heathen cultic practices." In the early Church, the exclusion
of eunuchs from the priesthood (particularly voluntary ones) was also an

attempt to discourage imitation of the Church Father Origen, who castrated himself in order to escape temptation. The ghost of that heterodox Church Father, whose name in Spanish furnished the double meaning (origin/Origen) of Lezama's famous review, *Orígenes*, seems to haunt these pages of *Paradiso*.

15. Allison Coudert, *Alchemy, The Philosopher's Stone* (Boulder, Colorado: Shambhala Publications, Inc., 1980), p. 144.

16. Coudert, p. 142.

17. Coudert, p. 145.

18. Coudert, p. 145.

19. *Aeschylus I Oresteia*, trans. Richmond Lattimore (Chicago: Univ. of Chicago Press, 1953), pp. 112-113.

20. See Gustavo Pellón, *"Paradiso:* un fibroma de diecisiete libras," *Hispamérica*, IX, Nos. 25-26, 1980.

21. For a discussion of this doctrine see Arnold, pp. 190-192.

22. Eloísa Lezama Lima, in her edition of *Paradiso* (Madrid: Cátedra, 1980), p. 477, n. 21, defines *dromomanía* as, "la manía de trasladarse incesantemente de un lugar a otro o necesidad exagerada de viajar."

23. Junco Fazzolari has already identified the undershirt with the *ouroboros*, p. 90. Souza, instead, has discussed the passage in terms of geometric symbolism as a movement from "inner confusion to inner unity... The sexual act becomes then one of many manifestations of the search for meaning in life and the control over chaos," pp. 61-62.

24. The passage reads: "Quizás la resurrección de los cuerpos sea el verdadero nombre de lo que Fronesis [sic] llamó la 'hipertelia de la inmortalidad,' " p. 378. Junco Fazzolari (p. 87) correctly ascribes the term and its homosexual definition to Foción.

25. Junco Fazzolari sees in Foción's defense of homosexuality, "el querer prolongar, con una falsa inocencia, una inmortalidad que se ha perdido irremediablemente con la caída" p. 86. In Foción's concept of homosexuality as a lost innocence I see a re-statement of Corydon's argument: "Tout comme je crois, excusez mon audace, l'homosexualité dans l'un et l'autre sexe, plus spontanée, plus naïve que l'hétérosexualité" p. 280.

26. I stress *Paradiso,* because *Oppiano Licario,* Lezama's posthumous novel, presents a somewhat more active José Cemí.

HAIDER ALI KHAN

Paz's Poetics: Textuality, Sexuality, Politics

(1)

In their study of Kafka, Gilles Deleuze and Félix Guattari raise a set of interrelated questions:

> How many people today live in a language that is not their own? Or not yet, even know their own and know poorly the major language they are forced to serve? This is the problem of immigrants, and especially of their children, the problem of minorities, the problems of a minor literature, but also a problem for all of us: how to tear a minor literature away from its own language, allowing it to challenge the language and making it follow a sober revolutionary path? How to become a nomad and an immigrant and a gypsy in relation to one's own language? (qtd. in Lawrence Venuti's "Simpatico," *Substance*, Vol. 20, No. 2, 1991, p. 3)

Two people who write in French may perhaps have some justification for raising such questions about the Czech Jew Kafka who wrote in German. But how can anyone raise these, or similar questions with regard to the work of Octavio Paz? Is he not an acknowledged master of the Spanish language? Has he not shown consummate skill in inhabiting all the modern forms and genres, utilizing them to produce dazzling effects? Is he not the cosmopolitan *pensadore* par excellence, a person of culture spanning the entire distance between not just Mexico and Madrid but also Paris and New Delhi? Is he not, after all, a poet of this century who embraced the modernist idea of universalism, rejecting the narrow provincialism of

36

Mexico? In a sense, the answer to all these questions, even to the last, Paz's edited anthology of Mexican poetry notwithstanding, could be yes. But that is really not the crux of the matter. Simply to juxtapose this list of questions with the ones raised by Deleuze and Guattari (which, I might add, do not stand as absolutes, but rather, to use their term, as "nomadic" strategies to counter a certain domination by other questions and other terms) is to confront a complexity that may otherwise be easily swept away. It is a conventional criticism with its usual litany of questions and strategies of reading may very well suppress: for it is the Oedipal anxiety to tame the text, to master its codes and its meaning that very often drives the conventional reader of (conventional) texts. One might even call it the grand cosmopolitan attempt at erasure, a move, often unconscious, to repress the uncomfortable traces of the other especially but not exclusively from the writings of women and non-Western people. Even when practiced in the name of the universal principles of modernism by the new criticism critics this has given a certain closure to texts which would otherwise open up spaces for a radical form of discourse. As I will argue, precisely such orthodox critical moves have been called into question by Paz's work even before the formal advent of post-structuralism or deconstruction. Without recourse to any currently fashionable literary labels, his work speaks in multiple voices about its own uncertainties as well as its discoveries.

It was perhaps Paz's good fortune that he came of literary age in the turbulent thirties, and found his own voice not only among the young poets in the self-consciously modernist journal *Contemporáneos*, but also in the confusion and turmoil of the dissolution and the reconstruction of reality surrounding him. It is true that the *Contemporáneos* and other dissident poets' European cultural curiosity led Paz to discover modernism in Spanish poetry from Gerardo Diego's *Antologia* (1932). The poetics of absolute interiority practiced by the contemporary Mexican poet Villaurrutia had tremendous initial impact at least from 1928 to the early thirties on the precocious Paz, so much so that even in 1973, Paz would recall that Villaurrutia "opened the doors of modern poetry for me." Indeed Villaurrutia and the *Contemporáneos* confronted the narrow cultural nationalism of Mexico during the 1920's and 1930's with the universalist approach to poetry and art. It is crucial for Paz and for much of the subsequent history of Mexican (perhaps even Latin American) literature that the European focus was continental, especially French, and unlike some other languages (for example, Bengali in India) not narrowly confined to the already established modernist English literature.

In going over Paz's literary production, one has to acknowledge his repeated confrontation not only with Time and History, but also with *time* and *history*. Among the Western readers of Paz's poetry, only Wilson comes close to grasping this aspect of Paz's struggle to be a poet.

> The active, bitter conflict between poetry and history generates moments of freedom, an epiphany that Paz calls 'poetic instants.' Consequently, the poet's reactions to history become a test of his moral fiber. *At this level Paz's desire to become a poet, to rebel against necessity has led him to explore the functions of the poet and poem in society, both Western and Eastern, almost anthropologically. This desire to work out his salvation as a poet inevitably invokes the fatality of having been born a Mexican. This implies belonging to the marginalized provinces of the great empires of the twentieth century (Europe, the United States, Russia, Japan).* Thus Paz's measuring himself with the world's great poets and thinkers takes on poignancy, he was not born in one of the centers of power and had to fight his way out of a limited nationalistic tradition to discover his true roots, his *mexicandad* . . . his contemporaneity with all who suffer history, his freedom. (my emphasis)

Leaving aside the inclusion of Japan among the empires (for it is another problematic non-Western, actually a non-Indo-European cultural formation), Wilson posits part of the problem of being a poet from the periphery accurately. However, Paz is also a poet of this acute, cruel, and infernally complex century when empires crumble and the old sometimes gives way to the new only for part of the old structure to reappear in another guise. Thus any polar confrontation, while a better way of bringing into relief a poet's inner landscape than the traditional interpretative criticism can only be a start. In Paz's case it is a promising start, as Wilson realizes.

> Paz's vueltas (return) from living abroad (Spain, the United States, France, India) to Mexico have engendered his most fertile thinking about values. This moral stance, tested by the accidents of history, travel, change, love, aging, reading, and so on, supplies a remarkable *coherency* to the *diversity* of his work. (my emphasis)

However, reading Paz in too 'coherent' a fashion carries its own dangers. It may not be the best way to reveal or even to know the site of conflicts that lend his poems such poignancy, resilience, and power. Wilson's reading of Paz, although insightful and admirable for its consistency, ultimately locks itself in the 'prison house of language' by not recognizing its own logocentrism. It ends up striving after the project of unearthing the changing but essential Paz, a presence which cannot be found because it is always already absent. I will try to show that Paz's own poetry grapples with this presence/absence/change problem in a way that reveals a field of forces running the entire gamut from the unconscious creative impulses to the politics of utopia.

It is remarkable that Paz's texts defy simple, interpretative gestures. By enmeshing multiple, sometimes parallel, always polyphonic linguistic collages together, Paz has, since the mid-fifties, moved beyond even the modified modernism of his early poems. In poems like *Blanco* and *Vuelta*, even in his repeated revisions of these and some other poems, Paz seems intent on teasing the readers on, but he also has a serious purpose. The textuality his work presents is not simple replication. Like Kierkegaard his problem is "how to repeat without replication?" Such an approach to his text plays down any notion of commentary as a hermeneutic exercise performed on an autotelic text. As Barthes has pointed out (such) a text has "other texts present in it, at varying levels in more or less recognizable forms: the texts of the previous and the surrounding culture." Barthes goes on to claim that:

> Any text is a new tissue of past citations. Bits of codes, formulae, rhythmic models, fragments of social languages pass into the text and are redistributed within it . . . . (Barthes, "Theory of the Text," in *Untying the Text*, p. 39)

Thus Paz seems to deliberately expose his poems to an intertextual field in the sense Jameson has defined the term. That is to say, far from denying the traces of the other (or in fact others), Paz seems intent on highlighting these traces as much as possible. Starting with *Piedra de sol*, or perhaps even before that with *¿Águila o sol?* in the beginning of the fifties, Paz invites (rather than suppressing for the sake of coherence) multiple meanings and offers a delirium of excess in his poems which is always already departing from both Anglo-Saxon modernism and simple varieties of surrealism. In Paz there is no simple economy of text, no simple political thematic organization, no transcendental signifier/signified that can be used to unlock 'the interpretation' of his works. In spite of this (or perhaps because of this), I would argue, his texts are densely packed with poetic/political subversion.

(2)

There are two overtly political periods in Paz's life. One belongs to the decade of the thirties, the other since his resignation from the Mexican diplomatic service as a protest against the massacre of students in Mexico City in 1968. In 1936-37, Paz broke off his formal education and went to Yucatan to set up a school near Merida. In his *Poemas* there is a 'final' version of a poem he first published in 1941, called "Entre la piedra y la flor" (Between the Stone and the

Flower). Paz began this poem during his stay in Yucatan. Explaining his later revisions, Paz insisted on the *political* intentions of the poem: an exposé of the rule of the dead hand of capital over living human bodies and spirits. Although Paz went to Spain the next year, he never fought in the Spanish civil war. However, he did observe in Spain a fusion of human spirit in revolt against terror, a unity that affirmed life against death. He would come back to this keenly felt experience of the possibility of a community of autonomous sub-jects (Foucault and Lacan notwithstanding) time and again. In the previously mentioned long, mythic poem *Piedra de sol* which marks a transition (but not from a political to non-political phase as some critics maintain), Paz is led to juxtapose the bombing in Madrid with lovers "fused together while making love."

> Madrid, 1937
> in the Plaza del Angel women
> were sewing, and singing with their children,
> when the siren sounded and the screams,
> houses kneeling down in the dust,
> towers splitting, façades gave in
> and the hurricane noise of the engines
>
> *(Poemas* 268-69)

This barbarity and utter destruction of fascism is contrasted with

> the two naked bodies make love
> to defend our share of eternity,
> our ration of time and paradise,
> to touch our roots, to recover ourselves,
> to recover our inheritance, stolen
> by the thieves of life a thousand centuries ago . . . .
>
> *(Poemas* 268-69)

Here Paz has already advanced beyond the politics of power, but not, as I have mentioned before, beyond politics. For, recovering the legacy of "the garden," another image used by Paz with increasing frequency, is not possible without fusing life and poetry—and life, social life, includes a political life. The triumph of fascism and the corruption of communism under Stalin left Paz in despair. For him renouncing party politics was easy, but it raised new problems of theory and practice. After all, can a man be a man in isolation? What is poetry, if not communication? *Soledad* (solitude) must be explored not for the sake of solipsistic self-justification, but to understand the limits of man and possibility of the community which Paz experienced in revolutionary Spain.

In 1941 Paz wrote "I want to find the deepest voice inside me . . . the insoluble solution . . . ."

This period also coincides with his reading of Nietzsche— "Only Nietzsche is capable of comfort."

When the retreat from direct politics is not an escape, it raises questions that are strategic in terms of life's choices. For Paz the strategic choice seems to have been a deeper exploration of the self through the medium of words. And here we come up against the question: how does a marginalized poet from the margins of the empires find his voice? Paz's answer to this question produced a polyphony of textured poems and essays. But at the most palpable level, that of poetry, we are led to see an exploration of the "moral sense" (Paz's term) in relation to natural freedom, human integrity, passion and sexuality. Why this occurs is also partly related to Paz's relationship with the French as opposed to the English modernists. But here, too, there are complications ahead.

(3)

Paz had come to surrealism through the influence of Luis Cernuda. When Paz wrote in 1942 that communion was still possible in poetry, he was exploring a psychic field that was possible because of surrealism. He also tried to project his own psychic landscape into the writings of modernists like Eliot. It is interesting that like many poets from the periphery, some of whom were left wing, he (mis)read Eliot's *The Waste Land* as a description of a historical reality, our own purgatory in our time. Ironically, Eliot himself never encouraged such a reading. On the contrary, he mobilized an interpretation along the lines of a spiritual journey. Paz also shows an appreciation for reality and aversion to systems that would certainly run counter to high modernism in the Anglo-Saxon world. At the same time, poetry becomes for him a dialogue with the world, moving between the two poles of solitude and communion. Paz's heterodoxy would evolve into a morality and politics of the body and not an escape from it. It is also important that he understood American capitalism directly by having been there. Thus, unlike some former revolutionaries, his renunciation of direct politics did not lead him to a reactionary status quo–oriented political stance.

Yet the stubborn problem of bringing poetry into life remained. In 1945 Paz published a poem called "La calle" (The Street). Here the poet is far from sure-footed, blindly tripping over stones that are dumb.

> where no one awaits or follows me
> where I follow a man who falters
>
> ("La calle")

Later Paz would talk about the phenomenon of *ningunuendo* (nobodying) in the industrialized, capitalist societies.

Perhaps it was lucky again for Paz that he went to a Paris that was humiliated. For a brief few years devastated Paris (or Berlin or Tokyo) would receive the citizens of the periphery on more or less equal terms. Although aware of a certain amount of exoticism with respect to Mexico, that country being the surrealist landscape par excellence, Paz attempted a synthesis rather than playing up his Mexican-ness. There may even have been an initial reversal of cultural oppositions which today, after Derrida, we might think of as being deconstructive. Yet Breton, while accepting Paz, made him represent mysterious Mexico, understandable in a man of Breton's temperament, but hardly an embrace without irony. Thus a return to Mexico on Paz's own terms would be necessary.

In ¿*Águila o sol*? Paz already declared his rupture with the earlier lyrical period. He also celebrated the discovery that poetry—surrealist poetry—can be action. Even at this stage he offered his anguished battle with language for the reader to feel the disturbing and palpable violence of a clash among thinking, feeling, and being. The language of the first part called *Trabajos del poeta* bears resemblance to Henri Michaux in its continuous leaps and metamorphoses of expressions. It is a language that is deliberately undomesticated, not put in the service of the poet. The fact that this attitude to the relation between the poet and the language was a conscious choice is revealed by Paz in his reflections on writing:

> Each time we are served by words, we mutilate them. But the poet is not served by words. He is their servant. In serving them, he returns them to the plentitude of their nature, makes them recover their being.
>
> (*El arco y la lira*, trans. Ruth Simms, 37)

The prose poems of ¿*Águila o sol*? (Paz would declare later: "There is no prose . . . everything is poetry in language," eliminating an unnecessary distinction much as John Cage did for music) confront the many selves in the itinerant Mexican Paz. One called "El ramo azul" (The Blue Bouquet) included in the second section called "Arenas movedizas" (Quicksand) is particularly interesting for dealing with the threat of mutilation and the ambiguities of being a Mexican.

A man (the poet-narrator) wakes up at night and walks off into a Mexican pueblo for a smoke. He soon realizes that someone is following him. A dialogue in "authentic" Mexican dialect takes place between him and an Indian peasant who apparently had followed him. The Indian demands the narrator's eyes as a bouquet for his fiancee. "She wants a little bunch of blue eyes," he explains. The narrator has to kneel down. A light is held up to his eyes as he stares dumbly at the machete. The ending is almost like that of a Maupassant short story. The Indian apologizes, realizing his mistake: "Well, they are not really blue, señor, please pardon me." For the narrator there is nothing left to do but to stumble back to his inn and then to flee.

Paz's very language of macabre fantasy/stark realism exposes the reader to the treacherous nature of any fixed notions about the identity of the poet-narrator and the integrity of the text. Next to the cosmopolitan European poet (Paz, whose eyes are, in reality, blue) or rather within this mask/reality there is also the reality/mask of *lo mexicano*. Indeed the *pachuco* and the *indio* are alive in Paz, threatening him and his text from becoming a universalistic, "modern" text, which will, in effect, reflect merely the dominance of the cultural imperialism of Europe. By contextualizing his surrealism and by letting the pores and fissures of his text show, Paz tends towards a radical form of discourse which stands apart from the conventional modern or even postmodern varieties.

Paz's long literary and intellectual *vuelta* (return) is accomplished in the truly epic and awesome poem *Piedra de sol*. Even the structure with the beginning and the ending stanza being identical reinforces the theme of eternal recurrence (Nietzsche's influence again?) which opens the poems:

> a willow of crystal, a poplar of water
> a tall fountain the wind arches over
> a deep-rooted tree but dancing away
> a river course that curves,
> advances, recedes, comes back again
> forever arriving . . . .
>
> (*Piedra de sol*)

Yet the poem itself is a meandering through a hall of mirrors, labyrinths, and traps. The body of a woman (several or the same, called Melusine, Eloise, Persephone, Maria and other names) merges surrealistically with various natural objects and the stone-goddess-nature comes alive at the end. This rich poem, densely packed with images and sonorous words, is made to perform a magic, the limits of which are also there as traces of palpable violence.

Thus the violence of history has to be acknowledged in the question

> Does nothing happen, only a blink?
> —and the feast, the exile, the primary crime,
> the jawbone of the ass, the opaque thud
> and the incredulous glance of the dead falling
> on an ash-covered plain, Agamemnon's
> great bellow, the scream of Cassandra
> over and again, louder than the screams of the sea,
> Socrates in chains . . . .
> . . . .
> the jackal discoursing in the ruins of
> Nineveh, the shade before Brutus
> on the eve of the battle, Moctezuma
> insomniac on his bed of thorns,
> the carriage riding towards death
> —the interminable ride counted
> minute by minute by Robespierre,
> his broken jaw between his hands—,
> Churruca on his casklike scarlet throne
> the numbered steps of Lincoln
> as he left for the theater,
> the death-rattle of Trotsky and his howl
> like a boar . . . .
>
> (*Piedra de sol*)

Notice here the inclusion of mythical, fictional, and historical sufferers of violence. Regardless of the geometry of spatiality ("real," three dimensional man, or imaginary zero/infinite dimensional characters) or the arithmetic of time (before/after, past/present) the deliberate mixing makes them all alike. There is violence in history and in reason, but also in imagination. This violence is the "rational" man's other, this is the goddess of stone, the teeth mother, or Kali drinking blood from human skull. After Lacan, and Deleuze and Guattari's Anti-Oedipus, we may want to change the metaphors to name-of-the-father or name-of-the-despot, though these are more prosaic. However, the fact remains that the darkness of history is deep within us. Suppressing this and trying to create a presence that is merely the appearance of the good life would be self-deception. Paz apparently has read Nietzsche all too well. Thus we are left with the image of the "foaming mouth of the prophet, his scream/the scream of the hangman and the scream of the victim . . . ."

In spite of the carefully chosen circular form and the marked transitions at the end, Paz is altogether too successful in impressing the reader with imagery like the following:

> afternoon of saltpeter and stone,
> armed with invisible razors,
> in red, indescribable script
> you write on my skin and the wounds
> dress me like a suit of flames
>
> > (*Piedra de sol*)

Even at the end, in spite of all his effort he cannot erase the trace of psyche which exclaims:

> I burn endlessly, I search for water,
> but in your eyes there is no water
>
> > (*Piedra de sol*)

The ending of this poem is a *tour de force* by a poet of the highest sensibility, and yet we know, after Barthes, Derrida, Lacan, Foucault, and Deleuze and Guattari that even the greatest of the writers cannot write a closed text, appearance to the contrary. Borrowing from Bakhtin I would observe that the text of *Piedra de sol* is "still warm from the struggle and hostility, as yet unsolved and still fraught with hostile intentions and accents." That, in my view, is also what makes this long poem such a powerful transitional text.

(4)

It is then not surprising that Paz's wrestling with the issues of identity/difference, text/context, morality in life/morality in poetry could not end with *Piedra de sol*. The turning point would not come until his long stay in India (1962-1968) and his immersion into both

Madhyamika and tantra. In this phase Paz also took a critical stance towards the structuralism of Levi-Strauss. Although he never articulated in prose the kind of critical readings that Barthes or Derrida would perform later, a discussion of his late poems will show a distinct post-structuralist tendency.

In India Paz most creditably rejected the way of the *Sadhu* and his self-involved way of inner salvation. Paz describes such a *Sadhu* as an *idolo podrido* (a rotten idol). However, confronting the mystical tradition, the suppressed other of the West, and though deformed and sometimes commercialized, a living cultural tradition in a peripheral community like India made the poet pose the previous problems more starkly in terms of words versus silence, invocation of the woman as the other in surrealism versus the woman as both woman in flesh and mother goddess, poetry or contemplation as a substitute for action versus moral action as being indispensable. India with its contradictions, its past of rich speculation and practice and its hopeless present of inaction jolted not just Paz the poet, but also Paz the man himself. In *Tumba de Amir Khusrú* he juxtaposed the brilliant poet-musician Amir Khusrú with the wandering dervish theologian Nizamuddin.

> Tombs, two names, their stories:
> Nizamuddin the travelling theologian,
> Amir Khusrú, tongue of the parrot
> the saint and the poet.

But the poem itself is a reflection and *partly* self-reflexive. Showing remarkable ambivalence towards poetry, Paz states, "Amir Khursú, parrot or mocking bird," ending the poem with the realization, "every poem is time and it burns!"

Another poem shows this oscillation between eternity and now, the contrast between the poet's temporality and the mystic's *nirvana* even more vividly.

> I am in the unsteady hour
> The car races between houses

By the light of a lamp I write
Absolutes eternities
and their outskirts
    are not my themes
I hunger for life and also for death
I know what I believe and that is what I write
Advent of the instant

                       (*Poemas* 425-26)

This is poignantly defiant and acknowledges the full frailty of art, especially poetry when confronted with the plentitude of being. Paz's solution is not to lapse into a mystical quiescence, or to find his way back to some political *vita activa*, although such explorations are not ruled out completely. Rather, he chooses to stay with and within his art and to give it as much life as possible at each moment with the full consciousness of the treacherous nature of the whole enterprise. Out of this Sisyphus-like striving comes a fuller realization of the role of Eros in life, and a need to demystify the surrealistic conception of woman as the ideal other half. Out of the imperative for showing the fortitude and moral courage to pursue the project of constructing a life and an art would also come the political phase after 1968. Paz's concern for the possibilities of unrepressed eroticism (the ideal of tantra) and the necessary human freedom runs parallel to his increased recognition that democracy has to be fought for actively in the most recent phase of his life and art. As mentioned previously, his contacts with Asia played no small preparatory role in this. I now want to focus on some specific texts to elaborate this point further.

(5)

Paz dealt at length with his first encounters with Asia already in "Mutra" in New Delhi and "¿No hay salida?" in Tokyo, both written in 1952. As Jason Wilson rightly observes

> "Mutra" is a crucial self-defining poem. The title places the poem in a town just south of Delhi and deals decisively with a 'temptation

49

to cede to Hindu or Buddhist mysticism.' Paz does not seek the 'dissolution' of his consciousness, but its active involvement with historical life.

Determined to be involved with time (history) at the same time as he condemns it, Paz did not allow the prolonged encounter with India to create in him a solipsistic surrender to quietism. At the same time he came to understand the limits of language and the possibilities of erotic love in even more poignant terms than he did during his surrealistic period. In both *Blanco* and "Carta de Creencia," two superb long poems, he uses language to reveal both its possibilities and its limitations.

In "Carta de Creencia" the very first thing that is called into question, by pointing out its uncertainty, is time itself.

> The uncertain territory
> between the night and day
> is neither light nor shadow
> it is time.

The uncertainty of writing on a darkening page, in a precarious temporal pause is underlined immediately after this. Writing/Speech/Words, all are uncertain.

> Words are bridges
> also traps, jails, wells.
> I speak to you: you do not hear me

Yet a poet who has chosen the social life must also participate in the making of poems with these uncertain bridges. He realizes that even love is an equivocal word ("*Amor es una palabra equivoca*"). The second and third parts of this poem, "Cantata," is a poetic reflection on the incertitudes as well as the multiplicities contained in the word *amor*.

> Desire invents it,
> Deprivations and lacerations give it life,

jealousy drives it
custom kills it.
     A gift
a punishment.
     Rage, beatitude
a knot: life and death.
     A wound
that is the rose of resurrection
A word:
     speaking it, we speak.

However, affirming that in speaking this word *amor* we speak ourselves cannot dissolve all questions. A series of further reflections and probes must follow:

Love commences in the flesh
where does it end?
     If it is a phantasm
it is made flesh in a body:
     if it is a body
it dissipates at a touch.

Meditations on love, especially the overcoming of the male-centered surrealist view helps him grasp that the word *love* is

Fatal mirror:
the image of desire disappears
you drown yourself in your own reflections.

To face the fact of earthly love without the benefit of mysticism; to explore *amor* through words and nothing but a poem exposes the poet to the ravages of time:

Time is evil
     the instant
is the fall

Yet the naturalistic position that love is a "permutation/ . . . in the history of primigeneal cells/ and their innumerable divisions

51

. . ." does not lead to any diminution of joy in its celebration.

On the contrary, in another image as striking as the ones in *Piedra de sol*, Paz recognizes the magical power of love to transmute:

> Invention, transfiguration:
> the girl becomes a fountain
> her hair—a constellation,
> a woman asleep an island.

This may be Nietzschean *amor fati*, but it is also deeper than that, for there is no need for a metaphysical justification. The coda to this cantata reveals with deceptive simplicity the depth Paz has reached since his earlier surrealistic conception of love and eroticism:

> Perhaps to love is to learn
> to walk through this world.
> To learn to be quiet
> like the oak and the linden of the fable
> To learn to see
> Your glance scatters seeds
> It planted a tree
>   I speak
> because you shake its leaves

The liberation that results from even an indirect confrontation with the logocentrism and phallo-centrism of (Western) civilization is not only the recognition of the limits and contingencies of language *à la Nagarjuna* or the Zen masters, but it is also an affirmation of the possibilities of our very contingencies and a willingness to surrender. It is to surrender that part we call ego, to part with the ego's psychological slogan "where there was id there will be ego." At the same time it is not a surrender to the chaotic forces of infantile strivings. Rather it is learning how to let go of narcissism and to return to something like the logic of the unconscious as Deleuze and Guattari describe it in *Anti-Oedipus* and *A Thousand Plateaus*.

It is indeed ironic, as Susan Suleiman points out in *Subversive Intent: Gender, Politics and Avant-Garde* that the avant-garde, including the surrealists, could not go beyond the patriarchal conversion of the woman as the other, the ideal partner of a split and alienated man. In some of his late poems, Paz seems to have progressed beyond the simple male/female polarity. In *Vuelta* there is a striking poem, *Nocturno de San Ildefonso* (Nocturne of San Ildefonso), which closes with the poet affirming the blood circulating in his head as he looks at his wife in flesh. She is alive, next to him, a *"fuente en la noche"* (fountain in the night). The serene surrender of ego is almost inaudible in the last line:

> I trust myself to her calm flow

Beyond love, it also seems that in *Vuelta*, Paz also returned to "real" (in the sense of Jameson, as that which hurts) life. Even as he recognizes that

> The good, we wanted the good:
>   to make the world right
> We did not lack integrity:
>   we lacked humility
>
> (*Poemas* 634)

Facing the wreckage of youthful dreams he is able to affirm:

> Fraternity over emptiness
>
> (*Poemas* 637)

Not respecting his own texts, but respecting the dynamic flow of the unconscious pulses and their conscious materialization, Paz revised a number of his earlier works. The comparison of some of the changes in the poem entitled *Vuelta* in its two versions in 1971 and 1976 shows the deepening protest against authority and opening up of even more space for an inner discourse. Not only is there addition (twenty-eight additional lines in 1976) but also respatialization through typographical reorganization ("language poetry" comes readily to mind as an analogy). Paz is more explicit in denouncing

53

escapism. For example, a section in 1971 which reads simply:

> Germination of nightmare
> in the stomach of the cinemas.

is expanded to read

> Germination of nightmare
> infestation of leprous images
> in the belly brains lungs
> in the sex of the temple and the college
> in the cinemas

It is possible to read in this use of synechdocical part-objects like "belly, brain, lungs" and a conceit-like expansion the criticism of the whole body of the society, but there is more. The nightmare germinates everywhere. Therefore, is the word immune from it? Given the radical doubt in which Paz has already thrown the surrealistic moves of equaling word with action, the answer implied would seem to be negative. Here we are brought face to face with the realization that history, real history (even putting both the words under erasure) involves palpable institutions and genuine suffering. Words can no longer stand in where moral action is necessary. It reminds one of Foucault's comments to Deleuze vis-à-vis the intellectuals in May 1968:

> . . . the masses no longer need him to gain knowledge: they *know* perfectly well, without illusion; they know far better than he and they are certainly capable of expressing themselves. But there exists a system of power that blocks, prohibits, and invalidates this discourse and this knowledge . . . . Intellectuals are themselves agents of this system of power—the idea of their responsibility for "consciousness" and discourse forms part of the system. (Foucault, "Intellectuals and Power," in *Language, Counter-Memory, Practice*, p. 207)

This, Paz has known all his life, Paz the wayfarer and the itinerant poet, at once the voice of *lo mexicano* and a human being with no country.

54

In his lifelong devotion to struggle with words and authorities, Paz, like Sor Juana Inés de la Cruz of an earlier period, the subject of his detailed study called *Sor Juana Inés de la Cruz o las trampas de la fe* (Sor Juana Inés de la Cruz or the Traps of Faith) had to confront the rituals, codes, hierarchies and dogmas of the twentieth century. Creating poems against despotism and the tyranny of time, Paz may have reached a tentative realization in *El mono gramático* with his resolve to explore *"mas ser sin yo"* (more being without ego). Given his earlier encounter with "the real," renouncing the "symbolic" stance of ego would seem to be another step towards freedom. Perhaps Paz can accomplish this and the West can accomplish what Paz suggested: "rediscover the secret of the incarnation of the poem into collective life, the fiesta." Perhaps all this and much more, but not without struggle. This is where the opacity of the text joins the opacity of life that has to be lived just as the text that has to be written over and over. Life, like the text, is a palimpsest.

Works Discussed:

Barthes, Roland. "Theory of the Text." *Untying the Text.* Ed. Robert Young. London: Routledge, Kegan, and Paul, 1981.

Deleuze, Gilles and Félix Guattari. *Kafka: Towards a Minor Literature.* Trans. Dana Polan. Minneapolis: University of Minnesota Press, 1986. Qtd. by Lawrence Venuti in "Simpatico," *Substance*, Vol. 20, No. 2, 1991.

Foucault, Michel. "Intellectuals and Power." *Language, Counter-Memory, Practice.* Ed. Donald F. Bouchard. Ithaca: Cornell University Press, 1987.

Wilson, Jason. *Octavio Paz.* Boston: Twayne Publishers, 1987.

EROS, SEMIOTICS OF SPACE, AND AVANT-GARDE IN OCTAVIO PAZ:
HOMAGE AND EROSIONS

Emil Volek

> Eyes that can see
> Oh what a rarity
> *William Carlos Williams*

Towards the end of the forties, Octavio Paz (b. 1914), who was already then considered one of the most distinguished Mexican writers, entered his „violent season": turning his back on the cherished mentors from the *Contemporáneos* group, he abandoned their brand of „pure poetry" - - following the postsymbolist line of Paul Valéry and Juan Ramón Jiménez - - for one of the most virulent and daring movements of the avant-garde: surrealism.[1] Actually, what is surprising is that it took him so long: as he himself recalls it to Guibert (213), he came in contact with surrealists as early as 1938; during the war (*Búsqueda* 63), he established close friendship with their „colony" in Mexico and, when the war ended, he associated himself with their group in France.

This was not the first time that surrealism was used by a leading Hispanic poet to exorcise a diehard tradition. In the late twenties, some of the brightest members of the so-called „Generation of 1927" - - like Federico García Lorca, Vicente Aleixandre, Luis Cernuda or Rafael Alberti - - took up its challenge and exploded the very same tradition of „pure poetry" which had shaped their poetic beginnings. In either case, the aesthetic lesson of „pure poetry" was not completely forgotten and left its imprint on the following surrealist phase.[2] However, the historical parallel ends here: while in Spain the surrealist craze was thwarted by the oncoming cataclysms of the thirties, for Paz, the „violent season" of the fifties was but a way-station towards an even more experimental and explosive period of the sixties and seventies.

I.

The cycles ¿*Aguila o sol?* (1951; *Eagle or Sun?*), *La estación violenta* (1958; Violent Season), and the essay *El arco y la lira* (1956; *The Bow and the Lyre*) probably offer the best of Pazian poetry and criticism from the surrealist decade. In the Mexican writer, both of these activities go hand in hand, as in so many cases of the postsymbolist literature, and together advance one of the most ambitious and self-conscious literary projects in Spanish America.

Arco is the first sustained attempt of Paz to formulate a kind of philosophy of modern poetry.[3] Romantic speculation, surrealist concept of art and its political stance combine under the Heideg-

---

[1] *Contemporáneos* (1928-1931; Contemporaries) emerged as one of the principal literary journals of the Mexican avant-garde.

[2] So far, Wilson's is the best account of the Pazian surrealist connection, although some of his information concerning the reception of surrealism in Mexico needs to be corrected; see, e.g., the special issue of *Artes Visuales* entitled *Surrealismo en México* 1974; Surrealism in Mexico).

[3] Paz understands the concept of literary modernity rather traditionally, as spanning the period roughly from romanticism to the end of the „historical" avant-garde of the twenties. In this way, he tacitly identifies *literary* modernity with the strand of our *historical* modernity extending from the Enlightenment. This is probably one of the intrinsic reasons why he has recently joined the clamor for the „end of modernity" - modernity reduced, for the convenience of its „postmodern" critics, to one of its threads - and why his criticism of this „Western modernity" has become more and more apocalyptic and exorcistic (*Hijos, Signo*). For a different approach see our *Cuatro claves* (9-17).

61

gerian umbrella. Poetry is viewed as an inquiry into being effected through language. But more specifically - - more romantically - - it is a search for transcendence, for the „other shore" (la otra orilla), and for the other. It is a mythical quest in which and through which fragmented man is reunited with his „other self" and, together, the splinters recover their original nature. Thus, leading man back to his lost paradise, poetry, as envisioned by Paz, transcends language and history (13).

Fortunately, this somewhat exalted dream of art is revitalized by a parallel drawn between poetry and eros, and, above all, by the mythology surrounding sexual union. The two emplotments mirror each other: eros is charted as an allegory - - as a metaphoric incarnation - - of poetry. Erotic love is the ecstatic moment in which man communicates with his original nature, with his lost self, alienated from him by the drudgery of everyday life and the repression imposed by his heritage. Like in poetrymaking, eros extends a bridge to the other and, through it, man achieves fulfillment and transcendence. Love can transcend, continues this poetic vision, only if it liberates, to the point of transgression and illicitness. In „Piedra de sol" 'Sun Stone', which is one of the most spectacular poems of Estación violenta, romantic mysticism and surrealist erotic revolution combine to give us the whole range of this liberating love. However, at this point of confluence of surrealism and mysticism, eros overflows the crystalline boundaries of allegory and manages to infuse the metaphysical skeleton with considerable flesh and blood. Indeed, this „surplus" rivals the eroticism of the major contemporary Hispanic poets, like Vicente Aleixandre or Pablo Neruda, who were also „liberated" by surrealism.

It will be interesting to observe how both emplotments will change and, especially, how the poetic discourse itself will begin to explore the possibilities obscurely plotted by the latter: how a metaphoric ploy will become a dynamic force shaping the very letter, the very textuality of Pazian discourse. One of the seminal passages of Arco will set us on the track to start following that change:

> ....in the amorous act consciousness is like the wave that, after overcoming the obstacle, before breaking rises to a crest in which everything - - form and movement, upward thrust and force of gravity - - achieves a balance without support, sustained by itself. Quietude of movement. And just as we glimpse a fuller life, more life than life, through a beloved body, we discern the fixed beam of poetry through the poem. That instant contains every instant. Without ceasing to flow, time stops, overflowing itself.(14)

This formulation is well worth underscoring as a kind of paradigm that will help us to highlight the subsequent changes. The resolution given here to the quest for the reunion with the other - - suspension of the flux of things by the poetic and erotic ecstasis is distinctly mystical and Schopenhauerian. This seems to be the earliest layer of mythologies framing Pazian philosophy of modern poetry, and corresponds to the „season" of „Poesía de soledad y poesía de comunión" 'Poetry of Solitude and Poetry of Communion' of the forties (Peras 117-31). In other parts of Arco, especially in its version from 1967 which spans the fifties and sixties,[4] and in his subsequent major critical contributions, this resolution is fulfilled by different philosophical concepts. A kind of „vertical," paradigmatic reading of Paz's critical work - - similar to the Proppian approach to the corpus of Russian fairy tales - - , uncovers, provisionally, the following framing myths that supersede one another: the Heideggerian trinity of Poetry, Language, and Being (Arco); the ahistorical, near Platonic structures fathered by Claude Lévi-Strauss (the eponymous book); the empty plenitude of Buddhist nirvana (Conjunciones) and the vacuousness and dispersion of textual meaning

---

[4] The second edition of Arco attempts to bridge the gap between this mystical vision and the technical and ideological input of French structuralism of the sixties. The two versions of Arco were aptly compared by Rodríguez Monegal. Rewriting - the overt and covert updating and „polishing" - of his texts is an obsession in Paz, and a possible nightmare for his critics (see Santí for some incisive remarks in this regard).

62

preached by the post-structuralist semiology of Derrida (*Mono gramático*). This shifting fulfillment of the quest keeps pace remarkably with Western intellectual developments as they swept through Europe from the forties to the early seventies; even the biography of the poet - - his long diplomatic service in India in the sixties - - coincides with the new upsurge of Western fascination with the East.

On the other hand, all these elements together sustain still another frame of Pazian thinking: his prophetic critique of the modern Western concept of Historiy - - of History as a lineal, teleological path of Progress and Perfection - as envisioned by Enlightened Reason.[5] Unlike many of his Spanish-American contemporaries, he does not stop at the comfortable criticism of the „bourgeois heritage" and the evils of capitalism, nor does he refrain from calling into question what was the sacred superstition of our times, the „scientific" Marxism - - also an off-shoot of the Enlightenment. What is so interesting and radical about him is that he goes on to question the very „roots" of Western tradition. Criticism, of course, at least implicitly, calls for other options. In Paz, the „West side" story will be checked and balanced by the „East side." We will turn to it in more detail shortly. Beneath Pazian work there lies yet another quest by Western man: a search for alternatives to the burden of his own tradition. The poet finds them in poetry, in love, in the rebellion of the body, in the dissolution of time, and the East will add some spice of its own, too.

All this may not supply nor replace a strong philosophy, but this intellectual and poetic vision certainly is a powerful *mythopoeia*, a necessary springboard towards any poetic and critical creation. Even the plight of contemporary philosophy, her Sisyphean task of demolishing the structures and traces left behind by mythology and by ideology in our social ritual and discourse, cannot fail to be transformed into such a *mythopoeia*, although negative and seemingly enjoying its „nihilism." Pazian critique of Western modernity and his poetic quest for alternatives not only creates the third emplotment of his universe, which will be fraught with as many myths and metaphors as the other ones, but it actually turns him into the most typical Western man.

.The ecstatic moment of love, „the time fulfilled in itself" (*Arco* 14; our trans.), also harbors an implicit denial of Time and of History. The momentary arresting of the metaphysical „will to life," invented for aesthetic purposes by Schopenhauer, is turned against their modern ideations. Violent shifts of time and space in „El himno entre ruinas" 'Hymn Among Ruins' and the cyclical universe of „Piedra de sol" reflect this criticism.

The poetic philosophy or philosophical poetics of love will be radically questioned in the sixties.

II.

Paz took full advantage of the possibilities that opened up to him in the early sixties, those delayed „happy years" after all sorts of wars and before other could break out with full force again. First came his close encounter with the East during the time, between 1962 and 1968, that he served as the Mexican ambasador to India.[6] He was not the only major Spanish-American writer to be exposed directly to the East. One would have to name at least one other Mexican, José Juan Tablada, as well as Pablo Neruda, the Ecuatorian Jorge Carrera Andrade or the Cuban Severo Sarduy; it would be a fascinating study to compare their experiences (see Durán for some hints). But, among all of them, he penetrated deepest into the web of Oriental thought and integrated it

---

[5] Goya, who saw considerable Napoleonic „progress" in his time, used an ambiguous phrase as a part of and also as a title for his engraving „The Dream of Reason Produces Monsters" (from *Caprichos*). Did he actually foresee that both the absence and the presence of *logos* produce monsters, only different kinds of them? Borges would say that our choice is purely aesthetic. On the other hand, Jung might remark that this invention of Enlightenment fits remarkably well into the Western pattern of extrovert tradition characterized by the need of Salvation from the outside: Utopia, Jesus, Progress, Light from the East, the Red Army-all the armies of the night of salvation.

[6] He resigned that post after the October 2 Tlatelolco massacre and broke with the Government of PRI-the Institutional Revolutionary Party-and with its mask of „institutionalized" revolution.

most intimately into his own literary and critical project. Even so, one can only wonder about the depth of his understanding. For example, *Conjunciones y disyunciones* (1969; *Conjunctionas and Disjunctions)*, which is the critical counterpart to the poems of *Ladera Este* (1969; East Side), is both dazzling and puzzling. It is even more so if we consider that, as Said or Todorov have shown, the Western „dialogue" with the „other" has not been precisely a history of success. *Conjunciones* displays erudition quite uncommon for a Western intellectual; but it also baffles one because all that knowledge and all the bridges opened toward the East follow the neat - - all too neat - - structuralist matrices of symmetries and inversions introduced by Lévi-Strauss.

One is tempted to paraphrase Borges and ask, if it is doubtful that history makes any sense, is it not even more so to have it draw, in the East and in the West, these rigorous calligraphis patterns? It might appear that the critic of the Western telos has been caught yet in another allegory and teleological trap. We could go one step further and question not only the methods of organizing that knowledge but the very attitude towards the East that transpires through *Conjunciones*. For example, to what degree does Paz succumb to the so-called „Eurocentrism"? Guided by his „natural" sense of centrality, Western man has imposed his views and disseminated his visions all around the globe. But there were differences: while in the New World his fantasy blended with Utopia, in the East, in the luxurious and sensual East, he deposited his libidinous dreams, his desire for individual fulfillment, and, later, his search for values that might bolter his own faltering tradition. This seems to be exactly what the poet is seeking and what he finds on the East side. As he himself lucidly says elsewhere, „It would be a mistake to believe that we are looking to Buddhism for a truth that is foreign to our tradition: what we are seeking is a confirmation of a truth we already know" (*Corriente* 102).

Whatever the value of the bridges that Paz engineered between East and West, the East influenced some of the key elements of his *mythopoeia*. Buddhist pantheism and Tantrist eroticism left the deepest imprint upon him. Buddhism subverted the concept of transcendence, of the „other shore": romantic mysticism had to yield to the empty plenitude and to the transcendence-in-the-presence of *nirvana*. Tantrism, in its turn, stressed in Paz the cosmic and violent dimension of erotic love; in this tradition, the surrealist subconscious and the experiments of Marquis de Sade were rescued from the „underground" and were elevated to and socialized by a public ritual of religious order.

The sixties were also the hey-day of the structuralist, semiological, and linguistic carnival which focused anew on social communication, on its codes, and on the semiotics of its messages. Paz was especially attracted to the work of Lévi-Strauss. He was fascinated by the latter's formulation of the latent structures of myths in terms of binary oppositions permitting him to put in order - - perhaps all too rigorous - - the storehouse of world mythologies, and welcomed the concept of structures (in French structuralism equivalent to codes) that seemed to defy, encompass, and annihilate History. In the volume dedicated to the French ethnologist, Buddhism surprisingly appears as a version of and as a complement to this structuralism, and *vice versa*. Through the fragile bridge built by the poet, they converge as critiques of the modern Western concept of History as Progress and, supposedly, abolish its very possibility. Here the poetic mythology becomes ritual exorcism. Of course, this plot is too neat - - too „classical" - - to effectively model any referential, historical reality - - whatever semiotic or ideological values we may ascribe to this concept - - , especially when both Buddhism and structuralism are accepted for their face value, without any criticism.[7]

---

[7] In Western tradition, this kind of closure has occupied a pivotal position. According to Aristotle, through the closure of *mythos* (plot), dramatic art does not merely imitate the appearance but captures the „essence" of things; hence, it is more „philosophical," „universal," and „valuable" than, e.g., historiography, factography, or science, as far as they are able to resist the irresistible temptation of some totalizing ideology. Logocentrism here turns Aristotelian *mythos* into a myth (see our *Metdestructuralismo* 161-82). In Western tradition, myth and *mythos* are inextricably intertwined.

64

The East thus turns into the fourth emplotment of the Pazian *mythopoeia*. It is the mirror image of the West in the sense that it supplements the deficiencies of the latter and ends up as the allegorical incarnation of alternatives sought by Paz, typically, outside and yet within his own tradition. It is even „read" through the eyes of surrealism and of structuralism. But, similar to the relation of eros and mysticism, the East overflows this allegory: its flesh and spice give a special touch to the fragile plots and, together with the structuralist connection, also furnish them with attractive makeup. All these allegorical, mythical, and modish frames and frame-ups that we have been joyfully excavating from the plot of his developing literary and critical project, should not mislead us: it is both with them and yet in spite of them – – thanks to the overflowing of metaphysical emplotments and exorcistic drives – – that Paz becomes a genuinely interesting and original thinker, not only of Mexican and Hispaic culture and tradition, but of contemporary Western culture at large.

Structuralism had yet more impulses in store for the Pazian literary enterprise. It is instructive to recall that in all its phases – – from Russian Formalism to the present – – , structuralism has always been related to successive faces of the avant-garde. For example, Formalism was stimulated by the futurism of Mayakovski and Khlebnikov (Pomorska); the Prague School was more „academic," but still entertained a close dialogue with the Czech avant-garde of the late twenties and thirties; or, among the French structuralists, the semiologists around Barthes helped to lay the ground rules for some neoavant-gardist experimentation of the „nouveau roman" in the sixties; in France this collaboration led its participants into „post-structuralism." The other side of the coin is that the antimimetic ideology of avant-garde – – as we show in our *Metaestructuralismo* (85-92) – – has molded in its own image even the alleged scientific projects of structuralist aesthetics, poetics, and semiotics. Indeed, it might now seem that, in „deconstruction," the expanding waves of the avant-garde have finally reached philosophy and have turned its discourse into one of the avant-garde's playful antimimetic literary genres. The *aporia* of „antimimetic metadiscourse," embraced by „deconstructive" criticism, has been both its driving and undermining force.

The neoavant-gardist experimentation and the structuralist and post-structuralist semiology set „in rotation" Pazian poetic and critical discourse. The manifesto „Signos en rotación" 'Signs in Rotation', published in 1965 and then added – – as an „epilogue" – – to the second edition of *Arco*, in 1967, conceptualizes this new face of his literary universe. In spite of quite an extensive rewriting of *Arco*, „Signos" does not blend with it easily (see also Santi), but is, so to speak, grafted on it. This concept of 'grafting' leads us to Derrida, who has shown how the „logic of the supplement" plays havoc with the assumed closure and unity of the „principal" text (144-45). On the one hand, the epilogue of *Arco* seems only to radicalize some of the earlier concepts and obsessions of Paz, for example, his modern preoccupation with „silence" as a part of poetic discourse;[8] on the other hand, it not only reopens the earlier conceptual framework and reveals it to be lacking, but it actually explodes it.

According to our „archeology," semiologial experiment creates the fifth emplotment of the developing Pazian *mythopoeia*. In this new framework, the word defies the traditional assumptions that "'language' has no exterior because it is not in space" (Lyotard 17), and becomes incarnate. The discourse attempts to empty its referential dimension and focuses more on itself. Instead of the „world", „feelings," „topics," or „transparent meanings," it highlights its own structure and material qualities. It stops being an allegory of the world and becomes a brave new playground of semiosis.[9] Unfortunately, as has alredy been said, this semiosis is firmly embedded in/ with the ideology of the avant-garde which has followed the Kantian siren or Mallarméan advice, „Exclus-en... / Le réel parce que vil" 'Cut the real out (... for it is cheap' (182-83). In *Le Plaisir du*

[8] See the subtle reading of this strand in Paz by Alazraki.

[9] Our *Metaestructuralismo* (68-71, 238-39, 251-54) charts the avantgarde background as well as some semiotic presuppositions of this process.

65

texte (1973; *The Pleasure of the Text*), Barthes ponders the *aporias* of this concept of discourse (50-53) and comes to the sad conclusion that it is not at all easy to exorcise the „world," the „outside"; „some" of it is even necessary because, otherwise, the text would be sterile. At least he inverts the terms: now it is the letter that views the world as its shadow (53). Just how this „shadow" should penetrate the virginal closure of the neoavant-gardist text remains the mystery of Barthesian *jouissance*.[10]

The sixties play havoc with Paz'an *mythopoeia*: while he plots the East side of his story of the West, his semiological attachment explodes these emplotments. However, similar to the surrealist season which shattered „pure poetry" and yet continued to be influenced by it, the debris of these emplotments flows in and overflows the semiological experiment, becoming that „something" needed for its fruitful, productive play.

The critical reflection in „Signos" turns on the famous Mallarméan poem „Un Coup de dés" 'A Dice Throw' (1897), and shows through its example how the „semiological mode," initiated *avant la lettre* by the French symbolist poet, has changed literary space and poetic language. Once again, without any visible anxiety, Paz faithfully misreads his subject, looking as he is for a confirmation of his latest poetic vision. Thus, the semiological conceptualization of „Un Coup" is faithful, but the ideology behind it, with all of its idealistic and somewhat esoteric metaphysics of „negativity," is completely disregarded:

> Space has lost, as it were, its passivity: it is not that which contains things but rather, in perpetual movement, it alters their course and intervenes actively in their transformations. It is the agent of mutations, it is energy. ... The change affects the page and the structure. ... Between the page and the writing is established a relation, new in the West and traditional in Far Eastern and Arabic poetry, which consists in their mutual interpretation. Space becomes writing: the blank spaces (which represent silence, and perhaps for that very reason) say something that signs do not say. ... The poet makes word of everything he touches, not excluding silence and the blanks in the text. *(Arco 258-60)*

In other words, modern poetry has transformed the typographic page into a kind of Einsteinian „timespace." The page has stopped being a mere simulacrum of virtual space, used - - as if from outside - - for conventional recording of speech that, as Lyotard or Wellek and Warren point out, „must be conceived as existing elsewhere" (*Theory* 142), and has no longer been left to chance, mitigated only by aesthetic touch-ups. Now it has become a concrete, protean, part of the new poetic semiosis, of the new, translinguistic poetic discourse.

In one of the games played in this broader playground, verbal text acquires the quality of pictorial sign: it symbolizes visually what it means verbally. Its limits are painting and pictographic or ideographic writing. Some of Apollinaire's *Calligrammes* - - like „Paysage" 'Landscape', „Lettre-Océan" 'Ocean-Letter', „Il Pleut" 'It's Raining', to name just a few - - exploit its mimetic potential. A host of cubo-futurists together with such master-poets as Pound, Cummings, Williams or the Chilean Huidobro, follow this path.[11]

In another game, it is the blank space that is, so to speak, drawn into the text: it becomes a special sign among verbal signs and acquires both its signifying form and meaning from their

---

[10] 'Sensual pleasure, enjoyment'. The English translation uses alternately 'pleasure' and 'bliss'. The ideology of the neoavant-gardist 'text' is summed up by Barthes in his post-structuralist manifesto „From Work to Text," writen in 1971.

[11] The semiotic play highlighted in the so-called „concrete poetry", which emerged from all these experiments in the 1950s, is even more complex and, in some cases, it abandons verbal discourse to turn into semiotics or painting *tout court* (for a perspicacious account see Steiner 197-218).

66

formal and semantic constellation.[12] „Un Coup de dés" sets out to explore the potential of this more abstract type. Some more involved examples of this game rely heavily on elaborate commentaries (in the case of Mallarmé, the preface to this poem and other "variations on a subject" serve this need). Barthes's differentiation between *representation* and *figuration (Plaisir* 88–90) may help us to better understand this second type. The abstract visual use of space does not put before our eyes specific objects created or recreated after „reality"; in contrast, it only plays with diverse figurative values of visual constellations. Abstract painting or collage come to mind first. The ornamental use of writing in Islamic architecture is another example. However, the effects are not only pictorial or sculptural. Thus, typographic „blow up" can influence the very literary semiotics of the text, and the „larger" volume experienced by the reader may enable it to make larger claims - - i.e., a poem may appear as a book, or a short story may sell as a novel.[13] Another case of the abstract figuration is that of the plurality of consciousness and of language - - i.e., of the paradigms of the language code - - which Blanchot glimpsed in the „new concept of literary space" of „Un Coup" (*Siren* 237–42).[14] Or Pazian *Blanco* (1967; *Blanco*) splendidly incarnates yet another figuration, that of Barthes's own understanding of this concept as „the way in which the erotic body appears ... in the profile of the text ... cleft into fetish objects, into erotic sites" (*Plaisir* 88–89; our adapt.). Among Paz's more experimental exercises, *Topoemas* (1968; Topoems) belong to the mimetic type; *Discos visuales* (1968; Visual Discs), to the abstract type. Yet, at the same time, the first edition of *Blanco, Topoemas,* and *Discos* all play with different values conferred upon them by the typographic „blow up."

Modern poetry most frequently uses both games simultaneously in order to generate an infinite variety of poetic „topograms." Some may show only a light trace of this new concept of literary space; others are more elaborate. But it would seem wrong to dismiss this whole poetic mode as though it were merely some „rare extravaganza" or „a fascinating historical curiosity" - - which are the characterizations that can be found, for example, in such discriminate authorities as Wellek and Warren (144) or Frank (13–14). It is also amusing to observe - - even within the limited scope of our study - - the contradictory moves of modern literature: how it exposes and subverts the forgery of traditional mimesis, especially that of the „realistic" art of the last century - - and yet how this alleged „antimimetic" art explores and forges other possibilities of imitation by words; how it questions and breaks up language, meaning, reference, and communication - - and, nevertheless, how it goes on to uncover new dimensions of verbal and topogrammatic semiosis.

If we now return to the critical vision of „Un Coup" by Paz, we note still another aspect: as he attempts to explain the significance of the Mallarméan experiment, he catches the first glimpse of

---

[12] The „empty" space, the typographic „silence," has a value of „zero sign." According to Jakobson, this is a special kind of sign which signifies precisely through the absence of the usual or expected „full" signs or as a „zero" part of the economy of some paradigms. „Zero sign" is thus a kind of „maverick" sign: it is „in" by being „out"; but it also is a „joker" sign because it fills the gaps of the system as the player needs it. E.g., in Sternian jokes, a „zero discourse" is pitted against the expectations raised in the reader and derives its significance, in each case, from its particular „environment" created by „full" discourse. „Zero sign" is one of those little „tricksters" that „lay bare" and explode the whole industry of „semiotic" trivia which flooded the academic marketplace in the wake of the structuralist „revolution."

[13] E.g., since fewer language elements fill the slots of lines and pages, their „weight" and „visibility" are enhanced; attention is drawn to more of their significant details (somewhat like the well-known Jakobsonian microscopic analyses of poetic texts); this slows down the tempo and forces us to put greater effort into the reading; etc.

[14] One could add to this interior polyphony yet another plural dimension, that of the dialogic polyphony of discourse, studied by Bakhtin, which is also reflected in the constellation of Mallarmé's poem.

the post-structuralist semiology in the making. On the other hand, this shows us how closely this semiology is related to the avant-garde experiments and ideology:

> There is no final interpretation for *Un Coup de dés* because its last word is not a final word. ... at the end of the journey the poet does not contemplate the Idea, symbol or archetype, but a space in which a constellation appears: his poem. It is not an image or an essence; it is an account being calculated, a handful of signs that are drawn, effaced, and drawn again. Thus, this poem that denies the possibility of saying something absolute... is ... the plenary affirmation of the sovereignty of the word. (*Arco* 252)

This semiological and *mythopoeic* criticism of meaning (the simultaneous nullity and sovereignty of the word) will reach its highest stage in a later experimental text, *El mono gramático* (1972; *The Monkey Grammarian*).

IV.

The poems from the volume *Ladera Este*, which highlights through its title the East as the „other side" of the West, play with all these new poetic myths and artistic devices. However, here the Pazian literary quest opens some unexpected ground. The semiological dynamization of literary space, pointed out in his reflection on Mallarmé, turns out to be only a way-station towards a more audacious goal. In „Carta a León Felipe" 'Letter to León Felipe' which is a kind of poetic, poematic manifesto, we read:

La escritura poética es
        Aprender a leer
El hueco de la escritura
        En la escritura
. . . .
La poesía
        Es la ruptura instantánea
Instantáneamente cicatrizada
        Abierta de nuevo
Por la mirada de los otros
. . . .
        La poesía
Es la hendidura
        El espacio
Entre una palabra y otra
Configuración del inacabamiento
        (91-92)
To write poetry
        Is learning to read
The hole of writing
        In the writing
. . . .
Poetry
        Is the instant rupture
Instantly healed
        Reopened
By the vision of the others
. . . .
        Poetry
Is the cleft

68

```
            The space
    Between one word and another
    Configuration of the unending
            (131-33; our adapt.)
```

„La poesía / Es la hendidura" 'Poetry / Is the cleft': 'hendidura' (cleft, crack, fissure, rift, split) is undoubtedly the key concept of this passage. But what is it? What does it stand for? The poem „Vrindaban" (the title comes from one of the holy cities of Hinduism) gives us the first hint:

```
    Tal vez en una piedra hendida
    Palpó la forma femenina
                Y su desgarradura
                    (61)
    Perhaps in a cleft stone
    He touched the feminine form
                And its rift
                (147; our adapt.)
```

The author's footnote to this place is more explicit: „certain stones are signs of the great goddess, especially if their form alludes to the sexual cleft (*yoni*)" (178; our trans.). Like Goya playing games with his gorgeous *maja* - - now dressed, now not - - , Conjunciones removes the last, albeit transparent, metaphorical veil of *maya* from 'hendidura' as 'yoni'. Describing the Tantric mandala of the human body,[15] Paz writes: „The two veins start at the sacred plexus, in which the penis (*linga*) and the vulva (*yoni*) are located' (76). In his inaugural lecture as a member of El Colegio Nacional de México (Mexican Academy of the Arts), entitled „La nueva analogía" 'New Analogy', from 1967, he calls Hindu temples „a sexual vegetation in stone, the copula of the elements, the dialogue between *lingam* and *yoni*" (*Signo* 13; our trans.). 'Hendidura' 'cleft' thus comes to symbolize, through the metaphor of vulva, one of the key sacred centers (*cakras*) of the Tantric mandala of the human body.

Another text from the same period, „La semilla" 'The Seed', relates the erotic concept of 'hendidura' to the earlier metaphysical and critical concerns of the poet:

> ... human time will then appear to be a divided present. Separation, a sharp break |*ruptura*|: now falls into *before* and *after*. This fissure |*hendidura*| in time announces the advent of the kingdom of man... As man's history unfolds, the fissure becomes broader and broader... But primitive man is a creature who is less defenseless spiritually than we are. The moment the seed falls into a crack, it fills it and swells with life. Its fall is a resurrection: the gash |*desgarradura*| is a scar; and separation is reunion. (*Corriente* 23-24)

This visionary text, roaming freely through art, time, history, and myth, sheds new light on one of the quoted passages from „Carta a León Felipe."

However, beyond the sexual metaphor of 'hendidura' and its esoteric and mystical symbolism, what is actually new in the Pazian erotic concept of poetry of the sixties? It is the fact that the former romantic mysticism establishes a surprising bridgehead on the typographic page: now, the blank page and the blank space between words open up into a kind of erotic cleft and dialogue. In „Carta a León Felipe," 'hendidura' - - identified with poetry - - is transformed, figuratively, into an image and a powerful symbol of the new literary space.[16]

In *Ladera*, 'hendidura' fuses a double heritage into a striking whole. In the first place, it assumes the image contexts developed earlier around 'herida' 'wound' and its synonyms. For example, in

---

[15] This picture is missing in the English edition.

[16] Other poems from *Ladera*, like „El día en Udaipur" 'The Day in Udaipur' or „Custodia" 'Monstrance', would lead us further in our search for other possible textual veils and unveils of 'hendidura'. The limits imposed on our study by the readers' endurance force us to forgo this path here.

69

the last sequel of „Diario de un soñador" 'Diary of a Dreamer', from 1945, the young poet raves; „Your are ... like a wound from which I drink the lost substance of creation, an imprevisible revelation..." (147; our trans.). The desired woman, compared to a wound, becomes a symbol of transcendence. At the end of his first surrealist text, „Trabajos del poeta" 'The Poet's Works', the wound is identified with the woman's sexual organ and the orgasmic moment becomes a symbol of poetic expression; both love and poetry resound with cosmic projection: „ ... pico que desgarra y entreabre al fin el fruto!, tú, mi Grito, surtidor de plumas de fuego, herida resonante y vasta como el desprendimiento de un planeta del cuerpo de una estrella" 'beak that tears and at last cracks open the fruit! You my cry, fountain of feathers of fire, wound resounding and vast like the ripping out of a planet from the body of a star' (Aguila 26-27). „Mutra," from Estación violenta, adds a telluric dimension through the metamorphosis of the split stone into a vulva. „Entrada en materia" 'Entrance into Matter', from Salamandra (1962; Salamander), powerfully sums up all the pieces of this strand, and introduces 'hendidura' as an equivalent of 'herida':

Ciudad
. . . .
Un reflector palpa tus plazas más secretas
El sagrario del cuerpo
El arca del espíritu
Los labios de la herida la herida de los labios
La boscosa hendidura de la profecía
. . . .
Y la juntura ciega de la piedra
Entre tus muslos ...
        (9-10)
   City
. . . .
A searchlight touches your most secret sites
The sacred place of the body
Ark of the spirit
Labia of the wound wound of the labia
Wooded cleft of the prophecy
. . . .
Blind junction of the stone
Between your thighs...
    (our trans.)

In turn, Ladera raises these images to a higher power by giving them, through the meeting with the East, a distinct symbolic closure (cleft stone/vulva as a symbol of the Great Goddes; the key center of the Tantric mandala of the human body; Buddhist sculpture, linga, and yoni as indexes of Buddhist culture, philosophy, and values). The emplotment of the image complex built around 'hendidura' in the Pazian work of the sixties becomes manifest in yet another way. Using the framework developed by Lévi-Strauss for the study of world mythologies, we can formulate the myth underlying this complex as follows:

S e p a r a t i o n		T r a n s c e n d e n c e	
Cleft Stone	Feminine Cleft	Eros	Poetry

Together, „feminine cleft" and „eros" mediate between Nature (the given, fatum) and Culture (the creation of man; freedom, although restrained here by „transcendence"). Through this mediation and closure, the myth also becomes mythos: a story, a tight plot.

But let us not repeat the mistake of structuralism - - which was to become too absorbed by symmetries, binary oppositions, and inversions to notice all the multifarious realities overflowing

Its strait, all too straight, generative *logos* - - and see in the mythic schema what it is not. It is not some latent, immutable mold of meaning that would, magically, hold in check the play of Pazian discourse and the metamorphoses of his *mythopoeia*. This mythic scheme is just one powerful and felicitous formulation of one facet of that play and of one moment of that flow. If we go back to the earlier stages, the terms change ('hendidura'/'herida') or disappear (cleft stone); if we go forward, poetry radically invades space and becomes material object, almost a part of Nature, and transcendence itself is challenged by Buddhism and changes its content. The East, paradoxically, grounds, enriches, and subverts different elements of the myth. Semiology, in turn, will explode it, but will retain its „shadow" as enrichment of its own game.

In this way, the context of *Ladera* - - and, more broadly, the whole Pazian work - - fulfills the Mallarméan vision of poetic discourse postulating, in the summary of Paz himself, „an ideal writing in which the phrases and words would reflect each other and, in some measure, contemplate or read one another" (*Arco* 251). Love and eros, once elements of the metaphysical *mythopoeia* or poetic themes, invade the typographic page and are dramatized, figuratively, in and through this new literary space. Literary discourse - - the semiotic dialogue of writing, print, and space - - acquires a body; and it is an erotic one.

V.

The erotization of literary space in Paz affects his very concept of poetry. The quest for transcendence, that characterized the earlier phase of his *mythopoeia* and is still fully present in the second edition of *Arco*, is now *textualized*. Transcendence is no longer a kind of meaning, reality or substance beyond the text: it becomes one of the shadows cast by the latter - - prefigured by the letter - - within the reading-spectacle. In this, the ideology of the avant-gardist text blends with and is reinforced by the interpretation given to the *aporia* of „immanent transcendence" by Tantrism: „Everything is real in Tantrism - - and everything is symbolic. Phenomenical reality is more than the symbol of the other reality: we touch symbols when we think we are touching bodies and material objects, and vice versa" (*Conjunciones* 68-69).

The long experimental poem *Blanco,* with its even visual textual labyrinths and erotic sites, powerfully develops this new concept of poetic space and of poetry itself. *Blanco* is a visionary poem and a visual play, a poetic speculation on love, language, reality and irreality of the world, all transposed into the textual metamorphoses on/of the page.[17] Among the types of erotic figuration of space pointed out in this tudy, it is the closest to the Barthesian concept of erotic figuration. As already in Tantrism, „scripture is *lived* as a body that is an analogue of the physical body - - and the body is *read* as a scripture" (*Conjunciones* 79). Once again, the light comes to Paz from the East and makes it possible for him to anticipate movement in the West.

In *Blanco,* according to the poet's introduction, „the space flows, engendering and dissipating the text" (*Ladera* 145).[18] Woman's body is transformed metaphorically into writing and writing plays with the figurative values of spatial erotic body. The textualized meaning and „transcendence," arising and vanishing in the act of reading, „make real the vision" only in the instant of contemplation. Poetic text becomes a correlate of the paradoxical plenitude and emptiness of *nirvana.* Tantric Buddhism, ideology of the avant-garde, and post-structualist semiology all blend into a dazzling *bricolage;* in *Mono gramático,* Paz has formulated it in the following way:

> ... the path of poetic writing leads to the abolition of writing: at the end of it we are confronted with an inexpressible reality. ... As I write, I journey toward meaning: as I read what I write, I blot it out, I dissolve the path. Each attempt I make ends up the same way: the dissolution of the text in the reading of it, the expulsion of the meaning through writing. ... the vision that poetic writing offers us is that of its dissolution. Poetry is empty, like the clearing in the

---

[17] See Ortega for one of the best commentaries on this involved poem.

[18] Omitted from *Configurations.*

forest... It is nothing but the *place* of the apparition which is, at the same time, that of its disappearance. (132-34)

When we read this, we can almost hear through it an echo of the earlier quoted passage from „Signos en rotación" (*Arco* 252). The theory developed there around „Un Coup de dés" is transposed here into a distinctly poetic and prophetic discourse which is an integral part of a long experimental poem in prose. In *Mono gramático,* the theoretical strand becomes an incarnation of the agonizing self-consciousness of the modern literary text reaching, as it assumes, in vain, for any kind of saving transcendence in/from the outside.[19]

Various claims of this visionary semiology of *nirvana* call for a closer scrutiny. Let us point to at least some of the issues involved. For example, if we take the quoted assertion in its broadest sense, it holds true of any text: all texts „flow," appear and disappear, before the reader's eyes, and no reading – – unless by some magic – – can transform the vision into a material world, only into another text. The difference between the traditional and the avant-gardist works lies, then, in how they use the media of transmission and by what *mythopoeia* they motivate that use. Beyond that, both the *mythopoeia* of the 19th century „realism" and that of the 20th century „avant-garde" are but two ideological forgeries – – to a great degree symmetrical and inverse – – which are „authenticated" only by the models and the molds they have forged to their image. In the beginning, it was useful for criticism to follow the avant-garde because its experimental character made it easier to rock the boat of traditional poetics; but, in the end, the privilege of one over the other is misleading because the „scientific" projects of contemporary poetics have become so irreparably entangled in the very ideological web of the avant-garde. Criticism cannot exist but in constant struggle with and as erosion of the entrapments of ideologies and of myths.

On the other hand, if these Pazian claims should represent a specific theory of textual meaning and of reading, present-day poetics would have to reject the metaphor of *nirvana* as another myth and mystification. For example, the text is a complex semiotic inscription: it is already filled with signs, verbal and non-verbal, alphabetic and non-alphabetic, coming in a certain order or configuration (this is, after all, what makes possible decipherment of unknown or coded scripts). The blank space itself is culturally – – i.e., semiotically – – conditioned: blank page or canvas are not „empty" but are „oriented" – – „read" – – differently in the West and in the East. Therefore, contrary to Barthes (*Critique* 57) and post-structuralists, the sense of a text is never empty; it is, so to speak, *preempted* in a certain way. Neither does the reading come close to the absolutness, closure, and introvertedness of *nirvana.* Rather, supplementing the text by social norms, values, conventions, and by the intertextual ties highlighted by its times, reading closes but temporarily and tentatively its horizon of meaning, and always leaves the door open for future readings and supplements.[20] The concept of „empty sense" can be salvaged only as a vague expression of the fact that there is no fixed, absolute meaning behind the text guaranteed by some Guardian Angel. What is important to note is that the realization of this lack of transcendence,[21] which slowly worked its way from philosophy to hermeneutics, was cheerfully embraced by the avant-garde and was put to use through its well-known concept of art as „intranscendent playing."

Those poets!, swearing on intranscendence, conjuring emptiness, and promising silence; and yet they continue to obscurely plot new works, new challenges, and new glorious shipwrecks in their – – declared and undeclared – – war on the absolute, that ever receding ritual horizon before the avant-garde literature. In the end, all this purported nihilism seems to be but a *defamiliarizing*

---

[19] See Alazraki for an inclsive comentary on this text.

[20] This point is made by the contemporary „reader-oriented" criticism.

[21] 'Leere Transzendenz/leere Idealität' 'empty transcendence/ideality' are the key concepts advanced as characteristics of literature from romanticism to present by Friedrich (*passim*).

- - polarizing and agonizing - - *ploy* of their literary game: of their ultimate quest for a new transcendence in and through artistic creation.

In the case of Paz, this struggle gives rise to yet another dazzling and puzzling literary and critical universe, comparable only to the most radical projects born out of the Spanish-American avant-garde, such as those of Vicente Huidobro, César Vallejo, Pablo Neruda or Jorge Luis Borges.[22]

WORKS CITED

Alazraki, Jaime. „The *Monkey Grammarian* or Poetry as Reconciliation." *World Literature Today* 56.4 (1982): 607-12.

„Para una poética del silencio." *Guadernos Hispanoamericanos* nrs. 343-45 (1979): 157-84.

Appollinaire, Guillaume. *Calligrammes: Poems of Peace and War (1913-1916).* Trans. A. H. Greet. Berkeley: U of California P, 1980.

Aristotle. *Poetics.* Ed. D. W. Lucas. Oxford: Oxford UP, 1968

Bakhtin, Mikhail. *Problems of Dostoevsky's Poetics.* Minneapolis: U of Minnesota P, 1984.

Barthes, Roland. *Critique et vérité.* Paris: Seuil, 1966.

„From Work to Text." *Image - Music - Text.* New York: Hill and Wang, 1977. 155-64.

Le Plaisir du texte. Paris: Seuil, 1973. *The Pleasure of the Text* Trans. Richard Miller. New York: Hill and Wang, 1975.

Blanchot, Maurice. *The Siren's Song.* Bloomington: Indiana UP, 1982.

Derrida, Jacques. *Of Grammatology.* Baltimore: The Johns Hopkins UP, 1976.

Durán, Manuel. „La huella del Oriente en la poesía de Octavio Paz." *Revista Iberoamericana* nr. 74(1971): 97-116.

Frank, Joseph. „Spatial Form in Modern Literature." *The Widening Gyre.* Bloomington: Indiana UP, 1968, 3-62.

Friedrich, Hugo. *Die Struktur der modernen Lyrik.* Hamburg: Rowohlt, 1956. *The Structure of Modern Poetry: From the Mid-Nineteenth to the Mid-Twentieth Century.* Evanston: Northwestern UP, 1974.

Guibert, Rita. *Seven Voices: Seven Latin American Writers Talk to R.G.* New York: Vintage Books, 1972.

Jakobson, Roman. „Signe zéro' ahd „Das Nullzeichen." *Word and Language.* Vol. 2 of *Selected Writings.* The Hague: Mouton, 1971. 211-22.

Jung, Carl G. „The Difference Between Eastern and Western Thinking." *The Portable Jung.* Ed. Joseph Campbell. New York: The Viking Press, 1971. 480-502.

Lévi-Strauss, Claude. „La structure des mythes." *Anthropologie structurale.* Paris: Plon, 1958. 227-55.

Lyotard, Jean François. „Interview." *Diacritics* 14. 3. (1984): 16-21.

Mallarmé, Stéphane. *The Poems: A Bilingual Edition.* Trans. Keith Bosley. New York: Penguin Books, 1977.

Ortega, Julio. „*Blanco*: Space of Change." *World Literature Today 56.4(1982): 635-38.*

Paz, Octavio. ¿*Aguila o sol? Eagle or Sun?* Trans. Eliot Weinberger. New York: New Directions, 1976.

El arco y la lira. 2nd ad. Mexico: F. C. E., 1967. Quoted after *The Bow and the Lyre.* Trans. Ruth L. C. Simmons. Austin: U of Texas P, 1973.

Blanco. Mexico: Joaquín Mortiz, 1967. *Ladera,* 143-69. Eng. trans. *Blanco. Configurations,* 177-95.

---

[22] We would like to thank Prof. Maureen Ahern and Miss Eileen Mahoney for their generous and repeated help with the English version of this study; and the former for the thorough discussion of our translations and adaptations.

73

La búsqueda del comienzo: Escritos sobre el surrealismo. Madrid: Fundamentos, 1980.

Claude Lévi-Strauss o el nuevo festín de Esopo. Mexico: Joaquín Mortiz, 1967. *Claude Lévi--Strauss: An Introduction.* Ithaca: Cornell UP, 1970.

Configurations. Trans. G. Aroul *et al.* New York: New Directions, 1971.

Conjunciones y disjunciones. 2nd ed. Mexico: Joaquín Mortiz, 1978. Quoted after *Conjunctions and Disjunctions.* Trans. Helen R. Lane. New York: The Viking Press, 1974.

Corriente alterna. Mexico: F. C. E., 1967. Quoted after *Alternating Current.* Trans. Helen R. Lane. New York: The Viking Press, 1973.

„Diaro de un soñador." *El Hijo Pródigo* nr. 24(1945):147-51.

Discos visuales. Mexico: Era, 1968.

Los hijos del limo. Barcelona: Seix Barral, 1974. *Children of the Mire: Modern Poetry from Romanticism to the Avant-Garde.* Cambridge: Harvard UP, 1974.

Ladera Este. 3rd ed. Mexico: Joaquín Mortiz, 1975. Engl. trans. quoted after *Configurations.*

El mono gramático. Barcelona: Seix Barral, 1974. Quoted after *The Monkey Grammarian.* Trans. Helen R. Lane. New York: Seaver Books, 1981.

Las peras del olmo. Mexico: Imprenta Universitaria, 1957.

Salamandra. Mexico: Joaquín Mortiz, 1962.

El signo y el garabato. Mexico: Joaquín Mortiz, 1975.

Topoemas. In *Poemas: 1935-1975.* Barcelona: Seix Barral, 1979. 497-504.

Pomorska, Krystyna. *Russian Formalist Theory and Its Poetic Ambiance.* The Hague: Mouton, 1968.

Rodríguez Monegal, Emir. „Relectura de *El arco y la lira." Revista Iberoamericana* nr. 74(1971): 35-46.

Said, Edward. *Orientalism.* New York: Pantheon, 1978.

Santí, Enrico Mario. „The Politics of Poetics." *Diacritics* 8.4(1978): 28-40.

Steiner, Wendy. *The Colors of Rhetoric: Problems In the Relation Between Modern Literature and Painting.* Chicago: U of Chicago P, 1982.

Surrealismo en México. Special issue. *Artes Visuales* nr. 4(1974).

Todorov, Tzvetan. *The Conquest of America: The Question of the Other.* New York: Harper Row, 1984.

Volek, Emil. *Cuatro claves para la modernidad: Andlisi semiótico de textos hispánicos. Aleixandre, Borges, Carpentier, Cabrera Infante.* Madrid: Gredos, 1984.

Metaestructuralismo: Poética moderna, semiótica narrativa y filosofía de las ciencias sociales. Madrid: Fundamentos, 1986.

Wellek, René, and Austin Warren, *Theory of Literature.* 3rd ed. New York: Harcourt Brace Jovanovich, 1977.

Wilson, Jason. *Octavio Paz: A Study of his Poetics.* Cambridge: Cambridge UP, 1979.

POETICS OF APOCALYPSE, SPATIAL FORM AND INDETERMINATION: THE PROSE OF OCTAVIO PAZ IN THE 1960s

ANTHONY STANTON
El Colegio de México

> Dans une société sans stabilité, sans unité, il ne peut se créer d'art stable, d'art définitif.
>
> Mallarmé

Criticism has only recently begun to analyze in depth the complex relationship that exists between the poetry and the prose of Octavio Paz. Daunted quite justifiably by the diversity and scope of the Mexican's work critics have, at the very most, tended to follow the line established by the writer himself, seeing in the poetry an illustration of the poetics and in the latter a rationalization of the former. What cannot be denied, of course, is the fact that there is a very close relationship between the two discourses. Yet this relationship is neither isomorphic, symmetrical nor self-explicative.

In the early phase of Paz's work, the period that stretches from 1931 to 1943, the prose certainly seems to perform a polemic role as a kind of exploratory justification of the kind of poetry the poet wants to write at that time, as in the case of the early essays of T. S. Eliot. Yet even at this moment there is an authentic dialogue between poet and thinker precisely because they are not identical. The essay that synthesizes this early period, "Poesía de soledad y poesía de comunión" (1943), sketches out a poetic ideal that is not successfully embodied in the poetry until several years later.[1]

Similarly, in the second phase of the Mexican's development, a period that goes from 1944 until the late 1950s, culminating in the poems of *La estación violenta* (1958) and in the extensive book of poetics *El arco y la lira*

71

(1956), it could be said that similar preoccupations are dealt with in both poetry and poetic thought: a metaphysics of temporal ontology that seeks forms of transcendence in eroticism and in poetry itself, seeing both as quasi-religious forms of experience capable of reuniting divided man with *otherness*, that supressed part of his lost wholeness. Nevertheless, here too it would be naive to seek to establish very rigid parallels between the two spheres: authentic poetry is ultimately irreducible to any form of conceptual rational-ization (including the poet's own attempts), while *El arco y la lira* explores problems that could never be fully dealt with within the generic limitations of verse.

A serious discussion of the problematic nature of the interaction between poetry and prose requires a careful *historical* description of the salient features of each before proceeding to compare and contrast. I emphasize the word "historical" in this case because "revisionism" is one of the most notable features of Paz's entire work. Not only has the poetry been rewritten, corrected, suppressed (especially some of the early poems), restructured (on a massive scale in the widely different editions of *Libertad bajo palabra*—1949, 1960, 1967, 1979—[2] and on a more limited scale in the recent verse); the prose too has undergone a similar process of "updating," as can be seen, for example, in the significant revisions introduced into the second editions of *El laberinto de la soledad* and *El arco y la lira*. When confronted by this scale of persistent revisionism, the critic who writes on Paz has no option but to take this historical aspect into account.

My intention in this essay is to identify, analyze and evaluate the most important ideas in what could be called the third phase of Paz's evolution as poet, critic and essayist. I limit my focus to the prose. This period of approximately 10 years starts in late 1950s and ends in the late 1960s. The dates coincide, as in the two previous phases, with certain changes in the writer's life: in 1959 he leaves Mexico and lives in Paris until 1962 and from 1962 until 1968 he resides in New Delhi as the Mexican Ambassador. Even though he does not return to his country until 1971, the period effectively comes to an end in 1968 when Paz resigns in moral indignation over the Mexican government's massacre of students at Tlatelolco. The events of 1968, not only in Mexico but throughout the Western world, provoke a serious reconsideration of historical and political matters and induce the need for a new reflection on Mexico—the subject of *Posdata* (1970) and the later compilation *El ogro filantrópico* (1979)—while the return to his native country marks the beginning of a new autobiographical and retrospective phase of Paz's poetry in *Pasado en claro* (1975) and *Vuelta* (1976). Yet the real justification for isolating this decade is due to a series of formal, intellectual and moral features that unify the somewhat external facts dictated by biography and/or geography.

The period represents an extraordinarily prolific and fertile moment in Paz's poetic and intellectual development. Retrospectively, it seems as though the poet himself had sought to enclose within the 1960 edition of *Libertad bajo palabra: obra poética (1935-1958)* a whole period of his life and work. In the following years two more volumes of collected verse appear: *Salamandra (1958-1961)* in 1962 and *Ladera este (1962-1968)* in 1969, in addition to experiments in spatial and visual poetry: *Discos visuales* (1968) and *Topoemas* (1968). His poetry reaches its most ambitious point in *Blanco* (1967), an "open" text which, like its prose equivalent, Cortázar's *Rayuela* (1963), begins with a kind of "tablero de dirección" that postulates different ways of reading the text or rather different texts to read.

This period of poetic experimentation coincides with an enormously varied prose output. In the short space of four years Paz publishes the following works: *Cuadrivio* (1965), *Los signos en rotación* (1965), *Puertas al campo* (1966), an important prologue to the collective anthology of Mexican poetry *Poesía en movimiento* (1966), a second and substantially revised edition of *El arco y la lira* (1967) that incorporates "Los signos en rotación" as the new epilogue, *Claude Lévi-Strauss o el nuevo festín de Esopo* (1967), *Corriente alterna* (1967), a second and drastically revised edition of *Libertad bajo palabra* (1968), *Marcel Duchamp o el castillo de la pureza* (1968), and finally *Conjunciones y disyunciones* (1969).[3] A sum total of eight full-length books: an astonishing achievement, even allowing for the fact that some of these were new compilations of previously published material.

Relatively little critical attention has been paid to these prose works. At most they have been used as explicative tools to elucidate the poetry of *Ladera este*. One source of difficulty in examining this wealth of production is the wide range of interests: essays on literary criticism, poetic theory and plastic arts; reflections on politics, comparative religion, anthropology; and the miscellaneous subjects treated in the final two sections of *Corriente alterna*. As it is impossible to analyze here the full breadth of these interests, I shall focus on the work that seems to me to be crucial to the elaboration of a poetic theory: "Los signos en rotación."[4] In the conclusion, however, I shall point out that the poetic is inseparable from a reflection on the other arts and from a vision of history, politics, morality and eroticism. In other words, a theory of the nature and the function of poetry forms an integral part of the cultural criticism of a poet and intellectual immersed in the currents of modern thought.

* * *

Three fundamental "encounters" shape this period: a careful reading of Mallarmé, a deep interest in the innovative theories of Structuralism, and a passionate study of the history and thought of Indian religion and civilization, especially those of Buddhism. In spite of their appearance as heterogeneous elements arbitrarily juxtaposed, these three "encounters" are experienced in a unitary way by the writer who sees certain analogies between underlying features. I shall explore some of these analogies later.

In order to understand the importance of "Los signos en rotación" we must retrace our steps back to 1956, the year in which *El arco y la lira* appeared. The first edition of this book can be described in general terms as an ambitious attempt to synthesize apparently irreconcilable ideas that stem from different disciplines of thought. Within this multiplicity of discourse three strands can be isolated: a Heideggerian philosophical stance that combines a temporal ontology with a view of poetry as a revelation of Being; a phenomenology of poetic experience based on the model of Rudolf Otto's phenomenolgy of religious experience; and a fusion of metaphysics, poetic theory and eroticism in what Paz has called "la metafísica erótica" (PO 168) of Antonio Machado. The book seeks to construct from these strands a poetic theory within a broad framework derived from the utopian programmes of a certain wing of Romanticism and their Surrealist disciples.

An important initial distinction is made between the poem as verbal object and what is called "la experiencia poética," a phrase that denominates something actually lived as part of the process of creation (in the author) and recreation (in the reader) of the poem. After exploring the distinguishing features of the poem and the similarities and differences between poetry, religion and eroticism as experiences that permit a revelation of the essential human condition, the final part of the book analyzes the tense and paradoxical relations between the poem, poetic experience and the historical and social dimension of existence. From the very beginning Paz adopts as programmatic the Surrealist equation between socio-political revolutionary aspirations and the absolute freedom demanded by poetry: "La sociedad revolucionaria es inseparable de la sociedad fundada en la palabra poética" (AL1 233).

The original epilogue in the 1956 edition transmits an ambiguous reply to what was declared to be the central question of the work in the initial "Advertencia": "¿no sería mejor transformar la vida en poesía que hacer poesía con la vida?; y la poesía ¿no puede tener como objeto propio, más que la creación de poemas, la de instantes poéticos? ¿Será posible una comunión universal en la poesía?" (AL1 7). Surprisingly, the epilogue describes the result of this attempt to "poetizar la vida, socializar la poesía" as "el fracaso revolucionario del surrealismo," compensated by "la luz de los poemas modernos" (AL1 245, 251). Yet if poetic experience, despite (or perhaps because of) its ambitious pretentions, has failed to transform reality, then the achievements embodied in certain poems must be deemed to be relatively modest compensation when compared with the text's urge to privilege poetic experience over and above the poem.

It is true that the failure of the attempt to reunite life and art is described as being due to the dominant historical conditions and to the corruption of modern revolutionary movements, yet even this explanation appears as an unconvincing tactic that merely passes the blame on to the antagonistic historical situation that has "resisted" transformation (a strange argument): "La posibilidad de encarnación de la poesía en la historia está sujeta a una doble condición. En primer término, la desaparición del actual sistema histórico; en segundo, la recuperación de la dimensión divina" (AL1 258). As neither of the two conditions has been fulfilled, the modern poet is left with no option but to retreat from his hopes for a collective transformation of society and content himself with the limited, personal transformation made possible (for creator and recreator) by the poem:

> la encarnación histórica de la poesía no es, sin embargo, algo que pueda realizarse en nuestro tiempo.
> . . . En cambio, el poema . . . sigue siendo una vía abierta. Puesto que la sociedad está lejos de convertirse en una comunidad poética, en un poema vivo y sin cesar recreándose, la única manera de ser fiel a la poesía es regresar a la obra. La poesía se realiza en el poema y no en la vida. (AL1 259-260)

Instead of acknowledging that the failure is due to some shortcoming in the utopian theory derived from Surrealism, this argument lamely asserts that poetic communion is dependent upon the prior transformation of history and of man. The central claim of the book, of course, is that poetry itself would be responsible for—and not dependent upon—these extra-artistic transformations. The argument in the epilogue seems to merely restate Breton's claim that historical conditions and Stalinist degeneration (not Surrealist doctrine) are to be blamed for the movement's failure to bring about a total revolution. Paz's unwillingness to abandon the Surrealist project gives rise to the ambiguous nature of the epilogue that tries to present as a victory what must be seen as a failure in the book's own terms.

Confined to solitude, the modern poet has one consolation: "este sentimiento de incertidumbre lo comparte el poeta con todos los hombres" (AL1 262). The tentative communion, however, is projected as a shared orphanhood holding out no more than a hypothetical promise of future reconciliation. As if to counterbalance these pessimistic implications, the final pages try to establish an optimistic note by advancing the prophecy of a future poetry that will celebrate human heroism as a model of collective freedom, in opposition to "el poema del poema," the Symbolist legacy of self-reflexive writing, a notion that although condemned here as an abandonment of history, will be vindicated in the later epilogue:

> Con demasiada frecuencia los poetas del siglo pasado y de la primera mitad del que corre consagraron con la palabra a la palabra, hicieron el poema del poema. . . . El nuevo poema nombrará a los héroes. Frente al nihilismo sin rostro de la técnica, el poema ha de consagrar a los héroes que asumen la libertad de todos frente al poder. El héroe: nuestro semejante. (AL1 263)

* * *

The second, revised edition of *El arco y la lira*, published in 1967, constitutes yet another example of the constant renewal, self-examination and updating of Paz's thought on poetry as part of a creative and critical revisionism that permits no notion of a fixed and stable answer. Emir Rodríguez Monegal has studied the general differences between the two editions: "entre la primera y la segunda edición el estructuralismo francés . . . irrumpe en el mundo occidental y no sólo cuestiona el concepto clásico de las humanidades sino que destruye el prestigio aún latente de las versiones sartrianas del existencialismo" (39). In the two editions two distinct moments of Western culture are reflected: firstly, French existentialism, with its reinterpretation of the philosophy of the early Heidegger, its inbuilt historicism and anthropocentric stance, and, secondly, the interdisciplinary movement known as Structuralism, renowned for its antihistoric and antihumanist stance. The modifications and changes in *El arco y la lira* are provoked by a new vision of the status of the human subject, of the nature of language and of the relations between creator, poem and language. In Rodríguez Monegal's words:

> Las supresiones de ciertos enfoques de Heidegger, como de todo lo que en el texto original asimila poesía y libertad, o antropomorfiza la creación literaria, insistiendo demasiado en el papel taumatúrgico del poeta, tiene[n] indudablemente que ver con una modificación en la perspectiva de Paz operada por el conocimiento del estructuralismo y de las nuevas teorías del lenguaje. (44)

Here I shall limit my attention to the importance of "Los signos en rotación," published first as an independent essay in 1965, an edition in which it is dated "Delhi, noviembre de 1964" and characterized by the editors as a "manifiesto poético," and later included in the 1967 edition of *El arco y la lira* as the new epilogue.[5] The essay does indeed have some of the elements of a manifesto, proclaiming a new vision of poetry that is hard to reconcile with the original or even the corrected text of *El arco y la lira*. Two opposing and ultimately irreconcilable views of man, language and poetry are forced to coexist. Enrico Mario Santí has observed how the 1956 edition represents not only "un cruce entre los atisbos filosóficos del surrealismo y la fenomenología existencialista" but also—and more revealingly—"una violenta reinserción del sujeto, de la conciencia individual, dentro de dos discursos (el surrealismo y el existencialismo) que postulan, o que al menos implican, todo lo contrario:

el empobrecimiento y límites de la conciencia ordenadora" ("Octavio Paz" 108, 111).

This dislocation at the heart of the text becomes much more pronounced in the second edition since the former discourses of surrealism and existentialism are still present, albeit in lower profile due to certain corrections and qualifications,[6] while the new discourse of Structuralism makes it even more difficult to hold on to the anthropocentric and humanist premises of 1956. Through its theory of language as an impersonal and unconscious system, its elimination of the human subject, and its view of the work of art as inwardly or self-referential, Structuralism would seem to imply a clean break with the philosophical props of the first edition, a break reinforced by the reading of Mallarmé in "Los signos en rotación." Yet the latter text attempts to fuse into a coherent totality (retrospectively valid for the whole book, since the new essay *replaces* the former epilogue) all of these conflicting doctrines with the net result that it appears as "la defensa de la presencia poética y del papel del creador a expensas de conceptos potencialmente subversivos; es decir, conceptos que plantean, desde su propio contexto filosófico, el desprestigio del sujeto y la necesidad de movilizar otros modos de análisis que rebasen sus límites" (Santí, "Octavio Paz" 113).

This uneasy juxtaposition seeks to combine two fundamentally different world views: a neo-Romantic credo (reinforced by Heidegger and by Surrealism) in which poetry, closely linked to magic and religion, is a sacred speech that articulates ontological presence, fullness of Being, the primordial unity of word and referent, of man and nature, of self and community; and a view derived from a "scientific," rationalistic and at times neo-positivist theory (Structuralism) which posits knowledge as something construed from the interrelations between the fixed elements of a synchronic system at any given point of time, instead of an etymological regression to a source of wholeness in the past.

It would seem, then, that "Los signos en rotación" merely dramatizes in a particularly forceful way the basic incompatibility—or series of contradictions—on which the text as a whole is based. There are, however, certain important factors which justify the necessity and even the internal cohesion of the new vision. In order to grasp these factors we must look carefully at the interpretation of Mallarmé. The new epilogue begins, like its predecessor, as an attempt to explain the failure of modern attempts at "transformación de la sociedad en comunidad creadora, en poema vivo; y del poema en vida social, en imagen encarnada" (AL2 254). This utopian view of a libertarian society modelled on poetry has remained a mere dream: "La conversión de la sociedad en comunidad y la del poema en poesía práctica no están a la vista" (AL2 254). The failure is explained partly, as in 1956, by the degeneration of modern revolutionary movements and by the conversion of Marxism into an official teleological dogma and a new instrument of opression in those countries where it has won power.

Yet the epilogue also describes three other closely related factors—
hardly explored in 1956—that obstruct the transformation of reality: the loss
of a traditional world view, the destructive effect of technology, and the crisis
of meaning. For Paz, the traditional world view was based on an archetypal
model of the universe as a harmonious and ordered whole that reflected
cosmic and natural rhythms and also each society's cyclical concept of time.
This organic scheme is fractured when the modern age eliminates the divine
presence and enthrones a linear and successive concept of time. With the
subsequent crisis of modernity there is a centrifugal dispersion and fragmentation of what remains of the former unified totality: "En un universo que se
desgrana y se separa de sí, totalidad que ha dejado de ser pensable excepto
como ausencia o colección de fragmentos heterogéneos, el yo también se
disgrega" (AL2 260). As authentic dialogue and communication depend on
the existence of others, poetry seeks to invoke and create this lost presence:
"La poesía: búsqueda de los otros, descubrimiento de la *otredad*" (AL2 261).

The world, then, has ceased to be a recognizable image or archetype.
Technology, the only modern reply to this loss, has only succeeded in
introducing a utilitarian and instrumentalist criterion of value, thus accelerat-
ing the fragmentation of the former unified system of analogical correspondences into a heterogeneous collection of objects that have no meaning apart
from their functions. This condemnation of technology as nihilistic destruction, as alienating exploitation due to a will to power, is obviously indebted
to Heidegger. The notion that the rationalistic-scientific adoration of
technology has led to a soul-destroying process of mechanization and
dehumanization is very prominent not only in "Los signos en rotación" but
also in "La nueva analogía: poesía y tecnología," an essay written in 1967. In
both essays, however, the condemnation of technology is followed by a
reflection on the positive ways in which modern art can use technology
without being controlled by it.

The traditional or pre-modern work of art could still be "una representación de la figura del universo, su copia o su símbolo" (AL2 262) precisely
because there was a stable and identifiable world view that provided a
mimetic model. If we accept that this archetype has been destroyed and that
technology cannot provide a metaphysical substitute because it is a means
and not an end in itself, then it is difficult not to accept the conclusion that
modern art must be non-mimetic and non-representational. Although it
seems to preclude the possibility of traditional, mimetic art, it could be said
that technology has a liberating effect. Free from the obligation to represent,
the modern artist can exploit the fragmentary signs and the empty space left
in the wake of technology's destruction:

> La técnica libera a la imaginación de toda mitología y la enfrenta con
> lo desconocido. La enfrenta a sí misma y, ante la ausencia de toda
> imagen del mundo, la lleva a configurarse. Esa configuración es el
> poema. Plantado sobre lo informe a la manera de los signos de la

> técnica y, como ellos, en busca de un significado sin cesar elusivo, el poema es un espacio vacío pero cargado de inminencia. No es todavía la presencia: es una parvada de signos que buscan su significado y que no significan más que ser búsqueda. (AL2 263-264)

Here we have the outline of a new aesthetic: the work as a configuration of signs hovering over an empty space, offering only a *potential* meaning subject to dynamic movement. In a way, of course, it could be said that this new art is representational in a negative sense: its formlessness mirrors the lack of any coherent world view.

The prophet of this fragmentary, dynamic and spatial art form is Mallarmé. It is interesting to note that in each phase of Paz's poetic thought different poetic models are erected as historical antecedents for the type of poetry deemed necessary in the present, thus construing a poetic tradition from the changing perspective of the present. In the early period the genealogy includes certain mystics, Romantics, *poètes maudits* and twentieth-century figures who embody the fusion of poetry with religious and erotic experience. In the 1956 edition of *El arco y la lira* the poetic family is expanded to include Eliot and Pound and certain figures from the Hispanic tradition (Unamuno and Antonio Machado but more for their prose than for their verse) while a privileged position is given to Breton and the Surrealists as the culmination of modern poetry. The 1967 edition broadens the scope of this tradition, especially in relation to modern Hispanic poetry (Spanish American poets are discussed in some detail), while Surrealism, although still granted a prominent position, is seen in more of a historical perspective. The sudden appearance of Mallarmé is the real novelty in this phase.

The Mallarmé who fascinates Paz at this moment is not the Symbolist poet who wrote occasional verse but rather the author of one late poem[7] which is seen as both apocalyptic and utopian: "*Un Coup de dés* cierra este periodo [de la poesía moderna] y abre otro, que apenas si comenzamos a explorar" (AL2 270). But why does Paz attach such enormous importance to a poem published in 1897? Why does he see it as both the culmination of modern poetry and the dawn of a new art? It should be pointed out that Paz had various models in this new reading of Mallarmé. In the first place, one should mention the theoreticians and practitioners of concrete poetry in Brazil, especially the members of the "Noigandres" group. Due to the traditional lack of communication between Brazil and Spanish America, Paz only discovered Brazilian concrete poetry in English translation in 1963, even though the group had begun its activities in the early 1950s. In a similarly indirect manner, Haroldo de Campos, one of the leading Brazilian theoreticians and practitioners, had read "Los signos en rotación" in a French translation (the essay first appeared as the new epilogue to *El arco y la lira* in the French edition published by Gallimard in 1965). Fascinated and excited by what he saw as the "postura radical" of the essay and its proximity to the theories of the Brazilian poets, Haroldo de Campos initiated a correspondence with Paz that was to culminate in a translation of *Blanco*.[8] Through independent but parallel routes both Paz and the Brazilian movement had come to see Mallarmé as the precursor of a new type of poetry.

The work of the French essayist Maurice Blanchot represents another antecedent. In *L'Espace littéraire* (1955) and in a later book quoted in "Los signos en rotación," *Le Livre à venir* (1959), Blanchot analyzes the way in which Mallarmé reaches a kind of ontological impersonality through a sacrifice of subjective personality to the objective reality of language. For Blanchot, the destruction of traditional language opens up a vast space in which the apparently negative residues of nothingness, absence, emptiness, silence and indetermination take on positive and affirmative values. His reading of the poem is seminal and worth quoting at length:

> *Un Coup de dés* est né d'une entente nouvelle de l'espace littéraire, tel que puissent s'y engendrer, par des rapports nouveaux de mouvement, des relations nouvelles de compréhension. Mallarmé a toujours eu conscience de ce fait, méconnu jusqu'à lui et peut-être après lui, que la langue était un système de relations spatiales infiniment complexes dont ni l'espace géométrique ordinaire, ni l'espace de la vie pratique ne nous permettent de ressaisir l'originalité. On ne crée rien et on ne parle d'une manière créatrice que par l'approche préalable du lieu d'extrême vacance où, avant d'être paroles déterminées et exprimées, le langage est le mouvement silencieux des rapports, c'est-à-dire 'la scansion rythmique de l'être.' Les paroles ne sont jamais là que pour désigner l'étendue de leurs rapports: l'espace où ils se projettent et qui, à peine désigné, se replie et se reploie, n'étant nulle part où il est. (286)

Blanchot views this work as marking the end of traditional literature and the beginning of a new kind of art: "Poème essentiel (et non pas un poème en prose), mais qui, pour la première et l'unique fois, rompt avec la tradition: non seulement consent à la rupture, mais inaugure intentionnellement un art nouveau, art encore à venir et l'avenir comme art" (283).[9]

Finally, the view that *Un Coup de dés*, through its dispersion and fragmentation of the unified solidity of mimetic art, embodies the birth of a new aesthetic can also be found in the early work of Umberto Eco. In *Opera aperta*, first published in 1962, Eco gives a now classic account of what he understood to be a series of characteristics shared by certain experimental works of modern art. He describes the formal and structural properties of those "open" or unfinished works that demand a plurality of different interventions by the active performer, reader or spectator. The open work is conceptualized (using scientific metaphors) as a "network of possibilities" which, due to its structural indetermination and essential ambiguity, has to be "completed" through a plurality of interpretations that are simultaneously generated and controlled by the structural properties of the work. Eco sees the theoretical model of the open work as an epistemological metaphor of our conceptual models of the universe that are made explicit in scientific theories of knowledge.

In his study of how cultural models express a world view, Eco draws a sharp distinction between the closed, unambiguous, static, monolithic, hierarchical order of a traditional universe governed by God and reflected by works of art with a limited number of prescribed and unquestionable readings and, in contrast to this, the model of modern art that expresses a world view governed by chance, ambiguity, indetermination and probability. Although his point of departure is information theory and modern music, the author identifies Joyce, Mallarmé and Kafka as the literary architects of the open work. Eco's interest, in the case of Mallarmé, is in the impossible project which constituted the dream and unfinished goal of the poet's life: what he called *le Livre* or *l'Oeuvre*. Envisioned as a perfect embodiment of the universe ("l'explication orphique de la terre"), the Work would be dynamic, in constant metamorphosis, a combinatory art with no fixed meaning and infinite possibilities of organization.

Although Eco discusses the problems associated with the open work, producing what could be considered a manifesto for a new avant-garde, similar to those produced by the Brazilian poets and by the French essayists already mentioned, there are certain crucial differences between his approach and Paz's reading of Mallarmé. Eco has described his book as "pre-semiotic" (5) and outlined his many points of contact with Structuralist analysis, although he does depart from orthodox Structuralism by giving a crucial role to the interpreter in the production of meaning. Nevertheless, in terminology, methodology and goals his approach aspires to be scientific. Science is privileged as the supreme type of knowledge which art can only hope to metaphorically express but never rival. His concept of the work as an epistemological metaphor gives art a secondary role, allowing it to do no more than work on previously elaborated scientific models. It is revealing, for instance, that Eco cannot contain his irritation at Mallarmé's mystic and hermetic claims to a superior form of absolute knowledge. Moreover, even though he has a great passion for literature (especially for Joyce), Eco's pervading interest, as confirmed by his later work, is the construction of a general theory of semiotics.

Although Paz's work at this moment is full of references to the other arts and the sciences, seeing in them common features such as discontinuity and indetermination, his passion is obviously poetry. Paz's fascination with Mallarmé and with Eastern religious ideas is due to the possibility he sees of constructing a *spiritual* art that would contain and release a new kind of wisdom (*sagesse* is the word used in *Corriente alterna*). His principal interest, as a creator and a thinker, is not in a scientific explanation of art but in the possibility of liberation (spiritual, collective, political) that a new art form could offer. Art is seen as inseparable from morality: it should provoke a

change in life. All of these concerns separate Paz not only from Eco but from
the Structuralist tendency in general. As we shall see, Paz's reading of
Mallarmé is not really Structuralist at all.

In his interpretation of *Un Coup de dés* Paz adscribes a dual value to
the poem: apocalyptic closure and prophetic aperture. It is apocalyptic
because it represents the impossibility of Mallarmé's Symbolist dream of
making the poem into a magical double of the universe. What it prophesizes
is a new spatial form that liberates a plurality of simultaneous readings
through a new kind of syntax or prosody: "El poema cesa de ser una sucesión
lineal y escapa así a la tiranía tipográfica que nos impone una visión
longitudinal del mundo" (AL2 271). As Paz's reading is extremely concentrated I shall briefly discuss some of the most striking features of this poem,
features which Paz takes for granted and therefore does not make explicit in
his text.[10]

The new syntax is both visual and acoustic. In the original preface
Mallarmé had identified the two codes that the poem admits: a pictorial code
which introduces "un espacement de la lecture," gives great importance to
the blanks or spaces that fragment and disperse the images into clusters or
"constellations," uses different typographical effects in order to suggest
"subdivisions prismatiques de l'Idée" (455), as if the Absolute could be
convoked by the virtually infinite number of visual combinations; and,
simultaneously, a musical code in which the spaces function as signs for
silence, while the different types of print, the recurring "motifs," and the
spatial layout in vertically superimposed "layers" create a symphonic effect of
density, resonance, rhythmical movement and temporal variation.

Capable of being experienced as both a visual representation and a
dynamic musical score, the poem also has two discernible semantic fields of
reference, both mirrored in the spatial layout: a "psychological" vocabulary
of seafaring, storm and shipwreck, suggesting emotional insecurity and the
threat of being engulfed by the vast chaos of the sea; and a metaphysical or
epistemological vocabulary which describes the failure of a search for
knowledge. The act of throwing the dice is analogous to the act of writing the
poem since both are attempts to impose order, necessity and destiny (the
Absolute Idea) upon chaos, contingency and chance (the empty void or abyss
of Nothingness). Although chance cannot be anulled by any act, Mallarmé
suggests it can be fragmented, dispersed or neutralized through an infinite
series of potential ramifications which each reader can construe into fragile
"constellations" which are dispersed again as the creative act of reading
moves on.

As both a finite negation and what Paz calls "un poema abierto hacia
el infinito," the text contains within it the generative principle of all future
interpretations. Although it can never name the Absolute number and
thereby annul random indetermination, each reading can be seen as a
"compte total en formation." Each reader, forced to relate horizontally and
vertically, visually and acoustically, mediating between the concrete and the

abstract, the psychological and the metaphysical, explores a virtually infinite network of simultaneously valid potentialities. The attributes of negation thus take on positive qualities. It is for this reason that Paz declares that "la novedad de *Un Coup de dés* consiste en ser un *poema crítico*," understanding the latter as "aquel poema que contiene su propia negación y que hace de esa negación el punto de partida del canto, a igual distancia de afirmación y negación" (AL2 271).

The "constellation" formed by future interpretations is not static but perpetually hypothetical. Paz suggests that Mallarmé's art of potentialities is made possible by a deep feeling that the cosmos has lost its consistency. In the face of chaos, the only reality that remains is language itself: an ideal, self-contained, relational system severed from its referential capability. The Absolute, if it exists, resides not in the external world or in the self but in the autonomous and dynamic interrelations of language itself. Mallarmé hinted at this in an earlier essay: "L'oeuvre pure implique la disparition élocutoire du poëte, qui cède l'initiative aux mots, par le heurt de leur inégalité mobilisés" (366). The Symbolist vision of the universe as an infinite system of analogical correspondences has been transposed to language itself. Mallarmé's awareness of the destruction of the traditional world view and of the total absence of any religious, metaphysical or scientific certainty allows for the creation of a new art form: "Aunque el horizonte de *Un Coup de dés* no es el de la técnica . . . el espacio que abre es el mismo a que se enfrenta la técnica: mundo sin imagen, realidad sin mundo e infinitamente real" (AL2 275).

The final section of "Los signos en rotación" charts the legacy of Mallarmé's poem. Paz sees elements of continuity in modern literature, especially in Surrealism's attempts—through automatic writing and collective creation—to dissolve the notion of the author and reestablish "la soberanía del lenguaje sobre el autor" (AL2 276). Although he favours these developments there is a rejection of the desirability of "eliminating" the creator. This notion, popularized soon after by Barthes' phrase "the death of the author" and by Foucault's proclamation of the impending disappearance of man, is dismissed as "una obsesión contemporánea: un miedo y una resignación," in which Paz sees "el proceso de sumisión espiritual del hombre" (AL2 277). The anti-humanism of Structuralism is rejected because it is seen as a nihilistic threat to one of Paz's basic convictions: that poetry and art should be instruments of communion between men, thus substituting the void left by the absence of religious and metaphysical faith. Indeed, one of the hopes that dominate this period of his work is that by using modern technology and by exploiting the model inherited from Mallarmé, poetry may once more recover some of its ancient properties as an art that is recited in an act of collective participation, a ritual performance, instead of the "arte mental" implied by the solitary and passive act of reading a printed text.

Mallarmé's poem is interpreted by Paz as a utopian prophecy of an art that could become a collective ritual of communion:

Toda escritura convoca a un lector. La del poema venidero suscita la imagen de una ceremonia: juego, recitación, *pasión* (nunca espectáculo). El poema será recreado colectivamente. En ciertos momentos y sitios, la poesía puede ser vivida por todos: el arte de la fiesta aguarda su resurrección. (AL2 281)

This ceremonial aspect of the new aesthetic should, of course, be read in conjunction with the poetics already developed in the first edition of *El arco y la lira*, where poetry is seen as analogous to myth ("todo poema, en la medida en que es ritmo, es mito") in so far as it rhythmically reenacts and recreates in the present archetypal or sacred time, "tiempo original que abraza todos los tiempos, pasados o futuros, en un presente, en una presencia total" (AL1 63). Just as a ritual reenacts the cyclical time of myth, a poem performs the same temporal operation on history: "Como en el mito, en el poema el tiempo cotidiano sufre una trasmutación: deja de ser sucesión homogénea y vacía para convertirse en ritmo, esto es, en tiempo original" (AL1 64). The denial of linear time and the corresponding recreation of a perpetual present are carried out in the temporal operations of writing and reading.

Yet the "negation" of history is paradoxical since the transcendence of linear time must occur within history. The two types of temporality (sequential history and cyclical myth) intersect in the poem, which thus becomes both linear sequence and suspended presence. Writing or reading the poem involves two mutually dependent operations: "trasmutación del tiempo histórico en arquetipo y encarnación de este arquetipo en un ahora determinado e histórico" (AL1 185). This definition is very close to Jakobson's later linguistic formulation of the poetic function: "The poetic function projects the principle of equivalence from the axis of selection into the axis of combination" (95). The linguist's language is more "scientific" and his definition is more precise, but the poet is trying to express a similar idea.

Since words have been emptied of their meaning and since we have no coherent world view, the modern poem can only be "un conjunto de signos que buscan un significado, un ideograma que gira sobre sí mismo y alrededor de un sol que todavía no nace" (AL2 282). Severed from the past and from an unimaginable future, poetry must inhabit "un presente fijo e interminable y, no obstante, en continuo movimiento" (AL2 283). As in the 1956 epilogue there is an attempt to reunite the solitary poet with the community: "La separación del poeta ha terminado: su palabra brota de una situación común a todos" (AL2 284), yet once again what the poet shares with his fellow men is orphanhood, exile and a search for meaning in a world devoid of meaning. The essay ends on an ecstatic note of climax: "Todo está presente: será presencia." Yet the reader knows that this presence is still absent and that the poem is no more than "una prefiguración: inminencia de presencia" (AL2 284).

* * *

If we accept that "Los signos en rotación" represents an attempt to substitute the Surrealist doctrine, that had identified revolutionary transformation and artistic freedom, with an alternative utopian model based on Mallarmé's open, spatial form that requires a creative collaboration on the part of the reader, then it remains to be shown just how this new art form can function as a prefiguration of not only individual but also collective, social, political and historical freedom. In order to do this we would have to examine at length the essays in *Corriente alterna*, where the full implications of this new aesthetic are sketched out. Yet this task would require a separate essay due to the complexity of the central theme that could quite plausibly be called one of the basic questions of late twentieth-century thought: the crisis of our linear concept of time that affects not only art but also the sciences, politics, history and morality. This cultural crisis of modernity is now widely accepted and debated under the name of *postmodernism*, but it was undoubtedly more difficult to perceive in the 1960s. Here, I can only mention some of the main issues that seem to have been generated by the aesthetic vision.

In *Corriente alterna*, as in the essay already examined, the apocalyptic tone coexists with the prophecy of a new art form which heralds a possible utopia: "Otro arte despunta"; "Otro tiempo alborea: otro arte" (CA 23, 39). The synchronic concept of time permits a return to the ancient idea of a combinatory art, a playful, collective ritual that seeks to accomplish the Surrealist dream of eliminating barriers between art and life: "La época que comienza acabará por fin con las 'obras' y disolverá la contemplación en el *acto*. No un nuevo arte: un nuevo ritual, una fiesta—la invención de una forma de *pasión* que será una repartición del tiempo, el espacio y el lenguaje" (CA 73). Yet how can this new art be achieved in practical terms? One possibility is that poetry should once more become an oral and auditory experience, a *performance* that involves collective participation. Modern poetry could perhaps achieve something similar through the use of the new technological instruments of reproduction: "Pero la futura poesía será oral. Colaboración entre las máquinas parlantes, las pensantes y un *público de poetas*, será el *arte de escuchar y combinar los mensajes*" (CA 71).[11]

The second and third parts of *Corriente alterna* trace the multiple analogies between this new aesthetic and other changes in the social, historical, political and moral spheres. Youth movements, the use of drugs in countries of the developed world, Nietzsche's nihilistic criticism of progress that results in a ludic aesthetic, Buddhism's negation of the Western notions of the self, static substance and historical change: these diverse phenomena are all interpreted as signs that confirm the end of modernity as a linear concept of time, thus reinforcing the implications derived from the reading of Mallarmé and Structuralism. The full importance of this for Paz's political thought is illuminated in those essays that dwell on the eclipse of the classical concept of revolution and the corresponding resurgence of the notions of collective revolt and individual rebellion. Here Paz identifies a phenomenon that proliferated in the 1960s and which he sees as representing a fracture in the monolithic discourse of Western reason: "la revuelta del tercer mundo." In more recent texts he has explored another development that also lies outside the previsions of classical Marxist doctrine: a religious and nationalist resurgence he has baptized "la revuelta de los particularismos."[12]

These multiple ramifications confirm the importance of Paz's reading of Mallarmé in the configuration of an aesthetic that is inseparable from an attempt to construct a new morality, a new vision of history and a new political philosophy. This wider project constitutes the very centre of Paz's endeavour as poet and thinker. It is, of course, a moving centre that constantly redefines itself in the light of its need to explain a volatile present. Each reformulation implies a rereading and re-vision of previous attempts. It is a tribute to the dynamic force of this moving centre that we can say today that the recurring obsessions of Octavio Paz are among the basic questions of modern thought.

NOTES

1. For a fuller view of the early prose see my article "La prehistoria estética de Octavio Paz" in the list of works cited.

2. For an overview of the changes in structure and content between these different editions see Santí's "Introduction" to his edition of *Libertad bajo palabra* and Paz's own declarations in an interview with me entitled "Genealogía de un libro: *Libertad bajo palabra.*"

3. The list is still incomplete. Among the several important essays collected in book form some years later: "La nueva analogía: poesía y tecnología", "Presencia y presente: Baudelaire crítico de arte" (both written in 1967) and "El soneto en ix" (this essay written in 1968 accompanies a translation of one of Mallarmé's sonnets). The three essays are included in *El signo y el garabato* (1973).

4. I include parenthetical references to Paz's work within the text using the following abbreviations: AL1 for the first edition of *El arco y la lira*; AL2 for the second edition of the same text; CA for *Corriente alterna*; PO for *Las peras del olmo*; OV for *La otra voz*. Full references are given in the list of works cited.

5. There are some variants between the original edition of *Los signos en rotación* (Buenos Aires: Sur, 1965) and the version published in the second edition of *El arco y la lira* in 1967. However, since they are insignificant I shall quote from the latter version.

6. One of the most revealing modifications is the elimination in 1967 of the phrase "No hay poema sin creador" (AL1 37), while the confident affirmation that "el lenguaje es algo exclusivo del hombre" is qualified by a footnote in 1967 (AL2 33).

7. I find it puzzling that H. Mondor and G. Jean-Aubry, the editors of the Pléiade edition of Mallarmé's works, should call *Un Coup de dés* "cette dernière des oeuvres en prose de Stéphane Mallarmé" (1581). Although it is radically different from most traditional verse, the spatial and typographical layout of the text makes it quite alien to prose.

8. The correspondence between the two poets from 1968 to 1981, together with the translation ("transcreation" as Haroldo de Campos would call it) of *Blanco* and of other poems by Paz, and an introductory note by Emir Rodríguez Monegal, have been published in Portuguese: Octavio Paz e Haroldo de Campos, *Transblanco (em torno a Blanco de Octavio Paz)*. The quote is taken from the first letter to Paz, dated 24. 2. 1968 (94). In his reply dated 14. 3. 1968 Paz refers to "Los signos en rotación" as "una refundición, ampliación y rectificación del antiguo 'Epílogo' de la primera edición" [my translation] (96). In the same letter Paz relates his late discovery of the Brazilian movement through English translations.

9. Blanchot coincides in this with the view of the early Roland Barthes who saw Mallarmé's destruction of "classical" writing as a liberating effect permitting the emergence of "neutral" writing or what he calls "le degré zéro de l'écriture" in the book of the same name published in 1953. This is one of the few instances in his whole work in which Barthes confers importance on a *poetic* text and one suspects it is due to the confessed influence of Blanchot.

10. My reading of Mallarmé's poem is indebted to the interpretations of Bowie and Davies in the list of works cited.

11. In his most recent book Paz has again commented on the immense possibilities modern technology offers to poetry, in particular the television screen that can combine visual, acoustic and dynamic effects: "En el poema venidero, oído y leído, visto y escuchado, han de enlazarse las dos experiencias. Fiesta y contemplación: sobre la página animada de la pantalla, la tipografía será un surtidor de signos, trazos e imágenes dotadas de color y movimiento; a su vez, las voces dibujarán una geometría de ecos y reflejos, un tejido de aire, sonidos y sentidos enlazados" (OV 123-124).

12. See especially "Revuelta y resurrección" in *Tiempo nublado* (85-103).

WORKS CONSULTED

Blanchot, Maurice. *Le Livre à venir*. Paris: Gallimard, 1959.

Bowie, Malcolm. *Mallarmé and the Art of Being Difficult*. Cambridge: Cambridge UP, 1978.

Davies, Gardner. *Vers une explication rationelle du 'Coup de dés'*. Paris: Corti, 1953.

Eco, Umberto. *Obra abierta*. 1962. Trans. Roser Berdagué. México: Origen/Planeta, 1985.

Jakobson, Roman. "Linguistics and Poetics." 1960. *The Structuralists: From Marx to Lévi-Strauss*. Ed. Richard T. de George and Fernande M. de George. New York: Anchor, 1972. 85-122.

Mallarmé, Stéphane. *Oeuvres complètes*. Ed. Henri Mondor et G. Jean Aubry. Paris: Gallimard, 1945.

Paz, Octavio. *Tiempo nublado*. Barcelona: Seix Barral, 1983.

_____. . *El arco y la lira*. México: Fondo de Cultura Económica, 1956.

_____. . *El arco y la lira*. 2ª ed. corregida y aumentada. México: Fondo de Cultura Económica, 1967.

_____. . *Las peras del olmo*. 1957. 2ª ed. revisada. Barcelona: Seix Barral, 1974.

_____. . *Corriente alterna*. México: Siglo XXI, 1967.

_____. . *El signo y el garabato*. México: Joaquín Mortiz, 1973.

---. *La otra voz. Poesía y fin de siglo*. Barcelona: Seix Barral, 1990.

Paz, Octavio e Haroldo de Campos. *Transblanco (em torno a 'Blanco' de Octavio Paz*. Rio de Janeiro: Guanabara, 1986.

Paz, Octavio y Anthony Stanton. "Genealogía de un libro: *Libertad bajo palabra*." (Entrevista) *Vuelta* Diciembre 1988: 15-21.

Rodríguez Monegal, Emir. "Relectura de *El arco y la lira*." *Revista Iberoamericana* 37 (1971): 35-46.

Santí, Enrico Mario. Introducción. *Libertad bajo palabra (1935-1957)*. By Octavio Paz. Madrid: Cátedra, 1988. 9-63.

Santí, Enrico Mario. "Octavio Paz: crítica y poética." *Escritura y tradición. Texto, crítica y poética en la literatura hispanoamericana*. Barcelona: Laia, 1988: 103-126.

Stanton, Anthony. "La prehistoria estética de Octavio Paz: los escritos en prosa (1931-1943)." *Literatura Mexicana* 2 (1991): 23-55.

LOS DOBLES EN EL PROCESO DE ESCRITURA DE *RAYUELA*

POR

ANA MARIA BARRENECHEA
Columbia University

El cotejo de *Rayuela* con el *Cuaderno de bitácora,* en el que Cortázar fue haciendo anotaciones de distinta naturaleza para registrar en forma no sistemática el proceso de construcción de la novela, me ayudará a iluminar el juego de dobles que pulula en ella. Mi propósito es estudiar *pre-texto* y *texto* con los supuestos de la nueva crítica genética, enfrentándolos y haciéndolos dialogar sin caer en el fetichismo finalista [1].

Los dobles surgen en el pre-texto en forma más parca. Aparecen algo desarrollados Horacio/Maga, Horacio/Traveler, Maga/Talita; otros figuran sólo mencionados y otros son reconocibles por el cotejo con el desenvolvimiento posterior de la novela.

Dos rasgos caracterizan *El cuaderno* cuando se lo confronta con *Rayuela.* Por una parte, la naturaleza peculiar del primero —con el esquematismo de las indicaciones— hace que estén sólo esbozados los personajes y las escenas, y que ofrezca un diseño menos rico y ambiguo que el de la novela publicada. Pero por eso mismo ayuda a precisar el esquema dual y los paradigmas que subyacen en la construcción de los dobles.

---

[1] En adelante citaré *El cuaderno* con la sigla *C* y *Rayuela* con *R* y el número de página. (Los subrayados están en el original siempre que no lleven indicación de que me pertenecen.) Sobre el primero véase mi artículo «La génesis del texto: *Rayuela* y su *Cuaderno de bitácora» (INTI,* IV-V, Otoño 1979-primavera 1980, pp. 78-92); para métodos de crítica genética: «Teoría y práctica de la crítica genética: el *Cuaderno de bitácora* de *Rayuela»,* en *Homenaje a Manuel Alvar* (Madrid: Gredos, en publicación) y los volúmenes colectivos de la escuela francesa actual: *Essais de critique génétique* y *Flaubert à l'oeuvre* (Paris: Flammarion, 1979 y 1980), y Jean Bellemin-Noël, *Le texte et l'avant-texte* (Paris: Larousse, 1972).

Por otra parte, *El cuaderno* plantea expresamente el fenómeno, su importancia y sus conexiones con la isotopía fundadora de *Rayuela*. En un pasaje —que luego citaré *in extenso*— expone la preocupación central revelada bajo la fórmula trópica $x \rightarrow y$ y su relación con la noción del doble[2]:

> *El doppelgänger* [...] Quizá *lo que ocurre es otra cosa,* que no vemos [...] Quizá hay una duplicación de signo inverso (por eso el sentimiento del doppelänger) *(C,* 125).

En otros momentos no está explícita la alianza y es necesario rastrearla en ciertos indicios. Por ejemplo, resulta significativo fijarse en la distribución de la página: la convivencia de dos tópicos en un mismo espacio indica que estaban relacionados en ese momento del proceso de la escritura aunque no aparezcan manifestados sus nexos.

La página 87 de *El cuaderno* registra una cita de René Daumal, autor cuya busca de trascendencia en la experiencia vital y en la escritura atrajo poderosamente a Cortázar. Debió de sentir que la aventura metafísica de su personaje tenía un aire de parentesco con la de Daumal, y lo señaló consignando la fusión de ambos: «Je ne veux pas mourir sans avoir compris porquoi j'avais vécu —dijo *Oliveira René Daumal»* (el subrayado es mío)[3]. En la misma página, inmediatamente después,

---

[2] El esquema trópico fundador aparece de diversas maneras en *El cuaderno* en una veintena de fragmentos *(C,* 50-53, 70, 71, 87, 89, 94, 99, 106, 107, 113, 120, 123, 125-127, 137). Se manifiesta en todos los niveles de la fábula (argumento) y del *sujet* (organización), en forma narrativa y discursiva, en la referencialidad y la autorreferencialidad. Se resuelve en una semiosis generalizada (x en lugar de y, $x \rightarrow y$), en una busca de relaciones que desemboca en la trascendencia (x está relacionado con y, x lleva a y). Es a la vez un ejercicio cognoscitivo empleado en el desciframiento de esos signos; una elección vital de la ruptura, la excentración, la inversión que traerá la plenitud y la unidad; un camino o mandala que se recorre hacia una realidad otra, es decir, hacia un centro, o una revelación súbita, que anuncian ambas la noción de figura; es finalmente una inquisición sobre el sentido secreto de la existencia y un ciego anhelo de encontrarlo.

[3] La cita está tomada de *Le Mont Analogue* (Paris: Gallimard, 1952, NRF), p. 56, y se repite entre frases de *jazz* en *R,* 80, sin la identificación Oliveira-Daumal. Véanse otros recuerdos del mismo autor en *C,* 69, 101 y 116. René Daumal (1908-1944) publicó en vida un primer libro de poemas, *Le Contre-Ciel* (Paris: Bibliothèque Jacques Doucet, 1936), donde se advierte ya el concepto de la poesía como una de las posibles vías de la trascendencia. «Le Père lumineux de la vrai connaissance, celui des initiés, est aussi celui des poètes, des vrais poètes» («De l'attitude critique devant la Poésie», en *Cahiers du Sud,* décembre 1929, apud A. Rolland de Renéville, «Préface» de la edición citada de *Le Mont Analogue,* p. 13). Más tarde, en *La Grande Beuverie* (Paris: Gallimard, 1938, NRF),

apunta este comentario sobre las relaciones que son transformaciones con inversión de signo contrario:

Extrapolación (palabra que no «existe» en español oh oh!)
   Todos los datos de un momento, de un espacio, ¿no son extrapolables a un otro plano que, así, se deja entrever?
   El «mundo» es signo de...
   Cierto Gran Desorden puede extrapolarse a un Centro: brusco cambio de — a +. Miguel de Mañara — + el Santo
      Loyola $\longrightarrow$
      Pablo

lo cual alude a su persistente utilización de los dobles como enlace de figuras opuestas pero complementarias y al movimiento trópico que las funda $(x \rightarrow y)$.

   Así se presenta (con la convivencia de la fusión Oliveira-Daumal y del concepto de extrapolación en una misma página) la plurivalencia del doble en el *pre-texto,* que luego corroborará el *texto.* Dentro de su variedad distingo tres tipos:

---

dio una parábola que exponía con imaginación y humor la crítica a un mundo «caótico, larval, ilusorio», enceguecido por el mecanicismo, el fetichismo de la intelectualidad y los bienes materiales. Su busca de trascendencia lo llevó al conocimiento de ciertos textos griegos y especialmente orientales, de la tradición mística, del ocultismo, de la *Kábbala,* de la alquimia, y aún más modernos como los de Gurdjieff. Estudió sánscrito para conocer más íntimamente las fuentes del hinduismo y realizó algunas traducciones de esa lengua. Daumal, siempre en lucha con la pobreza y la enfermedad, se caracterizó por exigirse una total autenticidad en la vida y en la escritura, la cual quería que fuese testimonio de una experiencia vital de la busca de la iluminación y no sólo un producto del intelecto. Antes de morir dejó muy avanzado un relato con el que pensaba completar *La Grande Beuverie,* con una visión positiva del hombre y del universo que contrabalancease el negativismo del anterior. Trataba de comunicar el camino que él y un grupo de amigos creían haber encontrado: «Ce récit sera sous une forme de roman d'aventures intitulé le *Mont Analogue:* c'est la montagne symbolique qui est la voie unissant le Ciel à la Terre; voie qui doit matériellement, humainement *exister,* sans quoi notre situation serait sans espoir» (apud A. Rolland Renéville, p. 19). Véase también aquí nota 9. El conocido símbolo de la montaña como eje del universo emparienta este libro con los símbolos del Mandala, del circo o la carpa, de la rayuela, del puente, diseminados en la novela de Cortázar. También los une la mezcla de tonos (humor y juego imaginativo, con seriedad y angustia) en el discurso. (Sobre las analogías y divergencias entre ambos escritores trataré en otra ocasión.) A la muerte de R. Daumal se publicaron: *Le Mont Analogue,* 1952; *Essais et notes. I: Chaque fois que l'aube paraît,* 1953 (del que se toma la cita de *C,* 116); *Poésie noire, poésie blanche,* 1954; *Lettres à ses amies,* I, 1958, todos en Paris: Gallimard, NRF.

1. *Complementarios,* desdoblamiento en opuestos que recompondrían la unidad perdida (Maga/Horacio, Traveler/Horacio).
2. *Gemelos,* identificación en figuras semejantes con leves variaciones (Maga, Talita, Pola; Horacio, Morelli; Talita, Traveler).
3. *Versiones deformantes,* lectura humorística, ridícula, grotesca y degradada de los héroes (Ossip, de Horacio; Berthe Trépat y la *clocharde* Emmanuèle, de la Maga).

En estos últimos la deformación no se limita a una función retórica (oposición de lo serio/lo humorístico) más que en el caso de Ossip. En Berthe Trépat y más claramente en la *clocharde* alude a la estructura simbólica global del libro, la antropofanía que se quiere alcanzar por la vía negativa del Gran Desorden. También encarna el peligro de esa busca, con la figura amenazante de la mujer castradora y devoradora (la Madre Terrible): de nuevo Eros/Thánatos, el vacío y la nada que corroen la imagen del Paraíso. Por razones de espacio disponible me limitaré a tratar ahora los dobles complementarios solamente.

Los complementarios

Oliveira, que es el centro y el héroe de esta historia, se bifurca formando dos parejas principales de opuestos complementarios, con dobles de distinto y de igual sexo: la Maga y Traveler.

La Maga

No me explayaré en detalle sobre la figura de la Maga en el *pre-texto* y en el *texto,* a la que dedico un estudio especial[4]. En ese trabajo he analizado: 1) los predicados que la definen; 2) la función narratológica; 3) la función semántica, y 4) la función simbólica. De todas ellas surge su perfil y su posibilidad de ser doble de Horacio, por las oposiciones: ignorancia/saber, intuición/razón, vida/no vida, consciencia/inconsciencia, naturaleza/cultura, materia/espíritu, concreción/abstracción. También por la coincidencia de que ambos intuyen (buscan) por caminos distintos un absoluto, y el poder de la Maga de simbolizarlo. Enfren-

---

[4] Véase «La Maga en el proceso de escritura de *Rayuela: pre-texto y texto*», que aparecerá en el volumen colectivo E. Dale Carter, Jr. (ed.), *La última casilla de la rayuela: veinticinco ensayos sobre Cortázar* (Los Angeles: California State University Press; en prensa).

tada a Horacio es, pues, la portadora de uno de los haces de elementos duales que configuran la dialéctica de *Rayuela,* y que el proceso del *pre-texto* va elaborando.

Ahora sólo me detendré en el comentario de la página 74 de *El cuaderno,* porque constituye el testimonio explícito de Cortázar sobre el carácter de doble que le atribuye a la Maga con respecto a Horacio.

> *Oliveira*
> Empiezo a verlo — a verme. Tenía que ser.
> Oliveira sube una escalera. Se siente como el bichito que recorre el canto ? de [la medalla] la moneda [5].
> De mi lado el reverso: la Maga
>   la dimensión poética (esa maravillosa entrega a los textos, a los cuadros poéticos, [al jazz] a los azares de la calle, a las suertes mágicas, al modo surreal de vida)
>   Todo eso es Nerval y Artaud — es decir asocialidad, miseria, soledad, muerte o suicidio. *Inevitablemente* si se quiere ser consecuente hasta lo último.
>   En él (su educación y sus medios)
>   el reverso:
>   la inteligencia
>   el don crítico
>   Wit
>   Esprit
>   Humour
>   Sentirse hombre en el sentido de los humanistas (Castiglione).
>   Todo está en eso.

La página se inicia con una confesión clara de que el autor (Cortázar) se identifica con el personaje (Oliveira), corroborando lo que varios críticos de *Rayuela* habían intuido basados en el análisis del *texto.* Luego expone sumariamente lo que deberá ser una meditación del personaje, alejado de sí mismo, capaz de verse y de ver a la Maga como las dos caras de una moneda. No existe otro lugar en *El cuaderno* —ni creo que tampoco en *Rayuela*— donde se inscriba con mayor nitidez que la Maga y Horacio forman una pareja de opuestos complementarios.

La disposición de la página esboza un paradigma aproximativo de rasgos encolumnados, muy marcados. La columna de la Maga en el paradigma se prolonga en el planteo del futuro desarrollo del sintagma.

---

[5] En mi sistema de transcripción del manuscrito, los signos [ ] abarcan palabras o frases anuladas.

Se reconoce que la dimensión poético-imaginativa, que rompe con las convenciones cotidianas y las leyes de la razón (magia, surrealidad), debe desembocar fatalmente en la muerte. Pero ¿quién lo reconoce en el *pre-texto?* ¿Cortázar, que se ha identificado con su personaje? («Empiezo a verlo — a verme»). ¿Horacio, que se ve a sí mismo frente a la Maga? Porque si el personaje Horacio incorpora a su configuración de inteligencia y razón la dimensión intuitiva e irracional de su doble, la Maga, caminará como ella hacia la muerte. Porque el autor, que controla el *pre-texto* y el *texto,* también decidirá que «si se quiere ser consecuente hasta lo último» *(se* quiere ser... ¿Cortázar, Horacio?) deberá enfrentar a sus personajes con el vacío final. Así se define para la Maga en primer término, y para Horacio, que es su doble, una de las constantes simbólicas: Thánatos, la cual ronda insistentemente a estos y otros personajes y sus acciones (Pola, Morelli, Rocamadour, enfermedad, accidente, suicidio) e impregna el esquema mismo de la trascendencia en el Mandala y la busca del centro (la plenitud o la nada; la carpa del circo o la morgue, cielo, kibbutz, Ygdrassil, o agujero, embudo, pozo).

No puedo pasar en silencio el final de la otra columna del paradigma, que corresponde a Horacio y que concluye en un anticlímax aparentemente inconsciente, exaltando la figura del Héroe: «Sentirse hombre en el sentido de los humanistas (Castiglione)». La frase contradice lo que anotará en páginas posteriores donde el autor se alerta a sí mismo sobre la exagerada dimensión que está tomando el personaje: «El problema es que todo tiende a centrarse demasiado en H. O. Caemos en el soliloquio excesivo, la desmesura egocéntrica» *(C,* 109); «Ojo! no hinchar a O. [...] O. no tiene ningún mérito ni grandeza» *(C,* 136). Sin duda este hombre renacentista, este Castiglione, está pidiendo a gritos la *hache* humorística correctiva del engolamiento aunque deba reduplicarse (hhumanista), para impedirle bordear el ridículo.

La Maga, como opuesto complementario de Oliveira, y ante el rasgo saliente de intelectualidad que lo define, representa el aspecto intuitivo e irracional que él anhela y no posee entre sus predicados definitorios. Ese rasgo no individualiza al héroe, por eso Cortázar necesita desdoblarlo en el personaje femenino. En cambio sí define a la fábula toda como crítica a la civilización occidental, sus dicotomías, su racionalismo, también como metáfora de la busca de una suprarrealidad, de una antropofanía, y como base de las discusiones estéticas y metafísicas que se insertan en ella.

Es necesario aclarar hasta qué punto es verdad que el héroe no lo posea. En los esquemas opositivos que figuran en *El cuaderno* —con la pareja Horacio/Maga o con otras—, el intelecto, el uso de la razón *versus* la intuición es el rasgo definitorio de Horacio, ya con ese nombre, ya con el de vida/no vida, conciencia/inconsciencia. Así, en *C,* 58, después de un párrafo sobre la «incomunicación» por la ignorancia de la Maga, escribe: «Oliveira, Monsieur Teste rodeado de seres más *vivos* que él. La *lucidez,* la *conciencia,* no son vida. La vida más viva es la más espontánea e inconsciente (la Maga, Traveler)». Dejo para otro momento el comentario de la identificación del héroe con el personaje de Valéry, que tan marcadamente está caracterizado como doble de su autor, como escritor y como paradigma del ejercicio del intelecto (caso en parte paralelo al de la identificación de Oliveira con Castiglione).

Junto a esta insistencia figuran, sin embargo, otros indicios que marcan de irracionalidad al mismo Oliveira desde el comienzo. Abundan en el monólogo de *C,* 47, que aunque es de sujeto no determinado parece atribuible al autor y a su héroe conjuntamente («bajo al volcán, me acerco a las Madres, me conecto al Centro»), y en *C,* 53, en las meditaciones de Oliveira en la *jazz session* [6]. Una corrección de *C,* 74, revela lo paradójico del perfil del protagonista. Después de haber anotado el *jazz* como preferencia que denota la irracionalidad de la Maga, Cortázar lo tacha, sin duda por darse cuenta de que no podía poner en el paradigma Maga/Horacio, como supuestamente privativo de la primera, un rasgo compartido tan ostensiblemente por ambos (y aún con mayor énfasis por Horacio), contraviniendo las reglas de todo sistema binario opositivo.

La misma contradicción puede leerse a cada paso en *Rayuela.* Por ejemplo, en pp. 40-41, se contraponen en Horacio el reconocimiento del acierto esencial de la Maga («cierra los ojos y da en el blanco») y el mantenerla marginada sin dejarla entrar en «el círculo de tiza» que aísla a los exquisitos, la crueldad con que califica su ignorancia (tener «aire o gofio en la cabeza») y la envidiosa valoración de sus hallazgos trascendentes (el asomarse «a terrazas sin tiempo que todos ellos buscaban dialécticamente»). Esta paradoja que caracteriza al personaje principal y a la ideología de la novela (quizá a la mayor parte de la obra de Cortázar) exalta conjuntamente al héroe intelectual poseedor de los valores

---

[6] El fragmento en primera persona no identificada en *C,* 47, figura en *R,* 458, como *Morelliana.* Todo el ambiguo espacio de las páginas 46-47 abunda en indicios que inclinan a atribuir lo registrado al autor y su escritura, otras veces al héroe y otras a ambos, con la característica fusión de los dos en varias instancias del *pre-texto.* Del *jazz* se habla en *C,* 46, también, y *C,* 47, registra: «Sí, el jazz es lo mismo; para mí es también el *intercesor.»* En cuanto al pasaje de *C,* 53, ocurre lo contrario al pasar al *texto;* ha sido copiado en *R,* 522, con escasas variaciones, sin atribuírselo a nadie.

culturales más refinados (incluyendo sin duda lo popular rescatado por ese mismo gusto) y al campeón de las vías de la irracionalidad, el juego y la magia[7].

Conviene cotejar *C*, 74, página antes citada para estudiar la función semántica de la Maga como doble de Horacio, con el pasaje de *R*, 116-117, también marcadamente dual, para anotar ciertas divergencias. En el *pre-texto* la conclusión era que el desorden de la Maga llevaba a la desintegración y a la muerte; en el *texto* se exalta su desorden: «Ese desorden que es su orden misterioso», mientras el de Oliveira —«enterrado en prejuicios que respeto y desprecio al mismo tiempo», según comenta de sí— no es más que «el falso orden que disimula el caos».

Se diría que esto refuerza mi interpretación de que en el *pre-texto* *(C*, 74) se mezclaba el punto de vista del autor sobre el curso coherente de su fábula. Aquí, en el *texto,* se ofrece sólo el punto de vista de Horacio en el momento de crisis en que, alejado de la Maga, corrige sus juicios sobre ella en forma que al mismo tiempo simboliza las dicotomías de la obra, la crítica al erróneo camino de Occidente y la busca mística del héroe, frente a la fuerte carga de discusión intelectual y de citas culturales.

Traveler

La pareja arquetípica de los complementarios es sin duda la de Oliveira y su amigo Traveler, la más destacada en el *pre-texto* y en el *texto* entre todos los dobles. Citaré los dos pasajes más significativos de *El cuaderno* por su forma explícita; en ambos figura Talita asociada a su marido en el juego de oposiciones:

Talita y Traveler	Piedras de toque
	Traveler: es más LIBRE. [*][8] Obra sin *reflexión*.
	Talita es como la Maga

....

[7] En *R*, 197-198, parece ofrecer una conciliación de la dualidad *intelecto/intuición, racionalidad/irracionalidad* fuera de la mentalidad occidental: «El absurdo es que no parezca un absurdo [...]. Yo no sé, che, habría que intentar otro camino. —¿Renunciando a la inteligencia? —dijo Gregorovius, desconfiado. —No sé, tal vez. *Empleándola de otra manera. ¿*Estará bien probado que los principios lógicos son carne y uña con nuestra inteligencia? Si hay pueblos capaces de sobrevivir *dentro de un orden mágico...*» (el subrayado es mío). En *C*, 130, anota la cita de Klages: «El espíritu juzga mientras la vida vive.» Ossip recuerda a Klages a propósito del erróneo camino seguido por la especie en *R*, 507, y Oliveira en *R*, 193 y 540, sin reproducir sus palabras.

[8] En mi sistema de transcripción, el asterisco (*) indica «fragmento ilegible».

Oliveira vela toda una noche esperando la muerte a manos de Traveler. Su doppelgänger, su forma fraternal *más realizada*. (C, 79).

Traveler y Oliveira son el mismo? El hombre y su doppelgänger Oliveira es el conocimiento, pero Traveler *vive*. Cada uno desea lo que es propio del otro. *Talita es ese símbolo*. Fábula de Ho y Mo en Daumal, «M. Analogue», p. 128 [9] *(C, 101).*

Identificación progresiva de Talita y la Maga.

La oposición en los dos fragmentos tiene por base el binomio *vida/ conocimiento,* que ya vimos que había servido para establecer, junto con otros, la función de doble de la Maga.

Traveler	*Horacio*
más libre	
obra sin reflexión	
más «realizado»	
vive	es el conocimiento

En la página siguiente se agrega otro rasgo que los separa: *humanidad/inhumanidad. El cuaderno* sólo habla de «la crueldad necesaria» *(C, 82),* sin atribuirla explícitamente a Oliveira, o como una alusión a la renuncia de sus convicciones: «Desesperación (¿piedad? ¿al fin?) de Oliveira» *(C, 123),* para no herir a los Traveler. En *Rayuela,* en cambio, Ossip le echa en cara su dureza en la prosecución del absoluto:

---

[9] Se refiere a un pasaje de la obra de R. Daumal *Le Mont Analogue.* La obra relata las aventuras de un grupo que decide embarcarse y partir en busca de ese monte desde cuya cima se contempla el universo en su unidad. En ella se intercala la leyenda «Histoire des Hommes-creux et de la Rose-amère», pp. 128-135. Dos gemelos idénticos, Ho y Mo, concluyen fundiéndose en un ser, Moho, a la muerte de Mo, que había intentado vanamente apoderarse de la Rosa-amarga. A pesar de que en vida eran iguales en su físico, cuando se unen en uno solo y éste emprende nuevamente la tarea que los justificará, se manifiesta una distinción entre ellos. La parte de Mo es la que conoce el camino (es el saber) y la parte de Ho realiza el gesto adecuado para alcanzar la Rosa-amarga (es la acción). La rosa (la flor del discernimiento) es el objeto del deseo y la busca. En toda la fábula el concepto del doble alude al peligro de la muerte en la figura de los Hombres-huecos. En la primera parte de la historia, Mo es convertido él mismo en Hombre-hueco después de su fracaso. El padre, al enviar a Ho para rescatarlo, le aconseja: «Va vers lui et frappe la tête. Entre dans la forme de son corps. Et Mo revivra parmi nous. N'aie pas peur de tuer un mort.» Esta leyenda se asemeja en algo a la de *El estudiante de Praga,* recordada en *C,* 107 (véase *Homenaje a Alvar),* y el encuentro en el espejo, pero aquí la fusión de los dobles no acarrea la muerte, sino la salvación de ambos en la unidad.

«si hubiera algo de humano en vos» *(R, 217)*. Frente a esto, *El cuaderno* presenta claramente a su doble como un ser marcado por notas de simpatía y humanidad: «Traveler: a tough guy ⟺ un tendre» *(C, 102)*. Es, pues, un hombre tierno, afectuoso, sensible, y al mismo tiempo un muchacho rudo, un tipo de agallas; es decir, un ser vivo ante ese inquisidor de la nada que es Horacio *(R, 237)*.

El *pre-texto* suele presentar la función de doble que le corresponde a Traveler en combinaciones con otros personajes. Por ejemplo, en *C, 79*, Traveler y Talita = Maga son un grupo opuesto por su soltura y afincamiento en lo real a Horacio, el hombre del intelecto y la busca, que se mueve en ámbitos enrarecidos. Pero en *C, 101*, el grupo se redistribuye.

La oposición Traveler/Horacio moviliza el tercer elemento, Talita, que es explícitamente el objeto del deseo, lo que uno no tiene y el otro posee, lo que se quiere alcanzar. *El cuaderno* lo expresa discursivamente y lo subraya con la mención de la obra de René Daumal, *Le Mont Analogue,* donde figura la fábula de Ho y Mo. La escena del puente o de «El tablón», registrada desde el comienzo, había desenvuelto en forma narrativa, a través también de una «fábula», la función de los dobles Traveler y Oliveira, y el papel simbólico de Talita. Volverá luego a poner en escena, en «Los hilos» o «El terror», el mismo triángulo, pero con las posiciones redistribuidas.

En «El puente», como se ha visto al estudiar el proceso de la secuencia narrativa [10], Talita ocupa la posición central, el fiel de la balanza, entre los polos extremos de Horacio y Traveler, que se la disputan en un episodio calificado de «juicio», de «cosa ceremonial» *(C, 45 y 50)*. En «Los hilos», los amigos ocupan el espacio cerrado de la habitación, que es el lugar de su enfrentamiento, y Talita (= Maga, Pola) ha sido desplazada a una posición lateral, en el patio, aunque siempre presente [11]. *C, 121,* fija la entrevista con las frases: «Traveler llega [al amanecer]. Estado de sitio. Diálogo con el doppelgänger». En un segundo plano se mueven las figuras duplicadas en el patio: Talita, Maga, Pola, Lilith, que pueden jugar ahora —como no ocurrió en «El puente»— superpo-

---

[10] Véase mi artículo de *INTI,* citado en nota 1.

[11] También Talita puede ocupar otra posición. Asociada a Traveler y situados en el mismo campo (cuando Traveler se ha desplazado al patio), funcionan ambos unidos frente a Oliveira (que sigue en el espacio de la habitación). Son capaces de sentir la atracción del amigo, o considerarlo afectuosamente desde lejos, y aun de intercambiar conductas con él, pero se hallan al fin de la saga de Buenos Aires en esferas que no se intersectan, como analizo más adelante.

niéndose, sustituyéndose, y ocupar el sitio del deseo en esa zona marginal.

No debe olvidarse que para comprender este ajedrez narrativo resulta altamente significativa la página 125, citada parcialmente al comienzo:

> *El doppelgänger*   Todo lo que *podría ser:*
> Quizá *lo que ocurre es otra cosa,* que no vemos
> Quizá hay como un segundo acontecer por encima o a través de lo que pasa.
> Quizá hay una duplicación de signo inverso (por eso el sentimiento de doppelgänger)
> Quizá la Maga está ahí, entonces.
> Quizá nunca hubo Maga y solamente Talita
> Quizá hubo solamente Pola, Lilith.

Como antes destaqué, este pasaje clave para iluminar la función del doble la conecta con la noción de *extrapolación,* de *analogía,* de *movimiento trópico x → y.* Aunque el concepto que se expone es el de «duplicación con signo inverso», la ejemplificación recae en personajes femeninos gemelos (Maga, Talita, Pola, Lilith) [12] y no se recurre a las parejas de opuestos complementarios (Maga/Horacio, Traveler/Horacio). Pero volviendo a considerar la distribución de la página, se ve que después de un blanco pequeño continúa insensiblemente con el diálogo de

---

[12] Esta evanescente figura de Lilith sólo aparece nombrada en *C,* 125, y nunca en *Rayuela.* Erich Newmann *(The Great Mother,* trad. R. Manheim, Princeton: Princeton University Press, 1963; original alemán de 1955, p. 82) la sitúa en su esquema III junto a Circe en el sector A —, polo negativo de las figuras mitológicas transformativas que representan más a la muerte psíquica y espiritual que a la física. Según Mary Daly *(Gyn/Ecology: The Methaetics of Radical Feminism,* London, 1979, p. 86), Lilith corresponde a la Lamia griega y romana, pero en la mitología asiria y hebrea primitiva (estudiada por Raphael Patay, *The Hebrew Godess)* precede a Eva y fue creada por Dios al mismo tiempo que Adán y con el mismo material, el barro, es decir, al mismo nivel que el hombre (apud Rosemary Jackson, *Fantasy. The Literature of Subversion,* London-New York: Methuen, 1981, pp. 148 y ss. y nota 5, p. 189). George MacDonald escribió la novela *Lilith* en 1895 y en ella el protagonista se pierde en un mundo detrás del espejo, el mundo vacío de la muerte, y enfrenta una figura femenina que borra todo instinto de vida, una muerte viva. No sabemos si Cortázar conoció esta u otras fuentes, pero la simple mención de Lilith en el *pre-texto* corrobora la sospecha de que el mito de la mujer devoradora estaba rondándolo durante el proceso de escritura de *Rayuela,* como lo muestra en su penetrante análisis Ana Hernández del Castillo en *Keats, Poe, and the Shaping of Cortázar's Mythopoesis* (Amsterdam: Purdue University Monographs in Romance Languages, 1982), basándose sólo en el texto publicado.

Traveler y Oliveira la noche de «Los hilos» en posiciones vitales anta-
gónicas: aceptación *versus* inconformismo y busca.

Toda pareja de dobles debe fundarse en ciertas semejanzas junto a
sus diferencias. La divergencia se acentúa sin duda en los dobles basados en rasgos contrapuestos; el punto límite entre Horacio y su amigo
(sus amigos), lo marca *C*, 106, donde se enfatiza la soledad, la insula-
ridad del primero y el concepto de excentración que define al personaje
y su empresa trascendente:

> *Tema*
> (1.ª persona) La intimidad de los Traveler. Es ahora que yo tendría
> que quedarme, *voyeur* sin deseo, amistoso.
> Alegoría de la incomunicación. Orbitas que se rozan (y eso es
> la amistad)
> La excentración inevitable, etc.

La página concluye —después de un interludio en el que planea una
reunión en el patio de la pensión— con otro fragmento sobre Oliveira
descentrado, *désaxé*.

Otras páginas de *El cuaderno* definen a Traveler con predicados que
lo asemejan a Oliveira y acentúan en ambos lo local. El *pre-texto* habla
de su afición porteña a los tangos y la fidelidad a la memoria de Gardel
con su lectura de las confesiones de Ivonne Guitry en la reunión del
patio *(C, 105)* [13]. Hasta se llega a extender en la elaboración de un código privado que utilizan Traveler y Talita para comunicarse, construido
con frases de tangos *(C, 55)*. La elaboración del código es un detalle
más de los rasgos que comparten Traveler (= Talita) y Horacio, los tres
preocupados por los juegos con el lenguaje, tan desarrollados en el
texto [14]. Oliveira fue caracterizado en *El cuaderno* por su afición al *jazz*,
mientras estaba en el espacio de París y asociado al Club de la Serpiente, hasta con el sentido metafísico de que era el «intercesor», el
camino abierto a una realidad otra. En Buenos Aires utiliza el tango
para fijarlo en el espacio porteño, unirlo a su juventud y a sus amistades
(de café), y re-ligarlo con Traveler, su doble localizado en ese espacio
y aquel tiempo que añora.

También Traveler coincide con Oliveira en compartir rasgos de hu-

---

[13] En *R*, cap. 111, se copia un pasaje de las confesiones de Ivonne Guitry en
La escuela gardeleana (Montevideo: Editorial Cisplatina); también se recuerda que
el libro fue tomado en préstamo por Traveler en *R*, 269 y 330, y la señora de
Gotusso lo reclama.

[14] De los juegos con el lenguaje trataré cuando comente la teoría literaria y su
práctica en el *pre-texto* y el *texto*.

mor y de excentricidad, gusto por lecturas esotéricas, textos de locos *(C,* 115), literatura popular:

> *Traveler:* demonólogo sonriente [15]
> —La solemnidad argentina, che... ¿Por qué no toman ejemplo de Macedonio, de Nalé, de César Bruto, de Oski?
> Traveler cultiva cosas como la confesión de Ivonne Guitry (reproducir *sic)* (C, 103).

Traveler, Talita y Horacio constituyen en Buenos Aires el círculo de los elegidos, moviéndose en esa zona preferida por Cortázar que incluye heterodoxamente la alta cultura y las alusiones literarias junto con la experiencia de lo popular urbano considerado como auténtico y rescatable por su función estético-humorística. Es un grupo definido por la imaginación, especialmente lingüística, y las actividades insólitas (trabajo en el circo, «el gato calculista y otras locuras» *[C,* 53], compra del manicomio), la excentricidad (lecturas y comercio con locos), magia, alquimismo y esoterismo burlón, los chistes a costa del prójimo.

Este grupo no está tan marcado como el de París por las alusiones culturales prestigiosas y los debates trascendentes. Se caracteriza más

---

[15] Fuera de la frase «demonólogo sonriente» el *pre-texto* no registra otro predicado de esoterismo para Traveler, ni tampoco su cómico intento de crear una mandrágora que figura en *R,* 261, con otros datos burlescos. En cambio abundan en el *pre-texto* y se amplían en el *texto* las alusiones a sabidurías mágicas y alquímicas, y ritos de pasaje. En *C,* 57, figuran expresamente atribuidas a Horacio y sus meditaciones conectadas con el manicomio, el Mandala, el circo: «*El manicomio y el circo:* Oliveira sospecha un Mandala (topografía). El manicomio sería un gigantesco trípode de sibila, el agujero de Eleusis, los Campi Flegrei: un *pasaje.* La carpa del circo, en cambio, es como un *Centro:* Oliveira-shamán tiene que subir.» En *C,* 99, aparecen como una lista de anotaciones tomadas de Seligmann para ser utilizadas más adelante, con predominio del simbolismo de transformación y pasaje: «*Analogía* [...] *Absconditorum clavis* [...] Invocación del diablo, La hierba meropis que abre los mares, Un *liber penitencialis [sic]* [...] La *prima materia* de los alquimistas [...] *Mundus Patet*» (tradición etrusca). Estas se repiten para Horacio en el montacargas del manicomio en *R,* 367; Horacio con Talita en *R,* 373; Horacio en la carpa del circo en *R,* 313. A ellas se agregan alusiones alquímicas burlonas con Berthe Trépat en *R,* 139, y el robo del *Liber penitentialis* por Traveler en *R,* 315. Algunas otras mandrágoras no conectadas con él aparecen en *Rayuela:* la cita de Achim von Arnim, *Isabel de Egipto,* «Discurso de la mandrágora» *(R,* 563) y la lectura asombrada de don Crespo de *Marco Antonio y Cleopatra* de Shakespeare, ante la reina que pide mandrágora para beber *(R,* 328). El esoterismo de Horacio oscila entre la versión humorística y la profunda; el de Traveler es siempre de tono festivo, como si funcionara con igual misión que la *hache* agregada para correctivo burlón al peligro de ampulosidad y retoricismo.

por habitar en un ámbito popular urbano (pensión «Sobrales», calle Cachimayo, Puente San Martín; *C,* 103 y 122), convivir con sus vecinos en el patio de la pensión y al mismo tiempo diferir de ellos. El círculo de los «selectos» se define fundamentalmente oponiéndose al de los «mersas», clase media pobre con «fallas» de lenguaje y de cultura que abarcan costumbres, estereotipos de conducta, prejuicios, vistos a través de los pre-juicios del autor.

Los del grupo que se rechaza están más desarrollados en *Rayuela,* pero ya figuran desde las primeras páginas en forma muy marcada en *El cuaderno.* En *C,* 43 (recuérdese que las anotaciones sobre la novela empiezan en *C,* 39, y que de 40 a 42 las hojas no tienen pasajes escritos), se dice «El hombre de la pipa (el administrador del circo). [Oposición total con Traveler, Talita y Oliveira.] Un capítulo contando la vida doméstica (gadgets, etc.) del hombre de la pipa.»

La escena de «El puente» entre Traveler, Talita y Horacio *(C,* 45) está diseñada con un segundo plano de vulgaridad que contrasta con su tensión «ceremonial» y su función de «Mandala». Lo forman la charla de Gekrepten con Horacio, las «escenas orgiásticas a través de una ventana del quilombo» (prostíbulo), luego suprimidas y sustituidas en *Rayuela* por las escenas de la calle, la visión de las vecinas, los comentarios de los niños, la salida de Horacio a buscar un tablón entre los habitantes de la pensión, la tan mentada «zona del café con leche» (anotada en *C,* 43, y repetida en *C,* 50) y el diálogo de Gekrepten con la chica de los mandados como resumen de la situación desde el punto de vista de la gente convencional *(C,* 50).

Más adelante el Director Ferraguto, su mujer la Cuca *(C,* 103), la señora de Gotusso y don Bunche *(C,* 106) vuelven a conformar el grupo (a los que se agrega don Crespo en *R,* cap. 46) de los que sirven de blanco para los dardos humorísticos de los selectos. En *C,* 113, se consigna otro tópico considerado vulgar, la discusión acerca de los granos con la Cuca Ferraguto, que curiosamente está clasificada entre las limitaciones del ámbito de la Argentina, entre sus rasgos negativos, como si estos temas caseros, de clase media pobre, no fuesen propios de todos los países. La visión de las cosas negativas y positivas de su tierra está muy polarizada en *El cuaderno* y merece ser comentada aparte.

Si entre los círculos opuestos se insertan como una cuña «las historias de fantasmas y de locos», irrumpe en el manicomio con toda libertad para descentrar la bipolaridad tan marcada de Traveler, Talita y Horacio por un lado y sus contrarios por otro. En la escena final de Buenos Aires, «Los hilos», se anotan para una etapa de su elaboración: «Intervenciones grotescas de la Cuca, Remorino, Ovejero, Ferraguto» y

Gekrepten, que «llega con tortas fritas» *(C,* 121), frente a la «Piedad de Talita y Traveler», interrumpidos por «Tiradas Piriz. Tiradas delirantes: muerte del perro. Ovejero: la visión científica del mundo.» Texto y pre-texto consignan para esta etapa del final de la parte de Buenos Aires (sin los capítulos prescindibles) la fraternidad grupal de Traveler, Talita y Horacio (que se sacrifica fingiéndose loco), y exaltan el triunfo de la amistad y de los lazos humanos *(C,* 123).

La escena del manicomio en la habitación de Oliveira constituye el punto crítico de las relaciones Traveler/Horacio como dobles arquetípicos. No hay que olvidar que en las tradiciones registradas por la mitología, el folklore y la literatura, el que se encuentra con su doble muere. El gesto ritual aparece insistentemente en *El cuaderno* consignando el enfrentamiento emblemático. Desde: *«El terror:* En la noche, Oliveira espera que Traveler venga a matarlo» *(C,* 57); también *C,* 79, 101, 111, 112, aun con la aclaración de su valor simbólico y no real: «Temor a ser asesinado: No se trataba de que quisieran matarlo físicamente» *(C,* 115).

La oposición *este mundo/un mundo otro* se encarna en Traveler (Talita) *versus* Horacio. No figura en ningún pasaje del *pre-texto* en forma paradigmática que los enfrente por rasgos distintivos, sino que se desprende de las acciones que se les encomiendan en la cadena narrativa de la última parte de Buenos Aires. Traveler representa en el relato la visión más positiva de este mundo («el territorio»), la forma más rica y fraterna que al fin Oliveira intenta salvar. Pero aun así, persiste la insatisfacción y el llamado de la trascendencia que se harán sentir fuertemente en Traveler y a veces más en Talita.

Las relaciones del triángulo y sus desplazamientos están claramente esquematizados en *El cuaderno,* aunque éste no registre, como *Rayuela,* la frustración de Traveler por su vida sedentaria. Talita, objeto del deseo de ambos *(C,* 45 y 101), está condenada por su condición femenina a oscilar entre uno y otro polo. Unas veces parece cerca de la destrucción por las tensiones a las que la someten: «Talita, harta, amenaza con tirarse a la calle. Oliveira tiene miedo» *(C,* 50); por momentos está peligrosamente más cerca de Horacio: «Talita y Oliveira: sentimiento del Mandala» *(C,* 105); o en el crítico centro según la imagen del puente y del fiel de la balanza *(C,* 45 y 51), actuando como intercesora en la ceremonia de pasaje. Pero siempre termina volviendo al lado de Traveler y ocupando «el territorio».

También el *pre-texto* registra los movimientos de la pareja en conjunto, ya sea arrastrados por el protagonista: «Choque de Traveler y Talita: *vuelven a sentir el llamado»* (C, 121), ya sea replegándose a la normalidad: «Todo vuelve-al-orden. Traveler y Talita se convencen de que Horacio está loco. Velarán por ese hermano enfermo» *(C, 123)*. En un detalle significativo, la que sintió más insistentemente el llamado es la que borra el camino mandálico y re-instaura el imperio del territorio, cuando se distribuyen tareas para volver a organizar la vida cotidiana: «Talita baja a borrar la rayuela. Destroza el dibujo» *(C, 123)*.

Cuando *El cuaderno* sigue tanteando para encontrar un final satisfactorio y aún no se ha decidido por las escenas prescindibles (breves, de aire «realista» [16], pero incongruentemente contradictorias y simultáneas), persiste en la unión de la pareja, como luego lo hará en *Rayuela*, aunque con otra propuesta. En *C*, 127, asistimos a una etapa en la que opta por la visión ambigua con aura de ensueño e irrealidad, con acumulación de los «tal vez», con un complejo vaivén de opciones. En ellas el triángulo ya se ha disuelto, Horacio y la pareja se miran uno a los otros, distanciados, sin posible re-unión. «Traveler y Talita lo velan de lejos. O él los mira mientras ellos empujan el tejo —» *(C, 127)*: las situaciones y las acciones pueden invertirse («lo velan a lo lejos» = afirmación del territorio ←→ «empujan el tejo» = busca de absoluto), pero ya nunca estarán juntos.

Lo que he analizado acerca del influjo de Oliveira sobre sus amigos puede extenderse hasta resultar un signo de la obra y su marco-estructura. *C*, 136, muestra las relaciones de los personajes como señales de una retórica que develaría la metafísica subyacente (o que se quiere que esté subyacente) en el relato:

Conciencia oscura de un drama
sin los resortes usuales
    no Edipo no Antígona
    no Swann
    no Sorel
  una *agitación molecular*
  una inquietud de la insatisfacción profunda
Así una conducta equívoca (Oliveira)
repercute en Traveler y Talita
y debió repercutir en Etienne, en Wong, en Ronald.

---

[16] Califico de «realistas» a las escenas anotadas para continuar el episodio final del capítulo 56, que concluye la saga de Buenos Aires por medio de los «capítulos prescindibles». Lo son si se las compara con el intento francamente fantástico que apuntó y desechó en *C*, 107, para resolver el periplo de la vida de Horacio (véase el artículo del *Homenaje a Manuel Alvar*, citado en nota 1). No lo son si, en lugar de atender a su tonalidad de vida cotidiana, se atiende a la alternancia de propuestas incompatibles que se ofrecen como aconteceres simultáneos en estructura fragmentaria e ilógica.

Ojo! No hinchar a O. No es *él* quien agita
sino sus conductas, el fenómeno que los otros
captan.
O. no tiene ningún mérito ni grandeza *(C,* 136).

El pre-texto muestra que es imposible separar la semántica y la sintaxis de los actantes: el punto de vista de la enunciación y la figura que dibuja el enunciado en el proceso generativo. La página diseña las relaciones dinámicas de los actantes (conducta equívoca de A que repercute en B, C, ..., N) y la metáfora narrativa (metáfora dinámica en sí y en su efecto) que quiere construirse para que repercuta en el lector (drama, inquietud, insatisfacción, agitación molecular), todo a partir del héroe Oliveira (ambiguamente activo-pasivo).

La misma página muestra también el forcejeo del autor en la concreción de su novela, su oscilar entre un proyecto grandioso y la conciencia de los peligros de ese proyecto: un héroe sin grandeza al que se le encarga encarnar una aventura sobrehumana entre Escilas y Caribdis de la metafísica y la ampulosidad, el reino milenario y la pensión «Sobrales», la retórica enjevecida y el humor.

Talita

Lo expuesto antes al hablar de Traveler muestra que Talita tiene una función ambivalente cuyo mecanismo se revela con claridad en *El cuaderno.* Es al mismo tiempo el doble gemelo de la Maga y el complementario de Horacio [17]. La primera función está directamente manifestada porque Oliveira funde a ambas en sus entrevisiones de Buenos Aires y la arrastra así a formar con ella una pareja de figuras intercambiables en una misma posición: el objeto del deseo, el absoluto anhelado. Pero la segunda función de oposición complementaria no aparece nunca explicitada en un pasaje del *pre-texto* que se focalice en Talita, como ocurre con la pareja Maga/Horacio. En efecto, la complementariedad de Talita está inscrita siempre en forma secundaria. O se produce a través

---

[17] Podría pensarse que Talita es con menor nitidez un doble gemelo de Traveler, pero esto aparece desdibujado porque el matrimonio y su armónico lazo «naturaliza» dicha función, y porque al convertirla en objeto del deseo para Horacio y Traveler la desgaja de este último. También se alude a la agrupación de la Maga y Traveler por el rasgo «espontaneidad»: «La vida más viva es la más espontánea e inconsciente (la Maga, Traveler)» *(C,* 58), pero ello se presenta como nacido de sus funciones con respecto a Horacio, lo cual los une en forma muy indirecta.

de la Maga, pues si es su doble paralelo puede sustituirla en la oposición con Oliveira (*«Identificación progresiva de Talita y la Maga»*,
C, 101) o a través de Traveler. Como lo hemos visto en los pasajes
citados al estudiar a éste en su función de *doppelgänger,* Talita figura
siempre en un segundo plano por la distribución de la página y por la
menor importancia de su desarrollo *(C, 79 y 101).*

El *pre-texto* define su función bivalente, determinando su posición
en el tablero de relaciones de los actantes:

$$\text{Traveler} + \text{Talita} \ (= \text{Maga}) \longleftrightarrow \text{Horacio}$$

Talita (por parecerse a la Maga, pero mucho más aún por ocupar la casilla de Traveler) es el complementario de Oliveira. En *C,* 101, aunque
se reconoce la función de gemelo y se la subraya (literalmente), se pri-
vilegia la imagen dinámica del discurso novelesco como una máquina
engendradora de relato.

Talita se convierte en una pieza móvil de este ajedrez narrativo, que
oscila en ocupar la casilla de Traveler o la de Oliveira, objeto del deseo,
símbolo a la vez de la busca del absoluto y de la plenitud de vida terre-
na. La misma movilidad del personaje la convierte en otra máscara del
puente (símbolo diseminado en pre-texto y texto), que *El cuaderno* foca-
lizó desde sus primeras páginas en la escena de «El tablón» [18].

Si la pareja Maga/Horacio se basa en la oposición vida/no vida,
intuición/intelecto, ambos se unen por la misma tensión hacia el absoluto, aunque la Maga lo entrevea a su manera por las vías irracionales
y poéticas. Considerada en el nivel más abstracto, la díada Traveler/
Horacio pareciera ser semejante a la anterior («la vida más viva es la
más espontánea e inconsciente [la Maga, Traveler], *C,* 58), pero no lo
es obviamente en el nivel concreto de los personajes (hombre/mujer,
amigo/amante), de los espacios (París, lo cosmopolita, el prestigio aventurero y cultural/Buenos Aires, la resonancia local, la vivencia memorable de la infancia y la juventud), de lo simbólico (la plenitud unitiva,
«lo otro»/lo terreno, la amistad, lo humano más valioso).

Si en la Maga = Talita (y Traveler) hay una libertad no reflexiva
que los acerca y puede agruparlos como dobles gemelos (aunque de ma-
tiz muy distinto), es indudable que el grupo porteño se afianza más en
la representación del «territorio» y del «lado de acá». El ámbito por-

---

[18] Para la escena de «El tablón», que llama también «El balcón» o «El puente»
en *El cuaderno* y que es la desarrollada en *Rayuela,* cap. 41, véase mi artículo
de *INTI,* especialmente p. 80 y ss. y nota 16.

teño, el matrimonio de Talita y Traveler, su restringida bohemia que no alcanza a perturbar su afincamiento, con los pies bien plantados en la realidad, el menor halo poético imaginativo de Talita establecen su diferencia. La conducta de los personajes con respecto a la experiencia metafísica es definitoria. La Maga encarna el impulso de Horacio, es la figura inspiradora que le señala inconscientemente el camino, bordea el límite del misterio y hasta se sugiere que lo traspasa antes que él. En cierto sentido se le asigna un papel activo de *inquietadora* de Horacio por su sola existencia. En cambio, Traveler y Talita son los *inquietados*, los que sienten el contagio y son arrastrados momentáneamente por el amigo, pero vuelven a su raíz humana, a este lado de acá, e intentan salvarlo.

El papel de Talita como objeto del deseo tiñe de erotismo la pugna de los complementarios Traveler y Horacio por lo que no se posee (plenitud terrena/plenitud metafísica) en el anhelo de unidad [19]. Y esta lucha, a su vez, tiñe de busca trascendente la pasión. En la saga de Buenos Aires, Talita va perdiendo su concreción carnal de objeto erótico, en un proceso que la va convirtiendo en un símbolo metafísico, pero en acentuada función vicaria de la Maga, que constantemente se le superpone junto con Pola, a la cual se agrega Lilith (sólo en *El cuaderno*).

CONCLUSIONES

Según advertí al comienzo, me he limitado a estudiar los dobles complementarios, pero la consideración de todos los otros tipos mostraría una red mucho más compleja de relaciones. Oliveira es el personaje central, del que se deriva el sistema de dobles que construye el *pretexto* y el *texto*. Los unos proceden de él por oposición complementaria (la Maga y Traveler), los otros por sustitución con figuras gemelas o transformaciones deformantes (Pola, Lilith, Trépat, la clocharde, Ossip), mientras Talita reúne en ella los caminos de la complementariedad y la identificación.

---

[19] Podría decirse que el nítido triángulo de Traveler-Talita-Horacio se corresponde con otro muy desdibujado de Horacio-Maga-Ossip, donde los dobles Horacio/Ossip se disputan a la Maga como objeto del deseo. Ni por la figura del doble (Ossip), ni por la relación de la Maga con él, la analogía alcanza un relieve comparable. Cabría enlazar esta simetría con otras: Maga/Horacio y Emmanuèle/Célestin *(R,* 242), y el paralelismo de Berthe Trépat-Valentin y la Maga-Rocamadour propuesto por Ana Hernández del Castillo. Todo ello constituye como una reduplicación de las parejas de dobles multiplicadas en visión especular.

La novela de Cortázar —como muy buena parte de la literatura contemporánea— ofrece dos tendencias polarizadas: una hacia la focalización de un *modelo* y otra hacia la concretización que trata de apagarlo sin borrarlo del todo. A cada autor se le plantea la dosificación y el tipo de equilibrio (o de desequilibrio) que desea establecer entre ambas y hasta la opción total por la primera. Esto lo conduce también a una oscilación entre la opacidad y la transparencia, entre entidades narrativas cerradas que se autoabastecen y acentúan lo metatextual *versus* entidades abiertas a la referencialidad.

Con su peculiar manejo de los dobles en *Rayuela,* Cortázar acentúa el modelo sin renunciar a una fábula y unos personajes, cuyos predicados los «naturalizan» en cierta medida. La constelación de dobles cumple en parte una función estructural que refuerza la organización cental del relato. Es multiplicación, fragmentación, diversificación caleidoscópica, y al mismo tiempo simetría, oposiciones bien delimitadas, esquema cerrado. Su inserción en una semiosis generalizada ($x \rightarrow y$) intenta convencer de que debe leerse el desarrollo de la historia contada como interpretación de los signos del universo y a la novela como *imago mundi.* Se trataría nuevamente de la noción de *figura,* que puede sugerir a unos lectores la promesa de una antropofanía, y a otros, en cambio, el orden de un juego con sus leyes marcadas.

A DIALOGUE OF GAZES: METAMORPHOSIS AND EPIPHANY IN JULIO CORTÁZAR'S "AXOLOTL"

by MAURICE J. BENNETT

The monster and the monstrous figure significantly in the work of the Argentine fictionist, Julio Cortázar. His narratives are notorious for their challenge to the categories of everyday existence — their contamination of the "real" with the "fantastic" until the two are indistinguishable. The Minotaur imprisoned in the Labyrinth and the human pursuer who will simultaneously destroy and liberate him are central to this aspect of his *oeuvre*, and the short story "Axolotl" recasts this ancient myth as an account of the mysterious transformation of a man into a kind of an aquatic lizard.

Carl Jung's theories of the psychological function of dreams about monsters offer a useful context in which to approach this narrative of what on the surface is troubling metamorphosis. Jung located the source of those images of terrifying beasts that have persistently haunted the human imagination in a biological memory that rebels against the separation of man from nature proposed by the rational consciousness by indirectly reminding him of his origins. Analyzing a patient's dream of being attacked by a dragon, half crab and half lizard, Jung wrote:

> our psychic structure, like our cerebral anatomy carries the phylogenetic traces of its slow and constant development that spread over millions of years. In a way, we are born into an immemorial edifice that we revive and that rests on millenial foundations. We have occupied every rung of the animal ladder; our bodies retain numerous vestiges ... we have an entire series of organs that are nothing but ancestral remains; we are, in our structure segmented like worms, whose sympathetic nervous system we also share.[1]

As a recapitulation of evolutionary forms and stages, man is necessarily a part of those forces and forms that appear monstrous to the waking

---

1. Carl Jung, "Du rêve au mythe," in *L'homme à la découverte de son âme*, préfaces et adaptation par Dr. Roland Cahen, 6ème ed. (Gèneve: Editions de Mont Blanc, S. A., 1962), p. 296. "... notre structure psychique, de même que notre anatomie cérébrale, porte les traces phylogénétiques de sa lente et constante édification, qui s'est étendue sur des millions d'années. Nous naissons en quelque sorte dans un édifice immémorial que nous ressucitons et qui repose sur des fondations millénaires. Nous avons parcouru toutes les étapes de l'échelle animale; notre corps en porte de nombreuses survivances ... nous avons toute une série d'organes qui ne sont que des souvenirs ancestraux; nous sommes, dans notre plan d'organisation, segmentés comme des vers, dont nous possédons aussi le système nerveux sympathique." All translations here are my own unless otherwise noted.

consciousness. Thus, the mythic and oneiric encounter with the monster, in a sense, becomes an introduction to that part of oneself that links him to the eternal universe. And in a neo-Romantic reformulation of the union of man and nature, Jung adds that "In plumbing his own depths, [the patient] would reach that level characterized by the saurian, those levels where flows a wave of eternal life, a wave that crosses nature, in which and through which all proper growth takes place, and where everything so perfectly completes itself that there remains neither covetousness nor extravagance."[2] The totemic and animistic practices of certain primitive tribes in their attempt to appease or absorb the forces that might otherwise dwarf and threaten consciousness can be traced to an intuitive perception of man's ineluctable ties with the cosmos; and even the more familiar hybrid forms of the Mediterranean — the fauns, satyrs, centaurs of Greek mythology — originate in a similar recognition. The monster, then, is both human and inhuman, man and the absolute other, and it is in the nexus of their dialectical interaction that Cortázar locates the present tale.

Cortázar has written that the central project of his fiction is the attempt to discover "a new ethic and a new metaphysic."[3] In the process, he has progressively refined his use of the Minotaur myth, transforming its explicit representation of the antithesis between man and animal, and their tenuous, uneasy union, into more extreme oppositions and, as a result, more profound reconciliations. "Axolotl" retains the labyrinth-monster trope as its fundamental conception, but the tale's power derives from its recognition and subsequent obliteration of absolute distinctions.

The outline of the story is simple: one day, while visiting the Jardin des Plantes in Paris, the narrator wanders into the aquarium building, where he becomes fascinated with a tank full of a species of Mexican salamander. A sudden fascination grows into a prolonged, inexplicable obsession, and when he is not actually staring at the creatures he lies awake imagining their world. These encounters and meditations result in his magical transformation into one of them. However, the tale's interest does not lie in narrative suspense. The first paragraph begins with the assertion, "There was a time when I thought a great deal about the axolotls," and ends with the declaration, "Now I am an axolotl" (p. 3).[4] The important considerations, then, are not what happens but the implications of the process and the result.

---

2. Ibid., p. 303. "En creusant ses propres profondeurs il atteindrait cette couche caractérisée par le saurien, ces parages où coule un flot de vie éternelle, flot qui traverse la nature, dans lequel et par lequel s'effectue toute croissance convenable et où tout s'accomplit de si parfaite façon qu'il ne reste plus ni convoitise, ni extravagances."

3. Quoted from *Arts*, Paris (July-August, 1963) in Nestor García Canclini, *Cortázar: una antropología poética* (Buenos Aires: Editorial Nova, 1968), p. 17. ". . . en todo lo que escribí hay una tentativa particular: descubrir una ética y una metafísica neuvas."

4. *End of the Game and Other Stories*, trans. Paul Blackburn (London: Collins and Harvill Press, 1963). All page references to "Axolotl" will be to this edition.

The narrator begins his tale with the invocation of recognizably conventional relationships. There is the sentimental *mis en scène* of Paris in the springtime — the traditional season of awakenings and transformations. As the city is blossoming after a bleak winter, he passes through the newly-green Jardin and remembers his "friendship" with the lions and panthers — every child's favorite animals. But these creatures are not up to their best form, and he turns to the tulips and then decides to enter the aquarium, which he has never visited before. After looking at a few ordinary fish, he suddenly espies the axolotls and is transfixed in epiphany: "after the first minute I knew that we were linked, that something infinitely lost and distant kept pulling us together" (p. 4).

The narrator consults a dictionary in order to gather just enough information to identify these strange creatures to himself and to the reader, but he rejects "specialized works" that would provide exact, scientific knowledge. The axolotls are associated with Aztec Mexico and with Africa, ages and geographies traditionally associated with dark, irrational forces that are the antithesis of European lucidity and rationalism. Thus, the rejection of scientific knowledge is the narrator's first unconscious step toward a union with these forces. Whatever knowledge he seeks is pursued not through rational investigation but by an effort of vision: "You eat them with your eyes," the aquarium guard says at one point (p. 7).[5] Significantly, a similar blank gazing characterizes the axolotls themselves; their eyes are the most vivid features of their anatomies and induce the hypnotic trance that captures the narrator. "And then I discovered its eyes, its face," he writes, "Inexpressive features, with no other trait save the eyes, two orifices, like brooches, wholly of transparent gold, lacking any life but looking, letting themselves be penetrated by my look, which seemed to travel past the golden level and lose itself in a diaphanous interior mystery" (p. 5).

Inevitably, the axolotls' strangely beautiful eyes are juxtaposed with more familiar gazes. In a crucial observation on difference and similarity, the narrator remarks: "In the standing tanks on either side of them, different fishes showed me the simple stupidity of their handsome eyes *so similar to our own*" (emphasis mine); and in the next paragraph he observes:

---

5. Cortázar's tale ultimately addresses the opposition and union of "seeing" and "saying." For the importance of these coordinates for modern literary practice, see Richard Kuhns, "Philosophy as a Form of Art," in his *Structures of Experience: Essays on the Affinity between Philosophy and Literature* (New York: Basic Books, Inc., 1970), pp. 215-272 *passim.*

> The anthropomorphic features of a monkey reveal the reverse of what most people believe, the distance that is traveled from them to us. The absolute lack of similarity between axolotls and human beings proved to me that my recognition was valid, that I was not propping myself up with easy analogies. . . . I think it was the axolotls' heads, that triangular pink shape with the tiny eyes of gold. That looked and knew. That laid the claim. They were not *animals.* (p. 6)

The syntactic ambiguity of the first quotation associates stupidity not only with the gaze of the other fish but also with the human; however, what distinguishes that of the axolotl is its communicative value: it *speaks* of "a different life, of another way of seeing" (p. 6). The axolotls' claim on the narrator is irresistible precisely because they are unlike the monkeys of the second quotation — or the lions and panthers with which the tale began, or other men — they are not "animals." As reptiles, their attraction transcends the more easily comprehensible appeal of phylogenetic fraternity.

The axolotls' eyes not only look, but *know*, and thus constantly tantalize the narrator with a mystery incarnate:

> The axolotls were like witnesses of something, and at times like terrible judges. I felt ignoble in front of them; there was such a terrifying purity in those transparent eyes. They were larvas, but larva means disguise and also phantom. Behind those Aztec faces, without expression but of an implacable cruelty, what semblance was awaiting its hour? (p. 7)

And in the middle of one of his visual efforts to "penetrate the mystery of those eyes of gold without iris, without pupil," he suddenly sees his own human face on the other side of the glass. It is only then that he understands the mystery, at the moment of his metamorphosis when he also realizes that for his human self no understanding is possible because "He was outside the aquarium, his thinking was a thinking outside the tank" (p. 8).

The narrator's first sensation as an axolotl is horror — a self-regarding human response that is consistent with his early anthropocentric commiseration with what he considered to be the axolotls' "hellish" fate in being confined to their narrow, watery universe, or his initial interest in their "humanlike" feet. He is appalled at the consideration that he is now a man buried alive, a human awareness condemned to a larval body and isolated in its consciousness, but the sudden touch and encountered gaze of a fellow axolotl produce the unexpected revelation that the other "knew also, no communication possible, but very clearly. Or I was also in him, or all of us were thinking humanlike, incapable of expression, limited to the golden splendor of our eyes looking at the face of the man pressed against the aquarium" (p. 9). The human narrator's silent, purely visual encounter with the reptile, the saurian of Jungian psychology, thus ends in his penetration to a realm of consciousness that is synonymous with life itself and that, while being antecedent to human awareness, continues to include it.

In his early play, *The Kings* (1949), Cortázar presented a more or less unretouched version of the Minotaur story, in which the monster was a symbol of those a-rational forces identified by Jung. The play repeated the opposition posited by the Romantics between the rational consciousness and nature, so that Theseus' destruction of the Minotaur was in some sense symbolic of the reason's assault on the a-rational self. Just before he dies, Cortázar's creature warns his slayer: "If you kill me, you will diminish yourself . . . you will fall into yourself, like crumbling cliffs and the dead. . . . You will remain here, alone within the walls, and there in the sea."[6] He thus prophesies the isolated, sterile, solipsistic consciousness against which Romantics and post-Romantics have long protested.

The "dark, humid" character of the aquarium building in "Axolotl" certainly assimilates it to the labyrinth archetype, and, like the Minotaur, the axolotl that awaits the narrator as an unsuspecting modern version of Theseus is a hybrid form with its humanlike feet and inhuman eyes. But the tale dismisses the Minotaur's union of man and animal as irrelevant to a civilization that has so domesticated nature that it can be sentimental about lions and tigers. It is the axolotl who is the absolute Other, with its pupiless, lidless eyes, its extreme immobility, and its association with barbaric cultures destroyed by rational Europe. As in Cortázar's early play, this monster, too, delivers Theseus a message: the choice to be made between plenitude and spiritual impoverishment. This time, however, it is Theseus who is destroyed by the monster as the axolotls consume the narrator "slowly with their eyes, in a cannibalism of gold" (p. 7). Jung wrote that such a devouring by the monster-dragon, the saurian, can be a symbol of resurrection and rejuvenation.[7] In this tale, the essential meaning of what may be regarded as a kind of transfiguration is suggested by the axolotl-narrator's closing words:

> I am an axolotl for good now, and if I think like a man it's only because every axolotl thinks like a man inside his rosy stone semblance. I believe that all this succeeded in communicating something to him in those first days, when I was still he. And in this final solitude to which he no longer comes, I console myself by thinking that perhaps he is

---

6. Quoted in Canclini, p. 21. "Si tú me matas, tú te diminuirás, al conocerme serás menos, tu irás cayendo en ti mismo, como se van desmorando los acantilados y los muertos. . . . Te quedarás, aquí, solo en los muros y allá dentro del mar."

7. Jung, *L'homme*, p. 293. ". . . le dragon est en même temps une possibilité de guérison, une possibilité de renaissance; lorsqu'un individu est englouti par un dragon, il n'y a pas là seulement un événement négatif. . . ."

going to write a story about us, that, believing he's making up a story, he's going to write all this about axolotls. (p. 9)

Cortázar thus retrieves the ancient idea of a fully sentient universe, where consciousness is not limited to man alone but is an essential attribute of the creation: the fundamental continuity between man and nature is thereby reestablished, however tenuously. Further, although the axolotls represent a nature that is conscious and knowing, they are also inarticulate, and the axolotl's closing words reveal a scheme whereby the human narrator has been made a vehicle of expression for their speechless awareness. Rational man, *homo sapiens*, is synonymous with *homo loquens*, the animal capable of speech; what distinguishes him among creatures is not what he knows but his capacity for elaborate communication. In these terms, humanity may be regarded as mute nature's attempt at self-expression. Modern man's separation from nature has left him with nothing to say, so that just as the axolotls' immobility complements the narrator's coming and going, so their *knowing* speechlessness complements his unknowing *speech*.

Thus, within the general context of Cortázar's aesthetic-ethics, it is significant that the momentary reunion of a fragmented ontology is embodied as narrative.[8] What begins as the presentation of two discontinuous realms of being becomes for a single transfiguring moment the node of a unitary awareness. Significant being is neither specifically "other" nor restrictively human, but derives from the mutual consciousness formulated between the axolotl's silent visual awareness and the human narrator's capacity for language. The intersection of the two produces meaning; the very story we read, co-authored by human and inhuman agents, testifies to the possibilities of a consciousness that is at once transcendent *and* articulate. Vision combines with Language to create Literature.

The atavism with which "Axolotl" confronts the modern sense of spiritual emptiness does not repudiate the rational mind so much as it attempts to recuperate a source of vitality. The tale responds to the perception of mankind's disjunction from nature with an image of its participation: the narrator's metamorphosis into a "primitive" life form; the shared awareness of man and axolotl promises a regained community. The final paragraph constitutes the peroration of what is essentially a homily on spiritually significant being. The metaphysical truth espoused here is the axolotl's conclusion, "if I think like a man it's only because every axolotl thinks like a man inside his rosy stone semblance." Equations of identity are, of course, reversible: if axolotl = man, then man = axolotl, and the circle of being is complete.

---

8. See Roberto Gonsalez Echevarria, *"Los reyes:* Cortázar's Mythology of Writing" and Sara Castro-Klaren, "Ontological Fabulation: Toward Cortázar's Theory of Literature," both in The *Final Island*, ed. Jaime Alazraki and Ivar Ivask (Norman: University of Oklahoma Press, 1981), pp. 63-72, 140-150.

THE TURBULENT FLOW:
STREAM OF CONSCIOUSNESS TECHNIQUES IN THE SHORT STORIES OF JUAN RULFO

PAUL W. BORGESON, JR.

Two principal tendencies have characterized Mexican prose fiction of the twentieth century. In the first few decades, the novel and short story generally reflected the country's socio-political turmoil, as in Mariano Azuela's *Los de abajo* (1915) or Martín Luis Guzmán's *El águila y la serpiente* (1926). Such social and historical analyses dominated for the first forty years or so. Meanwhile, in Europe, prose fiction was much more concerned with new trends in philosophy and psychology, in particular the ideas of Freud and Jung. These two tendencies (among others) finally came together in Mexico in the work of Agustín Yáñez (1904) and especially Juan Rulfo (1918). These writers, and others, also deal with the themes of the earlier social fiction, but with a significant difference. Rulfo, particularly, works with regional locales and characters, yet his best work is also highly universal in its portrayal of psychological issues, such as the problem of guilt, failure, and the consequences of socioeconomic dispossession. [1] On one level, his nar-

---

[1] On Rulfo's reconciliation of the regional with the universal, see Donald K. Gordon, "Juan Rulfo, cuentista," *Cuadernos Americanos* 155 (November-December 1967), 199-200; Carlos Blanco Aguinaga, "Realidad y estilo de Juan Rulfo," *Revista Mexicana de Literatura* no. 1 (September-October 1955), p. 60; and Hugo Rodríguez Alcalá, *El arte de Juan Rulfo* (Mexico: Instituto Nacional de Bellas Artes, Departamento de Literatura, 1965), p. 209.

ratives reveal the intimate circumstances of his land, suspended between growing cosmopolitanism and its rich indigenous heritage, and still in search of its identity. But Rulfo makes this process universal by exploiting the basic concept that at the center of one man lie all men, and his protagonists and their problems transcend their clearly national character. Given the dual nature of their role (general and specific), they have very few signs of individual personality. As Rulfo exposes the psyches of his fictional people, who share the same fundamental problems and live in similar circumstances, he also exposes the central core of their humanity, producing some of the finest, and most disquieting, literature in Latin America.

Rulfo's stories are unusually disturbing reading experiences. [2] His fictional world burdens the spirit, because it is devoid of the ordering elements of time, space, and personality, and even life and death themselves become blurred and largely meaningless. Additionally, his stories also explore radically original means of structuring fiction (in my view only Borges and Cortázar have been as successful at opening the Spanish-American short story to such new possibilities). With so many elements working against our means for imposing order on literature, Rulfo's narratives at times leave us feeling that in his fictional world absolutely nothing works,

Yet Rulfo's stories themselves, almost incredibly, do work. Rulfo leaves them trembling on the brink of literary self-destruction, but the reader, seeing his simu-

Yáñez's contacts with European literature incorporating new psychological ideas (specifically Joyce and Proust) are discussed by Domingo Miliani, *La realidad mexicana en su novela* (Caracas: Monte Ávila, [1968]), p. 59.

[2] Juan Rulfo, *Pedro Páramo*, 1955 (Mexico City: Fondo de Cultura Económica, 1971), and *El llano en llamas*, 1953 (Mexico City: Fondo de Cultura Económica, 1970).

lacra of reality crashing down about him—both in content and in literary form—cannot flee. He returns to Rulfo as does Kafka's "K" to his trial, or as Rivera's Arturo Cova returns to his jungles. How, then, does Rulfo make his stories function so effectively when what they portray is so desolate and powerless?

This paper seeks to identify the ways in which Rulfo's stories achieve this unsettling effect, and to analyze the balance between chaos and order in the world he depicts. To do this, I will focus on specific techniques which contribute to his stories' unique nature, and whose use reveals several of Rulfo's most significant achievements.

One of the principal experiments in the early twentieth century novel, in Europe and in the United States, was the stream of consciousness approach. For the purposes of the present essay, this narrative mode may be understood according to the characterization of Scholes and Kellogg:

> Stream of consciousness is any presentation in literature of the illogical, ungrammatical, mainly associative patterns of human thought. Such thought may be spoken or unspoken.[3]

I utilize this description among the many offered, because of its flexibility, its attention to technique, and for two more significant reasons: it recognizes that stream of consciousness may be portrayed either in speech or inward thought, and it gives us the insight that in such fiction, the subject matter is left apparently free from logical control. Scholes and Kellogg further help us to realize that there is not just one technique (interior monologue), but that a multitude of techniques constitutes the stream of consciousness mode, giving it richness;

[3] Robert Scholes and Robert Kellogg, *The Nature of Narrative* (New York: Oxford University Press, 1966), p. 177.

for what has survived has not after all been the mode itself so much as the techniques it developed.

The challenge of stream of consciousness fiction was as great as its opportunities: the writer needed to find a way to present coherently a psychological reality which was to be portrayed as chaotic; but when successful, such a portrayal could become itself, in form, a model of an illogical and fragmented reality. Juan Rulfo's fiction is based not only on the chaotic nature of the reality which surrounds his characters, but also on a general concept of the reality of the mind. Consciousness in Rulfo is portrayed as a dynamic and unstable synthesis of oppositions. On one hand are myth and irrationality; on the other are reason and order. His stories balance the two alternatives, and his problems and possibilities are then similar to those of the earlier stream of consciousness writers.

Some statements on Faulkner by Lawrence E. Bowling may help point out the technical relationship between Rulfo and stream of consciousness literature:

> The stream of consciousness technique tends to break down three stabilizing elements traditionally considered fundamental in narrative fiction: exposition, plot and chronological order. *The Sound and the Fury* is a novel abeut disorder, disintegration and the absence of perspective. The novel is essentially about the internal chaos of the characters—their intellectual, moral and spiritual disorder. [4]

The problem is to develop techniques which can be integrated into a narrative with some type of structuring (preferably all but invisible) yet reveal and even share in this disorder. A review of criticism on the stream of consciousness mode reveals that virtually all of the techniques used by these writers are also found in Rulfo;

[4] Lawrence E. Bowling, "Faulkner: Technique of *The Sound and the Fury*," *Kenyon Review* 4 (1948), 555.

yet most of them, rather than tending to destroy the narrative structure, actually contribute to his ordering of disorder. These techniques include the following: suspended coherence, sensory impression, repetition and several recurrent devices, disjunctive figures, narrative organization itself as a model of consciousness, and impressionistic or associative techniques. Such devices, understandably, tend to occur most frequently in the stories which most deeply enter into the protagonists' minds, such as in several of the classic Rulfo narratives: "Luvina," "La cuesta de las comadres," "En la madrugada," and "El hombre." More traditional tales such as "El día del derrumbe" or "Nos han dado la tierra" use only a few, and often for different purposes.

Association

If free or apparently free association may be taken as a basis for stream of consciousness, the critic must then find a text's thematic unity in the reasons behind such associations. In identifying the underlying relationships, one unlocks both the interior life of the characters, and the very theme and structure of the narrative itself. In order to discuss associative techniques in Rulfo's stories, it will be useful to evaluate and identify them in terms of their ordering or disordering effect on the surface narration. Thus, we may consider them as follows: conjunctive techniques, tending to bring surface cohesion; disjunctive devices, which give an appearance of disorder; and bridge techniques, which balance the two. It will be found that devices for bringing fundamental order dominate in Rulfo's fiction.

Sensory impression

The principal disjunctive device from stream of consciousness fiction also used by Rulfo is sensory impres-

sion, a technique which fragments and transforms perceived reality. This term was used for the first time (to
my knowledge) by Lawrence Bowling in 1948 and 1950. [5]
He describes sensory impression as the simple recording
in fiction of data perceived through the senses. He
writes that "sensory impression is the writer's nearest
approach to putting pure sensations on paper." [6] This
device, about as objective as can be found, is used by
novelists such as Woolf and Faulkner, and by Dos Passos
in his "Camera Eye." Although presented with objectivity,
sensory impressions are subjective in that they are not
confirmed by a narrator—they are merely the reactions
of a character, and may be at odds with others' perceptions. As Scholes and Kellogg have observed, "one
of the major trends in Twentieth century literature is
away from the attempt to penetrate an individual psyche
and toward a focus on the apprehension of 'impressions'
which claim no absolute validity as fact." [7] This is
precisely the case with Rulfo, whose use of sensory impressions results in a mosaic-like fragmentation of fictional reality into small bits and pieces. As Eric Auerbach
writes, this "is a method which dissolves reality into
multiple and multivalent reflections of consciousness." [8]
Sensory impression, then, is a major source of the apparent discontinuity which Rulfo, like the earlier stream
of consciousness writers, must delicately balance with
the need to be readable.

Carlos Blanco Aguinaga observes that Rulfo, "con
maestría asombrosa, ha ordenado la confusión en libertad aparente." [9] The constant play of sensory data is

---

[5] Bowling: "Faulkner," pp. 556-57; "What is the Stream of Consciousness Technique?," *PMLA* 65 (1950), 342.

[6] "What Is?," p. 342.

[7] Scholes and Kellogg, p. 203.

[8] Cited in Scholes and Kellogg, p. 203.

[9] Blanco Aguinaga, p. 77.

one of the principal ways in which Rulfo manages this.
And Hugo Rodríguez Alcalá deals extensively with what
he calls "experiencias de los sentidos" or "experiencias
sensoriales." [10] The reader will undoubtedly have observed the frequent and powerful use of sense-perception
in Rulfo: Rodríguez Alcalá's chapter discusses smell, feelings of cold and warmth, "internal sensations" such as
nausea or physical self-awareness, taste, touch and synesthesia.   Here, rather than further cataloging these sensations, it will be more to the point to demonstrate their
function in the narrative.

"Luvina" is an example of a *cuento* so full of powerful
sensory impressions, especially of sound (the "murmullos") and touch (such as the wind) that they overwhelm
the characters, who become hypersensitized to sense-
perceptions.   Sound, for instance, becomes so strong a
symbol of the village that the following dialogue occurs:

  —"¿Qué es? —me dijo.
  —"¿Qué es qué? —le pregunté.
  —"Eso, el ruido ése.
  —"Es el silencio. (p. 100)

Even the absence of sound becomes a type of sensory
impression.   Rodríguez Alcalá shows that the ghostly
Rulfian world is vitalized precisely by this kind of powerful and all-consuming sense-perception, in which even
silence is perceived by the senses.

One of the great frustrations which the reader often
shares with Rulfo's characters is a feeling of blindness.
Rulfo's visual descriptions are meager at best, and one
can scarcely discern what Luvina or Comala might look
like through the shadows.   Luvina, for instance, is a place
of wind, shadows and dust.   Dust reoccurs in "Talpa,"
here as the only characteristic of the land.   The Rulfian

[10] Rodríguez Alcalá, pp. 195-203.

protagonist, effectively blind, perceives his world through his other physical sensations alone, and he must communicate it to his auditor in the same way. Here, Rulfo perhaps improves on a Dos Passos; instead of simply enumerating the sensations, he is able to achieve a like effect while integrating them into a narrative context. Such an integration helps maintain the balance between order and chaos. [11]

The sensory nature of all perception in Rulfo's stories is so complete that at least two remarkable phenomena occur. One is that the verb *sentir* becomes a synonym of *pensar*, transforming mental perception into sensory apprehension: "Y yo comienzo a sentir como si no hubiéramos llegado a ninguna parte" (p. 65); "Y Tacha llora al sentir que su vaca no volverá" (p. 35). Reason and abstraction, in short, give way to the senses. Secondly, Rulfo's characters, who often make striking metaphors in their speech, occasionally transfer one sense to another synesthetically. Rodríguez Alcalá points out two such cases in *Pedro Páramo:* "olor verde" and "olor amarillo." [12] We find another in *El llano en llamas:* "Olía a eso: a sombra recalentada por el sol" (p. 67). It is revealing that these cases also involve the transference of *visual* sensations to other senses (smell, in the instances cited), thus further weakening the already meager sight-imagery, and contributing to the feeling of impotence projected by the protagonists.

There are also several cases of metaphors verging on full synesthesia in *El llano en llamas:* "un buche de coraje" (p. 70), "viento pardo" (p. 94), a wind stirs up

---

[11] Since people receive most of their information from sight, it is particularly disturbing that Rulfo should choose to minimize this particular sense (there is, for instance, essentially no physical description of Pedro Páramo).

[12] Rodríguez Alcalá, p. 201.

(*revuelve*) sadness (p. 96). Such cases of near synesthesia are far more common in Rulfo, and this type of manipulation of sensory apprehension is indeed one of his most common and effective devices. One should note in this regard that Rulfo's use of sensory descriptions is by no means a type of *preciosismo*. The characters perceive sensually, and we can only enter their world, therefore, through their senses. Sensory impression may be called *the* Rulfian descriptive technique. [13]

Suspended coherence

As mentioned above, bridge techniques serve to reinforce the appearance of disorder in the Rulfian narrative; the key word here, however, is "appearance," since they finally contribute to the reader's apprehension of the fictional world. "Suspended coherence," a favorite device of stream of consciousness literature, is Rulfo's principal bridging technique. The term, introduced by Robert Humphrey, denotes a device in which the explanations for certain statements are given to the reader only at a later point in the narrative. [14] The result is that the text is temporarily incoherent. When the reader comes to the explanation, a sudden revelation comes from putting the information together. The narrative content suddenly achieves perspective. The reader then sees the whole in a sort of internal overview which may at times bridge many pages of narrative. Suspended coherence is a flirtation between literary order and chaos.

In *El llano en llamas*, the technique of suspended coherence is used on at least two levels. At times only

[13] Another disjunctive device, chaotic enumeration, is revealingly absent in Rulfo, lending further credence to the thesis that total disorder is avoided, in favor of devices which give only an *appearance* of disarray.

[14] *Stream of Consciousness in the Modern Novel* (Berkeley: University of California Press, 1954), p. 66.

a few lines separate the complementary pieces of information. For instance, in "Luvina," the professor tells the invisible listener about the wind in the town, and says "Ya mirará usted ese viento que sopla sobre Luvina" (p. 94). A moment later he repeats, "Ya lo verá usted" (p. 95). At this point the reader does not know why the traveler will see it, but his momentary disorientation is resolved a few paragraphs late (p. 96), when the professor refers to the other as "Usted que va para allá." Other such momentary confusions abound.

But whereas Humphrey's discussion of suspended coherence limits itself to the level of random associations made by a wandering mind (and a consequent minor disconnection of elements), Rulfo's use of this device goes significantly further, as we shall see is the case with several other techniques. Suspended coherence becomes an essential structuring principle of stories such as "Talpa" and "Diles que no me maten." "Talpa" begins:

> Natalia se metió entre los brazos de su madre y lloró largamente allí con un llanto quedito. Era un llanto aguantado por muchos días, guardado hasta ahora que regresamos a Zenzontla y vio a su madre y comenzó a sentirse con ganas de consuelo. (p. 55)

The reader is completely unaware of what has taken place up to this point, since the story starts not even *in medias res*, but at the very end of the action. The rest of the story answers his question, "Why?" The frightful tale unfolds in fits and starts until it again reaches the end, with the "second" return of Natalia and the narrator:

> Ahora estamos los dos en Zenzontla. Hemos vuelto sin [Tanilo]. Y la madre de Natalia no me ha preguntado nada; ni qué hice con mi hermano Tanilo, ni nada. Natalia se ha puesto a llorar sobre sus hombros y le ha contado de esa manera lo que pasó. (pp. 64-65)

The fact that the end of the story marks a return to its starting point indicates the lack of real progression, stressed further by the line which follows the citation just above: "Y yo comienzo a sentir como si no hubiéramos llegado a ninguna parte." In "Talpa," as in so many of Rulfo's stories, nothing happens. The protagonists, in spite of their never-ending journeys, go nowhere.[15] The technique of suspended coherence is a major Rulfian strategy for communicating their fundamental immobility, the stagnation of his fictional world, and the discontinuity of human activities, on the level of narrative organization. It is in addition one of the ways in which Rulfo combats the linear nature of narrative, a point to be explored shortly.

Recurrent techniques

By recurrent techniques, which I consider conjunctive devices for reasons which will shortly be made clear, I refer to those devices which serve above all to provide order and coherence to a narrative, even when giving an appearance of fragmentation. They are abundant in Rulfo, and their frequent use affirms that he strives to present a coherent text. The jumpiness, the fragmentation of the text is effectively overcome through the use of these devices, which finally contribute to the reader's understanding and interpretation.[16]

The apparent discontinuity of Rulfo's narratives is particularly well expressed through several recurrent techniques: recapitulation, modulation, counterpoint, and

---

[15] Aside from the novel *Pedro Páramo,* many stories use the journey motif: "Talpa," "Nos han dado la tierra," "El hombre," "En la madrugada," "La noche que lo dejaron solo," "El llano en llamas," and "¿No oyes ladrar los perros?"

[16] The difference between a bridge technique such as suspended coherence and the conjunctive devices discussed here is simply one of degree. While both ultimately provide an element of unity to the Rulfian text, conjunctive images tend to do so more strongly.

what Rodríguez Alcalá calls Rulfo's "técnica de enfoques repetidos," which we will discuss first. [17]

Rodríguez Alcalá shows how Rulfo's narrative technique in "En la madrugada" presents the same scene as perceived two and even three different times by various narrators under differing circumstances. He plots the method's use in the story thusly:

1) La escena del castigo del becerro: partes 3, 4 y 5
2) La escena de don Justo con Margarita en sus brazos: partes 3 y 5
3) La "escena" de Esteban tendido en su catre después del homicidio: partes 4 y 6
4) La descripción de San Gabriel: partes 1, 2 y 8.
5) La "escena" de Esteban en la cárcel afirmando su amnesia: partes 4 y 7 [18]

This same device of repeated and changing focuses is used to a lesser degree in "Talpa" and even in "La herencia de Matilde Arcángel." It shows how Rulfo's narrative depends intimately on free association, and James East Irby notes that

La secuencia de eventos dentro del relato se pliega libremente al flujo del pensamiento del "testigo," quien, torpe para el análisis, va y viene entre el presente y el pasado y comunica sus impresiones "en bruto," sin elaboración, de acuerdo a una simple asociación de ideas, espontáneamente, tal como se le vienen a la memoria. [19]

The narrative device of repeated and alternating focuses (Alcalá says Rulfo "films" his stories) brings to mind the mosaic metaphor used earlier. Irby describes it as a

---

[17] This technique is the structural basis for numerous novels, such as Francisco Ayala's *El rapto* and Marco Denevi's *Rosaura a las diez*. Some of the density of Rulfo's stories comes from using such a technique, normally used in the longer novel form, in a short narrative, and the resulting condensation and more quickly changing focus.

[18] Rodríguez Alcalá, p. 19.

[19] *La influencia de William Faulkner en cuatro narradores hispanoamericanos* (México: UNAM, Escuela de Verano [Thesis], 1956), p. 135.

"mosaico de escenas fragmentarias." [20] The narrator puts the pieces into place, but the work of art is perceived, in a sense created, only within the reader. It is a kind of impressionism, reminiscent of the *pointilliste* technique. The device of repeated focus, so characteristic of Rulfo, is related to the next device: counterpoint.

Melvin Friedman, among others, discusses the application of musical counterpoint to literature. His observations shed light particularly on Rulfo. "The few successful attempts [at counterpoint] have constituted a literary rendering of the principle under the new relationship between time and space devised by Bergson," he writes. [21] The use of counterpoint in literature, then, implies a disjuncture of linear space and time arrangements, in that elements, instead of occurring in order, overlap and occur simultaneously. Applying this notion to Rulfo's writings, we see a strikingly integrated effort to liberate prose fiction from the bonds traditionally imposed on it by the discursive nature of language, a function, after all, of time and space.

Counterpoint is the structural basis for several of Rulfo's stories, such as "Luvina," "En la madrugada," and "El hombre." In these tales, Rulfo alternates the planes of time, space, and narrative presentation as musical tones alternate and overlap in counterpoint. In "El hombre," for instance, the point of view changes rapidly, alternating between the narrator and the two protagonists:

> Pasaron más parvadas de chachalacas, graznando con gritos que ensordecían.
> *"Caminaré más abajo. Aquí el río se hace un enredijo y puede devolverme a donde no quiero regresar."*

[20] *Ibid.*, p. 150.
[21] *Stream of Consciousness: A Study of Literary Method* (New York: Yale University Press, 1955), p. 13.

"Nadie te hará daño nunca, hijo. Estoy aquí para protegerte. Por eso nací antes que tú y mis huesos se endurecieron primero que los tuyos." (p. 41)

While Rulfo's technique is not truly simultaneous, it does achieve a notably simultaneous effect.[22] And combined with the technique of alternating focus and the other recurrent techniques we are about to examine, the effect is very like that of musical counterpoint. Irby, for one, recognizes Rulfo's use of counterpoint: "Rulfo delata cada vez más su deuda a Faulkner, alternando en contrapunto diferentes planos temporales y deslizándose entre varios puntos de vista..."[23] His counterpoint is not essentially fragmentary, in that it does not carry the tendency toward discontinuity to a total breakdown of the story, just as in music the use of this technique by no means destroys the composition. Rather, this device is another expression of the delicate balance between order and chaos so characteristic of Rulfo. Octavio Paz, in his preliminary remarks to *Corriente alterna*, seems to confirm the usefulness of what Rulfo has done:

> Espero que, a pesar de su aparente dispersión, sea visible la unidad contradictoria de estos fragmentos; todos ellos apuntan hacia un tema único: la aparición en nuestra historia de otro tiempo y otro espacio. Creo que el fragmento es la forma que mejor refleja esta realidad en movimiento que vivimos y que somos. Más que una semilla, el fragmento es una partícula errante que sólo se define frente a otras partículas: no es nada si no es relación. Un libro, un texto, es un tejido de relaciones.[24]

The other musical device which we will take up with regard to recurrent techniques is variously called "trans-

[22] One may see Ramón Pérez de Ayala's *El curandero de su honra* for a literally simultaneous narration in two planes (the two protagonist's, stories are set in parallel columns on the page, to be read at once).

[23] Irby, p. 136.

[24] Octavio Paz, "Advertencia" to *Corriente alterna* (Mexico: Siglo 21, 1967), p. 1.

position of leitmotif" or "modulation"; I prefer the second term, which Northrop Frye calls "the reappearance of an image in a different context."[25] In Rulfo, modulation is often a way of giving an appearance of chaos while again maintaining order. A few examples will illustrate his use of this apparatus. In "La noche que lo dejaron solo," we read that the narrator "se arrinconó en una esquina, descansando el cuerpo, aunque sentía que un gusano se le retorcía en el estómago" (p. 108). Later in the same story (p. 109), we read: "Feliciano Ruelas esperó todavía un rato a que se le calmara el bullicio que sentía cosquilleándole el estómago." This is an instance of the simplest reoccurrence of the image. A more subtle instance is this, from the same story:

1) "Luego se dejó resbalar en el sueño, sobre el cochal, sintiendo cómo se le iba entumeciendo el cuerpo." (p. 106)

2) "Llegó al borde de las barrancas. Miró allí lejos la gran llanura gris. 'Ellos deben estar allá. Descansando al sol, ya sin ningún pendiente,' pensó. Y se dejó caer barranca abajo, rodando y corriendo y volviendo a rodar." (p. 107)

3) "Luego sorbió tantito aire como si se fuera a zambullir en el agua y, agazapado hasta arrastrarse por el suelo, se fue caminando, empujando el cuerpo con las manos." (p. 109)

The connective elements between the three occurrences of the one image are: falling into a depth (*barranca*, *sueño*, and *agua*); feeling of relief and loss of control in the fall; and uncomfortable physical sensation. This type of modulation is less easily noted in reading than the more obvious type earlier noted. Yet another kind,

[25] The term "transposition of leitmotif" is Friedman's (p. 124); Frye uses the term "modulation" in "Literary Criticism," in *The Aims and Methods of Literary Criticism*, 2d ed. (New York: MLA, 1963), p. 77.

a bit more easily observed, depends on the use of a key word, as in "Luvina":

1) "Un viento que no deja crecer ni a la dulcamara: esas plantitas tristes que apenas si pueden vivir un poco untadas a la tierra, agarradas con todas sus manos al despeñadero de los montes." (p. 94)
2) [El viento] "se planta en Luvina, prendiéndose de las cosas como si las mordiera." (p. 96)
3) [los maridos de Luvina] "dejan el costal del bastimento para los viejos y plantan otro hijo en el vientre de las mujeres." (p. 102)

The key word of course is *planta*. It occurs three times, in quite different contexts. It also sets up a syllogistic relationship between the occurrences: it personifies the wind and the plants; it equates the husbands with the wind and the women with the earth; and it implies that the children of Luvina will cling to life just as do the plants and the wind. They will also live "un poco untados a la tierra," seized by the wind, and "agarrados con todas sus manos al despeñadero de los montes," a quick death awaiting them should they lose their grip. Modulation in Rulfo, then, may transfer elements from one image to another, and often does so without the reader consciously noting its effect. It can be, as in the case above, a particularly effective device.

The three recurrent techniques dealt with so far (repeated focus, counterpoint and modulation) are all means for restatement, a characteristic of almost all of Rulfo's fiction. Any reading of Rulfo reveals at once the frequent repetition, and Rodríguez Alcalá even uses it in parodying Rulfo's style. Such repetitions and restatements are one way in which Rulfo assures that the reader, like the protagonists, will "get nowhere" in his stories. More often than not, after struggling through the bog of repetitions, back-tracks ("eso le dije"; "y regresando a donde estábamos"), and unessential clarifications ("así es la cosa"), the reader comes to the end of the story only to find himself back at the beginning, as we saw in "Talpa." Rulfo uses repetition to slow down the narration as well, to stagnate the narrative progression even within a single paragraph. In "Nos han dado la tierra," there is a repetition in a single paragraph with the pattern ABBA:

> No, el llano no es cosa que sirva. No hay conejos ni pájaros. *No hay nada. A no ser* unos cuantos huizaches trespeleques y una que otra manchita de zacate con las hojas enroscadas; *a no ser* eso *no hay nada.* (p. 16)

The very first paragraph of "La cuesta de las comadres" also bogs down immediately. Here, the repetition is ABAB:

> Los difuntos Torricos *siempre fueron buenos amigos* míos. Tal vez *en Zapotlán no los quisieran;* pero lo que es de mí, *siempre fueron buenos amigos.* Ahora, eso de que *no los quisieran en Zapotlán* no tenía ninguna importancia. (p. 21)

On the surface level, such repetitions are a direct reproduction of the speaker's thought. On the level of the narrative technique, they further serve the same end as the other recurrent means used by Rulfo: to give voice to the consciousness which provides the stories' ultimate subject matter. And finally, they allow the insertion of fragmentary techniques (counterpoint, repeated focus) by slowing down the progression of the story, and "making room" for such procedures in a narrative of relatively little length.

Many of the techniques found in Juan Rulfo tend to disrupt the narrative line. [26] Yet in reading Rulfo serious-

---

[26] Here I may simply list some of the figures which, on the level of style, give further substance to the disjunctive nature of Rulfian narrative: polyptoton ("andar en andanzas"); intensifying repetition ("luego luego"); concretion of abstractions ("jorobado de sueño," "bajársele el sueño"); animation of the land-

ly (which is to say repeatedly), few feel that his narratives fail to hold together; rather, one asks, "How has this come about?" The unity of his stories is rather like that of a river, whose splashes, changes of direction and false channels in no way prevent it from being a river. This image was of course the one used by psychologist William James, who originated the term "stream of consciousness," later appropriated into literary criticism. [27] Later in his essay, James changes metaphors, and compares the shifting of conscious states with a kaleidoscope, whose very nature is change. The apparently disruptive nature of Rulfo's stories is actually inherent to their aesthetic unity.

Such a concept of fluid unity must be captured by the student of Rulfo; either one's consciousness must intuitively respond to the patterns found in the narrative, or (even better) one must achieve a simultaneous apprehension of the whole stream, manage to see it as a whole in spite of its unstable form. The story and the reader both, then, overcome the linear nature of narrative, shattered from the start by Rulfo's ordering of chaos. Enrique Anderson-Imbert alludes to these phenomena: "Por los agujeros abiertos en esa eternidad vemos y oímos a los muertos, son prendidos en instantes que no se suceden como los puntos de una línea, sino que están diseminados desordenadamente: sólo el lector va dándoles sentido." [28] And William James, in a footnote, reminds

scape; animalization of the protagonists; and an extensive group of rhetorical figures for repetition (including anadiplosis, conduplicatio and diacope) some of which are contrapuntal in nature.

[27] William James, *Principles of Psychology* (New York: Holt, 1890), particularly chapter IX (a re-examination of ideas he first published in 1884).

[28] Enrique Anderson-Imbert, *Historia de la literatura hispanoamericana* (Mexico: Fondo de Cultura Económica, 1966), 2:354. Much of Anderson-Imbert's description of Yáñez's *Al filo del*

us of Mozart, whose manner of apprehending his own creations recognizes the fullest unity of the work of art (and which directly applies to the musical nature of Rulfo's tales):

> I spread it out broader and clearer, and at last it gets almost finished in my head, even when it is a long piece, so that I can see the whole of it in a single glance in my mind, as if it were a beautiful painting or a handsome human being; in which way I do not hear it in my imagination at all in succession—the way it must come later—but all at once, as it were. The best of all is the hearing of it all at once.[29]

The procedure used by Rulfo in the 1950s has found substantial theoretical support and justification in the 1970s, particularly in work departing from that of Saussure and Barthes. Tzvetan Todorov, and especially Julia Kristeva's ideas on intertextual relations, are most useful in constructing the aesthetic behind Rulfo's procedures. Indeed: Rulfo's disjunctive and conjunctive devices provide excellent examples of Kristeva's *ideologema*, "el encuentro de una organización textual... con los enunciados que asimila en su espacio o a los que remite en el espacio de los textos exteriores."[30] Further, a work relates to "distintos tipos de enunciados anteriores y sincrónicos" (p. 15). The *ideologema* is the means by which the word relates to the whole text (see p. 16), precisely what we have been observing in Rulfo. His recurrent techniques seize the opportunities provided within the text itself, and use them to the fullest.

agua (especially p. 231) also illuminates the numerous points of contact between Yáñez and Rulfo (particularly his observations on failure, loosely-built plots, lack of a thesis, impressionism, fragmented and criss-crossing structure, the flow of conscious and subconscious, and interior monologue).

[29] James, p. 255.

[30] Julia Kristeva, *El texto de la novela*, Tr. Jordi Llovet (Barcelona: Editorial Lumen, 1974), p. 16. (Original title *Le texte du roman*.)

Additionally, Kristeva's "lectura transformacional," in which each segment "es leído a partir de la totalidad del texto," is precisely—indeed decisively—what is required in reading Juan Rulfo. Without such a reading, the text may in fact be incoherent because of its destruction of linear narrative and normal time and space relations. Rulfo had apparently realized what Kristeva now asserts: "no hay novela lineal" (p. 248), and he skillfully structured his texts to seize the opportunities presented by a non-consecutive narrative line.

Thus the structure of Rulfo's stories is such that it leads the reader, be it consciously or unconsciously, to pass through a process of instantaneous apprehension of the whole. [31] This process, shown to be aesthetically coherent and also based on the purest concept of the early stream of consciousness, is the ultimate justification for all of the disordering elements which we have been examining in Rulfo's tales. Through them he attempts to present a significant way to overcome the discursive nature of narrative, to create a text which steps outside of the "bourgeois" (i.e., ordered) nature of traditional narrative, to create a text which is revolutionary in its very language and structure. [32]

[31] John S. Brushwood observes in this regard that "Beyond the first few pages of this book [*Pedro Páramo*], any reference by the reader to either life or death is utterly useless... The book must be read with the subconscious. The reader cannot stay outside the novel. And he must do even more than just enter into the book. He must unite with it, entering into the book and allowing the book to enter him. Once the subconscious is open the reader's problem is resolved" (*Mexico in its Novel* [Austin, Texas: University of Texas Press, 1966], p. 32).

[32] See Jean Franco, "The Crisis of the Liberal Imagination," in which narratives by Sarduy, Fuentes and Cortázar are examined as to their "bourgeois" or "revolutionary" nature (*Literature and Ideologies*, no. 1 [December 1977-January 1978], especially p. 20.

Thought and speech

Interior monologue, often alternated with omniscient narration, is Rulfo's narrative mode *por excelencia*. It is also directly related to the characteristics of stream of consciousness fiction, in that interior monologue is the typical modal narration (so much so that the two terms, unfortunately, are often used interchangeably). Friedman notes that interior monologue proceeds, ideally, in the manner of musical counterpoint, by simultaneity. The juxtaposition of scenes that is one of Rulfo's contrapuntal devices is fundamentally an impressionistic technique, as noted above. On paper, Rulfo's stories are often a collection of brusquely juxtaposed fragments; they take form, as suggested earlier, only in the mind of the reader. As a consequence, it can be said that Rulfo has made narrative form mirror a concept of the human psyche. The inordinate and disturbing depth of his creations derives from this equation; it is as if the story were a nearly bottomless well, into whose depths we apprehensively peer, to see ourselves. Yet at the bottom of the well, which we sense more than we actually see, lies the universal core of human awareness as well.

One key to the nature of Rulfo's use of stream of consciousness devices lies in the phenomenon that his character's thought and their speech are fundamentally identical. He sets in motion a balance-wheel which moves between random and logical associations, which his characters express as they occur to them (as Irby says, "tal como se les vienen a la memoria"). Juan Preciado can "speak" in *Pedro Páramo* even while dead; we hear his protagonists' spirits think (again, *pensar* corresponds to *sentir*). The meaning of *Pedro Páramo's murmullos* is nothing less than this hearing of unspoken thoughts.

Irby has noted how Rulfo's simple and uneducated characters typically do not think before they speak, and do not, therefore, deform their statements through abstraction. Often, then, thought and speech, being one, are simultaneous in the narrative. "La noche que lo dejaron solo" provides a clear illustration of this identity between thought and speech in Rulfo. The narrator is omniscient, and the reader is provided with all his speech and thoughts:

> No serían muchas [noches] —pensó— si al menos hubiéramos dormido de día. Pero ellos no quisieron. "Nos pueden agarrar dormidos —dijeron—. Y eso sería lo peor."
> —¿Lo peor para quién?
> Ahora el sueño lo hacía hablar. (p. 106)

The protagonist's question responds to his own unspoken thought, in perfect sequence, and he speaks at the same instant in which the question occurs to him. It is revealing to note that in Rulfo, *decir* is frequently actually *decirse*, since his characters often speak only to themselves. Furthermore, their expression is stylistically indistinguishable from that of the narrators, so that in a real sense, almost all speech in Rulfo's stories is purely internal. This is especially true if we bear in mind that the narrated world is essentially in the mind of these characters in the first place, since we perceive it largely through them. The following lines, which occur shortly after our last citation, may illustrate this point (note that since the protagonist is alone, *dijo* here is *se dijo*):

> Se detuvo con los ojos cerrados. "Es mucho —dijo—. ¿Qué ganamos con apurarnos? Una jornada. Después de tantas que hemos perdido, no vale la pena." En seguida gritó: "¿Dónde andan?"

The shout here, following immediately the character's taking stock of his situation, is the only real act of external speech. It is significant also that the punctuation of these two cited passages follows the same pattern, further supporting the contention that speech is identical to thought here because we as readers are already inside the protagonists' minds. We hear the characters think, and it is purely coincidental to them that anyone may be present to hear them when they speak aloud.

Friedman observes that stream of consciousness fiction "characterizes the mind on the verge of dissolution into unconsciousness."[33] This is the magical, almost mythical, area where Rulfo's people dwell, and where thought and speech become one in effect. Rulfo has developed and used devices from stream of consciousness writing to create this very special and tenuous state of existence for his characters and their uncertain world.[34]

Objectivity in Rulfo

We have seen how Rulfo utilizes all of the important devices of stream of consciousness fiction, skillfully adapting them to his particular needs, and often in the process giving them a new or more extensive function. There is one major point of contact between Rulfian narrative and stream of consciousness writing yet to discuss: their "objective" nature.

Robert Humphrey notes that "one important achievement of Joyce's in *Ulysses* which is central to his whole

---

[33] P. 2.

[34] The equivalence between thought and speech is yet another breakdown of normal distinctions. Together with Rulfo's direct presentation (discussed below), this equivalence gives a most unique quality to Rulfo's fiction, and helps further explain its unusual impact. The thoughts and the words of the protagonists —and even of the narrators— seem to bypass the reader's intellect, already annulled, and to penetrate directly into his inner awareness to produce a direct and interior response. In this sense, it may be said that Rulfo's narrative structures are in essence anti-intellectual.

purpose and which is greatly dependent on stream of consciousness [is] the marvelous degree of objectivity which he achieves."[35] He goes on to write of Joyce's ideal narrator (as expressed in *Portrait of the Artist*), whose personality almost "refines itself out of existence." Indeed, the constant characteristic of stream of consciousness narration is an apparent total separation of the author from the narrator. The objective of this procedure is to present the character's psyche with no intermediaries between it and the reader. Yet this can never really be managed.[36] A theoretical impasse results between the goal—objectivity— and the necessarily subjective narrative modes by which the author must create this impression. The Rulfian paradox is that although his narrators have in a sense lost real faith in their own existence, they still tenuously perceive themselves; or perhaps what they see is their own limbo, in which cause and effect, subject and object, dissolve, to lose and then regain individual identity.[37] Irby has seen the subjective nature of Rulfo's narratives in spite of their frequently "objective" presentation, and writes of Rulfo's "concepción de forma narrativa como conciencia subjetiva de

[35] P. 15.

[36] See, for instance, Wayne Booth's widely-read *The Rhetoric of Fiction* (Chicago: University of Chicago Press, 1961), Part I *passim*. From a quite different critical vantage point, Todorov and Roland Barthes agree that "zero degree" writing does not really exist, that there is no naive or innocent writing; only an appearance of objectivity may be given. Rulfo's devices present just such an appearance. See Tzvetan Todorov, *Littérature et signification*. (Paris: Librairie Larousse, Langue et Langage, 1967), p. 97; and Roland Barthes, *Writing Degree Zero*, Tr. A. Laver and C. Smith (New York: Hill and Wang, 1968), especially p. 87.

[37] Irby speaks of "la visión subjetiva del autor" and says that "se pierde la relación normal entre sujeto y objeto" (p. 140). And later (p. 143) he writes, "Se disuelven las relaciones de causa y efecto que normalmente se expresan mediante la secuencia temporal."

una realidad caótica." [38]   All "objectivity" in Rulfo is but apparent, and it exists as a result of the very techniques we have been studying.

Psychologist William James, spoken of earlier, may help show just how close Rulfo is to the original concept of stream of consciousness. Both emphasize internal reality. "We shall see," writes James, "how inveterate is our habit of not attending to sensations as subjective facts, but of simply using them as stepping-stones to pass over to the recognition of the reality whose presence they reveal." [39]   In fact, subjectivity is enclosed in the very sentence in which the term "stream of consciousness" is first used:

> Consciousness, then, does not appear to itself chopped up in bits. It is nothing jointed; it flows. A "river" or a "stream" are the metaphors by which it is most naturally described. In talking of it hereafter, let us call it the stream of thought, or consciousness, or of subjective life. [40]

Rulfo's world, exclusively internal, fully conforms to this founding concept of the stream of consciousness. In the Rulfian world the only reality, being internal, is the very thoughts and sensations of the characters. It is highly ironic that such a subjective view of things should be presented in such an "objective" manner. In this paradoxical coexistence lies the essence of Rulfian narrative, and here lies also the reason for Rulfo's exploitation of the devices examined in this study: they allow the *cooperation* of the disparate elements of subjectivity and objectivity, order and chaos.

[38] *Ibid.*, p. 151
[39] James, p. 231.
[40] *Ibid.*, p. 239.

Conclusion

I conclude that Rulfo utilizes virtually all of the devices identified with stream of consciousness fiction, often on a very basic level of his narrative, and in several instances he extends their application significantly. His use of them, in fact, is closer to the original concept (as expressed by James) than many of stream of consciousness' other literary adaptations. Rulfo is not a stream of consciousness writer in the sense of the decades which preceded his work; rather, he has seized on the experiments of those times, integrating them into a narrative which shares many qualities with stream of consciousness fiction, but with far fewer limitations. In so doing, he has created a magnificently gloomy picture of his characters'—and mankind's—situation.

Juan Rulfo's use of stream of consciousness techniques allows him to produce stories whose structures support fully the image of chaos and desperation expressed through the tone of the characters' speech. He has managed to portray coherently an essentially chaotic vision by utilizing devices essayed by stream of consciousness fiction, which give an appearance of disorder, but making them contribute to the stories' unified structures. In the process, Rulfo thus moves beyond traditional linear narrative structures.

If Faulkner, according to Bowling, deals with the "intellectual, moral and spiritual confusion" of his characters, Rulfo goes a step beyond: into metaphysical despair.

University of North Carolina
Chapel Hill, N. C.

Las vidas de los héroes de Roa Bastos

Es posible que una de las marcas de la obra de Roa Bastos sea la falta de esa marca específica que se llama un estilo. Y esto es así porque cada vez que ha cambiado la noción de vida y de sujeto en la literatura latinoamericana, cambió también la escritura de Roa Bastos. O mejor: cada vez que se planteó el problema del uso de la literatura y su relación con la vida, la escritura de Roa Bastos ió como otro ciclo. Y en ese mismo momento construyó un tipo de representación que garantizaba la vida de lo referido, aun cuando esa representación se veía obligada a cambiar constantemente, a exhibir su historicidad. Y esto ocurre porque el centro de su representación es el cambio.

Me estoy refiriendo a la vida como concepto crítico (y por supuesto histórico): lo que queda cuando se eliminan las actividades especializadas, lo que se escapa, el resto, lo irrealizado, el sedimento, que se dice con un lenguaje donde no hay verdadero ni falso, universales ni trascendencias. Y me refiero al sujeto como algo que todavía nos cuesta definir: un conjunto de problemas ligado con la noción de fronteras, de temporalidades múltiples que coexisten, de ritmos, barbaries o minorías, nacionalidades y voces, exilios, diásporas, autoridades y resistencias. La combinación de vida y sujeto, cada vez variable, constituye el estilo cada vez cambiante de Roa Bastos.

El archivo de vidas y sujetos de Roa Bastos es doble: por un lado una serie de relatos de acontecimientos, guerras, derrotas y triunfos con sus héroes y fechas: la historia nacional. Por el otro, una serie de relatos de vidas, esas otras historias. Entre la historia y sus héroes y los héroes de las otras historias se dibuja uno de los campos fundantes de su obra. Y entre la vida de los héroes de la historia y la vida de los héroes de las otras historias se define la tensión cada vez cambiante de su escritura.

Las vidas trazan una serie de recorridos y constituyen lugares que son campos de discursos y cadenas de ficciones que los nombran. Esas vidas ligan lenguas, leyes y usos de cuerpos en sistemas narrativos específicos. Se trata casi siempre de historias de emancipación y de resistencia, es decir de vidas que se definen en relación

con el poder y sus dos posiciones extremas: enfrentarlo o representarlo. Y en la literatura de Roa Bastos, poder es simplemente poder (de) escribir y de decir yo. Por eso sólo desde *Yo El Supremo* pueden pensarse las vidas de sus héroes. El Supremo es la frontera de las vidas porque en él se constituye el sujeto como héroe y como historia nacional al mismo tiempo, y porque el yo escrito es a la vez el estado y la ley. Y sobre todo porque la condición de su discurso es la muerte. Esa muerte-vida de El Supremo aparece, entonces, como la frontera de las vidas de los héroes, su límite y su posibilidad. Dicho de otro modo: los héroes de Roa Bastos y sus relatos trazan un recorrido que va de lo oral a lo escrito, o en los términos mismos de su literatura, del él al yo. Se diferencian básicamente según cuenten o sean contados, según escriban o sean escritos.

I

El héroe contado, impersonal, el él, es el héroe popular, Solano Rojas de «El trueno entre las hojas» o Gaspar Mora de *Hijo de hombre*. El rasgo común que comparten es que los dos tocan (en acordeón o guitarra) «Campamento Cerro-León» el himno anónimo de la Guerra Grande. Y que esa música de la patria sigue oyéndose después de su muerte: el acordeón de Solano suena cada vez que se anuncia mal tiempo. Se trata del sonido, de la voz, del canto y de la tradición, es decir de la memoria. Los héroes orales y sus vidas sostienen la estructura de la memoria, o mejor, son su estructura significante. Se fundan en el sonido o la imagen, son como impersonales, retornan rítmicamente, contienen la posibilidad del cambio, se sostienen en las marcas en el cuerpo y aparecen como corte, frontera La historia de Gaspar, contada por el viejo Macario Francia, hijo de Pilar, es cada vez diferente, admite variantes, cambios «como quizá lo esté haciendo yo ahora sin darme cuenta», dice el que escribe, Vera. Esas historias, variables y abiertas como los cantos folclóricos, no se pueden plagiar porque lo oral es el lugar donde no hay propiedad. Ellos hacen sonar algo que retorna, como los ciclos naturales o como el mal tiempo, o algo que dice que sus vidas han dejado de ser vidas individuales porque el héroe popular representa una experiencia común y una identidad colectiva. Los ancianos cuentan esas vidas al que las escribe. Esos héroes sin yo carecen de infancia y de hijos porque ocupan la infancia de los que escriben y porque todos son sus herederos. Parecen haber nacido sin padre.

La estructura significante de la memoria se funda en la marca en el cuerpo. El centro de esas vidas es el sacrificio o martirio, el azote en el cuerpo, que las divide en dos partes. Solano enfrentó y quemó al norteamericano Way, pasó quince años en la cárcel, regresó ciego, tocó la música que perdura y murió ahogado en el río. La violencia del poder le dejó las cicatrices del látigo y el hachazo de la ceguera. Sostiene con su cuerpo tallado la memoria del origen de las luchas obreras, de la

.résistencia y la organización. Es el mártir que funda una historia de larga duración, la otra cara de la historia.

Lo mismo ocurre con Gaspar Mora, el otro mártir del azote en el cuerpo. Fabricaba instrumentos de música y enseñaba su oficio, hasta que la lepra corta su vida. Entonces se aísla y talla la imagen del Cristo leproso que después de su muerte enfrenta las imágenes oficiales de la Iglesia ligada con el poder. El Cristo leproso funda la tradición del cristianismo popular como resistencia. Encarna «una creencia que en sí misma significaba una inversión de la fe, un permanente conato de insurrección», un redentor hombre y no un Dios. Cíclicamente, cada Viernes Santo, la procesión popular lo saca del cerro y lo lleva al atrio de la iglesia, pero no entra, es su límite. Las vidas de los héroes populares, cortadas en dos por el sacrificio, representan un corte, una frontera, el lugar donde la historia se da vuelta y abre camino a las otras historias. Entre el martirio y la muerte final, es decir, entre dos muertes, en esa zona límite entre la vida y la muerte, o en la contravida, se construye su perdurabilidad y su condición de héroes de la memoria, fundadores de contrainstituciones y contrahistorias. El alma de Solano y su música, el cuerpo del Cristo hombre de Gaspar, son, por sus nombres mismos, el revés del otro Solano y del otro Gaspar, los dos héroes de la historia del Paraguay. Los separa de ellos el color de sus nombres: Rojas en Solano (la tradición de las luchas obreras), y Mora en Gaspar (la tradición del otro cristianismo, popular). Son cada uno el otro de los nombres de la historia.

II

Los héroes letrados o la otra parte del archivo, constituyen el centro de las novelas de Roa Bastos, los que las «escriben». Son Miguel Vera de *Hijo de hombre* y El Supremo. Hacen y son hechos por la historia política; la escriben en primera persona. La historia de Vera es lineal, desde los relatos orales de Macario Francia y desde el cometa hasta el fin de la guerra con Bolivia. La del Supremo va desde la colonia y la revolución hasta después de su muerte o aún hasta la actualidad porque es discontinua y sigue la expansión perpetua del texto. Pero las etapas de sus vidas no difieren demasiado porque pasan por todas las instituciones, desde la familia hasta el Estado. Tienen infancia, tienen madre y padre, y esto los diferencia de entrada de los héroes orales. La secuencia institucional y estatal de sus vidas sigue este orden: la infancia (alimentada por la oralidad popular), el viaje de iniciación (uno por río, el otro por tren) en el que nacen otra vez, la entrada en la institución de enseñanza, sonde se rebelan y la enfrentan: Vera participó de una rebelión en el liceo militar y estuvo a punto de ser fusilado, y El Supremo fue expulsado de la universidad de Córdoba por sedicioso, ateo y partidario de las doctrinas libertinas e iluministas. La secuencia continúa con la conspiración y la entrada en la historia política, la prisión y la guerra en Vera, y finalmente el acceso al poder. Vera llega a jefe: de destacamen-

to en la guerra y después a jefe político en su pueblo, y El Supremo accede a la dictadura perpetua y al poder absoluto. En este camino los dos construyen la escritura y el yo, un yo cárcel (en el caso de Vera, que comienza su diario en la prisión militar) o un yo-cráneo (en el caso del Supremo), que representa la estructura de la razón. Esa representación los constituye y constituye su escritura: reflexión, autorreferencia, división, desdoblamiento, la posesión de un código más, la capacidad de incluir y excluir, es decir, el poder de fundar instituciones. Su escritura, de entrada, es reflexiva y está dividida: los dos tipos de narración de *Hijo de Hombre* (algo así como la tradición de Sapukai y la de Itapé, del Cristo leproso y de las insurrecciones campesinas), y la Circular Perpetua y el Cuaderno Privado en *Yo El Supremo*. El héroe letrado está definido por la traición. Poder, uso del yo, posesión del código, división y traición son uno solo en Roa Bastos: sólo un telegrafista pudo delatar a los insurrectos en *Hijo de hombre*, y sólo el subordinado militar que escribe «Borrador de un informe» y divide su escritura entre crónica y confesión pudo hacer matar al Cristo femenino popular, la prostituta ciega. La traición de la escritura o del poder del yo escrito es la traición a lo que representan los héroes orales: la memoria de la resistencia en sus cuerpos.

Estos yo-Estado, yo-institución y razón, se acompañan de asistentes, secretarios, esclavos, hijos adoptivos. Con estos subordinados mantienen una relación mortal que alegoriza la relación de la razón con la memoria o de la oralidad con la escritura. Es la condena a muerte. En El Supremo el asistente condenado no es solamente Patiño, el que ejecuta el dictado y también asume la narración de la tradición oral, sino también Pilar, el esclavo al que El Supremo mandó matar. Su hijo Macario contará muchos años después la historia del héroe popular Gaspar Mora, su sobrino. Quiero decir con esto que de los asistentes condenados a muerte por el yo de la escritura parte una tradición o genealogía donde se inserta el héroe popular. En *Hijo de hombre* los subordinados de Vera están representados por la cadena significante de los mártires del cristianismo popular: Niño Nacimiento González o Pesebre, el hijo de Natividad, primer amor de Vera, al que da el tiro final, y después Cristóbal Jara, que lo salva de morir de sed, y a quien da también el tiro final. Y finalmente el hijo de Crisanto Villalba, el loco de la guerra, al que adoptó, es el que dará a Vera el tiro final. Los héroes orales son los asistentes del yo y del poder, y a Vera literalmente lo alimentan (en los dos sentidos) y lo salvan de morir de sed, con la leche de Damiana y el agua de Cristóbal. Esa pareja, o la relación entre los dos tipos de héroes, encarnan en la escritura de Roa Bastos la dialéctica entre la vida y la muerte. En el caso del Supremo él mismo se engendra del cráneo, se alimenta con los senos frontales y también se condena a muerte. Allí el yo del poder absoluto de la escritura ha llegado a la autoreflexividad absoluta.

Los héroes letrados, representantes de la historia política, o de la política del poder, de lo escrito, del yo, de la razón, de la contradicción y la escisión, aparecen como el fin de un proceso, como en una frontera del relato de emancipación y de acceso al yo. Allí lo íntimo y personal es a la vez político y público. Por eso el poder absoluto implica un yo absoluto y una escritura absoluta, totalitaria, que se funde con la reescritura de la historia. El Estado soy yo dice El Supremo, que no es sólo el héroe letrado por excelencia sino también el héroe nacional. Su escritura traza el mapa y las fronteras del Estado en forma de representaciones de lenguas, de espacios, y de leyes que incluyen o excluyen a los otros. Su función estatal (que es la función del yo y de la razón al mismo tiempo), es precisamente la de incluir y excluir, a la vez de sí mismo y de la nación.

III

Pero hay otra diferencia que se superpone a la separación entre héroes él y héroes yo, y que pasa por el interior de estos últimos y es uno de los factores fundamentales del cámbio en la escritura de Roa Bastos. La diferencia entre Vera y El Supremo, o entre las dos novelas, es la que va desde el testimonio a la historia: dos modos de la relación entre yo y él, dos concepciones del sujeto. En el testimonio de *Hijo de hombre*, el centro es la relación del sujeto con la verdad el yo que escribe se llama Vera. Y es el testimonio de un martirio, del valor de verdad del martirio, o del sacrificio de una vida (la de Gaspar Mora, pero también la de la cadena de los nombres cristianos, los pobres cristos) por una causa verdadera. El yo del que escribe es definido allí en términos de conciencia y de hegemonía del conocimiento sobre las otras instancias de la personalidad. Vera traicionó la insurrección popular cuando perdió la conciencia por el alcohol. Por eso la otra voz escrita, el otro yo que encuentra y publica sus escritos es una médica, la que encarna la verdad científica. Ella es la que puede juzgarlo incapaz para la acción y publicar su escritura como testimonio, sin las partes personales que le conciernen. Ese yo está enmarcado y constituido entonces por el él de los héroes orales de la resistencia por un lado, y por el otro yo de la ciencia, por el otro. Se encuentra entre el martirio y la verdad.

En el yo del Supremo, en cambio, no hay verdad, porque en la historia y el lenguaje, que es la materia que lo constituye, cada proposición tiene su contraria y cada verdad su contraverdad. Aceptar algo como verdadero o falso depende de la posición o de los intereses del que la postula o la juzga: la atribución de verdad es un acto interesado. Y en la historia y la lengua el yo ya no se reduce a la conciencia, sino que es un conjunto de estratos diversos y de pasiones encontradas. El cambio en la noción de sujeto en El Supremo y en la escritura de Roa Bastos multiplica y lleva al extremo los signos de la estructura de la razón para darlos vuelta: la historia ya no es lineal y su yo o poder masivo está atravesado y constituido por anacronismos, duplicaciones, discontinuidades, circularidades y significantes. El único que puede acusarlo de traición y juzgarlo es el perro y el único libre, el esclavo Pilar. Desde la tradición de los cínicos, los canes o perros (Diógenes, Luciano y su *Diálogo de muertos)* es decir, desde la tradición de la sátira, surge la voz otra que constituye una de las fronteras del yo. El filósofo cínico o el perro, que nada tiene, es el único que puede enfrentar el poder estatal. Lleva consigo todo lo que posee, su cuerpo, y piensa que la vida es más importante que la escritura. La otra voz o el otro yo escrito que encuentra sus escritos y los publica no es el yo de la ciencia y la verdad sino el yo del compilador, que es el de las parodias, inversiones, plagios, duplicaciones y también de los dobles, cráneos y mitologías que enmarcan esa vida y constituyen ese sujeto de la historia. Es el otro yo de la literatura. Allí no hay verdad sino perpetuamente otra voz, el lenguaje otro yo o el él del conjunto de la tradición y la memoria literaria.

Las vidas de los héroes de Roa Bastos, lo que es lo mismo, el juego de los yos y los ellos, que es también el juego de la dominación y la resistencia, ponen en relación la estructura de la memoria con la estructura de la razón. Y muestran que el estilo resulta de esa y otras combinaciones, y que cada crónica contiene una confesión, cada yo un otro yo, cada testimonio una historia y cada castellano un guaraní.

Josefina Ludmer

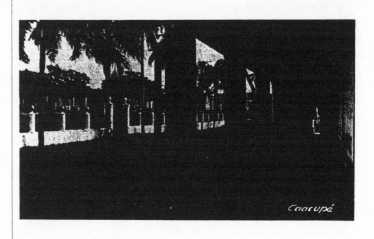

Caacupé

JOSÉ DONOSO: 'EL OBSCENO PÁJARO DE LA NOCHE' AS TEST CASE FOR PSYCHOANALYTIC INTERPRETATION

The work of Donoso, and in particular his best-known novel, *El obsceno pájaro de la noche*, seems to invite psychoanalytic interpretation. Donoso had himself been psychoanalysed before he began writing novels,[1] and, more significantly, in his work up to and including *El obsceno pájaro*, there are present what according to the Freudian book seem to be classic neurotic and psychotic symptoms. Critics have concurred in attributing to Donoso's characters, in particular to Humberto Peñaloza, a pathology capable of being fully explained in terms of psychoanalytic structures.[2] Donoso therefore provides an interesting test case for the interpretative value of psychoanalytic concepts.

For this purpose, the object analysed and the method of analysis must be kept distinct and examined carefully. Thus, for example, some of the attributions made by critics to Humberto Peñaloza are projections of a theory of interpretation, basically Freudian in its assumptions, which does not square with the kind of meanings generated by the text. However, the fact that Freudian concepts do not provide a 'key' does not mean they are simply irrelevant. In addition to opposing commonly-received versions of self and consciousness, the text proposes a view of the relations between the social and the psychological which reveals the contradictions of Freudian thought and produces an implicit critique of it. This counterthrust is not some tangential aspect of the text, but is embedded in its discourse.

Psychology and Sociology

El obsceno pájaro is a difficult work to write about because its own discourse seems to negate any model or procedure of rationality one might bring to bear. Within its own terms it appears to devour all possible *puntos de apoyo* outside its own convoluted enclosures. Cornejo Polar notes that the order which Donoso's work destroys 'parece confundirse con el horizonte total de la existencia', and complains that Donoso 'se olvida que ésta vive en la historia y que sobre las ruinas de un orden, que no es nunca el último, puede — debe — construirse una realidad mejor'.[3] But to handle the work in this way is to restore a division, which the text itself refuses, between the psychic and the social, phantasmagoria and history, inside and outside. If it subverts and distorts rational categories of time, space, and self, does it allow us merely to reconstruct them? Hernán Vidal, in his book on Donoso, proposes a similar division to that of Cornejo. He begins by reconstructing Humberto's biography and then gives a psychological description of Humberto which draws on Freud, Jung, and Adler. As a result, he separates Humberto's world from the social, treating it as an autonomous psychological world. In a final paragraph, he makes an

---

[1] George R. McMurray, *José Donoso* (Boston, 1979), p. 23.
[2] See Hernán Vidal, *José Donoso: surrealismo y rebelión de los instintos* (Barcelona, 1972); Silvia Martínez Dacosta, *Dos ensayos literarios* (Miami, 1976); Gloria Durán, 'La dialéctica del chacal y el Imbunche', *Revista Iberoamericana*, 95 (1976), 251–57; Isis Quinteros, *José Donoso: una insurrección contra la realidad* (Madrid, 1978); George R. McMurray, *José Donoso*; Pamela Bacarisse, '*El obsceno pájaro de la noche*: A Willed Process of Evasion', *Forum for Modern Language Studies*, 15 (1979), 114–29.
[3] Antonio Cornejo Polar, *José Donoso: la destrucción de un mundo* (Buenos Aires, 1975), p. 11.

exit from the world of dementia by appealing to a rationality outside the text: Humberto's 'schizophrenia' is ascribed to the fact that he is an 'intelectual pequeño-burgués' (Vidal, *José Donoso*, p. 235). This is actually a highly reductive statement: society is made into an ideological abstraction into which psychological structures can then be dissolved. Vidal's claim is that Humberto prefers fantasy to reality; but where is this reality, and how is access to it gained? In fact, why be conscious at all, if fantasy can be 'more satisfactory'? This is a question to which there is no simply social or simply psychological answer, and which reaches beyond Humberto considered biographically or individually.

The treatment of Humberto as a case of individual psychology, the interpretation of which will produce an interpretation of the text as a whole, in fact coincides with the attitude to Humberto which sees him as the single narrator of the whole novel. As Hugo Achugar rightly says, this text is characterized by 'la inexistencia del narrador como figura única'.[4] Achugar sees the indefinacy which rules the narrative as an 'ideological' principle, but uses the term ideology in a very abstract and general way, with the result that we do not find out what are the social implications of the destruction of the concept of single identity. What is needed is to bring the formal implications (that Humberto will not serve as a 'container' for the novel) together with the social implications.

Martínez Dacosta places Humberto within the classic constructs of ego psychology when she writes: 'La paranoia es el mecanismo de defensa que utiliza para protegerse de su sentimiento homosexual' (Martínez Dacosta, p. 74). The use of the word 'defence' is interesting; this type of statement is itself a kind of defence, against the subversiveness of the text. McMurray's treatment of *El obsceno pájaro* is more productive in that it confronts one with the argument that the states of altered consciousness manifested in the novel are merely pathological (McMurray, pp. 110, 111). Pamela Bacarisse's study of *El obsceno pájaro* similarly attributes schizophrenia to Humberto, taking 'El Mudito's life story' as 'a series of symptoms of schizophrenic ontological insecurity', and thus reconstructing the novel to fit an assumption of single truth and single identity.[5] Her assertion that 'the narrator is telling his story so that he will *not* be understood' sums up the main thrust of her argument, which aims to contain the novel within the premises of psychology. But when in one place she states 'the game . . . has got out of hand', this perhaps acknowledges the type of disruptive action which such containment attempts to control.

In an article published five years after his book, Vidal makes several references to Donoso, this time largely rejecting the idea that an irrational individual like Humberto can be the vehicle for effective social criticism.[6] However, he still adheres to the same basic model, positing a society which possesses (malign) rationality, that of repression, pushing the individual into irrationality. But the important point is not so much the positive or negative valuation of irrationalism or rationality as the distinction itself and how it is constructed. The terms may be reversed, but so long as they correspond with the division between society and individual, between conscious and unconscious, they sustain a construction which the text disallows.

Apart from Achugar, all the critics mentioned separate the psychological from the social, which raises the issue of how far the novel itself subscribes to such a

[4] Hugo Achugar, *Ideología y estructuras narrativas en José Donoso* (Caracas, 1979), p. 288.
[5] Bacarisse, '*El obsceno pájaro*', pp. 123, 125; see also pp. 117–18.
[6] Hernán Vidal, 'Narrativa del "boom"', *Arte, Sociedad, Ideología*, 2 (1977), 10–26 (p. 23).

separation. Theodor Adorno's essay, 'Sociology and Psychology', provides the best context for approaching this problem. Adorno shows how granting autonomy to the psychological is a political issue: 'The psyche that has been extracted from the social dialectic and investigated as an abstract "for itself" under the microscope has become an object of scientific inquiry all too consistent with a society that hires and fires people as so many units of abstract labour power.'[7] This taking away of the particular activity of the person, whether through labour or through ideological incorporation, should be compared with the continual metaphors of devouring and stealing (the bodies of others) in the novel.

The concept which most accurately engages with the structures of consciousness in *El obsceno pájaro* is in fact narcissism. This is for three main reasons. First, Humberto's action is basically narcissistic — rather, that is, than 'schizophrenic' or any other such term. Secondly, narcissism is a particularly appropriate concept for exploring the interaction of the social and the psychological. Thirdly, in Freud narcissism is used to account both for consciousness and for withdrawal of the self from the real world, in sleep or in pathological states, and also to account both for the capacity for love and for repression; in other words, it is a deeply ambiguous concept which reveals some of the contradictions of Freud's own thinking.[8] Since narcissism explodes the idea of the individual as the source of psychological structures, it is in this sense a self-destroying premise and therefore particularly appropriate to Humberto, whose individuality is both posited and destroyed by the text.

One of the ways Freud uses the concept of narcissism is to attempt to resolve the contradiction between ego instincts (or survival instincts) and sexual instincts. But the concept becomes deeply ambivalent: what is the self that is being loved? How far is it positive and how far a replica of destructive social systems? How far might it signify self-destruction? Adorno points to a main contradiction in Freud's thinking: what is socially permitted becomes what is desired, through a process which is kept unconscious in order to secure submission (Adorno, p. 87). So also the division between conscious and unconscious is a variable in which social and cultural organization shows itself.

The Action of the Text

In the analysis that follows it may appear that the assumption is being made that Humberto is the narrator-protagonist in a traditional sense. However, the assumption is made only tactically, precisely in order eventually to destroy it, in much the same way that the novel itself treats him as if he were a centre and an origin in order to explode this position.

The relationship between Humberto and Don Jerónimo exemplifies the pattern of domination and submission which runs through the novel. Humberto has an intensely ambivalent attitude to Don Jerónimo: on the one hand, he wants to participate in his power, in fact to become him, and, on the other hand, he wants to destroy him. Humberto's final revenge, in one of the key scenes, is Jerónimo's death by drowning in a pool presided over by the statue of a deformed and monstrous

---

[7] Theodor W. Adorno, 'Psychology and Sociology', *New Left Review*, 47 (1968), 79–97 (p. 81); see also p. 80.
[8] See Freud, Standard Edition, XIV, 94; XVI, 417, 473: Christopher Lasch, *The Culture of Narcissism* (New York, 1978), p. 36. Further references to Freud are to the Standard Edition.

'Diana Cazadora'. The mythological connexions of Diana = Artemis are relevant. Artemis made Narcissus fall in love, though 'denying him love's consummation', since he falls in love with his own reflection. Artemis has another victim, Actaeon, whom she changed into a stag and tore to pieces with his own hounds.[9] The metaphors are of self-enclosure and self-destruction, but mediated by the social in the form of mirror. Jerónimo puts on the mask of a monster in order to attend the dance given by the monsters he has installed in La Rinconada. But they are wearing masks of normal people, and he is the only one who is 'different'. The use of 'real' freaks as theatre recalls Todd Browning's film *Freaks* (1932), in which the parts were played by 'real' freaks. The disturbing result caused MGM to disown the film. Jerónimo's use of the freaks is turned against him in such a way that he himself emerges as the real freak or monster. He looks at himself in the pool:

Bajo los ojos para ver lo que sé que veré, mis proporciones clásicas, mi pelo blanco, mis facciones despejadas, mi mirada azul, mi mentón partido, pero alguien tira una piedra insidiosa al espejo de agua, triza mi imagen, descompone mi cara ... huyo tratando de arrancar con mis uñas esa máscara que no me puedo sacar aunque sé que es máscara porque esta noche es el baile de Emperatriz y yo me he disfrazado de monstruo, me rasguño la cara que sangra y sangrando me prueba que no es careta. (p. 104)[10]

Elsewhere Humberto states, 'si no ponemos una máscara no somos nadie'. But what are the rules of the system or theatre in which the masks are accredited with their roles? In this case, in the 'baile de disfraces', the rules are made by Emperatriz and Boy (Jerónimo's monstrous son) in order to trap Jerónimo in the same structure of illusion as he has placed them. This symmetrical reversal discloses Jerónimo's power as a member of the oligarchy to be dependent on the system which disguises social power by making biological features its symbols, thus providing it with the alibi of nature. Illusion-creating is power. To be excluded from power is to find that someone else controls the 'reality principle', or that it is irrational, or that there is no 'reality principle', or that all of these things are true simultaneously (the non-exclusive alternatives being a feature of the novel's logic). The breaking-up of the flat surface of the pool interrupts the appearance of rational space, revealing it as an agency of Jerónimo's superiority. The scene recalls Machado de Assis's short story 'O espelho' and takes its argument a step further. Once the surface is shattered, and the alibi of unconditional rationality destroyed, the masking and mirroring power of the social can be turned against Jerónimo. Face, mask, and mirror merge together; no gap is left between Jerónimo and the mask or reflection.[11]

Jerónimo's death is Humberto's invention, just as the social world which gives Jerónimo the mask of superiority is *his* (more accurately, his class's) invention. The difference between the aristocrat and the petty bourgeois is transformed, in order to reveal its secret arbitrariness and irrationality, into that between 'classical proportions' and physical monstrosity. Freud calls the process by which nations, castes, and classes construct mutual divisions 'the narcissism of minor differences' (Freud,

[9] Robert Graves, *The Greek Myths* (London, 1975), I, 287, 84–85.
[10] All references are to the fifth edition (Barcelona, 1977).
[11] Donoso's use of the mirror inevitably recalls Lacan's mirror-stage, which includes the statue and the fragmented body as opposites within the projected image of the self. Anthony Wilden, in Chapter 17 of *System and Structure* (London, 1972), argues that the alienation and violence which Lacan sees as structural within the constitution of the self are, in fact, characteristic of capitalist society. In this sense, Lacan does not provide, any more than does Freud, a rationality into which Donoso's text can be fitted.

XVIII, 101; XI, 199). The issue is how erotic energy is used to cement social antagonism.

In fact, La Rinconada both is and is not Humberto's invention, one of the characteristics of the text being that we do not know what is and what is not invented by him, or indeed how far he is the invention of others. Added to this, events (for instance, the birth of Boy) have multiple versions, and people (such as Humberto) multiple identities. In this sense, the text does not allow itself to be reduced to a rational reality. Its multiplicity connects with Humberto's refusal of literalness in his own writing and with the principle of over-determination, which Freud sees as characteristic of the unconscious: 'The principle of over-determination declares that there cannot be just one "true" interpretation of a symptom or symbol: it forbids literal-mindedness.'[12]

Humberto is trapped by what he has created: *vis-à-vis* the monsters of La Rinconada, 'él era el carcelero. . . . Él los había inventado a ellos, no ellos a él'; but 'estoy sellado dentro de sus intrigas y maquinaciones que yo urdo para ahogarme como si quisiera ahogarme' (p. 266). The question of agency, posed as who is author and who is actor, who is imprisoning and who is the prisoner, becomes blurred and ambivalent. Humberto is placed within a narcissistic action, which reveals its own bankruptcy. His writing was first an attempt to acquire a Name; the hundred copies of his book on Jerónimo's shelves signify to him the repetition of his name thousands of times. His subsequent book, which he writes and/or imagines, is concerned with cancelling the power of Jerónimo. But elimination of the other depends on self-elimination: 'Ahora me eliminaré yo para que te desplomes y te partas en mil fragmentos al caer' (p. 471). This would seem to have another meaning as well: to destroy Jerónimo implies destroying himself, so much does he depend on what he is struggling against; the two are parasitic on each other.

La Rinconada, the artifical world whose design is intended to prevent Boy's becoming conscious that he is a freak, repeats in miniature the topograpy of the novel as a whole. It consists in concentric circles of monsters (a social hierarchy of different classes) whose function is to provide a frontier which excludes any outside reality. Inside, dimensions of time and space are altered:

Boy debía crecer con la certeza de que las cosas iban naciendo a medida que su mirada se fijaba en ellas y que al dejar de mirarlas las cosas morían, no eran más que esa corteza percibida por sus ojos, otras formas de nacer y de morir no existían, tanto, que principales entre las palabras que Boy Jamás iba a conocer eran todas las que designan origen y fin. Nada de porqués, ni cuándos, de afueras, de adentros, de antes, de después. (p. 243)

There are similarities with the language of dream (p. 112), a single, flowing reality, whose images exist only in the instant. This translation of social space into abstract and unidimensional psychic space is a feature of the Freudian unconscious, which, as Adorno puts it, 'resembles the abstract society it knows nothing about, and can be used to weld it together'.[13]

Humberto, as El Mudito in the Casa, continually blocks up doors and windows, and then treats the surface so that it will look old and worn and thus homogeneous with the existing surfaces. This plugging of all holes has both totalitarian and

[12] Norman O. Brown, *Love's Body* (New York, 1966), p. 193.
[13] Adorno, 'Psychology and Sociology', p. 80. William Burroughs, in *Exterminator* (London, 1974), calls the Freudian unconscious 'this virus this ancient parasite' (p. 24).

paranoid aspects. It has been said, for instance, that one of the methods used by certain régimes in Latin America to disorientate political prisoners is to move the environment with the prisoner: the same enclosure (erected within a larger building) is dismantled and re-erected in a different part of the country. El Mudito imagines Inés in her final madness taken off in a straitjacket to a white room with no window, except for a photograph which masquerades as a window. The placing of boundaries which disguise themselves as outside world is part of a general control or blocking of the senses, which has its culmination in the figure of the *imbunche*, where all nine orifices of the body are sewn up. The *imbunche* is what witches do to the girls they steal for their orgies, or what the *viejas* will do to the imaginary miraculous child they are waiting for. Virgin birth reveals the wish for power and control, and witchery and motherhood-as-power show their connexion in terms of vampirism against children.

One of the functions of enclosure is the subversion of cognition: 'Boy debía vivir en un presente hechizado, en el limbo del accidente, de la circunstancia particular, en el aislamiento del objeto y el momento sin clave ni significación' (p. 243). Narcissus, Robert Graves suggests, is connected with narcotic: El Mudito and the *viejas* are in a sense drugged. The connexion between sleep, death, and mother-as-power has been pointed out by Igor Caruso.[14]

A repeated pattern of relationship between Humberto and Jerónimo is that of watcher and watched, and its main component is sexual. For instance, Jerónimo's potency depends on Humberto's being a witness to his acts. The parasitism also works the other way: having power over Jerónimo is a means of participating in his power. Moreover, in terms of narcissistic structures, watching the other would be a version of watching the self, so that, in watching Jerónimo, Humberto is in a sense watching himself as Jerónimo. This is reflected in the changing of pronouns and swapping of identities as Humberto narrates Jerónimo's actions. In the mutual exchange, the watcher's power is fed: 'Yo me quedé con la mirada cargada de poder' (p. 84).

Cannibalism and Catharsis

The exchange which occurs between watcher and watched is similar to the cannibalistic types of action and relationship that recur through the novel.[15] Unlike Freud, for whom cannibalism describes the ego's narcissistic incorporation of objects into itself, Donoso shows cannibalism to be a social product:[16] when Humberto first sees Jerónimo, he wants to devour him or be devoured by him; or there is the grotesque exchange in which Jerónimo, for political purposes, steals Humberto's wound, Humberto steals Jerónimo's potency, and Jerónimo Humberto's fertility. The exchange enacts the eroticizing of domination, while the connexion with eating is, as Lévi-Strauss puts it, that 'sexual and nutritional relations are . . . associated even today'.[17]

The cannibalism motif figures solely in the negative sense, that is, in being devoured or raided by the other. Humberto imagines Doctor Azula operating on him in order to steal all his organs: he will be turned into a hatchery for new organs; the defective parts of the monsters, grafted on to him, will become healthy: 'Nunca más seré una persona

[14] Igor Caruso, *Psicoanálisis para la persona* (Barcelona, 1965), pp. 137–38.
[15] For a study of the cannibalism motif in *El obsceno pájaro* and *Casa de campo*, see William Rowe, 'Donoso and Cannibalism', *Bananas*, 15 (1979), 34–35, 39.
[16] Freud, xiv, 249–50; see also Marvin Harris, *Cannibals and Kings* (London, 1978).
[17] C. Lévi-Strauss. *The Savage Mind* (London, 1972), p. 105.

sólo un terreno de cultivo para trozos de otras personas' (p. 292). Azula, himself a monster, is the doctor in residence at La Rinconada. What he does to Humberto, by making him monstrous, is in symmetrical opposition to the use of the monsters as theatre by making them 'normal'.

What enables parts of the person to be stolen and used as symbols of social power (the features appropriated as symbols of social hierarchy) is a system of social exchange — the same as that which is the source of the myth of the self as private property. The exchange is a type of substitution system. Donoso refers in an interview to his horror of substitution: 'La esencia de mi terror ante la existencia es que los seres son sustituibles; que una parte de un ser puede pagar las culpas de otro.'[18] The moral and religious aspects of substitution point to the need to define it as a destructive system which removes value.

Being in the power of the other is a fundamental theme of *El obsceno pájaro*. Humberto's response is systematic self-enclosure, similar to the shadow-world which Freud attributes to pathological narcissism: 'It seems as though in dementia praecox [i.e. schizophrenia] the libido, in its efforts once more to reach objects . . . does in fact snatch hold of something of them, but, as it were, only their shadows — I mean the word-presentations belonging to them' (Freud, xvi, 422). There is a correspondence here with Humberto's writing; he invented Inés so as to experience love, 'para tocar la belleza', as he says (p. 470), and he and Peta Ponce are people who can experience only the mechanics of love, not its consummation. Narcissism is revealed, finally, as the putting of Eros into the service of repression and power, and Freud's thinking not as scientific, in the way it would claim to be, but as a set of concepts, which themselves arise from the bringing of Eros into the service of domination and social power.

That Humberto's writing is non-linear and non-literal opens it both to positive and to negative forces. The non-literalism and multiplicity of planes dismantle the myths of single dimension, single identity, and society as rational; but the core is negative. Writing explodes his body, making it vulnerable to being raided: 'Mi obra entera va a estallar dentro de mi cuerpo, cada fragmento de mi anatomía cobrará vida propia, ajena a la mía, no existirá Humberto, no existirán más que estos monstruos, el tirano que me encerró en La Rinconada para que lo invente' (p. 263). The self is fragmented, raided, mutilated, taken over, cannibalized, and so on, and the concentric circles of monsters in La Rinconada are a figure of the layers of Humberto's imagination as successive magical defences through which to separate himself for ever from his point of departure. His imagination, which he describes as Jerónimo's slave, is shaped by the depredations of power structures.

Peta Ponce, who represents woman as witch, is the dark muse of Humberto's imagination: 'El prisma de la Peta Ponce refractando y confundiéndolo todo y creando planos simultáneos y contradictorios' (p. 263). She is responsible for the distortions of time and space, and embodies the danger of breaking rational structures. She has similarities with the Freudian unconscious: as the one who 'no muere jamás' and is 'un eco nacido en la pesadilla inicial' (p. 156). But the demonic as timeless is not the only version of Peta; the novel will not allow the separation of the demonic and the angelic,[19] the two are one: 'en el fondo de esa belleza de Inés

[18] *Revista Iberoamericana*, 76–77 (1971), 517–36 (p. 523).
[19] I am here indebted to an unpublished paper by Juan Ramón Duchesne.

joven habitabas tú, desde siempre, desde los siglos de los siglos, viva como las hogueras, variable como el agua' (pp. 470–71). Dismantling the boundary between the demonic and the angelic is analogous to the removal of those other boundaries, between conscious and unconscious, rational and irrational.

Humberto interprets the legend of the 'niña bruja' and shows that the feudal lord sustains his claim to legitimacy and rationality by keeping the irrational separate and hidden, and thus concealing the irrationality and monstrosity of his own power. Just as Peta and Inés fuse into one other, so Jerónimo is revealed as himself the source of the monstrous. The reinterpretation of the legend is a cognitive gain. Nevertheless, the positive and the negative are closely entwined, which is perhaps characteristic of cathartic processes. Humberto's writing, which reflects and comments on the novel itself as writing, has a major parasitic component in its continual borrowing or stealing the masks of the other. The bonfire sequence shows the negativity of this position and, at the same time, illustrates how, bound up with the negative, there is also a positive. The fire, which Humberto feeds with the pages of his own writing, is 'calor para combatir la intemperie aterradora' (p. 153), and it summons and convenes those who have no face, the people whose faces have been removed by surgery. Only when he becomes like one of them, who have nothing left that can be stolen, and has definitively eliminated his name, will he be able to get rid of Don Jerónimo.

But self-elimination has obvious limits. The process is of repetition and progressive emptying without change, or even renewal. Nevertheless, the destruction that Humberto is involved in, though it may seem to him to embrace 'el mundo entero', reveals itself to be an enactment of the destructiveness of a social system. The negative of the process is that it repeats the structures of the system it seeks to destroy, the positive that it removes the masks and covers, which hid the malignity of the system and its mode of operating.

Conclusion

The extreme negativity of *El obsceno pájaro* can be expressed in various ways. It presents a runaway system which can end only in complete self-destruction. The surface of consciousness is subject to infinite and malign manipulation and there is no 'depth' which is not capable of being similarly manipulated, nor any 'nature' which can be escaped to. Infinite manipulation, like infinite invasion or enclosure, is death. That these processes occur with the collaboration of the subject makes them particularly horrifying.

Clearly, it can be said that the text subverts bourgeois rationality, but it is essential to point to the unboundaried aspect of the destructive action. The key term is *infinite*, since infinite invasion and enclosure reintroduce transcendence into what is otherwise a thoroughly deconstructive process. What is quite absent from *El obsceno pájaro* is the possibility of minimal boundaries (such as the inviolability of body surface) necessary for the self to function and be in any way creative. This furnishes a clue: the lack of boundary indicates an equivalence between total invasion and total expansiveness. Invasion and enclosure are inversions of one another and, in so far as they tend to become total, mimic the unlimited expansiveness of the romantic self. This is the other side of the pure destruction enacted by the novel: the failure of a romantic project. In interviews, Donoso speaks of single identity as false and the recognition of the multiple self as liberating.

Nevertheless, in the novel, multiple identity emerges as negative and hellish — not through any inherent, narrowly psychological pathology but, rather, because it is open to the destructiveness of the social system. The close coincidence between liberation and alienation is parallel to the structures Marx saw emerging from the demise of feudalism and the establishment of capitalism.[20] *El lugar sin límites*, which grew out of an earlier version of *El obsceno pájaro*, traces the move from the fixed identities of feudal society as an experience of loss of boundary (in the figure of the male/female Manuel): hence the appropriateness of the title's reference to Marlowe, *Doctor Faustus* being concerned with a similar historical transition. As in *El obsceno pájaro*, the loss of boundary is experienced as hell, and in both books the transition from feudalism to bourgeois rule emerges as a negative liberation.

The negativity of the experience ends by destroying not the concept of multiplicity itself, but the individualist premises upon which it has been predicated. In this sense *El obsceno pájaro* closes the cycle of Donoso's novels which had begun with *Coronación*, and which had explored the irrational and grotesque egress of repressed energies. In *Coronación* and *Este domingo* the focus is manifestly on the individual as locus of repression. *El obsceno pájaro* modifies the terms, so that the theme is no longer the suppressed individual, and the focus shifts to the system of which individuals are products. This tendency is confirmed in *Tres novelitas burguesas*, with its play on maleness and femaleness as part of a system of social meanings, and in *Casa de campo* which investigates the rules by which identities are established during the formative phase of childhood. Freud's conceptualization, in terms such as 'omnipotence', 'cannibalism', and 'narcissism', of the loss of the boundaries of self is, therefore, relevant to the analysis of *El obsceno pájaro*. But it is not because these concepts provide a rational key to the action of the text. The Freudian concept of narcissism, juxtaposed with Donoso's use of metaphors which continually bring the social into the psychic and vice versa, reveals itself to be predicated on political individualism, and the reader is left with no way back to merely individual or merely psychological rationality.

WILLIAM ROWE

KING'S COLLEGE, LONDON

[20] Karl Marx, *Grundrisse* (London, 1973), p. 162.

Women's Expression and Narrative Technique in Rosario Castellanos's *In Darkness*

Naomi Lindstrom

This essay examines the ways in which Rosario Castellanos (Mexico, 1925-74), especially noted as a woman writer with feminist concerns, explores the problems of women's expression through the writing in her novel *Oficio de tinieblas (In Darkness)*. The 1962 work serves, at the thematic level, to convey particular social content. This content (a fictional exposé of the virtually feudal society of rural chiapas province; a sympathetic, intimate look at Tzotzil Indian culture) has often drawn the attention of critics.[1] The present study, though, is more concerned with a second aspect of the work. The construction of the novel serves to focus attention upon the ways in which a variety of women fail to express themselves, and, particularly, fail to express special problems arising from their situation as women.

To look at this special use of narrative technique, it would be well to review briefly the main tenets of Castellanos's literary feminism.[2] She did not write any programs or prescriptions for feminist writing. Her ideas appear here and there in her various writings, and many times she only gave them out orally to lecture audiences or students.

Fundamental to Castellanos's thought was a very broad definition of feminism in literature. To her mind, it was legitimate to seek an element of sex-role analysis in any complex literary work. She did not center her attention on work by avowedly feminist authors, but rather argued that any writer attentive to the nuances of social behavior would necessarily reflect feminist concerns. This included modern narrative works in which form and technique were highlighted. Such innovative texts, far from obscuring women's issues, could actually increase the reader's awareness of them.

Castellanos looked especially at works in which a woman or women speak and at works in which women characters fail to make their voices heard. Both possibilities fascinated her: the one, as showing woman's attempts to express her concerns, the other, as an illustration of woman's muteness, her inability or unwillingness to state her case.

Castellanos believed that such fictional devices as narrative voice and point of view, being closely related to the issue of "who speaks," were crucial in highlighting the problems of women. This analysis of *Oficio de tinieblas* follows from Castellanos's recommendation that works by women writers ought to be studied with the working assumption that these narrative techniques would reveal these writers' implicit statements about women's expressive difficulties.[3]

Before proceeding with the analysis, I should clarify a point of critical terminology. I am using the term *voice* more broadly than it is commonly employed in discussions of narrative technique. Castellanos's depiction of women's communication here often rests upon her use of *narrative voice* or *point of view*, the device studied by Wayne Booth, Ludomír Doluzel, Norman Friedman, et al. However, more is involved than a particular type of controlling narrative voice. One must also examine conversation between characters, soliloquies and other instances in which characters voice or conspicuously refrain from voicing their thoughts. *Voice*, then, refers to all devices that reveal either a good or a defective capacity for expression.

II

One of the first scenes in the novel narrates a tense encounter between an Indian man and his wife. Here, the chief goal of the narration is to reveal the deplorable communicational system that exists between man and woman in a relationship of non-equals. The woman is afraid to speak aloud, for fear of attracting attention to her failure to conceive; for lack of overt means of interchange, she relies on an interior fantasy, imagining the man's unuttered thoughts. The wife's imagined version of her husband's inner monologue is inaccurate, further damaging the situation. To show the reader this complex scenario of failed communication, the novel uses a variety of narrative techniques.

The wife in this scene is Catalina Díaz Puiljá, later to prove a dynamic and charismatic woman. At her first appearance, though, Catalina has not become a powerful figure able to rouse and command the population. She feels herself to be at an extreme of helplessness, and the way she speaks, or fails to speak, shows her as indeed a person of little importance.

Both partners appear in this scene, but the narrator only reveals Catalina's anxious thoughts. The husband remains a secret to both reader and wife. Catalina's distress, though, is revealed through a combined use of indirect interior monologue and editorializing summary by the narrator: "Out of the corner of her eye, while she was kneeling at the stone to grind up a day's supply of *posol*, Catalina kept watching her husband. When would he force her to repeat the separation vows? How long would he put up with the insult of a barren wife? Marriages like this one had no validity. One word from Winiktón and Catalina would be sent back to her family's hut out in Tzajal-hemel.

Why was it he kept her around? Fear? Love? Winiktón's face gave no clue. Without so much as a gesture of good-bye the man left the hut. The door closed behind him.

Catalina's features grew hard as an irrevocable resolve took hold of her. They would never separate, she would never be left alone, she would never be humiliated in front of everyone!"[4]

Here, Catalina's entire thoughts and behavior are dictated by a conflict-ridden circumstance. She would most like to know her husband's position with regard to their marriage; yet, she cannot. Indeed, she seeks to avoid speaking to him on any occasion, for fear she might remind him of her barrenness. Catalina dares not even exchange sociable pleasantries; she is afraid to greet her husband or say good-bye to him; she cannot look him in the face, but only observe him "out of the corner of her eye."

Catalina's inability to raise questions she clearly wants answered

72

has its counterpart in her husband's disinclination to give out information about himself. Despite her incessant spying, hypothesizing and speculation, Catalina ends this scene no better informed about her husband than when she began her attempt to divine his thoughts. Her problem, in this respect, is that her only way of interpreting her husband's blank muteness is to attribute to him the thoughts that are in her own mind. While he gives "no clue" she concludes that he, like herself, is obsessed with issues of childbearing and marital status.

Although the scene takes place in an indigenous household, it is easy to recognize certain features common to Western society. One sees the uncommunicative husband whose silence drives his wife to extensive interior monologues or fantasized dialogues. The narrator highlights Catalina's projection of herself as a failed wife "humiliated in front of everyone!" (p. 13), and her long, self-pitying unvoiced soliloquies. The narrative treatment of the scene emphasizes that women are often excessively verbal (in this case, unuttered verbiage) in ways that can hardly be favorable to them at the same time that they are unable to articulate concerns plainly.

Castellanos shows this blockage of expression as one result of the unequal distribution of power between man and woman. As in other Castellanos works, neither sex is assigned blame for this inequality. Rather, she carefully forcuses attention on whole society. Winiktón, although he terrifies his wife with his silence, is not really an oppressor figure; indeed, he will prove a heroic individual. Nor is Catalina any pathetically engaging victim. Her sullenness and continual brooding over grievances make her an unappealing character. Nonetheless, she is subject to her husband's rule. He could, if he cared to, deprive her of her wealth and standing. Emblematic of this inequality is the divorce ceremony Catalina obsessively fears. In the traditional rite, the man obliges the woman to speak words renouncing him, even though these words go against her true inclinations.

The next time the couple is shown together, the narrator utilizes a different procedure. Now there is a swing back and forth between man and woman, telling the reader what each is thinking, then summarizing and commenting. In this scene, the characters again speak much more to themselves than to each other. Catalina has brought an unknown girl to live with the couple, but Winiktón fails to respond even to this circumstance. Only Catalina's remark that "a white man raped her" (p. 29) draws a lively response from Winiktón. The following passage is a long interior monologue that reveals Winiktón seeking to formulate a fully-articulated concept of justice.

While Winiktón's mind works through the notion of justice, Catalina continues her practice of mentally reconstructing his thoughts. At the end of his inner monologue, the narrator gives Catalina's assessment of the man's inner state. Now it is clear how poorly Catalina's system works, for she concludes: "he's not thinking about anything" (p. 35). After transcribing this thought directly from Catalina's consciousness, the narrator steps back to comment ironically: "And she found it a comfort to know for sure."

What emerges from the narrative technique is an exposition of

73

man's and woman's stereotypical concerns. The man is mentally process-
ing abstractions, dealing with concepts, while the woman perceives the
girl's adoption as a means of altering the unfavorable balance of power in
her personal relations. One may well ask whether Castellanos has not
done women a disservice by showing the woman as a petty conspirer,
juggling household politics while the man increases his social awareness.
This same question is especially relevant to the second half of the novel,
where Catalina's internal monologues show her to be an ever more
hysterical and self-obsessed being.

The first argument against seeing antifeminism in Catalina's characterization is the novel's insistence on the social causation of Catalina's
malaise. The narrator, who is free to comment on the action when not
transcribing the character's thoughts verbatim, insists that Catalina developed her narcissistic, sly thought patterns because "her position as a
childless woman was so precarious" (p. 44). Because Catalina is subjected
to this strain and forced into silence about the matter, her voice is turned
inward, becoming an unproductive, obsessive monologue.

Throughout the novel, one finds women afflicted with this tendency to brood privately, especially over issues of womanhood and
maternity. This pattern appears not only in the uneducated Catalina but in
the worldly Latin woman, Isabel. The latter's inner, unuttered speech
reveals her fixation on the idea that her barrenness is divine punishment
for sexual misconduct. In her own essays and journalism, Castellanos
provided the model of a woman who could discuss any matter with
candor, including criticizing and eventually discarding as invalid the
concept of the presumed necessity of motherhood; in the novel *Oficio de
tinieblas* she offers the negative counterimage: women so terrified of
these concepts that they can only silently be obsessive about them. The
third-person narrator, however, breaks in on the accounts of these brood-
ings to undercut the women's self-pity with ironic remarks or to make
astute generalizations of which the women would not be capable. The
narrator's superior verbal performance constantly reminds the reader
how poorly these women voice their vital concerns, even to themselves.

It is significant that the favored mode of representing these
women's consciousness is through the narrator. Direct interior monologue
is used sparingly. The indirect monologue technique is more utilized
because it is another way to emphasize the women's low efficacy as users
of language: because their articulation of concepts is so inchoate the
narrator must help them along by organizing the representation of their
thoughts. The degree of the narrator's intervention corresponds to the
women's marked inability to be their own spokeswomen.

III

As well as showing the silent, brooding woman Castellanos shows
another manifestation of the same underlying problem; the stereotypical,
loquacious, and often devious female. This type is constantly willing to
employ language by her illogical, digressive talk marks her as a user of
frivolous "women's language," a person not to be taken into account. Like

74

Catalina Mercedes Solórzano is a "different" woman in a precarious and isolated position. She has saved herself from life on the streets by serving as procuress to the town's most powerful man. Unlike Catalina, Mercedes does not abstain from speech lest she jeopardize her standing. Her strategy is an overabundance of speech designed to create an illusory appearance of communication.

One first encounters Mercedes conducting a most tortured conversation. Having summoned an Indian vendor, ostensibly for a bargaining session, Mercedes deviates from the conventions governing such encounters. In that town, non-Indians are expected to be rude and distant to Indian vendors. Mercedes, however, addresses the girl in indigenous language and offers her a seat, leaving her "confundida por la amabilidad (confused by friendliness; p. 18)." After a few perfunctory remarks in her "buyer" role, Mercedes breaks with this role and speaks on topics inappropriate to the apparent situation. She reminisces about her youthful vigor and asks intrusive questions about the girl's marital status and prospects.

When the "buyer" returns to the bargaining theme, her rupture with expected behavior is still uppermost. Rather than replying to the asking price with a conventional protest, the buyer mocks the seller for demanding too little. The whole discourse is moved further into the realm of strangeness by her insistence that the Indian address her by her first name. Mercedes's disorienting conversation is a ploy designed to disarm and baffle the girl, who is being prepared to be an easy victim for the rich man. In addition, Mercedes must ascertain the girl's virginity without posing this question to her directly. Here the procuress is making use of language to disconcert her victim and to disguise the true nature of the encounter.

But when the woman remains alone, it becomes clear that she cannot halt her confusing voice even when it serves no easily recognizable end. The ironic narrator, characteristically, provides a "distancing" preface before immersing the reader into the flow of a character's thoughts. An "explanation" of the procuress's habit of soliloquizing is proffered: "El temperamento de doña Mercedes era comunicativo (Doña Mercedes was naturally communicative; p. 20)." This remark, which immediately follows Mercedes's display of verbal guile and obfuscation, places everything she is about to say under suspicion. The narrator also alerts one to the nature of Mercedes's expression. Rather than speaking to herself, she is addressing a being of her own invention, "imaginando un impreciso auditorio (imagining some vague listener; p. 20)."

The fictional listener may be vague, but Mercedes implicitly assigns him certain attributes. Speaking to this imaginary being, she uses the regional and familiar form of you, *vos*. No Mexican Spanish-speaker with serious pretensions to respectability makes such a linguistic deviation but the lax and "fallen" Mercedes flaunts the nonstandard form. She exploits it to create the illusion of intimacy outside the narrow primness of proper society, "como si fuéramos de confianza (as if we were old friends; p. 21)" and addresses him as "compadre (buddy; p. 20)." Mercedes's goal in creating this being and drawing him into collusion is to make him

75

accept a favorable account of herself. Her first tactic is to displace the listener's disgust from her own complicity to her employer's "unclean" desire for Indian girls. She virtuously intervenes to mitigate the impropriety; through her vigilance, she saves her indiscriminating employer from enjoying the more evidently unhygienic girls he might unthinkingly accept.

Later, Mercedes presents herself as a basically sensitive and noble individual to whom it "da remordimiento hacer estas cosas (is shameful to do these things; p. 20)." All consideration of verisimilitude is abandoned as the procuress states: "en la honra nadie me ha puesto nunca un pie adelante. Las señoras bien se pueden mirar en mí, que soy un espejo de cuerpo entero (as for maintaining your honor, nobody's ahead of me on that score. If those fancy ladies take a good look, they'll see I'm every bit as good as them; p. 21)."

A phantom listener is the only one who Mercedes can regularly have as the recipient of her outpourings, for this imaginary partner can never reject her discourse habits. The narrator underscores this point by observing slyly that the sociable Mercedes spent large portions of her time alone (p. 18).

In this scene, Mercedes speaks aloud rather than mulling over her thoughts in silence. Further, the narrative technique is Mercedes's direct voice, rather than indirect relay by the narrator. These features of the narrative treatment suggest a more verbal character, able to speak for herself. Yes this procedure ironically exposes the deficiencies of Mercedes's voice. In quoting the woman's *ipsissima verba*, the narrator has, in effect, allowed her the opportunity to betray her own incompetence.

This soliloquy, even with all the distortions and ramshackle arguments, makes two valid points. Mercedes recognizes that part of her problem is the lack of acceptable options open to women without wealth or male protectors. Without her employer's aegis, she observes, "¿adónde hubiera yo ido a parar? Estaría yo de atajadora, como tantas infelices que no tienen donde les haga maroma un piojo. O de custitalera, o de placers . . . a saber (What would have become of me? I'd be out robbing from the Indians, like so many poor women who can hardly keep body and soul together. Or I'd be living out practically in the same place as the Indians to try to sell them stuff, or out in the plaza . . . who knows; p. 21)." Mercedes also dimly realizes that too much depends on remaining in the good graces of her employer. The importance of this becomes increasingly clear throughout the novel as the unscrupulous boss repeatedly punishes those who offend him and rewards those who please him. He incarnates a male stereotype at least as negative as any of the female types who appear throughout the novel. The narrator is explicit about the relation between sex role and the man's reprehensible behavior, speaking on one occasion of "la insensibilidad de Leonardo, con ese orgullo del macho que no está acostumbrado a recibir dones sino tributos (the insensitivity of Leonardo, with that pride of the *macho* who's used to receiving tributes, not gifts; p. 197)."

Though able to glimpse the limitation of female roles and the

76

roblem of exaggerated male dominance, Mercedes cannot relate these issues to her devious habits of expression. When the reader places the two together, the result is essentially a sex-role analysis of female hypocrisy. Moreover, the third-person narrator plainly describes Mercedes as an oppressor as well as one of the oppressed, one who cannot be placed as a simple, appealing victim-prostitute. The narrator further alienates the reader from Mercedes's potential pathos by noting the laxity and indolence that facilitate her degradation: "Sus dos manos, acostumbradas al ocio, descansaban sobre el regazo (She kept her hands, which were used to lying idle, in her lap; p. 21)." and describing the coarse appearance Mercedes has developed: "cuarentona, obesa, con los dientes refulgiendo en groseras incrustaciones de oro (fortyish, obese, her teeth aglitter with tacky gold incrustations; p. 17)."

IV

The women discussed above have been revealed as notably poor users of human discourse. However, not all of Castellanos's portrayal of females and language is negative. On occasion, *Oficio de tinieblas* offers examples of women who experience limited liberation by making statements capable of clarifying difficult issues. Given outside support, the narrator makes clear, communication might have progressed from such beginnings.

An instance of this spark of illumination through language occurs when Marcela, the girl raped by Mercedes's employer, finds a verbal mode of comprehending this experience. The narrator has shown Marcela to be the most mute of women, unable to reply to simple questions or to express the most ordinary needs and desires. It has been amply revealed that her experience of language has not been one of increased awareness through speech. It is through confusing talk that she has been misled and betrayed. She is portrayed as the most uncomplicated example of oppression in the novel. In swift succession, she has been described as suffering entrapment and betrayal by Mercedes, being raped, and being expropriated by Catalina, who has taken over the running of the girl's life.

The narrator reports Catalina's assessment of Marcela: "esta muchacha insignificante y estúpida que ella usaba como un simple instrumento de sus propósitos (that insignificant, stupid girl she was using as a simple pawn in her game; p. 46)."

But one day as she listens to other persons discussing her case, Marcela has this reaction:

> Repitio mentalmente la frase, saboreándola: "un caxlán abusó de ella". Esto era lo que había sucedido. Algo que podía decirse, que los demás podían escuchar y entender. No el vértigo, no la locura. Suspiró aliviada.

> She repeated the sentence to herself, savoring it: "a white man raped her." That was what had happened. Something that you could say out loud and other people would listen and understand. Not a fall into dizziness or madness. She breathed a sigh of relief (p. 29).

77

The reader is here made aware of a particular lack. Marcela had not realized her traumatic encounter could be expressed and grasped through words and communicated to other people. The realization that her bewildering experience could be expressed in a sentence marks a move toward rational living. This straightforward message impresses upon the rape victim that her experience is not unique and eases her isolation.

Here, the message is optimistic: Marcela can learn from the articulation of experience. The narrative technique, though, warns the reader not to expect too great a breakthrough. It is significant that the entire episode is narrated by the third-person narrator, who summarizes all of Marcela's responses. The phrases "That was what had happened . . . madness" may or may not represent Marcela's own thoughts; they may be simply the narrator's summation of what Marcela felt. In either case, the narrator maintains control rather than allowing Marcela a voice of her own. There is no real indication that Marcela can formulate concepts in words, although she can clearly appreciate a formulation made by another.

The narrative treatment of this scene is prophetic of what is to come. Despite Marcela's insight into the possibilities for communication, she finds no opportunity to speak out. As Catalina's ward, she is next presented registering a series of wordless protests against her pregnancy. The narrator makes it known that she bases her actions upon a lack of understanding of the reproductive process. She does not comprehend that she is bearing a child, a child Catalina could not produce. Her confusion, the narrator tells the reader, is clear to Catalina, who is impressive in her refusals to enlighten her ward about the physical changes in pregnancy that terrify the girl. Bitterly jealous, the woman long avoids mention of the pregnancy. The narrator draws attention to Catalina's angry, aggressive withholding of communication: "calló (she fell silent), "enmudecía (she wouldn't say anything; p. 46)." "Desde afuera la miraba (She looked at her from without; p. 47)." Finally, the older woman screams at Marcela: "¡Vas a tener una hija! (You're going to have a baby! p. 46)." Thus delivered, the news sends the previously-unaware Marcela into a panic. Marcela's subsequent near-autistic behavior is unattractive, but the narrator is clearly not blaming her for it: "Marcela, a quien la adversidad había reblandecido los tuétanos, ya no protestaba (Life had beaten Marcela down to a pulp, and she gave up protesting; p. 47)." The narrator implies that if women are to become more articulate they must have support from their listeners and conversation partners.

Oficio de tinieblas expresses concerns common to many discussions of women's status. What makes this feminist statement so exceptionally interesting for literary readers is its mode of presentation. *Oficio de tinieblas* makes its points about women's voice, not simply through direct statement, but by the skillful design of narrative. It is the use of various forms of narration—characters speaking for themselves, direct and indirect interior monologues, and the narrator's commentary (often in cynical contrast to versions of events offered by the characters)—that are crucial in persuading the reader of the gravity of feminist issues. It is the rhetoric

78

of fiction, to use Wayne Booth's phrase, that allows this woman writer to express in fully literary fashion women's concerns.

University of Texas, Austin

NOTES

1. For examples of criticism of the novel's examination of indigenous culture and social inequity, see John S. Brushwood, *The Spanish American Novel: A Twentieth Century Survey* (Austin: University of Texas, 1975), pp. 236-37, which contains also commentary on the novel's treatment of time; his *Mexico in its Novel: A Nation's Search for Identity* (Austin: University of Texas, 1973), p. 166; Joseph Sommers, "Changing Views of the Indian in Mexican Literature," *Hispania*, 47 (1964), 47-55; "El ciclo de Chiapas: nueva corriente literaria," *Cuadernos Americanos*, 133 (1964), 246-261; "The Indian-oriented Novel in Latin America: New Spirit, New Forms, New Scope," *Journal of Inter American Studies*, 6 (1964), 249-265); "Rosario Castellanos: nuevo enfoque del indio mexicano," *La palabra y el hombre* (Xalapa, Veracruz), 29 (1964), 83-88; *After the Storm: Landmarks of the Modern Mexican Novel* (Albuquerque: University of New Mexico, 1968), 83-88; and "Forma e ideologia en *oficio de tinieblas* de Rosario Castellanos," *Revista de crítica literaria latinoamericana*, Nos. 7-8 (1978), 73-91. Other discussion of these themes includes Emmanuel Carballo, "Rosario Castellanos," in his *Diecinueve protagonistas de la literatura mexicana del siglo XX* (México: Empresas Editoriales, 1965) pp. 409-24; Walter M. Langford, *The Mexican Novel Comes of Age* (Notre Dame: University of Notre Dame, 1971), pp. 182-85): Günter Lorenz, *Diálogo con América Latina* (Santiago de Chile: Editorial Pomaire, 1972), pp. 185-211; César Rodríguez Chicharro, "Rosario Castellanos: *Balún-Canán*," La Palabra y el Hombre, 9 (1959), 61-67; and Alfonso González, "Lenguaje y protesta en *Oficio de tinieblas*," *Revista de Estudios Hispánicos*, 8, 3 1974), 413-17.
2. The best introduction to Castellanos as feminist is Maureen Ahern and Mary Vásquez, eds., *Homenaje a Rosario Castellanos* (Valencia: Estudios de Hispanófila, 1980). See also "Rosario Castellanos: Representing Women's Discourse," my article in *Letras Femeninas*, 5, 2 (1980), pp. 29-47. This essay examines in general terms Castellanos's ideas about and use of narrative technique without analyzing any work in detail. A very general and thematic study of Castellanos's literary feminism is Phyllis Rodríguez-Peralta, "Images of Women in Rosario Castellanos's Prose," *Latin American Literary Review*, 6, 11 (1977), 68-80.
3. See Naomi Lindstrom, "Rosario Castellanos: Pioneer of Feminist Criticism," in Ahern and Vásquez, pp. 191-92. The best sampling of Castellanos's feminist criticism is her 1973 *Mujer que sabe latin . . .* (México: SepSetentas); less literary, and more sociocultural, are the essays in *El uso de la palabra* (México: Excélsior, 1974).
4. Norman Friedman, "Point of View in Fiction: The Development of a Critical Concept," *PMLA*, 70 (1955), 1160-84; Wayne C. Booth, *The Rhetoric of Fiction* (Chicago: University of Chicago, 1961); Tzvetan Todorov, "Poétique," in Oswald Ducrot et al., *Qu'est-ce que le structuralisme?* (Paris: Seuil, 1968); Ludomír Doluzel, Narrative Modes in Czech Literature, (Toronto: University of Toronto, 1973), all examplify the type of terminological use I refer to. Castellanos's examination of all varieties of speech acts is closer to

79

the discourse analysis of Mary Louise Pratt, *Toward a Speech Act Theory* of *Literary Discourse* (Bloomington: Indiana University, 1977).

5. Castellanos, *Oficio de tinieblas* (México: Joaquín Mortiz, 1962), p. 13. Subsequent page numbers given in the text refer to this edition.

6. Wayne Booth, *The Rhetoric of Fiction* (cited in note 5 above), argues that all the structural features of fiction can be seen as devices to persuade the reader of the truth of what is being presented. This principle is especially well illustrated by Castellanos's novel, with its complex structure and pervasive social message.

Estrategias dramáticas del feminismo en *El eterno femenino* de Rosario Castellanos

Barbara Bockus Aponte

La posición central que ocupa Rosario Castellanos en la literatura contemporánea mexicana está perfilándose nítidamente en los estudios que han ido apareciendo después de su muerte inesperada en 1974.[1] Todavía objeto de poca atención crítica, sin embargo, es su drama, *El eterno femenino*,[2] a pesar de que resalta en el panorama teatral hispanoamericano por su tema abiertamente feminista y por su tono agresivamente satírico, y de que se destaca dentro de la obra misma de Castellanos por pertenecer al género que menos cultivó. Antes de *El eterno femenino*, publicado y estrenado póstumamente, solo había incursionado muy tentativamente en el campo del teatro.[3] Pero la experiencia de ser mujer, núcleo temático del drama, sí ha constituido, a lo largo de toda su obra, una corriente dominante. Este trabajo propone ver cómo esta tendencia temática, ya desarrollada por Castellanos en la narrativa, la poesía y el ensayo, se transforma y adquiere nuevas dimensiones en la forma dramática.

Para obtener una perspectiva clara, es indispensable comenzar por anotar, aunque sea someramente, los enfoques que la escritora ha dado en sus escritos anteriores a la problemática de la mujer en la sociedad mexicana. Ha recalcado su falta de identidad propia—la mujer "pasa de las manos de un padre a un marido, a un tutor y . . . jamás sobrepasa su estado de minoridad."[4]—y su pasividad ante tal situación: "La complicidad entre el verdugo y la víctima [es] tan vieja que es imposible distinguir quien es quien."[5] Pinta la angustia de tratar de ajustarse al papel que exige el sistema patriarcal: "Hasta que comprendí. Y me hice tornillo/bien aceitado con el cual la máquina/trabaja ya satisfactoriamente."[6] Y le atraen las que cuestionan de alguna manera esa tiranía de las costumbres, sean figuras históricas como Sor Juana, escritoras que comparten las mismas preocupaciones, como Virginia Woolf, creaciones ficticias suyas como Catalina Díaz Puiljá, o el yo lírico de los poemas de sus últimas colecciones. Arremete contra el concepto de matrimonio-maternidad como la única forma aceptable de realización femenina, y de allí salen algunas de sus frases más lapidarias. "La maternidad no es . . . la vía rápida para la santificación,"[7] dirá. La alternativa, la soltería, es eje de algunas de sus páginas más evocativas, las de sus cuentos, por ejemplo, cuyas protagonistas son seres aislados y solitarios. Estos hilos de la temática feminista se conjugan a veces, en la ensayística, con ideas para combatir esta sujeción. "La hazaña de convertirse en lo que se es—escribe— exige no únicamente el descubrimiento de los rasgos esenciales . . . sino sobre todo el rechazo de esas falsas imágenes que los falsos espejos ofrecen a la mujer en las cerradas galerías donde su vida transcurre."[8] Descubrimiento, y luego rechazo. Son las metas. ¿Y el arma escogida? Será, según anuncia en el mismo libro: "poner en evidencia lo que tienen de ridículas, de obsoletas, de cursis y de imbéciles. . . . Quitémosle al novio formal ese aroma apetitoso que lo circunda. . . . Quitémosle al vestido blanco y a la corona de azahares ese nimbo glorioso que los circunda."[9] Queda apuntado lo que será el plan de ataque en *El eterno femenino*.

La inclusividad temática es una de las primeras cosas que confronta al lector o al espectador de esa obra. Intenta reunir los múltiples aspectos de la estereotipación de la mujer que andaban dispersos en los ensayos, las narraciones y los poemas. Se debe tratar de identificar, entonces, estrategias unificadoras que impongan algún tipo de estructura funcional a esta materia si no dispar, sí fragmentada. Luego nuestro énfasis va a recaer en las técnicas de distanciamiento manejadas, porque son ellas más que nada las que dan a la temática feminista un ímpetu didáctico que no permitían las formas narrativas o líricas.

El eterno femenino no sigue las pautas estructurales del drama aristotélico. Sus tres actos no reflejan una trayectoria de presentación-enredo-desenlace. Son divisiones que podríamos llamar temáticas, en vez de dinámicas. El primer acto presenta etapas distintas de la vida de la mujer casada, cinco en total, desde la luna de miel hasta la vejez. El segundo acto destaca varias figuras femeninas históricas/legendarias. Y en el tercero se ven ejemplificadas las distintas alternativas abiertas a la mujer soltera. Así, la situación de la mujer contemporánea, la mujer mexicana de clase media, sirve de marco para la agrupación histórica.

El primero y el último actos reúnen imágenes estereotipadas negativas. Es un tipo de agrupación que la autora ha utilizado antes con, por ejemplo, las seis voces femeninas del poema "Kinsey Report," o las cuatro recreaciones de la mujer que constituyen los cuentos de *Álbum de familia*. En el primer acto se ven concretizadas las verdades humillantes que subyacen estas líneas de su poema, "Autoretrato":

> Yo soy una señora: tratamiento
> arduo de conseguir, en mi caso, y más útil
> para alternar con los demás que un título
> extendido a mi nombre en cualquier academia.[10]

Un tono satírico feroz y grotesco imbuye las representaciones del novio machista, de la novia inocente, la señora decente, la madre abnegada, la cabecita blanca. . . . En el tercer acto la soltera, la "otra mujer," la prostituta y la mujer de acción son tratadas con un humor menos agresivo quizá, pero igualmente satírico. En ambos, la mujer se ve sumisa a las normas sociales, claudicando o con el gozo macabro de una colaboradora, o con el patetismo de la víctima, pero siempre anulada por su situación, y nunca consciente de la posibilidad de "otro modo de ser."[11] Este no es el caso en el segundo acto. Las figuras presentadas, Eva, antes de la caída y seis figuras de la historia mexicana—la Malinche, Sor Juana, doña Josefa Ortiz de Domínguez, la Emperatriz Carlota, Rosario de la Peña y la Adelita—son tratadas con simpatía, porque ellas son las que se rebelaron, que actuaron en busca de autorealización. La mujer-estereotipo de los otros actos ha sido reemplazada por la mujer que funciona como símbolo.[12]

La heterogeneidad argumental de las muchas viñetas se inserta en un marco que impone otro elemento unificador además del de la división tripartita. Toda la acción del drama supuestamente surge de los sueños y de la imaginación de la protagonista, Lupita, mientras trata de peinarse en un salón de belleza el día de su boda. Se abre la comedia en el salón, y cada acto termina con un regreso de la protagonista a esta "realidad." Este marco, entonces, sirve de ancla tanto temporal como espacial. Además, el espacio escénico de un salón de belleza tiene significado simbólico con respecto al papel que se asigna a la mujer en la sociedad—el de adornar y agradar.

Ya esbozado el armazón estructural, las siguientes páginas de este trabajo se proponen analizar las técnicas de distanciamiento que son claves para una apreciación de *El eterno femenino*. Las que miramos primero son las que responden a una influencia brechtiana.[13] Esta modalidad teatral fundamentalmente didáctica ha sido característica de mucho del teatro hispanoamericano contemporáneo, especialmente en la década de los sesenta.

Hay analogías persuasivas que se pueden encontrar entre el concepto de alienación desarrollado por Brecht y el que es el subtexto del drama de Castellanos, y entre los propósitos del teatro épico y los que parecen animar *El eterno femenino*. "El concepto de alienación—explica Fernando de Toro en *Brecht en el teatro hispanoamericano contemporáneo*—significa el *extrañamiento* del hombre, su aislamiento y falta de conciencia de sí mismo y de su circunstancia histórica y finalmente su mutilación mental." Añade: "Toda la teoriá del teatro épico está dirigida a un solo objetivo: hacer consciente al hombre de su circunstancia y alienación y a la vez motivarlo a transformar . . . su situación presente."[14] El drama de Castellanos presenta a una mujer mexicana alienada y no concientizada e informa, como el teatro épico, sobre las relaciones sociales existentes. Se dirige a un público específico en un tiempo específico y quiere motivar a este público a cambiar. Como prueba intratextual de su intención didáctica se puede citar el diálogo a finales del segundo acto. Allí la Adelita de la Revolución se dirige a sus colegas históricas acerca del fracaso de ésta. Señala a Lupita y dice: "si hubiera triunfado ¿estaría esta muchacha aquí? ¿Existirían aún muchachas como ella con padres como los de ella, con novios como el de ella, con vida como la de ella?" (137)

Para lograr su propósito didáctico, "Brecht hubo de pensar en una forma para objetivizar la escena de tal forma que el espectador no pudiera identificarse con un personaje o con una situación";[15] de allí surgen sus técnicas de distanciamiento,[16] algunas de las cuales son utilizadas por Castellanos. *El eterno femenino* es un drama anti-ilusionista, es decir, no pretende recrear en el escenario la ilusión de la realidad, característica que comparte con el teatro épico y con muchas otras corrientes teatrales de la época post-realista. Las direcciones escénicas iniciales indican que no habrá posibilidad de que el actor se identifique con el personaje ni, como consecuencia, de que el espectador se identifique con él. "No tratará—dice—. . . de ser realista, sino de captar la esencia, el rasgo definitivo de una persona. . . . Es aconsejable la exageración de la misma manera que la usan los caricaturistas" (21-22). En el caso de Lupita, varias actrices toman el papel. Hay un momento, por ejemplo, de duplicación, donde una "Lupita" ve a otra en la televisión. Y hay un episodio cuando la Lupita vieja arranca su peluca de "cabecita blanca," se viste de china poblana y baila el jarabe tapatío, para luego volverse de nuevo vieja. Todas son funciones desrealizadoras.

Otra característica del teatro épico es que, paralela a la actuación dramática, hay una función narrativa que puede comentar, anticipar o resumir la acción. Ésta se halla ejemplificada en las mujeres históricas del segundo acto quienes cobran vida para re-representar teatralmente momentos críticos de su pasado. Todas ellas comentan aspectos de esta actuación, o entre ellas mismas o para el beneficio de Lupita, la espectadora dentro del drama. Otro mecanismo fundamental del teatro brechtiano, el actor que se dirige directamente al público y así rompe la cuarta pared, sólo lo aprovecha Castellanos en las últimas palabras del drama:

> LUPITA (Azorada, mirando el público como quien busca auxilio)—
> ¿Mi problema? . . . ¿Mi problema? ¡Chin! (196)

Aunque ella reacciona así ante la peluquera que le acaba de decir que su pelo es *su* problema, el público deberá entenderlo como refiriéndose no al desastre cosmético sino a su situación de mujer.

Las canciones y las proyecciones también operan como elementos narrativos en el drama épico en que complementan los acontecimientos representados en la escena. En "Cruda Realidad," la viñeta donde Lupita descubre que su marido tiene amante, la escenificación de este descubrimiento se corta bruscamente con la oscuridad, y el cantar de un corrido que narra cómo Lupita mata a los amantes:

> Cuquita la secretaria
> escribía con afán
> cuando entró por la ventana
> la mera mujer de Juan (49)

va acompannñado por una película muda que lo ilustra. Aquí el film y el corrido reemplazan la acción dramática, al mismo tiempo que recalcan su calidad de caricatura. En el cuadro, "Jornada de soltera," se combinan la película y la lectura de un poema. El poema, monólogo dramático de una voz lírica femenina, expresa un estado de soledad y sequedad. Las imágenes en la pantalla proveen el complemento narrativo: una secretaria produce sólo páginas en blanco, una enfermera cuida con esquisitez un muñeco, una maestra enseña el verbo amar a una sala vacía. El poema, que viene de la colección, *Lívida luz*, ha sido de esta manera transformado, objetivizado. Ambas viñetas distancian al espectador en el sentido de que rompen toda ilusión de realidad. El corrido vuelve a aparecer al final de drama donde funciona de epílogo.

Todos estos elementos del teatro épico se integran en una estructura a cuadros. En el teatro tradicional, se espera un desarrollo causal y continuo de una situación inicial. "En el teatro épico en cambio, cada cuadro tiene la función de desarrollar un aspecto en particular y el cuadro final nunca da una respuesta o solución."[17] *El eterno femenino* sigue este patrón. Cada viñeta presenta un aspecto distinto de la situación de la mujer, pero ninguna desarrolla una situación anterior. La estructura es abierta; no se sugiere ninguna solución. Se incita al espectador a buscarla.

Un hecho que distingue al teatro épico es el de "revelarse como *teatro* ante el público y no como algo real sucediendo por primera vez ante los ojos de aquél."[18] Todas las técnicas de distanciamiento contribuyen a este efecto. El teatro de Brecht es, por eso, metateatro, un término que se refiere no sólo a instancias del teatro dentro del teatro sino, según Lionel Abel, a todo drama que trata de la vida vista como ya teatralizada. *El eterno femenino* abunda en elementos metateatrales; el segundo acto se fundamenta en estos efectos. Allí Lupita entra en otro mundo cuyos habitantes *actúan* ante ella. Tanto espectador (Lupita) como actores (las figuras históricas) están conscientes de esta relación. Lupita anuncia que ha pagado su boleto y quiere ver "un espectáculo," y Carlota se alegra de tener la oportunidad de "representar" (87). El decorado apoya este ambiente doblemente teatral. Eva se exhibe en un circo, y como ella, las figuras del museo de cera forman parte de un espectáculo aun antes de empezar a representarse ante los ojos de Lupita (y los nuestros) como figuras históricas que voluntariamente van a dramatizar su retrovisión. Aun sin todo este aparato teatral la mera presencia de Sor Juana y sus compañeras en el drama sería elemento metateatral, porque, según Abel, hay metateatro cuando

> the persons appearing on the stage . . . are there not simply because they were caught by the playwright in dramatic postures as a camera might catch them, but because they themselves knew they were dramatic before the playwright took note of them. What dramatized them originally? Myth, legend, past literature, they themselves. They represent to the playwright the effect of dramatic imagination before he has begun to exercise his own; on the other hand, unlike figures in tragedy, they are aware of their own theatricality.[19]

Castellanos toma sus figuras del acervo histórico-mítico-literario mexicano e impone sobre estas figuras ya formadas su imaginación crítica. Ellas están conscientes de la peculiaridad de su situación. Sor Juana le explica a Lupita que tendrá dificultad en identificarlas "porque nos hicieron pasar bajo las horcas caudinas de una versión estereotipada y oficial. Y ahora vamos a presentarnos como lo que fuimos" (87). Estas mujeres conocen su "otra" existencia dentro de la mente popular. Aun Eva comenta: "Con esto del *Women's Lib* yo ando como chicle, de boca en boca" (74).

Los elementos metateatrales de la comedia no se limitan a esta situación de referencialidad histórica. En el primer y tercer actos, el móvil esencial de la acción es que Lupita juega los papeles de todas las otras mujeres, posibilidades futuras de su yo. Así que en cada cuadro se encuentra a Lupita en distinto disfraz. Además, en el último de estos cuadros, "Al filo del agua," Lupita es profesora quien, ante su clase de señoras respetables, su público, ataca al propio drama de Castellanos en que están actuando todas. Aquí, aun el núcleo argumental es metateatral.

Los procesos distanciadores susodichos que se originan en los postulados del teatro épico están complementados en *El eterno femenino* por las técnicas satíricas. Los que han escrito sobre este drama se refieren a sátira, ironía, farsa, parodia, caricatura . . ., pero no han hecho más que esbozar el posible funcionamiento de estas modas en la obra. Nos parece que el proceso retórico fundamental de que se vale Castellanos es la sátira, y que esto explica en parte la afinidad de la autora por los procedimientos brechtianos. Como explica Spacks en su estudio "Some Reflections on Satire," los comentarios de Brecht sobre los propósitos del teatro épico son sugerentes de los propósitos de la sátira.[20] Un factor determinante de los dos es la distancia mantenida entre el lector/espectador (y el autor) y la ficción que se presenta. Es nuestra hipótesis que la ironía verbal, definida como "The systematic use of double meanings,"[21] se usa en *El eterno femenino* principalmente como arma de la intención satírica imperante, y que es esta intención—"the ridicule of folly"[22]—la que mejor define la obra.

Si la sátira es una representación crítica (siempre cómica, muchas veces caricaturesca) de la realidad, ¿qué otra cosa son estos cuadros de los actos primero y tercero? En este caso la "realidad" satirizada se compone de las estructuras sociales, los prejuicios, las actitudes y los tipos que juntos conforman el papel de la mujer. Tomemos como ejemplo del esencial planteamiento satírico, la escena en el primer acto, "La Anunciación," cuyo título mismo satiriza el lugar sagrado que ocupa la maternidad en el código social mexicano. Signos visuales se combinan con el diálogo para destrozar sin piedad cualquier aura de felicidad o naturalidad que pudiera tener el momento de "anunciación." La escena se abre con "Lupita vestida con unos muy ceñidos pantalones toreros. Guapísima y exultante de dicha" (36). Con el trapo de sacudir ejecuta verónicas y otras figuras taurinas mientras en el trasfondo se oyen los olés de la multitud. Ese entusiasmo, en sí caricaturesco, y esa visión que tenemos de la Lupita bella y rebosante de salud sufren un revés inmediato con la llegada de su madre: "Una señora decente no tiene ningún motivo para ser feliz . . . y si lo tiene, lo disimula" (39) dictamina, y procede a arreglarle las cosas para que Lupita se conforme con lo que la costumbre dicta: "La toma, la despeina, le quita el maquillaje, la deja hecha un desastre y luego contempla, con la satisfacción del artista, su obra" (41). El contraste entre las dos Lupitas es sumamente cómico, tan rápida es la transformación, y la crítica feroz de la hipocresía con que la mujer busca manejar al hombre a través de su supuesto martirio—el pobre marido sufre el ataque furioso de las dos mujeres—revela la intención satírica. El último golpe está en las palabras finales del cuadro; naturalmente las tiene la madre: "Como ves—dice—no hay felicidad comparable a ser madre, Lupita. Aunque te cueste, como en muchos casos, la vida. Y siempre, la juventud y la belleza. Ah, pero ser madre . . . ser madre" (46).

Los cuadros satíricos más eficaces son los que se pueden resumir como éste, en una imagen visual: Lupita "hecha un guiñapo"; Lupita y Juan, como novios, ella "con el más convencional y pomposo traje de novia" con mancha de sangre visible en la cola y él, que "no tiene puesto más que el sombrero de copa, el cuello duro, la corbata . . ." (32-33); o Lupita de viejita, completamente sepultada bajo un montón de productos que ha ganado como premios de un programa de radio. Conjuntamente, hay momentos de gran genio satírico verbal, como en el último acto cuando Lupita, de "mujer de acción" entrevista a la astrónoma quien descubrió una estrella nueva. ¿Cómo? "Ah, pues por pura casualidad. Yo estaba como tortilla en comal, como dicen, porque estos benditos gatos no me dejaban dormir con sus maullidos. Y que agarro y digo: vamos a echarle un ojito al telescopio" (176). Y le sigue la celebridad, tan apoyada por su buen marido, quien dice, con orgullo complacido, que "¡ni siquiera la cuenta en el banco está a mi nombre!" (172). Nadie escapa su ojo y su oído despiadados. Se ve que no satiriza situaciones donde se contrasta lo encomiable y lo deleznable; por el contrario, el enfoque es siempre negativo.

Como señalamos antes, hay un trasfondo irónico que recalca la visión satírica básica. Puede ser puramente verbal, como el monólogo de Lupita de reportera quien, después de leer las instrucciones detalladas que tiene que seguir como entrevistadora—"No hacer mención de creencias religiosas . . . ni discutir su ideología política . . ." (169)—; ¡lee una invitación para un banquete para celebrar la libertad de prensa! Puede ser una ironía que surge cuando lo que se dice está en contraste cómico con lo que se percibe: Lupita, con tubos en la cabeza, cara embarrada de crema rejuvenecedora, bata que conoció mejores días" (46), que se dice, complacidamente, a sí misma: "Y en cuanto a mi persona, no he descuidado jamás mi apariencia. ¿Qué retiene al marido sino una mujer siempre bien arreglada, siempre esbelta, lucidora?" (48) Y es irónico dentro de la concepción total de la obra que el aparato conectado al secador, causa de las fantasías que vive Lupita, fue inventado para impedir que las mujeres pensaran.

Otra estrategia irónica surge de la estructura enmarcadora del drama, es decir, de la acción que toma lugar en el salón de belleza donde Lupita juega únicamente el papel de la novia que quiere peinarse, y, en este papel, representa el estereotipo de la mujer convencional. Esta Lupita puede ser considerada como víctima de la ironía dramática, que siempre "depends strictly on the reader's or spectator's knowing something about a character's situation that the character does not know."[23] A lo largo del drama y hasta el último momento, Lupita permanece completamente inconsciente de todos los elementos conflictivos del papel de la mujer que han sido representados en su vida onírica y fantástica, y lo único que le preocupa al final es su problema del principio—peinarse. Aun durante las secuencias del segundo acto se mantiene impávida ante los otros modelos de mujer que se le presentan, comentando, histéricamente, al final de este acto: "Pues cuando me comparo con Uds., con cualquiera de ustedes, pienso que tuve mucha suerte y que me saqué la lotería y que . . ." (137). El impacto irónico lo capta el espectador porque sabe que "su problema" es mucho más serio de lo que ella reconoce.

La ironía sin implicaciones satíricas escasea en la obra, pero es el proceso retórico que subyace la desmitificación de las figuras históricas.[24] Aquí el propósito no puede ser categorizado de satírico porque no es demoledor, sino positivo. El mecanismo retórico de que se vale es uno que se ha descrito en la obra de otra autora dramática mexicana, Elena Garro. Esa dramaturga, escribió Sandra Cypess, ''has inverted each sign function of the traditional system and offered new meaning for the signifiers that suggest new possibilities for the image of woman.''[25] Castellanos convierte símbolos que servían las metas de la sociedad patriarcal en otras que pudieran servir de modelos a la mujer liberada. Así la Sor Juana tradicional que entra en el convento, desilusionada por el amor, o la Josefa, que sacrifica todo por la patria, o la Rosario que causó el suicidio del poeta enamorado se convierten en mujeres de criterio independiente que actuaron por razones muy personales en busca de, o ya conscientes de su propio valor como individuos. Es una manipulación magistral de la ironía dramática. Aquí no es el espectador quien sabe algo que el personaje no sabe, sino el personaje quien conoce la verdad, y el espectador quien ve sus expectativas legítimas frustradas por la revelación del verdadero estado de las cosas. ¿Y qué sería esto? Pues en el caso de Josefa, que se metió en la conspiración no por patriotismo, sino porque la vida doméstica le aburría tanto. ¿Y el poeta enamorado? Se suicidó por saberse ridículo. Y así en los otros casos. El espectador siente el impacto intelectual, y quizá también emotivo, de la incongruencia entre los dos niveles de la ironía. La dramaturga tiene el cuidado de reforzar esta incongruencia, recalcando en sus acotaciones que las figuras históricas se encuentran ''representadas de la manera más convencional posible'' (85). A esta secuencia de inversiones irónicas se ciñe el tono del segundo acto.

Del haber hablado de la sátira y la ironía, sin tocar posibles elementos fársicos y paródicos en la obra no se debe inferir su ausencia, sino, sencillamente, que se juzgan menos importantes para la impresión total. Es cierto que Castellanos llama a su obra una farsa, y seguramente el tratamiento hostil que sufre Lupita al final, cuando le agreden las de la peluquería, crea el ambiente de ''comic mayhem'' típico de la farsa.[26] Y en cuanto a la parodia, entre varios momentos, podemos mencionar la recreación inspirada del estilo verbal del locutor de la televisión que entrevista a Lupita, La ''autoviuda.'' Es una obra, como se podría esperar de Rosario Castellanos, que maneja con destreza muchos aspectos de lo cómico.

Hay muchos matices de placer que se puede derivar de la lectura o del montaje de este drama y también de una meditación posterior sobre su impacto. Uno, íntimamente metateatral, viene de reconocer los *papeles* estereotipados que la sociedad ha asignado a las mujeres convertidas en *papeles* dramáticos que vemos presentados en el escenario. Virginia Woolf escribió en 1928 que nuestros valores están torcidos, demasiado influenciados por los valores masculinos, porque decimos: ''This is an important book because it deals with war. This is an insignificant book because it deals with the feelings of women in a drawing-room.''[27] ¿No es, en este raspecto, un placer ver cómo técnicas brechtianas han sido utilizadas para una temática de ''drawing-room''—o más de salón de belleza—en vez de una de guerra como él favorecía? Y es lícito dejar que el pensamiento ande por estos caminos, porque sabemos que Castellanos, gran admiradora de Woolf, le secundaba en esta opinión.[28]

Pero estas son especulaciones algo divagantes. Podemos dirigirnos a las preguntas propuestas al principio en cuanto a los procesos estructurales y las estrategias distanciadoras. Creemos que la división tripartita de la obra sí da forma y sentido al contenido. Se aprecia el efecto de contraste logrado por el encuadre de los modelos positivos del segundo acto entre los dos polos negativos. También es eficaz la separación de las situaciones de la casada de las peripecias de la soltera, separación que luego queda efectivamente anulada porque se ataca a las dos con la misma sátira demitificadora. Y la diferencia de tono entre el segundo acto—predominantemente irónico y más benigno—y el tono satírico de los otros dos realza los propósitos distintos que los animan y la diferencia en su manera de apelar al público. El drama adolece, sin embargo, de fallos estructurales. Se sabe que las repeticiones en el teatro épico tienen la función de subrayar el mensaje central. Pero hay aquí demasiada materia y la estructura libre no mantiene la atención a través de todos los cuadros de los tres actos.[29] Es posible imaginar una mejor obra más corta asemejándose quizá a estas revistas satíricas con las cuales empezó Brecht su carrera en los cabarets de la Alemania de la pre-guerra.

Con respecto a los efectos de las técnicas de distanciamiento, diría que por ellas la voz lírica, subjetiva de su ficción y su poesía se objetiviza y concretiza en el drama. La risa, nos advierte Castellanos al hablar de Isak Dinesin, "exige una especie de distanciamiento."[30] A través de esta risa ha hecho "el trabajo de exhibición de las motivaciones irracionales que se encuentran subyacentes en los símbolos tras los cuales enmascaramos nuestra conducta y de los valores a los cuales rendimos culto con cada uno de los actos de nuestra vida cotidiana."[31] Ha podido en esta obra de teatro hablar directamente y con mucho impacto didáctico al público y con una fuerza agresiva que ni en el ensayo—algunos también abiertamente didácticos y dirigidos a despertar conciencias—pudo lograr. Y con ello se inserta firmemente dentro de aquel panorama de la cultura mexicana reciente que tiene como propósito obligar al público a dudar de la validez de los mitos sagrados de su sociedad.[32] La sátira *anti-feminista* tiene una larga tradición histórica; postulamos que *El eterno femenino* de Rosario Castellanos, a pesar de sus defectos, es una adición memorable a una nueva tradición de sátira *feminista*. El valor artístico de este drama emana principalmente de la densidad de los elementos satíricos—e irónicos—que maneja.

Temple University

Notas

1. Vea *Homenaje a Rosario Castellanos*, eds. Maureen Ahern and Mary Seale Vásquez (Valencia: Ediciones Albatros Hispanófila, 1980).
2. México: Fondo de Cultura Económica, 1974. Se citará por esta edición. Estrenado en Mexico, D.F., 1976. El único estudio dedicado a este drama que conozco es el de Kirsten F. Nigro, "Rosario Castellano's Debunking of the *Eternal Feminine*," *Journal of Spanish Studies: Twentieth Century* 8, No. 1-2 (1980): 89-101.
3. Publicó "Tablero de Damas: Pieza en una acto" en *América: Revista Antológica* 68 (Junio 1952): 187-202. Escribió tres dramas en verso de un acto: *Judith, Salomé y Eva; Vocación de Sor Juana* en dos actos y *La creciente* en tres. Dos fueron publicados: *Salomé* y *Judith. Poemas dramáticos* (México: Editorial Jus, 1959). También aparecieron en *Poesía no eres tú; Obra poética: 1948-1971* (México: Fondo de Cultura Económica, 1972) 123-167. En años posteriores ella ha indicado que considera todos como tentativas fallidas. Para más información consulte los artículos de M. Seale

Vásquez y Kathleen O'Quinn y la bibliografía de Maureen Ahern en *Homenaje a Rosario Castellanos*.

4. *Juicios sumarios: Ensayos*. Cuadernos de la Facultad de Filosofía, Letras y Ciencias 35 (Xalapa: Universidad Veracruzana, 1966): 276.

5. *Mujer que sabe latín . . .* (México: Secretaría de Educación Pública, 1973) 38.

6. *Poesía no eres tú* 309.

7. *Mujer* 40.

8. *Mujer* 20.

9. *Mujer* 39.

10. *Poesía no eres tú* 298-299.

11. La frase viene del poema "Meditación en el umbral" donde se habla de la mujer como "otro modo de ser humano y libre." *Poesía no eres tú* 326.

12. Castellanos también ha reflexionado sobre la mujer como símbolo en su ensayo "Otra vez Sor Juana." El ensayo comienza así: "En la historia de México hay tres figuras en las que encarnan hasta sus últimos extremos, diversas posibilidades de la femineidad. Cada una de ellas representa un símbolo, ejerce una vasta y profunda influencia en sectores muy amplios de la nación. . . . Estas figuras son la Virgen de Guadalupe, la Malinche y Sor Juana." *Juicios* 26.

13. Kirsten Nigro comenta una posible influencia brechtiana en su artículo ya citado (98).

14. (Canada: Girol Books, 1984) 28.

15. Toro 28.

16. El dilema de la traducción correcta de la terminología brechtiana ha sido por muchos años tema de discusión entre los críticos. Ejemplo típico sería este comentario de Martin Esslin en la cuarta edición revisada de su *Brecht. A Choice of Evils*: "The producer must strive to produce by all the means at his disposal effects which will keep the audience separate, estranged, alienated from the action. That is the meaning of the famous 'Verfremdungseffekt', a term which has never been successfully rendered in English, because terms like alienation or estrangement have entirely different, and unfortunate, emotional overtones. In French *distantiation* is a happier term." (London: Methuen, 1984) 115. Para los propósitos de este trabajo he preferido usar "distancia-miento" por su cercanía al concepto aceptado de "distancia estética," y porque define mejor para mí lo que veo como diferencia clave entre la obra dramática de Castellanos y su trabajo en otros géneros.

17. Toro 51.

18. Toro 89.

19. *Metatheatre. A New View of Dramatic Form* (New York: Hill and Wang) n.p.

20. Patricia Meyer Spacks in *Satire: Modern Essays in Criticism*, ed. Ronald Paulson (Englewood Cliffs, NJ: Prentice-Hall, 1971) 362.

21. Matthew Hodgart, *Satire* (New York: McGraw Hill, 1969) 130.

22. Alan R. Thompson, *The Dry Mock. A Study of Irony in Drama* (Berkeley: U of California P, 1948) 5.

23. Wayne C. Booth, *A Rhetoric of Irony* (Chicago: U of Chicago P, 1974) 255.

24. Thompson comenta en *The Dry Mock* que no es cierto que la ironía es solamente una de las formas de la sátira, sino que la ironía dramática puede existir "without any satirical implication" (5).

25. "Visual and Verbal Differences in the Mexican Theater: The Plays of Elena Garro," en *Women as Myth and Metaphor in Latin American Literature*, eds. Carmelo Virgillo and Naomi Lindstrom (Columbia: U of Missouri P, 1985) 62.

26. Lupita encaja muy bien en la siguiente descripción de Jessica Milner Davis en su libro *Farce* (London: Methuen, 1978) 26: "In a farce, the victim is shown both inviting and suffering ridicule, and the insult is delivered directly and physically to the person of the victim."

27. *A Room of One's Own* (New York: Harcourt, 1929) 128.

28. Naomi Lindstrom nota que en un curso que siguió con Castellanos la escritora "tried to show her students how the relationship of reading public and literary work was skewed by our deep-seated notions about the importance of male things and triviality of all things female." "Rosario Castellanos: Pioneer of Feminist Criticism" en *Homenaje a Rosario Castellanos*, 73.

29. Estoy de acuerdo aquí con Kirsten Nigro quien comenta en el artículo ya citado que "the text badly needs a judicious pruning," p. 98.

30. *Mujer* 52.

31. *Juicios* 271.

32. David W. Foster, en su discusión de *El juicio* de Vicente Leñero menciona esta dirección en la literatura mexicana. *Estudios sobre teatro mexicano contemporáneo* (New York: Peter Lang, 1984) 68.

AVATARS OF INTELLIGENCE

Figures of Reading in the work of Gabriel García Márquez

by Alicia Borinsky

As the initial surprising effects of Latin American experimental narrative wear off, an interest in the construction of those texts as an end in itself for criticism gives way to other problems opened up by those structures. Readers blinded by the difficulties posed by ludic variations of time and attribution may have very well been mistaken in thinking that the dismantling and description of such games constitute a valid form of understanding what is at stake in the literary tradition initiated by Macedonio Fernández, Borges and Cartázar. For at the heart of these developments lies a contempt for the formalistic reading that some of those works have necessarily evoked due to the puzzling appearance of their pages.[1]

The work of García Márquez owes its popularity, in part, to the seemingly easy access it offers to naive readings, to the way in which it departs from the highly intellectualized mode that characterizes other fiction of the period. A new reader has been invited to the book. The pleasure of continued belief in the coherence of plot has been restored as a valid access to fiction. Hedonism—a complement to the need for immediate understanding of the facts narrated—is given a positive marking; the reading for plot derided by *Museo de la Novela de la Eterna, Hopscotch* and *62, Model Kit* to cite only a few examples, has returned with renewed intensities. Such a change in its most trivial aspects may be understood in terms of the attraction for conventional projections in characters and actions, a will to indulge in the many hallucinations provided by the unfolding of stories.

One hundred years of solitude and García Márquez' short stories provide the context for discussions of the uncanny and the marvelous as they are re-invented for the contemporary tradition through an abundant use of materials from the Medieval and Renaissance periods. While this is, undoubtedly, true, it is not the most important conclusion to be drawn from his literature but, rather, the result of a first reading still impressed, paradoxically, with the *newness* that the pleasures of plot development bring to a contemporary critical eye that aims to dismantle the effects of narrative conventions. Such a reading is as much a victim of the illusions elicited by transgression[2] as the formalistic views intent on explaining away the difficulty of novels through a description of their structures.

What is left if we take away the power that García Márquez' work has to silence the *beyond* of fiction sought by criticism?

—The conceit of the book

One Hundred Years of Solitude offers several answers to that question. One of them is optimistic. Once the reader closes the book it is possible not to feel that the plot is an obstacle to thinking. Because the conceit of the manuscript that has to be deciphered at the end has the general effect of re-weaving the beginning. The nostalgic ending of the book (the story of the family is over, the reader has *to leave* the scene of projection with the awareness that no continuation is possible given the apocalyptic ending) is intensified even further.

The reader has lost his/her innocence. Not only is the plot a fiction but the books read are also of questionable materiality. The realm of detachment has been founded. In leaving the book, the reader is nostalgic for the innocence lost through the realization that what he read was fiction. Thus, the loss is worked into the novel at two levels. The ending is the ending of the family (plot) and the beginning of critical awareness (because of the conceit of the manuscript being deciphered). It closes asking the reader to recover from the dizziness of fiction. The remedy seems to be the exercise of literary interpretation implicit in the awareness of translation.

Such is the optimistic side of *One Hundred Years of Solitude.* Its texture takes issue with the contempt for plot and celebrates criticism as a way out of its illusions *within* the framework of the book. A totalitarian intention underlies the project thus conceived. While the earlier formulation of the issue—as it appears in an exemplary way in Cortázar's *Hopscotch*—would have the reader choose between two avenues to be pursued with difficulty: the delight in the linear sequence of events with La Maga as a central node of meaning, or the disjointed critical eye stemming from Morelli's prophecies, *One Hundred Years of Solitude* masks the seams of its fiction until that crucial moment: the ending of the book where they become, in turn, the decisive element in the materiality of what is being read. In a literary figuration reminiscent of Borges' Aleph the facts of the book are thought of as being embodied in an instant: "The final projection, which Aureliano had begun to glimpse when he let himself be confused by the love of Amaranta Ursula, was based on the fact that Melquíades had not put events in the order of man's conventional time, but had concentrated a century of daily episodes in such a way that they coexisted in an instant"[3] (p. 382).

As it has been noted in other readings that this novel has elicited, this inscribes the book in a long tradition of self-conscious fiction. Nevertheless, the notation of this privileged instant that transforms reading into a fragile exercise of interpretation is not the most compelling ending for *One Hundred Years of Solitude.* The decipherer, alone in the room, arrives to his discovery through an active dismissal of a sector of reality: Wounded by the fatal lances of his own nostalgia and that of others, he admired the persistence of the spider webs on the dead rose bushes, the perseverance of the rye grass, the patience of the air in the radiant February dawn. And then he saw the child. It was a dry and bloated bag of skin that all the ants in the world were dragging toward their holes along the stone path in the garden. Aureliano could not move. Not because he was paralyzed by horror but because at that prodigious instant Melquíades' final keys were revealed to him.." (p. 381). The interpreter's task is, thus, rooted in an act of oblivion so violent that his gesture can hardly attempt to be all-embracing. Remembering his past is one with forgetting the immediate destiny of his offspring. The initial confidence in the affirmation of the re-reading of the novel as Melquíades' elusive truth disappears, giving way to the *gap* separating the time of interpretation from the present of pain.

The recognition of the gap locates interpretation in a temporal sequence where its looking back into the past becomes *simultaneous* with the oblivion of the facts

6

178

constituting it. The dismissal of the very level of experience it pretends to elucidate brackets the authenticity of its intentions as it redeems the book from the totalitarian—optimistic—effects through a reading distrustful of the illusions of completeness offered by the novel.

—The intelligent reader

The conceit of the book within the book in *One Hundred Years of Solitude* produces, as we have seen, the figure of a reader-decipherer who—from inside fiction—is charged with giving shape to events leading to his own inception as a character. His intelligence is not without bounds. The outer limit of its reach is indicated with precision in the dismissal of the immediate events that make up the concrete conditions for his act of interpretation.

While the decipherer incarnates the most recognizable figure for the act of reading in the novel, another character of a very different sort embodies the qualities attributed to the materiality of fiction itself. Remedios, the Beauty, has an evanescent presence. The nature of her intelligence is an object of discussion for the other characters who are divided in their opinion. There are those who think that she is retarded or simply stupid, and others, such as the Colonel Aureliano Buendía, who think of her as having a special lucidity that makes traditional forms of thought unnecessary. The nature of the passion she ignites in the males who pursue her make the reader understand her as the ever elusive object of a desire destined to be unsatisfied. Her figure is evocative of a long tradition in which female beauty is portrayed as dangerous and ultimately fatal to those who succumb to its spell. Her speech, unschooled in metaphor, works with a literality occasionally hilarious in its effects.

Remedios, the Beauty, is larger than life but has—as a fictional figure—an intensity that stands for the notion of reality itself. Her presence has an extreme carnality. One of the arguments against her intelligence is that she does not like to wear clothes. Her almost naked body is a constant reminder of her ahistorical nature. This refusal to participate in culture places her either above or beneath it. As the novel evolves, Remedios, the Beauty, levitates away leaving behind her a nostalgia for solving the doubts she inspired.

What is *the unknown* in the question about Remedios? The unfolding of her enigma brings us back to the way in which Melquíades' prophecy is deciphered. Her eloquence may be mistaken for lack of intelligent speech because of the inadequacy of her language in the context of everyday communication. Mequiades' manuscript remains virtually invisible until a revelatory moment sets the deciphering in motion. In very much the same way, Remedios' lucidity is accessible through an act of belief in the sophistication of her mind. The instantaneous perception of her beauty gives her carnality non-discursive meaning, her literal practice of language becomes a series of wise aphorisms. Her character encapsulates everything that may be said about the representational level in the novel conceivable as a grounding for the fictional weave. For she seems to exist in a *deeper* context beyond words, as a privileged image of the literary tradition preceding the novel, a powerful entity precipitating changes in the destinies of others by mere presence.

The other female characters are partial embodiments of the mystery of Remedios. They share with her the capacity for hiding part of their motivations, the design that portrays them as being part of a world of gravitating secrets. Such are

7

the traits of Amaranta, Amaranta Ursula, Pilar Ternera, Rebecca, Fernanda, who remain unknown to the readers in spite of the many anecdotes that they develop. The nature of their secrecy is, perhaps, their femaleness and is seen as constituting a potential danger to other characters who belong to the more recognizable world of adventure, where action is a measure of time.

Aside from the inevitable considerations linking this representation of women to the ideologies of the eternal feminine, it is worth noting that their power lies in their lack of participation in the world of discourse of the other characters. The reasons for the kind of gravitation they each attain are varied: Fernanda has a mysterious ailment and, like Rebecca, a past unknown to the reader. Ursula sees through her blindness and intuition beyond any reasoning about the origins of her power; Pilar Ternera's physical energy is matched only by nature itself; Amaranta has an uncanny apathy that grants her the qualities of a patience turned obsessive strategy; Amaranta Ursula is a combination of the two other female characters present in her name. Her powers are enormous and her physical energy is portrayed as being almost impersonal because of its similarity to a "natural" force. The rapid inventory of traits provides the register in which the notion of Remedios, the Beauty, becomes a cipher (*cifra*) for understanding the role that this privileged energy plays in the assessment of how the novel works.

The female characters, as described, possess something beyond intelligence, ways of understanding and interacting through what appears as a leap in which the rational is acknowledged but always marginalized. Remedios, the Beauty, is the most hyperbolic figuration of the process that turns these women into emblems of a secret source of energy. When she levitates out of the novel, Remedios, the Beauty, intensifies the kind of nostalgia created by the other female characters. Her loss is the absence of something that takes on the virtuality of a gravitating reality because of the insistence of the carnality that grants her presence for the reader.

Melquíades' manuscript is an object attuned to the nature of Remedios, the Beauty. Its language is not discursive (sequential) although abundant in effects sustaining the desire to understand it. Remedios, the Beauty, may not be part of this world but her otherworldliness attracts characters to a fatal destiny. The manuscript to be deciphered has, as the love generated by Remedios, the Beauty, a frightening capacity for causing violence. The decipherer, alone in a room, forgets about his own child as he starts to understand Melquíades' message. Paradoxically, in forgetting his offspring, he has the hope of finding himself:

> "Fascinated by the discovery, Aureliano read aloud without skipping the chanted encyclicals that Melquíades himself had made Arcadio listen to and that were in reality the prediction of his execution and he found the announcement of the birth of the most beautiful woman in the world who was rising up to heaven in body and soul, and he found the origin of the posthumous twins who gave up deciphering the parchments, not simply through incapacity and lack of drive, but also because their attempts were premature. At that point, impatient to know his own origin, Aureliano skipped ahead." (p. 382).

8

He skips aheadßßßAureliano's "intelligent" reading feeds on partiality. His being a reader as a character is not a device that facilitates a projection for the reader of *One Hundred Years of Solitude*. Aureliano strives to find *himself* through the betrayal of two poles that sustain the fiction in which he participates. In forgetting his offspring he is being unfaithful to that level of the plot that might give him a future, as a member of an extinct family; he does not perform the funeral rites for his son because his refusal constitutes the objective ending for the adventures that led to him; he also betrays the reader of the novel—that other implicit entity in every book—by not being interested in following every avatar of the manuscript. As he skips passages in order to find his own origins, he ceases to be a neutral embodiment of reading to become more explicitly what he has always been: a fictional character whose limitations are the result of hedonistic self-interest.

—Objects to be read

In thinking of Aureliano's "intelligent" role as a decipherer and Remedios, the Beauty, as an embodiment of a non-discursive enigma, we have constituted a basic scene of reading and writing. The reader (Aureliano) on the one hand and the subject (Remedios, the Beauty) on the other. The stability of this arrangement disappears as Aureliano's unfaithful reading of the manuscript emerges in the novel. The will to partiality as a means of self-understanding puts him at the same level as the other characters in the book.

What is the proper manner of annotating that level? What is entailed by this question? In attempting to answer it, we should rephrase it as a boomerang that questions the place of the reader in the novel. For the awareness of the shared ground makes it necessary to find another ground for the critical reading, it destroys the system of illusions through which one character, less fictional than others, would be entrusted with a decisive say about the limits of fiction and the nature of its detached assessment by a reader.

In *Autumn of the Patriarch*, the totalitarian power of the dictator stems precisely from his capacity to draw on the mystery that his persona has created. The issue of whether he is alive or dead is discussed by "the people"; the uncertainty of his reactions grants him a specificity that intensifies the sense that his being is beyond the grasp of the common man. As we go through the novel we are made aware, though, of the fact that his power is sustained by a complicated system of illusions. The substantial presence attained by the dictator in the eyes of his contemporaries is shown from the inside of the machine of power as a machine of conventions.

There are some hilarious moments, such as the one in which the dictator's own mother says that had she known the high position her son would hold, she would have made sure that he learned how to read and write. Aside from the situational humor and the abundant social comment that may be drawn from the statement, we should reflect on how this figure of the dictator is given the attributes of a power deprived from all intelligence.

The texture of the novel allows the reader to see two strands of the repressive tapestry woven by the dictatorship: one is the ruthless violence exercised against the opposition replete with shifts in motives for striking out t the hastily defined enemies; the other is the seams that hold the image of the ictator together in front of "the

9

people." What are the tricks that shape the image of the dictator toward the outside world? A suspicion of repeated doublings maintains his own identity in the dark; his speeches—made out of cliches—save him from the horrors of originality in language; his love-sickness for a female character who spurns him with her final disappearance grants him a sense of humanity, insofar as she represents the beauty of the poor ("la belleza del muladar") and the kind of vulnerability associated with classical demagogy.

The dictator is an elusive object whose language and very being are the subject of interpretation. *Autumn of the Patriarch* brings back in a new framework the problems of how to translate (interpret) the kind of presence of character who, devoid of intelligence of his or her own, precipitates, nevertheless, everything of importance that takes place in the narrative. Because the dictator does not have an analytical system, he is the ideal object for analysis. His silence (let us remember at this point that his most eloquent speeches are his own taped interventions that mix the commonplaces belonging to all) triggers the need for the speech of others.

Autumn of the Patriarch is an extended meditation on the authority granted a character because of the ignorance of his origins; the less the reader knows about the reasons determining the character, the more attracted he/she is to study him and fall within his aura. The illusion of depth that such a development gives to fiction is seen in the novel in its political aspect of cruelty and its ludic literary consequences.

The system that was put into play in *One Hundred Years of Solitude* reappears here establishing the limits of the objects to be read with increased analytical clarity: the reader is drawn to *a secret*. The dictator, Remedios, the Beauty and Melquiades' manuscript offer several faces: one is an all-embracing intelligence, the other is staggering stupidity and ignorance. The reader has, as in the previous novel, an entity where he may project himself: in *Autumn of the Patriarch* it is no longer the last of the Buendías but "the people" who see the dictator from afar, as he passes in a car without their being able to tell whether it is really he, what his face looks like but sure, nevertheless, of the pressing nature of the question. In that partial system of projections, the reader is less fortunate than he was in *One Hundred Years of Solitude* because this time there is no way out from the space of reading. While it was possible to frame Aureliano's reading of Melquíades in a specific room and look at it from another level, an *outside*, in this novel that beyond does not exist. For it is the world itself, and the reader is drawn from this dictator to all others, outside the book but within the system that turns mystery and stupidity into absolute power.

—The evidence

In *Chronicle of a Death Foretold* everybody knows that somebody will die. The novel does not deal with a mystery but with a matter self evident. A fact, more tangible than comprehensible, initiates the narrative. A man has been murdered. The characters of the novel compose a gallery whose opinions and previous knowledge of the event are not enough to have stopped it. The context for the death is a tightly knit community; the motive is simple and classical. It involves a marriage a virginity lost by the bride at the wrong time, an explanation that may not have been true

10

and the death of the male culprit at the hand of avenging males.

How does this novel produce its illusions of suspense? What does the reader expect from its pages? The pleasure involved in reading this book is a celebration of reality. The murder acquires the necessity of a privileged object. It has taken place. It is there. The role of the characters in the book is none other than attesting to the existence of the event that holds them together by making it "happen" over and over again. The reader contemplates the fabrication of presence for the event and ends up convinced of its inevitability. In this case, as in many others, inevitability is to be confused with necessity. The grounding subject of the book is the *necessity* of the event. While the novel starts by stating what happened, its suspense is built around the credibility given to its occurrence, its *weight* for a reader. The success of the book resides in silencing that level of reading that might want to question the event, that is, the silencing of a more intelligent and suspicious look at the information.

—Conceits of books, conceits of facts

These thoughts have taken us from the conceit of the book in *One Hundred Years of Solitude* to the conceit of the fact as a grounding for fiction in *Chronicle of a Death Foretold* through a meditation on the power attained by an aging patriarch whose very existence becomes the subject of a novel in *Autumn of the Patriarch.*

In drawing the figures of reading as they appear in each of these texts we have found a need for a distinction between reading and readers as they appear within fiction (as part of a plot) and reading and readers in the sense commonly understood as critical. Following closely such developments in *One Hundred Years of Solitude*, a model for reading emerged where intelligence was equated with the mystery of Remedios, the Beauty's silence as a grounding for fiction; while a hostile reaction to Aureliano's partial interest in deciphering the past embodied the beginning of critical awareness on the part of a detached reader.

Autumn of the Patriarch intensifies these problems by making of the mystery (eloquence and elusiveness) found in Remedios, the Beauty, a haunting and urgent political problem in the figure of the dictator. In *Chronicle of a Death Foretold* the celebration of conformity creates a fissure through which a critical reader, performing his task *against* the grain of the book, understands his own exclusion as central to what is being narrated.

How does this kind of reading mesh with current ways of literary analysis? By putting three major works by García Márquez into play, we have generated a prism of analytic effects seemingly borne out of individual readings but with a dialogical encounter strongly dependent on the tradition of reading forged by Macedonio Fernández, Borges and Cortázar. Perhaps the clearest answer to this last question may be found in that which the analysis has refused: a methodological jargon that would take away from reading that intense effect of lucidity generated by fictions analyzing other fictions.

Boston University

11

183

NOTES

1   The effacement of the difference between the discourses of history, philosophy, sociology and fiction is at the root of these works. Nevertheless, the initial difficulties posed by the interpretation of their textures, created a realm where literary criticism saw itself as being exempt from the ludic bracketing it was trying to uncover. Such an error created a formalistic approach to texts that wished nothing better than subverting the difference between play (seen as frivolous) and science (seen as non ludic).

2   *One Hundred Years of Solitude* has invited thoughts on how, after its appearance it is no longer possible to read without being wholly involved in the minimal avatars of plot development as they elicit representations of the outside world and the literary tradition. Such a stand gets a great deal of its energy from the transgressive gesture it has to make in rejecting contemporary interests in the function of structural patterns.

3   All quotations from the novel follow G. Rabassa's translation: Gabriel García Márquez, *One Hundred Years of Solitude* (Chicago: Avon Books, 1971).

12

The Storyteller and the Carnival Queen: "Funerales de la Mamá Grande"

Debra A. Castillo

¿Cómo puede estar acabado [mi libro] si aún no está acabada mi vida?
(Ginés de Pasamonte in *Don Quijote*)

The archaeologist or historian of Macondo would find it difficult to date the reign of the Mamá Grande in relation to that of the Buendía dynasty. For although her name is briefly mentioned in *Cien años de soledad*, the Mamá Grande does not fit easily into the pages of Melquiades's text and seems to belong to another level of fictional reality altogether. It is the narrator of the short story, "Funerales de la Mamá Grande," who indicates most clearly that this is indeed so. In the opening paragraphs of the story, the narrator defines himself as the representative of a period of transition, a time in which the life and death of the Mamá Grande is already, in terms of the story, passing from common knowledge into the reconstructions of historical or mythic representations. The narrator, nevertheless, still remains in that period of flux, "antes de que tengan tiempo de llegar los historiadores"[1] to impose a rigid order on the memories and fix them in official narrative. The narrator, thus, situates himself temporally and establishes a site from which he is to construct his tale, a site which is determined physically ("ahora es la hora de recostar un taburete a la puerta de la calle"), temporally (now, in this unsettled period of transition), and philosophically ("ésta es, incrédulos del mundo entero, la verídica historia" [p. 127]).

In a few brief lines, the narrator establishes his authority and the audience's ignorance, his truth and our incredulity, his choice of a specific form of expression: "verídica historia" which does not acknowledge itself, which denies all ties to the (as yet unwritten) official history.[2] What he rejects, then, from this chosen position, is what Bakhtin calls the "conceptualizing discourse that had made a home for itself in all the higher reaches of national ideological thought processes,"[3] that is, the conceptualizing framework of a history within which all acts and events find their proper, officially sanctioned place. The strangeness of this story is due precisely to this election of a place which is no proper place, to this rejection of the conceptualizations of official discourse, a problem in which the readers' angle of vision—our place or displacement in the text—is a crucial element. The inevitable recognition that the place of the narrator will be usurped exacerbates rather than relieves this strangeness. The historians will arrive, and this discourse will give way before another, a conceptualization in which the proper place will be decreed by law: the true history, and no longer the "verídica historia," which dissipates the incredulity of a naïve populace.

The opposition between the two histories is not as simple, however, as the narrator expects the more credulous of us to accept. Luis de Arrigoitia is correct in his recognition that even non-conceptualized history is heavily dependent on the detritus of official histories, on memories of "la 'danza de la muerte' medieval, el teatro jesuita y calderonsiano del siglo XVII, los desfiles de carnaval, la propaganda comercial del siglo XX."[4] Indeed, the narrator of this story draws his material from just such detritus. His story sifts this jumble of half-forgotten festivity, this refuse heap of the conceptual, mediating the interval between the death of the Mamá Grande—which after all signals the passing of a historical epoch—and the official reinstitution of the myth of her life and reign under the approving eye of the historian.

The narrator, we recall, sets his stool against "la puerta de la calle," assuming the traditional pose of the storyteller and indicating by this position his openness to still other elements of historical detritus: the voices from the street, the gossip rejected by the traditional historian who prefers to consult the textual evidence in libraries and archives. In so doing, the storyteller identifies an ideological place for his tale as well as spatial and temporal ones, and he indicates his objections not only to the conceptualizations but also to the univocity of historical discourse. His story is, implicitly, a dialogic one, which establishes a conscious opposition to and a polemical stance against the centralizing, reductionist forces functional as the official historical ideology. An oral tale rather than a written history, it is both more flexible and more ambiguous; it is also, however, as a tale based on the anonymous voices of popular report, subject to the deformations, distortions, and confusions of all gossip.

Clearly, such deformations are the very substance of a dialogic account of the past in Bakhtin's sense of the word. The narrator who organizes the elements of the story into the text we read does so in a manner that is patently incomplete and frequently contradictory. His tale, unlike that of the historians, does not produce or reflect a single predetermined meaning; instead, it emphasizes the decisive moment of the tale's reception. Such a text, in Bakhtin's words, "is not a dialogue in the narrative sense, nor in the abstract sense; rather it is a dialogue between points of view, each with its own concrete language that cannot be translated into the other."[5] The dialogue, then, takes place between the bits of gossip jostling for priority in the tale and occurs as well between the storyteller on his stool and the audience (of gossipmongers?) at his feet, an audience whose delight in the tale remains unaffected by the proximate infringement of stabilizing convention.

At the same time, while he reveals the bankruptcy of the conceptualizing discourse of historical writing, the narrator, like the historian, shapes the story by his telling of it. The disparate voices he manages, however incomplete their message, never dissolve into cacophony or mere noise. In this shaping impulse, the "positionalities"[6] of historian and storyteller begin to approximate each other. Beneath his rejection of the distortions of history is his own ironic acceptance of the importance of concurrence in the adoption of a single story, "la verídica historia," a concept which he, no less than the other, later historians, arrogates to himself. The narrator rejects history, but also, albeit parodically, mimics its norms, methods, and style and reveals history's rhetorical function as an organizational metaphor. Furthermore, this oral tale reaches us, its current public, in a written form, and in that respect too the story is incorporated into historical discourse. It remains, however, a historical discourse which maintains a constant self-critique of its own presuppositions. Robert Sims, then, errs in his statement that "in 'Los Funerales de la Mamá Grande,' García Márquez succeeds in restoring to myth its primary function of speaking narratively about important subjects."[7] The situation, the site, and the function of this narrator are far more complex; the parodic nature of his stylistic undertaking indicates once again that he places himself to one side of any such facile identifications, whether historical or mythic. Just as temporally he locates himself between the "reality" of Mamá Grande's reign and the arrival of the historians, so ideologically he is placed between the voices of the street (which will eventually evolve into myth) and the voices of the historians, for both history and myth are handicapped by their inability to recognize or accept the transformatory power of language as it distances reality from the public. The narrator's position between or beside both myth and history, both language and the object of analysis, allows him to uncover (or recover) both language and the object and to reveal that the site of analysis conditions all such imaginative reconstructions, whether mythic or historical.

The incredulous reader is not likely to forget that, at least since Cervantes, a story's claim to be the "verídica historia" is almost automatically a signal of fictionality, and in relating history and gossip through the mediations of his text the narrator points to the underlying similarity of gossip and history as rhetorical strategies and, further, to the fictionality of both these radically opposed options for discourse about a perceived reality. The storyteller, in revealing the fundamental identity of the historians' and the gossips' desire to recapture and hypostatize past events now fading into inaccessibility, destroys two myths of authority: that of hegemonic history and that of nonreflective myth. In their decomposition he is finally able to resolve the problem of his own parodic stance in relation to the Mamá Grande.

It should come as no surprise, therefore, that the Mamá Grande defies all attempts at insertion into narrative. Even in life, "se esfumaba en su propia leyenda" (p. 133), and through her death she passes into history, but at the same time escapes reality and the possibility of any reconstruction except any admittedly imaginative one, exceeding her "proper" limitations of time and space. Macondo is the navel of the universe (an undecipherable dream's navel in Freudian terms), and the Mamá Grande, equally undecipherable, "durante el presente siglo . . . había sido el centro de gravedad de Macondo" (p. 129). Because she is so essentially insubstantial, her function as a centering presence is highly problematic. Whereas representational literature has always been premised on a recognizably extraliterary reality, the story of the Mamá Grande denies us this assumed anteriority to representation, displacing the extraliterary origin of the text and leaving the author (comically) compromised by a centerless form.

The Mamá Grande, an unreal and semi-divine figure in her lifetime— the narrator notes that on her birthdays "se vendían estampas y escapularios con [su] imagen" (p. 132)—is even less accessible as a biographical subject as her image fades still further into an absolute otherness created in the tumult surrounding her death. Her very name serves only as a social marker, indicating her standing in the community, and offers no proper, unequivocal reading. Her proper name, María del Rosario Castañeda y Montero, vanishes with her accession to the role and power of the Mamá Grande, and even that name, which signals her place in the social hierarchy, is subject to slippage. The woman herself, "que fue dotada por la naturaleza para amamantar ella sola a toda su especie, agonizaba virgen y sin hijos" (p. 133), and her name "se ignoraba en el resto del país hacía pocas horas, antes de ser consagrada por la palabra impresa" (p. 138). Neither "mamá" nor "grande," except in physical size, the matriarch achieves greatness only in the fickle and ephemeral light of the attention of the press. Yet, at the same time, she is a totalizing presence in the story, annihilating the biographer, depriving him, except for the scrambling for fragments of a parodic vision, of his authoritative place. The *mise en abîme*, frequently pressed into service by scholars to model other decentered fictions in which the originary force is endlessly displaced, seems inappropriate in application to these radically parodic displacements of the Mamá Grande, a woman whose vast, ephemeral bulk obliterates abyssal perception.

Her image, the image recreated through news reports and offical communiqués, is, nevertheless, clearly the focal image of the story, and her death represents a moment of crisis on all levels. "El orden social había sido rozado por la muerte" (p. 138), says the narrator, and the President of the Republic, the representative of social and political power, pays homage to her passing by his presence at her funeral. Joined there by the Pope, the representative of religious power, the spiritual and terrestrial forces converge, inevitably, inexorably, at the hidden source of their authority, at the carnival surrounding the funeral of the Mamá Grande whose moral patrimony includes the seal of their legitimization. Significantly, the narrative proclamation of the death of the Mamá Grande replaces the death itself in importance, and this fictional construct rather than the raw event inspires the narrative. Distance from the actual (absent) event serves as a limiting or destabilizing force on the narrative form, but it is also a critical enabling factor in the production of meaning(s). Ginés de Pasamonte's observation to Don Quijote that death is essential to completing the picaresque biography is well taken in terms of the biographical mode in general. "Funerales" carries out the implication of such an observation, and, in a parodic reversal of the typical biography, the narrator concentrates not on the "life and works" but on the crucial period of the "death and funeral" as his subject. The ultimate narrative fantasy, it seems, would be for readers to pretend that there was once a moment prior to this death, or, indeed, that there will be a moment that we could reach posterior to the funeral celebration.

The problem for the narrator, clearly, is how to force this fragmentary, ambiguous, yet totalizing presence to disclose itself and assume a form and a meaning. Since legend and the passage of time already obscure the reality of the Mamá Grande's existence and her reign, and since the very existence of any raw event anterior to the symbolizing impetus is at question, the narrator resorts to hyperbole, the rhetorical trope that functions on the boundary of objective reality, to force that "reality" which is beyond the limits of the objective to reveal its secrets. The Mamá Grande, a presence which can be glimpsed just beyond or outside the reach of the narrator, is unavailable in any absolute sense to historical reconstruction. Thus, the narrator of this tale elects the medium of exaggeration and irony, operating always on the borders of a semiotic collapse. Weeks are "interminable," Nicanor is "titánico" (p. 128), the Mamá Grande is "infinitamente rica y poderosa" (p. 130); instances are multiplied throughout the text. Such expressions, by virtue of their very magnitude coupled with semantic vagueness, have a disconcerting effect, as the magnificence of the subject is both declared and subverted in the same phrase. Interminable time, titanic size, and infinite riches are dismissed with the same gesture that eventually discounts the Mamá Grande's claim to universal moral hegemony.

In representing the figure of the matriarch from a hyperbolic and ironic perspective, the narrator sacrifices positive and positivistic attempts to represent what once was; instead, irony and exaggeration are recuperated for a negative dialectic—the story's "way of covering over the instability of its form, a way of acknowledging and denying in the same gesture the presence/absence of the organic totality it strives to achieve."[8] The opening of "Funerales," with its juxtaposition of "incrédulos" and "verídica historia," makes just such a gesture of affirmation and negation. The narrator clearly demonstrates his ironic totalizing aspirations in the closing lines of the story by repeating, from a point just prior in time to the opening of the story, the motivations expressed in the opening sentence: "Sólo faltaba entonces que alguien recostara un taburete en la puerta para contar esta historia . . . y que ninguno de los incrédulos del mundo se quedara sin noticia de la Mamá Grande" (p. 147). With the repetition of the key words "taburete," "historia," and "incrédulos," the storyteller reaffirms his position just before releasing the tale, appropriately, not to the conceptualizations of history, but to the rubbish heap from which he garnered his detritus. And this tale, like the detritus which composes it, is as transitory as the transitional place from which it is told: "mañana miércoles vendrán los barrenderos" (p.147).

Since the Mamá Grande, however distorted or traduced by the storyteller's hyperbolic text, is the titular focus of the story, the question that remains to be explored is that of the relation between her and the storyteller. What can be discovered between the lines of the parodic or ironic text of the position, place, situation of this ambiguous woman? The storyteller, like the traditional historian, *does* provide an accounting of the important events in the life of the matriarch, describing these events in the form of biographical references. Thus, "a los 22 años" she assumed power, "hasta los cincuenta años" she was still rejecting passionate suitors (p. 133), "hasta cuando cumplió los 70," her birthday was celebrated by "las ferias más prolongadas y tumultosas de que se tenga memoria" (p.131), and she "vivió en función de dominio durante 92 años," her death breaking a dynastic chain that extended in direct line for descent for two centuries (p. 129). These few temporal references, imprecise, linked on the whole to the body's biological clock rather than the historian's extrinsic calendar, provide the standard of temporality in the story. Only rarely is calendar time evoked: the Mamá Grande dies "un martes del setiembre pasado" (p. 127), and her grandmother confronted a patrol of the Coronel Aureliano Buendía during "la guerra del 1875" (p. 130).

Yet even these scant references to biological or historical time are rendered ambiguous. The date of the Mamá Grande's death fades away during the "horas interminables" of the "blablablá histórico" of the Congress (p. 141) and the "semanas interminables y meses alargados" in which the holy Father waits out the "insomnio sudoroso" (p. 143) prior to the funeral itself. Even the reference to the direct line of descent in the rulers of the kingdom of Macondo is confused by the practice of incest, which "convirtió la procreación en un círculo vicioso" (129). In a story where "interminable" is the preferred adjective of time, it is not surprising that the few numbers we are given become rarified by the atmosphere of eternal waiting.

If the Mamá Grande assumed power at age twenty-two and reigned ninety-two years, if her grandmother, who lived to over one hundred, recalls (at what age?) the war of 1875, what year is it now, in the present of the story? And how can we correlate the amount of time that, logically, must have passed, as suggested by the amazing longevity of these women, with the presence of the veterans of Coronel Aureliano Buendía who have come to the funeral "para solicitar del presidente de la república el pago de las pensiones de guerra que esperaban desde hacía *sesenta años*" [my emphasis] (p. 144)? The reader's struggle to create a historical narrative against the grain of García Márquez's text responds to the appeal of the rhetorical mode of history as a meaningful ordering system in modern life. The narrator tantalizes this desire for order in the readers by providing just a few of the dates and references that Peckham calls "indicators of pastness"[9] in historical narrative. At the same time, the undermining of such indicators, which becomes a covert structural imperative in the text, responds to the narrator's recognition that, in Peckham's words, "such indicators— historically authentic details—are not only symptoms of the rhetorical overdetermination of history. They can also become ends in themselves. . . . "[10] García Márquez's indicators are *underdetermined*; no matter how our rage for order compels us to rearrange the scattered facts, the result is inevitably a recognition of discontinuity. Clearly, time itself is deformed by irony; the sequence which can be derived from the story reveals no law, no access to meaning, no culmination of a teleological historical endeavor.

At the age of twenty-two, María del Rosario Castañeda y Montero becomes the Mamá Grande, a recognized anachronism from the moment of her accession to power. From the day of her father's funeral, she becomes "aquella visión medieval" that "pertenecía entonces no sólo al pasado de la familia, sino al pasado de la nación" (p. 133). The Mamá Grande's reign is indeed a medieval one; fairs mark her birthdays, yet another fair accompanies her long death struggle, her funeral is nothing if not a carnival celebration, and even her picture, as reproduced in the newspapers of the capital, is mistaken for that of one more "nueva reina de belleza" (137). These celebrations follow what Bakhtin has described as the traditional medieval pattern: "the feast is always essentially related to time, either to the recurrence of an event in the natural (cosmic) cycle, or to biological or historic timeliness. . . . [F]easts were linked to moments of crisis. . . . "[11] The storyteller's ambiguity about specific dates and places, his reluctance to impose a fixed form on the hyperbolic material, is highly appropriate to the carnival mood that pervades the story. For, as Bakhtin finds, "carnival was the true feast of time, the feast of becoming, change, and renewal. It was hostile to all that was immortalized and completed."[12] We incredulous readers are distanced in both time and space from these medieval celebrations, but the storyteller's allusive-elusive text makes at least one point clear: the Mamá Grande is the archetypal "reina de belleza," the carnival queen.

The last carnival, that of her funeral, marks the final vanishing of the medieval vision. The moment of crisis signalled by her death and funeral intimates the appearance of a new order; the queen is dead, long live the queen! The Mamá Grande, beauty queen at age twenty-two, virginal still in her final appearance, must yield her place to the new "reinas nacionales de todas las cosas habidas y por haber." The queen who exercised moral hegemony over her subjects is replaced by many queens, queens who, in this new epoch, can now "casarse y ser felices y engendrar y parir muchos hijos" (147).

The narrator's description of the final carnival scene, a description exuberantly rehearsed in the briefer references to the fairs surrounding other key events in the life of the Mamá Grande, culminates in another negative vision, related to but distinct from the now customary negative dialect of ironic hyperbole. Here, the question of representation resurfaces in another form. The narrator (or is this a different, more omniscient persona?) carefully enumerates the list of what the people "no determinó," what "nadie vio," and "nadie advirtió" (p. 146), subverting his words in a carnivalesque or parodic statement, negating his perceptions at the moment of their expression. Yet, this unseen reality becomes, by the author-narrator's acknowledgement of it, part of the readers' reconstruction of the scene. What is real, or what becomes for us the reality of the story, is not so much what is seen as what is told or left untold, a series of events, unseen and unforeseen, swept away with the detritus of history or with the inattention of the excited crowds.[13]

Like the funeral procession, the other great enumerative list of the story, the Mamá Grande's last testament, fills a similar subversive function. In both, orderly progression and a form sanctioned by custom, tradition, and an awareness of dynastic obligations is evoked and then, smoothly, deprived of significance and emptied of substance. Significantly, in the funeral procession, the people ignore all that which does not fit the decorum of the occasion, the list of forgotten sights reaffirmed in the storyeller's negative recounting of them. In an exactly contrary manner, the decorum of the testament invites speculation on the origin of such spectacular riches, and the same eyes which, blinded by the decorum of the funeral, refuse to see the vultures hovering nearby, when encouraged by the decorum surrounding the Mamá Grande's place in society, see all too clearly the reaches of her vast patrimony: "Nadie conocía el origen, ni los límites, ni el valor real del patrimonio, pero todo el mundo se había acostumbrado a creer que la Mamá Grande era dueña de las aguas corrientes y estancadas, llovidas y por llover, y de los caminos vecinales, los postes de teléfono, los años bisiestos y el calor . . . " (pp. 129-30). The narrator, significantly, again uses a negative structure to introduce the hyperbolic list, cuing the reader once more to a subversive reading of the text of the *vox populi*; "todo el mundo" is blinded by magnificence.

Our dependence on the whims of the narrator is nowhere so clear as in this interplay of significance and irrelevant observation, this negative recording of the seen and unseen. While the Mamá Grande's own enumeration of her holdings is, apparently, no less extensive and hyperbolic than that of her townspeole (she requires three hours to detail her vast material holdings), the storyteller dispenses with the general outline of the testament in a single paragraph. He attaches far more importance, however, to the "enumeracíon minuciosa de los bienes morales" to which the Mamá Grande dedicates the last of her fading strength. Her heterogenous list of her moral privileges includes: "los colores de la bandera, . . . las cartas de recomendación, . . . las reinas de belleza, . . . la pureza del lenguaje, . . . el peligro comunista" (pp. 136-37). This spoken list of her invisible patrimony would seem to ratify her family's claim to hereditary custodianship over the signs and symbols that form the heart of official discourse, but the unfinished list, through the subversive agency of the hyperbolic narrator and his incredulous readers, dissolves itself in the moment of its utterance. The nephews, supposed heirs of both material and moral goods, suffer, like the inhabitants of Macondo in *Cien años de soledad* or the lonely old dictator eking out his waning years in *El otoño del patriarca*, from the plague of forgetfulness which descends upon them at the moment of the matriarch's death.

The contagious plague of forgetfulness spreads thoughout the village of Macondo, throughout the entire country, throughout the world, and even reaches past the pages of the text to affect us, its readers. We tend to forget that it is not the power of the Mamá Grande which is absolute but, despite hints as to the constitutive powers of the written word, that of the narrator. This storyteller, who filters the whole of the story through his perception and controls it with his imaginative recreation, is at the same time a curiously reticent figure. Despite his eagerness to define his position in traditional storytelling terms, the narrator remains anonymous, "remains unidentifiable."[14] His position is one of effacement. This ruse, for we must see it as such, of choosing a site and then refusing efforts at situation, defines the storyteller's art which, as suggested earlier, ostensibly chooses one site while mediating (or occupying simultaneously) two places: that of history and that of myth. It is a position he cannot maintain easily; in fact, he could not maintain it at all without the readers' forgetfulness, our unconscious complicity in his ostensibly overt placement of the story's center and in his devious usurpation of that place.

It is impossible to forget, though the reader forgets much, that this story, at once official history and oral tale, also parodically re-enacts both these possibilities and more. As González Echevarría very rightly points out, "If anything, the story is a reflection upon language, told in the clichés of journalese and government prose, written almost exactly as it would have been reported in the newpapers and the mass media."[15] Is there, then, in this adoption of journalistic prose, evidence of a secret alliance of the narrator with history, an alliance which would forward the process of disintegration of the presumed reality of the Mamá Grande? Yes and no. The two speakers (oral storyteller and journalist), the two languages (gossip and journalese), the two places of storytelling (small town stool and capital-city news office) are incompatible ones. Yet, the "almost"—"almost as it would have been reported"—provides the clue for their coexistence, the forgetting and the forgetting about forgetting that eases over both internal and external contradiction. Yes, the journalist as historian subverts reality and converts it into official history. Yes, the storyteller's imaginative reconstruction of the life and death of the Mamá Grande traduces that life and death. At the same time, the narrator engages in an active dialogue with both these possibilities; almost a journalist, not quite a mythic oral storyteller, his dialogic, carnivalesque retelling both reaffirms and subverts the tale and the various points of view for telling it.

This subversive, parodic tale of a carnival queen that "se esfumaba en su propia leyenda" (p. 133) seventy years before the insistently anonymous narrator arrives to set up his stool and tell his story, alerts the reader once again—as in so much of recent Latin American narrative—to a recognition of the representational duplicity of art. It offers, moreover, food for reflection on the theme of the mediation between text and reality, between text and text, and, ultimately, between the reader of the story—audience to gossip, reader of newspapers—and this mediated realm: a reader or a critic equally interpreted by the text as interpreter of it. Yet precisely because of its parodic character, a subliminal recognition of the reality from which the carnival provides only a brief interregnum accompanies this inward-turning movement from text to narrator to reader. The reader must, finally, turn outward again from the dream of carnival to the gritty social reality that is repressed by the dream: "mañana miércoles vendrán los barrenderos y barrerán la basura de sus funerales, por todos los siglos de los siglos" (p. 147). The historians have already arrived in Macondo, and while García Márquez's history is not official history, his historical sodality with the reality of his country is clear.

CORNELL UNIVERSITY

1. Gabriel García Márquez, "Los funerales de la Mamá Grande," in *Los funerales de la Mamá Grande* (Buenos Aires: Editorial Sudamericana, 1973), p. 127. Further references will be contained within the text.

2. The conflict of oral and written (official) history is a continuing concern in the works of García Márquez. In the retelling of the episode of the massacre of the banana workers, for example, *Cien años de soledad* develops the theme in a similar, though somewhat less complex, manner. The omniscient narrator's tacit support for the unofficial versions of the massacre represented in the stories told by José Arcadio Segundo and the unnamed child makes the question of oral history unproblematic in outline, though often unreliable in specific detail—e.g., in the discrepancy about

the number of dead carried by the hallucinatory train. Curiously, García Márquez's fictional account has historically served as an impetus to permit the unwritten episode to be recognized and reinserted into the offical history of Colombia. In *El otoño del patriarca*, the roles of history and oral recounting are somewhat more radically polarized than in either *Cien años* or "Funerales." "History" tells of the immaculate conception of the patriarch, of his incommensurable size, of his heroic accomplishments. Oral legend once more, as in *Cien años*, unearths the reality behind this official mythologizing. In "Funerales," the oral narrator is a less reliable figure than his counterparts in the novels. However, it is precisely the highly qualified mediation between the speaker and his listening (reading) audience that renders this oral (written) version of history so ambiguous.

    3. M. Bakhtin, *The Dialogic Imagination*, trans. Caryl Emerson and Michael Holquist (Univ. of Texas Press, 1981), p. 77.

    4. Luis de Arrigoitia, "Tres cuentos de Gabriel García Márquez," *Revista de Estudios Hispánicos* (Puerto Rico) 6 (1979), 152.

    5. Bakhtin, p. 76.

    6. "Positionality" is defined by Susan Stewart ("Shouts on the Street: Bakhtin's Anti-Linguistics," *Critical Inquiry* 10 [1983]) as "the place of the subject within the social structure, a place where subject and structure are mutually articulated" (277). This approximation is not meant to suggest a nostalgia on the part of the narrator for the certainties of history; rather, the parodic adoption of history's forms is another aspect of the essentially dialogic nature of the tale.

    7. Robert Sims, "The Creation of Myth in García Márquez' 'Los funerales de la Mamá Grande,' " *Hispania* 61 (1978), 21.

    8. David Carroll, "Representation of the End(s) of History: Dialectics and Fiction," *YFS* 59 (1980), 213.

    9. Morse Peckham, *Romanticism and Behavior* (Univ. of South Carolina Press, 1976), p. 61.

    10. Peckham, p. 62.

    11. M. Bakhtin, *Rabelais and His World*, trans. Hélène Iswolsky (Cambridge, MA: MIT, 1968), p. 9.

    12. Bakhtin, *Rabelais*, p. 10.

    13. García Márquez uses this device elsewhere in his fiction. In *Ontoño*, for example, the dictator's mother tries to reveal the "true" story of his conception and birth to her inattentive son, a story which diverges radically from the accepted historical version of his immaculate conception and miraculous birth. Once again, it is the essential that is ignored in this episode of another dying matriarch: Bendición Alvarado "trataba de revelarle al hijo los secretos de familia que no quería llevarse a la tumba, le contaba cómo le echaron su placenta a los cochinos, señor, como fue que nunca pude establecer cúal de tantos fugitivos de vereda había sido tu padre, trataba de decirle para la historia que lo había engendrado de pie . . . , pero él no le ponía atención . . . " (Barcelona: Plaza & Janes, 1975 [135-36]).

    14. Sims, p. 15.

    15. Roberto González Echevarría, "Big Mama's Wake," *Diacritics* 4.2 (1974), 56.

THE DEATH OF ARTEMIO CRUZ:
THE FALSE GODS
AND THE DEATH OF MEXICO

By V. Émilio Castañeda

NO ONE DOUBTS THAT ARTEMIO CRUZ, main character of the novel by Carlos Fuentes, *The Death of Artemio Cruz*,[1] is an incarnation of Mexico: the nation of the past and of the present, Mexico considered materially and spiritually. According to Walter W. Langford, the novel is a study of the fate of Mexico in this century.[2] True, one may say, a study of the present Mexico as a product of its 1910 revolution; Mexico is seen throughout its history, from its independence of Spain, and even farther back, from its original conquest. In his search to interpret the past and his quest for a Mexican identity, Carlos Fuentes deals with what he calls Mexican Mythology[3] and the voice-conscience of Artemio Cruz throughout the novel is but a mere reflection of what could be better called mythical history:

> You will advance down the nave to the conquest of your New World. Heads of angels will pass, prodigal grapevines, many-colored flowers, red globular fruits captured in golden nets, mortized white saints, fright-faced saints of the heaven the Indian created in his own image and likeness: angels and saints with faces of the sun and the moon, . . . with the cruel, empty, useless eyes of idols and the rigorous lineaments of the cycles (31).

Artemio Cruz is Mexico crucifying itself. He is also the symbol of the cyclical condition of the Mexican History which has produced over and over failure in many of its social programs. Artemio is the cross that Mexico carries and becomes its scaf-

---

[1]Carlos Fuentes, *The Death of Artemio Cruz*, transl. Sam Hileman, (New York: Farrar, Straus and Giroux, 1982). References to this edition will be indicated by page number in the text.

[2]Walter M. Langford, *The Mexican Novel Comes of Age* (Notre Dame, Indiana: University of Notre Dame Press, 1971), p. 139.

[3]Langford, p. 130.

folding, over and over the same way and because of the same reasons. Carlos Fuentes focuses in that condition and Artemio Cruz as the sad vision of what has become of the Mexican Revolution of 1910; nevertheless, that is not an exclusive characteristic of Artemio, he is also the symbol of the failure of other social revolutions: Juarez fails, Mexico in its history fails him. Then and now, the now of the novel, the dream becomes a nightmare. For Maximilian and Santa Ana the nightmare also became a reality.

If the focal point of the novel is the Mexican Revolution of 1910, it is only because it is convenient, it is something close at hand for Carlos Fuentes; that revolution is the prototype of all the failed revolutions in Mexico, just as Artemio is the prototype of the many millionaires doing dirty business in Mexico, according to Vasquez Amaral;[4] and in a more specific way Anderson-Imbert refers to Artemio's cancerous putrefaction as the symbolic putrefaction of the social body of his country.[5]

The death of the country is seen clearly when one of the nation's representatives is the symbol of its deaths: just as the murder of six million Jews is understood more clearly in its tragedy when one considers each person separately. The continuous self-examination of Artemio, and that voice, continuous and omniscient in its accusation always in the present, make us aware of the loss. All Mexico — its history, its people, religious and political leaders — lives in the vivid evocation of Artemio's conscience: "what is it called when you give everything in order to receive everything" (262). Destruction and peace are contrasted so that the latter is perceived as a possibility of success:

> you will be the boy-child who goes to the land and finds the land, who leaves his beginings and encounters his destiny, today when death

---

[4]Jose Vasquez Amaral, *The Contemporary Latin American Narrative* (New York: Las Americas Publishing Company, 1970), p. 34.

[5]Enrique Anderson-Imbert, *Spanish American Literature: A History 1910-1963* (Detroit: Wayne State University, 1970), 2nd Ed., Vol. 11, p. 719-720.

is the same as beginning and ending and between the two, in spite of everything, is strung the thread of freedom (271-272).

The fact that Mexico is sacrificed to the cruelty and ambition of Artemio is almost a necessity, as Carlos Fuentes himself explains: "The true vengeance of Montezuma is the permanent feeling of sacrifice in Mexico to be able to maintain the order of the cosmos. That has been the ultimate victory of the Indian world in Mexico."[6] Thus, according to that, Artemio thinks of the advantages brought about by the death of Gonzalo Bernal, and his conclusion is clear: "he thought to himself, the deaths of others is what lengthens our own life" (39). But throughout the novel it becomes very plain that Artemio and those he represents are not ready to be the ones to give their own for others; he says: "I don't care to die as the last sacrifice in a victorious cause" (178).

From very early on in his career, Artemio, as well as Don Gamaliel and the others who benefit personally in Mexico, has learned the art of political accommodation: "Yes, yes, yes: how fortunate that our ideals coincide with our interests" (112), says Artemio's tape-recorded voice. And in the end, those who one time might have considered themselves driven by the hope of a better country, they all come to create a nation of slaves whose revolution was betrayed as Diaz-Lastra states in his article,[7] Carlos Fuentes affirms in the words of his character Gonzalo:

> I don't know whether you remember the beginning. It was such a short time ago, but it seems so far away now. Leaders didn't matter then. It wasn't a war to raise up a caudillo, but to raise up all men (185),

and the contemporary Mexican history teaches us. The Mexican Revolution was not made for all; it elevates one man every six years, it elevates one party perpetually.

[6]Emir Rodriguez Monegal, "Carlos Fuentes," *Homenaje a Carlos Fuentes*, ed. Helmy F. Giacoman (New York: Las Americas Publishing Co., Inc., 1971), p. 30. (English version by the author of this essay).

[7]Alberto Díaz-Lastra, "Carlos Fuentes y la revolución traicionada," *Cuadernos Americanos*, 185 (1965), 369-375.

Artemio has been elevated in two ways, opposite extremes. On the one hand he thinks of himself as being in a high place: "up here where I am now: only here I tell them, is dignity possible, not below in the middle of envy and monotony and standing in lines: all or nothing" (113). On the other hand is the opposite extreme of his human condition, equated in the novel to a failed Christ:

> ...someone has nailed a long cold dagger in my stomach,...someone else has driven a spike in my guts: I reach out my arms, I make an effort to raise myself and there are their hands holding me down ... (211).

In that ambivalent situation Artemio sees himself lowered, in as much as he considers himself to be a god who needs no one to be, and has power without limits: "Heaven that indeed exists and belongs to me. This is to be God, truly" (155). And like the serpent of the Garden of Eden, Artemio is fallaciously truthful, twice expert in lies and falsehoods in his ability to deceive others and himself, because as he says: "we desire the greatest possible good for our country, so long as it accords with our own good" (117).

Those continuous manipulations of Artemio, directly and indirectly related to the moral deaths of his wife's family are a vivid contrast to all the killings, and pillaging for booty which occur in the novel and are repeated in the history of Mexico; Artemio is a Cain, a brother killer. In spite of all such descriptions loaded with propaganda, there is no doubt of the message Carlos Fuentes gives: the Mexican Revolution is attacked because it failed in its vigorous and faithful prosecution of the initial goals, it is attacked because it did not put aside those opportunists who got bigger and thrived in the fight, and took from it most of its initial spirit of reform in favor of the dispossessed. But again, we know from history that the Mexican Revolution of 1910 was not the only one to produce such hindrances and leeches of society; other revolutions in that cyclical history of Mexico had already produced such fruits.

The old woman Ludivina, who enters the novel close to its end, throws in her son's face the evil done in the past, and that man, a cowardly ancestor of Artemio, cannot escape his mother's barrage in a series of questions:

> Know what? That nothing lasts? That power founded on injustice must perish at the hands of injustice? That the enemies we shot, whose tongues we cut out, whose arms we cut off, whose lands we raped so that we could be the great family . . . that some day they would find revenge and destroy us, take from us what was never really ours, what we held by strength and not by right? (290)

The old mother's attack is not only against the cowardly son, it is also the repudiation of a false social program which elevates an individual and not the people. The old mother knows with familiarity all of the lies used to justify wrongdoing. Those lies are also familiar to those who have studied the history of that nation.

In the political arena, the actions of Artemio mirror his double posturing and his ultimate goal: the personal benefit. For Artemio the ideals of the Revolution are now just sketches, like dirty laundry turned inside out before the wash: "That good old Mexican Revolution!" (53), he says when an excuse is needed to defend his interests, to justify his robberies. Thus when the foreigner, the North American character in the novel, tries to make a parallel between the Mexican and the Cuban Revolutions, Artemio does not hesitate for a second and uses his influence — money — so that the result be that the Cuban Revolution is far below the Mexican, not because of the truth of the matter, but because of the need to justify what he Artemio gained in the Mexican (197). In another example of Artemio's callousness when confronted with the human misery which the Revolution had promised to solve, he first decides not to pay a debt he had with a poor Indian community

201

and then he orders the insult: "Tell the manager of the ejido to clamp down on them. That's why I pay him" (156).

In that sad ironic form Carlos Fuentes avoids barely being more explicit and maintains a literary level in his novel. Fuentes controls his reader the same way Artemio controls public opinion; thus Fuentes in one of his many voices, this time outside the work of fiction, speaks at length of the need to impose art to reality, so reality becomes logical: "the type of novel that I want to write is one in which the external reality is valid in terms of the novel itself."[8] That is the kind of thinking which makes of Carlos Fuentes an "elequent and unsubtle"[9] writer as *Time* says and Carlos Fuentes explaining of himself: "I am a putter-inner, not a taker-outer."[10]

One vital part of that — put-in — is the voice "tú" (a Spanish grammatical second person familiar) which speaks to Artemio throughout the novel in the grammatical future tense. That voice is a sort of Virgil guiding Artemio through the twelve circles of his hell, which is nothing else but the other side of the coin-mirror in which Artemio sees himself to hide his daily lies.[11] In that way the options he had and did not take are contrasted to the choices he made, closing thus the door to others. That literary technique allows the reader to be a judge, helped by that voice, of Artemio's deeds during his life, and his behavior towards himself and others. To confirm even more the inescapable judgment to which Carlos Fuentes has guided the reader, a parallel is made between Artemio Cruz and his son Lorenzo, who had gone to fight in the Spanish Civil War; the selfless actions and courageous valor of the son are contrasted to the cowardly and totally selfish actions of the father. Thus when Artemio thinks of his son killed in the Spanish conflict, he thinks of him along with

8Emmanuel Carballo, *19 protagonistas de la literatura mexicana del siglo XX* (Mexico: Empresas Editoriales, S.A., 1965), pp. 429-430. (English version by the author of this essay).

9"The Marxist Myth of Mexico," *Time*, June 5, 1964, p. 104.

10Rodriguez Monegal, p. .43.

11Carballo, p. 440.

those who died to keep him, Artemio, alive, and this time, perhaps without any self interest he says:

> ... thank you because you taught me what my life could be. ... Thank you. I could have died in Perales. I could have died with that unknown soldier. I could have died in that empty room, in front of that man. I survived. You died. Thank you (235, 236, 237).

But that lifestyle of selfish acts and cowardice had been chosen earlier in his life after the death of the only person perhaps loved by Artemio. The thought of that death stays within him always and he tries to occupy his mind making money, taking control of others, being proud to be the one mover, the one who controls the rest of those poor who still find consolation and strength in the Church; he is a god, as his mind tells him continually: "This is to be God, isn't it? to be feared and hated, this is indeed to be God, isn't it?" (235).

In the two sides of the choice there always will be something or someone to put a limit to Artemio's life. In the same manner in which he killed or allowed others to kill or die, the actions of Catalina, his wife, are a reciprocal counterpart of his life: she is the one who morally-spiritually and almost physically, kills him (48). This other side of the coin is the presentation of Catalina as a possible path for Artemio's redemption; as Carlos Fuentes says of that relationship, if the two had opened up to each other and spoken openly, Artemio would have done things differently, would not have lived as he did, would not have died as he did;[12] but of course that option had been discarded when Artemio had earlier decided to marry Catalina, and then, she already had decided to do him in in order to avenge many wrongdoings.

In the death of Artemio many other deaths take place also: the death of Mexico, the death of a corrupted and adulterated God — the Church represented in the priest who is at Artemio's bedside is as pale and deathbound as Artemio —, the

12Ibid., pp. 441-442.

death of good intentions, the death of the Mexican Revolution.

In the episodes of the novel which take place in the present, Artemio's consciousness is keenly aware of his smell of rotting matter, he distinguishes the smells of the physical functions of his body, and receives also the smell of incense (church) from the priest, all sensations and smells mixed up in an indication of ruin and putrefaction; the sacred and the profane in a symbolic reminder of gods, but gods in decadence. That strong smell of incense which Artemio identifies so clearly is vividly contrasted with the smells of his own body in cruel paradoxical impotence. Too late the awareness of a possible salvation! Too late the awareness that his body would have an end! Both the body and the church impotent when most needed!

During his moments of lucidity in that deathbed, when the desire of continued life, good moments — happy moments, is stronger, Artemio angrily rejects the smell of the hated priest and his rites and pantomime, because of what religion had done to him and the country, yet stronger over the other smells is the acrid urine smell of his loss of bladder functions, and in that mixture Artemio makes a connection between past and present and is able to single out, and put blame in past actions because they are the cause of present conditions, thus his responsibility gets heavier. In one of his memories of the past, Artemio sees himself in the war and subconsciously he links that past action with his present situation: "His forehead wrinkled as he thought about the familiar death of brave men who die with a wet spot on their uniforms at the crotch." (182), and he dies with that image of the past-present, a probable subconscious desire of redemption in its last accusation.

Carlos Fuentes gives in his novel a glimpse of a future which begins and is a promise for the nation, but that glimpse is so short that one tends to forget it. The character Gloria, the girl who comes to Artemio in his deathbed and is quickly taken away, is perhaps the symbol of a new generation who will remember the past with its many wrongs and selfishness, who will remember that dream which is about to end, and will have a strong repugnance to what it embodies: symbolically the corrupt nation dying, left alone so that the new nation which begins will not be tainted; therefore the new Glory, with a promising future ahead, is separated from that old glory which has to die.

In his novel, Carlos Fuentes suppresses the before and the after, and according to Octavio Paz, there is no historical time in it, "there is no succession, all the historical times and places coincide and come together in that instant when Artemio Cruz questions his life."[13] Nevertheless, there are moments in the book, when the reader is aware that Artemio does perceive time as sequential and causing in its passing, subsequent events: Artemio's memories of the past are clearly at times, stabs at his conscience. But in the final analysis, that hieroglyphic which is Artemio, as Octavio Paz calls it, is not solved; that road of alternatives has to be walked all over again. Walter M. Langford, speaking of Fuentes' work affirms that it has meaning only in terms of life, since death, the death of Artemio is seen only as negation of life.[14]

If one takes the novel as simply a novel, Langford's statement is absolute, but if one takes Artemio as symbol of a nation, then the conclusion is inescapable: the only salvation for that country is the human spirit. God is lost for Artemio, religion has no meaning, others count egotistically in so far as they benefit oneself materially, so the only hope of a better future for Mexico is in that prophetic-cryptic voice "tú" which speaks to Artemio throughout the novel, and close to the end tells him "you will reach out your hand, . . . you will reach out your hand" (241). The hope of a future action! But the ultimate decision is always ours.

[13]Octavio Paz, "La mascara y la transparencia," Homenaje a Carlos Fuentes, p. 19 (English version by the author of this essay).
[14]Langford, p. 147.

Gringo viejo / The Old Gringo:
"The Rest Is Fiction"

Jonathan Tittler

UNTRANSLATABILITY IS by now a critical commonplace. Whether we speak of moving from one language to another, as from Spanish to English, or moving from raw experience into any symbolic medium (language is of course but one of the more familiar sign systems available to us), despite appearances or reveries to the contrary, nothing emerges quite so clearly from the attempt to bridge the difference between the original and translated versions as the difference itself. When, in Cabrera Infante's *Three Trapped Tigers,* at the end of the long verbal joyride that constitutes "Bachata," Silvestre equates translation with betrayal, he is certainly referring to this very phenomenon.[1] Borges's spoofs on the notion of originality in *Crónicas de Bustos Domecq* (Chronicles of Bustos Domecq) and "El inmortal" (The Immortal) as well as Octavio Paz's meditation in *Literatura y literalidad* (Literature and Literalness) on the reduction implicit in translation, and Walter Benjamin's inquiry into "The Task of the Translator," likewise evoke the ultimate vanity of trying to render anything in terms other than its own.[2]

It should come as no surprise, then, that a fictional work such as Carlos Fuentes's *Gringo viejo* does not maintain a word-to-word (or even page-to-page) correspondence with its English translation, *The Old Gringo,* even if—or especially if—one of the co-translators is the author himself.[3] The author of a work such as *Gringo* (the one word which both titles bear in common), with its perspicacious account of the cultural barriers separating Latin America from its Anglo neighbors to the north (as well as a few aspects held in common), must be sensitive to the needs and desires of readers in these respective linguistic and cultural zones. Despite the inevitable divergence between the two texts, much may be gained from scrutinizing the particulars of the case. After all, not every difference in meaning constitutes a loss, and no two losses are identical. The questions I shall be asking at the outset are: In what significant ways do the versions differ and how do their differences potentially affect the text's meaning for or impact on its readers? The problematics arising from Fuentes's reading of himself—broadly formulated as the relation of history to fiction—leads us to consider not only some persistent motifs in the author's ample repertoire but also several matters of import to contemporary critics and general readers alike.

The textual features in question involve, first, a half-page appendage to the Spanish-language version, located at the end of the novel and bearing the sobriquet "NOTA DEL AUTOR" (Author's Note, 189). In it one finds a very brief sketch of the novel's historical setting: Ambrose Bierce, the misanthropic American journalist and short-story writer, old and tired, left some letters for his friends in which he stated his preference as to the matter in which he would die. Rejecting falling down the stairs as an unworthy end, he characterized dying before a Mexican firing squad, in contrast, as a form of euthanasia. The following paragraph, on which we shall concentrate and from which this paper draws its title, reads: "Entró a México en noviembre y no se volvió a saber de él. El resto es ficción." (He crossed into Mexico in November and was not heard of again. The rest is fiction.) There is also a concluding sentence that announces where and when the book's writing process began and ended (a surprising twenty-year span ending in 1984), and an italicized tag that reads "*México, febrero de 1985*" (Mexico City, February 1985). Apparently, some months separate the writing of the Author's Note from the end of the novel proper.

This entire document is missing from the English-language version (such a formulation is preferable to "translation"; in private conversations Fuentes has revealed that Harriet's and the Old Gringo's dialogue lines were written first in English, a datum that should exempt the English-language version from the subordinate status to which translations are normally relegated). Instead—and here is the other main feature to consider —we are regaled with an extra chapter (number 23), whose entire contents consist of the following words: "Now she sits alone and remembers." To be sure, there are other textual differences, including an abundance of parentheses and italics in the English version and an inverse ordering of chapters 18 and 19, which I hope to study at some other time. For now I wish only to isolate these final, most telling differences.

"The rest is fiction": What are some of the assumptions that permit one to make that sort of statement? To begin with, of course, one presupposes the existence of a discourse that is veridical, with a verifiable historical referent. Second, there is posited a binary distinction between such a discourse and another sort, not so anchored in the world beyond books and commonly called fictional. And third, it is implied that the very words conveying both the historical discourse and its fictional other or supplement are themselves part of that same historical discourse, that is, they denote something observable and susceptible of corroboration. In such a tidy common-sense scheme, the Author's Note may be taken as an informative aid in the Spanish-language reader's contextualization of the novel, allowing him or her better to appreciate the cultural significance of the novel's titular figure. Bierce's status as a pundit on the U.S. scene, conversely, would thus explain the absence of a need for such explanatory material in the New York edition. Instead, U.S. readers would be expected to benefit from a reminder that the entire novel is sedentary, recollective. Knowing that it takes place within the memory of the female protagonist allows an enhanced sense of spatial and temporal closure, as well as of formal symmetry.[4]

Let me not be cunning: what follows is largely dedicated to showing the invalidity of the above scheme. A close reading of *Gringo* reveals that a face-value acceptance of the categorical language in the Author's Note fails to account for too many of the novel's textual features. A familiarity with Fuentes's general concerns as a narrator and thinker, moreover, points toward a radically different understanding of both the passage in question and the nature of the rapport between fiction and history in the abstract.

An alternative explanation of the same passage would take account of the following complexities: 1) History is rife with fictionality. Bierce's letters, for instance, cannot be accurate or complete reflections of his state of mind. Surely such lapidary statements as "Oh, to be a gringo in Mexico; that is euthanasia" smack of literature, of the writerly desire to shock with uncommon concepts uncommonly expressed. 2) The Old Gringo's view of Mexico during its great upheaval is mythical and idealized, as romantic as is his desire to determine autonomously his own destiny. For both Harriet and him, Mexico represents an alternative to the known, routinized, historical world of the United States. Mexico is exotic and fresh, somehow authentic, a place where glory and individual self-realization can still be attained. Mexico is the timeless land that Juan Dahlmann visits in Borges's "The South" and The Final Island to which Marini aspires in Cortázar's "The Island at Noon."[5] Which is to say that, for those from north of the border, Mexico is the space of myth, of fiction, the locus of their dreams. 3) The thumbnail biography Fuentes provides of Bierce is so terse as to constitute a caricature, a stylized and distorted construct that both reduces (in the number of features it attributes to a figure) and exaggerates (those few aspects then acquire disproportionately great importance). Calling such a discourse "historical" would surely degrade that term beyond recognition. 4) The authorial voice that conveys the stereotyped vision in the Author's Note, alleged to be unproblematically historical, is neither the same as the novel's narrator (whose tone is decidedly other) nor, obviously, a direct presentation of Fuentes the man. We witness, rather, a masterful performance of the author "playing himself," a gambit that entails donning a translucent mask, reminiscent of the epilogue in *The Hydra Head*.[6] There the novel closes with a resonant *boutade* on "straight talk," as if one might somehow cut through the complex mechanisms of narrative technique, halt the text's interplay of signifiers, and penetrate to the heart of what the work is about. 5) "The rest is fiction" has another sense that we are perhaps too eager to overlook, but should not in the context of the games with mirrors and masks being played in the Author's Note. The rest, remainder, or supplement—part of the standard baggage of post-structuralist discourse—

is here equated with fiction. But in what sense? In that of a discourse distinct from non-fiction, that which recounts what "official" histories dare not or will not tell. But that sense should not stand to the exclusion of the notion of the "rest" as a critical fiction as well. Supplementarity is a metaphor of almost ubiquitous currency that enables attentive readers to stand both within and without the tradition of Western metaphysics, to go beyond the mere logocentric understanding of texts, to "overstand" them (the term is Wayne Booth's), to unravel and dismantle them.[7] Ever conscious of the intellectual winds, Fuentes gives evidence here of having anticipated our critical moves and, as it were, turned deconstruction upon itself. By creating a supplement (the Author's Note) which portrays the rest of the novelistic corpus as a supplement (*the rest,* that which is neither historical nor critical), he puts to us the undecidable question as to where the margins lie and from where our fiction-ridden discourse may emanate.

These considerations mandate our abandoning the simple antinomial scheme advanced earlier. But how do we know they invoke more valid criteria than the first approximation? To answer that question, and mindful that the Author's Note seeks to be both a part of and apart from the novel (constituting in itself a structure antagonistic to discrete, absolute dualities), let us look at some of the ways in which history and fiction interact in *Gringo.* That interaction requires us to address questions of literary genre, of the ways in which fiction permeates history even as it exhibits its fictiveness, and of the historical models proposed within the fiction. After dealing with these issues we shall be in a better position to assess the nature of the difference between *Gringo viejo* and *The Old Gringo.*

Gringo belongs to that sub-genre known as the historical novel, a relatively long narrative work set within a recognizable framework, some of whose characters, individual traits, or events may be taken from historical actuality. The limiting adjective "historical" tells us that the work is a hybrid, a product of both knowledge and imagination with respect to a period in the past, one of whose principal attractions lies in the reader's uncertainty as to which elements are factual and which invented. Quite salient in this regard is Fuentes's extremely delicate handling of his protagonist's identity. Although there are many insinuations as to the continuity between the striking figure of the Old Gringo and the celebrated writer Ambrose Bierce, only once in the novel proper, and very late in its development at that, is that identity made explicit. Whereas Pancho Villa is decidedly historical and Harriet Winslow is utterly fictional, the historicity of Bierce/Gringo remains tenuous, equivocal. This ambiguity as to historicity is reflected also in the pivotal character's dual occupation as journalist and short-story writer.

Fiction has of course long taken for granted its right to appropriate history for its own purposes—Roa Bastos's treatment of Doctor Francia in *I the Supreme,* Carpentier's portrayal of Henri Christophe and Mackendal in *The Kingdom of This World,* and Fuentes's recreation of Felipe II and company in *Terra Nostra* are only three recent examples, but one can easily cite the medieval Spanish *Poem of the Cid* without stretching the claim.[8] It is hardly noteworthy, then, that names such as LaFollette, Sinclair, Taft, Pershing, Roosevelt, Wilson, Hearst, and others of early twentieth-century U.S. history should appear as background references in *Gringo.* Less conventional, however, is the commingling of these figures with their Mexican contemporaries: Carranza, Obregón, Zapata, Madero, and Villa. The implicit question raised by this juxtaposition is why these heroic figures of the Mexican Revolution are not part of U.S. history (and, of course, why those sons of Manifest Destiny are not part of Mexican history). And, consequently, how is our understanding of our own past affected by the others' view, by a vision, such as Arroyo's, of the U.S. as the foreign and distant and curious, eccentric, marginal world of the Yankees who did not enjoy good food or violent revolution or women in bondage, or beautiful churches, and broke with all tradition just for the sake of it, as if there were good things only in the future and in novelty (128)? When we claim something is historically verifiable, to which histories (plural and relativized) are we referring?

At times, in contrast to these interdisciplinary matters, the novel partakes of the quintessentially literary. Occasionally such moments obtain through highly sophisticated and self-conscious devices, such as the contrived hall of mirrors, which suddenly gives the ingenuous characters their first full-length view of themselves. Or the numerous, emphatically posited, psycho-analytically inspired substitutions, repetitions, and reversals among paternal and filial figures (Arroyo replaces Harriet's bland lover Delaney as well as the Gringo's lost son, the Gringo is both lover and father figure for Harriet and is eventually buried in her father's grave, and so on).[9] Else-where, however, one finds the more facile techniques of Arroyo's transparent naming (he is characterized as an "arroyo fluido y parejo de sexo") and of the black horse he melodramatically mounts alongside the Gringo's white steed. Or the soaring lyricism (largely preserved in the translation) in passages such as the following amorous description: "a sea of slow cool tides and sudden flashes of heat from the unsuspected depths where an octopus could move in senseless fear and clouds of black sand would funnel upward, warming the waters with the suddenly revealed fever of the unmoving, breaking the mirrors of the cool sea, splintering the surface of reality" (127). Despite the novel's frequent incursions into and out of the historical, there is never a moment when the reader loses sight of the text's intimate conjunction with the fictive.

Yet that markedly fictional reality is taken very seriously, both by the characters and by the solemn-voiced narrator. Paradoxically enough, the novelistic universe acquires opacity—credible depth and texture—through the incorporation of multiple layers of human experience, including

211

dreams, phantasmatic presences, and myths, all of which elements involve a degree of fictionalizing, of image making. Most representative of the way in which fiction permeates existence in *Gringo* is the role of memory. The entire novel, of course, is related doubly in retrospect, both with respect to the narrator and to Harriet. Without Harriet's desire to recover her past, to recreate a sense of Mexican time, love, and death, the work would be drastically different and impoverished. We have no reason to impugn the narrator's powers of recollection (which seem conventionally absolute), but what about Harriet's? The novel itself asks that question by juxtaposing her literate memory to Arroyo's unschooled, oral powers of retention. The indeterminate accuracy of Harriet's reminiscences is further underscored by the disclosure that both Harriet and the Old Gringo have invented aspects of their past—he, the episode of his father's fighting for the Confederacy in the U.S. Civil War, and she, her father's supposedly heroic death in Cuba during the War of 1898 between Spain and the United States. Memory is of course the element common to history and stories, *la historia* and *las historias* in Spanish. In the case of *Gringo,* fiction, in addition to giving represented reality a palpable concreteness, shows the limits of history, memory, and narrative—revealing the ultimately unrecoverable, unseizable, unknowable nature of the past, the present, and the imaginary.

In two of its leading characters the novel proposes, through opposition, competing models for a predominant vision of history. General Tomás Arroyo, a vehicle and perhaps a victim of history in one of its most violent manifestations, has a linear, progressive view of history. It is his hope to bring about an abrupt and fundamental change in Mexican history, to snap the tyrannical line of the dictatorship of Porfirio Díaz, and to usher in an era of revolutionary social justice. Harriet Winslow, a pragmatic, proper, Protestant woman, has a cyclical, deterministic view of history. Her fear that not only Mexico but all of history is unchangeable perhaps motivates her decision not to have children, thereby foreclosing a repetition of her experience. In this connection the differences in the versions of the novel become most significant. The English-language edition (which returns to the leitmotif "Now she sits alone and remembers") closes upon itself and in more ways than one gives Harriet the last, fatalistic word. The Spanish-language edition, in contrast, refuses to inscribe a neatly closed arc, leaping directly from the novel's anecdote into the unsettled space of history occupied by the Author's Note.[10] Accepting the Spanish version and choosing Arroyo's linear model—albeit interrupted—implies sacrificing Harriet's vision of cyclical repetition. Favoring Harriet's circle, conversely, means disregarding Arroyo's vision of unique human experience and change wrought by action. Is the Spanish version of the novel the original, authoritative one? Did Fuentes alter his view of history in the time it took to work out an English text with Margaret Sayers Peden? And should we not also give credence to the atomistic, disintegrated perspective of the iconoclastic Gringo, or perhaps the four-stage spiral synthesis elaborated in Vico's *New Science?*[11] My focus constrains me from going into detail, but many of Fuentes's other fictions (*The Death of Artemio Cruz, A Change of Skin,* and *Terra Nostra* principal among them) and several essays in *Tiempo mexicano* (Mexican Time) indicate his validation of the last, Vichien alternative.[12] It is sufficient to note that the binary opposition between Harriet and Arroyo, like that between the past and the present, man and woman, Mexico and the United States, Bierce the journalist and Bierce the fabulator, and so on, is only the starting point for a dialectic whose prime aim is to transcend dualism itself.

In the end, it is tempting to say that Fuentes has misread himself not once but twice (first in the Author's Note and then in its elimination) and that the English version of *Gringo,* in eschewing ceaseless internal tension for a reassuring but astonishingly pat resolution, just means less. At once a decapitation and—perhaps—a capitulation to market forces, removing the Author's Note appears to have an impact that can best be appreciated if we try to imagine Cervantes's *Don Quixote,* the novel's most frequently mentioned textual archetype, with one or another of its prologues expunged. And yet, decapitation is not the same as lobotomy and need not render a text inert. Without the glaring lack in *The Old Gringo,* it is unlikely, for instance, that the Author's Note in *Gringo viejo* would have acquired sufficient relief to provoke the foregoing analysis. Taking our cue from the self-deconstructed, decentered, multiply encoded text we have fondly dubbed *Gringo* (a term of both rancorous derision and no little respect), we should resist the temptation to take that always premature decision to dismiss a problematical text or fragment. For in the very effaced supplement, the absent "rest," one has the telltale sign of the untranslatability we so readily accept as a point of departure.

NOTES

1 Guillermo Cabrera Infante, *Three Trapped Tigers,* trans. Donald Gardner and Suzanne Jill Levine in collaboration with the author (New York: Harper & Row, 1971), 481.

2 Jorge Luis Borges and Adolfo Bioy Casares, *Crónicas de Bustos Domecq* (Buenos Aires: Editorial Losada, 1967); Jorge Luis Borges, "El inmortal," in *El Aleph* (Buenos Aires: Alianza/Emecé, 1971 [1949]), 7-28; Octavio Paz, *Literatura y literalidad* (Barcelona: Tusquets Editores, 1971); Walter Benjamin, "The Task of the Translator," in *Illuminations,* trans. Harry Zohn, ed. and intro. by Hannah Arendt (New York: Schocken Books, 1969), 69-82.

3 Carlos Fuentes, *Gringo viejo,* (Mexico City: Fondo de Cultura Económica, 1985); Carlos Fuentes, *The Old Gringo,* trans. Margaret Sayers Peden and the author (New York: Farrar Straus Giroux, 1985). All page references to the

novel correspond to the English-language version and will appear parenthetically in my text. There is also a British edition of the English translation (London: Deutsch, 1986) that does not differ significantly from the U.S. version treated herein.

4 Since giving an earlier, oral version of this essay I have discovered that in some printings of the first Mexican edition a *fe de erratas* has been incorporated that seeks to reintroduce a twenty-third chapter into the book. Such a gesture, as it reinscribes the notion of intentionality into critical exegesis, clearly threatens to erode the value I ascribe to the absence. Whether future editions follow the printer's trivializing lead or, in view of the novel's favorable reception by the reading public, accept the meanings reasonably imputed to the text as first discovered, remains to be seen.

5 Jorge Luis Borges, "The South," in *Ficciones,* ed. and intro. by Anthony Kerrigan (New York: Grove, 1962), 167-74; Julio Cortázar, "The Island at Noon," in *All Fires the Fire and Other Stories,* trans. Suzanne Jill Levine (New York: Pantheon, 1973), 90-98.

6 Carlos Fuentes, *The Hydra Head,* trans. Margaret Sayers Peden (New York: Farrar Straus Giroux, 1978), 291-92.

7 Wayne C. Booth, *Critical Understanding: The Powers and Limits of Pluralism* (Chicago: Univ. of Chicago Press, 1979).

8 Augusto Roa Bastos, *I the Supreme,* trans. Helen Lane (New York: Knopf, 1986); Alejo Carpentier, *The Kingdom of This World,* trans. Harriet de Onís (New York: Collier, 1957); Carlos Fuentes, *Terra Nostra,* trans. Margaret Sayers Peden (New York: Farrar Straus Giroux, 1976); *The Poem of the Cid,* trans. Lesley Byrd Simpson (Berkeley and Los Angeles: Univ. of California Press, 1957).

9 Another level of meaning of the same phrase, to be sure, may be parodic. "The rest is fiction" enacts a playful inversion on the cliché "the rest is history," normally an anecdotal tag where conclusions have become knowledge too common to bear repeating. In this sense the phrase thus serves also as a post-facto confirmation of the ironic, acutely self-reflexive status of such narrative motifs as the mirrors and the seemingly patent Freudian archetypes.

10 See note 4.

11 Giovanni Battista Vico, *The New Science of Giambattista Vico,* trans. from the 3rd ed., 1744, by Thomas Goddard Bergin and Max Harold Fisch (Ithaca: Cornell Univ. Press, 1948).

12 Carlos Fuentes, *The Death of Artemio Cruz,* trans. Sam Hileman (New York: Farrar Straus Giroux, 1964); Carlos Fuentes, *A Change of Skin,* trans. Sam Hileman (New York: Farrar Straus Giroux, 1968); Carlos Fuentes, *Terra Nostra,* op. cit.; Carlos Fuentes, *Tiempo mexicano* (Mexico: Joaquín Mortiz, 1971).

When Unamuno, in his Life of Don Quixote and Sancho, comes to the chapter in which the priest and the barber scrutinize the gentleman's library, he dismisses the episode with these brief and sententious lines: "All of which is literary criticism, which should be of little concern to us. It is about books, not life. We will omit it." It is not our purpose to analyze the Basque author's twisted interpretation of a liberal and humanist thought totally contrary to his own (which, I might add, has much more in common with Quevedo's world view than with Cervantes's). Others have already done that analysis, and we refer the reader to their work.[1] We will only make the observation that when he expresses himself in terms of "life" and "books" inside the literary space of the novel, Unamuno seems to fall into the mind-set of the vulgar realism which he so rightly detested. When life enters a book, it is immediately transformed into literature, and we should judge it as such. Actually, the sixth chapter ("The Inquisition in the Library")[2] plays a fundamental role in the novel, to the extent that without it, the Quixote would not exist. What Unamuno omitted was nothing less than Cervantes's marvelous gallery of mirrors, that game at once destructive and creative with respect to the different literary codes of his time. Unamuno's error once again demonstrates--as if it were still necessary--his total insensitivity to a work as different as it is infinitely superior to his own.

A novel, let us remember, is not tied solely to the social and historical context out of which it is born. It also, and above all, responds to the laws of the genre to which it pertains: to the requirements of its own discourse. Although for an appreciable majority of novelists, critics, and readers what is most important is its relation with the "reality" it pretends to represent--novel as a mirror of life's path, characters destined to compete with those whose civil records are on file--the novel's link with the body of works published previously is always stronger and more decisive than that which connects it to "reality." The Quixote is precisely the best proof that a text cannot be studied in isolation, as if it had come from nowhere or were a simple product of the world, but rather must be examined in connection and correspondence with other texts, with a whole system of values and meanings which already exists. As the Russian formalists said in their day, the function of every work is in its relation to the rest. Every work is a differential sign.

Cervantes's great novel is an extremely complicated literary discourse which is clarified and ultimately makes sense because of its links with the literary models of the epoch. This intertextuality plays a primary role in the work, just as it does in the French and English literature it most influenced, from Sterne to Flaubert. Chapter six permits Cervantes to introduce literary discussion into the lives of his characters and launch his theory within the confines of the novel itself. As is true for a sector of contemporary novelistic production--which "cervantizes" without realizing it--characterized by its suspicion of traditional "forms" and "contents," the Quixote is, simultaneously, criticism and creation, writing and a questioning of writing, a text which constructs itself and never ceases its self-evaluation.

But the relation of Cervantes's novel with the literary corpus of his time is not limited, as Unamuno leads us to believe, to the very important sixth chapter; on the contrary, it manifests itself from the prologue to the end of the work. Américo Castro saw this clearly when he wrote:

> Much has been said about the literary sources of the Quixote, and very little about the presence and function of books within the

216

creative process of the work itself. The acts of reading or writing are tasks of many of the characters who populate the pages of the Quixote, tasks without which some of them would not exist.... It could be said that the Quixote is a book forged out of and derived from the active material of other books. The first part essentially comes out of the books read by Don Quixote; the second part is, in turn, an outcome of the first: it does not limit itself to the continued narration of new events, but rather incorporates into the life of the character the awareness that that life already is the subject of a published narrative. The Don Quixote of the second part continues himself, as well as the literary interpretation of Cide Hamete.[5]

With his usual vision, long before the publication in the West of the formalists' discoveries, the author of El pensamiento de Cervantes was able to perceive the decisive role of intertextuality in the Quixote and of the play of the written word in the psyche of the characters. As we will see, within the constraints of this brief essay, Cervantes's masterpiece illustrates better than any other novel the principle formulated by Shklovsky, which maintains that every literary work "is created in parallel and opposition to some model. New form does not appear in order to express a new content but rather to replace an old form which has lost its aesthetic character."[4] In the prologue of the novel, Cervantes suggests that we contemplate it as a new and original literary work which on the one hand activates all or almost all of the latent possibilities of novelistic discourse, and on the other proposes a unique combination, irreducible to any previous model.

Some Cervantes scholars, following in the footsteps of Unamuno in his efforts to disassociate the Quixote from its creator and consider him an unschooled genius, tell us, as does Mr. Rodríguez Marín, that the book contains many excellent features, but "its own creator was unable to see them.... It has been we readers who have discovered the best of the great book's treasure." This, of course, is ridiculous, and the saddest part is that the author reveals nothing except his own incredible presumption when he indirectly takes credit for "discovering" the hidden treasures of the book. Nobody was more aware than Cervantes of the value and originality of the literary object he offered his readers. Just as Juan Ruiz boasts about writing "strange verses" because he was the first poet to use the zéjel with internal rhyme of the Arab poets, Cervantes defines himself as a "rare inventor" and takes care to indicate from the beginning that his book is absolutely different from those which at that time are being published and are gaining public favor. Starting with the prologue, he begins an imaginary dialogue with the common reader, designed to emphasize the sign which would differentiate his novel from the literary system of his time.

The Quixote does not reflect only, as is commonly said, the contradiction and dialectical play between reality and fiction, being and appearance, through the prism of its hero's madness. That opposition-- inns/castles, windmills/giants, basin/helmet, flourmills/fortresses, etc. --is, of course, extremely important, but it shouldn't distract us from the capital fact that Cervantes brings us into a fantastic gallery of mirrors, a subtle web of signs corresponding with opposing realities. We are reminded of the specificity of the literary phenomenon at every step as we penetrate the book's verbal labyrinth. While in ordinary communication the language code is taken for granted, to the point that the speakers use it automatically and put it, so to speak, in parentheses, literary language is distinctive in that it offers us some degree of information about its own structure. In the former case, the linguistic structure is simply a mode of transmitting information; in the latter, the literary structure puts emphasis on its own message, rather than on the referent, and the peculiar thing is precisely the information offered to us about its own construction:

> So he decided not to insert any tales, either detached or con-
> nected, in this second part, but to include some similar episodes
> arising out of the actual happenings themselves; and even these
> should be sparing and no longer than their bare narration required.
> So, being confined and enclosed within the narrow limits of the
> story, though he has the skill, the knowledge and the capacity for
> dealing with the whole universe, he begs that his pains shall not
> be under-valued, and that he shall be praised not for what he
> writes, but for what he has refrained from writing.   (746)

Like the author--or authors--of the work, the characters of the
Quixote demonstrate great concern with language and the manner in which
the facts are related. In one example, we find Don Quixote criticizing
Sancho for violating the language's code and the rules of good narrative
discourse:

> "Go on with your story, Sancho," said Don Quixote, "and leave
> the road we are to follow to me."
> "I tell you, then," Sancho resumed, "that in a village in
> Estremadura there was once a shepherd--a goatherd I should say,
> for he kept goats--and this shepherd or goatherd, as my story
> tells, was called Lope Ruiz. Now this Lope Ruiz fell in love with
> a shepherdess called Torralba, which shepherdess called Torralba
> was the daughter of a rich herdsman; and this rich herdsman..."
> "If you tell your story that way, Sancho," said Don Quixote,
> "and repeat everything you have to say twice over, you will not
> be done in two days. Tell it consequentially, like an intelligent
> man, or else be quiet."
> "The way I'm telling it," replied Sancho, "is the way all stories
> are told in my country, and I don't know any other way of telling
> it. It isn't fair for your worship to ask me to get new habits."
> (152-53)

Far from limiting itself to the scrutiny of Don Quixote's library by
the priest and the barber, the literary discussion occupies whole chapters
throughout the work: in the first part, the innkeeper mentions a suitcase
"forgotten" by a guest in which two chivalric romances and the history of
the Gran Capitán, Gonzalo Fernández de Córdoba, are found. This device,
very commonly used in the narrative of the epoch to insert new stories,
provokes an extremely interesting discussion about the concept of
verisimilitude. The debate is reopened later with a defense by the canon
of what is artistically credible and a response from the priest which
expands upon his earlier point of view. During this exchange, the canon
criticizes the structure of the books of chivalry in such a way as to
emphasize the contrast between them and the wise and harmonious architecture of the object Cervantes offers us. In the second part, we find a
discussion with the gentleman in green about poetic art and a curious
debate about translations and the art of translating when Don Quixote,
during his stay in Barcelona, visits a printing house:

> "Yet I dare swear," said Don Quixote, "that you are not appreciated
> by the world, which is always loath to reward intellect and merit.
> What abilities are lost here! What talents neglected! What virtues
> unappreciated! But yet it seems to me that translating from one
> tongue into another, unless it is from those queens of tongues
> Greek and Latin, is like viewing Flemish tapestries from the wrong
> side; for although you see the pictures, they are covered with
> threads which obscure them so that the smoothness and gloss of the

fabric are lost; and translating from easy languages argues no talent or power of words, any more than does transcribing or copying one paper from another. By that I do not mean to imply that this exercise of translation is not praiseworthy, for a man might be occupied in worse things and less profitable occupations." (877)

The most interesting controversy is perhaps the one in chapter forty-eight of the first part, in which the canon, after finishing his criticism of the unbelievable parts of the books of chivalry, attacks the "plays being presented these days," that is to say, Lope de Vega. As Vicente Llorens has noted, Cervantes's attack on the books of chivalry would be disproportionate if it didn't also imply a critique of Lope's plays, which perpetuated the anachronistic ideals of the Amadis, presenting them to the public as contemporary and applicable values in the context of that time.[5] In addition, the canon's assault on Lope's popular art points out the opposition of Cervantes's subtle literary engineering to the literary canon of the epoch, affirming, in this way, its specific kind of "difference."

The dense correlation of the Quixote with the literature of its century manifests itself on all levels of the work, from the most superficial to the most profound. On the one hand, the book is full of allusions to and quotes from the Romancero, the books of chivalry, the Latin poets, Ariosto, Garcilaso, etc.; on the other, it presents itself to us in its totality as an exclusively literary object, not as a slice of life or of "reality." Cervantes doesn't tell us, as does Galdós in the prologue to Misericordia or Cela in that of La colmena, that he found the plot of the novel in life, basing himself on observations and studies of his model. Cervantes says he found his story in notebooks written in Arabic by one Cide Hamete Benengeli, for which he paid a few reales and which the last author--that is to say, the compiler--had translated into a Moorish Castilian for a hundred pounds of raisins and two bushels of wheat. The work's different artifices appear enveloped in mist, and it can be rightfully said that the entire fabric of the novel is based on the dialogue of "the authors" with a "second author"--the compiler, who, in turn, discovers the work of a third--Cide Hamete Benengeli, who is called nevertheless "first author"--a work translated and adapted by a fourth author--since this last one tells us on occasion that he doesn't limit himself to the role of a translator and takes on the tasks of censor and even explicator--with which the reader is lost in a labyrinth of conjecture as to the identity of the narrators, confronting a text of a text of another text: the same technique of infinite inclusion of Russian dolls or Chinese boxes.

One of the most notable particularities of the novel is that its characters are themselves and are also the literary projections of one of the narrative genres then in vogue. The gentleman from La Mancha has been influenced by literature to such an extent that he becomes a protagonist of the books of chivalry, which means that the norms of a very precise and concrete literary code become part of the complex texture of the hero. In his essay on the structure of the Quixote, Castro astutely observes that Cervantes introduces metaphor into the body of the novel, not as mere rhetorical figure, but as part of the lived experience of his protagonists: "The windmills are not only giants, but in addition are the contents of the experience of someone who lives them as such, near other lives that continue to see them as windmills. The metaphor is no longer the property of the lyric poet and is converted into metaphorized existence." Exactly: when Don Quixote takes the basin for a helmet or the inn for a castle, he is living the metaphor from the inside, and something similar occurs, as we shall see, with other characters in the novel.

219

The irresistible contagion of literature does not affect only the gentleman from La Mancha and the books of chivalry. In Cervantes's work almost all the characters show themselves to be avid readers of stories and tales: the innkeeper, his wife, and Maritornes passionately tell us of their literary tastes and fantasies; other figures inform us about their libraries, as does the gentleman in green, or confess to us, as does the canon, that they have attempted to write a novel and have "more than one hundred pages finished." Literature has made an idiot of Don Lorenzo, as his own father, the gentleman in green, tells us. Some characters Don Quixote runs across are mere projections of the bucolic genre, such as Marcela, Crisóstomo, Eugenio or Anselmo. This general receptivity on the part of the heroes of the work to the persuasive magic of reading and their innate propensity to assume traits of the characters of other literary genres explains the anger of Don Quixote's niece at not only the books of chivalry but at the novelistic genre in general:

> He opened one, and saw that it was Jorge de Montemayor's Diana, and supposing that all the rest were of the same kind, said: "These do not deserve burning with the rest, because they do not and will not do the mischief those books of chivalry have done. They are books of entertainment and can do no one any harm."
> "Oh, sir," cried the niece, "your worship should have them burnt like the rest. For once my uncle is cured of his disease of chivalry, he might very likely read those books and take it into his head to turn shepherd and roam about the woods and fields, singing and piping and, even worse, turn poet, for that disease is incurable and catching, so they say." (61)

It must be admitted that facts bear her out. Momentarily distracted from the business of righting wrongs, Don Quixote is transformed, at the duke's castle, into a character from an Italian-style novel of love and adventure of the type Lope and María de Zayas would later cultivate, and which Cervantes himself tried out in the novelettes inserted in the first part of the book, such as "The Tale of Foolish Curiosity" or the story of Cardenio and Dorotea. Loved by the damsel Altisidora, he asks for a lute and decides to respond to her proposition in verse, according to the requirements of the genre. In the same way, at the end of the work, when, defeated by the bachelor Sansón Carrasco he must renounce the exercise of his knighthood, he resolves to become a shepherd and live in the country-side, that is, change from a character of the chivalric genre to one of the bucolic genre and trade in the habits and conventions of the Amadis for those of the Diana.

In the Quixote's universe, the power of literature is absolute, and almost all the characters adhere to the literary conventions necessary for the credibility of the genre they represent, whether because of their natural inclination or merely a sporting spirit: the priest, the barber, Sansón Carrasco and Dorotea disguise themselves as enchanter, damsel, knight errant and enchanted princess and express themselves as characters in a book of chivalry would. The duke and duchess, the damsel in distress, Altisidora, and a company of extras and servants do the same in the castle. In this way Cervantes presents us with a sampling of the different literary codes of his time, with the arsenal of techniques peculiar to each, and then proceeds with the malicious game of destroying them in the name of the unheard-of, dazzling literary reality which he creates. With respect to the genre of chivalry, the parody is continuous; one need only remember that the gentleman was dubbed a knight by the innkeeper and two prostitutes. The Italianate genre fares no better: when Don Quixote responds to the damsel Altisidora accompanied by the music of the cittern, his song is interrupted by the racket caused by some cats with bells tied to their tails that scatter around the room and cover the unlucky knight with scratches. In another passage, Don Quixote comes across some shepherdesses framed by the conventional landscape of the bucolic novel and, suddenly, a herd of wild bulls with their lead oxen trample the delicate and distinguished characters of the scene and annihilate the unreal atmosphere of that false Arcadia with burlesque violence.

The intertextual game of the work is revealed in a special way in the second part, by way of a continuous dialogue between what the final editor is giving us and the already published texts of the first part and of Avellaneda. The gentleman from La Mancha and his squire are now characters of Cide Hamete Benengeli's chronicle, printed and sold in thousands of copies, and are recognized as such by the other protagonists of the second part. The literary discussion, extended before to include genres as diverse as the books of chivalry, the bucolic novel, Lope's plays, etc., now also includes the first part of the novel. Don Quixote and Sancho often appear to be worried about the image they are projecting as literary characters in Cide Hamete's chronicle, and other characters, such as Sansón Carrasco and the Duchess, ask them about things that happened in the first part in order to clearly understand confusing or insufficiently explained situations, or to point out contradictions or errors into which knight and squire fell.

But Cervantes's extraordinary gallery of mirrors acquires a new dimension when the gentleman and his squire not only are recognized and recognize themselves as characters of the first part but also as characters of the work published by Avellaneda. The latter's attack bothered Cervantes a lot, and in the prologue to the second part he responds with irony to the accusation that his references to Lope were products of envy. He isn't content, however, to polemicize from the outside, and according to his habit, he introduces the debate into the world of the novel itself, beginning a new, audacious and ingenious dialogue between his two heroes and those described by Avellaneda. In this way, the Don Quixote and Sancho of the second part have full consciousness of their double projection, at one and the same time as characters of Cide Hamete and of the apocryphal novel, which permits Cervantes to weave a subtle web of relations between the literary projections of the heroes of both works, and in the process point out the manifest inferiority of the one written by his rival.

When Roque Guinart plays host to Don Quixote in Barcelona, he makes clear his preference with respect to the two books, and the knight himself, upon discovering a copy of Avellaneda's work on his trip to the printer's, disdainfully condemns it to the purifying flame. In Don Quixote's exchange with the damsel Altisidora, she tells him she saw his enemy's novel thrown into the fires of hell, and the knight responds: "If it were good, faithful and true it would have centuries of life; but if it is bad, its passage will be short from its birth to its burial" (918). Even more marvelously, the gentleman from La Mancha rebels in a way we today would call Pirandellian, or like Augusto Perez of Niebla, against the destiny that Avellaneda has woven for him, and he modifies his travel plans in order to wrest all authority from the apocryphal author, clearly showing his story to be false. But the moment when Cervantes's literary game is deployed with the greatest effect is in the passage in which Don Quixote and Sancho come across a character from the false Quixote:

"My name is Don Alvaro Tarfe," replied the guest.
"Then I take it," said Don Quixote, "that you are no doubt that Don Alvaro Tarfe who features in the second part of the History of Don Quixote de la Mancha, recently printed and published by a modern author."
"I am he," replied the gentleman, "and this same Don Quixote, the principal subject of that same history, was a very great friend of mine. It was I who drew him from his home or, at least, persuaded

him to go to some jousts which were being held at Saragossa, where I was going myself. And to tell you the truth, I did him many kindnesses and saved him from having his back tickled by the hangman for his foolhardiness."

"And tell me, Don Alvaro, do I in any way resemble this Don Quixote you speak of?"

"No, certainly not," replied the guest, "not at all."

"And this Don Quixote," said our one, "did he have a squire with him called Sancho Panza?"

"Yes, he had," replied Don Alvaro, "and though he had the reputation of being a comical fellow I never heard him say anything at all funny."

"I can very well believe that," broke in Sancho Panza, "for it's not everyone that can say good things, and this Sancho Panza you mention, sir, must be a very great knave and a dolt and a thief, all rolled into one. For I'm the true Sancho Panza, and I have more wit than ever rained from the sky." (926-27)

Cervantes's novel is purely a story about different stories, discourse about earlier literary discourses which at no time hides the process of enunciation; on the contrary, it makes it clearly evident. The tale of the character driven mad by books of chivalry thus turned, insidiously, into the tale of a writer driven mad by the prodigious power of literature. If the "constant play of relations between the parts and the whole on the one hand, and the words and the structure on the other is presented in the form of a spiral in which the number of turns is proportional to the fullness and complexity of the system," in the case of the Quixote the helicoidal movement is practically infinite. Cervantes has touched all the keys and registers of the game. For this reason, when today's avant-garde, abandoning restricting "realism" predominant in these last centuries, try to return to the novel possibilities of expression lately lost or left fallow, deliberately or not, they are following in Cervantes's footsteps.

An analysis of Three Trapped Tigers by the Cuban novelist Guillermo Cabrera Infante provides us with an excellent example.

A hurried reading of Three Trapped Tigers has led a good number of readers and critics to the mistaken conclusion that it is an uneven work, full of brilliant pages and partial narrative successes, but chaotic and badly planned on the whole. Since its publication, the book has been greeted as a novel of great significance, and rather arbitrarily compared with Rayuela.[6] These same admirers, after lamenting its verbal juggling, its confused assembly, the lack of a general scheme, etc., have often extracted certain passages or chapters, for example "She Sang Boleros" or the monologues of "The Debutantes," at the expense of the rest, considering it little more than simply fill-in material, inane joke, a digression that can be done without: an opinion shared, we must admit, by a considerable number of readers.

At first glance, the facts seem to back them up: the general structure of TTT does not emerge easily on a first reading. The scattered order, or better, the strictly regulated disorder of the novel often leads us astray. In a volume dedicated to Cabrera Infante's work, for example, we find an essay containing several important errors: its author confused Cuba Venegas with Minerva Eros; he doesn't see that Ribot, the cartoonist, and Eribó, the bongo player, are the same person; he attributes the brief monologue at the end of the novel to La Estrella, on her deathbed under an oxygen tent, and he judges the dialogue of the last 150 pages between Silvestre and Cué, in which fundamental keys to the book are revealed, to be "an exercise in tedious inauthenticity," all splashed with quotes from Mallarmé, Dubuffet, Umberto Eco and other samplings of Buenos Aires erudition, a la page.

Obscurity, said Jean Genet on one occasion, is the author's courtesy to the reader. TTT is a good example of those works which, instead of bowing to the rules of a game known to the reader, creates its own rules as it goes along. It is precisely the final victory of the author over the habits of conformity and routine, which in their wily way slip into every reading exercise, that brings to the reader, confused and perturbed at first, an informed participant later, an aesthetic emotion. As we advance along the twisted path of the book, we little by little reconstruct the elements Cabrera Infante had introduced in such an unconnected way. Thus, our reading is an active one: it is we, the readers, who must solve the jigsaw puzzle. Cabrera Infante's courtesy consists in allowing us to reconstruct the novel with our talent and sensitivity.

In order to reach his objective, the novelist ably plays with "anachronism"--the relations existing between plot time and the time of the narrative instance which contains it. Critics have been correct to point out the influence of Sterne: the indirect use of the excusatio propter infirmitatem, narration perpetually interrupted by inopportune digressions and in many passages, following in the footsteps of Tristram Shandy, the puns, circumlocutions and word plays become the authentic texture of TTT, erasing all vestiges of plot from the novel. In addition, the work's magnificent "gallery of voices" introduces a series of discourses in which intonation, mime and sonorous gesture play a role of the first order. In his introductory remarks, Cabrera Infante advises the novel be read aloud, a hearing instead of a reading: in this way the rich wrapping of the word, its acoustic character, acquires a significance independent of its meaning. Often the anecdote is less important than mime and gesture, comic or grotesque variations, shocking or unheard-of syntactic arrangements. Cervantes had seen this clearly. "The stories," he wrote in El coloquio de los perros, "some are charming in and of themselves; others, in the way they are told; I mean that some give pleasure although they are told without preamble; there are others which must necessarily be dressed with works, with facial expressions, gestures and changes in the tone of voice, so that something is made from nothing, and a weak-kneed piece becomes bold and pleasurable."

The aforementioned elements, as well as the influence of the cinema, radio, television and the hit parade of the times, have been pointed out by most responsible critics. But the novel's web of connotations does not only extend--as is the case, for example, in the works of Manuel Puig--to popular culture of the mass media. TTT also, and above all, embraces the world of books, and, like the Quixote--whose path it follows many times, perhaps unknowingly--is an extraordinary example of intertextual dialogue.

Cabrera Infante's novel is offered to us as an elaborate and complex literary discourse which is defined and becomes meaningful by way of its closely woven net of relationships with different contemporary models. Bustrófedon's amusing pastiche of the principal Cuban narrators reminds us at an opportune moment that the literary text cannot be judged in isolation, but rather in relation and correspondence with other texts, with a whole system of values and norms that precede it and predetermine its identity, by way of its imitation, parody or rejection of them. Like Cervantes, Cabrera Infante introduces a literary discussion into the body of his novel and creates a work that, as it advances, comments on itself, parodies and destroys rival models and erects on their ruins the prodigious framework of its fabrication. The game of correspondences is manifested equally at all levels of the book: TTT is full of literary quotes, allusions to writers and works, discussions about the art of translating, etc. --exactly like the Quixote. The references to Joyce, Hemingway, Faulkner, etc., are abundant (for example, the jokes and word plays about "For Whom the Balls Tell" and "Across-the-river-and-into-the-trees"). One of the narrators, Codac, even dreams about The Old Man and the Sea.

If the world Don Quixote sees is described to us in terms of the
Amadis, the heroes of TTT must also pass through the filter of their
literary culture (Conrad, Lorca, André Gide, p. 342; Huxley and Hemingway
again, p. 392, etc.). Silvestre and Cué debate what is or should be
literature, just as the priest and the canon discuss the verisimilitude
of the books of chivalry and of Lope de Vega's plays (357-58). We saw how
Don Quixote makes fun of the repetitive way in which Sancho tells his
never-ending story; in a very funny passage, Cabrera Infante employs a
similar technique when he shows us his heroes, during the evening drive
with Magalena and Beba, parodying a version of the "never-beginning story"
(419-20). Cervantes's characters frequently talk of their readings and
their libraries and, like the canon, confess to us that they have tried
to write; Cabrera Infante's trapped tigers seem to be really obsessed by
writing and interrogate each other about their writer's calling: "Someday
I'll write that story," says Silvestre. The dialogue between him and Cué--
an interrupted dialogue, and for that very reason more significant as it
reveals a profound preoccupation--is a good example:

> --Why don't you write? I asked him suddenly.
> --Why don't you ask me rather why don't I translate?
> --No. I think you would be able to write. If you wanted.
> --I used to think so once too, he said and fell silent. (337)

> . . . .

> He had been talking. We still were and we ordered a sixth round
> because the conversation had gotten around once more, of its own
> accordion, to what Cué called El Tema, and which was neither sex
> nor music nor even his incomplete Pandects this time. I believe we
> arrived there on the Gulf Stream of Consciousness, going around
> and around the subject of words without ever getting to the ques-
> tion, the one and only question, my question. But it was Cué who
> landed first, insisting that I follow him ashore.
> --What would I be then? Just one more average reader? A transla-
> tor, another traitor? (367-68)

Let us remember that during his visit to a printer's in Barcelona,
the gentleman from La Mancha comes upon a translator and discusses the art
of translation with him. This topic--translation--is one of the essential
ingredients of Cabrera Infante's novel. In the dialogue just cited, Cué
responds to his friend's question, and then both discuss writers and
novels:

> ...--Aside from that there is this Montenegro fellow: his Men
> Without Woman would be O.K. if his prose wasn't so underdeveloped;
> then there are two or three short stories of Novás Calvo, who is a
> great translator.
> --Lino? Excuse me! Have you ever read his version of The Old Man
> and the Sea? There are at least three serious mistranslations on
> the first page alone and it's a very short page. Man, did I feel
> sorry for him, so I didn't look for more. I hate disappointments
> but just out of curiosity I looked at the last page. I found that
> he managed to transform the African lions in the memory of Santiago
> into sea lions! Morsas, which is not a morsel but a mouthful of
> shit! (369)

Still, later on, Silvestre repeats his attack:

> Ferocious barbarhythms, translated of course from the American. He
> also says afluente instead of próspero, moron for idiota, me luce
> instead of me parece, chance for oportunidad, controlar instead of
> revisar and things like that. Qué horror el Espanglish. Doctor

224

Esperanglish, I consume. We'll take good care of you one day, Lyno
Novás. (399)

At this point, the "Story of a Stick (With Some Additional Comments
by Mrs. Campbell)"--a tale inserted in the body of the novel as Cervantes
inserts "The Tale of Foolish Curiosity" or the story of Crisostomo and
Marcela--makes sense: this Mr. Campbell, whom we hear of first thanks to
the bilingual MC of the Tropicana, is the author of a story, very
Hemingwayesque, of which we are offered two versions in the section
entitled "The Visitors." The first one, presented second, is a succession
of expressions and turns of phrase literally translated from English,
which infect the linguistic structure of the Spanish and produce an
irresistible comic effect in the reader, while at the same time, very
effectively, and without the annoying rhetoric we are used to, denounces
the imperialist penetration of English into the Spanish-speaking world.
But the second version, corrected, we later find out, by Silvestre himself, is also, in its way, a betrayal: "It was terribly hot. There was a
low ceiling of fat gray clouds, actually more black..." ("Habia un techo
bajo de gordas nubes grises, negras más bien"). As Emir Rodríguez Monegal
says: "How can one fail to recognize, in the string of adjectives, without
a comma, precisely one of the notorious characteristics of the English
style of William Faulkner, which his translators (from Novás Calvo to
Jorge Luis Borges) acclimatized to Spanish, inevitably betraying the
natural course of the language?"[9]

In a very Tristramshandyesque way, Cabrera Infante gives us the key
to Silvestre's obsession with the art of translation only in the final
pages of the book, an important episode not only because Cabrera Infante
slips himself into the novel as the editor-in-chief of the Havana weekly
Carteles--a job he actually held--but also because it motivates the insertion of Mr. Campbell's story, an addition that otherwise would have been
arbitrary. This obsession follows Silvestre until the last lines of his
tale, when, exhausted, he goes to bed: "...dreamiendo soñing of the sea
lions on page a hundred and a one in the Spanish varsion: Morsas:
re-Morsas: Sea morsels. Tradittori" (481).

Faithful to Cervantes's example, Cabrera Infante presents us with a
showcase of narrative models with which he wants to confront his novel,
and throws himself into the burlesque game of mimicking them in the name of
the differential reality he creates. The target of these parodies is not
in this case books of chivalry or the pastoral novel but rather the works
of outstanding Cuban writers. In order to comprehend the purpose of the
pastiches of Bustrófedon, it is indispensable to refer to the already-
mentioned literary discussion of "Bachata," when Silvestre and Cué successively recite the names Montenegro, Novás Calvo, Piñera, and Carpentier,
or the passage in the same section in which Silvestre expresses his
opinion about Martí:

--Is that what it cost to bury Bustrófedon?
--No, that's what it cost to bury Martí. Sad, isn't it?
He didn't answer. I'm not a Martian. Neither of us was. I used to
have a great admiration for Martí, but there was all that stupid
fuss about him, everyone trying to make a saint of him and every
politico saying he was his son and sole heir, that I got sick of
the sound of the word Martian. I liked the word Martian--or even
Marxian--or even, heaven help me, Maritain!--better. (437)[10]

"The Death of Trotsky as Described by Various Cuban Writers, Several
Years After the Event--or Before" contains imitations of Martí, Lezama
Lima, Virgilio Piñera, Lydia Cabrera and Nicolás Guillén; some are very
funny; others ironically affectionate, such as those of Piñera or Lezama.
The cruelest, without a doubt, is that of Carpentier's ornamental style,
which so often overdecorates the scene as if with icing or papier-mâché,

although one must recognize that Bustrófedon carries the joke too far, and at times, it gets away from him.

Even in those passages of the novel that make reference to the movies, TTT repeats, voluntarily or not, Cervantes's scheme: Silvestre and Cué are transformed into film characters, just as the protagonists of the Quixote are converted into characters of books of chivalry or bucolic novels. During his visit to Livia's apartment, Cué identifies with Andy Hardy and David Niven; in the drive of "Bachata," with Robert Montgomery. At other times, in a spirit of fun, they parody in a very Cervantine manner scenes from well-known films, following the lead of the priest, the barber, Sansón Carrasco and Dorotea when they play the roles of enchanter, damsel, knight errant and enchanted princess: the dialogue of Vincent van Douglas in Thirst for Life, of Gary Cooper and Katy Jurado in High Noon, of Abbot and Costello Meet the Ghosts, etc.

The author or authors of Cervantes's novel, just as the last name of the protagonist (Quijada, Quesada, Quejana?), are offered to us in a doubtful and problematic way. The final compiler of the book works with what others have written and the extent of the participation of the different authors is never clarified (Cide Hamete, the translator and those alluded to in the first chapter). As we shall see, the same lack of precision concerning who relates the multiple tales which make up the final structure of TTT also affects our reading of Cabrera Infante's novel. To solve the puzzle, we will take a closer look at the section titled "Bachata." Almost all of the fifty pages it covers--except two dedicated to the eleventh session of the mysterious woman being psycho-analyzed--refer to the drive taken by Silvestre and Cué, involved in a long and sinuous conversation whose verbal fireworks attempt to hide, without doing so, the secret anxiety and anguish of the two trapped tigers. The point of view of the narration is that of Silvestre, and the conversation of the protagonists--elusive, full of breaks--reveals little by little the keys, pieces whisked away by the author--that will permit the reader to finally put together the whole jigsaw puzzle of the novel (the inclusion of Mr. Campbell's story, the personality of Magalena Crus, Cué's last narration found in "The Debutantes," etc.).

Cué has recounted a dream to Silvestre (338) and, one-hundred pages later, the latter again touches on the theme and, in his turn, tells the dream of his friend: "my friend, our friend," "this cryptic girl friend... who's as secret as yours and almost as obvious" (455). The revelation of the identity of the friend happens fourteen pages later:

> --I'm going to tell you the name of the woman of the dream. She's called Laura.
> I was expecting him to hit the ceiling. I'd been expecting it for weeks, I'd been expecting it all day, all through the evening and the early part of the night. I no longer expected it. He didn't even jump up. But I had something you don't: his face opposite me.
> --It was she who dreamed that dream.
> --So?
> I felt like a fool, more than ever.
> --It was her dream.
> --You've already said it. What else?
> I fell silent. I tried looking for something better than the usual pat sayings and catchphrases. A phrase to catch. Words and sentences scattered here and there. It wasn't either baseball or chess, it was a seesaw puzzle. Crisscrosswords.
> --I've known her for days. A month or two, rather. We've been going out. Together, that is. I think, I believe, no: I'm going to marry her. (469-70)

In order to understand the secret tension in this dialogue we must go back, according to the usual method of Cabrera Infante, almost 300 pages, to the story Cué tells in "The House of Mirrors" (146-47). In a deliberately elliptical way, Cué mentions his history with Laura Díaz:

> No, there was no love lost between Laura and me that evening, not as yet. There was love, there is, there will be as long as I live, now. Livia knew it, my friends knew it, the whole of Havana/ that is to say the whole world/ knew it. But I didn't know it. I don't know if Laura ever knew it. Livia, sure, she knew it I knew she knew it because she insisted that I come in when I went to look for Laura on June 19, 1957. (150)

. . . .

> I remember now (when the door of Livia's new house opens) another door that closed and the handy, hardy words Laura said and which her suddenly icy tone rendered truly dramatic: Next time see that you close the door and she left. I remember her ever-present indifference whenever I called her, called on her, whenever I went to see her at the TV station and the affectionate coolness in which our relationship ended: phrases like How're you and See you soon and So long for now taking the place of all our previous expressions of warmth, of affection--of love? (153)

The scene in which Laura surprises Cué in a situation of embarrassing intimacy with Livia, and after which she definitely distances herself from him, occurs on the 19th of June, 1957, in other words one year before the automobile drive on which Silvestre announces his plans to marry her--from there comes the hidden violence of the friends' conversation. But what is of interest now is a number of scattered elements in the characterization of Laura Díaz, as it appears in Cué's narration: "...tall girl, poorly dressed...simple, down-to-earth and open beauty...she was a widow...a small blond and ugly girl. It was her daughter...today when she is famous...she works in television..." (147-53). Let us remember also that Silvestre is a writer, and Laura's dream that Silvestre told on page 456, and let us go on to the Mysterious Woman's psychoanalytic episodes:

First: "Did you know that my husband is a writer?"
Second: A dream.
Third: "Doctor, do you think I should go back to the theater?"
Fourth: Childhood memory. Implicit poverty.
Fifth: Story of the courtship. What is important is the encounter with the childhood friend, schoolmate in the village, with whom she sat at night on the sidewalk of the house. Compare this data with the first sequence of "The Debutantes" and the two girls' inclination to tell stories, show off and do theater (11-15).
Seventh: "I told you a lie on Friday, doctor.... That boy I was telling you [the rich one] we never got married. I married another boy who I didn't even know."
Eighth: Another dream.
Ninth: "Didn't I tell you I'm a widow?" The dead husband's family took the little girl from her, alleging that she lived "the immoral life of an artist."
Eleventh: Childhood trauma. A new reference to the husband.

This scattered data allows us to identify the mysterious woman undergoing psychoanalysis, who is none other than Laura Díaz, Silvestre's future wife. I say future because when "Bachata" ends, Silvestre and Laura haven't married yet. This indicates to us, without a doubt, that the sessions of psychoanalysis are set in a time subsequent to that of the plot of the rest of the novel. Laura is not only the wife of Silvestre but in addition she has abandoned the theater, as we learn in the third sequence. This sending us to a subsequent period seems to me to be very important since it gives us the key to the structure of the book and the role Silvestre plays in it.

In "Bachata," Silvestre--like a character of Cervantes or from La lozana andaluza--looks for paper and pencil to jot down an anecdote (324), or affirms: "Someday I'll write that story," and Arsenio--likewise as if he were a character in a Cervantes or Delicado novel--alludes to his future condition as character. After a reference, which is a long way from being coincidental, to Don Quixote, "a perfect example of an early contrary," we read:

> --What about you and me?
> I thought of telling him to be more modest.
> --We aren't literary characters.
> --What about when you write down our night deeds?
> --Even then we won't be. I'll be a scribe, just another
> annotator, God's stenographer but never your Creator. (442)

As we see, in this passage Silvestre characterizes himself, defining his later work in terms of scribe, annotator, God's stenographer, "but never your Creator." The observation seems fundamental to me since, as any coherent literary text, TTT provokes us with information about its own structure:[11] the role of the novelist in it will be that of a scribe, annotator, stenographer--not the omniscient narrator of the nineteenth-century style, Jehovah, God and Creator. The time following that of the action contained in the work thus includes the stage of Laura Díaz's psychoanalysis and of Silvestre's work as scribe, annotator or stenographer, while he constructs or deconstructs for us the admirable edifice of the novel. Silvestre's privileged role is first revealed to us by way of these frequent references to the act of writing ("and I'm taking more time to write it than he took to do it"); in addition, he is the only character to conceive of the work as a volume, a printed novel, with numbered pages, published or ready for publication ("Titles by commentator," 348).[12]

The identification of Silvestre as editor or compiler of the work is still more precise when he refers to the definitive pagination of the novel that we, the readers, have in our hand: "He told me everything. Or almost everything. The story is on page fifty three"; "I was sleeping dreamiendo soñing of the sea lions on page a hundred and one in the Spanish varsion" (481).

The story that Cabrera Infante "omits"--the quintessential piece necessary in order to complete the jigsaw puzzle and decipher its disorderly order--is none other than the process of structuring the novel at a time later than that in which the plot develops, just as the "omitted" story of the Quixote is the one which would have clarified for us the process of its successive fragmentary creation. With this I don't pretend to affirm that the repetition of the Quixote's blueprint in TTT is always conscious. In my opinion it is not: as my experience with Don Julián proved to me, I didn't discover until later, when I had concluded the book, that the episode of the flies in the library of Tangier played a role in the internal structure of the book similar to the function of the examination of the gentleman's library by the priest and the barber; in other words, it is possible to "Cervantize" without knowing it. Undoubtedly this is the case because of the fact that Cervantes implicitly explored the latent possibilities of the genre with which he had chosen to express himself, and whoever conceives of the novel as an adventure, not less problematic for being necessary, has to refer to the immense field of strategems he passed through. If to this we add that--in theme (Tiempo de silencio) or structurally (Juan sin tierra)--some of us Spaniards intentionally connect ourselves with his "strange" invention, it is the proof that, by the paths of Borges or Américo Castro, the lesson of the Quixote has finally forged a path and presides on both sides of the Atlantic over the contemporary resurgence of our novel.

In TTT, Cabrera Infante has presented us with the facts in a scattered form that nevertheless fosters the effort to order them. He has maliciously shuffled the materials like a card player and, with a truly praiseworthy courtesy and respect for our intelligence and sensibility as readers, has permitted us the exquisite pleasure of their reconstruction.

--Juan Goytisolo

NOTES

1 Carlos Peregrin Otero, "Unamuno y Cervantes," Letras I (Barcelona: Seix Barral, 1972), 171-90.
2 Miguel de Cervantes, Don Quixote, trans. J.M. Cohen (Penguin, 1950), 56. All further citations are from this edition; page numbers are noted in the text.
3 Américo Castro, "La palabra escrita y el Quijote," Hacia Cervantes (Madrid: Taurus, 1958). Translation by N. Helsper.
4 In Théorie de la littérature: Textes des Formalistes russes, collected, presented and translated by Tzvetan Todorov, prologue by Roman Jakobson (Paris: Editions du Seuil, 1965), 76-97.
5 Vicente Llorens, Literatura, historia, politica (Madrid: Revista de Occidente, 1967).
6 Although I am not in agreement with the severity of Juan Benet's criticism of Cortázar, expressed in an interesting interview published in the Uruguayan weekly Marcha (now closed down by government order), there is no doubt that he hits the nail on the head when pointing out some of the voluminous novel's defects and insufficiencies. In any case, the critics' inadequate comparison of the two works serves only to emphasize the indisputable superiority of TTT. Cabrera Infante can rightly claim his kinship with Cervantes and Sterne; Hopscotch's laborious construction--in spite of some brilliant sections, whose goals are achieved with perfection--is more closely related to the experimentalism of Gide's Les faux monnayeurs.
7 Julián Ríos, ed., Guillermo Cabrera Infante (Madrid: Fundamentos, 1974). See especially the excellent articles by Emir Rodríguez Monegal and Julio Matas.
8 Guillermo Cabrera Infante, Three Trapped Tigers, translated from the Cuban by Donald Gardner and Suzanne Jill Levine in collaboration with the author (New York: Harper & Row, 1971). All further citations are from this edition; page numbers are noted in the text.
9 Article included in the volume cited in note 7.
10 Something similar is happening today in Spain with the process of "beatification" of Antonio Machado, "the Good,"--beatification which demonstrates a total lack of comprehension on the part of its authors of Mairena's teachings. How long will our so-called literary historians persist in the prehistoric custom of dividing writers into the Bad and the Good?
11 The same structural information and indirect references to the process of their own creation are found in two fundamental novels of our post-war period: Camilo José Cela's La familia de Pascual Duarte and Luis Goytisolo's Recuento.
12 It is true that on page 290 Códac refers to himself as "an anonymous scribe of latter-day hieroglyphs," but we know that it was Silvestre who gave him Bustrófedon's "memoirs" to copy, and we can deduce that they, once transcribed, returned to the hands of their former owner.

Editor's Note: This essay originally appeared in Goytisolo's Disidencias (Barcelona: Seix Barral, 1977). It is here translated by Norma Helsper and appears by permission of the author.

The Fiction of Popular Design and Desire: Manuel Puig's *Boquitas pintadas**

❦

Lucille Kerr

Boquitas pintadas, Manuel Puig's second novel, opens with a display of death—an obituary notice that announces the demise of Juan Carlos Etchepare (the small-time, small-town Don Juan who, as we shall see, functions as both a seductive model and a model of seduction in the text).[1] This written verification of closure on the life of the novel's protagonist seems to offer us a sign of the finite nature of a text which might otherwise appear ready and able to go on forever. For, along with proliferation of distinct narrative and discursive forms within its pages, the generic model which the formal design of *Boquitas pintadas* is supposed to replicate—the serial(ized) novel (i.e., *folletín*) named in its subtitle—suggests a text potentially out of control, a text which might threaten to regenerate itself without end.[2] Yet, as it turns out, *Boquitas pintadas* is in many ways a very controlled text, one whose constituent parts have been very carefully organized and articulated by an authorial figure whose own ludic performance and position are also brought to light by it.

It is within this meticulously and, yet, playfully ordered network that we come to see a kind of "perfect match" between thematic material and structural machinery. It is, however, a match that ultimately reveals the author, as well as his protagonist, caught in the act, as it were, orchestrating a set of slippery maneuvers that finally signal their own undoing. In fact, *Boquitas pintadas* seems to be constructed as a kind of play among formal, discursive and thematic paradoxes which provocatively implicate both the author(ity) behind and the literary and cultural traditions which surround the whole text.

It is evident from the novel's first chapters or, rather, installments (we should remember that the text repeatedly asserts its generic origins in all sixteen chapter headings, where the word "entrega" appears) that the narrative techniques of the novel are also manipulative strategies deployed by an author whose relation to his reader is ultimately as significant as the relationships among his fictional characters.[3] Like some of Puig's other works, *Boquitas pintadas* is a complex and variegated text which presents

MLN Vol. 97 Pp. 411-421
0026-7910/82/0972-0411 $01.00   © 1982 by The Johns Hopkins University Press

several kinds of reading problems—problems which concern readerly interpretation as much as performance.[4] For—as is true of any text, of course—when we pose the question of how to read this novel we potentially call into play a set of distinct but interconnected operations through which various types of meaning might be constructed.

Boquitas pintadas is composed through the juxtaposition, or virtual grafting together, of a set of anecdotally related but formally and discursively dissimilar texts.[5] Each of the novel's chapters (with the exception of one, perhaps—Chapter XIII) appears as a collection of diverse narrative techniques and forms of discourse; moreover, in many segments, or even whole chapters, there is little or no mediation by an organizing and privileged narrator. This novel, in fact, represents well the narrative heterogeneity characteristic of all of Puig's work: included in *Boquitas pintadas* there are letters, diary entries, magazine and newspaper articles, official (legal, medical, police, and government) documents; in addition, there are interior monologues, dreams and stream of consciousness segments, hidden dialogues, immediate direct dialogues, and a variety of texts in which an undramatized omniscient narrator reports on the characters' actions and thoughts, or describes objects and places of significance within the fiction.

Given the fragmentary nature of the novel's text, and the intermittent appearance of the omniscient narrator only within some of its sections, there seems to be no position from which an immediately accessible narrative unity might be offered the reader. Rather, it is the reader's task to bridge the various gaps between separate texts and distinct modes of discourse, to continually shift perspective on and change his/her relation to that text in order to follow or understand its movements. The reader would thereby attempt to create meaning from the text—that is, domesticate and control it. Moreover, readers' abilities to understand, and thus master, the relationships among all of the text's fragments also depend on their capacity for perceiving and then overcoming the disjunctions between story and plot—disjunctions that are created mainly by the temporal inversions and nominal, as well as narrative, elisions which proliferate throughout the novel's pages.[6]

To read *Boquitas pintadas* therefore entails a kind of dialogic engagement with a textual strategist who plays with, by also regulating, the reader's desire for knowledge. That desire is periodically satisfied, yet sustained, by the narrative tactics deployed in essence by two textual authorities—that is, by the author and his narrating surrogate (the omniscient narrator who intervenes only sporadically). Both of them control our appropriation of the text by offering at once too much and too little information about the novel's fictional events and characters. What is of particular importance here is that this play between authorial and readerly desires, as well as performances, is connected in two significant ways with the story around which that relationship is developed. For the story of *Boquitas pintadas*, we must remember, is a tale of romance and mystery, whose anecdotal complexity is, in its own way, matched with the complicated narrative structure and devices used to (re)present it. Moreover, in their plays for power and pleasure, the novel's protagonists offer themselves as fictive analogues for the textual figures who appear to hover over them on either "side" of the text.

The novel's story is composed as a network of interconnected and coetaneously developed stories which can be summarized but, because of their very complexity, never represented or retold in the form of a single, purely linear narrative sequence. That tale deals with the lives and loves of Juan Carlos and several other characters from Coronel Vallejos, the provincial town which also serves as the stage upon which Puig's first novel, *La traición de Rita Hayworth*, is set. It is primarily in Coronel Vallejos (a transparent "cover" for General Villegas, the Argentine town in which Puig himself grew up[7]) that the story of Juan Carlos, his family (his mother Doña Leonor and his sister Celina), his friend (Pancho), his girlfriends and lovers (Nené, Mabel and Elsa DiCarlo), and his acquaintances (Raba) is told. That story spans three decades; it moves from the 1930s to the 1960s. However, the episodes upon which the narrative text dwells, and which thereby constitute the tale as such, unfold mainly between the years 1935 and 1941, and additionally surround the dates of Juan Carlos' and Nené's deaths (1947 and 1968, respectively).

All of these characters' lives are interconnected in such a way that to tell the story of one is to tell the story of several others, perhaps even that of all of them together. Thus, the (hi)story of Coronel Vallejos is presented as the network of intertwining lives (here that means essentially the lies told, the loves won, and the losses suffered) that construct, according to Puig, the typical actions and activities which serve to fill up, and even kill, time in the petty, everyday world of that era's provincial life. However, we must remember that *Boquitas pintadas* is more than a chronicle of life in the provinces. It is also a tale of popular romantic intrigue whose sentimental portraits and episodes, as well as dramatic orchestrations or movements, serve to remind us that this text is also about other texts, and, particularly, about forms of "high" and "low" art or culture. In episodes reminiscent of Golden Age and nineteenth-century drama, as well as of tragic-ironic tango sketches and episodic soap opera intrigue, Juan Carlos and his partners in romance and treachery become the meeting ground for all sorts of traditions and models with which the novel engages in dialogue.[8] In fact, it is particularly the novel's dealings with a literary legend or cultural myth (i.e., the Don Juan figure) and a specific form of popular art (i.e., the *folletín*) with which we are concerned here. For it is in the development of these dialogues that the "perfect" (but, as we shall see, also paradoxical) "match" between intra- and extrafictional performances, as well as between thematic and structural patterns, is so provocatively established in *Boquitas pintadas*.

In Puig's representation of Coronel Vallejos and its characters (and especially in what we might call his "anatomy of the Don Juan/macho syndrome") we become witnesses to a variety of plays for power and pleasure that are both typical of the popular forms of culture from which the novel's episodes, characters, and even languages seem to be drawn, and, moreover, representative (as Puig would himself assert) of the provincial reality he wishes to dissect.[9] It is especially in relation to the various plays with, and around, the question of knowledge in several registers of the text that those interconnections might be discovered. The facts about the characters' secrets—their romantic, and even criminal, entanglements—are revealed in such a way that it is not until we have completed the novel that we can put them all in place and fully understand the story that has been told. The revelation of important details is regulated so as to control our access to the novel both as narrative structure and fictional story. Thus, we are only gradually shown and eventually (or finally) allowed to see all the causes and consequences of the relations among the figures who matter most: Nené, Juan Carlos, Mabel, Pancho and Raba.

To trace out the relationships interconnecting these principal characters would mean to diagram a set of parallel, and yet crisscrossing, paths among them—paths that would remind us of the impossibility of sketching a neat diachronic account of their (inter)actions. However, one of the ways we might in fact attempt to represent that complex network is, paradoxically, to think in terms of a linear model—to summarize the story not as a chronology of actions, but as a set of separate, but conjoined, relations among its actors. Thus we might use a nominal sequence (the enumeration just employed here, that is: Nené, Juan Carlos, Mabel, Pancho, Raba) that the novel's own segments explicitly suggest to us, in order to translate into a virtually linear form what is in fact a synchronic network within the text.[10]

In this series of names, the secret seductions and betrayals that inform the characters' movements are brought to light by the very order and grouping it overtly displays. In effect, we see the men surrounded by the women they desire and/or reject, and the women linked to the men they agree, or are forced, to love and/or leave. For in this sequence we see Juan Carlos embraced, as it were, on one side by Nené (the girlfriend he tries but fails to seduce; the one who, in her own way, remains faithful to him until the end), while, on the other, he is held by Mabel (his secret lover and partner in deception; the girl who almost outdoes him at his own game). Next we see Pancho (Juan Carlos' friend, "student" and imitator who also becomes his rival) flanked on one side by Raba (the girl he succeeds in seducing, but whom he quickly abandons after fathering her child; the one who avenges his various betrayals of her by murdering him), and on the other side by Mabel (the girl who becomes also Pancho's secret lover; the one who operates as his accomplice in the betrayals of both Raba and Juan Carlos).

While the truth of these as well as other relationships is revealed to the reader by the end of the novel, it is not necessarily, nor entirely, revealed to the characters themselves. For, the success of Juan Carlos—that able imitator of his own legendary and literary predecessors—depends not only on his powers to seduce others, but also on his ability to induce them to play along with him, to remain silent about the pacts, promises and ploys for which they all serve as participants or witnesses. Juan Carlos' secret powers are therefore contingent upon his power to keep a set of secrets, as well as to persuade others to follow his example. In fact, as the description of some of the links among Nené, Juan Carlos, Mabel, Pancho, and Raba implies, secret pacts and pacts of secrecy abound in Coronel Vallejos—the place wherein both the economics and erotics of romantic, and ultimately criminal, plots are certainly underscored.

In this town, and in the text that presents its inhabitants, everyone has, or pretends to have, something to hide. Furthermore, everyone seems ready to pay a price, or to extract payment from others, in order to keep the truth (of transgression) from being revealed or to construct a fiction to take its place. What Juan Carlos and almost everyone else seem to discover, however, is that their powers and pleasures are in fact limited; each must pay, either in life or in death it seems, for the transgressions through which, we see in the end, they wind up betraying mostly themselves. By the end of the novel, which closes with a kind of ceremonious awarding of "prizes and punishments" (pp. 235-42) typical of many serial novels, we see that each character has been "poetically" rewarded or chastised for his/her actions.[11] When we arrive at Nené's death in 1968 (p. 235), only Mabel and Raba survive within the fiction; and each, along with those who have already been done away with in the text, either continues to suffer or finally reaps the benefits of payments already made for treacherous acts. Behind this apparently judicial and economic ritual of the popular art form there lurks the image of an authority who, like the seductive figure to whom he is so intimately connected, cannot, in the end, elude the mechanisms which ensnare all of his fictional characters.

Juan Carlos is, of course, the focal center of this popular and dramatic network in which seduction and betrayal are the structuring maneuvers, fantasy the principal means of escape, and punishment or disillusionment the main reward for its players' actions. He is the organizing principle, the powerful figure, in or through whom everyone else seems to meet. Whether loved romantically by his various women, or faithfully emulated by his friend and rival, or worshipped blindly by the family that seeks to defend his image of innocence—Juan Carlos plays a central role in the lives of all those around him. However, this character—recuperated, it seems, from a long line of Latin lovers, and, perhaps, both (intentionally) criticized and (unwittingly) admired by the text—is not without either accomplices or imitators in both the text and story of *Boquitas pintadas.*[12]

As the previous comments about the novel's story would perhaps already reveal, Juan Carlos has a lot of help indeed in authoring the relationships

in which he functions as a privileged character. In fact, like the
literary/legendary figure whose seductive and rebellious behavior he
regenerates in many ways, Juan Carlos is the perfect model—that is, the
exaggerated paradigm—of the subject who is always maneuvering to get
what he wants, the subject who is determined to negate the laws or limits
which would deny him his desired goals. Moreover, he is not unique here;
he is not the only one who manages to live by strategic moves and plots in
Puig's novel. For the tactics employed, and some of the goals set, by Juan
Carlos are virtually duplicated in the designs and desires of the other
characters, as well. We come to realize, therefore, that everyone in Coronel
Vallejos is out to get some kind of satisfaction; all use whatever means at
hand to attempt to control those upon whom their own satisfaction and
success may depend. Moreover, here the power of one may mean the
pleasure of another character, and vice versa, in a novel wherein, we
eventually realize, the complicity of all the participating parties is what
keeps everything, including the text itself, moving.

    We might finally be able to see—once the authorial figure, we
remember, has allowed us that vision—that the kinds of strategies, as well
as goals, informing the relations of power and pleasure among these fictive
entities may actually provide an aid for the interpretation of not only the
real world to which that fiction would at some level refer, but also, and
more important for this discussion, the narrative structures supporting
that fiction. For the novel that presents a story of romantic intrigue
wherein strategic arts and artful strategies are highlighted, is itself a text
orchestrated to seduce and betray, perhaps even to control and to please,
its readers. In *Boquitas pintadas* we might therefore perceive the
convergence of several patterns of desire and power, as well as the
coincidence of both fictional and textual plots. In effect, the reader who is
lured on by, and thus agrees to submit to, the plays of romantic mystery is
the reader whose desire to find out the truth is but the desire to learn all
the details about the desires of others. And the authority who apparently
sets up that text, constructing its erotic and political fictions, is the author
who would seem to desire a certain control over, and at the same time
agree to play with, the reader upon whom his own projected power, and
perhaps even pleasure, must of course also depend. Their dialogue is, to
say the least, a provocative one.

    This coincidence of the patterns of textual and fictional desire, as well as
the uncanny duplication of tactics designed to satisfy and also sustain
them, should not surprise us. For, as we realize from the beginning of
Boquitas pintadas, Puig's novel pretends to be an example of the very genre
in which not only romance and mystery (and thus seduction and betrayal)
are likely to predominate, but also the one in which the author-reader
dialogue, and of course its politics and pleasures, are put into relief—that
is, the *folletín.* One of the most interesting and problematic aspects of Puig's
version of the popular form is that it appears to do the impossible, as it

were. Contrary to what that subtitle and the word "entrega" in each heading would affirm, *Boquitas pintadas* lacks precisely what would seem to be the *sine qua non* of serial fiction. Given that the text's installments are not, in fact, installments—they are not separated by the regular temporal gaps that, along with certain narrative devices, would produce the kind of indeterminacy typical of the genre; and, given that the reader's appropriation of the text is therefore not coincident with, nor determined by, the temporality of publication, as is characteristically the case; *Boquitas pintadas* virtually renders impossible the identity its subtitle and chapter headings insist upon affirming.[13]

The possibility of that very impossibility is, paradoxically, demonstrated throughout Puig's novel. Through the complex defamiliarization of an originally complicated story, and through the spatialization of temporal and narrative gaps achieved by that same deformation, Puig's novel is able to (re)produce the problematics and effects of the very genre his text names.[14] The gaps of indeterminancy created by the many temporal inversions and elisions of significant details; the proliferation of heterogeneous discursive forms; the juxtaposition of dissimilar narrative techniques and fragments; and the absence of a single and continuously represented narratorial or authorial position within the text—all these aspects of the novel serve to place its readers in precisely the kinds of positions characteristic of their role in "real" serial fiction.[15] Although we know that this story must end, and soon, because we are presented with a single book with a finite number of pages and chapters, in the first of which, we must remember, we are already told of the protagonist's own end, Puig's novel would seem to resist acknowledging that fact. It seems to be able to (make us) forget that originally fatal scene, the limits of its own pages, and the clearly visible contiguity of all of its "installments."

The virtual recuperation of the *folletín* and the potential attack on the Don Juan figure are thus concurrent with, and dependent upon, one another.[16] The genre from which Puig's novel is clearly distanced is also the one it succeeds in regenerating; the legendary figure whom it would kill off, especially in its opening pages, and whose ultimate demise it thereby both predicts and promises, is also the one the novel succeeds so well in resurrecting. Both models are, in effect, both replaced (perhaps virtually suppressed) and yet revived by new versions. However, it is not only in this interplay of potentially recuperative and repressive operations that we might discern just how good a match Juan Carlos is for the novel, or just how perfect a vehicle Puig's *folletín* is for the story of a provincial but popular Don Juan. We might consider as well some key structural analogues between the typical Don Juan's life story and the basic pattern of the *folletín*, as well as the parallel changes Puig effects in each of those models in order to produce the text of *Boquitas pintadas*.

The backbone of the serial(ized) novel and the legendary figure's classic biography is (as the popular genre's name in English reminds us) the notion of a series—a pattern which informs both the story told and the method of telling, the latter being cruical to, and exaggerated in, the popular form. Puig seems to work with a paradox inherent in the serial progression itself. For the diachronic movement which underlies the notion of a series as we see it developed in the *folletín* and the donjuanesque story is also a movement of repetition and return. Given the typicality of the kinds of scenes and relationships, as well as narrative devices, which make up popular serial fiction, for example; and, given the way in which the erotic relations in which the donjuanesque character serially participates are, in their essence, similar to, and thus virtual repetitions of, one another; we can see that in these series and serials it is as if there were virtually no progression whatever. That is, just as or, paradoxically, because everything keeps moving, nothing seems to move at all. In effect, what Puig has done in *Boquitas pintadas* is to transform into a relatively synchronic network of relations the typically successive or serial events, as well as the temporally spaced episodes, that inform the various models with which he works. In so doing, he both differentiates his story and text from their virtual or actual sources and, yet, highlights, by returning (us) to, the very essence of the fictions and narrative structures which originally determine them.

The outcome of this project is the production of a self-reflexive and self-critical text whose position vis-à-vis its models, or even itself, seems ever double and, thus, unstable. To attempt to stabilize its position or voice, so to speak, and reduce the text to a "monologue" of sorts is, in fact, to wind up demonstrating yet again its paradoxical and ambivalent nature. One concluding observation about the interplay of dialogues within the novel might further illustrate this point. If we accept that Puig draws attention to various forms of popular culture for which he has expressed his appreciation; that he also examines the legendary model of male behavior which, according to his views, Western culture would valorize and he would here criticize; we must also admit that, at the same time, he cannot avoid revealing the uncontrollable and, therefore, intriguing problematics intrinsic to that combined enterprise.

It could be argued that, in order to succeed in one of his projects, Puig seems to have to sacrifice himself to the other; in order to save, or defend, one model he may unwittingly undermine the suppression of, or attack on, the other. As emphasized here already, the author-reader dialogue is indeed an important part of the whole text. Its development in *Boquitas pintadas* demonstrates that the success of Puig's *folletín* is in more ways than one grounded in the successes of the donjuanesque model—a seductive, unstable and problematic pattern that binds, as we have seen, fictive and textual figures alike. For, to become the author of a *folletín,* to assume the apparently privileged and stable position of the one whose power and, perhaps, pleasure are determined by one's ability to manipulate and deceive, laugh at while also playing with, one's accomplice(s) and even victim(s) is, of course, to follow in another way (and therefore keep alive or resurrect) a donjuanesque model of performance. It is the kind of performance which, we now see, has the power to seduce even the subject who would also attempt to diffuse its attraction. Here in *Boquitas pintadas,* then, it never becomes quite clear who or what is really in or out of control, or whose "voice" might finally be heard. For, the text that would ultimately assert its own ambivalence or instability, the text that would resist our readerly mastery until, and beyond, the end, would also seem to control the author(ity) or master-manipulator who seems to hover above and lurk behind that text, but who is, of course, only another mobile fiction created by it.

University of Southern California

NOTES

* The present essay is a revised version of papers read at Louisiana State University (23 February 1981), the Louisiana Conference on Hispanic Languages and Literatures, held at Tulane University (26-28 February 1981). and the University of Kansas (23 April 1981). I wish to thank the Departments of Spanish and Portuguese at both Tulane University and the University of Kansas, and the directors of the La Chispa for the opportunity to present this work. I should also like to express my gratitude to the American Philosophical Society, from which I received a research grant that enabled me to complete part of this study.

1 Manuel Puig, *Boquitas pintadas: folletín* (Buenos Aires: Sudamericana, 1969); hereafter page references will be made parenthetically within the text.

2 Cf. the remarks related to the notion of control in another of Puig's novels (*El beso de la mujer araña*) by Alicia Borinsky, *Ver/ser visto: Notas para una analítica poética* (Barcelona: Bosch, 1978).

3 The novel is composed of sixteen chapters, divided equally into two parts; there are no titles other than the successive ordinal numbers and the word "entrega" at the head of each chapter. Puig has asserted in several places his desire to "seduce" his (real or imagined) reader, whose participation in his texts is virtually required by the narrative methods employed in them; see his two discussions with Ronald Christ: "An Interview with Manuel Puig," *Partisan Review,* 44 (1977), 54, and "Interview with Manuel Puig," *Christopher Street,* April 1979, p. 30.

4 The extreme discursive and formal heterogeneity of this novel is also characteristic of Puig's next work, *The Buenos Aires Affair;* moreover, the complex narrative design of each helps to retard as much as promote understanding of the events it relates. The reader's "hermeneutic activity" involves coetaneously an effort to make (logical) sense of the narrative and to determine its meanings; see Frank Kermode, *Novel and Narrative,* W. P. Ker Lectures, 24 (Glascow: Univ. of Glascow Publications, 1972), pp. 9-10, for comments on reading as a "hermeneutic activity."

5 This view of *Boquitas pintadas* as a network of texts "grafted" together is suggested by Severo Sarduy, first in "*Boquitas pintadas:* parodia e injerto," *Sur,* No. 321 (November-December 1969), pp. 71-77, and then in "Notas a las notas a las notas . . .: A propósito de Manuel Puig," *Revista Iberoamericana,* 37 (1971). 555-67 (the latter is in fact an expanded version of the first essay).

6 The terms "story" and "plot" have been supplied by translators as approximate renderings of *fabula* and *sjužet* (or *siuzhet*), the terms first used by the Russian Formalists and later elaborated (as *fable* and *sujet*) by some French Structuralists. The basic theoretical or critical considerations of these categories include: Victor Shklovsky, "Sterne's *Tristram Shandy:* Stylistic Commentary," and Boris Tomashevsky, "Thematics," both in *Russian Formalist Criticism: Four Essays,* ed. and trans. Lee T. Lemon and Marion J. Reis (Lincoln: Univ. of Nebraska Press, 1965), pp. 25-67 and 61-95; and Victor Shklovsky, "The Mystery Novel: Dickens' *Little Dorrit,"* trans. Guy Carter, in *Readings in Russian Poetics: Formalist and Structuralist Views,* ed. Ladislav Matejka and Krystyna Pomorska (Cambridge: MIT Press, 1971), pp. 218-26. Temporal inversion or deformation, used by Puig in several of his texts, is one of the most visible signs of the transformation of story into plot.

7 See, among others, Puig's autobiographical account in "Growing Up at the Movies: A Chronology," *Review,* Nos. 4-5 (Winter 1971-Spring 1972), pp. 49-51.

8 The notion of a text in dialogic relation with other texts, languages, or traditions is developed by Mikhail Bakhtin in *Problems of Dostoevsky's Poetics* (1929), trans. R. W. Rotsel (Ann Arbor: Ardis, 1973), and in *The Dialogic Imagination: Four Essays* (1975), trans. Caryl Emerson and Michael Holquist, ed. Michael Holquist, Univ. of Texas Press Slavic Series, No. 1 (Austin: Univ. of Texas Press, 1981); see also Julia Kristeva, *Le texte du roman: Approche sémiologique d'une structure discursive transformationnelle* (The Hague: Mouton, 1976).

9 See, for example, Christ, "An Interview with Manuel Puig," p. 54, and Emir Rodríguez Monegal, "El folletín rescatado," *Revista de la Universidad de México,* 27, No. 2 (1972), pp. 26-30, for Puig's views on the relation between his novel and the extra-literary world upon which it would comment. In a personal interview (22 and 25 January 1979), Puig emphasized his desire to call into question, even criticize, the Don Juan/macho figure through his novel; cf. Danubio Torres Fierro, "Conversación con Manuel Puig: La redención de la cursilería," *Eco,* 28 (1975), 511, and Christ, "An Interview with Manuel Puig," p. 61.

10 In Chapters IV and V, for example, the activities of each of the characters during a single day (23 April 1937) are narrated successively in exactly this order; see also Chapters IX (27 January 1938) and XVI (15 September 1968). A departure from this ordering occurs in Chapter XIV, where, because of the focus on the day of Juan Carlos' death (18 April 1947), Juan Carlos precedes Nené in the sequence.

11 See Carlos Raúl Yujnovsky, *"Boquitas pintadas ¿folletín?" Nuevos Aires,* No. 8 (August-October 1972), p. 53.

12 Among other sources, the following provide basic information about the development of the Don Juan figure and legend over the years: Leo Weinstein, *The Metamorphoses of Don Juan* (Stanford: Stanford Univ. Press, 1959); Oscar Mandel, ed., *The Theatre of Don Juan: A Collection of Plays and Views, 1630-1963* (Lincoln: Univ. of Nebraska Press, 1963); Otto Rank, *The Don Juan Legend* (1924), ed. and trans. David G. Winter (Princeton: Princeton Univ. Press, 1975; Saint-Paulien, *Don Juan: Mythe et réalité* (Paris: Plon, 1967); H. G. Tan, *La matière de Don Juan et les genres littéraires* (Leiden: Presse Universitaire de Leyde, 1976); and Armand E. Singer, *The Don Juan Theme, Versions and Criticism: A Bibliography,* Rev. ed. (Morgantown: West Virginia Univ. Press, 1965).

13 Cf. Alicia Borinsky, "Castration: Artifices; Notes on the Writing of Manuel Puig," *Georgia Review,* 29 (1975), 106; Alfred J. Mac Adam, "Manuel Puig's Chronicles of Provincial Life," *Revista Hispánica Moderna,* 36 (1970-71), 61-62; and Yujnovsky, *"Boquitas pintadas ¿folletín?"* pp. 53-56.

14 In addition to Shklovsky's basic statements concerning the term "defamiliarization" ("making strange")—"Art as Technique," in *Russian Formalist Criticism*, pp. 5-24—see R. H. Stacy, *Defamiliarization in Language and Literature* (Syracuse: Syracuse Univ. Press, 1977), for a theoretical and historical discussion of the concept. It is in part because of its variety of defamiliarizing techniques that this novel can be read as a special case of "spatial form" in modern fiction. For, it is not only in the various disjunctions between story and plot, but also in its peculiar relation to its generic model, whose characteristic temporality is spatially manipulated, that *Boquitas pintadas* would represent such modes. The notion of spatial form is developed first by Joseph Frank in his well known essay "Spatial Form in Modern Literature" (1945), *The Widening Gyre* (Bloomington: Indiana Univ. Press, 1968); see the essays by Rabkin, Holtz, Kermode and Frank himself, in *Critical Inquiry*, 4 (1977-78) and 5 (1978-79), for a recent polemical discussion through which an expansion and clarification of the theory has been attempted.

15 Wolfgang Iser uses the serial novel as a prime illustration of the kinds of narrative techniques that create indeterminacy in a text, forcing the reader's participation in it; see his "Indeterminacy and the Reader's Response in Prose Fiction," in [English Institute] *Aspects of Narrative*, ed. J. Hillis Miller (New York: Columbia Univ. Press, 1971), pp. 14-17.

16 Rodríguez Monegal has emphasized the notion of recuperation vis-à-vis this and other popular models (with which Puig agrees), in his "El folletín rescatado." See also Saúl Sosnowski, "Entrevista con Manuel Puig," *Hispamérica*, No. 3 (1973), p. 73.

TESTIMONIO Y AUTOR/IDAD EN
HASTA NO VERTE JESUS MIO,
DE ELENA PONIATOWSKA

Cynthia Steele
University of Washington

La publicación consecutiva de *Hasta no verte Jesús mío* (1969) y *La noche de Tlatelolco* (1971)[1] convirtió a Elena Poniatowska en la figura más destacada entre los escritores comprometidos de México, lugar que ha venido ocupando a lo largo de los últimos veinte años. Además de gozar de una recepción entusiasta entre los críticos, estas novelas se sitúan entre las obras más leídas en la historia de las letras mexicanas[2]. La popularidad de estos libros responde en gran medida a su implicación en urgentes problemas sociales y políticos que adquirieron relevancia a partir del movimiento estudiantil de 1968.

Si *La noche de Tlatelolco* ha servido como celebración y vindicación de ese movimiento, además de portavoz de la indignación provocada por su violenta represión por el gobierno, *Hasta no verte Jesús mío* tiene una función semejante respecto a los problemas que aquejan a los pobres del Distrito Federal. La obra está basada en la historia oral de Josefina Bórquez (1900-1987), llamada Jesusa Palancares en el texto[3], una lavandera que atrajo a la autora por su carácter vivaracho y contestatario. Poniatowska entrevistó a Bórquez todos los miércoles durante un año, durante 1963 y 1964. En ensayos publicados en 1979 y 1984, la escritora describe la relación íntima aunque difícil que existía entre entrevistadora e informante en las primeras etapas de su colaboración. Después las dos mujeres fueron amigas a lo largo de dos décadas, hasta la muerte de Bórquez en mayo de 1987[4].

En los dos ensayos, la autora escribe sobre su estrecha identificación con su informante, cuya fortaleza y vitalidad admiraba y cuya mexicanidad llegó a reconocer como suya. Resume la naturaleza de su colaboración así: "Ella y yo teníamos una relación personal muy amorosa, pero un poco conflictiva" ("Testimonios" 158). Hasta cierto punto este conflicto podría haber derivado de las diferentes agendas de las dos mujeres al construir la historia oral y del papel editorial agresivo que tomó Poniatowska. Ella describe el proceso editorial en términos que combinan metáforas de la domesticidad 'femenina' con otras de la violencia 'masculina': "Utilicé las anécdotas, las ideas y muchos de los modismos de Jesusa Palancares pero no podría afirmar que el relato es una transcripción directa de su vida porque ella misma lo rechazaría. Maté a los personajes que me sobraban, eliminé cuanta sesión espiritualista pude, elaboré donde me pareció necesario, podé, cosí, remendé, inventé" ("Hasta" 10). Luego explica que su interés en la vida de Bórquez se centra en su combatividad e independencia, precisamente lo que la diferenciaba del modelo estereotipado de la mujer mexicana pasiva y sumisa, y encontró un foco para estas características en la participación de Bórquez como soldadera en la Revolución. Para Josefina Bórquez, por otro lado, la ejemplaridad de su vida está en su ilustración de conceptos religiosos; además, habló muchísimo de las difíciles condiciones materiales de su vida. La transcripción de la primera entrevista entre Poniatowska y Palancares (véase la próxima sección de este ensayo) comienza así:

> Yo quiero empezar por hablar de lo que he sufrido aquí en México, porque de cuando fui chica no interesa. Ya pasó tiempo. Así es de que yo ahorita voy a hablar únicamente de cuando yo llegué aquí a México sin amparo más que el de Dios porque no conocía a nadien y tuve que andar sufriendo por las calles[5].

Por otra parte, Poniatowska se tomó muchas libertades al recrear el lenguaje de Bórquez, combinándolo con los dialectos de trabajadoras domésticas de diferentes partes de la república que había conocido a lo largo de los años, para crear una especie de denominador común del habla femenino popular. No es de extrañar, entonces, que, al enfrentarse con el manuscrito final, Bórquez haya negado su autenticidad: "Usted inventa todo, son puras mentiras, no entendió nada, las cosas no son así" ("Testimonios", 160). Sin embargo, cuando vio su santo patrón, el Niño de Atocha, en la portada del libro impreso, pidió ejemplares para que sus compañeros del taller leyeran sobre su vida. Es decir, Bórquez parecía dispuesta a aceptar la veracidad del texto una vez que éste estaba asociado con lo que para ella era el máximo símbolo de autoridad religiosa. Como veremos, esta autoridad era esencialmente patriarcal, una extensión del considerable poder que su padre y su marido habían ejercido sobre ella durante su juventud.

Por la insistencia de Bórquez en mantenerse anónima, nuestra única fuente de información sobre ella han sido los ensayos escritos por Poniatowska, el primero de los cuales no se publicó hasta catorce años después de que tuvieran lugar las entrevistas en que se basó el texto. Esto ha complicado todo intento de determinar hasta qué punto el libro es ficticio y hasta qué punto discrepa con el sentido que habrá dado Bórquez a su propia vida. Estas dos cuestiones están relacionadas pero no son intercambiables, ya que la visión que tiene cualquier persona de su vida, cualquier autobiografía, es hasta cierto punto una ficción. Poniatowska ha observado que "Jesusa inventaba una vida anterior e interior que le hacía tolerable su actual miseria" ("Hasta", 7); aunque este comentario se refiere específicamente a su fe en la reencarnación, quizás podría aplicarse a su historia entera. Cualquier narración necesariamente es selectiva y parcial, un invento de lo que fue, entrelazado con una crónica de lo que pudo haber sido. Una solución cada vez más popular al dilema del crítico de la novela testimonial (y especialmente de este libro) es pasar por alto la dimensión biográfica y tratarla como una novela cualquiera. Pero esta solución atribuye implícitamente toda la autoridad creativa a uno de los dos autores del texto. Para parafrasear la advertencia de Stephen Tyler sobre la etnografía, completa el proceso de robarle la voz al informante (128), reduciendo la especifidad de vidas e identidades humanas a la seguridad de la abstracción.

Nuevas fuentes: Las entrevistas

Durante septiembre de 1988 y abril y mayo de 1989, Elena Poniatowska me dio acceso a transcripciones de algunas de sus entrevistas con Bórquez (la primera de las cuales está fechada el 4 de marzo de 1964), además de varios borradores, tanto tempranos como tardíos, del texto del testimonio. El primer borrador aparentemente es de 1963 o 1964, si nos atenemos a la declaración de la informante de que nació en 1900 y ahora tiene 63 años; el último está marcado "penúltima versión" y lleva la fecha de diciembre de 1967. En algunas entrevistas se incluyen las preguntas y otras intervenciones de Poniatowska; en otras, y en todos los borradores del libro, éstas han sido suprimidas.

Lo que revelan estos materiales es que, en el libro, Poniatowska se mantuvo extremadamente fiel tanto a la historia de su informante como a su lenguaje. No hay duda de que Josefina Bórquez fue una informante elocuente aunque difícil. En muchas ocasiones se irrita cuando la autora le hace la misma pregunta en dos o tres ocasiones, para buscar clarificaciones o verificar que ha comprendido algo. A veces Bórquez repite una declaración contradictoria y luego se enoja con Poniatowska por confundirse o señalar las contradicciones. En gran medida, la tensión entre las dos mujeres parece derivarse de sus diferentes sistemas de valores y maneras de comprender la psicología, lo que tiene sus raíces en su educación y experiencias vitales ya que pertenecen a clases sociales tan distintas. Mientras Poniatowska busca motivaciones y reacciones complejas, Bórquez encuentra explicaciones y sentimientos sencillos y, para ella, obvios. Por ejemplo, cuando ésta habla del deseo que tenía su marido de matarla, Poniatowska aparentemente interrumpe para preguntar sobre sus motivos. Josefina responde, "¿Que por qué me quería matar? Porque no quería que me quedara viva". Ante

una pregunta semejante sobre por qué el compañero de su hermana la quiso asesinar, Bórquez contesta, "Pus porque son locos los
hombres". En otro momento declara que los hombres son innata-
mente infieles: "Lo train de herencia". Josefina también insiste que
no le dolió cuando su marido fue matado en la Revolución: "Yo no
sentí feo. No. ¿Pa' qué? ¿Pa' qué sentía yo feo si yo quería que él se
muriera?"

En otra parte de la conversación, se hace evidente que hay un
desacuerdo fundamental entre las dos mujeres sobre la autenticidad e importancia del amor romántico. Poniatowska insiste que
Bórquez debía haber estado enamorada en algún momento de su
vida, y Bórquez contesta una y otra vez que, mientras ha sentido
"aprecio" o "estimación" por sus amigos, por ejemplo, en el caso del
chofer (Antonio Pérez), nunca ha estado enamorada de nadie, ni
siquiera de su marido. Por otro lado, ella reconoce haber sentido celos y rabia hacia las amigas que la han dejado para irse con "otros
hombres", un comentario que subraya el carácter masculino de su
auto-imagen. Pedro Aguilar, su marido, sí la había amado, dice,
pero ella no le había correspondido por su egoísmo y falta de sensi-
bilidad: "Yo no lo quise ... Porque no, no, no. Era un hombre de muchas mujeres, muy mujerero, y muy parrandero, y muy celoso".
Explica que no cree en el amor romántico, que las historias de
amor que se escuchan en la radio son mentiras. Cuando Poniatowska sugiere que no es normal el no sentir amor, Bórquez se defiende, contestando que la anormal será su entrevistadora por creer
en un concepto falso, o señalando que la definición de la normalidad es variable: "Pues no será normal, pero para mí sí es normal
porque yo no los sé querer, pues..."

Una entrevista fechada el 11 de mayo de 1964 contiene este elocuente discurso sobre las desventajas del matrimonio para la mujer (pobre), en contraste con la independencia y la felicidad de la vida de soltera:

> .... es muy bonito vivir sólo sin que nadie le reclame a uno. La vida es
> más bonita así solito uno, sin quien le pegue a uno un grito. Va uno
> por la calle muy feliz sin que haya ningún reclamo. Pero vaya usted
> por ése que tiene su mujer y sus hijos, y luego muy felices andan
> paseándose ellos, sin saber que sus hijos tienen hambre, sus mujeres
> están careciendo de lo más indispensable, y éso no es de justicia. Por
> eso no tiene uno que meterse en danzas. Por eso mismo vivir sólo sin
> buscarse compromisos ajenos [sic].

En la misma conversación Poniatowska cuestiona el rechazo de
Bórquez hacia su marido, sugiriendo que él no siempre se había
portado tan mal con ella, ya que, cuando andaban en la Revolución,
una vez le había curado las piernas quemadas por la nieve, y en
otras ocasiones le había traído mascotas. Bórquez contesta que los
hombres son "convenencieros" (hacen lo que les conviene); que Pedro la había curado por el que dirán, y que no le había traído ningún animal; se los habían regalado a él y eran mascotas suyas.

Describe su papel como esposa de Pedro Aguilar en estos términos: "...pos era su gata del, su criada, su gata sin sueldo. La mujer no es más que la gata sin sueldo. Limpia el suelo, vete al mandado, lava los trastes, haz la comida, y dale de comer a tu marido, lávalo, plánchalo, y sin ningún centavo que uno gane. Eso es la gata de balde. ¡Mejor no ¡Pus qué! ..."

Aunque estas entrevistas y borradores no contienen información que cambie fundamentalmente nuestra comprensión del texto literario o de la informante que sirvió de modelo para Jesusa Palancares, sí expresan algunas características y creencias de forma más rotunda: concretamente, su aceptación del aspecto hostil y violento de la conducta humana, especialmente la masculina; y su rechazo categórico del matrimonio y del concepto del amor romántico. Además, revelan nueva información sobre la dinámica de las entrevistas y la dialéctica de las ideologías conflictivas que engendraron el texto final.

La historia oral como confesión

Si el escepticismo de Bórquez con respecto a la veracidad del texto refleja, hasta cierto punto, su personalidad combativa, probablemente derive también de la naturaleza problemática de la relación etnográfica, que tiene sus raíces en importantes diferencias de clase y, por consiguiente, de acceso al poder. Algunos críticos de la historia oral como género, entre ellos Langness y Frank (46-47), señalan la transferencia, la contratransferencia y la identificación como fenómenos comunes en este tipo de relación. Además, los comentarios de Poniatowska indican que Bórquez llegó a depender de ella emocionalmente, mientras que se rebelaba a la vez contra esta dependencia. Al mismo tiempo, Poniatowska dependió de Bórquez para sentirse mexicana. Esta dinámica, junto con la profunda religiosidad de Bórquez, sugieren una relación terapeútica o confesional. Como sostiene Michel Foucault:

> [d]esde la Edad Media por lo menos, las sociedades occidentales han establecido la confesión como uno de los ritos principales en que dependemos para la producción de la verdad ... hemos pasado de un placer para ser contado y escuchado, centrado en la narración heroica o maravillosa de 'pruebas' de valentía o santidad, a una literatura ordenada según la infinita tarea de extraer desde lo más profundo de uno mismo, de entre las palabras, una verdad que la misma forma de la confesión ofrece como un espejismo destellante (*The History* 58-59, mi traducción).

Según Foucault, la confesión cristiana, como la 'cura hablada' freudiana, ha tomado como su tema predilecto el sexo; la obligación de esconder el sexo en la vida cotidiana se ha complementado con el deber de revelarlo en la confesión privada (*The History*, 61). Si vemos *Hasta no verte Jesús mío* como una confesión, entonces es una confesión que toma la violencia, en vez del sexo, como su enfoque narrativo. De hecho la sexualidad puede verse como el centro ausente de la vida de Jesusa Palancares, el silencio ensordecedor que emana de la auto-censura. Mientras la narradora se extiende hablando de las vidas sexuales ajenas, lo hace principalmente con el propósito de condenar su inmoralidad y egoísmo y así establecer un contraste implícito con su propio comportamiento pudoroso. Niega rotundamente el haber tenido deseos carnales jamás ni haber tenido contacto sexual desde que enviudó a los diecisiete años. Por lo tanto el lector confiado se sorprende cuando menciona su sífilis avanzada, un episodio que describe en un tono exento de emoción. En este y otros pasajes de la novela, la inocencia intencionada y el desencanto de Palancares parecen coexistir con una inocencia auténtica.

La colaboración entre Poniatowska y Bórquez, entonces, fue complicada por conflictos ideológicos y una dinámica difícil caracterizada por una dependencia mutua y una fuerte ambivalencia de parte de la informante con respecto a la autoridad de su entrevistadora. Como veremos, la formación de Bórquez había engendrado una internalización del autoritarismo, la violencia, el racismo y el rechazo de lo femenino. Por lo tanto, su percepción de Poniatowska como autora y 'confesora' (blanca, rica, educada, poderosa) femenina era profundamente ambigua. En cuanto a Poniatowska, a la vez que se frustraba al no encontrar un sistema de valores semejante a su propia cosmovisión, buscaba –y encontraba– en su informante la sabiduría popular. La siguiente descripción proviene de la transcripción de una entrevista no grabada, fechada el 11 de mayo de 1964:

> A José, le ha nacido un pollito negro y a cada rato se asoma a verlo. Se ve muy contenta con su pollito. Tiene sus trenzas hechas un nudo, a modo de chonguito y la cara muy risueña. Sigo con los ojos su sonrisa, la curvatura de sus labios; a veces los encoge en una sonrisa muy especial, maliciosa, de lado, y pienso que así debía sonreir cuando era una muchachita ... Bajo su piel morena, se levantan los músculos; fuertes duros, duros los pómulos, dura también la quijada. Los ojos negros miran con cierta ansiedad, como buscando algo, como que salen al encuentro. Encogida sobre su sillita de madera, José es como un idolito; y pienso que me está dictando una lección muy profunda; dice cosas de una sabiduría grave, adolorida...Y quisiera que en su libro se reflejara esto; que no simplemente fueran anécdotas añadidas las unas a las otras más o menos entretenidas, sino que todo adquiriera otro sentido, que los conceptos pudieran translucirse a través de la acción; que la filosofía de la vida de José, se viera, y se viera cuán valiosas son sus ideas y su actitud ante todas las cosas.

La familia y la personalidad autoritaria: La identificación masculina, el autodesprecio racial y la violencia

Es convincente el argumento de Edward H. Friedman de que la protagonista de *Hasta no verte Jesús mío* admira a los hombres por su estado privilegiado, no por su moralidad. Sin embargo, discrepo con su opinión de que "a Jesusa no le gustan los hombres y, de hecho, hace todo lo posible por eludirlos" (181, mi traducción). Al contrario, la vida de Palancares está marcada por la competencia y los conflictos con otras mujeres, comenzando con su madre y su hermana, una actitud que encuentra su complemento en su fuerte identificación con e idealización de los hombres, comenzando con su padre y su hermano Emiliano, y culminando con sus guías espirituales masculinos. Esta preferencia de género se transfiere a las actitudes de Jesusa hacia la homosexualidad; su tolerancia hacia los hombres homosexuales se extiende hasta Manuel el Robachicos, mientras su condena del lesbianismo es categórica (184-87, 261).

Después del capítulo introductorio, que coloca la narración en el marco del espiritualismo, la historia oral de Palancares comienza con el fin prematuro de su niñez, como resultado de la temprana muerte de su madre en un contexto de miseria. Ella describe cómo brincó a la sepultura en un intento inútil de proteger la cara de su madre para que no le cayeran los montones de tierra, y como expresión de su duelo y deseo de morir: "Quería que me taparan allí con mi mamá" (17). La fuerza conmovedora y la posición enfática de este episodio llaman la atención del lector hacia la pérdida de su madre y la tragedia de su niñez truncada: "Mi mamá no me regañó ni me pegó nunca. Era morena igual a mí, chaparrita, gorda y cuando se murió nunca volví a jugar" (20). Sin embargo, hay pocas menciones posteriores de su madre, y éstas enfatizan su preferencia por el padre; él es sin duda la figura central en su economía psíquica. Aunque su deseo de morir surgirá otra vez después de la muerte de Emiliano, ella permanece impasible ante la muerte de su padre (según ella porque no la presenció). No obstante, la intensidad de su duelo por la muerte de una mascota suya varios años después se puede interpretar como una reacción retardada a la pérdida anterior y mucho mayor.

La identificación de Jesusa Palancares con la etnicidad despreciada de su madre es, en muchos sentidos, central para su autoimagen e ideología. Después de la muerte de ésta, su hermana mayor Petra volvió a vivir con la familia y a reemplazar a la madre, pero Jesusa la rechazó. Al comentar su desafío a Petra, Jesusa ofrece dos explicaciones. En primer lugar, no la quería porque no se había criado con ella: "Ya estaba acostumbrada a mano de hombre, a la mano de mi padre". Además, su hermana, a diferencia de su padre, era morena (aquí y a lo largo de la novela, se contradice con respecto a su propio color): "Petra era trigueña, más prieta que yo. Yo tengo la cara quemada del sol pero no soy prieta, pero ella sí era oscura de cuerpo y cara. Salió más india que yo. Dos sacamos el color de mi papá y los otros dos fueron prietitos. Efrén y Petra, Emiliano y yo, mitad y mitad" (31)[6]. Por lo tanto, ella asocia el color moreno y los rasgos indígenas con su madre, y la ascendencia europea con su padre; de acuerdo con la ideología mexicana domi-

nante, valora su abolengo europeo por encima de su linaje indígena. Quizás no es casual que, después de que han muerto todos los
miembros de su familia inmediata y ella se ha convertido al espiritualismo, sólo recuerda con cariño al hermano claro, Emiliano, e
incluso imagina que él vuelve de la muerte para salvarla de sus borracheras: "Emiliano ... siempre fue bueno conmigo. Durante años
me cuidó cuando anduve de borracha en las cantinas. Se materia-
lizaba, se servía de otros cerebros y me sacaba de las juergas. Se
me presentaba en otro señor y me decía –Vámonos. Y yo me le que-
daba mirando: –Pues vámonos, le decía yo muy dócil" (15-16).

En cuanto a su hermano mayor, Efrén, Jesusa asocia su tez
morena con su alcoholismo e inmoralidad: "Era muy prieto, muy
borracho y muy perdido" (27). El auto-desprecio racial que está implícito en su caracterización de sus relaciones familiares se hace
aún más evidente cuando habla del consejo dado a su marido mu-
jeriego en el sentido de que, si le va a ser infiel, por lo menos debe
escoger amantes menos prietas que ella:"–Siquiera cuando se meta
a hacerme guaje, búsquese una cosa buena, que no sea igual a mí
de india ... Una cosa que costiée ..." (104).

Palancares reconoció y manipuló el poder del cual gozaba sobre
su padre a lo largo de su niñez y adolescencia: "Mi papá hacía lo
que yo quería" (21). Según ella, tanto él como su madre eran permi-
sivos pero no cariñosos. Sin embargo su narración revela maneras
en que él indirectamente expresaba su afecto, peinándola o hacién-
dole sus pocos y primitivos juguetes, la mayoría de ellos típicamente masculinos (canicas de piedra, una flecha, una honda, una mu-
ñeca hecha de una ardilla muerta). Este vínculo entre padre e hija
a través del juego y el placer fue roto, en gran medida, por la muerte de la madre: "Después nunca me volvió a hacer nada. Nunca
más. Se hizo el sordo o todas las cosas le pasaron como chiflonazos"
(18).

Después de la muerte de su madre, la conexión emocional de
los niños con el padre se da por medio de la naturaleza; Felipe
Palancares llevaba a sus hijos a buscar huevos de tortuga en la pla-
ya de Salina Cruz por la noche, y luego, durante la Revolución, llevaba a Jesusa a nadar en el río. Además de este placer que ambos
encuentran en el mundo natural, Jesusa sugiere que ella y su padre compartieron otras características, todas ellas tradicionalmen-
te consideradas como masculinas: la inteligencia, la autosuficiencia, incluso la incapacidad de cocinar (22, 26, 28).

La fijación edípica de la protagonista se expresa vívidamente a
través de la actitud posesiva hacia su padre, la cual es más aparente cuando, al morir la madre de Jesusa, él comenzaba a traer mujeres a cuidar a los niños y compartir su cama. Jesusa no toleraba
sus relaciones sexuales con ellas; además, literalmente estaba
siendo reemplazada, ya que ella solía dormir en la misma cama
con su padre. La narración de los eventos revela una inocencia intencionada que es característica de la voz narrativa de Jesusa: "Yo

dormía con mi papá, pero como es tierra caliente, nos tendíamos en una hamaca, y nunca dejé que se fuera a acostar con la mujer esa. Entonces ella empezó a emborracharse con lo del mandado, váyase a saber por qué" (21). El día después de que esta mujer acusó implícitamente a Jesusa de cometer incesto –acusación que sería hecha explícita por otras compañeras posteriores de Felipe– Jesusa la corrió a pedradas, utilizando como pretexto el alcoholismo de la mujer (a la vez que toleraba las borracheras de los hombres de su familia).

En gran medida Jesusa desempeñaba el papel de protectora y vengadora matriarcal como contrapartida al papel que había adoptado Felipe Palancares de padre irresponsable e inocente víctima de las mujeres oportunistas y manipuladoras. Estos son roles asociados con los géneros sexuales que, según Fromm y Maccoby, prevalecían entre los residentes del pueblo mestizo que ellos estudiaron durante los años sesenta; los psicólogos sugieren que la ineficacia masculina es un síntoma de la desintegración del sistema patriarcal tradicional, en el contexto del empobrecimiento del campo bajo el Porfiriato[7]. En su forma más extrema, este síndrome se alterna con el masoquismo sádico (el cual lleva a la violencia doméstica que encontramos en la casa de los Palancares) (115, 151). De acuerdo con este modelo, Jesusa nos dice que su padre reconocía el derecho que ella tenía, de hecho su obligación, de golpear a sus queridas:

> Siempre tuvo sus mujeres y eso sí, yo siempre les pegué porque eran abusivas, porque eran glotonas, porque se quedaban botadas de borrachas, porque se gastaban el dinero de mi papá...Eso era lo que a mí me daba más coraje, que se acabaran el dinero de mi papá, eso sí que no, por eso le golpié a sus queridas ... Él sabía que yo tenía que pegarle a todas sus mujeres, menos a mi madrastra (67-69).

Una contradicción clave en la narración que hace Palancares de su niñez emerge de su presentación de salvadores masculinos falsos. En la superficie la narradora parece tener una visión caballeresca de los hombres (la cual probablemente aprendió de la ideología popular y las novelas de romance) como rescatadores de doncellas en peligro; sin embargo, una y otra vez su historia revela que el 'salvador' es un lobo disfrazado de cordero. Por ejemplo, después de que Efrén, el hermano mayor de Jesusa y un alcohólico, regresó a la casa familiar, golpeaba a su mujer, Ignacia. Jesusa (quien atacó a la primera amante de su padre y también pegaba a su hermana Petra) defendió a su cuñada, a pesar de que ésta regularmente la golpeaba a ella. Cuando Ignacia abortó a causa de los golpes de Efrén, su padre, por su cuenta, le pegó a éste y corrió de la casa a la pareja. Al hacer esto, alegaba que estaba protegiendo a su nuera, pero en realidad solamente se tranquilizaba la conciencia al alejar a esa pareja violenta de su presencia y ahorrarse la posible intervención. Después de que Efrén se cayó borracho en una zanja y se ahogó, Felipe aceptó a Ignacia en la casa, otra vez presentándose como su salvador. Sin embargo, la embarazó, revelando así su interés en la situación; había cambiado su protección por acceso sexual. Es interesante notar que este es uno de los pocos incidentes sobre el cual Jesusa expresa alguna duda, empezando la última parte de la anécdota con la frase, "Según cuentan"; parece que le cuesta aceptar el hecho de que su padre se haya aprovechado de su cuñada. Su mayor preocupación, sin embargo, no es por el bienestar de Ignacia; más bien lamenta que la relación haya producido un pariente (un medio hermano y sobrino a la vez) que no se da cuenta de su parentesco con ella. Para Jesusa el episodio es importante no porque ejemplifica el abuso sexual sobre las mujeres desprovistas del poder, sino porque contribuye a la desintegración del linaje Palancares y a la dispersión de la familia.

La historia de Petra es semejante. Fue raptada a los quince años por un extraño quien mantuvo con ella una relación opresiva durante tres años. Jesusa le echa la culpa a su madre, en vez de a su padre, por no haber protegido a Petra, ya que ésta se encontraba haciendo tareas domésticas–recogiendo una manta recién lavada–cuando fue secuestrada: "... por eso de la recochina limpieza le birlaron a su hija" [32]. Por otro lado, no se le ocurre echarle la culpa a ninguno de sus padres por no hacer nada por encontrar y rescatar a su hija desaparecida. Le toca a otro extraño, Cayetano, liberar a Petra de su secuestrador; luego ahorró su salario durante un año para devolverla a sus padres y al mismo tiempo pedirles permiso para vivir con ella sin casarse. Por consiguiente, su comportamiento caballeresco resulta ser tan engañoso como la actuación de Felipe con Ignacia; era una manera de hacer que Petra contrajera una deuda con él, deuda que pagaría con el sexo y la sumisión. Además, Cayetano resultó aún más peligroso que su suegro; tres o cuatro meses después de comenzar a cohabitar con Petra, intentó asesinarla mientras dormía. Como en el caso de Ignacia, era un hermano (Emiliano), en vez del padre, quien salvó a la mujer en peligro; pero Petra, como su madre (la madre de Jesusa), finalmente murió del susto.

Asimismo, el aparente poder que tiene Jesusa sobre la vida de su padre, incluyendo sus relaciones sexuales y su dinero, enmascara el poder real y completo que tenía él sobre la persona de ella, incluyendo la autoridad de escogerle marido y así determinar su futuro. Es una autoridad que él cedía y asumía arbitrariamente. En un nivel psicológico, ella interpreta la intervención de Felipe como prueba de su cariño; además, como mujer, a ella no se le permitía llenar el vacío de poder que deja el abandono paterno. Hasta cierto punto el comportamiento irresponsable de Felipe Palancares parece ser motivado por sus celos de los pretendientes de su hija predilecta (o, por lo menos, la narradora quiere hacernos creer que ello es así). Como se comentó antes, su conducta no es atípica aparentemente y puede indicar una desintegración de los patrones tradicionales del poder patriarcal.

En todo caso queda claro que el deber de Felipe estaba definido por un sistema patriarcal y que Jesusa era objeto del tráfico de mujeres[8]. En la narración de su niñez ella describe repetidamente sus interacciones con hombres en términos de propiedad e intercambio. Por ejemplo, más de una vez su padre fue castigado por no protegerla del abuso físico de los demás. Durante la Revolución ella y cuatro mujeres carrancistas fueron capturadas y retenidas durante dos semanas en el campamento de Zapata sin ser tocadas, antes de ser devueltas a sus maridos. Así Zapata probaba su superioridad militar sobre los carrancistas y al mismo tiempo demostraba su honor masculino al no aprovecharse de su botín de guerra. Además, el general apelaba al honor de Felipe Palancares al pedirle que defendiera a las mujeres de los celos de sus maridos ofendidos. Estos por fin se contentaron con arrancar de sus mujeres la promesa de guardar el secreto de su prisión, protegiendo así el honor de sus maridos. Al cumplir con la promesa durante cincuenta años, Jesusa implícitamente expresa su aprobación de este código caballeresco del intercambio de mujeres.

El tráfico de mujeres también funcionaba –en menoscabo de Jesusa– en el caso de su matrimonio con Pedro Aguilar. Su padre había abandonado su autoridad paterna por la rabia provocada cuando Jesusa habló zapoteca con un grupo de soldados (lo cual indica su racismo, celos y compulsión por controlar su propiedad femenina) y luego por la negativa de Jesusa a dejarse castigar. Ella buscó la protección de un hombre más poderoso, el superior militar de su padre (antes una amiga de su madre no había tenido suficiente poder social para defenderla de la violencia de su madrastra). Cuando Pedro Aguilar, cuyos intentos de controlar a Jesusa habían resultado vanos también, le propuso matrimonio, ella lo rechazó y pidió que la mandaran a Oaxaca. Entonces le tocaba al general, el substituto de su padre, determinar su futuro. Él no basó su decisión ni en los deseos de Jesusa ni en los de su familia, sino en una desconfianza general en la agresión masculina contra las mujeres. En vez de ponerla a merced de la tripulación masculina del barco que la llevaría a Tehuantepec, prefirió entregarla a un solo hombre.

Antes, la insistencia de Aguilar en pagar toda la mercancía que compraba Jesusa, contra sus vehementes reparos, había sido una manifestación de bravata machista y un intento claro de comprar a la pretendida endeudándola con él. Una vez que había tomado posesión de su presa a través de la decisión patriarcal del general, se vengó de ella por sus desaires, manteniéndola encerrada bajo llave, golpeándola y "ocupándola" sexualmente sin reparar en los deseos de Jesusa. Por su cuenta, a lo largo de su narración Palancares se niega a reconocer que haya tenido tal deseo. Su padre y su marido pueden haber logrado o no hacerla renunciar a la sexualidad –una pregunta que el texto contesta ambiguamente. De lo que no hay duda es de que ellos, y la sociedad en general, sí la convencieron de que reprimiera el discurso sexual femenino. Sin embargo, como veremos, estos deseos resurgirán en la forma de revelaciones espiritualistas. Inicialmente Jesusa adoptó el papel obediente y sumiso que se esperaba de ella. Cuando por fin se rebeló contra los abusos de Pedro, durante su ausencia, comportándose precisamente como él temía (administrando un bar y comprándose un vestuario suntuoso; es decir, tomando, coqueteando, experimentando el placer en su ausencia y por lo tanto fuera de su control), él la castigó exigiendo que se vistiera de hombre y prohibiéndole que se bañara. En otras palabras, respondió a sus acciones agresivas y típicamente masculinas forzándola a renunciar simbólicamente a su sexualidad femenina, haciendo que su aspecto estuviera de acuerdo con su conducta "masculina y cochina"9. Su segundo acto de rebelión directa fue cuando ella se defendió de sus ataques físicos; no obstante, siguió sirviendo a su esposo desde una posición de inferioridad (marcada por el uso de "usted" al dirigirse a Pedro, mientras él le hablaba de "tú")10.

Las únicas memorias positivas que Palancares conserva del hombre que brevemente fue su marido son las noches en que él le leía novelas. El placer que le da la narración y específicamente el contar sus revelaciones espirituales y sueños tuvo sus orígenes aparentemente en estas experiencias (y, como veremos, antes en la cárcel de Tehuantepec). Sin embargo, aún en este contexto Pedro insiste en ejercer un control absoluto sobre su mujer, contradiciendo sus interpretaciones imaginativas y exigiendo que respete sus propias interpretaciones como válidas. No es de sorprender que Pedro no le enseñe a leer. En cierto sentido él es como un guía religioso predicando dogma a los ignorantes; como veremos, en la Obra Espiritual Jesusa encontrará finalmente otra fuente de autoridad patriarcal, aunque esta sea un poco menos inflexible.

Tanto estos episodios como otro incidente que revela las raíces psicológicas y sociológicas de su crueldad evitan que Aguilar sea presentado como un villano estereotipado. Jesusa cuenta que, cuando ella y su marido fueron a visitar a la abuela de Pedro, ella observó el tierno reencuentro entre su marido y una chiva que había sido su nodriza y, en efecto, había reemplazado a su madre (nos dice que la chiva murió -aparentemente de pena- un día después de que terminó su visita). Es característico de la falta de comunicación entre los dos esposos que Jesusa nunca supo qué había sido de los padres de Pedro. Este retrato patético de la carencia emocional está de acuerdo con los perfiles psicológicos de los hombres violentos; el clásico caso del hombre que golpea a su mujer es el de una persona que ha sufrido abuso físico, descuido extremo o abandono durante su niñez y que intenta ejercer un control total sobre otra persona, subconscientemente para compensar su anterior experiencia. Ya que es imposible, no se diga indeseable, obtener tal control sobre otro, su frustración puede desembocar en violencia (Shupe, 36-37). Esta dinámica puede exacerbarse si el objeto del control se rebela, como lo hizo Jesusa. Además de esto, la violencia familiar puede ser el resultado de sentimientos reprimidos de rabia y frustración en otra dimensión de la vida adulta del hombre, como un ambiente laboral alienante, o el desempleo y la incapacidad de cumplir con sus obligaciones masculinas de mantener a su familia.

Por haber atestiguado y experimentado en carne propia la privación emocional y el abuso a lo largo de los años, Jesusa, por su cuenta, adoptó la tendencia masculina hacía la violencia que prevalecía en su cultura, especialmente el abuso físico y emocional de mujeres y niños[11]. Los investigadores han notado la frecuencia de una estructura extremadamente autoritaria entre las familias mexicanas campesinas, en las que se utiliza el castigo corporal severo para inculcar en los niños la obediencia y la sumisión (Fromm y Maccoby 186; González e Iracheta, 124). De niña a Jesusa le gustaba matar a pedradas las lagartijas e iguanas, una actividad que ella describe como típicamente masculina (19-20). Después de que había corrido a la primera querida de su padre, él los dejaba a ella y su hermano atados y encerrados cuando iba a trabajar. Además, él, a diferencia de su madre, golpeaba a sus hijos, especialmente al hijo mayor, Efrén (27). Es de notar que, en vez de culpar a su padre por su maltrato de Efren, Jesusa le echa la culpa a éste por su maldad. Incluso observa que ella misma siguió el ejemplo de su padre cuando empezó a tener problemas con Perico, su hijo adoptivo (cuyo nombre verdadero es Lalo), golpeándolo y encerrándolo. Lo que no reconoce es que, irónicamente, su abuso de Perico logró los mismos resultados negativos que produjeron en Efrén los castigos de su padre[12]. De hecho, ella no reconoce ninguna relación de causa y efecto entre el maltrato de los niños y su rebeldía; al contrario, atribuye el problema a la fatalidad del destino: "Mi papá quiso evitarle las malas compañías, como yo a Perico, pero con todo y eso, él siempre las agarró. Así es que ya el que nace de mala cabeza, ni quien se lo quite" (27).

Al comentar su conducta y la de otros personajes, Palancares suele recurrir a un sistema de lógica dual. Por un lado, ella repite creencias cristianas sobre la bondad y la maldad: que la docilidad y la obediencia son buenas y serán premiadas, mientras que la agresión y la terquedad (que en algunas situaciones se podrían interpretar más adecuadamente como fortaleza y firmeza) son malas y serán castigadas por Dios. Sin embargo, estas declaraciones casi siempre son seguidas por expresiones contradictorias de una sabiduría popular que ella ha aprendido de sus experiencias: que si uno no se defiende (si "se deja") de las fuerzas de maldad y agresión en el mundo, uno es tonto y, de hecho, merece el sufrimiento que inevitablemente nace de la sumisión y la resignación. Un ejemplo de esto son sus comentarios sobre la docilidad de su hermano Emiliano. Según Jesusa, él era el más bueno de sus hermanos: "Era un hermano tan manso ese Emiliano; un pedazo de azúcar no empalagaba tanto". Sin embargo, ella reconoce que su exagerada deferencia a la autoridad patriarcal, en contraste con su propia terquedad, lo llevó a la muerte: "Pero de nada le sirvió ser el único que nunca le contradijo a mi papá ... Con razón dicen: caballo manso tira a malo y hombre bueno tira a pendejo" (53).

Esta ambivalencia también es aparente en el auto-retrato que nos hace Palancares de sí misma como una rebelde franca y testaruda; cuenta que ella y sus parientes llegaron a aceptar estas características como innatas e inmutables, una convicción que le permite a ella sentir cierto orgullo por tener cualidades que no son aceptables en las mujeres. Mientras Jesusa no fue maltratada físicamente por sus padres biológicos (ya que se defendió del único intento de su padre de pegarle), sí fue golpeada repetidas veces y, en una ocasión, apuñalada por su madrastra, Evarista. Además, ella atestiguó y a veces participó en ataques contra sus parientes, especialmente mujeres. Ella se resignó a ser maltratada porque quería quedarse al lado de su padre y en todo caso no tenía adónde ir. A este respecto, la suya era una reacción común a la dependencia psicológica y económica. Además, aceptaba la racionalización de Evarista en el sentido de que la golpeaba por su propio bien; Jesusa hasta llega a expresar su gratitud por esta disciplina extrema, a la cual ella atribuye su conocimiento de las tareas domésticas que después fueron esenciales para su supervivencia (52). De igual importancia, estas tareas le permitían mantener una independencia económica, la cual la protege de otros abusos. Cuando a su madrastra se le pasó la mano y le dio una puñalada en una rabieta, Jesusa primero reprimió el incidente, "olvidando" que había sido herida hasta que alguien se fijó en la sangre, y después intentó proteger a su agresora (de manera semejante, repetidamente intentó proteger a su padre del conocimiento de las relaciones violentas en que ella se encontraba, supuestamente porque en su ausencia él no podía defenderla, pero probablemente también porque ella sabía a través de la experiencia que, de saber, él no intervendría). Así, según la lógica de Palancares —la cual es la racionalización que suelen usar los que abusan de los niños— el castigo corporal severo es justificado por la desobediencia del niño y es necesario para reformar su conducta.

Los críticos han tendido a enfocarse en las exaltadas autodefensas de Jesusa, comenzando con el momento en que se defiende de los agresivos vituperios de la amante de su marido, luego contra las palizas cada vez más brutales de Pedro, y finalmente otros incidentes en que ella da el primer golpe en vez de someterse al abuso, especialmente de los hombres. Mientras esta agresividad es claramente una de las cualidades que la hacen atractiva a los lectores, especialmente a las feministas, no se puede pasar por alto su repetido y a veces gratuito recurrir a la violencia a lo largo de su vida, lo cual sugiere que su estrategia de supervivencia incluía la adopción de una ideología y de una conducta machistas. "Yo era rete fina para pegar", se jacta en un momento dado, "... antes, hasta comezón sentía en las manos" (150-51). En vista del extenso maltrato de mujeres y niños que atestiguó Jesusa y que sufrió en carne propia, no es de sorprender que ella misma abuse de su propio hijo adoptivo[13]. Tampoco se puede ver su participación en la Revolución, y después en la Guerra Cristera, como un elemento neutral en la formación de su carácter; los sociólogos han documentado el hecho de que los ambientes militares fomentan la violencia doméstica (Shupe, 85). Aunque ella comenta en más de una ocasión que ha tenido una vida 'mala', emborrachándose y peleando demasiado, parecería que su conversión a la Obra Espiritual ha mitigado esas tendencias. Los dogmas católico y espiritista proscriben estas y otras actividades con las cuales ella gozaba –entre ellas el baile–, y el ambiente urbano empobrecido (tanto material como estéticamente) le ha negado el contacto con la naturaleza, otro de los pocos placeres constantes de su vida. Para cuando ella narra la historia, le quedan solamente tres fuentes de placer: la comida[14], las revelaciones espirituales y la conversación. No es de sorprender, entonces, que dos focos de su narración sean la comida y los éxtasis espiritualistas o que estas descripciones cuenten con una sensualidad y un erotismo que están ausentes o reprimidos en otras áreas de su narrativa y de su vida.

La cárcel como hogar y capilla

Gran parte del cuarto capítulo se dedica a la descripción del trabajo que hacía Palancares a los diez años en la prisión de mujeres de Tehuantepec, un episodio de su vida que ilustra las relaciones de poder articuladas por varias instituciones en la provincia mexicana a comienzos del siglo. En este capítulo aparece una mujer anónima que ha sido encarcelada por siete asesinatos. La construcción de la prisión anticipa la del Panopticón, tal como la describe Foucault; se aproxima más al modelo del calabozo. Las habitaciones de Jesusa, su madrastra Evarista y Fortunata, la madre de ésta, se encontraban entre la calle (la esfera pública) y la larga fila de celdas, la mayoría de ellas vacías. Palancares interpreta este arreglo como necesario para la seguridad, el encierro y la exclusión de la sociedad, e implícitamente de la vigilancia: "Así es de que no había por donde fugarse" (34). Además, había una jerarquía entre las prisioneras. Mientras las borrachas pasaban la noche en las celdas que estaban más cercanas a la calle y se les permitía acceso a la luz y apertura relativa del patio, a la asesina se la confinaba a la oscuridad constante, al calor y encierro de la celda más lejana.

Proscrita así del contacto social en virtud de su 'deuda' más grande a la sociedad ("debía siete muertes"), esta presa pidió que se le permitiera a Jesusa dormir en su celda porque ella tenía miedo (Palancares no especifica de qué: ¿de lo sobrenatural? ¿de la soledad?) Aún más notable es el hecho de que Evarista, la hija de la rectora, dejara a Jesusa hacerlo. Esto sugiere, en primer lugar, que su madrastra se preocupaba poco por el bienestar de Jesusa. Hasta cierto punto esto puede deberse a una actitud generalizada hacia los niños como sirvientes; quizás también refleje la ausencia de lazos de sangre entre Evarista y Jesusa, los cuales probablemente habrían acarreado un mayor sentido de responsabilidad. En todo caso, si no vemos la acción como sádica (y la interpretación adulta de Jesusa parecería no apoyar esta posibilidad), el consentimiento de la carcelera implica un mayor grado de confianza en la presa de lo que se esperaría. Esta confianza, por su cuenta, sugiere que la dinámica de poder en la prisión no es estrictamente jerárquica. Al contrario, hasta cierto punto se conforma a la descripción que hace Gilles Deleuze de las sociedades 'primitivas', en las cuales

> ... la red de alianzas ... no se puede reducir a una estructura jerárquica o a relaciones de intercambio entre grupos filiales. Las alianzas tienen lugar entre pequeños grupos locales, los cuales constituyen relaciones entre fuerzas (regalo y contra-regalo) y el poder directo ... las alianzas hilan una red flexible y transversal que es perpendicular a la estructura vertical ... y forman un sistema físico inestable que está en un desequilibrio perpetuo en vez de un ciclo cerrado y recíproco (35-36, mi traducción).

La descripción que hace Jesusa de la enormidad de la prisión y de su arreglo nocturno ("La cárcel era inmensa de grande. Dormíamos pegadas a la reja") sugiere que ella también tenía miedo, pero no de la asesina cuya celda compartía. Al contrario, fue de ella de quien Palancares aprendió primero el placer de la narrativa, mientras la presa le contaba su vida: "...le gustaba hablar en voz alta y me contaba su vida y yo le fui tomando el gusto" (38). Es un placer que años después, cuando se lo dosifica su esposo/carcelero, le permitía a Jesusa escapes temporales de la cárcel de su matrimonio; cuando está vieja y ha cambiado el papel de escucha por el de hablante, tal praxis se hace un vehículo de autorrevelación, de intimidad –aún de inmortalidad, a través del texto que nosotros leemos.

En última instancia tanto la asesina como Jesusa eran presas, atrapadas por instituciones sociales que no permitían ninguna movilidad y aisladas del resto de la comunidad carcelaria, tal como lo estaban en la sociedad más allá de las rejas (la presa no tenía familia; el padre de Jesusa la había abandonado dejándola con su madrastra abusiva). Cuando un terremoto hizo caer el techo de la prisión, los carceleros evacuaron el edificio pero se olvidaron de las dos personas atrapadas en la celda más lejana. Así que lo que podría haber sido una metáfora del colapso de las estructuras sociales anacrónicas se convirtió en otra muestra del desamparo de las víctimas. Además, la extrema indiferencia de Palancares al contar el incidente –pues describe una conversación tranquila que tuvo con su madrastra después del desastre– enmascara su rabia y miedo. Después liberaron a todas las borrachas pero dejaron a la asesina en la prisión, donde ahora se sentía aún menos segura. En una inversión irónica del Panopticón, en el cual los carceleros crean la impresión de estar vigilando a los presos sin dejarse ver por estos, ella pide que la cambien a la celda más cercana a la calle para poder vigilar a sus carceleros y así disminuir su soledad y temor: "...se pasaba todo el día cerca de la reja para mirar a la gente" (39). A través de la narración Palancares postula las oposiciones de oscuridad vs. luz, y de calor y encierro vs. apertura y movimiento; pero el calor es también el pobre calor humano al cual la presa se siente atraída, como a una llama, mientras huye de la oscuridad opresiva de su celda.

De la misma manera que Jesusa aprendió los deleites de la narración con esta mujer, también aprendió de ella la dimensión utópica de los milagros. El Niño de Atocha, quien después sería el santo patrón de Palancares (y quien vigilaría su historia desde su trono en la portada del libro), respondió a sus oraciones, las cuales fueron comunicadas a través de velas financiadas por pequeños préstamos de su carcelera. Estos préstamos aportan una clara evidencia de que la relación entre carcelera y reclusa se caracterizaba no sólo por la jerarquía y la opresión sino también por una alianza implícita basada en la pobreza y la fe compartidas.

Primero, el santo apareció en la comunidad presidaria en forma de un niño misterioso que le llevaba cestos de comida a la asesina. Mientras la importancia de la comida en una situación de pobreza podría parecer obvia, si aceptamos las descripciones que ofrece Palancares tanto carceleras como presas comían extremadamente bien: "Era media res la que se cocinaba a diario. Un día se hacía guisado en verde con pepita de calabaza y hierba santa, otro día en jitomate y chiles colorados. Les dábamos también **gina do shuba** que en otras partes le dicen cuachala, un mole de maíz tostado" (35). Fue después, al hacerse criada en el Distrito Federal, cuando Palancares supo lo que era el hambre. Estas comidas compartidas sugieren otro sentido en que la vida carcelaria no era estrictamente jerárquica y punitiva. Sin embargo, la comida también tiene significados psicológicos que la narradora reconoce en otro contexto: "Dicen que el huérfano no tiene llenadero porque le falta la mano de la madre que le dé de comer y a mí siempre me dio guzguería. Comía desde las cinco de la mañana hasta las ocho de la noche" (42). Vistos así, los regalos del santo, como las complicadas y suntuosas comidas de la cárcel, negaban el hecho de la pobreza y a la vez consolaban a la asesina emocional y espiritualmente.

Después, al reaparecer en forma de un joven abogado, el Niño de Atocha misteriosamente hizo que la mujer fuera perdonada y la transportó milagrosamente al estado de Zacatecas para que diera gracias en su altar (las revelaciones espirituales de Palancares también tienen a su salvador en forma del niño Jesús o de un joven guapo; para ella éste representa a Cristo o al Diablo; es un símbolo altamente erótico). El último regalo que el santo le hace a la presa, entonces, es el de su libertad y movilidad —las dos cosas van muy unidas en la imaginación de Jesusa- pero en este caso, irónicamente, la que recibe el milagro percibe la movilidad como otra forma de encierro -o más precisamente, de destierro-, una exclusión de la única comunidad que ella conoce, la de la cárcel de Tehuantepec.

Este episodio se parece mucho al primer milagro supuestamente efectuado por el Niño de Atocha, tal como está descrito en la "Novena y triduo dedicados al milagrosísimo Niño de Atocha" promulgada por la iglesia católica mexicana. Según este panfleto, los fieles pueden incurrir en el favor del santo llevando a cabo obras de caridad, especialmente cuidando a los enfermos o a los niños pobres abandonados (un consejo que Jesusa Palancares tomó a pecho a lo largo de su vida). Se supone que el Niño hizo este milagro en la ciudad de Durango en febrero de 1829, cuando misteriosamente apareció, disfrazado de galán, para liberar a una presa que había sufrido largos períodos de encarcelamiento sin gozar de ninguna defensa. Aunque el Niño le dijo a la mujer que lo siguiera, ella lo perdió de vista, sólo para encontrar su efigie en el santuario dedicado a su adoración en Fresnillo, Zacatecas (6-8). La estrecha semejanza entre esta leyenda y la historia de la presa en Tehuantepec plantea interesantes preguntas sobre la relación entre la doctrina religiosa, la memoria y la narración. Parece probable que Josefina Bórquez haya inventado la historia, por lo menos parcialmente, conscientemente o no, basándola en su conocimiento de la literatura eclesiástica, o que su informante, la presa, haya hecho lo mismo al relatarle sus propias aventuras a Jesusa[15].

Al darse cuenta de que había sido liberada por un santo (más específicamente, por una encarnación de Cristo), la presa dice que se empeñó en ahorrar suficiente dinero para regresar a casa -un tema que recurre varias veces en la narración de Palancares- y que, cuando finalmente llegó al Istmo, las primeras personas que buscó fueron sus ex-carceleras, Evarista y Fortunata. La escena se describe más como una reunión de viejas vecinas o amigas que de viejas antagonistas. Parece claro que, a pesar de la negligencia que ha sufrido, y a pesar de su profunda soledad, la asesina sentía que pertenecía, de una manera perversa, a la comunidad presidiaria, una sociedad de mujeres pobres que había reproducido, en forma de microcosmo, la estructura de poder de la sociedad mexicana en general, pero con importantes diferencias. Como ha señalado Foucault, la cárcel es sólo una manifestación de una estructura que cala en la sociedad contemporánea en formas tan diversas como la escuela, la fábrica, el hospital y el cuartel (con todas las cuales la vida de Palancares se cruzará, con la excepción de la escuela). En vista de su radical soledad, entonces, por qué no iba la presa a sentir nostalgia por la celda donde, por oscura y calurosa que fuera, ella había comido bien y su miedo existencial era amortiguado por la compañía de una niña que le escuchaba fascinada. Y, atrapada en la metrópolis anónima y alienante muchos años después, sola en el mundo como la asesina, por qué no iba a recordar Jesusa a su vieja compañera de celda en algún nivel y, por lo tanto, por qué no iba a hacer lo posible por regresar una y otra vez a la cárcel, preparada a retomar la narración de su propia historia ante sus colegas -del sistema penal y de la pobreza femenina- y ante ese emisario de la sociedad privilegiada que le habría parecido su Niño de Atocha particular, Elena Poniatowska.

La apropriación del poder patriarcal a través de la religión.

El tipo de pensamiento que Palancares aplica para justificar el maltrato de los niños -la teoría de que el castigo y la expiación severos purifican al pecador, salvándolo de futuros pecados- es fortalecida por las enseñanzas de la Obra Espiritual. Por ejemplo, cuando Jesusa se sintió traicionada por Antonio Pérez, y él luego se enfermó de sífilis avanzada, ella interpretó este hecho como un castigo divino. De la misma manera en que, durante la Revolución, un curandero había pedido el consejo de Jesusa para decidir si Pedro debía curarse y, en el caso afirmativo, cómo esto debía hacerse, su guía espiritual la incluyó en la decisión de cuán severo debía ser el castigo de Antonio por su mala conducta; ella pudo negociar, en varias etapas, un período de sufrimiento cada vez más breve para su amigo infiel. Es de notar, sin embargo, que ella no pidió que Dios perdonara del todo a Pérez; al contrario ella parecía disfrutar al observar la dificultad que él tenía al caminar y al imaginar la desintegración de su pene o "animal". Además, Palancares dice que ella sospechaba desde el principio que la otra mujer tenía sífilis, y por haber trabajado en un hospital de mujeres ella conocía bien los efectos devastadores de la enfermedad (típicamente, ella se había compadecido no de las pacientes sino de los hombres que habían tenido contacto sexual con ellas; en ésta y otras situaciones, ella seguía el dogma cristiano según el cual la mujer es la instigadora y el hombre la víctima del pecado). Sin embargo, ella no intentó advertirle a Antonio que estaba exponiéndose a una enfermedad grave. Jesusa explica su no intervención diciendo que él no le habría creído, que él habría atribuido la advertencia a los celos. Mientras, por un lado, esta percepción revela un conocimiento de la psicología humana, también es coherente con su pesimismo sobre la capacidad humana de efectuar cambios. Cuando Antonio se recuperó milagrosamente de la enfermedad, sin aparente intervención médica, la fe de Jesusa fue confirmada; Dios lo había castigado por su insensibilidad hacia ella, y a la vez había mostrado misericordia hacia Antonio y hacia Jesusa al no llevárselo. Después, cuando Palancares misma contrae sífilis, expresa (¿finge?) sorpresa e inocencia, sin ofrecer ninguna explicación fisiológica ni religiosa de su enfermedad.

La atracción del espiritismo para Jesusa Palancares, entonces, proviene de la ilusión de control sobrenatural que le da. Cree que lo que no puede llevar a cabo directamente lo puede lograr -general-mente con más efecto dramático– a través de sus guías espirituales. La imposición del sufrimiento en los demás le provee un perverso consuelo por su propia desgracia. Al mismo tiempo, su manipulación del poder divino le trae una compensación por su profundo sentimiento de impotencia (un sentimiento que tiene sus raíces, por supuesto, en sus severas limitaciones sociales como mujer pobre y vieja).

El espiritismo fue introducido por las élites latinoamericanas durante el siglo diecinueve y eventualmente llegó hasta las clases desposeídas de los ámbitos rural y urbano, donde se sincretizó con el catolicismo popular. Esta religión ocultista, basada en las teorías de Allan Kardec (el seudónimo de Leon Denizarth Hippolyte Rivail [Francia, 1804-1869]), se parece en muchos sentidos al cristianismo ortodoxo, particularmente en su concepto de la naturaleza dual (material y espiritual) de la humanidad y en su énfasis ético en la buena conducta como motivo de recompensa. La mayor diferencia está en su creencia en la posesión (en algunos casos, a través de mediums y sus ayudantes, los mediudinades) como un medio de comunicación entre espíritus encarnados y seres incorpóreos. Según Alan Harwood, "[L]a metafísica de la psiquiatría ... proviene del protestantismo; la metafísica del espiritismo tiene sus raíces en el catolicismo popular ... Como el catolicismo, atribuye la última responsabilidad a los poderes del mundo sobrenatural" (190-91, mi traducción)[16]. En su estudio del espiritismo en una comunidad puertorriqueña de Nueva York, Harwood encontró que el mundo espiritual es jerárquico en dos sentidos. La jerarquía moral consta de cinco niveles: 1) los espíritus intranquilos; 2) los espíritus de la gente normal; 3) los espíritus de los líderes venerados; 4) los espíritus moralmente perfectos, como los santos, los ángeles y los serafines; y 5) Dios. Además, hay otra jerarquía vertical dentro de cada nivel o cuadro de espíritus. Un ángel guardián le toca a cada espíritu encarnado, al nacer; éste es ayudado también por espíritus incorpóreos de categorías menores, llamados protectores y guías. Según las enseñanzas de Kardec,

> ... los espíritus pasan por una serie de reencarnaciones, cada una de las cuales permite que el espíritu realce su pureza moral sobreponiéndose al sufrimiento y a los dilemas éticos implicados en la vida terrestre. Por lo tanto, la vida se ve como una prueba del espíritu que, si es aprobada, le permite ascender en la jerarquía celestial. El suspender la prueba no acarrea ningún descenso de categoría pero puede ocasionar una prueba más dura en la próxima encarnación (Harwood, 41-45, mi traducción).

Esta jerarquía espiritual, sin embargo, se complementa con cierto carácter igualitario, ya que se cree que todos los espíritus pasan por todas las categorías. Por lo tanto, la situación de un espíritu encarnado en cierto plano moral (y material) en la jerarquía no impide que él ocupe un plano superior en otra encarnación. De ahí la creencia de Palancares acerca de que fue reina en una vida anterior y que la pobreza y el sufrimiento son castigos por mala conducta, y también su esperanza implícita de que sus futuras encarnaciones sean más felices.

En su estudio de la comunidad espiritista puertorriqueña en Nueva York, Harwood encontró un número desproporcionado de mujeres, sobre todo de más de cuarenta años. Él y otros investigadores han concluido que las iglesias espiritistas y espiritualistas tienden a atraer a individuos y comunidades en proceso de transición y readaptación social. La iglesia provee un sentimiento de comunidad, en efecto es un grupo de terapia para individuos aislados y, al prometerles contacto con parientes fallecidos, puede ser una manera de trascender la muerte simbólicamente. Al ofrecer diagnósticos concretos y curas de las enfermedades y los problemas sociales, el espiritismo provee al creyente un sentido de certeza y control en situaciones inciertas. El fenómeno de la posesión también constituye un realce del prestigio social para personas como Jesusa que de otra manera tendrían poco. Al mismo tiempo, la posesión ofrece un contexto para un comportamiento que de otra manera no sería aceptado por la sociedad o para el individuo; en el caso de Palancares, sirve como foco de la fantasía y el deseo.

Además, el espiritismo le permite a Jesusa depender emocionalmente de una nueva serie de figuras patriarcales, como su protector (Manuel Antonio Mesmer, el médico alemán que inventó la teoría del magnetismo animal o el mesmerismo [1734-1815]) y sus guías, todos los cuales son considerados como más puros moralmente, y por lo tanto más autorizados y poderosos que ella. Raymond Prince ha explicado que la religión espiritista opera como lo que él llama "psiquoterapia primitiva":

> [N]o hace ningún intento de proveer al paciente con una comprensión de su propia personalidad ni de hacerlo independiente. Por el contrario, la técnica común consiste en colocarlo dentro de un cono de autoridad por decirlo así –se le asigna al cuidado y control de un espíritu benévolo ... A cambio de la protección y el socorro, el paciente debe proveer al espíritu con comida y otras ofrendas, debe comportarse de ciertas maneras fijadas y observar ciertos tabúes. Hay un intercambio de la libertad por la protección ... el conocimiento profundo es la prerrogativa del curandero y no del paciente (33-34, mi traducción).

Prince caracteriza así el "cono de la autoridad" (el cual recuerda la estructura piramidal de la sociedad mexicana):

> Considérese un cono de luz en cuyo vértice hay un espíritu omnisciente que es la fuente de la luz. Todos los hombres que están dentro del cono de luz son sanos, fértiles y prósperos; más allá, en la oscuridad, los hombres están muriéndose, están enfermos o son sujetos a todo tipo de ansiedades. Para entrar en el cono de luz se requiere la purificación y para quedarse allí se requiere la obediencia. A medio camino entre el vértice y la base del cono esta el círculo de curanderos-sacerdotes quienes, por su proximidad, pueden comunicarse directamente con el espíritu, pero el hombre común que reposa en la base del cono sólo puede comunicarse a través del curandero. Bajo circunstancias especiales, el espíritu puede descender del ápice y montar o entrar en el cu-

randero y hablar de cosas espirituales con los hombres de abajo; o el espíritu puede montar directamente a los legos, generando dentro de ellos y sus compañeros-en-luz acciones salubres (34, mi traducción).

En su estudio de las sectas religiosas protestantes en Guatemala, Bryan Roberts ha notado la importante función social que éstas desempeñan entre los residentes urbanos de pocos recursos y sin parientes en la ciudad, especialmente las mujeres que están separadas de sus maridos o han sido esposas de alcohólicos (145). En su opinión, Peter Fry ha superado este análisis en su estudio del Pentecostalismo y la Umbanda (una variante del espiritismo que tuvo sus orígenes en Africa) en el Brasil contemporáneo, al sostener que la función de estas sectas no es meramente social, sino ideológica también; ellos ofrecen "un marco para interpretar los eventos cotidianos de maneras que son básicamente congruentes con la posición social y económica y los prospectos del individuo". Según Roberts, Fry constrasta la ética puritana predicada por los Pentecostales, y su coherencia con los valores de la clase media y la clase obrera calificada brasileñas, con la jerarquía autocrática de la Umbanda, que tiende a atraer a gente con menos recursos económicos:

> La Umbanda está organizada alrededor de centros de culto que están controlados autocráticamente por los líderes del culto; tiene una cosmología ecléctica y variable en la que tanto la bondad como la maldad son partes necesarias de la eficacia ritual y por medio de la cual los individuos desarrollan relaciones particularistas con sus espíritus. Los devotos exigen ayuda contra fuerzas malévolas que les han afligido sin motivo, tales como la mala salud, el desempleo, frustraciones en el amor u otros problemas básicos de la vida urbana. La Umbanda, entonces, está organizada por un sistema de clientes y se especializa en dar soluciones rituales a corto plazo a las dificultades e inseguridades de la vida en las ciudades y las área rurales (Roberts 145-46, mi traducción).

Para Roberts el autoritarismo y particularismo de la Umbanda constituyen "la otra cara del capitalismo industrial en los países subdesarrollados"; esta religión "es posible porque las relaciones particularistas que se establecen con los espíritus con la esperanza de ganar favores son homólogas con las relaciones reales establecidas para el beneficio de los hombres en la sociedad". Aún el lenguaje utilizado por los seguidores de la Umbanda es tomado de las relaciones económicas capitalistas (Fry 196, mi traducción).

Sola en la ciudad, sin familia y abandonada por una serie de hijos y mascotas adoptivos malagradecidos (con la excepción de Perico, quien finalmente ha regresado pero, según ella, por interés en vez de amor), traicionada por varias instituciones sociales 'revolucionarias', vieja y enfrentada con un futuro de enfermedad y muerte, Palancares vuelve al espiritismo en busca de compañía, poder y esperanza. La promesa de la reencarnación ofrece una recompensa concreta por sus obras buenas que no han sido reconocidas: una nueva vida, la oportunidad de comenzar de nuevo en mejores términos. Por otra parte, su religión le ofrece la ilusión de participar en el castigo divino de los que la han lastimado o desilusionado, además de la fantasía de una rica vida erótica: "Yo tengo tres [protectores] ... al final de la curación, llega mi protector Luz de Oriente que es el más guapo de los tres. Pero yo los quiero igual a todos. Nomás que Luz de Oriente me mira con mucha hambre. Tiene hambrosía en los ojos a todas horas. Y me deja pensando" (14).

Esta dimensión erótica de la religión tiene cierta ambigüedad, aún en la imaginación de Jesusa. En la escena onírica que abre la novela, el mismo guapo espíritu se convierte en su marido explotador, Pedro, quien está determinado a ejercer el último control llevándola consigo a la muerte: "Cuando yo la vea perdida, te mando a ti por delante y acabo contigo", le había dicho Pedro (11). En su sueño, como en su vida consciente, Jesusa reconoce que es su miedo (e implícitamente su propio valor y agresividad) el que la ha salvado tanto de sus protectores terrenales como de los espirituales. Sin embargo, en otras ocasiones, cede control enteramente a sus guías espirituales: "Mi protector Mesmer ... me tiene dominada ahora. Me levanta, me hinca, hace lo que quiere conmigo .... No me mando yo. Así es de que todo lo que el protector quiere, pues que lo haga en mi envoltura. Yo no puedo oponerme" (302). Cuando la congregación espiritista comienza a despreciar a Jesusa, ella desarrolla la capacidad de comunicarse con el espíritu de Mesmer sin la intervención de un medium; el círculo se cierra cuando ella se retira de la comunidad espiritista que le había brindado compañía a practicar la posesión en forma solitaria. Esto le permite recuperar el poder que ella había cedido a los mediums que actuaban como sus intermediarios, al mismo tiempo que sigue atribuyendo la responsabilidad de su vida al reino espiritual, siempre sin dejar de gozar de un control vicario sobre su vida.

En el contexto de esta soledad, la conclusión del texto sintetiza la peculiar mezcla de individualismo vivaracho y dependencia implícita, tal como está dirigida al interlocutor, a quien ella parece tener cierto resentimiento por haber logrado (con su cooperación) penetrar en su intimidad. También capta el pesimismo y la misantropía que caracterizan su evaluación de la naturaleza humana y de las relaciones interpersonales, pero que entran en contradicción con sus acciones continuadas a favor de otros: "Yo no creo que la gente sea buena, la mera verdad, no. Sólo Jesucristo y no lo conocí. Y mi padre, que nunca supe si me quiso o no. Pero de aquí sobre la tierra, ¿quién quiere usted que sea bueno? Ahora ya no chingue. Váyase. Déjeme dormir" (316). Al concluir su novela con esta declaración de autosuficiencia (inventada por Poniatowska), la autora se vuelve la acusación implícita de su informante en contra de sí misma y, por extensión, en contra del lector. Uno se queda con un ligero sentimiento de culpa por haber escuchado la confesión de Palancares, por haberse entrometido en una vida desesperada que se ha hecho menos privada al ser contada, pero que al mismo tiempo se ha hecho menos anónima y solitaria. Este fin, un desafío implícito, se abre a la colectividad que Jesusa Palancares, como su contraparte real, Josefina Bórquez, rechazó categóricamente a lo largo del siglo veinte mexicano que fue su vida.

NOTAS

1. *Hasta no verte Jesús mío* fue publicada por Ediciones Era en 1969, luego por la Secretaría de Educación Pública en 1986. La traducción al inglés ha sido completada pero aún no se ha publicado. *La noche de Tlatelolco* fue publicada por Ediciones Era en 1971; la traducción inglesa de Helen R. Lane, *Massacre in Mexico*, publicada por Viking Press en 1975, ya está agotada.

2. La última edición que sacó Ediciones Era de *Hasta no verte Jesus mío* consiste en cuatro mil ejemplares, mientras que la de *La noche de Tlatelolco* es de ocho mil.

3. Entrevista personal con Elena Poniatowska, México, julio de 1987.

4. Entrevista personal con Elena Poniatowska, México, julio de 1984.

5. Según Poniatowska, Josefina Bórquez:

> hablaba mucho de su situación actual, de lo mal que estaba su vivienda, de la gente en el vecindario, de lo mal que estaba el país, era una visión muy pesimista. De a dónde íbamos a dar, que la comida era pésima, que la leche tenía agua, que las tortillas tenían papel periódico, que el pan costaba demasiado caro. Entonces eso era una cosa que ella repetía mucho, mucho, mucho. Y claro que se lo quité; porque el estar hablando todo el tiempo de eso ... Para ella la novela habría sido sólo el espiritualismo y la carestía, y la mala situación actual (Steele, "Entrevista").

6. En julio de 1987, tres meses después de la muerte de Josefina Bórquez, Poniatowska me mostró una fotografía de su informante que se había tomado cuando ésta tenía unos cuarenta años. Era de una mujer morena, guapa sin ser bonita, orgullosa y de mucho carácter.

7. Véase González e Iracheta sobre la relación entre la pobreza y la violencia en el campo mexicano a comienzos del siglo.

8. Véase el ensayo de Gayle Rubin sobre el sistema sexual/de género y "el tráfico de mujeres".

9. En otra parte de la narración Palancares ofrece otra explicación de su costumbre de vestirse de hombre, diciendo que ello le permitía seguir a Pedro en situaciones de combate cuando no se les permitía a las mujeres acompañar a sus maridos (109).

10. Compárese la combinación de sumisión y rebeldía (expresadas en el cambio del *usted* por el *tú* y por la aparente imitación de la letra de un bolero) en esta carta dictada por una mujer campesina analfabeta y dirigida a su marido abusivo a comienzos del siglo:

> Apreciable Sr.: ... despues de saludar a ud. con el respeto devido, ... le doi mis mas rendidas gracias por los dias que estube tomando un pan en su dichosa casa ... un millon de gracias por todo y por los porrasos que Ud. me dio tanto que sufri con Ud. no podria estar ni un momento a gusto con Ud. tal vez porque era llo pobre ... En fin deje Ud. el mundo rodar y puede encontrar otra megor que llo. Ni llo para Ud. ni Ud. para mi ... Adiós ingrato. Dios quiera que te cases pronto para que maltrates a tu mujer y te aga lo mismo (sic; citada en González e Iracheta 141).

11. En entrevistas que le hizo en 1984 a un grupo de mujeres en Ciudad Neza-hualcóyotl, el cinturón de miseria más grande de América Latina, Gisela Espinosa Damián encontró que: "Más de la mitad de las mujeres son gol-peadas, y aunque muchas de ellas se defienden con la misma violencia, la idea también prevalece que si una mujer 'se porta mal', está bien golpearla" (40, mi traducción) .

12. Compárese la descripción que hace Poniatowska de la costumbre de la an-ciana Josefina Bórquez de encerrar sus animales cuando iba a trabajar: "En aquellos años Jesusa no permanecía mucho tiempo en su vivienda por-que salía a trabajar temprano a un taller de imprenta en el que aún la em-pleaban. Dejaba su cuarto cerrado a piedra y lodo, sus animales adentro as-fixiándose, sus macetas también" ("Hasta", 5).

13. Los sociólogos coinciden en que los patrones de violencia tienden a ser aprendidos durante la niñez. Por ejemplo, véanse McCall (114) y Shupe (36).

14. En varias ocasiones Palancares describe con muchos detalles y evidente gusto los placeres de la comida (36, 41, 67, 87-88).

15. Una conversación con la autora eliminó la tercera posibilidad, de que ella haya sido la responsable de incorporar la leyenda del Niño de Atocha en la obra (Entrevista personal, Seattle, febrero de 1989).

16. En su artículo en *Vuelta*, Poniatowska identifica la religión de Bórquez co-mo el espiritualismo; según ella, ésta se diferencia del espiritismo al estar asociada con los pobres. Las fuentes sociológicas que he consultado conside-ran que el elemento distintivo del espiritismo es la reencarnación; a dife-rencia del espiritualismo, esta religión (como Jesusa Palancares) predica la creencia en múltiples vidas. Además, mientras comenzó en América La-tina como un fenómeno de élites, el espiritismo "se filtró a las clases bajas urbanas y al campesinado" (Macklin 393, 415-17). Jesusa Palancares mis-ma se refiere a su religión como el "espiritismo" (160).

BIBLIOGRAFIA

Deleuze, Gilles. *Foucault*. Trad. Séan Hand. Minneapolis: University of Minne-sota Press, 1988.

Espinosa Damián, Gisela. "Feminism and Social Struggle in Mexico". *Third World-Second Sex*. Ed. Miranda Davies. Tomo 2. London: Zed Books, 1987. pp. 31-41.

Foucault, Michel. *Discipline and Punish: The Birth of the Prison*. Trad. Alan Sheridan. New York: Vintage Books, 1979.

-----. *The History of Sexuality*. Tomo 1. Trad. Robert Hurley. New York: Vintage Books, 1980.

Friedman, Edward. "The Marginal Narrator: *Hasta no verte Jesús mío* and the Eloquence of Repression". En su *The Antiheroine's Voice* (Columbia: Uni-versity of Missouri Press, 1987), pp. 170-187.

Fromm, Erich and Michael Maccoby. *Social Character in a Mexican Village: A Sociopsychoanalytic Study*. Englewood Cliffs, New Jersey: Prentice-Hall, 1970.

Fry, Peter. "Two Religious Movements: Protestantism and Umbanda". *Man-chester and Sao Paulo: Problems of Rapid Urban Growth*. Ed. John D. Wirth y Robert L. Jones. Stanford: Stanford University Press, 1978. pp. 177-202.

González, Soledad y Pilar Iracheta. "La violencia en la vida de las mujeres cam-pesinas: El distrito de Tenango, 1880-1910". *Presencia y transparencia: La mujer en la historia de México*. México: El Colegio de México, 1987. pp. 111-41.

Harwood, Alan. *Rx: Spiritist as Needed: A Study of a Puerto Rican Community Mental Health Resource*. London: John Wiley and Sons, 1977.

Langness, L.L. y Gelya Frank. *Lives: An Anthropological Approach to Biography*. Novato, California: Chandler and Sharp Publishers, 1981.

Macklin, June. "Belief, Ritual, and Healing: New England Spiritualism and Mexican-American Spiritism Compared". *Religious Movements in Contemporary America*. Ed. Irving I. Zaretsky y Mark P. Leone. Princeton: Princeton University Press, 1974. pp. 383-417.

McCall, George M. y Nancy M. Shields. "Social Structural Factors in Family Violence". *Violence in the Home: Interdisciplinary Perspectives*. Ed. Mayr Lystad. New York: Brunner/Mazel, 1986. pp. 98-122.

Novena y triduo dedicados al milagrosísimo Niño de Atocha. N.p.: n.p., n.d. Comprada en un puesto de literatura católica en frente de la catedral de Mazatlan, Sinaloa, septiembre de 1988.

Poniatowska, Elena. Entrevistas personales. Chimalistac, México, D.F., julio de 1984 y de 1987, septiembre de 1988, y abril y mayo de 1989; Seattle, febrero de 1989.

-----. *Hasta no verte Jesús mío*. México: Ediciones Era, 1969.

-----. "Hasta no verte Jesús mío". *Vuelta*, noviembre de 1978. pp. 5-11.

-----. *La noche de Tlatelolco*. México: Ediciones Era, 1971.

-----. "Testimonios de una escritora: Elena Poniatowska en micrófono". *La sartén por el mango: Encuentro de escritoras latinoamericanas*. Ed. Patricia Elena González y Eliana Ortega. Río Piedras, Puerto Rico: Ediciones Huracán, 1984. pp. 155-62.

Prince, Raymond. "Psychoanalysis and the Chronically Poor".*Culture Change Mental Health and Poverty*. Ed. Joseph C. Finney. Lexington: University of Kentucky Press, 1969. pp. 20-41.

Roberts, Bryan. *Cities of Peasants: The Political Economy of Urbanization in the Third World*. London: Edward Arnold, 1979.

Rubin, Gayle. "The Traffic in Women: Notes on the 'Political Economy' of Sex". *Toward an Anthropology of Women*. Ed. Rayna R. Reiter. New York: Monthly Review Press, 1975. pp. 157-210.

Shupe, Anson, William A. Stacey y Lonnie R. Hazelwood. *Violent Men. Violent Couples*. Lexington, Massachusetts: Lexington Books, 1987.

Steele, Cynthia. "Entrevista con Elena Poniatowska". *Hispamérica* 1990 (en prensa).

Tyler, Stephen A. "Post-Modern Ethnography: From Document of the Occult to Occult Document". *Writing Culture: The Poetics and Politics of Ethnography*. Ed. James Clifford y George E. Marcus. Berkeley: University of California Press, 1986.

Jean Franco

Self-Destructing Heroines

To describe someone as a "public woman" in Latin America is simply not the same as describing someone as a public man — and therein hangs a tale. The public woman is a prostitute, the public man a prominent citizen. When a woman goes public, she leaves the protected spaces of home and convent and exposes her body on the street or in the promiscuity of the brothel.

> Blacks, mulattoes, mixtures of all kinds, drunks, somnolent or frightened half-breeds, skinny Chinese, old men, small groups of young Spaniards and Italians walked through the patios out of curiosity. They walked to and fro passing the open doors of the bedrooms, stopping to look in from time to time. The prostitues, dressed in cotton clothes, were sitting at the back of the rooms on low boxes. Most of them sat with their legs apart, showing their sex, the "fox" which sometimes they had shaved and sometimes they hadn't.
>
> (José María Arguedas, *The Fox Above and the Fox Below*)

You have only to look at the gridiron plan of a traditional Hispanic town to know how important the distribution of space is and how completely public space — the cafes, the park benches, the civic buildings — are male preserves, places where they make speeches, run businesses and argue about literature. Women's space is far more privatized — the enclosed world of the home or the convent, both of which are turned away from the street to look inwards into a series of patios. Women and men meet in church or at the market but seldom casually. This division of the traditional city into public (male) spaces and private space where women's power derives from motherhood or virginity has deeply affected both political life and the imaginary repertoire on which literature draws. The Latin American novel came into being as a national endeavor programmed by masculine phalansteries and feminine marginality. More than poetry (which allowed for male erotic fantasy and hence "feeling"), the novel is centered on the drama of male enterprise or impotence, the search for male identity that depends on the allergorization of women characters in their virtually invariant positions of mother, prostitute or love object. Even the great historical novels of contemporary Latin America — *Terra Nostra* by Carlos Fuentes, *The War of the End of the World* by Mario Vargas Llosa, *The Supreme I* by Roa Bastos, *The Autumn of the Patriarch* by Gabriel García Márquez, novels which are extraordinarily detailed models of societies with their histories, their social classes, their art and literature, their battles and deaths — take as given the contrast between male (activity and enterprise) and female (passivity and reproduction). These novels are such efficient machines that we forget that there isn't an intelligent woman in any of them or that the most common form of male and female intercourse is rape.

Obviously these are giant generalizations which do not take into account a certain "feminization of discourse" (notably in the novels of Manuel Puig). But exceptions do not alter the fact that women in reality as well as in literature are overwhelmingly identified with fixed terrorities. In one of his poems, for instance, Vallejo turns his mother's body into a building which is both house and temple. Father and son pass

> Between the colonnade of your bones
> that cannot be brought down even with lamentations
> and into whose side not even Destiny
> can place a single finger.[1]

In this poem, reproduction is valued; the mother takes the place of Christ who is invulnerable to the gesture of doubting Thomas. Yet her body does not speak. It is a mute vessel whose role is to offer the transient male his only security in life. The mother does not *say*. She *is* a place, a house and a temple. The mother's body offers a return to childhood before the entry into the symbolic order of language. Women are prior to language and therefore to literary creation. To sanctify motherhood, even ironically, as Vallejo does, only reinforces the taboo on creation, a creation that seems to involved risk, mobility and the male's alienation from the female, and from the motherly qualities of connectedness and caring.

In Vargas Llosa's novel *The Green House*, there is an even more powerful and devastating form of female silence—the silence of the woman who has been mutilated as a direct result of violence. A brothel owner, Anselmo, conceives a passion for an adolescent girl Antonia, who had once been abandoned in the desert after a robbery and murder and whose eyes and tongue had been pecked out by vultures. Blind and mute, she is apparently docile and at the same time mysterious. Anselmo kidnaps her and hides her in a tower in the brothel, supplying her with his voice and his sexual fantasy to which she eagerly responds. Long after Antonia's death in childbirth, her memory continues to haunt Anselmo. Yet Antonia epitomizes female mutilation rather than romantic love. Her mute blindness graphically illustrates the fact that the virtuoso male fantasy depends on women being the blank page on which male writers can write their own story. In Vallejo's poem, women are ineluctably associated with reproduction; in Vargas Llosa's novel, they are the docile performers of a male script which they may interrupt but in which they play no creative part.

These narrative fantasies and resolutions are obviously fueled by myths of creativity like those described by Sandra Gilbert and Susan Gubar in *The Madwoman in the Attic*. As long as women's creativity can be reduc-

ed to reproduction, men can freely usurp intellectual and literary creation, presenting it either as the virile activity of the father or, with equal
audacity, as a form of male birthing. Latin American writers are
astonishingly blatant in their usurpation of creative power. In a recent
play by Mario Vargas Llosa, *The Señorita from Tacna*, the protagonist
Mamaé is an incontinent old woman who pees all over the stage.
Women's bodies are unreliable (the same author's *Aunt Julia and the
Scriptwriter* has another incontinent female letting her husband down in
public) and thus provide a comic form of subversion of respectability, a
kind of latter-day carnivalesque. Further, the uncontrollable body is
linked to Mamaé's unbridled romantic memory which flows as freely as
her bodily liquids. But far from subverting the traditional subordination
of female creativity, the play reaffirms it. The real protagonist turns out
to be Mamaé's great-nephew who boasts the all-conquering name
Belisario, and who sits at the side of the stage agonizing over his writing
and his decision to give up a law career. What bothers him most,
however, is that he is inexplicably drawn to writing about his great-aunt
and using her "women's material" in his own writing. It is as if the old,
public "male" themes of death and heroism have been played out so that
the writer is now forced to incorporate formerly despised material. The
play is unusually blatant in revealing a yearning for feminine feeling
although the author can only present this in comic form.

Latin American women, like their counterparts in Europe and North
America, have thus been faced with powerful taboos on literary creativity whilst their own cultural forms — gossip, romantic narrative,
lullaby — have been devalued or usurped. It is not surprising that the poet
Gabriela Mistral, writing half a century ago, should come to sense that
poetic creation was abnormal, a monstrous substitute for the "real" creation of human life. In the last decade, though, this situation has radically
changed, not only because of the emergence of many women writers in
Latin America but also because women have been thrust into the public
sphere. The politics of death, fear and disappearance, the destruction of
the immunity formerly accorded to the Church and to middle-class
women, the transformation of popular culture by a ruthless "modernizing" capitalism using the mass media as its instrument — all these have
radically changed the older structures of everyday life. In the vacuum left
by the outlawing of political parties, new movements have come to the
fore, many of them under the aegis of women and the clergy. In Argentina, the mothers of the disappeared began to hold demonstrations in the
Plaza de Mayo in Buenos Aires, inaugurating a symbolic action that has
been imitated in Chile and in El Salvador. These women took over public
space, their only weapons being white headscarves and photographs of
disappeared children. They refused to stay in the privatized space of the
home, nursing their grief behind four walls and were not afraid to
display their sorrow, to show the mutilation of loss. In Chile, families of

the disappeared chained themselves to public buildings; in Mexico, they held fasts and vigils.[2] In countries in which women's public behavior has been carefully circumscribed, they made spectacles of themselves.

There are many parallels in literature to this occupation of public space. But what interests me here are not so much the novels that deal with torture, violence and political themes,[3] but rather the emergence of certain *topoi*—in particular, the *topoi* of the stigmatized female body and that of the liberated artist or performer. Both *topoi* respond to a system of representations found in works by male authors; in the first caste to the representation of sado-masochistic relations and in the second case to the "immobile" and fixed spaces of femininity (house, brothel, convent) which the actress alone transgresses. Yet performance is also a problematic metaphor for liberation. In *Ways of Seeing*,[4] John Berger pointed out that women are always performing, always self-conscious because they are subject to the judging male look. Women can never forget their looks as males can. Thus, for women writers to depict creativity in terms of a performance inevitable exposes the painful contradiction that, to be creative, she must become a public woman, a public woman whose shame and failure are exposed to ridicule.

In Griselda Gambarro's play *The Camp*,[5] first published in 1967, the female fantasy of performance is subjected to devastating exposure. Obviously, that fantasy is not peculiar to Latin America. Doris Lessing's Anna in *The Golden Notebook* (to mention only one example) has a similar fantasy. But in *The Camp*, all structures are at the point of breakdown and madness. The setting of the play is Auschwitz. Its title, *The Camp* (El Campo), is ambiguous since in Spanish *camp* means both "countryside" and "concentration camp." The play uses both meanings simultaneously. Both concentration camp and countryside are offstage, heard by the audience through offstage sounds—singing peasants and playing children to suggest country pastoral; screams sirens and dogs to suggest inhuman oppression. Characters refer to the outside either as nature (fox hunting) or to comment on the barbed wire and the smell of burning flesh (people or animals). Onstage, some characters wear S.S. uniforms and one of them is said to resemble Menengele, the notorious operator of the Auschwitz ovens. However, the set always suggests a certain "normal" everyday life, for it is by turns an office, a dining-room, a concert hall or a private house.

Briefly summarized, the plot is about the incorporation of a liberal individual, Martin, into the authoritarian state through his "seduction" by a prison-inmate, Emma, and by the force and persuasion of a camp commandant, Franco. At the end of the play, Franco has apparently freed Martin from the camp, but he is branded by officials who thus incorporate him into the totalitarian society. And the play can be taken as an allegory of "man's eternal inhumanity to man" or as an allegory of the subjection of the individual to the totalitarian state, in which case Martin can be considered the protagonist. But it is the figure of Emma which is most interesting. She is, from the first, presented as totally subjugated by the camp commander, Franco, who barks orders, manipulates her, wheedles, promises and threatens by turn but always orchestrates the situation. He incarnates the Subject with a capital S, the system itself, which by turns appears benign, homely, authoritarian and savage (e.g., Franco takes off his jacket, puts his feet on the table, kisses Emma's hand or appears with a hunting rifle). His only consistency is that like the State his actions are never predictable. Emma, on the other hand, bears the visible signs of her subjection. She is barefooted, wears camp uniform, has a shaved head, a wounded hand and is branded. Her body is totally out of gear with her words. She has an itch she cannot control. Ordered by Franco to behave seductively to Martin, she can only arouse his pity and disgust — which, however, are as potent a method of seduction as the erotic.

Now quite clearly in this play, Franco attempts to use desire in order to captivate Martin; yet desire cannot be enjoyable. Relations of authority and power encourage sado-masochistic positions: hence Emma's abjection, her insistence that Franco is really a friend of the family and that she has been branded because she was always getting lost. Outwardly Emma connives with the system but her body signals its rebellion through the constant itching which also prevents her from being made into a love object. Body and speech have no natural connection. Emma sometimes speaks as if she were a society lady or an ambitious concert pianist or a seductress. But her appearance and her body do not cooperate in this masquerade. Gambarro thus presents us with a dysfunctional system in which subjects like Emma are forced to adopt contradictory positions, in which there is no fixed identity except the permanent identity of abjection. This is brilliantly illustrated by the stage directions. For instance, when Franco kisses Emma's hand in order to suggest his conventional respect for a lady, the directions read, "the gesture should slowly lose its genteel character and should become a gesture of domination." Ordered to seduce Martin, Emma half-heartedly attempts to do so while Franco, at the other side of the stage, beats the ground with a whip. With every blow, Emma cries out as if the whip had been laid across her body. It is "as if" Emma had been beaten, for she has an imaginary relationship with real repression.

The climax of the first part of the play is Emma's concert, which is attended by S.S. guards, camp inmates and by Martin and Franco. However, Franco sabotages the performance. There are no programs, Emma wears a wig which falls off, Franco tears her dres and the piano tuner hastily called in at the last moment untures the piano. When Martin protests, the S.S. guards rough him up and he is forced, out of compassion for Emma, to admit that he had "enjoyed" the concert. In the second act, Martin and Emma are thrown together in a room from which they can hear the sound of hunting. Again the ambiguity of camp/countryside affects our understanding of events: Franco appears in hunting clothes and orders Emma to go and see the animals that he has killed though, plainly, the animals could also be people. Inexplicably, he also orders Martin to take Emma home and the stage is immediately converted into a private house. Though there is nothing to suggest domesticity, Emma begins to act in a different way; her memories are no longer the Franco-inspired memories of friendship and childhood but "real" memories of her arrival at the camp, of the dogs that bit her in a certain place — "guess where . . . . It was a bit of luck because there is not much flesh there . . . all the same it hurt." Clearly this is a reference to her symbolic castration by the State. Yet even though she fragmentarily grasps the fact that she has been subjugated, she cannot form an alliance or relationship with Martin and cannot even remember his name. She is still hooked on the sado-masochistic relationship with Franco. Even so, she tries to lay claim to some semblance of normal life. She unpacks her suitcase and takes out a change of clothes only to find that it is a prison uniform identical to the one she is wearing. Finally, when the camp employees come to brand Martin, she tries to account for her stigmatized body and to rationalize her abjection: "I had to bear some kind of mark. We have to know who we are—a little mark." It is in this final desperate moment, when the liberal Martin is about to be marked by the State, that she finally remembers his name.

Gambarro's plays are not written as feminist works; but they are important because they allow us to understand that the social construction of the feminine position within the overall sexual politics of sado-masochism is symptomatic of the State's manipulation of the erotic in order to secure obedient subjects. Female sexuality is a lure. Further, women incline to perform this script written by the State because their creativity is often a desire for performance. Indeed, the concert performance in *The Camp* is one of the most powerful and pitiless representations of women's desire seeking to liberate itself from sado-masochistic performance only to find all other forms of expression closed. The performance is, after all, the State's gift to Emma for seducing Martin (which she cannot really accomplish because of her unpleasant, subjected appearance). Emma herself desires neither love nor motherhood, though she obediently performs Franco's script; rather she aspires to the kind of power known as art. She does not aspire to create in the true sense but rather to perform on a public stage. But Emma not only has to perform in a prison camp atmosphere to an audience of drilled prisoners but is also the butt of their jokes, so that the performance becomes a ritual of humiliation. Nothing is genuine except the disharmony produced by the piano. Worst of all, her body betrays her and she cannot play for itching, an itching that is made worse by the lotion that Franco provides. Because the piano does not work she is forced to *pretend* to play on soundless keys; to suppy the want of sound, she hums a Chopin polonaise.

The audience of prisoners demands an encore. In Gambarro's stage directions, "Emma sits down and repeats the same performance. At a given moment, the S.S. guard gives a signal and the prisoners begin to hum, softly at first, but gradually they increase the volume with the obvious intention of drowning Emma's voice. She sings more loudly but despite her increasingly desperate efforts, the chorus of prisoners drowns her voice. At another signal from the S.S. officer, the prisoners abruptly stop singing. Emma goes on pretending to play but though she tries to open her mouth, only a hoarse murmur can be heard. Franco begins to applaud. The audience mechanically demands an encore." Following this fiasco, Franco kisses her hand, thanks her, forces a bunch of flowers on her but when she mutely tires to shake Martin's hand, Franco brutally reminds her that her own hand is wounded. Meanwhile, Franco also comments on the smell of burning bodies that now penetrates the auditorium. As Emma throws herself to the ground, unable to bear her itching body any longer, Franco hysterically forces Martin to admit that he had indeed enjoyed the performance.

Emma is caught in the double bind that harnesses women to repressive social orders. Yet there is a way in which she also seems to be the author's scapegoat, a figure of shame and self-hatred. Similarly, that woman as creator easily turns to self-parody can also be observed in some of the short novels and stories by the Puerto Rican writer, Rosario Ferré. In "Sleeping Beauty,"[6] Ferré's heroine is a dancer, María de los Angeles, who has a tragicomic fixation on the film *The Red Shoes*. Using letters, newspapers reports, interior monologue, Ferré parodies the language and limitations of Puerto Rico's Beautiful People (the BPs). Like Emma, María de los Angeles wants to perform but finds herself up against the State — in this case, her own industrialist father, the convent in which she has been educated, and her own social class. But dancing is also a metaphor for the bodily freedom which has been denied women. This can best be understood in the light of another of Ferro's stories, "The Youngest Doll," which, under an apparently comic surface, presents a ferocious satire on women's immobility. The protagonist of the story is a maiden aunt who as a young woman had been bathing in a flooded river with her hair streaming towards the sea when a chigger entered her body, lodged in her thigh and caused it to swell to immense proportions. To compensate for her unmarried state and her immobility, the aunt makes life-sized dolls and presents on to each of her nine nieces when they marry. The youngest niece marries an ambitious doctor whose father had made a fortune out of the aunt's leg and on her marriage she receives a special doll with diamonds for eyes. The greedy doctor takes out the eyes and ants crawl inside the doll, which had been stuffed with honey. But as the years pass, the doctor's wife comes more and more to resemble the doll; on the day that she appears to relapse into porcelain-like immobility, the doctor applies his stethoscope to her chest as the angry chiggers reach out to attack him from the empty eye sockets.

The dolls are clearly like upper-class women who are made of honey and spice and all things nice, but who are both deprived of movement and inwardly resentful. Because their only function is to reproduce, these women are identified with nature; but the chiggers are also part of nature. So nature is double-edged — honey and devouring ants, the river and the chiggers. Women are forced to be like nature, but also to be narcissistic, because they are evaluated by the male look. Even their self-expression is a form of narcissism. Thus it is particularly appropriate that the aunt should pay attention to the doll's eyes which (except in the case of the youngest doll) she has imported from Europe. The eyes are then soaked in the river "so that they could learn to recognize the slightest movement of the chigger's antennae." Men deprive women of eyes. They rob them of the look that is power, and reduce their knowledge to the instinctual. To be "blind' in a society where the eyes is the most important source of knowledge means to be shut off from positive knowledge and hence from the symbolic order. It means that women are thrust back into nature, but a nature that is not simply good motherhood but also a furiously angry chigger.

"The Youngest Doll" with its angry immobile woman helps us to account for María de los Angeles' fascination with dance in "The Sleeping Beauty." In this *nouvelle*, Rosario Ferré constructs a collage out of letters, newspaper reports, wedding invitations, the announcement of a birth, the captions written under wedding photographs and all the other minor documents of everyday life. The action of the story covers a brief period of two years when María de los Angeles, an aspiring dancer, leaves convent school, attempts to dance in defiance of her family, marries because she thinks her husband will encourage her dancing, but finds herself pregnant when the husband rapes her in order to consummate the marriage. María de los Angeles gives birth to a son but plots revenge. Her alter ideal is the daring circus performer and her father's former mistress, Carmen Merengue. María de los Angeles' fantasy relationship with Carmen acknowledges a suppressed part of her father's life and valorises a marginalized class. Since María de los Angeles is forbidden to dance, she hires a hotel room and practises Carmen Merengue's high wire act there. At the same time, she fabricates her own death by writing anonymous letters to her husband in which she encourages him to believe that she is being unfaithful. The husband bursts into the hotel room, finds María de los Angeles with a man she has picked up from the street and kills himself and his wife. The son and heir will be taken in by the grandparents to continue to true line.

"The Sleeping Beauty" is written as farce, yet the joke consists of the twist it gives to the usual love triangle. María de los Angeles fabricates the triangle because she is unfaithful not with a man, but with art. Dancing is her husband's rival because it is taboo for a woman. It is thus interesting that "adultery" and illicit love, once a favorite theme of women writers, should have become a pretext that enables women writers to deal with the forbidden passion for creativity: yet more than individual creativity is involved. In two works written about Argentina, the woman artist and performer finds herself participating in a different kind of public performance. In Luisa Valenzuela's "The Fourth Version,"[7] an actress called Bella (another Beautiful Person) negotiates her way from party to party and into an Ambassador's bed. The Embassy is a haven in the midst of political turmoil, but a haven that is soon invaded by political refugees. Valenzuela's story is the "fourth version" of a narrative about Bella that the author is trying to write, one in which the true story, the story of the disappeared, of terror and political exile, cannot be told. By pretending to write Bella's love story, the narrator is aware that she is *not* telling this other story, the story in which Bella is *not* a protagonist but "one more pawn in the game." In the course of the overt narration which eventually fuses with the censored and clandestine narration, Bella becomes the Ambassador's lover: she stars as the only performer in a dramatic monologue, is offered a tour in the Ambassador's native country (somewhere in Central America), and during the tour her apartment in Buenos Aires is ransacked by the police. When she returns home, she again takes up her affair with the Ambassador, whose wife has now left him, and moves in to the Embassy. But the affair comes to an abrupt end as the Ambassador is recalled because of his policy of offering exile to political prisoners. He and Bella throw one final party in which Bella invites families who are seeking diplomatic immunity in order to escape the terror. But before the party ends, the police enter the Embassy and Bella is killed. In this way, the story registers the breakdown of sanctuary which had once protected embassies and churches in Latin America and which the killing of nuns, priests, the bombing of cathedrals and embassies has brought to an end.

Beneath the telling of Bella's story, however, there is a sub-text. Whenever the Ambassador wants to communicate something that cannot be communicated in ordinary speech, he tells a story about his mythical Uncle Ramon. Bella's story is part of a similar device. what cannot be "narrated" because it is fear, terror and oppression has to be displaced onto a love story which demands a certain kind of protagonist, a protagonist who can hook the reader because she is beautiful, seductive and independent. But of course this is also a feminine fantasy, a fantasy of a heroic "free" woman who, like Emma in *The Camp*, projects female fantasy as performance. The actress is able to cross boundaries; in traditional terms, she uses the influence of the "bottom sheet" — that is, the influence of the courtesan. But in Valenzuela's story, such seduction is both parodied and finally undermined by "real" events.

The ambivalence of the performance metaphor is also starkly exposed in Marta Traba's novel *Conversation in the South*.[8] One of the women who participate in this conversation is an actress, an older woman whose son is missing in Chile. She confronts a younger friend, Dolores, who had participated in underground movements, had been arrested, and had aborted a child under torture. The novel is, however, less a conversation and more a meeting of memories on the eve of death. The memories of the actress include one particular traumatic moment during a visit to Buenos Aires. Her friend Elena had lost a daughter, Victoria, who is now numbered among the "disappeared." Elena takes the actress to the demonstration of the "madwomen" of the Plaza de Mayo, a demonstration that horrifies the actress and shows her a different kind of performance. Here the women wear white handkerchiefs and perform their grief to a silent city square. They hold up photographs which no one will see and shout questions that no one will answer. Naked grief has abolished distinctions of social class and all feeling of shame or respectability. To her horror, the actress also finds herself screaming; but hers is a different script.

Clearly the figure of the performer provides these women writers with a device for referring to both sexual and public politics. In contrast to some male writers like Gabriel García Márquez, who wishes to keep the masculine and feminine sphere strictly separated and who recently declared in a *Playboy* interview that women make toffee animals so that men can go off to the wars (even as a joke this is dubious), these women writers have had to find ways of overcoming the limitations imposed by restricted female territories. By "territories" I mean both the privatized spaces (convent and home) allowed women, and the feminine connotations that have accrued to their immobility and passivity because of this restriction. The "deterritorialization" of the feminine and of the indigenous has occurred not only in recent literature but also in society at large. There has been massive migration into cities, the uprooting of entire populations, the removal of indigenous peoples from their traditional territories as well as the destruction of hitherto "sacred" territories such as embassies, churches and middle-class homes and hence the dismantling of the imaginary repertoire on which writers draw. Once the state invades homes, converts mothers into madwomen and bombards cathedrals and embassies, we know that the hegemonic discourse has undergone a change. "Home," "family," "church" can no longer underpin regimes which attack these territories. What authoritarian discourse attempts to do is to displace the meaning of these spaces, to make them both more abstract and more restricted in meaning. Thus they qualify them so that church implies "loyal and traditional church" and family means "disciplined and obedient" family. But by qualifying these terms, they wrest universality from the hegemonic discourse. They also create exclusions, forcing the excluded to regroup themselves in spaces which the military ignore or leave open. Literature registers such changes as shifts in the imaginary repertoire or as sterotyped gestures which are now only available as traces of the past. Whereas many male writers tend to conceal the stereotype by veiling it as history (this is the way things *really* were), women writers are forced to parody the stereotype for otherwise they would have to deny the possibility of any breakthrough. The figuration of woman as performer thus becomes a device that permits them to explore the traditional limitations on creativity even though, as I have shown, it also opens up ambiguities that invite parody. In trying to influence the public as performers, Emma, Bella and María de los Angeles become "public" women. Their desire to create is at once passionate but grotesquely distorted, for they are still besieged by the negative eros of death and destruction that tears apart Latin American political life and has its roots in *machismo*.[9] The sado-masochism that underpins *machismo* allows space to performers because it is itself highly theatrical. By liberating themselves from the fixed spaces to which Latin American women have traditionally been condemned, Emma, María de los Angeles and Bella find themselves performing a sado-masochistic script in which their originality can only take the form of abjection or death. They are self-destructing heroines, but their failed performance should not deter us from envisioning a society that would give them room.

NOTES

[1] Poem LXV from the collection *Trilce* (1922). The translation is my own.

[2] See, for instance, Hernan Vidal, *Dar la vida por la vida: La agrupacion chilena de familares de detenidos desaparecidos* (Minneapolis, Institute for the Study of Ideologies and Literature, 1982).

[3] These have been constant preoccupations in women's writing over the last few years. See, for instance, Elena Poniatowska, *La noche de Tlatelolco*, Elvira Orfée, *La última conquista del Ángel*, and Luisa Valenzuela, *Donde viven las águilas*.

[4] John Berger, *Ways of Seeing* (Penguin, 1972).

[5] *El Campo* (Buenos Aires, Ediciones Insurrexit, 1967).

[6] Both of the stories I discuss, "La bella durmiente" and "La muneca menor," are included in *Papeles de Pandora* (Mexico, 1976).

[7] Included in *Cambio de armas* (Ediciones de Norte, 1982).

[8] Marta Traba, *Conversación al sur* (Mexico, Siglo XXI, 1981).

[9] This essay is part of a chapter on "The Sado-Masochistic Text" which will appear in a collection of essays on contemporary Latin American culture now in preparation.

La guaracha del Macho Camacho:
The Novel as Dirge

℁

Carlos J. Alonso

> From these facts . . . I infer the capacity of
> music to give birth to *myth* (the most signif-
> icant example), and particularly to *tragic*
> myth: the myth which expresses Dionysian
> knowledge in symbols.
>
> —F. Nietzsche, *The Birth of Tragedy*

An examination of present-day literary production in Puerto Rico
allows one to realize that the publication of *La guaracha del Macho
Camacho* in 1976 was a significant turning point for Puerto Rican
cultural production. We need only to confront Luis Rafael Sánchez's novel with earlier canonical works such as Antonio S. Pe-
dreira's *Insularismo*, Luis Palés Matos's pronouncements on Afro-
Antillean culture or René Marqués's crucial essay "El puertorriqueño dócil" to establish the particular heterodoxy represented by
this text. Even when compared to stylistically similar and almost
coetaneous works like *Figuraciones en el mes de marzo* by Emilio Díaz
Varcárcel, the idiosyncratic dimension of *La guaracha del Macho
Camacho* can be readily appreciated. With its rambunctious portrayal of contemporary island reality as a form of entropy, the
novel constituted a relentless dismantling of the ponderous and
solemn meditations on the problematics of Puerto Rican cultural
specificity that had characterized—indeed, become synonymous
with—the country's intellectual and artistic endeavors. Spurred by
the intractable and engulfing American hegemony over the island,
Puerto Rican writers and intellectuals have periodically endeavored to produce formulations of cultural autochthony to counter
that ominous presence. Sánchez's work represents an attempt to

question and dislodge the concept of culture that had provided the foundation for the previous debate on the specific character of the Puerto Rican cultural predicament. Faithful to the presuppositions of nineteenth-century *Kulturgeschichte*, these earlier interpretive efforts invariably managed to subsume the variegated aspects of cultural life under a privileged category or event, whether geographical (insularity), psychological (docility), or historical (the island's spiritual and linguistic roots in the Hispanic world). *La guaracha del Macho Camacho* advances the claim that the operant idea of culture that underlied such formulations cannot serve as an epistemological instrument to encompass the heterogeneous cultural reality of contemporary Puerto Rico. In its stead, the novel proposes the examination of the contradictory and decentered role played by the channels of mass communication in the projection of a cultural space, a role that is practically irreducible to a homogeneous and totalizing conception of cultural analysis.[1] In this enterprise, Sánchez's work is consonant with a number of recent efforts by other Latin American writers such as Mario Vargas Llosa and Manuel Puig, whose texts incorporate diverse elements of mass culture in an explicit and decidedly ironic fashion. In this context *La guaracha del Macho Camacho* is perhaps the more ambitious text, given its evident aim to appropriate indiscriminately the totality of the multifarious discourses engendered by the means of mass communication.

The abandonment of the static and reductive concept of culture signaled by Sánchez's novel has inaugurated a discursive space that younger writers have laid claim to enthusiastically. The best examples of this phenomenon are two works by Edgardo Rodríguez Juliá whose characteristics preclude the possibility of an unambiguous generic filiation. The first of these, *Las tribulaciones de Jonás*, is an heterogeneous text that revolves around an eyewitness account of the obsequies for Luis Muñoz Marín, Puerto Rico's preeminent modern political figure. The second, *El entierro de Cor-*

---

[1] There are two excellent articles that develop specifically the issues raised in the foregoing discussion: "La vida es una cosa *phenomenal: La guaracha del Macho Camacho* y la estética de la novela actual," (in *Isla a su vuelo fugitiva: Ensayos críticos sobre literatura hispanoamericana* [Madrid: Porrúa Turanzas, 1983]) by Roberto González Echevarría, and "En el principio fue el ruido: *La guaracha del Macho Camacho*" by Aníbal González, forthcoming in *Revista Interamericana de Bibliografía*. The first is an attempt to read Sánchez's novel as a mock epic of nationality and the second proposes to use categories derived from information theory in its analysis of the text.

tijo, describes the wake and burial of a revered band leader, an event that is especially significant for the island's black population.[2] In these texts, Puerto Rican culture and identity are portrayed as a collection of conflicting and utterly contradictory gestures that emerge most saliently in a moment of collective grief. There is, however, no attempt to impose coherence on these impulses by means of an overarching interpretive scheme, allowing them instead to retain their unmitigated contradictory force. Even the traditional self-assured stance of the cultural interpreter is unsettled in these works. In an effort to explain his attitude towards Muñoz Marín, the narrator of *Las tribulaciones de Jonás* proposes the following: "Pero bien que estaba encarcelado en dos sentimientos opuestos: No podía solidarizarme ni con el resentimiento de sus enemigos ni con el amor de su pueblo; difícil me resultaba lo mismo la admiración que la denuncia."[3] In this fashion, the meditation on Puerto Rican culture becomes a poignant yet celebratory acceptance of internal contradiction and unwieldy heterogeneity.

The text of *La guaracha del Macho Camacho* projects itself as the most consummate embodiment of this centripetal conception of cultural reality. From its jagged, fragmentary structure to the disparate linguistic registers that it appropriates, the novel appears to resist the drive towards a synthetic formulation of culture and nationality that characterized earlier works. This aspect is underscored by the parodic inclusion in the novel of shibboleths and rhetorical formulae wrenched from that previous textual tradition: Fragments of works by Zeno Gandía, Palés Matos and René Marqués, for example, are echoed in Sánchez's text as disenfranchised instances of cultural detritus. Instead, by following the meandering and decentered dissemination of Macho Camacho's *guaracha* through the means of mass communication, the text seemingly eschews the will to power of such attempts, imitating in its attendant excesses the uncontrollable gyrations that seize the *guaracha*'s most ardent admirers.

Nevertheless, if *La guaracha del Macho Camacho* represents a radical departure from the preceding conception of literary discourse as a vehicle for cultural self-definition, it is no less true that the novel does not renounce completely its status as an epistemological

---

[2] See Aníbal González's incisive review of *El entierro de Cortijo* in *Sin Nombre*, 13, No. 4 (julio-septiembre 1983), pp. 82-86.

[3] *Las tribulaciones de Jonás* (Río Piedras: Ediciones Huracán, 1981), p. 54.

instrument. One can ascertain this in the broadest of terms through the existence of an evident allegorical intention that envelops the text. The disembodied nature of names such as El Nene and La Madre are only the most salient instances of a more extended allegorical structure that dominates the novel: The pro-American senator, his son Benny, doña Chon and the other characters are transparently abstract and stereotypical figures as well. It seems clear, moreover, that their mutual interaction is meant to suggest an extensive and endemic network of exploitive relationships determined along class, gender and race lines. This allegorical component is clearly at work, for instance, in Benny's killing of El Nene: The half-witted son of the poor black woman is murdered by the irresponsible son of the well-to-do family. Through similar developments the novel advances, then, an interpretation of contemporary Puerto Rican society that is totalizing both in its consideration and its critique of that society. The predominantly sociological nature of the critical commentary on the novel attests to the efficacy of this discourse of social criticism in *La guaracha del Macho Camacho*.[4]

Even more significant from this perspective is the novel's desire to achieve simultaneity in its depiction of the island's contemporary reality. *La guaracha del Macho Camacho* endeavors to offer a synchronic picture of Puerto Rican society by portraying itself as taking place in a single instant: throughout the novel it is forever five o'clock on a Wednesday afternoon in San Juan, as the oft-encountered refrain "a las cinco de la tarde, tarde de miércoles hoy" repeatedly asserts. The spatial correlative of this temporal

[4] See, for instance, the following works on the novel: Randolph Pope, "*La guaracha del Macho Camacho* y la contaminación de la mente," *The Bilingual Review/La Revista Bilingüe*, 5 (1978), 152-55; "Puerto Rico entre amos y guaracha: novelas de Enrique Laguerre y Luis Rafael Sánchez," by María Solá Márquez, *Sin Nombre*, 10, No 2 (julio-septiembre 1979), pp. 84-95; José Luis González's "Plebeyismo y arte en el Puerto Rico de hoy," in his *El país de cuatro pisos* (Río Piedras: Ediciones Huracán, 1980), pp. 91-104; José J. Beauchamp's "La novela puertorriqueña: una estructura de resistencia, ruptura y recuperación," *Casa de las Américas*, Año 21, No. 124 (enero-febrero 1981), pp. 67-82; "Sexo y mulatería: dos sones de una misma Guaracha," by Carmen Vázquez Arce, *Los Universitarios*, No. 187 (julio 1981), pp. 22-24; "*La guaracha del Macho Camacho*, la novela del 'aquí'," *Revista Chicano-riqueña*, Año 9, No. 1 (1981), by Elpidio Laguna-Díaz. There is also an entire number of *Revista de Estudios Hispánicos-P.R.* devoted exclusively to Sánchez's work (Año 5, [1978]), as well as two illuminating interviews with Sánchez himself: "Entrevista con Helen Calaf de Agüera," *Hispamérica*, 8, No. 23-24 (1979), pp. 71-80, and "El oficio y la memoria: Luis Rafael Sánchez," (interview with Arcadio Díaz Quiñones) *Sin Nombre* 12, No. 1 (abril-junio 1981), pp. 27-38.

paralysis is the monumental traffic logjam that ensnares the characters along with—it would seem—almost the entire population of the island. Thus, the frenzied movement that characterizes the text's language, and the disjointed, episodic nature of the narration are only mirages that belie the essential organicity determined by the novel's temporal stasis. Combined with the strong allegorical component described above, this attempt at simultaneity evinces the text's desire to encompass Puerto Rican reality as a comprehensive totality.

There is, nonetheless, in *La Guaracha del Macho Camacho* a dimension of the text that dismantles the pretensions to totality and organicity evinced at all levels of the novel. This dimension takes the form of a parallel subtext that is revealed through the existence of an essential indeterminacy at the core of *La guaracha del Macho Camacho,* one that we propose to examine in the remainder of this essay.

Few critics have perceived that the title of the novel *La guaracha del Macho Camacho* encompasses a momentary ambiguity that can only be settled contextually each time it appears in the text. This arises from the fact that the label "La guaracha del Macho Camacho" refers both to the text, the novel, as well as to the musical composition, the *guaracha,* whose universal success and effect on Puerto Rican life are documented in the narrative. Nowhere is this equivocation more explicitly demonstrated than in the "Advertencia" or Foreword with which the text begins:

> *La guaracha del Macho Camacho* narra el éxito lisonjero obtenido por la guaracha del Macho Camacho "La vida es una cosa fenomenal," según la información ofrecida por disqueros, locutores y microfoniáticos. También narra algunos extremos miserables y espléndidos de las vidas de ciertos patrocinadores y detractores de la guaracha del Macho Camacho *La vida es una cosa fenomenal.* Además, como apéndice de *La guaracha del Macho Camacho* se transcribe, íntegro, el texto de la guaracha del Macho Camacho "La vida es una cosa fenomenal" para darle un gustazo soberano a los coleccionistas de todos los tiempos.[5]

The "Advertencia" would appear to suggest the possibility and desirability of distinguishing clearly between the two compositions

[5] *La guaracha del Macho Camacho* (Buenos Aires: Ediciones de la Flor, 1976), p. 11. All subsequent references are to this edition and will be noted parenthetically in the text.

to which the title "La guaracha del Macho Camacho" alludes: the novel and the song. Indeed, as the "Advertencia" explains, the text of the song "La guaracha del Macho Camacho" is appended to the text of the novel *La guaracha del Macho Camacho* in an unequivocal position of supplementarity.[6] At the same time—and notwithstanding the attempts at typographic differentiations—the playful style of the passage previously read is founded just as clearly on the equivocality in the referential value of the expression "La guaracha del Macho Camacho." The label "La guaracha del Macho Camacho," then, confronts us with an instance of what Paul de Man calls a moment of undecidability between the constative and performative functions of language: "The grammatical model . . . becomes rhetorical not when we have, on the one hand, a literal meaning and on the other hand a figural meaning, but when it is impossible to decide by grammatical or other linguistic devices which of the two meanings (that can be entirely incompatible) prevails."[7] In Sánchez's text, the expression "La guaracha del Macho Camacho" denotes the literal meaning of song, at the same time that it proposes the metaphoric identity of text and musical composition. Thus, even though rhetorically the title "Advertencia" could be interpreted in its acceptation of prologue or introduction, it could also be read as a warning or advice to the reader not to confuse his *guarachas,* even if the injuction is itself built on such a confusion. I have decided to heed this duplicitous warning in all of its paradoxical force, taking the liminary act of bad faith it represents as the point of insertion for my commentary on the text. This coincidence of titles has been remarked by others before, particularly by Efraín Barradas, who interprets it as a means of suggesting in the "Advertencia" the pre-existence of the song vis-à-vis the text the reader is about to begin.[8] I would like to attempt

[6] "El texto final de la guaracha es un documento, no un texto narrativo. Aunque éste cumple una función narrativa en la obra . . . no es un texto narrativo per se, sino una especie de falso objeto arqueológico." Efraín Barradas, *Para leer en puertorriqueño: Acercamiento a la obra de Luis Rafael Sánchez* (Río Piedras: Editorial Cultural, 1981), p. 115.

[7] "Semiology and Rhetoric," in *Allegories of Reading: Figural Language in Rousseau, Nietzsche, Rilke, and Proust* (New Haven: Yale University Press, 1979), p. 10. The debt to de Man's work in general is, as it will become evident, central to this essay.

[8] "[E]l título de la novela se confunde con la mención de la imaginaria guaracha del Macho Camacho. Lo que nos remite otra vez al lema: si tenemos un texto en nuestras manos que comienza con unos versos de una guaracha—y sabemos que los lemas se toman de otras fuentes—, entonces esa guaracha existe." Quoted from Barradas, p. 107.

a more radical reading, examining in more detail the way in which this ambiguity is sustained throughout the text, in order to explore ultimately the conflation of the literary and the musical on which it is predicated.

The commingling of the novel and the song begins, in fact, earlier than with the "Advertencia." The latter is preceded in the text by an epigraph to the entire novel that appears under the heading of "Lema." It consists of the first two lines of the song "La guaracha del Macho Camacho," which read: "La vida es una cosa fenomenal / Lo mismo pal de alante que pal de atrás." In this fashion, the text of the novel *La guaracha del Macho Camacho* begins with a transcription of the beginning of the song "La guaracha del Macho Camacho," blurring from the outset the distinction that will be attempted immediately afterwards in the "Advertencia." This conjunction is underscored further at the broadest possible level by the totalizing reach shared by both song and narrative. The novel attempts the portrayal of Puerto Rican society in its entirety, mirroring the way in which "La guaracha del Macho Camacho" has invaded all strata of the social order, leaving no one unperturbed in its wake. The rich, pro-American senator; his frigid and neurotic wife; his black, lower class mistress—all are denuded by the probing narrator and all are seduced as well, willingly or not, by the pulsating lyrics of "La guaracha del Macho Camacho."

Moreover, in stylistic terms the language of the novel is used in ways that suggest rhythmical patterns, cadences and leitmotifs. Take, for instance, the following passage: ". . . Las trompetas hienden los surcos, las trompetas hablan de ritos clandestinos, las trompetas hablan de cuerpos montados, las trompetas hablan de cálidos encuentros de una piel con la otra, las trompetas hablan de ondulaciones lentas y espasmódicas: el trío de trompetas trompeteras" (p. 20-21). And by the same token: "Beberle el jugo del bolsillo es lo que yo quiero. Pelarlo como un pollo es lo que yo quiero. Hipnotizarle la cartera es lo que yo quiero. Exprimirlo para que suelte cuanto bille tenga encima o debajo es lo que yo quiero. Chuparle hasta la última perra es lo que yo quiero" (p. 83). This analogy with musical form could be perceived to be the structuring conceit for the narrative in its entirety. In point of fact, the novel is constructed through the reiteration of a scheme that can be described as contrapuntal in nature. Each vignette devoted to a particular character is invariably followed by a fragment from the radio transmission of an excited disk-jockey who extolls the virtues of "La guaracha del Macho Camacho" and his creator, in an ever-growing linguistic paroxysm:

> Acaban de empezar a oír mi acabadora Discoteca Popular, que se trans-mite de lunes a domingo de doce del mediodía a doce de la medianoche por la primera estación radiodifusora y primera estación radioemisora del cuadrante antillano, continúa en el primer e indispensable favor del respetable público, después de ocho semanas de absoluta soberanía, absoluto reinado, absoluto imperio, esa jacarandosa y pimentosa, la-xante y edificante, profiláctica y didáctica, filosófica y pegajosófica gua-racha del Macho Camacho "La vida es una cosa fenomenal." (p. 39)

This formal arrangement mimics—one could argue—, the *soneo*, the dynamic relationship between the melody and the chorus or refrain that is so predominant in popular Caribbean music. More-over, the sections that deal with each protagonist in turn follow one another always in a rigorous order—*la China Hereje*, Senator Vicente Reinosa, his wife Graciela Alcántara del López y Mon-tefrío, La Madre/El Nene, Benny—as if to imitate the stanzaic arrangement of the lyrics in a song. In addition, the text of the novel repeatedly quotes excerpts from the lyrics of "La guaracha del Macho Camacho," so that if one were to collect all of these quotations strewn throughout the novel, a reconstruction of the entire text of the *guaracha* could be accomplished with ease.

Culling all of these instances, one must reach the inevitable con-clusion that the undecidability perceived in the "Advertencia" is neither an isolated nor a fortuitous double entendre, but rather the telltale symptom of an ambiguity that permeates the entire text. If we are attentive to the logic proposed by this dimension of the text, it becomes apparent that the transcription of the *guaracha* that is appended as a supplement to the body of the novel acquires a highly problematic status. For the novel systematically puts in check precisely the possibility of determining where the text ends, and where the song begins. If we turn to the appendix where the *guaracha* is included, we realize that the indeterminacy is rigorously sustained there as well. At the top of the page there is a heading that announces that what follows is the "TEXTO INTEGRO DE LA GUARACHA DEL MACHO CAMACHO." Therefore, the text of the novel exhibits many of the attributes of the song, and the musical composition is blatantly marked with a rubric that des-ignates it as text, notwithstanding the evident desire to distinguish between the two through the obvious act of exclusion that yielded the appendix.

This state of affairs allows us to identify in the novel the surreptitious postulation of an indissoluble link between music and writing. The conjunction of the two registers (using the word in its musical sense as well) provides—as we shall attempt to demonstrate—an opening into a subtext in the novel where *La guaracha del Macho Camacho* provides a critical commentary on its own coming into being. I would like to suggest that the presence of this subtext is also articulated through the veiled allusions in the novel to Nietzsche's work *The Birth of Tragedy*.

The relationship between the two texts perhaps becomes clearer when we note that the original title of Nietzsche's treatise, subsequently shortened by the author, was "The Birth of Tragedy Out of the Spirit of Music." As is well known, in this work, Nietzsche proposes the essential identification of music with the Dionysian, and its subsequent vanquishing by the forces of the Apollonian spirit in the later Greek tragedy. In *La guaracha del Macho Camacho* the Nietzschean text can be felt lurking in the background, as the passage that will be reproduced presently makes evident. The scene portrays El Nene, the monstrous idiot child, accosted by a swarm of children who treat him as a plaything:

> Bajo un sol irritado por su propia candencia, ¿Apolo rubicundo avecindado in spite of himself en una ciudad llamada San Juan? ¿Apolo rubicundo taumaturgo de los soles truncos?, ¿Apolo rubicundo por la combustión de otro día nuestro?, relumbra tamaña la burla: juegos de escarnio, juegos de pullas y puyas representados sobre una tarde aparatosa: ... relinchada y malsana felicidad, cuando una varita seca hace su entrada en el lóbulo y El Nene se achica como un gongolí, pasteurizada mala leche y hervida en veinte ojos abiertos a todo mal, mala leche revuelta con aullidos; cacareos de intención homicida de los niños que halan los bracetes toninos y deshuesados del Nene. Hasta que el empeño de romperlo se rompe y se frustra. (p. 176)

The fragment is particularly interesting on account of the economy with which it incorporates the two Nietzschean categories. The Apollonian is represented explicitly by the Sun, and by the curative powers repeatedly ascribed to it by the child's mother and her lover. By the same token, the attempted dismemberment of El Nene by the children clearly alludes to the Dionysian frenzy that culminates in the ritual *sparagmos* or dismemberment of the sacrificial victim.

Poised as he is between the Sun and his tormentors, between

Apollo and Dionysus, El Nene appears in this scene as emblematic of the text itself. For *La guaracha del Macho Camacho* encompasses simultaneously two contradictory and irreconcilable conceptions of writing: the first, a mystification that projects what could be referred to as the totalizing power of writing; the second, the knowledge that such a mystified conception of writing is an illusive gesture. The first of these undergirds the novel's attempt to portray itself as taking place in a single moment. This is also the plane that legitimizes the novel's claim to encompass Puerto Rican culture and society in its entirety, in much the same way in which, according to Lukács, the Greek epic reflected the organicity of the Greek world, regardless of the former's episodic structure.[9] This conception of writing is predicated, therefore, on a language that is devoid of its temporal dimension. The resulting projection of an atemporal discourse constitutes the ground and possibility of the vertiginous stylistic movement that characterizes the text. Opposed to this conception there is also in the text a plane where these pretensions are radically challenged and ultimately overturned. This dimension of the novel is constituted by the subtext to which I alluded earlier, in which *La guaracha del Macho Camacho* delivers a critical commentary on its own presuppositions.

It should come as no surprise that the protagonist of this critical mise en scène should be El Nene, the teratological being who becomes a haunting presence throughout the novel. Like the text, he exists in an unfathomable world of temporal stasis and selfsame identity:

> Como un reptil manchado por escamas y llagosidad abrupta; ... lentitudes, torpezas: como un reptil desperezándose, poniéndose de pie y despatarrado, vómito y baba bajando, vómito y baba escurriendo, obsequio los ojos al mosquero ..., despierta la idiotez, despierta y amenizada con cubos de más baba y más legaña: en medio de un cayo en que verdece el desamparo. (p. 115)

But also like the text, his monstrous nature bespeaks the aberration of his contradictory engenderment. When we reach the end of the text, we suddenly realize that El Nene is the propitiatory victim of a tragic plot that concludes with his death in the last page of the novel. Thus, the end of the text coincides with the demise of the

---

[9] *The Theory of the Novel*, tr. Anna Bostock (Cambridge: M.I.T. Press, 1971), pp. 29-39.

monster/child, reinforcing the metaphoric association that links the two. Moreover, the death of El Nene is provoked, significantly, by a moment of specular confrontation with the self: Terrified of his own deformity in a mirror, the child runs into the path of Benny's oncoming car. But this death in the final lines of the novel constitutes also a beginning, a veritable *prelude*, when we consider that it is immediately followed by the transcription of the "TEXTO INTEGRO DE LA GUARACHA DEL MACHO CAMACHO" that is appended to the novel. It is here, perhaps, that we begin to understand the full force of the ambiguity that confounds both text and song. In this ending of "La guaracha del Macho Camacho" that also constitutes the beginning of "La guaracha del Macho Camacho," the novel paradoxically places us at its inception precisely at the moment of its attempted closure. In this fashion, the text reenacts its own beginning as the conjunction of writing and a violent act that both precedes and subtends it. This violent act alludes, of course, to the instauration of the figural mystification of writing at work in the novel, the same that underwrites the text's desire to engender total simultaneity and closure. Through this tragic subtext, the novel underscores what the founding act of violence has repressed: the radical temporality inherent in signification and the heterogeneity and discontinuity that in effect constitute the text.[10]

We can finally fathom the ultimate meaning of this ritual death when we discover the mythical antecedent that it appears to recall, and its relation to the Nietzschean allusions in the novel. For this subtext inaugurates a space where the novel reenacts a distorted but still recognizable version of the founding myth of the Orphic movement, that is, the tale of the murder of the infant Dionysus by the Titans. In the myth, the Titans distract the child by offering him toys, and when the victim is distracted by his own image in a mirror they hold to him, the sacrifice is consummated.[11] In *La*

[10] On this subject see the following two works by Jacques Derrida: "La Difference," in *Marges* (Paris: Minuit, 1972), pp. 1-29, and "Force et signification," in *L'Ecriture et la différence* (Paris: Seuil, 1967), pp. 9-49, especially pp. 27-49.

[11] I have consulted a number of sources that study this myth and its importance to Orphism in particular, and the figure of Dionysus in general. Only the most relevant ones are offered here: *From Orpheus to Paul*, by Vittorio D. Macchioro (New York: Henry Holt, 1930); J. R. Watmough's *Orphism* (Cambridge: Cambridge University Press, 1934); *The Orphic Hymns*, ed. A. Athanassakis (Missoula: Scholars Press, 1977); *The Asiatic Dionysos*, by Gladys Davis (London: G. Bell and Sons, 1914); *Dionysus: Histoire du Culte de Bacchus*, by H. Jeanmaire (Paris: Payot, 1951); *The Greeks*

Guaracha del Macho Camacho the original mythical narrative is transformed into the passion of El Nene at the hands of the band of children who use *him* as a plaything, as the scene quoted earlier depicts. The most significant parallel with the myth is, of course, the role played by the mirror in both narratives.[12] Whereas in the myth the young Dionysus is fascinated by his image, in the novel, the child is overwhelmed by the monstrosity of his own deformity:

> Puñado de manos, puñado de voluntades, tropelío, algazara de dedos, el espejo elevado como un cáliz, el pedazo de espejo elevado como una forma sagrada. Hasta que la cara del Nene se vacía en el pedazo de espejo, incontenida. Levantada, erguida, sostenida la gran cabeza por diez manos. El Nene, despertando al horror de su propio horror se arranca de la garganta un tañido protestante envuelto en llanto. Entonces, todo el dolor del mundo se le espeta en el corazón y el cielo se aparda como un piso de madera sin lavar: vetoso y ruin . . . Correr es grato y libre, lo descubre sin descubrirlo, correr, desaparecer como un punto, inalcanzable por los gritos que gritan a las cinco de la tarde, tarde de miércoles hoy. (pp. 244-45)

Moreover, the dismemberment of the child's body that follows the sacrificial moment in the myth has an echo in the description of El Nene's death: "Yo no tuve la culpa a unos sesos reventados en la puerta del Ferrari y a unos ojos estrellados por la cuneta como huevos mal fritos." (p. 255) Thus, the text represents—valga la palabra—a mythical narration of its own repressed beginnings in terms of the violent suppression of the Dionysian impulses that must be held in check for the novel to achieve its desire for totality and closure. This dimension of the text that we have endeavored

---

and the Irrational, by E. R. Dodds (Berkeley: University of California Press, 1951); Park McGinty's *Interpretation and Dionysos: Method in the Study of a God* (The Hague: Mouton, 1978); and, of course, *The Birth of Tragedy* by F. Nietzsche, tr. Walter Kaufmann (New York: Random House, 1967).

[12] The mirror is one of the most salient aspects of the original myth, and as such, it has given rise to multiple interpretations: "Certainly the Neoplatonists saw in it [the mirror] an allegory of the nature of mankind. Proklos of course, when he sees in the picture of Dionysus looking at his reflection in the mirror an image of the opposition between the eternal intelligible world and the unreal world of birth and decay, is introducing Platonic notions which could not have been in the minds of the creators of the story. Nevertheless they too had a religious doctrine to propound, and it may well be that in the same picture we are meant to see a foreshadowing of the double nature of mankind, his heavenly nature which is his real self, and his earthly or Titanic which is no better than a shadow." Quoted from W. K. C. Guthrie's *Orpheus and Greek Religion: A Study of the Orphic Movement* (New York: Norton, 1966), pp. 122-23.

to examine becomes then an instance of the demystifying capabilities that Nietzsche ascribes to the Dionysian, its capacity to produce a myth that expresses the knowledge of contradiction and difference. In this fashion, the novel uncovers its own passage from the knowledge of a dangerous supplementarity in language—associated figuratively with music and the Dionysian—to the closed economy of signification on which the novel's epistemological pretensions are grounded; from "La guaracha del Macho Camacho" to *La guaracha del Macho Camacho*.

Nietzsche's essential identification of music with the disseminatory powers of the Dionysian spirit perhaps suggest that Sánchez's attempt to use a song to project his totalizing view of Puerto Rican reality would result in the contradictory and problematic self-knowledge that the novel evinces.[13] Indeed, if we read attentively the lyrics of "La guaracha del Macho Camacho," we find that the song already spoke of its disturbing and unsettling nature from the outset, particularly if we keep in mind the novel's persistent association of the song with a famous Puerto Rican vedette. I therefore would like to conclude with the last three lines of that slippery and peppery, purgative and instructive, prophylactic and didactic, scatological and eschatological guaracha del Macho Camacho, "La vida es una cosa fenomenal":

> "que la cosa no puede reposar,
> que la negra quiere sudar,
> que la negra se va a alborotar." (p. 256)

Wesleyan University

---

[13] Marcel Detienne makes a similar point regarding the corrosive presence of Dionysus in the bosom of Orphic religion: "One can still ask if the split inflicted by Orphism on the body of Dionysiac religion is not menaced by the very thing that makes it possible, that is, by Dionyso's inveterate oscillation between the twin poles of savagery and paradise regained. By conferring pride of place on a divine power whose royalty at the beginnings of the world is based on his privileged ability to reunite in himself the most diverse forms and elements, Orphism was unmistakably drawn into the orbit of the Dionysiac phenomenon and caught up in the whirl of metamorphoses that Dionyso's constitutive, ever-renewed madness indulges in throughout the course of history." In *Dionysos Slain*, tr. M. and L. Muellner (Baltimore: Johns Hopkins University Press, 1979), pp. 92-93.

RENE PRIETO

THE AMBIVIOLENT FICTION OF SEVERO SARDUY

"La muerte—la pausa que refresca—forma parte
de la vida."

Severo Sarduy, *Cobra*

C'est en somme d'un codage de la pulsion de
mort, dont Freud nous dit qu'elle est antérieure à
l'objet et à l'amour, qu'il s'agit dans le récit
obscène.

Julia Kristeva, *Histoires d'amour*

To SAY THAT AMBIVALENCE, exaggeration and multiplicity play a major
role in the recent novels of Severo Sarduy is to belabor a point for
reasons which only the temper of these very works can justify. Saturation
and redundance, even critical, are as topical to Sarduy's fiction as
transformation and evolution are typical of his characters.

The narrative subject in *Cobra*[1] as well as in *Maitreya*[2] develops
through a transmutational process in every way antithetic to the classical
notion of character unity. Its kaleidoscopic nature becomes clear only in
the light of Lacan's maxim, "Je ne pense pas là où je suis, et je ne suis
pas là où je pense." Furthermore, the impermanence of Sarduy's
subject-in-process is made evident at all levels: sexual, nominal, and
morphological. La Tremenda, the protagonist of *Maitreya*, is also la
Colosal, la Monumental, la Masiva, la Contundente, la Diva, la Prima,
la Obesa, la Toda-Masa, la Delirium, la Divina and la Expansiva. Cobra
is a transvestite, a castrato, male, female, square root of itself, and, after
many upheavals, a whimsical prima donna in a Moroccan nightclub
where she shares the spotlight with la Divina, la Adivina, la Di Vina, and
Lady Vinah. The protean characters of *Cobra* and *Maitreya* even coexist
with their own images, sometimes stunted (Pup: Cobra), sometimes
reflected , such as the fabulously identical twins la Tremenda and la
Divina: "eran tan idénticas y gritonas que había que marcarlas con
puntos de colores en la frente para saber cual había ya mamado y a cual
había que darle dos cucharadas de cocimiento de yerbabuena o dos
nalgadas suavecitas para que se durmiera" (p. 87).

Referring to the evolution and expenditure[3] characteristic of the narrative subject in *Cobra* several critics, among them Emir Rodríguez Monegal, have mentioned the affiliation between Sarduy's fiction and the work of Georges Bataille.[4] However, while it is true that in the figuration of eroticism and dilapidation the work of both authors is immediately comparable, no one will deny that their respective portrayals of death (which is both the driving force and seminal feature of their narrative universe) differ dramatically.

For Bataille eroticism is "L'approbation de la vie jusque dans la mort."[5] It is through the erotic act that two individuals are joined together and communicate. But eroticism, claims Bataille, "ouvre à la mort. La mort ouvre à la négation de la durée individuelle" (p. 29). Therefore, in fiction at least, and always through the body, the protagonists of Bataille's universe are relentlessly driven to their own end, whereas those of Sarduy's novels brandish death as a beguiling plaything which always signals a new beginning. Since death and life are histrionically (and logically) wedded in Sarduy's conception, the ontological process of *Cobra* and *Maitreya* unfolds as an ostensible contradiction which I propose to analyze and summarize here in one question: how can violence, castration and death function as a kind of tectonics of the body, as a generative magma begetting fecundity from barrenness and growth from decay? Having noted that the process of character expenditure in both novels serializes its hermeneutic complexity along three rungs—rejection, discontinuity and transformation—I propose to open discussion by examining each of these features in detail.

The protagonists of *Cobra* and *Maitreya* are maimed from the outset by what should be labelled (in keeping with Sarduy's iconoclastic parody) a "tragic flaw" essentially amounting to an undisguised mockery of the inherently failed human condition. As Biblical man turns to his maker besmirched by the onus of original sin, so does Cobra, frenzied by the unsightly feet which deface her otherwise dazzling beauty: "'¿Por qué me hiciste nacer si no era para ser absolutamente divina? . . . ¿De qué me sirve ser reina del Teatro Lírico de Muñecas, y tener la mejor colección de juguetes mecánicos, si a la vista de mis pies huyen los hombres y vienen a treparse los gatos?'" (p. 11). In the same manner, in *Maitreya*, La Tremenda laments: "Dios o Big bang. . . . ¿Por qué . . . me has hecho vulnerable, blanco indefenso de los rayos, y permites que con revigidos artilugios birriagen el dibujo de la voz que te loa?" (p. 142). Furthermore, in both novels the initial flaw is merely a prelude to the eventual and inevitable breakdown of the entire bodily machine: "Mas poco duraba la majestad de la engreída diosa paquidérmica: a los primeros estentores trompetados caía en un stress germánico: resacas, come repletas de crustáceos, en la cabeza, relámpagos úricos en las bisagras mandibulares, fuacatazos en la campanilla, nudos vocales y tizones en la garganta, cuyas cenizas tupían los canales del laberinto."[6] All does not function as it should in *Cobra* and *Maitreya*; things fall apart. But the ubiquitous flaws and universal inadequacies should be seen for what they really are. In Sarduy's fictional portrayals insufficiencies are clearly symptoms of a profound dissatisfaction, deceivingly featured as a rejection of part of the body (the feet or the sexual organs) when in fact they signal an overall negativity, a rejection of the entire self which the discarded appendage (Cobra's sex, for example) will come to symbolize, metaphorically. Furthermore, as Freud has made amply evident, negativity (*Nachfolge*) should be seen as the equivalent of expulsion or, more exactly, of the instinct of destruction (*Destruktionstrieb*).[7] And this equivalence explains why Cobra's rejection of his feet heralds a wish to negate or annihilate his whole self. Fueled by desire, Cobra enacts the primal fantasy of the dismembered body which, according to psychoanalysis, masks castration anxiety. Wishing to reduce the size of his tormented extremities ("los pies de Cobra eran su infierno" [p. 29]), the protagonist ends up shrinking his entire body and becomes Pup, the "white dwarf." Then, to attain the summit of wish-fulfillment after being shamed in part by his own dwarfness, he submits his own parts of shame, his "residuo grosero, lo que de tí se desprende informe" (p. 115) to the eager blade of Doctor Ktazob" que en taimado raspadero tangerino arranca de un tajo lo superfluo y esculpe en su lugar lúbrica rajadura" (p. 85).

Mutilation and decay are pervasive figurations of both *Cobra* and *Maitreya* but should not be seen as signs of discontinuity, however. As the narrator of *Maitreya* indicates: "un don perdido implica el surgimiento de otro" (p. 91). This is why the faithful Tibetan followers who cast the rest of their dismembered Master to the air discover that "la cabeza, como un planeta desorbitado que al caer volviera al estado de lava, de cal o de nácar, en un despliegue helicoidal y luminoso, quedó convertida en una concha marina tornasolada y gigante" (p. 23). This process in which expenditure is a requisite ingredient of transformation and, therefore, of production, is also dramatically different from the Bataillean notion of negativity. In Bataille's fiction the "negativité sans emploi"[8] turns out to be an affirmative dispersion in which the characters (such as those of *Histoire de l'œil* or *Ma Mère*) engage in an unfettered passage towards death, the one and only rebuttal of human isolation (what Bataille terms "l'ipseité").[9] In linguistic terms, Bataille portrays negativity as a series of ellipses (the blank pages of *Mme Edwarda*) where all and nothing are equally unspeakable.

In contrast to Bataille in these respects as well, Sarduy turns his back on verbal avarice, on the white page, and his own process of *dépense* generates a widespread sense of prodigal squandering. So too, mutilation in his novels functions as a confirmation of the heterogeneous nature of his narrative subjects always portrayed in a complex verbal system which can be labelled "motivated," if we abide by the term coined by Russian Formalism.[10] By this I mean that in *Cobra* and *Maitreya* the polyvalence of signs is a reflection of the ontological plurality which is one of the major themes of both novels. And this polyvalence is created by means of two mechanisms: the paragrammatic movement, and what I label hybridization to betoken an agglutination of signifiers.[11]

One of the most significant uses of hybridization in *Cobra* stems from the very name of the surgeon who "arranca de un tajo lo superfluo" (p. 85), Dr. Ktazob. This patronymic simultaneously contains and delivers a network of signs axiomatic to the capital problem in the text: castration anxiety. First and foremost, *zob* designates the phallus in Arabic and is a word freely used in current French jargon.[12] Furthermore, *cazzo* [Katzo] in Italian is a synonym for *zob* and, finally, a phonetic reading of the surgeon's name [K] [ta] [zob] would define in Spanish one who castrates (i. e., "quita" *zob*).[13]

The "superfluo" mentioned in the text is what is never specifically mentioned in Spanish in this section of the novel: the *zob* or [katzo] which the protagonist is missing and which the surgeon (whose signifier is male organ by definition, i. e., [katzo] and *zob*), severs with one blow, "arranca de un tajo" (p. 85). We might add that the phallus is conspicuously absent, and its absence directly parallels the lack or loss in Cobra's own castrated body.

We must not forget, either, the significant role of the consonant "Z" for any student of Roland Barthes such as Sarduy. As Barthes has demonstrated in *S/Z*, the letter "Z" is "l'initiale de la castration" housed in the medial axis, the vital center of Sarrazine, protagonist of Balzac's short story.[14] Like Sarrazine, the one who [K] [ta] [zob] displays in the very heart of his name, which is his textual body, the "Z" emblematic of the emasculation which Cobra desires. Offering his body as an oblation to Ktazob's blade, the protagonist denies his virility, in the general and abstract sense, as well as the object which represents it and which he is about to discard. And it is not surprising that he rejects this one part of his body, the phallus, because metaphorically speaking it is the very emblem of his identity. The synonymity of both signifiers—phallus/Cobra—is manifest in the section immediately following the castration scene in the chapter entitled, "La Conversión." After the suture which puts an end to the·operation, Cobra's pillow remains smeared with "almidón límpido o semen" secreted by "lengüetas acanaladas, ásperas" (p. 118). And immediately after the operation Cobra's behavior is described with an ambiguous terminology which could equally refer to the male organ and to the reptile: "Se yergue . . . Se desdobla . . . la cabeza triangular que corona un arco . . . esa ojiva de bulbos babosos . . . Con la respiración del durmiente se contrae y dilata la cuenca estriada . . . (p. 119) and "enchumbarán, apretadas las esponjas . . . chorros de jugos corrosivos, salivazos fénicos . . . (p. 120).

The nexus between phallus and reptile is not only evident in the text describing the castration ceremony but throughout the entire novel as well. On page 89, for example, it is said of the Alexandrian saint who emasculates himself in a static rapture: "amputóse de un tajo el basilisco." The text is equally explicit when it identifies Totem's organ to a reptile: "Le fosforece enroscada en el sexo, una serpiente. Al glande se adhiere blanda, la cabeza. Afilada, goteando leche, penetra la lengüeta." (C, p. 142).

Occasionally identified with other male characters in the novel, the phallus is, nonetheless, most emphatically and most often coupled with Cobra himself and is in every way the sign of (what becomes after the castration scene) his/her identity. We are further convinced of this identification when the protagonist loses his/her name after the castration ceremony to retrieve it only during the initiation in "Cobra II." Besides his name, after Ktazob's operation the protagonist loses its alter ego, Pup, the white dwarf which is a reflection, "un otro yo" of itself.[15] As the surgeon informs Cobra in a sentence which clearly identifies the dwarf alter ego with the severed organ: "ella . . . no es más que tu desperdicio, tu residuo grosero, lo que de tí se desprende informe . . . cuerpo de tí caído que ya no eres tú (p. 115).

The process of hybridization which foregrounds the topic of discourse by its very absence corresponds, therefore, to the lack which denotes in this instance the loss of the male organ and also, as we have noted, the loss of identity or, more exactly, of specificity. Cobra is essentially kaleidóscopic and Sarduy portrays its plurality by continuing to represent the facets or personae which it ostensibly discards through what Kristeva has defined as the paragrammatic movement. As Gerardo Vázquez Ayora indicates, this movement is based on "mecanismos de generación y selección que exigen la figuración de cada elemento citado por lo menos con dos referencias."[16] Aside from the "linear" reading which reveals the stream of events, Sarduy's system fosters a discontinuous communication whereby the reader can link one clause with its recapitulation in a dramatically different context. In *Cobra*, for example, the paragrammatic movement permits the contiguity of two antithetic fictions. Sarduy structures the text so that the protagonist can be both masculine and feminine, not in succession but conjointly.

In the chapter entitled "¿Qué tal?" which follows the castration scene Cobra appears "envuelta en una capa negra, cubierta por un sombrero de cardenal" (pp. 126-27). This description becomes codified as a leitmotif which reappears later in the novel: "Un sombrero rojo cuyos cordones, cayendo hasta una capa negra, del rostro ocultaban las flores de oro" (p. 143) and comes to represent Cobra as a female character. However, at this point in the narrative (the chapter entitled "La iniciación") the protagonist's sexuality has evolved once again. When the leitmotif was codified Cobra had just been emasculated and he was indeed she. But in "La iniciación" he has reverted to his male persona: "con los nudillos se acarició la barba" (p. 135). Thus, the paragram used to portray Cobra as female shares the narrative space in which he is undisguisedly male. In this manner, Sarduy convincingly portrays two antithetic fictions simultaneously: Cobra as he is and Cobra as he wishes to be.

The protagonist's castration fantasy extemporizes his will to be "other." This is a yearning he satisfies by transforming his inmost being into a prurient furrow of flesh, an empty space which allows her to house and therefore to possess the phallus she covets. Ktazob's operation permits the protagonist to evolve from being to having; it is only by virtue of her newmade womb, in other words, that Cobra will legitimize the possession of the phallus inside her body in a culminating paroxism of narcissism.[17] This is why it is helpful to remember at this point how, according to Freud, the decisive element in the genesis of homosexuality is a fixation on the mother whose body is a receptacle by definition and therefore embeds and reclaims the male organ. As Julia Kristeva so pertinently observes: "Son corps plein, réceptacle et répondant des demandes, tient lieu de tous les effets et satisfactions narcissiques, donc imaginaires: c'est dire qu'elle est le phallus."[18]

I have already noted how phallus and Cobra are metaphorically substitutable in Sarduy's novel. Now, I should like to discuss how the loss of the protagonist's name after the castration scene further corroborates this synonymity. After Cobra loses his masculinity he is never identified by his signifier (which he has, we could say, "perdido de un tajo") but rather by four of the signifieds which define him: "copenhague bruselas amsterdam"; "appel alechinsky corneille jorn"; "serpiente venenosa de la India"; "recibe en la pagaduría su salario" (pp. 136-37). The loss of the phallus motivates the lack of signifier and the loss of identity; as Kristeva notes in *Révolution du langage poétique*: "pour qu'il ait énonciation il faut que l'*ego* se pose dans le signifié, et ceci en fonction du sujet manquant dans le signifiant . . ." (p. 45).

The protagonist recovers his missing identity only after affirming himself as subject of the novel. Until the initiation, Cobra is object of the text, third-person pronoun, the voice that Emile Benveniste defines as the "non-personne."[19] However, after the ceremony begins the protagonist speaks in the first person: "ahora da vueltas alrededor de mí, mirándome" (p. 140), that is to say, he takes possession of the text since, as Benveniste has demonstrated, the first person is the voice that appropriates the narration: "les indicateurs *je* et *tu* ne peuvent exister comme signes virtuels, ils n'existent qu'en tant qu'ils sont actualisés dans l'instance du discours, où ils marquent par chacune de leurs propres instances le procès d'appropriation par le locuteur" (p. 255).

The text describing the initiation is, therefore, Cobra's own. This possession by the first person can only take place after the subject elucidates (enacting it) the fantasy of castration since, as Kristeva indicates in *Révolution du langage poétique*, "la découverte de la castration détache le sujet de sa dépendance vis-à-vis de la mère, et, à travers ce manque, fait de la fonction phallique une fonction symbolique—*la* fonction symbolique" (p. 45).

The use of the first person, following the castration scene, emblematizes access to the symbolic function which is language and, in this instance, the act of writing. Becoming "yo" Cobra becomes the text, the "boca que obra," emitter of the symbolic discourse which dresses itself as parody of mimetic representation.

Furthermore, the affirmation of the narrative subject is the culminating moment of the initiation ceremony during which the protagonist receives a name, that is to say, the only sign he is still lacking:

> le trazó en el jacket, sobre la espalda, un arco vertical que se abrió en la piel, chorreando, embebido por la felpa, retorciéndose como una serpiente macheteada.
> "¿Cobra?" pregunta Escorpión.
> "Cobra: para que se envenene," responde Totem. (p. 154)

But even the investiture of the male Cobra does not hinder the periodic figuration of the protagonist in his female incarnation as a constant return of the repressed. The previously quoted paragram, "un sombrero rojo cuyos cordones . . . ." underscores the plurality typical of this novel and makes amply clear that in *Cobra* the thematic development is a process affirming the heterogeneous nature of all narrative characters.

As is amply evident, the heterogeneous subject of *Cobra* and *Maitreya* is mirrored by the polyvalence of signs underscoring the multiplicity of sense contained in both novels. In *Cobra*, Eustaquio's colossal "tube" dazzles la Señora in a Turkish bath house. The sight of it stirs her deeply as a potent reminder of Ganesha, the legendary elephant god of India.[20] Later on, when more than the mere view of this member thrills to gayness the dancers of the "Teatro Lírico," la Señora exclaims: "Dios mío, . . . a esta casa la ha perdido la trompa de Eustaquio" (p. 25). By means of this intertextuality (the elephant's trunk figuratively likened to the Eustachian tubes which metaphorically mask the maleness of the Indian makeup man) Sarduy forges yet another paragram which fully corresponds, in its plurality, to the kaleidoscopic characters of his novel and contrasts with the element of expenditure represented by violence and mutilation. In other words, the novel is composed of ever-expanding (ever ambiguous) signs, ostensibly in contrast with the rampant erosion disabling the characters. In *Cobra*, Pup tears off the ears from a little girl so she can steal "unos aretes de caramelo" (p. 97). Totem slices off his tongue (p. 170), and Cobra's feet succumb to a "morado lezamesco" followed by "grietas en el tobillo, urticaria y luego abscesos subiendo de entre los dedos, llagas verdinegras en la planta" (p. 34). In *Maitreya* characters are scourged, raped and mutilated even after death. The Leng sisters "raspaban, de un cadáver, las viruelas; con una lima, le desgastaban los dientes" (p. 30). Later in the novel other characters "jugaban con excrementos . . . con agua sucia . . . se entregaban a los oprobios prescritos" (p. 156).

But characters are not exclusively disabled, demolished and spent in these novels. For the most part, they turn away from any fruitful enterprise as well. Intercourse is conspicuously absent from *Cobra* and *Maitreya* although it figures in the fantasy conceived by the characters themselves. For example, at one point in the later novel Iluminada describes a couple she sees reflected in a mirror: "lo que aquello apretaba entre los brazos, con dedos separados y curvos, sin presión, era su pareja blanquísima, patiabierta y vuelta hacia él, senos enormes y cintura estrecha, caderas grandes que movía lenta, cubierta de coronas pesadas y pulseras de piedra sin brillo, mientras se dejaba hundir entre las piernas un falo rojo y enorme, sin venas . . ." (p. 46).

The wanton voyeurism of this scene may well obscure the lack of creative urge actually portrayed in the text. But careful reading soon reveals that what *Iluminada* describes is a mere hallucination brought on by infusions of laudanum. In addition, both the dehumanized subject of the sentence, "aquello," as well as the description of a phallus "rojo y enorme, sin venas" put the overt sensuality of this passage in proper perspective allowing us to see the alleged love tryst as a sterile allegory of the sexual act and not as the act itself.

Sexual communication is avoided in *Cobra* as well; the erotified tableau of the four "blousons noirs," for example, culminates in a total

lack of contact, in a rejection of all partners: "Totem: Nos mastur-
bamos; Tigre y Tundra; Escorpión y yo. Cada uno terminaba solo.
Nadie toca la leche de otro. No nos miramos" (p. 167). Leng mastur-
bates as well and only as a last resource does he squeeze his body between
that of his partners, avoiding all genital contact: "Ya cuando sentía que
la centella germinadora subía por los alambiques ovillados, entonces se
acercaba a la frazada que envolvía a los bultos simétricos y, entre su ropa
sudada, como un jabalí en la gruta, se escurría ligero. Las estremecidas,
vueltas una contra otra, lo incrustaban entre sus volúmenes . . ."
(pp. 96–97).

Given the pervasive sterility of *Cobra*, it is not surprising that the major erotic fixation in the novel which comes after it should be sodomy,
and specifically what Sarduy labels in *Maitreya* "f.f.a." or "el consuelo
digital" (p. 161) which violates "los anales del imperio" (p. 156). In
Maitreya the homing hand ("En ano metía primero las yemas unidas de
los dedos, como para cerrar una flor o acariciar el hocico de un tapir"
[p. 156]), functions just as much on the thematic level (as an emblem of
perversion and sado-masochism) as on the symbolic. We have seen how,
in *Cobra*, the reptile metaphorically designates the phallus. The same
transference of sense from one sign to another is at work in *Maitreya*,
with one difference, that to decode it we must refer to the doctrines of
Tantrism which play such a pivotal role in Sarduy's narrative conception. According to Kundolini yoga, the hand can symbolically emblema-
tize the phallus. We learn in the *Satcakranirupana* that Kundolini is the
serpent residing in the median line of the body (*dehamadhyaya* in San-
skrit).[21] When it is properly awakened with Hatha yoga, Kundolini
travels through the six vital centers, or *cakras*, of the body until it reaches
the seventh, *sahasrara cakra*, the lotus of a thousand petals, found at the
crown of the head. Only when Kundolini reaches this center does the
disciple attain enlightenment (*mukti*).

What is particularly interesting about this process is that the second
cakra, svadhistana, is situated at the base of the male organ, lotus with
six vermillion-colored petals, and, according to the dogma, it is associated with an element (water), a color (white), one of the senses (taste),
and a part of the body (the hand).[22] This symbolic equivalence between
the hand and the phallus would convincingly clarify the otherwise mysterious parthenogenesis of la Tremenda in *Maitreya*:

> Entonces el iranio, escupiéndose la mano, los dedos reunidos en un
> cono, la hundió hasta las falanges, en el túnel que se iba delatando
> a su paso . . . La Tremenda amaneció cosiendo y cantando . . . Esa
> misma noche empezó a hincharse . . . Agarrada al árbol plástico . . .

la Tremenda dió un gran pujo. Sobre una colcha . . . cayó parado,
como sobre una flor de loto, la mano derecha alzada y abierta, sonriente y rojo, como de sangre fresca o de porfirio, el engendro . . . .
(p. 181)

But being born on his feet is hardly the only idiosyncracy of the
marvelous child who "presentaba una protuberancia. El pelo, trenzado a
la derecha, era azulado . . . El lóbulo de la oreja tres veces mas largo que
lo normal. Cuarenta dientes sólidos y parejos protegían una lengua larga
y afilada . . . y una fina membrana le unía los dedos de las manos y los
pies" (p. 181). In fact, all these features correspond to the thirty-two
which distinguish the last historic Buddha (who precedes Maitreya) born,
like Tremenda's infant, *per angostam viam*.

Even such brief excursion into Tantric thought demonstrates how the
polyvalence in *Maitreya* functions on two levels at all times. On the symbolic plane Tremenda's "hijo caudal" confirms the generative power of
the hand and the nexus between this extremity and the phallus, whereas
on the thematic level, the hand corroborates the difference between the
Bataillean notion of *dépense* and Sarduy's prolific conception.

The characters in the work of both authors are portrayed in a context
of expenditure. However, in Sarduy's fiction, violence, castration, and
death are decorative mannerisms, rhetorical figures along a generative
chain. The prodigal squandering of self in both *Cobra* and *Maitreya*
simply signals the beginning of one and all transfigurations. Being is
forever becoming and the body defamed, rejected and mauled is soon
after the germ of a fledgling creation. As Sarduy says in *Cobra*: "La
muerte—la pausa que refresca—forma parte de la vida" (p. 230). Before
all, therefore, destruction in his works is always ambiviolence, gateway
of change.

Middlebury College

1. Severo Sarduy, *Cobra* (Buenos Aires: Editorial Sudamericana, S.A., 1973). All
subsequent parenthetical page references are to this edition.
2. Severo Sarduy, *Maitreya* (Barcelona: Editorial Seix Barral, S.A., 1978). All subsequent parenthetical page references are to this edition.
3. I use this term in the sense Georges Bataille gives it in his theory of a general
economy. Georges Bataille, "La notion de dépense" and "Le principe de la perte," in
Œuvres complètes, I (Paris: Éditions Gallimard, 1970), pp. 302–08. For Bataille *dépense*
or expenditure refers to all forms of unproductive squandering antithetic to the bourgeois
notion of utilitarian accumulation. *Dépense* is always typified by a gratuitous loss or, as
Bataille puts it, by *"la perte* qui doit être la plus grande possible, pour que l'activité prenne
son véritable sens" (p. 305).

4. Emir Rodríguez Monegal, "Las metamorfosis del texto," in *Severo Sarduy* (Madrid: Editorial Fundamentos, Colección Espiral, 1976), p. 35.

5. Georges Bataille, *L'Érotisme* (Paris: Les Éditions de Minuit, Collection 10/18, 1957), p. 15.

6. *Maitreya*, p. 139.

7. Sigmund Freud, *la Négation* (Paris: *Organe Official de la Société psychanalytique de Paris*, VII [2], 1934). Julia Kristeva expands upon these notions in both *Polylogue* (Paris: Éditions du Seuil, 1977) as well as in *Recherches pour une sémanalyse* (Paris: Éditions du Seuil, 1969). In *Polylogue* she discusses the enjoyment of destruction or death wish and its nexus with the sublimated and repressed anal drive (p. 70). In *Recherches* she notes that negativity, "le mouvement même de la matière hétérogène," can only produce a subject in process (p. 105). Both negativity—specifically the notion of scission—and the heterogeneous subject which results from it are fundamental to the understanding of Sarduy's work. In their appetite for destruction (the anal fixation in *Maitreya* is only one example) Sarduy's characters are involved in a process of negativity which, as it turns out, proves to have at least two positive aspects. On one level the negating subject of *Cobra* and *Maitreya* is, in its very formulation, an affirmation of the work of art, or, in other words, the most convincing testimony of creation. But so too, and more importantly, the ostensible negation of life in both novels is truly an affirmation of the complementarity of life and death and thus, negation in these instances turns out to be what Kristeva calls "une dissolution productrice": "Si ce mouvement matériel de scission, de rejet, reste un 'négatif' pour l'entendement kantien, il est pensé par la dialectique et parce qu'il est inséparable de l'être, comme une *positivité* fondamentale . . . tout en maintenant les oppositions kantiennes, la dialectique hégélienne s'achemine vers leur refonte fondamentale qui, à la place de 'l'être' et du 'néant,' instaurera une *négativité affirmative*, une *dissolution productrice*" *La Révolution du langage poétique* (Paris: Éditions du Seuil, 1974), p. 105.

8. Georges Bataille, *Œuvres complètes*, V (Paris: Éditions Gallimard, 1973), p. 369.

9. According to Bataille man lives in absolute isolation in a "nuit universelle" which is tantamount to an absence of being (since being in his system precludes the recognition of and communication with others). Men are like isolated particles which can become part of an ensemble only by transcending the very life which maintains the barriers of this isolation. Georges Bataille, "Le labyrinthe" in *Œuvres complètes*, I (Paris: Éditions Gallimard, 1970), pp. 433–41.

10. The Formalists argue that the content of a given work could well motivate its form. In a text about madness (a work by Artaud or Lautréamont, for example) the syntax would be impaired, the meaning precarious and the discourse ambiguously incomplete.

11. Kristeva expands upon the Saussurean notion of paragram in both "Pour une sémiologie des paragrammes," *Tel Quel*, 29 (Spring, 1967) as well as in *Recherches pour une sémanalyse*. She refers to the polyvalence of poetic language ["l'absorption d'une multiplicité de textes (de sens)"] as *paragrammatisme* and explains how the poetic signified, "renvoie à des signifiés discursifs autres, de sorte que dans l'énoncé poétique plusieurs autres discours sont lisibles" (*RPUS*, p. 255). In contrast, by hybridization I refer to the multiplicity of texts (or meanings) contained in a given *signifier*.

12. In the event that identifying a word as Arabic in a Cuban novel written by a Frenchified writer should appear far-fetched to some readers, I refer them to page 108 of the Editorial Sudamericana edition for other examples of the vocabulary which is presently exerting such a major influence on spoken French.

13. Sarduy hinders the reading of *Ktazob* by bringing together two consonants, [k] and [t], in a phoneme which is illegible and therefore unacceptable in Spanish. [Kt] obstructs the access to the third syllable, represses the signified of the surgeon's name and thus hides the presence of the phallus or *zob* behind the mask of the unsayable.

14. Roland Barthes, *S/Z* (Paris: Éditions du Seuil, 1970), p. 113.

15. According to a branch of Tantrism known as Kundalini yoga, the name of the white lingam is *itara* which literally means "the other." Mircea Eliade, *Yoga, Immortality and Freedom* (Princeton, N.J.: Princeton University Press, 1969), p. 243. Needless to say, Pup

herself is the "other" Cobra, the Cobrita that "se desprende . . ." from his body (i.e., the phallus).

16. Gerardo Vázquez Ayora, "Estudio estilístico de *Cobra* de Severo Sarduy," *Hispamérica* (23-24, 1979).

17. As Freud points out: "Homosexuals are persons who, owing to the erotogenic importance of their own genitals, cannot do without a similar feature in their sexual object." This is the case of Cobra, attracted to the very feature he rejects from his body in order to undergo the transformation which will allow him to accommodate his desire. See Sigmund Freud, "Analysis of a phobia in a five-year-old boy" in *The Standard Edition of the Complete Psychological Works*, X (London: The Hogarth Press, 1955), p. 109.

18. Julia Kristeva, *La Révolution du langage poétique*, p. 45.

19. Emile Benveniste, *Problèmes de Linguistique générale* (Paris: Éditions Gallimard, 1966), p. 256.

20. Ganesha is one of the most popular Hindu divinities "made by Parvati from the dew of her body mingled with dust." He has the head of an elephant and rides around on a steed which is nothing but a rat. What is most pertinent to the elaborate intertextuality in Sarduy's novel, however, is that, according to legend, Ganesha's belly burst open one day after a fall from his steed when the latter scurried away frightened by a huge snake. Of particular interest to us is the fact that thereafter, Ganesha took hold of the snake "and rolled him around his damaged stomach . . . to repair the damage he had caused." *New Larousse Encyclopedia of Mythology* (London: Prometheus Press, 1959), p. 378. As we can see, therefore, even the pairing of "trunk" and reptile is a direct allusion—in the inexhaustible system of references which is *Cobra*—to yet another textual framework.

21. Sir John Woodroffe, *The Serpent Power* being the *SATCAKRANIRUPANA* and *PADUKA-PANCAKA* (Madras: Ganesh and Company, 1978).

22. As could be expected, intertextuality in Sarduy's conception embraces his own work as well as the mythology and literature of several continents. The fist, we have seen it, is the object of desire in *Maitreya* and the metaphorical substitute of the phallus, while the phallus in *Cobra* is a reptile disguised as *zob* and *cazzo*. What I have not mentioned, however, is that *cazzotto*, in Italian, means fist. We see, therefore, how with a mere shake of the hand in terms of sexual metaphor Sarduy links together his two novels. In fact, such wordly disguise convinces us that the most notable transvestites in *Cobra* and *Maitreya* are linguistic signs and not characters, as readers are wont to believe. With only one thing in their heads, moreover, these transvestite signs cannot help bringing to mind one of Philippe Sollers's most astute observations: "L'art qu'est-ce que c'est? C'est de la métaphorisation sexuelle bien sûr." Philippe Sollers, "Jazz," *Tel Quel*, 80 (Summer, 1979), 18.

LA POSMODERNIDAD DE *COMO EN LA GUERRA* DE LUISA VALENZUELA

CYNTHIA TOMPKINS
University of Wisconsin-Parkside

Tal como lo evidencia la "sesión de tortura" que fuera omitida "como parte de la censura del Rodrigazo" (García Pinto, 245), pero que precede el texto en la versión inglesa,[1] *Como en la guerra* (1977) se inscribe en la "narrativa del proceso" (Masiello), la cual constituye una implícita denuncia contra la represión militar que tuvo lugar en la Argentina de 1976 a 1982. *Como en la guerra* trata la crítica situación personal del exiliado mediante cánones típicos de la posmodernidad. Considerando la continuidad de la diáspora argentina, forzoso es admitir que la obra no ha perdido vigencia a pesar del tiempo transcurrido desde su publicación. *Como en la guerra* se deconstruye en el curso de la lectura ya que versa sobre cuestiones de autoconocimiento y definición del ser nacional a la par que descarta el concepto tradicional de un sujeto unitario mediante la exploración del concepto posmodernista de la "difusión del ego" (Hassan, 41).

Al principio, *Como en la guerra* se presenta como un informe psicoanalítico que incluye textos escritos por la analizada. Sin embargo, la irrupción de una voz narrativa autorreflexiva indicada gráficamente mediante el empleo de bastardillas lo torna ambiguo porque se distancia tanto del psicoanalista como de la analizada al anunciar, "me gusta seguirlo con el dedo por el plano de la ciudad" (43) y "yo que ahora escribo esto no la puedo seguir constantemente porque tengo un ancla que me fija a una única sucesión de imágenes" (83). Sin embargo, poco después la voz narrativa adopta el punto de vista de la analizada al afirmar, "se habría asombrado ante tanto papel escrito... cuartilla sobre cuartilla hasta llegar a estas hojas que ahora estoy llenando... para enredar aún más la madeja y complicar la historia" (93). De modo que las aparentes muestras se convierten en el texto principal. Además de transformarse en un personaje ficticio de la analizada, el psicoanalista se asemeja al narrador autorreflexivo al preguntarse, "existo? Es decir en la misma intensa medida de existencia de esos seres que tejen y destejen la trama de la fábula?" (97), y decide, "eso ya no nos importa: ni la trama ni ella que intentó meternos dentro de su fábula" (97). Por otra parte, la voz narrativa confirma la condición ficticia del psicoanalista al

© 1991 NUEVO TEXTO CRÍTICO Vol. IV No. 7 Primer semestre

afirmar, "una muerte sobre papel impreso significa una muerte repetida tantas veces como lo crean necesario los lectores" (131).

El informe psicoanalítico concluye al final de la segunda parte, "salió sabiendo y no pudo escribir más... porque la verdadera sabiduría es incomunicable" (130). Asimismo, desaparece la voz narrativa autorreflexiva señalada mediante el empleo de bastardillas. Sin embargo, mientras se refuerza el concepto de la difusión del ego mediante la juxtaposición de pronombres, la voz narrativa toma el punto de vista del profesor/psicoanalista. Dice, "son mujeres reviejas las que los reciben (me reciben) y él que ya es yo empieza poco a poco a identificarse, a rejuntarme, el él-yo yo y mi Otro... me toman, lo toman (nos toman)" (135).

En el plano del contenido, la primera aproximación al concepto posmodernista de la difusión del ego surge de la relación dialógica establecida entre el psicoanalista y la analizada. Aunque ambos comparten la ideología lacaniana, sus puntos de vista, "la posición integral de sus personalidades" (Bakhtin, 93) difiere, a tal punto que el objetivo manifiesto de producir un informe "científico" de la terapia se ve subvertido no sólo por el hecho de que ella intuye la estratagema de grabar las sesiones, sino también por su rendición paródica de conceptos lacanianos tales como *l'hommelette*, el estadio especular, y el Nombre-del-Padre, además de conceptos freudianos tales como Totem y Tabú y el hombre de los lobos (Hicks, 59). Hasta cierto punto el dialogismo, a su vez, se ve subvertido por un acuerdo implícito ya que ninguno de los dos manifiesta interés alguno en descubrir el nombre del otro; además, los disfraces del profesor (marinero, viejo travestista, agente de una compañía de seguros), se ven replicados por los avatares de la analizada (campesina, anticuada cocotte).

En primera instancia y tal como lo hemos indicado, el texto se postula como un informe psicoanalítico basado en la indagación de las razones que pudieron haber llevado a la protagonista a la prostitución. No obstante las tácticas empleadas, la analizada logra guardar el secreto, al igual que todo lo concerniente a su mítica hermana y a su relación con Navoni, dirigente de un grupo subversivo, quien no sólo la ha abandonado sino que también parece haber traicionado a sus camaradas, causando así la detención y el posterior exilio de la protagonista. El hecho de que la analizada está dispuesta a "cambiar de piel cuantes veces fuera necesario" (60), además de su teoría de las muñecas rusas que consiste en "meternos unos dentro de otros y mezclarnos las vidas para intercambiar experiencias" (86), que el profesor malinterpreta como una justificación de la prostitución, hacen alusión a la difusión del ego.

Además del discurso psicoanalítico, arraigado culturalmente en la obsesión de los argentinos con la terapia, un "cafisho" (proxeneta) articula el código neofeminista de la "brujería", mediante el cual presenta a la protagonista como una castradora, una devoradora de hombres, cuyo poder real reside en subvertir la moral burguesa al defender la integridad de sus colegas (46-47). La finalidad de este discurso es encubrir la amenaza económica que le implica el hecho de que la protagonista haya logrado convencer a sus compañeras a declararse en huelga a menos que él acceda a sus demandas que consisten en la reducción de la jornada de trabajo y la provisión de Seguridad Social (46).

La naturaleza dual de la búsqueda (autoconocimiento e identidad nacional) se hace explícita en términos de la analizada, ya que al profesor le preocupa pensar, "que la uso de espejo, me pongo máscaras para verme mejor y ella tiene que restituirme mi verdadera imagen" (72). Asimismo, notando que "todo a su alrededor grita Argentina, Argentina" (23) se pregunta, "qué tiene este país que todos le huimos y nos quema por dentro? ¿Qué hay de nosotros por el mundo, linyeras del amor sin siquiera querer reconocernos, negándonos los unos a los otros? ¿Qué es ser...?" (23).

La desaparición de la protagonista desencadena el proceso de la búsqueda. La Barcelona "secreta" (García Pinto, 244) se vuelve surrealista y el profesor comienza a experimentar una serie de transformaciones. A pesar de que se lo haya considerado como una versión paródica del héroe del relato tradicional definido por Propp como un sujeto unificado que experimenta una serie de situaciones previsibles (Hicks 55-57), me inclino a enfatizar la indeterminación psíquica y sexual del protagonista. Sin ir más lejos, al considerarlo una creación ficticia de la analizada, argumentaría que "la heroína novelística... inscribe lo femenino silenciado (representado por la prostituta) en la historia al representar la oposición heterosexual como arbitraria y en última instancia intercambiable por medio del vestuario" (Bauer, 9). El experimentalismo posmodernista (Hassan, 43) de *Como en la guerra* nos permite interpretar la obra como "a feast of becoming", (Hassan, 171) es decir, una celebración de la transformación, en tanto el proceso mismo de la búsqueda adquiere tanta importancia como el desarrollo del protagonista. En otras palabras, tal como en la novela de aventuras, en lugar de sustentarse en las características innatas o en la posición social del héroe, la narrativa lo hace "en base a lo que no es, a lo inesperado y no predeterminado" (Bahktin, 104).

Inicialmente el proceso de búsqueda interior permite una lectura jungiana ya que el objetivo del profesor/psicoanalista es lograr la incorporación de su contraparte femenina/ánima. La aparente homogeneización del discurso heteroglósico reforzaría esta interpretación; sin embargo, los distintos niveles de la búsqueda reafirman la polifonía del texto. A semejanza de la búsqueda espiritual feminista, el proceso de autoconocimiento desarrollado en *Como en la guerra* presupone asumir la nada existencial ("nothingness", Christ, 120); además, tal como en *Surfacing*, la novela de Margaret Atwood (Guédon 104-111), el proceso descrito por Valenzuela comparte ciertas características de la tradición shamánica de los indígenas norteamericanos. El profesor recurre al onanismo (¿erotismo posmodernista?, Hassan, 42) mientras se concentra en las fotos de la analizada a modo de mandala. Al desgaste físico se le suman los efectos del ayuno y de la vigilia; sin embargo, intuye, "estoy porque está ella [y] estoy siempre con ella aunque nadie lo sepa, ni ella misma" (128).

Al buceo secular del inconciente se le contraponen imágenes de la tradición judeocristiana presentadas en términos nuevaolescos (New Age), en tanto el protagonista, como víctima sacrificial, es llevado en andas por telúricas ancianas latinoamericanas que tienen "el mismo color de las montañas y hablan lengua de rocas" (136). A la procesión judeocristiana se le contrapone un rito de purificación nahuatl el cual, a su vez, se completa con visiones inducidas por hongos alucinógenos.

El concepto de la difusión del ego se ve reforzado por las constantes redefiniciones del proceso de búsqueda interior, ya que la interpretación jungiana va seguida por una formulada en términos iconográficos cristianos, "radiante debe de estar en alguna parte, y a mí me corresponde encontrarla así, como con halo. Y allá voy. Allá voy, allá" (129). De regreso en latinoamérica la búsqueda se torna proceso de autoconocimiento, definido como "una parte de sí mismo, la verdad, el conocimiento, la felicidad" (154). La "transgresión del sexo" (159) que experimenta en la tercera parte se refuerza mediante la siguiente proposición: ella "puede ser todas y se convierte en todos. El también ha sido todos/as para ella" (157). Finalmente, el protagonista afirma: "busco la búsqueda, la razón de la búsqueda. Busco a una mujer, me busco a mí mismo, a mi contraparte femenina. Busco la verdad, la realidad" (184).

En el ámbito europeo, la relativa marginalidad de los personajes en cuanto a nacionalidad (argentinos) y profesión (profesor/psicoanalista, prostituta, "cafisho"/proxeneta) constituye una crítica solapada al capitalismo. En el contexto latinoamericano, se hace referencia al "estado militar" —concepción tecnocrática nacida en la década del 70 debido a que la estructura democrática liberal no pudo contener las "contradicciones internas" aparejadas por el capitalismo multinacional en los países en vías de desarrollo. Es decir que a fin de asegurarse la hegemonía, la oligarquía financiera recurre a las fuerzas armadas a fin de que, fundamentadas en la doctrina de la Seguridad Nacional, instituyan el orden necesario para la reinserción en el circuito del capitalismo. Innecesario es acotar la dependencia con respecto a los Estados Unidos, tanto en lo político-militar como en los modelos económicos (Duhalde, 22-24).

Como en la guerra ilustra la lucha por el poder mediante el dialogismo resultante del contrapunto del discurso de las fuerzas armadas con el de la izquierda. A pesar de la indeterminación del texto, el hecho de que los miembros del grupo guerrillero están de duelo debido a la muerte de uno de sus integrantes, y de que sean "más atacados que atacantes" (165), son indicios que connotan la "guerra sucia". Asimismo la referencia a "la selva misionera, los esteros de Formosa" (163), teatro de la acción de la historia de Navoni, hace alusión a la represión sistemática de la "Operación Independencia", llevada a cabo en Tucumán en 1975 y que se constituyera en modelo para el "proceso" (Rock, 366).

La indeterminación y fragmentación típicas de la carnavalización comparten los aspectos lúdicos y subversivos de la posmodernidad, ya que en ambos casos el objetivo se subsume en promover la renovación" (Hassan, 171). Además, considerando que el "carnaval ... permite una relación interpersonal original caracterizada por la sensualidad y que sus aspectos lúdicos posibilitan la juxtaposición de realidad y fantasía" (Bahktin, 123), se infiere que la comunidad de actores llevaba a cabo el objetivo subversivo de indoctrinamiento mediante la representación de bailes caracterizados por la improvisación y el empleo de la mímica. Finalmente, dado que "el sentido carnavalesco del mundo implica el *pathos* resultante de transformaciones y desfasajes, de muerte y renovación" (Bahktin, 125) se deduce que el Auto Sacramental de la gorda constituye otro caso de carnavalización, ya que a pesar de que los actores vacilaran entre considerarla "bella" o "una morcilla obscena" (168), se convierte en víctima sacrificatoria del rito comunitario (170-171).

A renglón seguido las escenas de carnavalización, cuya función es la de connotar la lucha de clases, se desplazan a Buenos Aires (García Pinto, 243): "hay espíritu de carnaval con algo fúnebre pero carnaval al fin en un silencio con barreras para que no pasen los coches" (181). La tradicional oposición entre unitarios y federales —representantes de los intereses portuarios frente a los del interior, respectivamente— que ha caracterizado a la Argentina desde sus orígenes, se presenta mediante una relación dialógica expresada por medio de representantes de la población rural que "necesita(n) ser entendidos" y los porteños, que "necesitan entender" (184). "El diálogo de la lucha de clases... en el que discursos diametralmente opuestos se enfrentan dentro del marco general de un código compartido" (Jameson, 283), se efectúa cuando el protagonista se transforma en un avatar de Navoni, ya que respaldado por un grupo subversivo participa en un enfrentamiento con las fuerzas armadas a fin de llevar a cabo un milagro que puede ser interpretado como la utopía del "tiempo nuevo de la recuperación" (182). Logra volar las "paredes de [una] fortaleza" (194) de las cuales emerge un avatar de Evita, "allá arriba en lo alto sobre una tarima blanca, toda resplandeciente, irradiando una luz sorda pero intensísima, majestuosa en su ataúd de vidrio que es como un diamante" (195).

El dialogismo implícito entre el pensamiento occidental y el realismo mágico latinoamericano se desarrolla especialmente en la tercera parte. Pese a la aparente indeterminación del texto se postula la necesidad de que los argentinos redescubran sus raíces latinoamericanas (Garfield, 28). Además, se hace alusión a una serie de figuras legendarias tales como Ceferino Namuncurá, el Che Guevara, y Evita (Garfield, 25) que en última instancia constituyen mitos fundamentales para cimentar el "ser" nacional.

Como hemos mencionado, la página cero que fuera omitida de la edición argentina pero que precede al texto en la versión inglesa contiene una escena de tortura experimentada por el protagonista con posterioridad a los hechos narrados (García Pinto, 245). De modo que además de sugerirse que la supresión de la oposición es inevitable en un estado militar, se refuerza el concepto posmodernista de la difusión del ego al juxtaponer "la desintegración shamánica del cuerpo seguida por la del yo" (García Pinto, 245). En resumidas cuentas, además de "cierta caracterización y apoyatura argumental a fin de posibilitar el cuestionamiento de la subjetividad" (Herrmann, 5), *Como en la guerra* incorpora el amplio espectro de la realidad latinoamericana al abocarse al paradójico intento de la búsqueda del autoconocimiento y del ser nacional a la par que se descarta, por ficticia, la noción tradicional de un ser unificado y se explora el concepto posmodernista de la difusión del ego.

NOTA

1. Luisa Valenzuela añade: "creo que cumplo con esa necesidad de hablar de la violencia de Buenos Aires" (García Pinto, 245).

OBRAS CITADAS

Bakhtin, Mikhail: *Problems of Dostoevsky's Poetics*. Trans. Caryl Emerson. Minneapolis: University of Minnesota Press, 1984.

Bauer, Dale M.: *Feminist Dialogics: A Theory of Failed Community*. New York: State University of New York Press, 1988.

Christ, Carol P.: *Diving Deep and Surfacing: Women Writers on Spiritual Quest*. Boston: Beacon Press, 1980.

Duhalde, Eduardo Luis: *El Estado Terrorista Argentino*. Buenos Aires: Ediciones El Caballito, 1983.

García Pinto, Magdalena: "Entrevista con Luisa Valenzuela" en *Historias Intimas: Conversaciones con Diez Escritoras Latinoamericanas*. Hanover: Ediciones del Norte, 1988.

Garfield Picón, Evelyn: "Interview with Luisa Valenzuela", *Review of Contemporary Fiction*, 6.3 (Fall 1986): 25-30.

Guédon, Françoise Marie: "Surfacing: Amerindian Themes and S hamanism" en *Margaret Atwood: Language, Text, System*. Grace, Sherrill E. & Lorraine Weir, eds. Vancouver: University of British Columbia Press, 1983.

Hassan, Ihab: *The Postmodern Turn*. Ohio State University Press, 1987.

Herrmann, Anne: *The Dialogic and Difference*. New York: Columbia University Press, 1989.

Hicks, Emily: "That Which Resists: The Code of the Real in Luisa Valenzuela's 'He Who Searches'". *Review of Contemporary Fiction*. 6.3 (Fall 1986): 55-61.

Jameson, Fredric: *The Political Unconscious*. New York: Cornell University Press, 1981.

Masiello, Francine: "Cuerpo/presencia: mujer y estado social en la narrativa argentina durante el proceso militar". *Nuevo Texto Crítico*. 2.4 (1989): 155-171.

Rock, David: *Argentina 1516-1982*. Berkeley: University of California Press, 1985.

Valenzuela, Luisa: *Como en la guerra*. Buenos Aires: Editorial Sudamericana, 1977.

— —: "He Who Searches", en *Strange Things Happen Here*. Trans. Helen Lane. Harcourt Brace Jovanovich: New York and London, 1979.

TRANSLATION AND PROSTITUTION: ROSARIO FERRE'S
MALDITO AMOR AND *SWEET DIAMOND DUST*

JANICE A. JAFFE

"[E]mpieza con la llegada de los americanos en 1898 y termina con su salida en el año 2000" (González, 18). This summary, which Rosario Ferré offered of her novella *Maldito amor* when the book first went to press in 1986, reflects the preoccupation with understanding and overcoming Puerto Rico's colonial status which characterizes much of the writer's work. It is surprising, therefore, that *Maldito amor* pictures Puerto Rico as destroyed by, but never freed from, colonization by the United States. More surprisingly, Ferré's own translation of *Maldito amor* into English, entitled *Sweet Diamond Dust* (1988), views U.S. dominion in Puerto Rico in a conciliatory light and even celebrates some of the legacy of U.S. occupation on the island. In light of her statement of the novella's content and her negative portrayal of the United States' colonization of the island it seems that by altering her text when translating her own work into English, Ferré "prostitutes" herself as a Puerto Rican writer. I use "prostitute" deliberately, because through *Sweet Diamond Dust* and an essay Ferré wrote about translating her own fiction, the writer accords prominent and parallel cultural roles to the translator and the prostitute as emblems of linguistic and sexual marginalization and mutability. This paper will suggest that through her subversive construction of these two figures, in the passage from Spanish to English, Ferré begins to articulate a positive identity beyond colonialism for Puerto Rico.

312

This study begins with a brief look at statements by Ferré that characterize the prostitute, the translator and the people of Puerto Rico according to the same metaphorics of mutability and, therefore, motivate the present investigation. I am interested in how Ferré's representations resemble analogous notions of the prostitute and the translator present in translation studies and discourses on prostitution, particularly insofar as her depictions of these two intersect in relation to questions of colonial identity. With these questions in mind, the second part of my paper compares the differing pictures of Puerto Rican identity presented in *Maldito amor* and *Sweet Diamond Dust*.

My use of the term metaphorics above is informed by Lori Chamberlain's incisive survey of the metaphorics of translation which, she shows, has contributed to relegating the translator to a secondary, "reproductive" status, hence, dependent and lacking authority. "The metaphorics of translation," she argues, "is a symptom of larger issues of western culture: of the power relations as they divide in terms of gender" (66). Exposing how translation work has come to be pejoratively feminized, Chamberlain calls for subversion of this process and looks for women to create new and liberating "metaphors of cultural production" beyond these "gender binaries" (72).

I refer to Chamberlain's study for two reasons. First, her examination of the metaphors that have historically been associated with the work of translation discloses the connections that have been drawn between translation, colonization and the oppression of women, all central issues in Ferré's writing. Referring specifically to *Maldito amor* Ferré herself has emphasized the relationship between "el colonialismo de estado" and "el colonialismo de la mujer, que vive una vida fragmentada y dependiente del orden patriarcal" (*Coloquio* 109). Second, consistent with recent feminist approaches to these topics, Ferré's metaphorics of translation and prostitution constitutes an attempt at liberation from the binarism which has placed the prostitute and the translator, and, by implication, herself and her compatriots in the secondary status in dualistic representations of identity.

Ferré's portrayal of the translator and the prostitute highlights their capacity to transcend linguistic and cultural barriers separating Puerto Rico and the United States. She idealizes her identity as a translator who discovers that her "verdadera morada" is "ni Washington ni San Juan, ni el pasado ni el presente, sino el pasaje entre ambos" (*Coloquio* 69). Similarly, in *Sweet Diamond Dust* one of the female protagonists defines the body of Gloria, the prostitute who dissolves cultural and linguistic boundaries through intercourse with Puerto Ricans, North Americans and South Americans as a unifying passageway: "In her body, or if you prefer in her cunt, both races, both languages, English and Spanish, grew into one soul, one wordweed of love" (76). Significantly, Ferré also emphasizes the ability to pass back and forth between cultures as the core of Puerto Rican identity. In her preface to the second edition of *Maldito amor* (1991), published after her translation of the novella, the author reconciles a list of binary opposites that have described Puerto Rico throughout its history with the following: "País e*squisinfrénico* con complejo de Hamlet, nuestra personalidad más profunda es el cambio, la capacidad para la transformación, para el valeroso transitar entre dos extremos o polos" (13).

While in the above characterizations Ferré purports to praise the mutability of the translator, prostitute and colonized Puerto Ricans, she also indicates how such qualities have been construed pejoratively. I will return in more detail to the connections Ferré herself draws between these figures, but I cite these examples and the ambivalence they reflect to illustrate the intimate tie between Ferré's vision of the prostitute and the translator and the colonialism which has placed Puerto Ricans in a similar limbo. As articulated by the Puerto Rican historian Juan Angel Silén, the colonial power "aims at liquidating the subject people's traditions, at replacing their language with another, at destroying the culture of the colonized while withholding that of the colonizer — and thus at brutalizing within a net of ambivalences and contradictions" (21-22).

These contradictions are clearly presented by Ferré. In the first passage, from her essay about translation, a string of negatives precedes Ferré the translator's location of her true home. Then, in *Sweet Diamond Dust*, while envisaging the prostitute as a powerful vehicle for intercultural understanding, the female voice in Ferré's text consciously employs the most vulgar image of a woman as solely a sexual object as she addresses a conservative male interlocutor. Finally, in her preface, "Memorias de *Maldito amor*," though Ferré represents Puerto Ricans as heroic in their capacity for change, her image also recalls the tragic figure of Hamlet and the frequency with which Puerto Rico's situation has been described as schizophrenic in negative terms. Ferré incorporates and interrogates these contradictions as a necessary step in her search to overcome them, as can be illustrated by examining her metaphorics of the prostitute and the translator from the perspective of theories of translation and prostitution.

Fidelity and license are the binary terms that perhaps most obviously reflect the damaging analogues that have long been established between the translator and the prostitute, and, hence, are useful for initiating the theoretical discussion of Ferré's treatment of these figures. These terms, rethought in Ferré's writing, are also consistently questioned by feminist theorists of translation, including Chamberlain, Barbara Johnson and Susan Bassnett. The fidelity/license opposition, where fidelity has been positively valorized and license condemned, has traditionally been employed to celebrate or condemn the translator's work as well as to regard the prostitute as contemptible in contrast to the faithful wife. This polarity is implicit in the Italian expression which views translators as treasonously unfaithful, "traduttore-tradittore."[1] I emphasize these opposing terms because they are central for Ferré, and because they aptly describe the problematic notions of fidelity vs. freedom, or assimilation/independence in the relationship between the colonizer and the colonized.

Another trait at issue in Ferré's texts concerning Puerto Rico's colonial situation is the denial of personal identity imposed upon the translator and the prostitute in their work. Even as he calls on the translator to reject invisibility as a goal, Lawrence Venuti's title for his history of translation, *The Translator's Invisibility*, appropriately sums up the situation of one who, in the name of fidelity, regularly sacrifices authority to communicate the voice of another, whose originality "rather lies in self-effacement, a vanishing act" (*Rethinking Translation* 4).[2] The work of prostitution also involves self-effacement as the prostitute submits to the demands of the client.[3] As Simone de Beauvoir, whose discussion of prostitutes in *The Second Sex* informs Ferré's construction of Gloria in *Maldito amor*, asserts, the prostitute works "in her pure generality — as woman" (565). If, however, as with the translator and the prostitute, the individual identity of a colonized people is often unrecognized or denied, such is not the case for the resources these figures provide.

Fundamental to Ferré's vision that the translator and the prostitute play prominent cultural roles, evident in her image of the "pasaje entre ambos," is the idea that they disseminate knowledge, whether sexually or linguistically, that has potentially transformative power for society. The translator, as the word's etymology suggests, is an agent entrusted to linguistically uncover and "carry across" into his or her homeland the secrets of a foreign culture. The prostitute has been ascribed a parallel knowledge of the soul of a culture or the secrets of sexuality, according to Simone de Beauvoir (178, 192), whose writings, as mentioned previously, inform Ferré's construction of the prostitute. This characterization surfaces in Ferré's essay about the prostitute Isabel la Negra, the model for her story "Cuando las mujeres quieren a los hombres," as Ferré recalls that "gracias a ella se aclaraban toda una serie de misterios que aparentemente eran muy importantes" (*Coloquio* 112).

The knowledge and mysteries transmitted by the prostitute and the translator are represented positively in the preceding paragraph, but the purveyors of such knowledge are simultaneously perceived as undermining a culture's integrity and stability. In terms evoking both sexual exploitation and colonizing conquest, Victor Hugo refers to this threatening stereotype of the translator whose work is seen by the "target" culture, at least initially, as "a violation of frontiers," "a forced introduction" (qtd. in Lefevere 18). Though radically different in that the translator's profession is legal and that of the prostitute often criminalized, a similar fear exists of the prostitute's potential power to destroy society's moral and political order.[4] The fear, still persistent, that prostitution forms a "counter-society" which, consequently, poses a "threat that is at the same time moral, social, sanitary, and political" (Corbin 5), helps explain the existence of United States laws that forbid entry, residency or citizenship to anyone who has ever been a prostitute. A similar concern underlies laws enacted in this country to forbid entry to Communists or other individuals who the U.S. government feared would be political subversives.

That societies attribute to the translator and the prostitute the power to affect cultural identity becomes especially significant when a culture confronts situations of enormous flux, such as Puerto Rico faces today. Simone de Beauvoir and Priscilla Alexander (co-director of the prostitutes' rights group COYOTE Call Off Your Old Tired Ethics), note societies' increased recurrence to prostitution during moments of social disorder or change (Beauvoir 559, Alexander 186). Likewise, case studies have confirmed that translation occupies a more prominent role in "marginal, new, insecure or weakened" cultures (Bassnett xii). The translator who "challenges cultural forms of domination, whether nationalist or elitist" (*The Translator's Invisibility* 147) simultaneously threatens colonizing authority and advances the struggle to forge an identity beyond colonialism. Ferré's "pasaje" appropriately reflects societies' tendencies, in response to these allegedly rebellious forces, to try to control or limit the translator and the prostitute's access to power within the social body by marginalizing them or, as in the case of U.S. immigration laws regarding prostitutes, to deny them "pasaje" altogether.

Ferré's image of the "pasaje" is also suggestive of movement and the final parallel between the translator and the prostitute that I want to emphasize. In the margins of society, both the translator and the prostitute are linked with transitoriness, and this freelance movement, from client to client or voice to voice, also contributes to the image among some, both inside and outside these professions, that their practitioners enjoy great freedom. Transitoriness, however, equally suggests powerlessness. Without a clear space of their own, the voice of the translator and the prostitute remain unheard. The translator, for example, speaks through many and varied other voices but rarely his or her own. In parallel fashion, the fact that prostitutes move not only from one client to another, but with equal frequency, in and out of prostitution in search of a space beyond the margins of society, is stressed in several studies of prostitution (Ellis 261, Bullough 285-86). The fact that many prostitutes associate prostitution with transitoriness as a symptom of powerlessness is also borne out by the fact that WHISPER, the prostitutes' rights group, was founded with the purpose of helping individuals leave prostitution (Bell 123).

Ferré underscores the link between the transitory character of the translator and prostitute and of Puerto Ricans in their presumably temporary "commonwealth" status by using terms such as "cambio," "transformación" and "transitar entre dos extremos o polos" to portray the core of Puerto Rican character. At once emblematic of traditional notions of fidelity and of license, of powerlessness and power, what emerges perhaps most prominently in the above discussion of the prostitute and the translator is enormous ambiguity of identity. In *Maldito amor*, Ferré suggests that for Puerto Ricans this uncertainty is ultimately destructive, but she envisions the positive possibilities of this fluidity through her emplotment of herself as translator and of Gloria Camprubí as prostitute in *Sweet Diamond Dust*.

The title of Ferré's essay about translation, "Ofelia a la deriva en las aguas de la memoria," manifests the parallels she draws between the translator and the prostitute and her questioning of the binary oppositions applied to these figures. In portraying her role, rather than adopting the persona of a translator, Ferré appropriates the image of Shakespeare's Ophelia, who, though faithful in her love for Hamlet, is accused by him of employing her beauty as a harlot.[5] Ferré's mention of Ophelia evokes the suspicion that as translator she engages in prostitution and at the same time intimates that such an accusation is unwarranted.

In linking prostitution to translation, as the essay's title suggests, Ferré also reflects the identity crisis she experiences as a translator. Shakespeare's Ophelia suffers madness as a consequence of her "maldito amor" for Hamlet and perishes by drowning, and Ferré indicates that in translating her own work she risks such madness or fatal loss of personal identity. The Ophelia in Ferré's essay recalls her image, cited earlier, of Puerto Rico's protean character, "país esquisinfrénico con complejo de Hamlet." Like the Ophelia in *Hamlet*, Ferré, floating in a dream down the middle of Washington's C & O Canal, with San Juan on her left and D.C. on her right, is "a la deriva," adrift in confusion or madness. Yet in this marginal space she is also free, not forced to either cultural bank. Considering the etymology of "deriva" and "derivar," she is also, like the translator who "carries across" cultural mysteries and the prostitute characterized by de Beauvoir, at the source or origin, possessing the secrets of both cultures, and potentially transforming them by giving new cultural meaning to words. "A la deriva," both in the act of translating and in her examination of her own role as a translator, Ferré responds to Lori Chamberlain's call for "new metaphors of cultural production," which derive from rethinking the binaries traditionally used to define and evaluate translation.

Conscious of the charge that as a translator she prostitutes herself by rewriting into English and "adulterating" her work by omissions and additions, Ferré both challenges and celebrates the equation of translation with prostitution. In self-defense she cites both the Italian expression "traduttore-traditore" and the French equation of translation with female licentiousness, "plus qu'elle est belle, elle n'est pas fidèle" (*Coloquio* 78). In translating, "deriving" her own work, she claims that treason or license is necessary in the name of fidelity to the writer, who changes or gives new meaning to words and in the process improves upon the previous version. Therefore, taking full license in translating, articulated in sexual terms by Ferré, "como si se estuviese hundiendo en el pecado," she experiences not guilt but euphoria (*Coloquio* 79). Implicitly undermining the production/reproduction opposition also critiqued by Chamberlain, Ferré "a la deriva," tampering with the "original," participates in the work's perpetual process of becoming, the "solemn drift and derivation [*dérive*] of literary works" called for in "Translating" by Maurice Blanchot (84). This process, for Ferré, is inseparable from that of articulating Puerto Rican identity and, more specifically, her own identity as a Puerto Rican writer.

As a Puerto Rican writer who represents her nation first in Spanish and then in English, Ferré seems anxious about the charge of prostitution, while she justifies the license she takes with *Maldito amor*. Does she "sell herself" for economic gain as she markets her wares in English, not her native language but the language of Puerto Rico's current colonizer, "[e]l lenguaje de la tecnología y del capitalismo," which demands a dividend (*Coloquio* 76)? At issue in this criticism is the idea that her translation constitutes submission or fidelity to a colonizing power. In fact, Ferré acknowledges making changes as she consciously adapts her writing for a technological, capitalist mentality. She reasons, though, that this apparent prostitution, these changes, are central to reaching her intended audience; she translates for English-speaking Puerto Ricans on the mainland, to save them from cultural suicide "al devolver la memoria a su verdadera morada" (80). Implicitly attacking English as the language of hegemony, Ferré asserts that she is restoring their country and culture to her people, "aunque sea en inglés" (*Coloquio* 80). Like the prostitute who, according to de Beauvoir, lays bare the hypocrisy of official virtues, and the translator who challenges the linguistic domination of one culture over another, Ferré implies that translation is an act of rebellion, as it is for the Quiché-speaking Rigoberta Menchú, who learns and orally translates the narrative of her life into Spanish as a weapon against repression by the Spanish-speaking colonizers of her people in Guatemala (Menchú 9).

Yet, it can be argued that as a translator Ferré "prostitutes" her Puerto Rican identity in the negative connotation of that act. When she translates her essay about translation, she omits the pejorative image of English, "aunque sea en inglés" which I quoted above. Furthermore, where her essay in Spanish speaks of Puerto Ricans on the mainland confronting a "lucha por integrarse a una sociedad que discrimina cruelmente contra ellos" (*Coloquio* 79), the essay in English eliminates any mention of discrimination and also refrains from criticizing the goal of assimilation among these Puerto Ricans who "struggle to integrate with and become indistinguishable from the mainstream" (163). It may appear that Ferré adopts one cultural identity in Spanish and another in English. In Spanish she recognizes and critiques the discrimination that Puerto Ricans experience as Hispanics in the United States and, for that reason, views English as threatening to Puerto Rican identity. By contrast, in English she seems to become an assimilationist, silencing both her native language and the non-technological vision of the world that Spanish represents for her. To dismiss or reject Ferré's work in translation on this basis, though, is to misunderstand the "verdadera morada" that Ferré discovers through the transitoriness of her work, in the passage from Spanish to English.

The translator who constantly passes between different cultures and in the process searches for her own space and voice, says Ferre, "[l]ucha por conciliar culturas diferentes, salvando las barreras que establecen esos prejuicios y malentendidos que son el resultado de costumbres muy distintas y de diferentes maneras de pensar" (*Coloquio* 70). "Salvando las barreras" can mean overcoming or destroying barriers, but it can also denote saving or preserving them. As a translator it seems that Ferré finds her "verdadera morada" by doing both; that is, overcoming cultural barriers precisely by preserving the tensions between both cultures as integral to contemporary Puerto Rican identity. This notion of home is corroborated by Ferré's characterization of the translator as the "pasaje entre ambos," that is, a space to pass between both cultures, which also defines the translated text, a literary passage through which diverse cultures can meet. Through a comparison of *Maldito amor* and *Sweet Diamond Dust* I will illustrate first how the translated text might raise the negative suspicion of translation as prostitution and then show how by a process that involves "salvando las barreras," Ferré identifies a "verdadera morada" for Puerto Ricans.

As I noted earlier, Puerto Rico's colonial legacy is the central theme of *Maldito amor*, in which five conflicting narrative voices reconstruct the nation's struggles under Spanish and North American dominion as experienced by the De la Valle clan of sugar cane planters. A story of each generation's loves and losses, the narrative also brings to light the oppression of women, blacks and mulattos and their increasing defiance of unjust social codes from generation to generation. What motivates these narrators, all members or friends of the De la Valle family, to speak is a desire to articulate their own identity and, implicitly, their nation's destiny. Unfortunately, their contradictory perspectives, none of which establishes clear authority from the reader's perspective, suggest a miserable truth about Puerto Rican identity, summed up in the novella's title. Whether recounting Puerto Rican domination by Spain or by the United States, or the parallel domination of women by men, the title *Maldito amor* refers equally to the doomed romances in the novella and to a frequently misdirected and thereby accursed love of country. At the novella's conclusion Gloria Camprubí, the prostitute, who narrates the final section, burns down the plantation to end the cycle of ill-fated loves and the lies about Puerto Rico's past that they spawn. With this action she destroys the other surviving narrators, perhaps including herself, but particularly the historical novelist who, like Puerto Rican authors of the "novela de la tierra" in the 1920s and 30s and politicians of that era such as Puerto Rico's first elected governor Luis Muñoz Marín, nostalgically idealizes Puerto Rico's past under Spanish dominion. While most of the novella's narrators view the U.S. domination of Puerto Rico negatively, as suggested by Ferré's comment at the beginning of this article which envisions North Americans finally leaving the island, in *Maldito amor* Ferré seems unable to articulate that departure or any positive future for Puerto Ricans beyond colonialism.

In *Sweet Diamond Dust* Ferré does not alter the plot of the novella, yet in certain "passages" a positive vision of Puerto Rico's future is expressed. This is reflected first in the new title, which erases the image of doomed love. In rewriting Ferré also takes the opportunity to correct chronological inconsistencies, as she renders paradoxes and intricacies of Puerto Rican history more vividly for readers. As I stated above, Ferré regards such changes to her Spanish text as a simple attempt to improve upon the previous version. However, just as in the translation of her essay about translation, in certain instances Ferré modifies the anti-Yankee tone of the Spanish text, particularly in one of the four lengthy additions to the English text not present in *Maldito amor*. I see these cases of apparent "prostitution" to a Yankee clientele differently, as central to Ferré's conception of a destiny for Puerto Ricans outside the common pro or anti-Yankee dichotomy.

The section entitled "El rescate," or "The Rescue" in the English version, which represents the novelist *Don* Hermenegildo's version of how the De la Valle's sugar plantation escapes purchase by North American investors, clearly evidences the softening of the creole/Yankee opposition. Hermenegildo's words in Spanish proudly proclaim the rescue of the Puerto Rican plantation from the predatory force of the North American mills, that is, from "las garras de la Central Ejemplo" (55). By contrast, in English the sense of an identifiably Northern threat is eliminated and the *criollo* mill is saved "from being blown away by the wind" (52). Soon after this, Hermenegildo and Ubaldino de la Valle discuss the risks of losing the sugar mill in the pleasantly messy and somewhat chaotic atmosphere of a typically Puerto Rican café "lejos de aquella manía de orden y de limpieza que cundía desde la llegada de los extranjeros en todos los centros oficiales del gobierno de Guamaní" (57). The Spanish text evinces obvious resentment for this quality associated with the imposition of North American culture on the island, whereas in English the orderliness and cleanliness neither infiltrates the government, nor is associated with foreign intervention. Rather, order is a feature "that had come lately over most of the town" (57). One risk of not selling the mill, according to Hermenegildo, is that "los extranjeros podían tomar represalias" (61) which could jeopardize Ubaldino's political career. The risk of reprisals remains in the English *Sweet*

Diamond Dust, but the foreigners as agents of such reprisals disappear: "there were sure to be reprisals against us" (61). These three examples reflect a more conciliatory attitude toward U.S. intervention in English than in Spanish, for which Ferré could be accused of betraying her Hispanic heritage. But this less dichotomous, 'us' versus 'them' representation of Puerto Rican reality may be seen more constructively as transcending binarism in the passage toward a new understanding of what Puerto Rican identity means at the close of the twentieth century.

Ferré's four substantive additions into the English text which are not present in *Maldito amor* reflect this more positive depiction of Puerto Rican cultural reality and are also consistent with Ferré's stated purpose of restoring some of their culture to English-speaking Puerto Ricans within the United States. Instead of "selling herself" like a prostitute, Ferré "sells" Puerto Rico to English-speaking Puerto Ricans by enticing them with details about Puerto Rico's landscape, particularly as it has shaped the Puerto Rican character, picturesque anecdotes about legendary heroes, notes about Puerto Ricans' artistic achievements and, finally, complexities of the island's history from the time of the Spanish conquest to the present. The English version condemns the injustices wrought by the Spanish conquest, including the *criollos'* enslavement of blacks and mulattos and the Spanish view of the Taíno Indians as inferior, but the positive legacy of Spanish dominion receives equal attention. Similarly, while some of the interpolations to the translation manifest overt praise for North American contributions to education, transportation and technology on the island, both versions denounce the early efforts to impose English on the island. Also, the Spanish and the English texts alike espouse the conviction that the sugar mill and land should forever remain in Puerto Rican hands. Readers of *Sweet Diamond Dust*, not *Maldito amor*, learn in some detail about how Puerto Ricans fought bravely against the North Americans in 1898, and they also read that some members of the same family fought to defeat North American troops while others aided the Northerners in their campaign to occupy the island. In the end, especially with the amalgamation of pro and anti-Yankee sentiments within the same family, the reader recognizes in *Sweet Diamond Dust* a new portrait of Puerto Rican identity effected by "salvando las barreras" of the Hispanic and Anglo heritages that merge in Puerto Ricans today. The prostitute, Gloria Camprubí, embodies that new vision.

In a previously cited sentence drawn from one of the extended additions to the English text, Laura, Gloria's mother-in-law, identifies the new Puerto Rican, bequeathing the plantation to Gloria because, "In her body, or if you prefer in her cunt, both races, both languages, English and Spanish, grew into one soul, one wordweed of love" (76). The emphasis in this statement on the relationship between identity and language, especially with "wordweed," a neologism suggestive of a new language which in its prolific growth resists boundaries and a linguistic garment that marks one's identity, underscores the parallel roles of the translator and the prostitute. It is significant, therefore, that Ferré creates this vision of the prostitute only through the act of translation which requires constantly passing back and forth linguistically and culturally between Spanish and English. That this positive vision of the prostitute, emblematic of Puerto Ricans' future destiny, is inseparable from the work of translation is further illustrated by the fact that in *Sweet Diamond Dust* Gloria's prostitution is central to Laura's decision to leave the plantation to her, while Gloria's prominence in the narrative structure and the plot of *Maldito amor* resides not in her identification as a prostitute but, more generally, in the oppression she has experienced as a mulatto woman.

In *Maldito amor*, the idea that Gloria is a prostitute is only insinuated, and solely by male characters. They raise that suspicion, together with her racial heritage, to deny her legitimacy within the De la Valle family, to deny her credibility and to emphasize that she is unworthy of inheriting the plantation. Arístides de la Valle, admitting in his embittered narrative his unrequited love for Gloria, refers to her as "la puta del pueblo" (54), but the family's black servant, Titina, denies such an accusation (29). In *Maldito amor* neither Gloria's mother-in-law Laura nor Gloria herself ever suggests that she is a prostitute. The historical novelist and Spanish sympathizer, *Don* Hermenegildo Martínez, expresses concern that the rumors he has heard about Gloria are true, even though he hears them from unreliable sources. Gloria's marriage to Arístides' older brother Nicolás, named after the saint who reputedly gave three women bags of gold for marriage dowries to rescue them from prostitution, perpetuates a pejorative concept of prostitution as transitory work that any woman would want to abandon. The exclusively negative light cast on prostitution in *Maldito amor*, a compendium of the worst stereotypes about this profession, is not the most prevalent view in *Sweet Diamond Dust*.

The representation of Gloria in *Sweet Diamond Dust* preserves the deprecatory attitude toward the prostitute represented by the male characters in the novella, but simultaneously envisions the potential for freedom in this mutable identity. In this different construction the links between the transformative power embodied in the translator and the prostitute emerge. I noted above how Laura's characterization of Gloria recalls Ferré's depiction of herself as translator. In addition, like the translator who transmits the mystery of cultures, "a la deriva" in Ferré's terminology, Laura portrays the prostitute Gloria as "the priestess of our harbor; pythia of our island's future; of a time when a scanty, meager land that for centuries had condemned us to immobility and backwardness will ultimately have no importance and where our souls, our very lives will be determined by transformation and daring, in other words, by change" (76). The emphasis on transitoriness in this characterization constitutes another point of convergence I have emphasized between the prostitute and the translator's cultural vocations. Transitoriness is a necessary pathway toward freedom, Ferré suggests here as well as in the other parallel between the translator who purports to restore *their* country and culture to Puerto Ricans living on the mainland and to Gloria. Laura bequeathes the plantation to Gloria with the expectation that the latter will sell the land bit by bit, not to North Americans but to Puerto Ricans moving to the mainland, "as well as to those who will undoubtedly return, perhaps after spending half their lives reaping California grapes, or driving a taxi through the cement jungle of New York, but with enough money in their pockets to buy a piece of their lost paradise back" (76-77).

The connections Ferré draws between the translator and the prostitute, evident in her references to future change and restoring Puerto Rican heritage to Puerto Ricans, stress their function as agents of cultural transmission, specifically of a new vision of Puerto Rican identity. In this capacity, they are both reproductive, in the sense of giving birth, and productive of something entirely new, conceived of amorous union rather than antagonism between cultures. Gloria's son Nicolasito, fathered by Nicolás or possibly one of her clients, "the child of all" (76) is the son of the union between north and south, much as Ferré's *Sweet Diamond Dust* can be seen as the offspring of this love for both the positive North American and Hispanic aspects of her heritage. The images of the C & O canal in Ferré's essay on translation evoke this idea, as the canal recalls the birth canal. In her essay "Las dos Venecias" Ferré herself constructs this equation between the canals of Venice, writing as giving birth and her own birth canal: "un lugar de tránsito y de cambio, de canales misteriosos por los cuales las vidas de otros seres, así como las palabras que intentan describirlas, fluyen y desembocan unas en otras" (16). According to Laura in *Sweet Diamond Dust*, Gloria, in whom Spanish and English unite, embodies the passage that will make Puerto Rico "a chink in the wall" through which the North and the South will talk and finally arrive at mutual understanding (76). Ferré's text mentions the allusion to *A Midsummer Night's Dream* here, reminding the reader that for the lovers, Pyramus and Thisbe, the hole, like the translator's "pasaje," both exposes and weakens the barriers to forbidden love, in Puerto Rico's case between the Anglo and Hispanic legacies to Puerto Rican identity. The chink, which exists only if the wall remains as well, is also a textual manifestation of Ferré's goal of "salvando las barreras," a fitting image with which to conclude.

In the end, Ferré never reaches the concluding moment of freedom she promises: "termina con su salida en el año 2000" (González, 18), either in *Maldito amor* or *Sweet Diamond Dust*. Indeed, both versions of the novella end with the incendiary destruction of the De la Valle plantation, which indicates that for Ferré the question of Puerto Ricans' identity and the island's future destiny remain far from resolved. It is, after all, only in a dream that Ferré experiences a vision of the "verdadera morada" described in her essay on translation. She, and, her writing suggests, her fellow Puerto Ricans, cannot yet dwell in the home Ferré attempts to articulate, but at least she has derived a "pasaje," a space for exchange and dialogue about Puerto Rican identity, which is itself a pathway to freedom.

BOWDOIN COLLEGE

NOTES

[1]At least as early as the seventeenth century Dillon Wentworth, the Earl of Roscommon, overtly equated unfaithful translation with the licentiousness of a prostitute, while expressing his disdain for unskilled translation done out of economic necessity: "I pity from my Soul unhappy Men/Compelled by Want to prostitute their Pen, /Who must, like Lawyers, either starve or plead, /and follow, right or wrong, where Guineas lead" (qtd. in Lefevere 45).

[2]In *After Babel*, the oft-quoted study of translation, which is also the most influential source for Ferré's writing on translation, George Steiner describes this precarious character of the translator with reference to Borges' famed tale of translation, "Pierre Menard," and the author's crisis of identity portrayed in "Borges and I": "The translator too 'must live on in Borges' — or in any other author he chooses — not in myself — if indeed I am anyone — though I recognize myself less in his books than in many others'" (73).

[3]Evelina Giobbe, a former prostitute and founder of the prostitutes' rights group WHISPER, decries how the prostitute in her work faces the "absence of identity, the theft and subsequent abandonment of self" (qtd. in Bell 128).

[4]In his oft-cited and exhaustive study of prostitution in nineteenth-century Paris, Alexander Parent-Duchâtelet expresses the anxiety of many when he pleads for regulation of prostitutes because "they surround us...they gain access to our homes" (qtd. in Corbin 4).

[5]Hamlet articulates his charge in language that likewise serves to discredit translations which display fidelity to beauty over honesty: "Ay, truly; for the power of beauty will sooner transform honesty from what it is to a bawd than the force of honesty can translate beauty into his likeness" (3.1.111-114).

WORKS CITED

Alexander, Priscilla. "Prostitution: A Difficult Issue for Feminists." *Sex Work: Writings by Women in the Sex Industry*. Ed. Priscilla Alexander and Frédérique Delacoste. San Francisco: Cleis Press, 1987. 184-214.

Bassnett, Susan. *Translation Studies*. Rev. ed. New York: Routledge, 1991.

Blanchot, Maurice. "Translating." Trans. Richard Sieburth. *Sulfur* 10:1 (1990): 82-86.

Bell, Shannon. *Reading, Writing and Rewriting the Prostitute Body*. Bloomington: Indiana University Press, 1994.

Chamberlain, Lori. "Gender and the Metaphorics of Translation." *Rethinking Translation*. Ed. Lawrence Venuti. New York: Routledge, 1992. 57-74.

Corbin, Alain. *Women for Hire*. Trans. Alan Sheridan. Cambridge: Harvard University Press, 1990.

de Beauvoir, Simone. *The Second Sex.* Trans. H. M. Parshley. New York: Knopf, 1983.

Ellis, Havelock. *Sex in Relation to Society.* New York: Random, 1936. Vol. 4 of *Studies in the Psychology of Sex.* 1906.

Godard, Barbara. "Theorizing Feminist Discourse/Translation." Bassnett and Lefévere 87-96.

González, José Luis. *El país de cuatro pisos.* Río Piedras: Ediciones Huracán, 1983.

— *Nueva visita al cuarto piso.* Madrid: Minuesa, 1987.

Ferré, Rosario. *El coloquio de las perras.* Harrisonburg: Banta Co., 1990

— *Las dos Venecias.* México, D.F.: Joaquín Mortiz, 1992.

— *Maldito amor.* 2nd ed. Río Piedras: Ediciones Huracán, 1991.

— "On Destiny, Language, and Translation; or, Ophelia Adrift in the C. & O. Canal." *The Youngest Doll.* Lincoln: University of Nebraska Press, 1991. 153-165.

— *Sweet Diamond Dust.* New York: Random House, 1989.

Johnson, Barbara. "Taking Fidelity Philosophically." Difference in Translation. Ed. Joseph F. Graham. Ithaca: Cornell University Press, 1985. 142-48.

Lefevere, André. Introduction. *Translation, History and Culture.* Ed. Susan Bassnett and André Lefévere. New York: Pinter, 1990. 1-13.

Lefevere, André, ed. *Translation/History/Culture.* New York: Routledge, 1992.

Menchú, Rigoberta and Elizabeth Burgos. *Me llamo Rigoberta Menchú.* Mexico: Siglo veintiuno, 1988.

Shakespeare, William. *Hamlet.* 1600-1. London: Orbis Publishing, 1978. Vol. 3 of *The Annotated Shakespeare.* Ed. A.L. Rowse. 3 vols. 1978.

Silén, Juan Angel. *We, the Puerto Rican People.* Trans. Cedric Belfrage. New York: Monthly Review Press, 1971. 157-210.

Steiner, George. *After Babel: Aspects of Language and Translation.* London: Oxford UP, 1975.

Venuti, Lawrence. Introduction. *Rethinking Translation.* Ed. Venuti. New York: Routledge, 1992.

— *The Translator's Invisibility.* New York: Routledge, 1995.

PARODY OR PIRACY: THE RELATIONSHIP OF
THE HOUSE OF THE SPIRITS
TO
ONE HUNDRED YEARS OF SOLITUDE

ROBERT ANTONI

While the first few sentences of *The House of the Spirits* seem to belong to García Márquez and *One Hundred Years of Solitude*, the last few—which, ironically enough, are much the same—belong to Isabel Allende. "Rarely has a new novel from Latin America consciously or unconsciously owed more to its predecessors; equally rare is the original utterance coming out of what is now a collective literary tradition."[1] That this is Allende's first novel does not excuse the presence of García Márquez (as the critics suggest), though it might explain it, perhaps in terms of a problem facing all post-Boom Latin American novelists, new and other-wise, who wish to follow in the tradition of magical realism: How does one get beyond *One Hundred Years of Solitude*, since all writing in the genre would seem, in the end, a rewriting of this novel?[2] Allende begins with this premise—consciously or unconsciously—and in the rewriting she discovers her own novel, one very different from *One Hundred Years of Solitude*, [*Cien años de soledad*]. *The House of the Spirits* [*La casa de los espíritus*] reads, initially, like a parody of García Márquez's novel, though not a *conscious* sort of parody. We may consider, for example, M. M. Bakhtin's definition of conscious parody, which is always a "doubled-voiced," a premeditatedly "double-languaged" phenomenon: it is the rather brutal confrontation of two distinct languages within the same utterance, a parodied language which is stylized and represented (in this case belonging to García Márquez), and the stylizer's own language which does the representing (and which *should* belong to Isabel Allende).[3] The former dissolves in the process of illuminating and affirming the latter. But Allende does not use García Márquez's language as an expose to destroy it, speaking *through* it in her own language; rather, Allende uses his language as a means to discover her own language, which she *substitutes* for García Márquez's.[4] In other words, we would have trouble isolating a representing discourse which is simultaneously present, and at odds with the represented discourse: there is no obvious wink at the reader. We can, however, contrast an "initial" discourse with a "final" discourse, which *are* at odds with each other. Allende begins speaking in a represented language—a language not her own, but García Márquez's, though perhaps she is not aware of it—and through this language she discovers her own representing language.[5] It is as though Allende "unconsciously" parodies García Márquez early in the novel, then stumbles happily onto her own language—her own story—in the end. But is there unconscious parody (Bakhtin does not speak of it), or are we simply speaking here of inattentive writing? Are we simply comparing an established master with a first novelist?

330

A consideration of the structure of this novel indicates that it is more the result of planning than a happy accident. Allende knew from the onset—at least intuitively—that she was dealing with two stories, two languages, and that one would ultimately replace the other. Let us begin with the first:

> *Barrabás came to us by sea*, the child Clara wrote in her delicate calligraphy. She was already in the habit of writing down important matters, and afterward, when she was mute, she also recorded trivialities, never suspecting that fifty years later I would use her notebooks to reclaim the past and overcome terrors of my own.[6]

> Barrabás llegó a la familia por vía marítima, anotó la niña Clara con su delicada caligrafía. Ya entonces tenía el hábito de escribir las cosas importantes y más tarde, cuando se quedó muda, escribía también los trivialidades, sin sospechar que cincuenta años después, sus cuadernos me servirían para rescatar la memoria del pasado y para sobrevivir a mi propio espanto.[7]

This, quite obviously, is the language of magical realism, the language of García Márquez, and we note similarities in tone and technique; there is even a striking resemblance between Allende's first sentences and the well-known first sentence of *One Hundred Years of Solitude*: "Many years later, as he faced the firing squad, Colonel Aureliano Buendía was to remember that distant afternoon when his father took him to discover ice;"[8] "Muchos años después, frente al peloton de fusilamiento, el Coronel Aureliano Buendía había de recordar aquella tarde remota en que su padre lo llevó a conocer el hielo."[9]   But there are two conspicuous differences between this sentence and Allende's, which alert us immediately that she is doing something quite different.   Most obvious is Allende's first-person reference; instrumental to García Márquez's technique is the use of a God-like, third-person-omniscient narrator, though this narrator is identified in the last pages of the novel as Melquíades, a character of the story. Similarly, Allende informs us in her Epilogue that the unnamed "I" is Alba, as well a character in the story. Melquíades, however, always remains distant. A less obvious difference is Allende's specification, in her first sentences, that the present moment of writing is fifty years after the events; in García Márquez's novel we learn that Melquíades wrote of the Buendías prophetically, one hundred years before the events, thus grounding the story, in the end, in the realm of mythological time. Allende, on the other hand, fixes her novel from the onset in a time which seems more historical than mythical, more *un*spiritual than spiritual.

For the remainder of the first section (pp.9-25), Allende narrates from a third-person-omniscient point-of-view, in a voice much like that of García Márquez; the unnamed "I" disappears, and Allende's language is the language of magical realism: synchronic, hyperbolic, crowded with metaphor, oxymoron, synesthesia, personification. This narrative voice is the "feminine" voice in the text. Gérard Genette's term "focalization" may be helpful here in identifying this voice, which is "internal" and "variable," belonging simultaneously to Clara (through her notebooks) and to Clara's granddaughter, Alba, (the unnamed "I" of the second sentence).[10] There is a sense in which this voice belongs also to Blanca, Alba's mother, the third of the novel's heroines. Clearly such information as Blanca's love affair with Pedro Tercero, or her marriage to the Count, could have come to Alba only through Blanca herself; Blanca, like Clara (neither actually speaks in first person), narrates *through* Alba. More precisely, the "focalization" of this "feminine collective" voice shifts in propriety among the three heroines.

Initially however, Clara takes precedence: the first voice in the story, the voice of magical realism, belongs to the spiritualist. *The House of the Spirits* begins as a family saga—Clara's story—with occasional vague references to politics and history. Language, technique, characters, and events all have correlations in *One Hundred Years of Solitude*, another family saga. A passage from each text illustrates their likeness:

from *One Hundred Years of Solitude*:

> When the gypsies came back, Ursula had turned the whole population of the village against them. But curiosity was greater than fear, for that time the gypsies went about making a deafening noise with all manner of musical instruments while a hawker announced the exhibition of the most fabulous discovery of the Naciancenes. So that everyone went to the tent and by paying one cent they saw a youthful Melquiades, recovered, unwrinkled, with a new and flashing set of teeth. Those who remembered his gums that had been destroyed by scurvy, his flaccid cheeks, and his withered lips trembled with fear at the final proof of the gypsy's supernatural power. The fear turned into panic when Melquiades took out his false teeth, intact—a fleeting instant in which he went back to being the same decrepit man of years past—and put them back again and smiled once more with the full control of his restored youth. p.17

> Cuando volvieron los gitanos, Ursula había predispuesto contra ellos todo la población. Pero la curiosidad pudo más que el temor, porque aquella vez los gitanos recorrieron la aldea haciendo un ruido ensordecedor con toda clase de instrumentos músicos, mientras el pregonero anunciaba la exhibición del más fabuloso hallazgo de los naciancenos. De modo que todo el mundo se fué a la carpa, y mediante el pago de un centavo vieron a un Melquíades juvenil, repuesto, desarrugado, con una dentadura nueva y radiante. Quienes recordaban sus encías destruidas por el escorbuto, sus mejillas fláccidas y sus labios marchitos, se entremecieron de pavor ante aquella prueba terminante de los poderes sobrenaturales del gitano. El pavor se convirtió en pánico cuando Melquíades se sacó los dientes, intactos, engastados en las encías, y se los mostró al público por un instante—un instante fugaz en que volvió el mismo hombre

decrépito de los años anteriores—y se los puso otra vez y sonrió de nuevo con un dominio pleno de su juventud restaurada. p.12

from *The House of the Spirits*:

The intrepid traveler was laid to rest in a grandiose funeral. His death made him a hero and his name was on the front page of all the newspapers for several days. The same multitude that had gathered to see him off the day he flew away in his bird paraded past his coffin. The entire family wept as befit the occasion, except for Clara, who continued to watch the sky with the patience of an astronomer. One week after he had been buried, Uncle Marcos, a bright smile playing on his pirate's mustache, appeared in person in the doorway of Nivea and Severo del Valle's house. Thanks to the surreptitious prayers of the women and children, as he himself admitted, he was alive and well and in full possession of his faculties, including his sense of humor. Despite the noble lineage of his aerial maps, the flight had been a failure. He had lost his airplane and had to return on foot, but he had not broken any bones and his adventurous spirit was intact. p.14

Enterraron al intrépido viajero en un funeral grandioso. Su muerte lo convirtió en un héroe y su nombre estuvo varios días en los titulares de todos los periódicos. La misma muchedumbre que se juntó para desperdirlo el día que se elevó en la pájaro, desfiló frente a su ataud. Toda la familia lo lloró como se merecía, menos Clara, que siguió escrutando el cielo con paciencia de astrónomo. Una semana después del sepelio, apareció en el umbral de la puerta de la casa de Nívea y Severo del Valle, el propio tío Marcos, de cuerpo presente, con una alegre sonrisa entre sus bigotes de pirata. Gracias a los rosarios clandestinos de las mujeres y los niños, como él mismo lo admitió, estaba vivo y en posesión de todas sus facultades, incluso la del humor. A pesar del noble origen de sus mapas aéreos, el vuelo había sido un fracaso, perdió el aeroplano y tuvo que regresar a pie, pero no traía ningún hueso roto y mantenía intacto su espíritu aventurero. p.20

The characterization of Tío Marcos quite clearly originates in García Márquez's Melquíades: both characters die and are resurrected (the Melquíades passage above is a foreshadowing of what is to happen in fact); both are adventurers, world travelers, conveyors of great inventions, bearers of magical books; both are alchemists, astronomers, entrepreneurs. They are even similar in appearance: Melquíades with his "untamed" beard and "flashing" smile, Tío Marcos with his "pirate's" mustache and "sharklike" smile. But Tío Marcos is only one of several characters early in the novel modeled after characters in *One Hundred Years of Solitude*: Rosa the Beauty is based on Remedios the Beauty, and, to a lesser extent, Clara on Ursula, Esteban on José Arcadio, Blanca on

Amaranta. Allende's narrative technique early in the novel as well comes from
One Hundred Years of Solitude. Both authors make use of extensive
foreshadowing and flashbacks (seen also in the first sentences) to establish
verisimilitude and temporal discontinuity. Allende, like García Márquez, speaks
in hyperbole, including extravagant documentation, with the naming of "old-
world" historical figures: Melquíades' false teeth are "the most fabulous
discovery of the Naciancenes," and Tío Marcos' "noble" maps (we know from
the previous page) "he had traced himself based on various theories of Leonardo
da Vinci and on the polar knowledge of the Incas"; "había trazado basándose en
las teorías de Leonardo daVinci y en los conocimientos australes de los Incas."
There is a striking similarity in narrative tone; it is a tone which is unemotional,
unhesitating, even while speaking of the most improbable events—a tone García
Márquez tells us he learned from his grandmother, who told utterly fantastic
stories with a "brick" face.[11] Finally, Allende's language comes from García
Márquez's novel; in addition to the abundant use of figures of speech already
noted, the prose style in both novels is characterized by a "simple eloquence,"
interrupted occasionally by a flourish of convoluted, "antiquated speech":
compare García Márquez's "in full control of his restored youth," with Allende's
"in full possession of his faculties" and "his adventurous spirit was intact" (two
of several formulaic phrases which Allende seems to have taken directly from
García Márquez's novel).

The point is not hard-pressed; there is little in Allende's first pages which
does not have its correlation in *One Hundred Years of Solitude*, and García
Márquez may be felt as a palpable presence well into the novel.[12] Admittedly,
there are isolated instances in which Allende seems *consciously* to be parodying
García Márquez: for example, Clara's insistence that names should not be
repeated in the family because they "created confusion in her notebooks which
bore witness to life" (p.223); "crean confusión en los cuadernos de notar la vida"
(p.107) .In *One Hundred Years of Solitude* García Márquez repeats names and
traits to the extent that the characters become almost interchangeable. Such
instances of intentional parody are few, however, and García Márquez's novel is
not so much destroyed in *The House of the Spirits*, as gradually replaced, as
though the literary model were slowly abandoned under the weight of powerful
memories.

Yet even in her first chapter, Allende indicates that this displacement will
occur, alerting us that she is doing something more than rewriting García
Márquez's novel; in Chapter 1—unlike anything which occurs in *One Hundred
Years of Solitude*—Allende alternates her third-person-omniscient, magical
realist narrations with the shorter, first-person testimonies of Esteban Trueba.
His is the second voice in the text, the "masculine" voice, and Trueba is the
novel's hyperbolic macho—dictator in his home, patron and rapist on his estate,
and bastion of "democracy" in government house. Trueba's narrations are jarring
because they interrupt the narrative flow, and disconcerting because his character
is disagreeable. Such narrations, however, provide a strong counterpoint with
the "feminine" voice; they establish a dialogue (in Bakhtin's terms, the
confrontation between an "authoritative" discourse and an "internally persuasive"
discourse).[13] Although Trueba's voice cannot be identified as the political,

historical voice early in the novel (such *information* does not come from him entirely), he is at least *representative* of that voice—one well known in Latin America; furthermore, Trueba's voice opposes the magical, "feminine" voice: "He maintained that magic, like cooking and religion, was a peculiarly feminine affair" (p.117); "Sostenía que la magia, como la religión y la cocina, era un asunto propiamente femenino" (p.124). The historical narrative, however, does *not* belong to Estaban Trueba, though his voice is recognized early in the novel as the "historical" voice: this narrative belongs to Alba, his granddaughter, the political activist.

Perhaps to her benefit, Allende abandons the technique of alternating Trueba's testimonies with the main narration after the first chapter (she comes closest in Chapters 6 and 10, both of which are divisions in the novel); Allende keeps the dialogue alive, however, by giving Trueba occasional sections for the rest of the novel. Nevertheless, the question arises as to why Allende chose to write in Trueba's voice at all. Such a narrative strategy seems risky, if not conspicuously dangerous: by breaking the narrative flow, by providing a contradictory viewpoint, Trueba's narrations work to destroy any "magic" her omniscient narrations create. An early statement in the novel (coming in the midst of a passage which reads like pirated García Márquez) indicates that this is Allende's objective: "It is a delight for me to read her [Clara's] notebooks from those years, which describe a magic world that no longer exists" (p.72); "Es una delicia, para mí, leer los cuadernos de esa época, donde se describe un mundo mágico que se acabó" (p.78). In this sentence, like the second sentence of the novel, the unnamed "I" surfaces from the collective-feminine, omniscient viewpoint to transport the reader for the instant to the present moment of writing. It is this "moment" which the book is working toward, the present-tense moment of the Epilogue in which the same "I" states: "At times I feel as if I had lived all this before and that I have already written these very words, but I know it was not I: it was another woman, who kept her notebooks so that one day I could use them. I write, she wrote..."(p.367); "En algunos momentos tengo la sensación de que esto ya lo he vivido y que he escrito estas mismas palabras, pero comprendo que no soy yo, sino otra mujer, que anotó en sus cuadernos para que yo me sirviera de ellos. Escribo, ella escribió...." (p.379). Not until the Epilogue is this "I" (with whom the reader may have identified Isabel Allende for most of the novel) named specifically as Alba Trueba, the posited author, though the reader is well aware of this by the last pages. What is also clear is that even though the words of this Epilogue may, in part, belong to Clara—by virtue of owning a share in the collective-feminine voice—they belong almost exclusively to Alba, simply because Clara does not belong to *this* reality: a reality in which "magic" does not exist. Similarly, though the words of the old notebooks may, in part, belong to Alba—by virtue of a shared inheritance—they belong almost exclusively to Clara. *The House of the Spirits* begins in the tradition of magical realism, but as it continues it becomes less and less Clara's (or García Márquez's) book, and more and more Alba's (Allende's) book, until finally there is no longer magic but only realism, and the novel becomes the tragic political history of Chile.

Chapter 1 then reads as a kind of "Prologue", with a confrontation between the polar languages of the novel (masculine and historical, feminine and magical). Significantly, the title of this chapter—"Rosa the Beautiful"—refers to the character who, together with Tío Marcos, is most reminiscent of García Márquez's characters. Rosa dies at the end of this first chapter, leaving behind her only the memory of a "mythological creature;" there is a sense in which Rosa "originates" the Trueba line, in opposition to the final Aureliano who dies in the last pages of *One Hundred Years of Solitude*, "the mythological animal that was to bring the line to an end" (p.383); "el animal mitológico que había de poner término a la estirpe" (p.334). Also significant is Tío Marcos' final "disappearance" at the end of Chapter 1, leaving behind him only the chest of "magical" books. Chapter 2, Trueba's chapter, begins the historical narrative of the text. Even though there are political and historical references in the first chapter, such references are not for the most part identifiable, and they are farcical, reading like similar references in García Márquez's novel:

> Severo's political designs began to take shape. He had worked for years toward this end, so it was a personal triumph when he was invited to be the Liberal Party candidate in the upcoming Congressional elections, representing a southern province that he had never set foot in and that he had difficulty finding on the map. p.23

> ...comenzaron a concretarse los planes políticos de Severo. Había trabajado durante años con ese fin. Fue un triunfo para él cuando lo invitaron a presentarse como candidato del Partido Liberal en las elecciones parlamentarias, en representación de una provincia del Sur donde nunca había estado y tampoco podía ubicar fácilmente en el mapa. p.29

Trueba is the focus of two other chapters in *The House of the Spirits*, Chapters 6 and 10, both of which contain several of his testimonies: these three chapters divide the novel. As has been stated already, the feminine-collective voice belongs primarily to Clara early in the novel, with Alba and Blanca present in an obscure way (again, neither Clara nor Blanca speak in first person). As the book continues, however, there is a gradual shift in the focalization of this voice—from Clara, to Blanca, to Alba—as the book slowly shifts in subject matter—from family saga (fantasy), to love story, to political history. The author conceived an individual narrative for each of her three heroines, and each narrative reflects the way in which, according to Allende, that character attempts to escape the "mediocrity" of her destiny as a Latin American woman: "[Clara] escapes through her contact with the spiritual world, through her charitable work....Blanca, who is a less flamboyant character, has the experience of great love. She lives this experience as if it were a novel and escapes living a humdrum life. Alba, of course, becomes an activist."[14] With Chapter 1 as "Prologue", Trueba's three chapters (2, 6, and 10) then divide the novel into the three narratives of its heroines:

Chapter 1: Rosa the Beautiful   "Prologue"
                                (confrontation of polar voices)

Chapter 2: The Three Marias   Trueba

Chapter 3: Clara the Clairvoyant
Chapter 4: The Time of the Spirits   Clara
Chapter 5: The Lovers   (family saga)

Chapter 6: Revenge   Trueba

Chapter 7: The Brothers
Chapter 8: The Count   Blanca
Chapter 9: Little Alba   (romance)

Chapter 10: The Epoch of Decline   Trueba

Chapter 11: The Awakening
Chapter 12: The Conspiracy   Alba
Chapter 13: The Terror   (political history)
Chapter 14: The Hour of Truth

Chapter 15: Epilogue
                (first-person, present-tense)   Alba

Of course, there is a sense in which all narratives overlap, just as there is a sense in which the feminine voice is a "collective" focalization; a glance at the chapter titles indicates, however, that Allende conceived of her novel with these three divisions, these three epochs. Chapters 3 through 5 consist of Clara's "family saga," the magical realist story, as though it were a continuation of the first chapter without the intervention of Trueba's testimonies. Clara again takes charge of the collective female voice, with the "I" surfacing momentarily toward the beginning of each chapter (as though the unnamed Alba wished in some way to differentiate herself) and with Trueba's "historical" narrative now taken up by the same feminine voice: Trueba narrates only one section among all three chapters. Significantly, in Chapter 5 (the last of Clara's chapters), the earthquake occurs, "[which] signaled such an important change in the life of the Trueba family that from then on they divided all events into before and after that date" (p.139); "[que] marcó un cambio tan importante en la vida de la famila Trueba, que a partir de entonces dividieron los acontecimientos en antes y después de esa fecha" (p.147). Toward the end of the chapter Blanca—who gradually takes charge of the narrative as it shifts toward romance—notices how their lives have changed:

> Blanca noticed that in the course of all these chores not a single ghost
> appeared from behind the curtains, not a single Rosicrucian arrived
> on a tip from the sixth sense, nor did any starving poet come running

in summoned by necessity. Her mother seemed to have become an
ordinary down-to-earth woman.
   "You've changed, Mama," Blanca said.
   "It's not me who's changed," her mother replied. It's
      the world."15

Blanca notó que en todos esos afanes, no apareció fantasma alguno
detras de las cortinas, no llegó ningún Rosacruz advirtido por su
sexto sentido, ni poeta hambriento llamado por la necesidad. Su
madre parecía haberse convertido en una señora común y silvestre.
   —Usted ha cambiado mucho, mamá —observó
   Blanca.
   —No soy yo, hija. Es el mundo que ha cambiado
   respondió Clara. p.151

Trueba again becomes the focus of Chapter 6, and it is at this point in the novel
that the "historical" narrative becomes referential: Trueba's mutilation of Pedro
Tercero's hand identifies the latter with Victor Jara, the folksinger whose hands
were similarly mutilated a few days after Chile's military coup. It is also at this
point in the novel that the "magic" begins to disappear, slowly displaced by the
"historical" narrative.
     Blanca is the focus in Chapters 7 through 9, which tell of her brother's
romances, of her own marriage and separation from the Count, of Alba's birth,
and of Blanca's clandestine meetings with her lover, Pedro Tercero. The
unnamed "I" seldom surfaces from the omniscient viewpoint (as though Alba
were no longer as far removed) and the voice becomes more the voice of Alba in
the Epilogue. In the last of Blanca's chapters (Chapter 9), two significant events
occur: the death of Clara "[which] completely transformed life in the big house
on the corner. Gone with her were the spirits and the guests" (p.251); "[que]
transformó por completo la vida de la gran casa de la esquina. Los tiempos
cambiaron. Con ella se fueron los espíritus" (p.262); and, toward the end of the
chapter, Trueba's pledge to send his bastard son to the police academy (he is to
become Colonel García, Alba's rapist and torturer in the end of the novel).
     Chapter 10, the third of Trueba's chapters, marks a second turning point in
the novel. After Chapter 10 the magic dissipates, and *The House of the Spirits*
becomes a novel of *historical* realism. Significantly, this chapter is titled "The
Epoch of Decline"; it marks the turn toward tragedy in the novel. In addition to
Pedro Tercero (Victor Jara), other recognizable figures have been introduced
into the text—most conspicuously "the Poet," Pablo Neruda, whose burial is
transformed in the novel into a freedom march—but not until the final third of
the book do these figures become fully fleshed-out. Not until the final third of
the novel do the historical events become identifiable, and not until the magic is
gone does the history evoke any real sense of tragedy.
     As stated already, however, this historical, political narrative is not the
property of Esteban Trueba: it belongs to Alba. In the final third of the novel
Trueba's authoritarianism is slowly subdued, and Alba slowly surfaces from the
feminine-collective voice to take charge of the novel's historical narrative, as

though one voice were gradually consuming the other (Trueba has only two testimonies in the last four chapters). But not only does a "feminine" historical voice emerge in the novel to coincide with the well-known "masculine" historical voice, a "feminine tradition of writing" is instituted to coincide with the "masculine tradition of writing," also firmly grounded in Latin America. The Latin American canon is bound up with the masculine word—from the conquistadores to the patriarchs to the revolutionaries—a masculine tradition of writing originating on the continent (and a tradition represented in *One Hundred Years of Solitude*). In *The House of the Spirits* Allende asserts her own feminine tradition, handed down from Clara through her notebooks, and established in Alba's torture chamber, when Clara appears to her suggesting "that she write a testimony that might one day call attention to the terrible secret she was living through, so that the world would know about this horror that was taking place" (p.251-2); "que [ella] escribiera un testimonio que algun día podría servir para sacar a la luz el terrible secreto que estaba viviendo, para que el mundo se enterara del horror" (p.362). It is at this point in the story which Alba begins to write the novel which is *The House of the Spirits*. But before Alba is taken away to the torture chamber, a meaningful event occurs in the novel: Colonel García builds a bonfire in the courtyard of the Trueba house which he feeds with all of their personal documents, including a chest of forgotten "magic" books found in the basement. It is from these magic books belonging to Tío Marcos (Márquez?) that both Clara and Alba (Isabel?) have learned to read. In *One Hundred Years of Solitude* it is Melquíades' magical parchments which survive the destructive passage of time. In *The House of the Spirits*, however, it is Clara's magical notebooks which survive, and it is Melquíades' parchments and Tío Marcos' books which Colonel García (García?) destroys.

There is a series of opposing parallel movements which define this novel thematically. Trueba's *machismo* is slowly subdued under the influence of the novel's three heroines, and though it remains "intact" (to borrow an expression from García Márquez via Allende) at the end of the novel, Trueba has won a legitimate claim to humanity. Feminine consciousness evolves over the course of the novel, from Clara who responds to life's atrocities by regressing into silence, to Alba who becomes a political activist. Finally, history replaces magic, tragedy replaces comedy. The same opposing parallel movements occur in the novel structurally, to mirror the thematic movements. Trueba's authoritative discourse is subdued by the internally persuasive discourse of the feminine-collective focalization. Clara's distant, third-person-omniscient voice slowly surfaces, ultimately becoming the first-person, present-tense voice of Alba in the Epilogue. Finally, historical writing replaces magical writing, tragic sentiments replace comic sentiments. All this amounts to a novel which—more consciously than unconsciously—may begin as an attempt to rewrite *One Hundred Years of Solitude*, but which discovers itself as a unique statement.

University of Iowa

NOTES

1   Alexander Coleman, "Reconciliation among the Ruins," *The New York Times Book Review*, 12 May 1985, p.1.

2   There are of course other Latin American magical realists (Carpentier, Asturias, Rulfo, Vargas Llosa, etc.), and other magical realist novels. *One Hundred Years of Solitude*, however, is a landmark text in the genre, in addition to assimilating many other Latin American writers and novels, magical realist and otherwise (e.g. Borges and Cortázar). Allende would also have been drawn to García Márquez's novel in that it is the story of a Latin American family, precisely the type of story she set out to tell. (Interestingly enough, García Márquez first thought to title his novel *La casa* [The house].

3   M. M. Bakhtin, "Discourse in the Novel," in *The Dialogic Imagination*, tr. C. Emerson & M. Holquist (Austin: University of Texas Press, 1981), pp.259-422. Bakhtin defines the novelistic hybrid as an "*artistically organized system for bringing languages into contact with one another*," (p.361), and he speaks of "stylization" as the "most characteristic form of internally dialogized mutual illumination of languages" (p.262). "Every authentic stylization...is an artistic representation of another's linguistic style, an artistic image of another's language. Two individualized linguistic consciousness must be present in it: the one that *represents* (that is, the linguistic consciousness of the stylizer [Allende]), and the one that is *represented* [García Márquez?] which is stylized. Stylization differs from style proper precisely by virtue of its requiring a specific linguistic consciousness (the contemporaneity of the stylizer and his audience), under whose influence a style becomes a stylization, against whose background it acquires new meaning and significance" (p.362). Parody, according to Bakhtin, is a particular kind of stylization in which the represented language opposes the representing language: "[In certain] internally dialogized interillumination of languages, the intentions of the representing discourse are at odds with the represented discourse; they fight against them, they depict a real world of objects not by using the represented language as a productive point of view, but rather as an exposé to destroy the represented language. This is the nature of *parodic stylization*" (pp.363-4). Bakhtin continues: "In order to be authentic and productive, parody must be precisely a parodic *stylization*, that is, it must re-create the parodied language as an authentic whole, giving it its due as a language possessing its own internal logic and one capable of revealing its own world inextricably bound up with the parodied language" (p.364). The problem, initially, is that Allende does not present García Márquez's language as a separate entity, but confuses it with her own language (i.e., Clara's).

4   In fact, Bakhtin does account for such a process: "We have in mind first of all those instances of powerful influence exercised by another's discourse on a given author. When such influences are laid bare [and this may be Allende's

downfall], the half-concealed life by another's discourse is revealed within the new context of the given author. When such an influence is deep and productive, there is no external imitation, no simple act of reproduction, but rather a further creative development of another's (more precisely, half-other) discourse in a new context and under new conditions" (p.347).

5 This, according to Bakhtin, is one of the main functions of novelistic discourse, one of its most attractive features: "What is realized in the novel is the process of coming to know one's own language as it is perceived in someone else's language....There takes place within the novel an ideological translation of another's language, and an overcoming of its otherness—an otherness that is only contingent, external, illusory" (p.365).   Although Bakhtin does not refer specifically to "unconscious" parody (he considers only those works in which all is quite purposeful), he comes encouragingly close: "One's own discourse and one's own voice, although born or dynamically stimulated by another, will sooner or later liberate themselves from the authority of another's discourse....A conversion with an internally persuasive word that one has begun to resist may continue, but it takes on another character: it is questioned, it is put in a new situation in order to expose its weak sides, to get a feel for its boundaries, to experience it physically as an object.   For this reason stylizing discourse by attributing it to a person often becomes parodic, although not crudely parodic— since another's word, having been at an earlier stage internally persuasive, mounts a resistance and frequently sounds with no parodic overtones at all. Novelistic images, profoundly double-voiced and double-languaged, are born in such soil, seek to objectivize the struggle with all types of internally persuasive alien discourse that had at one time held sway over the author" (p.348).

6 Isabel Allende, *The House of the Spirits*, tr. M. Bogin (New York: Knopf, 1985), p.3. All other references to the novel are to this edition.

7 Isabel Allende, *The House of the Spirits* (Barcelona: Plasa & Janes Editores, S.A., 1982), p.9. All other references to the novel are to this edition.

8 Gabriel García Márquez, *One Hundred Years of Solitude*, tr. G. Rabassa (NewYork: Avon, 1970), p.11). All other references are to this edition.

9 Gabriel García Márquez, *One Hundred Years of Solitude* (Barcelona: Editorial Argos Vergara, S.A., 1975), p.7. All other references to the novel are to this edition.

10 Gérard Genette, *Narrative Discoure*, tr. J.E. Lewin (New York: Cornell University Press, 1980), pp.189-94. Avoiding the limitations of "point of view," Genette takes up the slightly more abstract term "focalization," which corresponds to "focus of narration." The focalization of a narrative may be "external" if "the hero performs in front of us without our being allowed to know his thoughts or feelings" (p.190), or it may be "internal" if we are given access to such thoughts and emotions.   An internal focalization may be (a) "fixed," if

everything passes through a single character to whose perspective we are restricted (b) "variable,." if the focal character changes, and (c) "multiple," if the same event is evoked several times through the perspectives of several characters. "The commitment as to focalization is not necessarily steady over the whole length of a narrative," and it may change according to the character observing or being observed: "Any single formula of focalization does not, therefore, always bear on an entire work, but rather a definite narrative section, which can be very short. Furthermore, the distinction between different points of view is not always as clear as the consideration of pure types alone could lead one to believe. External focalization with respect to one character could sometimes just as well be defined as internal focalization through another" (p.191).

[11] Gabriel García Márquez, *The Art of Fiction LXIX*, interview published in *The Paris Review*, Vol. 23, No. 82, Winter 1981.

[12] Clearly elements reminiscent of García Márquez persist until the end of the novel (the forshadowing technique, the repetition of family traits, the solitude of Trueba and Alba, etc.), but such elements become meaningful and productive specifically in terms of Allende's own text, and they no longer stand apart as grafted from another.

[13] Bakhtin describes authoritative discourse as the word which "demands that we acknowledge it, that we make it our own; it binds us, quite independent of any power it might have to persuade us internally; we encounter it with its authority already fused to it. The authoritative word is located in a distanced zone, organically connected with a past that is felt to be hierarchically higher. It is, so to speak, the word of the fathers. Its authority is already *acknowledged* in the past" (p.342). Bakhtin notes that the role of pure authoritative discourse, excepting parody (and Allende is clearly parodying the authoritative patriarchical figure), is insignificant in the novel as it cannot be dialogized (which is the obvious reason Allende departs from her technique of alternating Trueba's testimonies with the main narration after the first chapter). Internally persuasive discourse, however, is "affirmed through assimilation, tightly interwoven with 'one's own word' " (p.345).

[14] Isabel Allende, *Imagine*: *International Chicano Poetry Journal*, interview (Boston), Winter 1984, pp.42-56.

[15] My point is further illustrated here by the translator's switching, perhaps inadvertently, to Blanca's point of view: she replaces "—respondió Clara" with "her mother replied" (p.144).

Re-Escribir y Escribir:
Arenas, Menard, Borges, Cervantes, Fray Servando

No sin cierto humor, Borges conjetura una y otra vez que el universo es una biblioteca, que sus escritos deben entenderse como el testimonio de un lector atento, que la "verdad" de la literatura reside en la repetición de algunas metáforas privilegiadas pertenecientes, siempre, a otros. La escritura borra la individualidad del texto particular y lo integra a la gran biblioteca común, una entidad carente de autores. El gesto tiende a mostrarnos que la "novedad" de los textos es simplemente una ilusión para enmascarar su verdadera naturaleza, la de ser repetición de una instancia de la biblioteca. El arte consistiría en la recurrencia de ciertas insistentes metáforas o historias (estas últimas, también metáforas desde una perspectiva como la de Macedonio y Borges) presentadas en un tono cada vez más simple, más claro. La obra "individual" se convierte en el testimonio de una lectura que propone otra. Existe como una figura de su propia inestabilidad; sólo es posible por una relación de analogía con algo distinto y, sin embargo, para efectuar la ilusión de su propia presencia (*visibilidad*, como diría el reseñador de Menard) debe indicar la fisura que la separa de aquello que desea imitar, de aquello con lo cual desea confundirse.

La obra de Macedonio es, fundamentalmente, una galería de juegos para materializar una literatura de la nada con el objeto de desenmascarar las ilusiones creadoras de la ficción. Sus juegos son redes con una función estrictamente negativa: destruir toda lectura que no vea el texto como re-escritura de otra lectura. Macedonio jugó con personajes que llamaba "ausentes", "inexistentes" y nombró una condición de existencia para sus propios trabajos. Esa condición era un lector de naturaleza especial, alguien capaz de despojarse de ilusiones con respecto a su existencia individual y preparado para materializar la nada a medida que leía, alguien que pudiera leer *sólo* el ejercicio de lectura. Este era su lector *fantástico* y, simultáneamente, el escritor ideal.

Existe un entrecruzamiento interesante entre Macedonio y Borges. Para esa red necesitamos un tercer lector (o, por lo menos, uno al que podamos referirnos ingenuamente como tercero por el momento; se multiplicarán más adelante) que fue "creado" por el lector fantástico de Macedonio, Borges. Se trata de Pierre Menard [1].

[1] "Pierre Menard, autor del Quijote." La paginación corresponde a: Jorge Luis Borges, *Ficciones* (Alianza-Emecé, Madrid, Buenos Aires, 1971)

que ceder y asumir las creencias corrientes en su propio momento. La artificiosidad de Menard es su mayor éxito; la *mismidad* de sus palabras con respecto a las de Cervantes es una elaborada máscara que esconde una compleja diferencia en la repetición. Distancia, otredad, travestismo son sus virtudes; su maestría es mayor porque sabe producir artificios. Pero todo esto se repliega sobre sí. El reseñador es criticado por medio de su propio discurso, hecho de pedantes lugares comunes, frases intelectualoides una estrecha admiración por el "Arte". Al querer repetir a Cervantes como autor, Menard reproduce la emulación de los caballeros andantes de don Quijote. El juicio acerca de Menard está inscripto en la obra que intenta reproducir, ya que Menard está contenido en ella. Hay una cadena de imitadores: Don Quijote—caballeros andantes/Cervantes—sabiduría de su época/Menard—Cervantes, que nos devuelve a la relación entre D. Quijote y los caballeros andantes.

"Pierre Menard, autor del Quijote" es, también, una complicación de las nociones de Borges sobre el valor de la repetición en la literatura. Leemos una exageración de su propio proyecto. Si el valor de la literatura reside en la repetición de ciertas metáforas privilegiadas y si consideramos obras enteras como una metáfora, no podríamos pensar que es *un gran logro* generar la repetición de una obra maestra por medio de un fragmento que es, también, una repetición?

Pierre Menard y el reseñador participan de la ilusión de creer que la literatura construye hermosos artificios y verdades esenciales; el juego textual de que ambos son efecto parece indicar que estas verdades no existen o, por lo menos, que son de una naturaleza muy modesta. Escribir es reescribir, leer. El ejercicio debe carecer de solemnidad, consiste en someterse a una recurrencia. Es un modo de inscribir el movimiento de imitar algo que es, ya, una imitación.

Pierre Menard es un autor que trata de ser él y otro simultáneamente (*El otro, el mismo*, como dice Borges en el título de uno de sus libros) y es presentado por un reseñador cuya admiración sirve para denigrarlo. La imitación que Menard hace de Cervantes es tan completa que demuestra que Cervantes era, como él, *otro* autor. "Pierre Menard, autor del Quijote" es una metáfora del juego textual entre acercamineto y distancia con respecto al texto "original" en el ejercicio de leer (reescribir). El lector pasivo ha sido exagerado al punto de convertirse en su opuesto; ceder a la fuerza del "original" se convierte en el deseo de generarlo. *Ficciones* pone entre paréntesis *el* género más explícitamente practicado por los lectores: las reseñas. Está compuesto de reseñas acerca de libros inexistentes escritos por autores apenas existentes. Los reseñadores se implican en los textos por medio de un discurso desconfiable. ¿En qué consiste esta desconfianza? Es un reconocimiento del texto como *manipulación*; su mayor efecto consiste en crear la duda acerca de todo lo dicho en él; la red que convierte al comentarista en personaje produce la noción de que no debe esperarse ninguna verdad privilegiada de lo que dice. Los autores no son los "dueños" de su discurso; Menard no puede ser Cervantes porque Cervantes no era él mismo, del mismo modo que Menard no es el mismo. Esta crítica radical del yo, de la individualidad, que parte del "almismo ayoico" de Macedonio produciría, idealmente, una literatura escrita por nadie, leída por su reflejo y que no transmitiría otra cosa que este intercambio. Esta es la literatura de la materialización de la nada. (Existen juegos análogos en la obra que firman juntos Borges y Bioy Casares bajo los seudónimos de Suárez Lynch, Bustos Domecq y,

Delinear la figura de Pierre Menard como autor es engañosamente fácil. Se propone escribir *Don Quijote*; una de las alternativas abiertas para hacerlo es convertirse en Cervantes. Su lista de publicaciones muestra a las claras los esfuerzos que debe realizar. Pierre Menard es un poeta del simbolismo francés; debe aprender un idioma extranjero de una época ajena y perder su identidad para ser Cervantes, pero, aún así, el camino parece demasiado fácil:

> Ser, de alguna manera, Cervantes y llegar al Quijote le pareció menos arduo -por consiguiente, menos interesante-que seguir siendo Pierre Menard y llegar al Quijote a través de las experiencias de Pierre Menard. (Esa convicción, dicho sea de paso, le hizo excluir el prólogo autobiográfico de la segunda parte del don Quijote. Incluir ese prólogo hubiera sido crear otro personaje—Cervantes—pero también hubiera significado presentar el Quijote en función de ese personaje y no de Menard. Este, naturalmente, se negó a tal facilidad. (p. 53)

Finalmente Pierre Menard logra completar su proyecto: genera unos fragmentos de *don Quijote*. Se nos aconseja que leamos un fragmento transcripto dos veces y el "análisis de texto" suministrado por el reseñador nos persuade de las diferencias enormes que hay entre ambos dependiendo de quién sea el autor. Como leemos esto en *Ficciones* sabemos que el mismo reseñador es un personaje desconfiable cuya "información" debe tomarse con cautela. Escribe sobre un Pierre Menard de Nimes que publicó entre principios de 1920 y fines de 1930, y firma su artículo también en Nimes, 1939. La lista de las publicaciones de Menard, suministrada con admiración servil, es una parodia de ciertos amanerados gustos argentinos de fines de la década del veinte, y el intento de escribir *Don Quijote* es otra instancia de la noción del mapa de tamaño natural como imagen de una literatura que entiende la imitación como confusión total con el referente que quiere nombrar.

El fragmento de *Don Quijote* transcripto en la reseña es: ..."la verdad, cuya madre es la historia, émula del tiempo, depósito de las acciones, testigo de lo pasado, ejemplo y aviso de lo presente, advertencia de lo por venir." (p. 57) Habla acerca del tiempo y la Historia, los dos factores que parecen separar nítidamente a Cervantes de Menard. Al mismo tiempo, vuelve a dibujar el camino tomado por Menard para ser, simultáneamente, él mismo *y* Cervantes. El fragmento es la indicación de un puente en el que parecen fusionarse. Se nos pide que lo leamos dos veces para descubrir aquello que lo hace plural; no *un* texto sino varios, por lo menos dos. *Por lo menos dos*, como intuimos en *La Modestia de la Historia*,[2] ese otro texto de Borges. El fragmento se convierte en plural y es en esa pluralidad donde reside la maestría de Menard. Ha sido capaz de crear una convención, de mentir. Según el reseñador, Cervantes simplemente copió, repitió lo que en su época era un corriente prejuicio con respecto a la Historia. Menard, en cambio, debe construir una intrincada madeja para, en primer lugar, creer lo expresado en el fragmento y, más tarde, generarlo. Menard debe ser otro, traicionar su época; Cervantes sólo tuvo

---

[2] "La Modestia de la Historia" es un texto interesante para consider la recurrencia de imágenes o metáforas en la literatura.

acaso, Montenegro).

Un texto se convierte en el texto ideal si se desenmascara como ficción; debe mostrar el andamiaje que lo hace posible. "Pierre Menard" ataca la noción de autor desde su propio título y, como notamos, efectúa un vacío que impide la fijación de un referente en la narración. Según Macedonio, estos textos constantemente autorreplegándose existirían para ser inmediatamente olvidados, ya que su función es la del provocar *el efecto* de lectura. El lector perfecto debería darse cuenta de que el texto no dijo nada, no creó nada y, como consecuencia, no recordaría nada. El texto autodestructivo ideal construiría una red para mostrar la naturaleza secundaria de sus argumentos y personajes, reduciéndolos a simple apoyos para la lectura. Obviamente, *Ficciones* y gran parte de la obra de Borges y Bioy Casares son ejemplo de estas prefiguraciones. "Pierre Menard" trata de repetir precisamente el momento de *don Quijote* en el cual su autorazgo parece cuestionable: el párrafo que escribe Menard es de la Parte I, Capítulo IX de *don Quijote*. Es el momento en que el narrador nos dice que ha encontrado de casualidad unos papeles escritos en árabe, los hizo traducir y leyó la historia de don Quijote escrita por Cid Hamete Benengeli. Este fragmento es precedido por una nota acerca de cómo todos los moros son mentirosos pero, acaso, los historiadores sean diferentes. Don Quijote es presentado como un texto escrito por un moro y filtrado por una traducción.

Al leer "Pierre Menard" hemos diseñado una escena básica: la insistencia de palabras que reaparecen en un texto sin productor fijo. Este vacío de productores es efecto de un juego textual; Pierre Menard repite el movimiento de repetición ya presente en *don Quijote*. Su proyecto reaparece en *El mundo alucinante*[3], novela del joven escritor cubano Reynaldo Arenas. *El mundo alucinante* es, también, una reescritura. Los textos "originales" son, a primera vista, de naturaleza diferente. Se trata de las *Memorias* y *Apología* de Fray Servando Teresa de Mier, un texto autobiográfico y su defensa política en respuesta a sus enemigos. Se necesitan unas breves notas sobre la curiosa vida de Fray Servando Teresa de Mier.

Nació en el entonces Nuevo Reino de León en la Nueva España (Monterrey) en 1763; se hace sacerdote dominicano en 1780 y recibe el título de Doctor en Teología. Su fama como orador hace que lo elijan para hablar en los funerales de Hernán Cortés y también lo lleva a ser comisionado para dar un sermón acerca de la tradición de la aparición de la Virgen de Guadalupe. Este sermón-dado el 12 de diciembre de 1794- causa un gran escándalo y ocasiona denuncias de herejía ante el tribunal de la Inquisición. No entraremos en los detalles del sermón pero será útil recordar las causas por las cuales Fray Servando sufriría penosas consecuencias. Ha habido una cadena de malentendidos en el asunto y los mismos escritos de Fray Servando luego de las acusaciones de sus enemigos han servido para diluir el sentido inicial de sus palabras, si alguna vez lo hubo. Fray Servando negó la tradición hispánica de la aparición de la Virgen de Guadalupe y sugirió (el énfasis depende del modo en que leamos el sermón) que la Virgen de Guadalupe era una máscara de Quetzalcoatl, cosa que sería probada por unos jeroglíficos presentes en su imagen. Quetzalcoatl, desde esta perspectiva, podría haber sido una deidad cristiana revelada a la gente de la región antes de la llegada de los españoles. Toda la visión de las religiones

---

[3] La paginación corresponde a: Reynaldo Arenas, *El mundo aluci.ante* (Editorial Diógenes, México, 1969).

precolombinas debía ser revisada por el descubrimiento y, como consecuencia, sería minimizado el papel de los españoles como introductores de la verdadera religión siendo este sustituido por un reconocimiento —como más adelante ocurre en la obra de Fray Servando— de su función de conquistadores y opresores de los pueblos americanos.

Los cargos contra Servando son denunciados el día siguiente al sermón y unos días más tarde es puesto bajo arresto en su propia celda del Convento de Santo Domingo. El año en que esto ocurre, 1795, señala el comienzo de los viajes, juicios y evasiones que han hecho de Fray Servando un personaje tan curioso. De Méjico pasa a un convento en Burgos. Su primera evasión exitosa lo lleva a Francia (alrededor de 1801) donde hay testimonio de discusiones teológicas con rabinos en una sinagoga de Bayonne. En París, adonde se traslada seguidamente, se hace amigo de Simón Rodríguez, el maestro de Bolívar. Trabaja enseñando español y —según su *Autobiografía*— traduce *Atala*, de Chateaubriand.

Fray Servando dice una y otra vez en su *Autobiografía* que el mundo está lleno de farsantes y mentirosos. Un farsante habría robado su traducción y notas de *Atala* para publicarlas, alteradas, con otro nombre. Fray Servando pasa su vida escribiendo contra sus enemigos y haciendo querellas legales. Después de conseguir su secularización del Papa viaja de Francia a España y de allí a Italia. En 1816 se une a las fuerzas que luchan contra los españoles; cae en prisión nuevamente y escapa de un continente a otro. Después de la independencia mejicana regresa a Méjico de su prisión en España pero es encarcelado nuevamente debido a sus discursos contra Iturbide. Los últimos tres años de su vida transcurren en una atmósfera comparativa tranquila. Es representante de Nuevo León en el Primer Congreso Constitucional Mejicana después del triunfo de las facciones anti-Iturbide. Pero aún entonces, juega un papel de opositor; sus opiniones son de tal naturaleza que se convierte en una figura aislada. Su último discurso público en noviembre de 1827 (muere el 3 de diciembre de ese año) es, en parte, una defensa contra acusaciones que se le habían hecho.

Fray Servando Teresa de Mier fue un escritor prolífico. Reynaldo Arenas ha elegido leer varios de sus trabajos para su novela. Son la *Apología* (escrita en 1819), donde habla fundamentalmente de sus evasiones y otros hechos curiosos como su negativa de casarse con una hermosa judía, un intento de evasión en el cual usó un paraguas como paracaídas, descripciones de los países por donde viajó (sus "observaciones" de la vida cotidiana le permiten retratar a los españoles, por ejemplo, como libertinos con mujeres semidesnudas por las calles y al clero como una banda de analfabetos), estafas tales como hacerse pasar por Obispo de Baltimore, peleas con varias burocracias; y la *Carta de despedida a los mexicanos escrita desde el Castillo de San Juan de Ulúa* (1821), donde intenta elaborar una teoría de interpretación de jeroglíficos capaz de testimoniar la esencia cristiana del Méjico precolombino.

El juego entrevisto en Menard era una complicación de la problemática que surge al intentar fijarle un productor al texto que leemos. Este juego de complicación de la noción de autor comienza por una novela, *don Quijote*. Leeremos estas preguntas en Arenas referidas a un discurso que es, aparentemente, de naturaleza distinta, un espacio donde el problema de la "verdad", de un referente *anterior* al texto se revela con mayor insistencia. *El mundo alucinante* comienza con una carta que propone, desde el principio, el proyecto de Menard burlándose del tipo de identidad expresado por la firma-Reynaldo Arenas-que la sigue:

> ...No obstante, la acumulación de datos sobre tu vida ha sido bastante voluminosa; pero lo que más útil me ha resultado para llegar a conocerte y amarte, no fueron las barumadoras enciclopedias, siempre demasiado exactas, ni los terribles libros de ensayos, siempre demasiado inexactos. Lo más útil fue descubrir que tú y yo somos la misma persona. De aquí que toda referencia anterior hasta llegar a este descubrimiento formidable e insoportable, sea innecesaria y casi la deshechado por completo. Sólo tus memorias, escritas entre la soledad y el trajín de las ratas voraces, entre los estallidos de la Real Armada Inglesa y el tintinear de los mulos por los paisajes siempre intolerables de España, entre la desolación y el arrebato, entre la justificada furia y el injustificado optimismo, entre la rebeldía y la huída, entre el destierro y la hoguera; sólo ellas aparecen en este libro, no como citas de un texto extraño, sino como parte fundamental del mismo, donde resulta innecesario recalcar que son tuyas; porque no es verdad, porque son, en fin, como todo lo grandioso y grotesco, del tiempo; del brutal e insoportable tiempo que en estos días te hará cumplir doscientos años. (pp. 9-10)

A pesar de la afirmación "que tú y yo somos la misma persona", el descubrimiento es que ambos son *otra persona*. El intercambio entre *tú* y *yo* no consiste de una pluralidad no problemática que preserve la identidad de cada uno para sí. Es, por el contrario, el descubrimiento del cambio constante de un pronombre por otro, no simplemente el pasaje de un *tú* a un *yo*. Esa *misma persona* que parecen devenir es una figura de la circulación dentro del sistema de pronombres personales. Esa *misma persona* es *nadie*; es, al mismo tiempo, todas las personas. Por eso leemos la consecuencia, aparentemente paradójica, de que el libro contiene a las Memorias de Fray Servando como parte fundamental, pero con un papel distinto del de una cita. ¿Dónde reside la paradoja? El texto elegido de toda la bibliografía de y sobre Fray Servando para figurar explícitamente (sabemos que hay otros dos incluidos) en la novela son sus memorias. Las memorias parecen rescatar aquello que fuera destruido: la identidad de Fray Servando con respecto a sí mismo en la forma de una autobiografía. Su "vida" en un texto está contenida en *El mundo alucinante*, un libro con un nombre distinto del suyo, con una diferencia que denota el pasaje de lo singular al plural. De Fray Servando (un nombre propio) al sustantivo que más abarca, el mundo. De la individualidad del nombre propio a una palabra que nombra al mundo.

Otra vez, el Borges de "El Aleph" y "El Zahir" implica y está implicado en este texto. El problema reside en la simultaneidad de nombrar. Dicho de otro modo, si la otra persona no es *yo* ni *tú* sino una constante oscilación de los pronombres personales que simultáneamente los presenta y borra, ¿cómo construir un discurso que asuma esa oscilación? ¿Cómo sería un texto que partiera de un entendimiento del proyecto de Pierre Menard como disolución de los autores en una forma análoga al modo en que el intercambio de pronombres personales termina borrando la noción de persona anterior al discurso? Las respuestas dibujarán una figura para esa *otra persona* creada por la lectura de las memorias de Fray Servando. Nuestra primera lectura considerará a la novela como una elaborada reescritura de las Memorias, dándole a éstas el papel de una fuente "originaria".

La primera pregunta que formulamos es: ¿en qué juego participa el autorazgo de las memorias al integrarse a la novela? Seguiremos un camino análogo al primer movimiento de "Pierre Menard"; se tratará de descubrir cómo el productor se convierte en *otra persona*.

La novela tiene tres capítulos número uno, tres rapítulos número dos y un curiosamente espaciado y plural número tres. La aparición de cada capítulo número uno cerca del otro ayuda a intensificar el efecto de oscilación en la elección de cómo comenzar la lectura de la novela. Los tres capítulos número uno tienen los siguientes títulos en este orden: "De cómo transcurre mi infancia en Monterrey junto con otras cosas que también transcurren"; "De tu infancia en Monterrey junto con otras cosas que también ocurren", "De cómo pasó su infancia en Monterrey junto con otras cosas que también pasaron". Recurre el *de* en las tres versiones y hay un cambio en los verbos usados para cada caso: *transcurrir, ocurrir, pasar*.

Estos títulos son *subtítulos* para distintos capítulos número uno; son *casi* el mismo subtítulo. La diferencia entre ellos está dada por el pronombre personal y los verbos usados para indicar el pasaje del tiempo. El comienzo de cada subtítulo con *de* sugiere que se nos va a decir algo acerca de algo, la existencia de un *tema*. El tema sería una infancia que *transcurre, ocurre, pasa*. Cada subtítulo parece estar implicado y luego desplazado por el otro. La variación de los pronombres personales y los verbos muestra la función de enmascarar que asume la insistencia del *de*. No hay, en verdad, tema sino la presentación del movimiento que crea temas como efecto de un juego textual. La mismidad de lo "dicho" en cada uno de los subtítulos implica diferencia, la existente entre *transcurrir, pasar, ocurrir* y la que hay entre los pronombres. Cada uno de los verbos se convierte en *traducción* del otro; la oscilación creada por el hecho de que cada uno lleva el número uno da la ilusión de la posibilidad de elegir distintos comienzos para la novela; de una elección que pueda sustraernos de la ambigüedad de un comienzo dividido en tres intentos del mismo gesto, condenado a la pluralidad y la fragmentación. *Otro* comienzo que no se cuestione como el *único* número uno.

Cada subtítulo está, también, *dividido* en dos partes que forman la figura de la traducción (*traducción* como un ejercicio que, bajo el gesto de decir lo mismo, repetir, se inscribe como separado de aquello que nombra). La segunda parte repite la primera parte del subtítulo en un plural referido a "otras cosas". El verbo usado es el mismo, cada parte es un juego con distintas formas de ese verbo: el singular y el plural. (Significativamente, el segundo capítulo número uno, el que usa *ocurrir*, no tiene esta división y sugiere, así, unidad en el hecho que *ocurre*). Elegir uno solo de los subtítulos no superará la pluralidad porque cada uno es una pluralidad en sí mismo. Los tres números uno se burlan de la noción de comienzo y sugieren una elección frustrada por cada uno de los subtítulos. Los verbos utilizados nombran al tiempo. Pero, no obstante, leemos la parte más "ahistórica" de la novela; parece una continuación de esa otra novela "prelógica" de Arenas, *Celestino antes del alba*. Hay una coexistencia entre vivos y muertos, un espacio común donde la supresión del tiempo parece posible:

Yo eché a correr por entre los troncos de las matas de corojos, llamando a mi madre. Pero en esos momentos mi madre estaba desemillando algodón--para sacarle el hilo--para hacerlo tela para venderla--para comprar un acocote para cuando llegara el tiempo de sacar al aguamiel--para sacarla--para hacerla pulque--para venderlo--para comprar cuatro maritates--para regalarlos al cura--para que nos volviera a bendecir el ganado--para que no se nos muriera como ya se nos murió. Además: también ella estaba muerta. (p. 12)

La repetición de *para* enfatiza la sucesión: una cosa debe ser hecha de modo que otra siga; los guiones de separación intensifican el efecto. Pero la cadena se interrumpe por la presencia del tiempo: ella estaba muerta. La cadena es, en verdad, inexistente. Muestra el movimiento ilusorio de la sucesión: la madre, el cura, el ganado, cada una de las tareas, todo existe simultáneamente. Pero, aún así, la clave para la realización de este efecto es la causalidad: la simultaneidad se logra por un juego textual que contiene sucesión.

Las primeras palabras del primer capítulo número uno siguen a un subtítulo escrito en la primera persona del singular. Es un *yo* quien habla:

Venimos del corojal. No venimos del corojal. Yo y las dos Josefas venimos del corojal. Vengo solo del corojal y ya casi se está haciendo de noche. Aquí se hace de noche antes de que amanezca. En todo Monterrey pasa así: se levanta uno y cuando viene a ver ya está oscureciendo. (p. 11)

¿Quién es ese *yo*? Primero hay un *nosotros* que viene con las dos Josefinas, las Hermanas Iguales. Pero no lo hace. Se presenta como individuo, ya que tiene la posibilidad de compartir un plural con sus hermanas. Una vez que ha mostrado que es una primera persona en el sentido de que funciona así en relación a otros, una vez que ha logrado diferenciarse como pronombre, niega la afirmación: ''Vengo solo...'' Reaparece la negación de la sucesión por medio de su uso, que habíamos notado. Los capítulos reproducen el movimiento de los subtítulos. Son, como ellos, presentación de alternativas que impide la elección de cualquiera de ellas en detrimento de las otras. El juego precisa la orquestación de alternativas, lo importante es el juego textual y no cada uno de los elementos por separado.

Yo, tú, él, nosotros, vosotros, ellos. Estos son los términos puestos en juego en los tres capítulos que llevan el número uno. Si esto debe ser entendido como un juego textual entre los pronombres que impide la definición de cada uno de ellos como entidades separadas, el problema del productor del texto se integra al sistema de interdependencia ya que él no es otra cosa que uno de esos pronombres. Esta fluctuación tiende a construir un discurso descentrado.

El capítulo dos ocurre, también, tres veces y representa un juego pronominal. Los subtítulos son: ''De mi salida de Monterrey''; ''De la salida de Monterrey''; ''De tu salida de Monterrey''. Los textos se apartan de la apariencia ''ahistórica'' de los anteriores ya que el camino a la cuidad de Méjico se enriquece con alusiones que ayudan a fijar el momento de la partida (entre ellas la fecha de la construcción de la Catedral de Méjico). Fray Servando emerge como una figura histórica. Comienza la construcción de un lenguaje que hará una suerte de mímica con respecto a las *Memorias*; este aspecto aproxima a Menard y Arenas. La partida de Monterrey no es sólo la recurrencia de los juegos pronominales indicados sino, también, otro comienzo porque introduce a la Historia como una determinante con importancia en el discurso. La partida de Monterrey es un camino hacia Méjico; es, además, el camino hacia la "vida" pública de Fray Servando.

El comienzo de una vida histórica parece sugerir que la figura de abolición del tiempo por medio de la orquestación de distintas alternativas para el acto de comenzar ha llegado al momento decisivo de elegir entre una de esas alternativas. Pero no es así. Por el contrario, las alternativas reaparecen de modos más interesantes e intensos. Los capítulos que llevan el número dos han integrado en sus tres partes conflictivas el juego entre los capítulos número uno. El capítulo número tres, "Del panorama de la cuidad" aparece sin el ya obvio movimiento de los otros expresado por la repetición de los números. Es una puesta en escena de la cadena sugerida por una de sus oraciones: "siguió a la turba que seguía a la vez a una mujer, que seguía a una soga que la llevaba arrastrada por el cuello." (p. 20); la prolija sucesión de quién sigue a qué es parodiada por: "También el mantenimiento de la hoguera era un gran problema y para ello se empleaba a un millar de indios, que debían abastecer aquellas llamas día y noche, sacando leña de donde fuera, y en situaciones críticas servían ellos mismos de combustible. Pero algunos no esperaban a que se tomasen tales resoluciones y, cansados de tan continua búsqueda, se lanzaban (con la poca leña que habían encontrado) a las llamas y de esta manera la iban atizando por un rato." (p. 21) Aquellos que prenden el fuego se arrojan a él para hacerlo arder. La distinción entre el productor y su producto es oscurecida por un sistema básicamente inestable en el cual sus funciones se intercambian; esto surge del movimiento del texto. No necesitamos el ejercicio de traducción de los capítulos número uno y dos porque este número tres está dividido, en sí mismo, en por lo menos tres partes. Y es nuevamente la violencia de los pronombres personales en su tendencia a desplazar al otro y, de ese modo, cancelarlo la que produce el vacío.

El mundo alucinante trabaja con datos históricos, sigue lo que puede ser considerado como la "vida" de Fray Servando pero, sin embargo, destruye constantemente la linealidad cronológica por medio de la oposición de elementos contradictorios como, por ejemplo, el momento en el cual Fray Servando se pasea por la calle que lleva su nombre. La imposibilidad de elegir entre alternativas opuestas no ordenadas jerárquicamente existe en todos los capítulos de la novela y cumple la función de poner entre paréntesis la noción de progreso narrativo.

El capítulo número siete es, otra vez, tres capítulos. También es otro comienzo en el sentido en que es el punto de partida de ese otro libro que la novela intenta ser: las *Memorias* de Fray Servando Teresa de Mier. Las *Memorias* son precedidas por la *Apología*, texto en el cual Fray Servando se defiende de los ataques provocados por su sermón acerca de la Virgen de Guadalupe y sugiere que su "vida" es consecuencia del sermón. Los tres números siete tienen los siguientes títulos en este orden: "De las consecuencias del sermón"; "De la consecuencia del sermón"; "De la consecuencia del sermón". El capítulo número seis tiene una imagen que califica la naturaleza plural de este nuevo comienzo: "y el cielo haciéndose pedazos, daba acceso a Las-Nuevas-Imágenes-Recuperadas." (p. 39) Las imágenes son nuevas y recuperadas. Son plurales pero pueden efectuar oblicuamente la ilusión de su singularidad; cada punto de partida es simultáneamente, un ir hacia atrás. El exceso de material cronológico produce un vacío histórico.

El texto se convierte en un movimiento que no lleva hacia ningún lado en línea recta sino que se difunde en múltiples direcciones.

"Consecuencias" en plural en el primer capítulo número siete parodia el singular que sigue. Pero, ¿qué sabemos de aquello que produce la consecuencia, del sermón? En el capítulo "Del conocimiento de Borunda" leemos acerca del encuentro con un personaje que es "algo así como una gran pipa que se movía y hablaba, pero más gorda" (p. 33). Esa gran pipa tiene una teoría que redefine la tradición de la Virgen de Guadalupe. El encuentro ocurre en una cueva; Fray Servando y Borunda hablan sentados sobre esqueletos, rodeados de murciélagos. Borunda le dice a Servando *su* sermón; le cuenta que "la imagen de Nuestra Señora de Guadalupe es del tiempo de Santo Tomás a quien los indios llamaban Quetzalcoatl" (pp. 33-34. Ese es el sermón de Fray Servando. Adquiere el status de una cita de un libro que no leyó, ya que Borunda alude a la existencia de un texto donde sus teorías están fundamentadas pero Fray Servando no tiene acceso a él. El sermón sólo le pertenece a Fray Servando en apariencia, no es responsable de él; su voz produce el efecto de un autorazgo que, en verdad, no existe.

El plural del primer capítulo número siete refleja la pluralidad de productores--por lo menos dos--del sermón. El sermón le "ocurre" a Fray Servando. Sus palabras son "un largo combate entre los antiguos dioses y las nuevas leyendas" (p. 38). Fray Servando, Borunda, el público se sustituyen los unos a los otros. Hay un movimiento que produce la ilusión de un discurso con productores fijos pero, al intercambiar sus posiciones, crean una continuidad que supera las identidades individuales, destruyéndolas y reemplazándolas.

Así como la Virgen de Guadalupe contiene y es contenida por Quetzalcoatl, *El mundo alucinante* contiene y es contenido por otros libros. ¿Qué papel cumplen las *Memorias* y la *Apología* en la novela? ¿Hasta qué punto pueden ser entendidas como "fuentes originarias" de la novela? Fray Servando asegura en esos trabajos que, por un lado, el sermón no le pertenecía y que, por otro, fue malinterpretado. Dio el sermón por influencia de Borunda pero ni bien tuvo la oportunidad de leer el libro de Borunda disintió con él. (No es inútil recordar que en su *Carta de despedida a los mejicanos desde el Castillo de San Juan de Ulúa*, también contenida en la novela, Fray Servando desarrolla una teoría no menos disparatada que la de Borunda; se basa también en una cierta interpretación de jeroglíficos para sacar consecuencias sobre la ortografía de algunas palabras. Los entrecruzamientos con la tesis de Borunda son múltiples.) A pesar do todo esto, Fray Servando sostiene que el sermón no fue un error. No decía lo que el público creyó oír (sugiere que su tono sobre lo dicho no fue positivo y desarrolla una compleja teoría sobre la necesidad de predicar cosas posibles, no necesariamente ciertas) y, en todo caso, quien hablaba era Borunda a través de su propia voz, con un discurso ciertamente oblicuo, ya que Fray Servando no había leído su libro en el momento de su prédica. Simultáneamente, Fray Servando se une al público en la condenación de Borunda.

La Apología es un texto que trabaja en múltiples direcciones. La primera persona que escribe esta defensa y las *Memorias* se delinea como tal en un combate contra sus enemigos pero comparte sus opiniones y se confunde con ellos; estos textos son el producto de un *lector*. En ambos Fray Servando culpa a sus enemigos por no estudiar lo suficiente si pertenecen al clero y por desconocer los escritos de Bartolomé de las Casas y otros si son políticos racistas. La inferioridad que ve en los españoles la atribuye a que leen poco y a que, en verdad, son un pueblo analfabeto. Sus enemigos lo son por ignorancia; Fray Servando se ve a sí mismo como una figura construida por el prejuicio y la falta de lecturas.

El mundo alucinante es metáfora de la oscilación de los textos de Fray Servando, de su "vida" entendida como la reescritura de una teoría que no conocía del todo pero que está, no obstante, implicada en su biografía. *El mundo alucinante* juega con la figura de las atribuciones de Borges al negar la posibilidad de distinguir un solo productor del texto. Pierre Menard eligió ser él y Cervantes al mismo tiempo y en esta fusión diseñó un movimiento oscilatorio entre el S. XVII y el S. XX; *El mundo alucinante* parece intentar un gesto de fidelidad histórica que, sin embargo, se subvierte constantemente.

El reseñador de "Pierre Menard, autor del Quijote" nos dice que Pierre Menard decidió dejar de lado las etapas intermedias de su tarea y que sólo leeremos un fragmento de sus logros. ¿Qué falta? ¿Cuáles fueron esas etapas intermedias? Precisamente las que permiten la lectura doble del fragmento, las que marcan la oscilación entre Menard y Cervantes, el momento en el cual Menard está por convertirse en *otro*. Esas etapas intermedias *son El mundo alucinante*. El juego intertextual entre pronombres es lo que la novela ofrece como ilusión de su productor y eso es precisamente lo que Menard oculta. Menard no muestra las dificultades de pasaje de su lengua nativa al español del Siglo de Oro; su aprendizaje es simplemente mencionado por el comentarista. En el heterogéneo discurso de *El mundo alucinante* hay una coexistencia, una fluctuación entre el español contemporáneo y el de la época de Fray Servando. El juego de palabras por el cual *fraile* repetido se convierte en *fraude* (fraile/fraile/fraude) es un modelo reducido del discurso de la novela, hecho de palabras que están en el proceso de convertirse en otras pero que, no obstante, tienen un resto que las preserva (en este caso, la similitud de sonido inscribe la posibilidad de esa preservación).

En "Pierre Menard, autor del Quijote" encontramos el juego de atribuciones existente en la parte del Quijote de la cual toma su fragmento representado (en el sentido teatral del término) en la forma de notas al pie y trabajos individuales de Menard (las traducciones literales de traducciones literales, transposiciones, etc.) Los últimos capítulos de *El mundo alucinante* repiten este movimiento que consiste en establecer núcleos en la narración que repliegan el texto sobre sí. Esto aparece en la forma de un político--Victoria Guadalupe--cuyo nombre sintetiza simultáneamente la vida de Fray Servando y la novela; también en la frenética escritura de *Apologías* que ocupa a varios personajes y en la parodia que Heredia escribe acerca de un poema aún no escrito. *El mundo alucinante* parece partir de un género con una relación directa con "la verdad": autobiografías escritas por un historiador. Pero al delinear la relación de Fray Servando con la *Clave para los Jeroglíficos Americanos* de Borunda hemos develado el mismo gesto de Menard: la imposibilidad de distinguir un productor único del texto creada como efecto de la atribución de autorazgo al productor de otro texto, igualmente cuestionado. (Acaso debiéramos recordar que el autor de la *Clave para los Jeroglíficos Americanos* no posee una identidad más clara que Cid Hamete Benengeli.)

Estos textos se constituyen como tales por repetir otros que son, a su vez, repeticiones. De este modo se ofrecen como obras que sólo producen el *efecto* de lectura desde una perspectiva como la de Macedonio Fernández.

Ha llegado el momento de preguntarnos cómo hablan estos textos e en contra de sí mismos, en contra de su teoría de develar la máquina de la ficción replegándose sobre su propio discurso al mismo tiempo que parecen diluirse en una repetición infinita que no reconoce ninguna fuente originaria. La base del intento es, nuevamente, la ''verdad''. Esta sospecha, esta desconfianza con respecto a textos que ocultan cómo están constituidos, esta escritura de obras radicalmente autorreflexivas supone una teoría tan convencional y proclive a la producción de ilusiones acerca de sí misma como la de los textos que se propone negar. El sueño del texto perfecto que sólo produzca el *efecto* de lectura, es decir, que sugiera el lenguaje en pura fluidez, también implica una máquina de ilusiones. La distancia radical con respecto a la ''vida'' y los referentes fijos presupone una oscilación que crea sus propias convenciones para materializar la ausencia. Esta ausencia está en conflicto constante consigo misma ya que al constituirse en un texto individual se convierte en su propio opuesto.

Reynaldo Arenas en *El mundo alcinante* y Borges en ''Pierre Menard, autor del Quijote'' crean máquinas que tienden a enmascararse como una lectura vista como reescritura. Este efecto de repetición implica una ilusión tan fuerte como la de la tradición realista que pretenden negar; no se nos pide que pensemos que en vez de libros leemos ''vida'', se supone, en cambio, que olvidemos el libro, lo borremos y creamos que es la teoría del lenguaje que lo hace posible.

The Johns Hopkins University   ALICIA BORINSKY

LA VIDA NOS HA ENSEÑADO: RIGOBERTA MENCHU Y LA DIALECTICA DE LA CULTURA TRADICIONAL

David E. Whisnant
Univ. of North Carolina, Chapel Hill

> [Nuestro] hijo va a conservar, en la medida de todas las posibilidades, las costumbres de nuestros antepasados.
> —*Me llamo Rigoberta Menchú*

Se ha discutido una y otra vez el papel de la cultura tradicional en las situaciones de cambio económico, político y social.[1] En *Las venas abiertas de América Latina*, Eduardo Galeano muestra cómo actuaban los conquistadores hacia las culturas indígenas: para ellos las culturas indígenas eran absolutamente dispensables frente a la cultura "más avanzada" de los Europeos. Bernard Sheehan ha relatado una historia muy parecida en cuanto a los conquistadores que a principios del siglo XVII lograron someter a los indios en Norteamérica.[2] Para los "desarrolladores" que han tomado prestada la bandera del "progreso" (con tanta gratitud), la cultura tradicional es algo que vale, pero que no vale mucho. Les da pena destruirla, pero como funciona como una barrera contra la modernización, hay que destruirla.[3]

Lo interesante del caso es que tales concepciones de la cultura no son elementos centrales a dichos proyectos de colonización o modernización, sino que elementos periféricos a un sistema cuyo propósito es principalmente económico. Para acercarnos a concepciones más aplicables al testimonio de Rigoberta Menchú, tenemos que pensar en los análisis que han sido propuestos sobre la cultura en términos más explícitamente políticos. En relación a tales concepciones se puede decir que desde un punto de vista puramente lógico, en el contexto de una lucha revolucionaria, la cultura tradicional puede funcionar como freno contra una lucha efectiva, como un fundamento esencial de confianza y poder para los que luchan, o como algo que poco o nada tiene que ver con los propósitos políticos.

En todo caso, cuando se estudia la cultura tradicional desde un punto de vista político, surgen algunas preguntas importantes: ¿Qué papel juega la cultura tradicional en la formación de una identidad personal y un sentido de comunidad que se puedan usar para capacitar a una persona o a una comunidad para lograr los objetivos de su lucha? ¿Qué utilidad tienen los valores antiguos y fijos en un mundo relativista y materialista? Y sobre todo, ¿qué importancia debe tener el localismo y el regionalismo en una política concebida estructuralmente en términos necesariamente globales? En este contexto, uno de los propósitos de este ensayo es tratar de desarrollar una tipología de las funciones de la cultura tradicional en los procesos de cambio social.

Me llamo Rigoberta Menchú nos ofrece una oportunidad para analizar muy especificamente tales asuntos en cuanto a la cultura tradicional de los Quiché en el altiplano de Guatemala.[4] Afortunadamente tenemos aquí en vez de un análisis erudito y abstracto, el relato directo de una muchacha Quiché que a lo largo de su narración se concibe a sí misma cada vez más como una persona esencialmente política. Además, la narrativa trata muy explicitamente de la relación entre la cultura tradicional y (a) la formación de la conciencia política de Rigoberta y (b) la vida y la lucha de su comunidad. Pues en verdad la lucha revolucionaria de Rigoberta y sus compañeros se presenta principalmente en términos de un intento para resolver la disonancia cognoscitiva entre el mundo sagrado de "nuestros antepasados" y el mundo que cada día más Rigoberta y su comunidad entienden en términos materialistas.

Por tanto quisiera mostrar que *Me llamo Rigoberta Menchú* sugiere (1) que la cultura tradicional tiene un papel fundamental en el nacimiento de la conciencia

I&L 4:1 Spring 1989

política; (2) que tal conciencia funciona fuertemente en la percepción y el análisis de la explotación; y (3) que a pesar del hecho de que algunas de las funciones de la cultura tradicional son negativas (es decir, desfortunadas o contrarias en cuanto a la lucha política), al mismo tiempo hay funciones positivas que facilitan la lucha.

Más especificamente, se puede mostrar que la cultura tradicional funciona en varios niveles: funciona a veces para aumentar la vulnerabilidad de individuos y comunidades, pero también proporciona un sentido de continuidad, comunidad y seguridad. Además, una vez que empieza la lucha activa, la cultura tradicional permite levantar a un nivel más alto el sentido de solidaridad político-social y la voluntad de resistir, crea (paradojalmente) una orientación hacia el futuro, aumenta la capacidad comunal y personal para ser pragmática y flexible, orienta la imaginación hacia la invención de nuevas formas de supervivencia, y conduce a un sincretismo muy útil en términos de los objetivos políticos finales. Y sobre todo la cultura proporciona una capacidad de lograr autotrascendencia.

LA CULTURA TRADICIONAL Y EL CRECIMIENTO DE LA CONCIENCIA

La cultura tradicional de los Quiché está fundada sobre todo en "la pura natureza"(30). "Nosotros, los indígenas," dice Rigoberta, "tenemos más contacto con la naturaleza" (80). Sólo se puede herir la tierra cuando uno tiene que cultivarla, y además en tal caso hay que pedir permiso (81). Cada niño "tiene que dialogar con la naturaleza", de modo que cada uno tiene su "nahual" (es decir su "sombra" o ser paralelo), el cual "casi siempre es un animal" (39). La comunidad tiene tanto cariño hacia los animales que no quiere matarlos (227). Por necesidad y también por preferencia la mayoría de las medicinas son naturales, y "el chimán" es al mismo tiempo un sacerdote y un médico (236, 238). Como en muchas culturas tradicionales,

I&L 4:1 Spring 1989

hay "un diálogo constante entre la tierra y la mujer" (245), especialmente cuando la mujer está embarazada:

> Se levanta [la madre] a las tres de la mañana ... sale
> a caminar, se encariña con los animales, se encariña
> con toda la natureza, llevando en mente que el niño lo
> está recibiendo y empieza a platicar ... con su hijo,
> desde cuando está en su vientre ... Es como como si es-
> tuviera acompañada de un turista, donde le explica
> las cosas (28).

Por tanto "No es parte aislada el hombre," dice Rigoberta, "que hombre por allí, que animal por allá, sino que es una constante relación" (41).

La relación entre la gente y la tierra está reflejada también en el arreglo del tiempo. El maíz es el "centro de todo" en la cultura (77). La madre de Rigoberta, quién siempre tiene "sueños con la naturaleza", le explica cuales son "los días fértiles para sembrar" (237). En el calendario de la comunidad hay más de setenta días sagrados, así que casi "todas las cosas tienen un día sagrado" (90).

La sabiduría sobre la naturaleza —como la de las leyes de la sociedad y de los modelos de cómo vivir— procede de los antepasados. Desde el principio hasta el fin, todo está referido a los antepasados. "Nunca," dice Rigoberta, "hacemos una cosa fuera de las leyes de los antepasados" (85). Para cada niño el eje de la vida es que "tiene que vivir como vivieron sus abuelitos" (34). Cuando una mujer se da cuenta que va a tener un hijo, le cuenta a su marido "ese hijo va a conservar, en la medida de todas las posibilidades, las costumbres de nuestros antepasados" (27). Por tanto, al llegar a la pubertad, Rigoberta sabe plenamente que su libertad como mujer tiene límites: mis padres, ella dice, "me ponían libertad de lo que yo quería hacer con mi vida, pero obedeciendo en primer lugar, a las leyes de nuestros antepasados" (84). Este aspecto de la cultura también sirve para organizar a la comunidad, la cual está encabezada por "un señor elegido" que funciona como el padre simbólico de todos. Tales señores se los llama "abuelitos" (27).

Pues resulta que las costumbres establecidas y los "secretos" culturales tienen mucho valor entre los indígenas. Cuando se prepara una fiesta, se sacan los instrumentos de música maya que ha guardado la comunidad desde siempre (180). Son tradicionales también muchos aspectos de las vestimientas indígenas (especialmente la de las mujeres) (29, 35, 236). Cuando un indígena deja de llevar tal ropa, ha señalado que ha rechazado la cultura— como las prostitutas (58) o los indígenas "ladinizados". Muchas costumbres están relacionadas con las ceremonias, de las cuales hay tantas: del nacimiento (27-38), de los diez años (70), de la siembra y de la cosecha (73), del casamiento (86), de la muerte (226), de San Miguel Uspantán (231), y otras.

Se puede ver, pues, que la cultura de los Quiché tiene una orientación muy tradicional. De modo que no debe ser una sorpresa que el nacimiento y crecimiento de la conciencia estén vinculados muy estrechamente a la cultura tradicional. Cuando Rigoberta habla sobre "el hecho de que amamos mucho a la naturaleza," habla en primer lugar de cómo *actúan* concretamente los indígenas; pero cuando añade "y tenemos gran cariño a todo lo que existe" (41), nos damos cuenta de que tales modos de acción están también ligados a valores y conceptos abstractos de una entelequia que define la percepción de la realidad y orienta el desarrollo personal. Es decir, la cultura tradicional tiene muchísimo que ver con el nacimiento de la conciencia política de que habla Rigoberta.

En casi cada momento que se amplía la conciencia de Rigoberta, tal ampliación es facilitada por la cultura. Como sirvienta en la casa de los ricos, empieza a hablar —gracias a su cultura y condición económica compartida— con la otra sirvienta, quien le proporciona su primer modelo de resistencia activa. Después de escuchar hablar a los ricos (durante la cena de navidad) de que los indios son pobres solamente porque no trabajan, Rigoberta logra desobedecer una orden (126). También logra entender que hay otros indígenas parecidos en otras tierras—y por consiguiente dice "el problema no era sólo mi problema". Ella comprende esto no a través de preguntas sobre la geografía o las ideas políticas, sino que preguntando "¿Cómo hacen el desayuno?" y "¿Qué comen en el almuerzo?" Al oir "En la mañana comemos tortillas con sal," dice Rigoberta "Eran lo mismo, pues" (144), y su mundo adquiere una dimensión más amplia.

Pasa lo mismo con los padres. Cuando está en el hospital, el padre de Rigoberta se da cuenta que todos los médicos son ladinos, pero al mismo tiempo a través de la plática con otros enfermos indígenas, él ve que "habían muchas cosas que eran comunes a los indígenas en otros lugares." La cultura compartida le da la posibilidad de comunicarse con ellos, y a su vez la comunicación que ocurre le da "otra visión, otra forma de ver todo" (140). Más tarde, Rigoberta explica cómo su madre "no sabía expresar su conocimiento sobre política pero tenía una gran politización a través de su trabajo" en las fincas y con otras mujeres en la comunidad. A su vez el sentido político que tiene la madre pasa a los niños:

> Desde muy chiquitas, teníamos [nosotros los niños] que andar con ella, como para aprender el modelo de mi madre o copiar de ella todos los detalles que nos enseñaba sobre política. (243)

Por tanto, la cultura tradicional es la cuna y el primer paso hacia el sentido político, aunque no sea una política *consciente* o expresada verbalmente. Sin embargo, la cultura de Rigoberta y sus compañeros campesinos del altiplano está en el último peldaño del sistema jerárquico cultural del país. Sirve fuera de la comunidad principalmente para justificar la explotación y marginación.

Muy temprano en su vida Rigoberta adquiere conciencia de los patrones de explotación que afectan a los indígenas en las fincas—en el mundo ladino de los caporales, los contratistas, y los terratenientes. En primer lugar, la explotación toma formas físicas y económicas (el trabajo duro, la comida de perros, las tiendas y cantinas que roban el poco dinero que pueden ganar los indígenas, las deudas, la violación de las muchachas—págs. 43, 48, 76), pero siempre hay también una dimensión cultural de la

I&L 4:1 Spring 1989

explotación. Por ejemplo, hay un contraste dramático entre la imagen del mundo del altiplano, donde cada persona tiene su nahual (lo que a menudo es un animal), y la imagen de los Quiché y los animales apretados en el camión que los lleva hacia la finca (42). "No se soportaba", dice Rigoberta, "el olor de toda la suciedad, de animales y de gentes." Lo que es insoportable aquí es , al mismo tiempo, el propio olor y cómo *se ve* (y se huele) una cultura del punto de vista de otra. O sea, el olor es un olor *"cultural"* que procede de una disonancia cognoscitiva.

Tal sentido está presente de alguna manera en cada ejemplo de explotación, desde la fumigación de los niños en las fincas, la molestación sexual de la sirvienta en la capital (121), y el encarcelamiento del padre de Rigoberta (128), hasta las tonterias de la "reforma agraria" (183) y la masacre de los 106 campesinos de Panzós (186). De modo que cuando Rigoberta llega a la ciudad —o sea al centro o a la esencia de la cultura dominante— le parece como "un monstruo". Al decir "éste es el país de los ladinos, pues" (53), Rigoberta emite un juicio que procede al mismo tiempo de una inocencia e ignorancia profunda y de una sabiduría superior de las diferencias entre una cultura "moderna", brutal y destructiva, y una cultura antigua, llena de cariño y creadora.

Lo que sufre Rigoberta, pues, es la explotación política, social y económica, y "la opresión cultural" (144). "He sufrido," ella dice, "el marginamiento hasta lo más profundo, lo más hondo de mi ser" (70). Por tanto, es apropiado que uno de los ejemplos más destacados de explotación/marginación ocurre en la forma de un "gran folklore" que cada presidente monta para "grandes gentes... senadores, personalidades de otros países, embajadores" y (por supuesto) "una serie de turistas" que toman "todas las fotos que quieran" y que "les hacen actuar [a los indígenas] como hacen los artistas de los ricos" (233). Se presentan los bailes tradicionales en el traje nativo. Y para que todo se presente de una manera aceptable, se dan instrucciones a las reinas indígenas, "porque se considera que el indígena no sabe". Tienen que memorizar [forzosamente, en castellano] saludos para el presidente y

I&L 4:1 Spring 1989

los militares. Entonces se presenta el festival tan lindo de "la cultura tradicional".

Hasta este punto hemos examinado lo dado de la cultura tradicional de Rigoberta, el papel de la cultura en el nacimiento de la conciencia política y la función de tal conciencia en la percepción de la explotación (y las reacciones ante ella). Ahora pasamos a considerar las funciones que tiene esa cultura una vez que empieza la lucha política. Tenemos que tener siempre en cuenta que al fin la cultura tradicional no es solamente un tesoro enterrado en las cabezas y vidas de los indígenas, sino un tipo de moneda corriente cultural, trocada en un mercado controlado por los que tienen poder y cultura "alta".

Inmediatamente después del festival que acaba de mencionarse, por ejemplo, los portadores de la cultura se convierten en algo desechable. Tienen que hosperdarse en una pensión donde entran los borrachos y las putas. "Y eso," dice Rigoberta

> es lo que ... nos duele más. Quiere decir, que el traje sí lo ven bonito porque hace entrar dinero, pero la persona que lo lleva es algo como si fuera nada... Sacan mucho dinero con la presentación de la reina. [Asi que sólo] pueden entrar gentes con dinero. (234)

Esto es un ejemplo bastante claro y concentrado de la interpenetración e interdependencia de la explotación cultural y la de los otros tipos (económica, política, social). También muestra como se puede usar una "valuación" formal de la cultura tradicional para explotar y controlar a la gente.[5] La cultura tradicional como *artefacto* tiene del punto de vista de la cultura dominante un valor positivo, pero como *modo de vivir* tiene un valor negativo.[6]

Como artefacto, es plasmable y vendible; se puede poseer y exhibir por los ricos como evidencia de su "posesión" de "raices" culturales que ya desde hace muchos años han rechazado como barrera contra su propia movilidad socio-económica, y (a la vez, paradojicamente) como evidencia de su sabiduría cosmopolita sobre culturas exóticas. Como modo de vivir, por otra parte, la cultura tradicional se percibe por la clase dominante como una carga no deseada (darle servicios sociales a la gente cuesta dinero), como una complicación ética (al fin de cuentas los pobres tienen derechos humanos), y como impedimento político y social (necesitan tierra; tratan de organizarse como trabajadores).

Por tanto, a un nivel muy básico la lucha es una lucha en la cual la cultura se ve por ambos grupos como arma y armadura. Pero como veremos, no es una lucha en igualdad de condiciones.

LA CULTURA Y LA LUCHA POR LA LIBERACION

Como se mencionó al principio, la cultura tradicional tiene varias funciones en la dinámica de cambio que se ubica al centro del testimonio de Rigoberta. A pesar del hecho de que muchas de estas funciones son positivas, hay funciones negativas que son ineludibles, de modo que la cultura tiene que verse de una manera dialéctica.

La mayoría de las funciones negativas están relacionadas con un aumento de la vulnerabilidad. En efecto, la naruraleza dialéctica de la cultura tradicional se puede ver claramente cuando la otra sirvienta en la casa de los ricos le sugiere a Rigoberta que se haga una pequeña huelga contra la arrogancia y la dureza de la mujer rica. A pesar de que la rica le ha causado a Rigoberta tanto dolor y vergüenza, Rigoberta dice:

> Yo tenía pena. En ese tiempo yo no era capaz. Tal vez por la misma formación con mis padres. Yo no era capaz de desobedecer. Y estos patrones abusaban de toda mi obediencia. Abusaban de toda mi sencillez. Cualquier cosa, la hacia, tomándolo como un deber mío. (124)

En este caso su "formación" aumenta la vulnerabilidad de Rigoberta. Desgraciadamente, hay muchos otros ejemplos.

En primer lugar, el mundo de Rigoberta es muy pequeño y su comunidad está de alguna manera barricada detrás de una cultura que es admirable pero rígida también. "No tuve la oportunidad de salir de mi mundo," nos

I&L 4:1 Spring 1989

dice Rigoberta. Aunque el país está lleno de enemigos, le falta al mundo hasta *el concepto* de un enemigo (149). Y la iglesia también le enseña a la gente a soportar el abuso y a esperar el reino de los pobres en el cielo (147).[7] Claramente es más fácil enseñar tales cosas ("adormecer al pueblo", 148) si la gente no sabe nada sobre como funciona el mundo fuera de la aldea.

Pero la situación es peor todavía. Cuando Rigoberta habla sobre las riquezas de la cultura, dice que cada una de las 22 o 23 étnias en Guatemala "tiene su forma de expresarse" (36). Pero una forma de expresarse también resulta ser una manera de aislarse y separarse de otra gente con quien uno tiene intereses políticos en común. De modo que una y otra vez Rigoberta habla sobre "las barreras" lingüísticas y étnicas (60, 61, 170, 190). "Existimos en un pequeño lugar," dice ella,

> y tanta barrera no permite el diálogo de unos a otros.
> Al mismo tiempo ... decimos aquí está mi étnia y aquí
> tengo que estar, pues. (170-171)

Además, tal situación es muy útil para los enemigos: estas son "Todas las barreras que el mismo régimen alimenta cada vez más," nos explica Rigoberta.

Al dar los primeros pasos hacia una visión más amplia del mundo, Rigoberta siente deseos tan fuertes de aprender el castellano (lo que codifica las reglas del sistema opresor). "Yo quiero, yo quiero aprender," dice ella. Pero su padre —quién iguala (no sin razón) el proceso de aprender con una "ladinización", o sea como una pérdida de la identidad cultural, dice que no: "mejor sufrimos juntos" (115). Tenemos así que las barreras dentro de la comunidad son tan fuertes como fuera de ella.

Al salir de la comunidad, Rigoberta y sus vecinos están automáticamente marcados por sus vestimientas tradicionales. Así, la rica le dice a Rigoberta, "me da vergüenza... tienes que cambiar de como estás" (119). Destacados así, los indígenas tienen que soportar el asco que sienten los ladinos hacia ellos—hasta los que son de la misma clase y situación: "Somos pobres, pero no somos

I&L 4:1 Spring 1989

indios" (145). Por tanto los indios, careciendo del lenguaje dominante y llevando las vestimientas tradicionales como una estrella amarilla, andan marginados, amenazados y engañados, despachando sus pequeños asuntos a través de abogados, oficiales públicos e intermediarios que también son engañadores (130, 136). Por tanto, a través de las acciones de ocultar, conservar, y practicar ciertos aspectos de su cultura, los indios se convierten en víctimas cada vez más vulnerables.[8] Afortunadamente, hay otros aspectos más útiles a la lucha política.

Continuidad

Cuando en un cierto punto empieza Rigoberta a relatar la historia consensual (o sea, el mito), dice lo siguiente:

> Que dicen que eran así nuestros abuelos, que hicieron tal cosa los blancos y así empiezan a culpar a los blancos. Que nuestros antepasados sembraban bastante maíz. Que no hacía falta maíz para ninguna tribu, para ninguna comunidad y que era todos juntos. Y ... teníamos un rey y el rey sabía distribuir todas las cosas con todos que existían ... Antes no estábamos divididos en comunidades ni en lenguas. Nos entendíamos todos. Nuestra medicina eran las plantas ... [y] los animales ni siquiera nos picaban ... Todos caminábamos a pie, pero todos vivíamos bien. (94-95)

De modo que el tiempo de los antepasados era una época de abundancia, de igualdad social y económica, y de una relación simbiótica entre la gente y el ambiente.

Quizás la historia sea un poco idealizada (como todos los mitos), pero hay que notar también que los antepasados no han retenido sencillamente una serie de imágenes románticas, sino que han guardado al mismo tiempo una versión *analítica* de sus experiencias históricas. Es decir, el mito incluye un análisis estructural de donde proceden los problemas de desigualdad, de enfermedad, de escasez, de división social y política. Por tanto, mantenerse en contacto con los antepasados no es sólo protegerse y ha-

I&L 4:1 Spring 1989

cerse invulnerable, sino también liberarse y adquirir un mayor grado de poder. Esto es la dialéctica central de la narrativa en cuanto a la cultura tradicional.

Se debe notar además que aunque los antepasados son antepasados, están paradojicamente muy presentes y a disposición de la comunidad. Rigoberta dice que "El tiempo que estamos viviendo lo tenemos que vencer con *la presencia* de nuestros antepasados" (220; el subrayado es mío). Esto se refiere en primer lugar a los abuelos ya vivientes, pero también a la herencia total del pasado, la cual se transmite a través de un proceso muy consistente y conciente. Entre los ejemplos que abundan en el libro está el de la muerte como una ocasión para transmitir cosas muy concientemente (las leyes, las creencias, las esperanzas) del pasado al presente y del presente hacia el futuro. "En el momento en que [una persona] va a morir," nos cuenta Rigoberta,

> [la persona] llama a la persona que más quiere ... [para] transmitirle ... el secreto de sus antepasados y también transmitirle su propia experiencia, sus reflexiones. Los secretos, las recomendaciones de cómo hay que comportarse en la vida, ante la comunidad indígena, ante el ladino ... La persona que recibe las recomendaciones guarda el secreto y las va transmitiendo, antes de morirse, de generación en generación (226).

Por consiguiente, los indígenas tienen siempre en cuenta que "nos toca multiplicar las costumbres de nuestros antepasados ... [Nos] comprometemos a que nuestros antepasados van a seguir viviendo con nuestros hijos," así que "pasarán las generaciones y las generaciones y seguiremos siendo indígenas" (92-93). Y este proceso les proporciona una fuente de poder potencial que procede de las imágenes de la época primaveral y una claridad analítica que está basada en el conocimiento —preservado y transmitido por los antepasados— de lo que han estado haciendo los blancos siglo tras siglo.

I&L 4:1 Spring 1989

Comunidad y seguridad

Desde el principio hasta el final, la vida del indígena es vida en comunidad. Y a su vez el concepto y la estuctura de la comunidad están afincados en la cultura tradicional del grupo. De modo que la propia vida es vida compartida, la vida como ha sido definida y refinada generación tras generación. La comunidad recibe y entrena a un bebé; la comunidad enseña a los niños; la comunidad previene que cualquier persona esté o se sienta aislada en su vida; la comunidad les proporciona a todos los propósitos y compromisos comunes. "Lo que simpre nosotros tomamos en cuenta," nos informa Rigoberta, "es la vida en comunidad" (242).

Tal entrenamiento empieza antes de que nazca el bebé. Si se come algo delante de una mujer embarazada, hay que compartirlo con ella. Si no se comparte la comida, "se teme que la señora aborte al niño o que el niño sufra internamente porque no puede comer lo que uno está comiendo" (36). Al describir qué pasa cuando nace un bebé en la comunidad, Rigoberta distingue explícitamente entre las intenciones de los indígenas y las de los burgueses:

> [En] las clases burguesas, inmediatamente que nace, se piensa que ese niño tiene que educarse, que tener un nivel de vida. Entonces, nosotros los indígenas, inmediatamente pensamos que la escuela del niño tiene que ser la comunidad, que el niño tiene que vivir igual con los demás. (36)

Se enseña de una manera muy precisa y dramática la diferencia entre los dos conceptos de vida. El verbo central de la vida burguesa es *ganar*, pero el de la vida indígena es *compartir*. Por tanto al principio

> se le amarran las manos [del niño] ... para que no acumule cosas que la comunidad no tiene y que sepa repartir sus cositas, que sus manos tienen que estar abiertas. Las mamás se encargan de abrirles sus manos. (36)

La vida de manos abiertas es una vida en que la comunidad comparte sus bienes y dialoga en forma permanente. En cada comunidad, nos dice Rigoberta, hay una casa grande para los oratorios, las reuniones y fiestas, o lo que sea. En esa casa

> se va a reunir toda la comunidad y celebramos nuestra
> fe ... Nos reuníamos a rezar y, al mismo tiempo, muchas veces nos reunimos a platicar nada más. Para contarnos las experiencias de cada uno ... Es un diálogo entre nosotros. Al mismo tiempo rezamos y juegan un ratito los niños. (78)

Como en la ceremonia que se celebra cuando se cumplen los diez años, tal charla con la familia y la comunidad es como "si estuviéramos rezando a Dios" (72).

Por tanto, el concepto de comunidad y de lo que se comparte en forma constante entre los miembros de la comunidad, están estructurados y mediados por la presencia de los antepasados (o sea la cultura tradicional). Además, está la integridad de la comunidad simbolizada por "un elegido" o "representante" que "toda la comunidad considera como padre". También hay una "señora elegida", igual "como si toda la comunidad fueran sus hijos" (27). De modo que tenemos otra vez lo dialéctico cultural: una comunidad de *iguales*, encabezada (no obstante) por dos *líderes*, los cuales son nada más que símbolos de una cultura *igualitaria y consensual*.

En su calidad de "los elegidos" de la comunidad, los padres de Rigoberta entienden como se puede transformar el sentido de comunidad en una capacidad de lucha contra su explotación y destrucción. Sus padres, dice Rigoberta, usaban su tiempo "por amor de la comunidad" (131). Enfermo y perseguido por las autoridades, el padre les recomendó a sus "hijos" que "no confiáramos sólo en él sino que confiáramos en la comunidad. 'Ahora soy su padre', decía, 'pero después la comunidad será el padre'" (140). Cuando empezó la autodefensa, se celebró una "ceremonia de comunidad donde nosotros pedimos al dueño de toda la naturaleza, que es el dios único para nosotros, que nos ayude" (151). Cuando el gobierno, a través

I&L 4:1 Spring 1989

de la "reforma agraria", trata de ubicar a la gente en parcelas separadas, ellos lo resisten, sabiendo que "[tenemos] que vivir en comunidad" (184).

Ultimamente, sin embargo, la brutal opresión militar de la comunidad es inaguantable, y la gente se da cuenta de que tiene que abandonar su aldea. Para que el cambio sea marcado temporalmente y sea aceptado sicológicamente, la comunidad arregla una "fiesta de despedida". En la ocasión de la fiesta, se ve muy claramente la vinculación dialéctica entre el sentido de comunidad y la necesidad de luchar. "Todo el mundo lloraba," dice Rigoberta., "y, a veces, se reían porque estaban contentos y no sabían como expresar su alegría" (181). Para salvar algo (para retener la posibilidad de reirse y estar alegre) es necesario aceptar el riesgo de perder todo. Para orientar a la comunidad hacia la lucha que viene, el padre de Rigoberta (o sea de la comunidad) saca de la sabiduría de los antepasados un dicho corto y simple: "La cabeza de un hombre no sólo [sirve] para el sombrero". En ese dicho se condensan los hechos dados (y durables) de la cultura, el conocimiento de la posición social de los campesinos (o sea de las estructuras explotadoras de la sociedad), y el sentido de uno mismo como uno que sabe hechos antiguos y fundamentales que no conocen los explotadores. Con las conciencias de todos enfocadas por esta imagen, con todos ante el hecho de la disperción inminente y total de la comunidad, el padre le da a la gente un mensaje clásico de principio y de desafío:

> Hijos,... es posible que el enemigo nos vaya a quitar la pequeña vida que tenemos, pero tenemos que cuidarla y defenderla hasta lo último. Pero si no hay remedio, confíen y tengan esperanza de que el padre de ustedes es el pueblo, porque el pueblo se dedicará a cuidarlos como yo los cuido. (181)

Luego empieza la lucha.

Y ¿cómo funciona la cultura tradicional una vez que empieza la lucha?—cuándo les toca al padre y a la madre y a los hijos dispersarlos e "ir a otro lado"?

Solidaridad y resistencia

Al empezar la lucha, los indígenas tienen que ser capaces de diferenciar lo que pertenece a su mundo (lo que apoya sus intereses) de lo que les amenaza. Esto requiere un proceso de construir y también eliminar barreras. Es decir, hay que buscar y definir —a pesar de las barreras históricas— una solidaridad con otra gente que comparte la misma situación, y hay que marcar como enemigos y opresores a los demás. También hay que estimular la fuerza y determinación para luchar y liberarse.

Para lograr la solidaridad, es muy útil la cultura tradicional. Cuando subió al poder el general Kjell (gracias a los votos de los campesinos, obtenidos a la fuerza), él hizo muchas promesas: les iba a dar a los campesinos salud y carreteras y escuelas y "una serie de cosas" (183). También les prometió "pan". Pero para los indígenas, él que promete "pan" es una señal de peligro. "Estábamos en el pueblo," recuerda Rigoberta,

> Era un día domingo. Y Kjell hablaba mucho que iba a dar pan, iba a repartir tierra. Es que ellos dicen pan, ni siquiera decir tortilla. Muchas veces ni saben qué es lo que come un indio ... Nuestra alimentación es tortillas. (183)

Aquí, pues, la misma palabra es un marcador de clase, de poder, de ignorancia de la mayoría de la gente. Una persona que ni siquiera conoce la comida de la gente no puede tener en cuenta sus intereses.

Otro ejemplo parecido es la llegada de la Coca–Cola— muchas veces la primera cuñita del capitalismo internacional y de la ubicua cultura imperialista norteamericana. Saben perfectamente los abuelitos lo que es, lo que hace físicamente, y lo que significa cultural y politicamente. Dicen

> hijos, nunca van a enseñar a nuestros hijos a tomar esta porquería porque es algo que trata de matar nuestras costumbres. Son cosas que pasaron por máquinas y nuestros antepasados nunca usaron máquinas

I&L 4:1 Spring 1989

... Es comida de los blancos y los blancos se sienten ricos con estas cosas. (97)

Se ve entonces que la cultura —aunque sea a un nivel
(como sugerí antes) un fuente de vulnerabilidad— proporciona no obstante medios para juzgar cosas para que se
retenga, se proteja y se incremente el grado de solidaridad
interna.

Más especificamente, la lucha organizada de la comunidad cuando empieza—está basada en grupos naturales
ya existentes entre la gente y emplea directamente la sabiduría de los antepasados. "Existían ya," nos dice Rigoberta,
"nuestras organizaciones, así, nuestros grupitos de niños,
grupos de jóvenes, grupos de mujeres, grupos de cate-
quistas. Entonces empezamos a alimentar todos esos grupos que existían " (146). Cuando se forma el Comité de
Unidad Campesina (CUC), se forma a partir de un "grupo
de comunidades" (185). Además, empiezan a usar —para
protegerse, para confundir y luchar contra el ejército—
"las trampas" de los antepasados (145, 149). "Cuando empezamos a organizarnos," recuerda Rigoberta, "empezamos a emplear lo que habíamos ocultado" (196). Usan las
trampas; usan el conocimiento de la naturaleza; construyen una red de información; golpetean al ejército con
piedras, con machetes, y hasta con el agua caliente, el
chile, y la sal (155). Cuando una anciana mata a un sol-
dado, Rigoberta ve el acto como "el triunfo de nuestros
secretos" (173). "Pobre del ejército, pues" observa Rigoberta, "porque ni siquiera sabe qué es un guerrillero; entonces se lo imaginan como un monstruo, como pájaros o
cualquier tipo de animal. Entonces, tienen miedo meterse
en las montañas" (153).

Y finalmente la solidaridad y la capacidad para resistir
proceden del concepto de los antepasados no sólo como
guardadores pacíficos de los secretos, sino también como
luchadores. "Nuestros antepasados," dice el padre de Rigoberta, "nunca se sintieron cobardes," así que "tenemos
que seguir luchando" (183). En verdad, la narrativa que les
dan los abuelos de Rigoberta a sus hijos y nietos es una
narrativa de la lucha de *sus* antepasados contra los espa-

ñoles: "Dicen que hacían trampas ... cuando llegaron los conquistadores" (149). De modo que la *herencia* de los Quiché de hoy es la de una lucha que se ha perpetuado unos 400 años; el concepto de ellos mismos como luchadores infatigables quizás sea el hecho más profundo de la cultura.

Orientación hacia el futuro

Porque la lucha ocurre en un mundo que va cambiando cada momento, para los Quiché no es solamente un asunto de *resistir*, sino de cambiar. Por consiguiente es interesante notar que, en una cultura tan fuertemente orientada hacia la sabiduría y las leyes de los antepasados (es decir hacia el pasado), los indígenas tienen que mantenerse (dialécticamente, otra vez) orientados también hacia el futuro. Por tanto, la gente resulta capaz de imaginar y construir cada día métodos nuevos para luchar y sobrevivir, y de conocer y aceptar tranquilamente las fronteras experienciales y un futuro que sin duda va a ser tan diferente del pasado como del presente.

¿Cómo ocurre esto? Parcialmente del hecho de lograr conocer y aceptar el hecho de que las cosas tienen naturalmente un comienzo y un fin es una parte importante del entrenamiento (lo que es completamente tradicional en la comunidad, y una característica estructural de ella) de los niños y jóvenes en la dialéctica inescapable de la vida. Nos dice Rigoberta, por ejemplo, que una muchacha, después de su casamiento, tiene que ir para siempre a vivir con la familia de su esposo. No obstante, la muchacha, "cuando sale de la puerta de su casa no puede mirar para atrás" (103). De una manera más amplia, ocurre algo parecido cuando la comunidad tiene la fiesta de despedida: ellos tienen que decir adiós —quizás para siempre— a la aldea, y lo dicen sin mirar para atrás. Pero de alguna manera el adiós es irónico, porque llevan (y llevarán) todo el pasado (o sea el presente) consigo. Entonces los indígenas están de alguna manera orientados muy fuerte y claramente tanto hacia el futuro como hacia el pasado.

Al discutir las fiestas que se celebran en Guatemala, Rigoberta se refiere muy en especial a la de Tecún Umán, el héroe de la lucha Quiché contra los conquistadores. Pero es chocante cuando ella nos dice, "pero nosotros eso no lo celebramos". ¿Pero por qué no se celebra entre los Quiché el día de su héroe más sobresaliente? Fíjense, nos dice Rigoberta, "en primer lugar... ese héroe no está muerto," y en segundo lugar "Se celebra [en las escuelas] su aniversario como algo que representó la lucha en aquellos tiempos. Pero para nosotros existe la lucha todavía" (229).

A través de esta distinción salen otros aspectos destacados de la cultura tradicional: su pragmatismo y flexibilidad, su orientación sincrética, y (al fin de cuentas) su capacidad de autotranscedencia.

Pragmatismo y flexibilidad

Al principio, señala Rigoberta que "la vida nos ha enseñado" (158). La importancia de este hecho —de la orientación pragmática fundamental de la cultura— se ve una y otra vez. Llegó un día, recuerda Rigoberta, "un oportunista" de tipo intelectual que les dijo a los trabajadores "Es que ustedes los campesinos son tontos, no leen, no estudian." Pero los campesinos le dijeron "Te puedes ir con tus libros a la mierda" (248). Los campesinos tienen una confianza muy fuerte en su capacidad de aprender directamente de la vida lo que necesitan. De tal manera Rigoberta distingue explícitamente entre si misma y la rica de la ciudad: Rigoberta llega a la casa de la rica sin saber nada de nada, pero nos dice "Me sacaba todos los oficios en un rato. Para mi no era difícil" (120). Al contrario, pensando luego en "el ambiente humilde de nosotros y el ambiente relajoso de ellos," ella observa que "Triste es la gente que ni siquiera sabe hacer ni mierda" (126). De modo que la capacidad para enfrentar los hechos, para aceptarlos y para aprender de ellos —o sea el pragmatismo— es algo fundamental en la cultura de Rigoberta.

El pragmatismo conduce a una flexibilidad muy útil— la cual es un característica inesperada en una cultura basada tan fuertemente en las leyes de los antepasados. Al hablar en la casa de la rica con la muchacha de otra étnia, "Completamente se me cambiaron todas las ideas," dice Rigoberta, "se me venían muchas ideas" (114). Además, pasa algo parecido a nivel comunal. Cuando llega la represión, la gente tiene que actuar de una manera muy pragmática y flexible. "Allí," nos dice ella, "fue precisamente cuando rompimos con muchos esquemas culturales, pero, sin embargo, tomando en cuenta que era una forma de salvarnos" (154).

Ultimamente, a pesar de su preferencia de conservar el pasado y mantener la cultura tan pura como sea posible (recuérdese que la ladinización se ve siempre como un peligro), la cultura es también profundamente inventiva e incorporativa. Por ejemplo, se pueden ver las características inventivas e incorporativas muy claramente en el Baile de la Conquista (231), la ceremonia de autodefensa (151) y la fiesta de despedida (180). El Baile de la Conquista se inventó para celebrar la lucha de los antepasados, la supervivencia de la comunidad, y su capacidad para incorporar a la vida de todos —de una manera imaginativa y trasformadora— la pena y la pérdida colectiva. Además, en la fiesta de la despedida se inventa una manera de incluir dialécticamente en la visión del futuro el renacimiento del pasado. El futuro esperado es aquel en el cual "nosotros pudiéramos expresar nuestros sentimientos, hacer nuevamente nuestras ceremonias como lo hacíamos" (181).

Sincretismo

A su vez el pragmatismo, la flexiblidad y la capacidad de inventar e incorporar están basadas en un sincretismo que funciona como el modo operativo básico de la dialéctica cultural. Hay muchisímos ejemplos —simples y complejos— en la narración. A un nivel muy básico, cuando alguien en la comunidad está enfermo, se usa el rosario y las letanías para rezar, pero también se usan "nuestros medios indígenas" (112). De hecho, si se sigue cómo funciona el catolicismo dentro de la cultura, se comprenderá más facilmente el sincretismo.

En un momento muy temprano en la narración, Rigoberta habla especificamente sobre "la mezcla de la Religión Católica y de cultura o, así, costumbres católicas" (71). Al principio, esta mezcla parece un poco esquizofrénica. "Nuestra reunión cultural como indígenas, la teníamos el viernes," dice Rigoberta, y "Nuestra reunión como católicos, el lunes" (111). Pero no es esquizofrénica, porque hay integración al nivel de costumbre y sentimiento, pero más importante a un nivel *conceptual* . Se tiene tranquilamente en cuenta la dualidad: "Nos sentimos muy católicos, porque creemos en lo calólico," nos dice ella, "pero al mismo tiempo nos sentimos muy indígenas, orgullosos de nuestros antepasados" (108). Por tanto la Biblia se ve como un texto de ambas, la nueva religión y la cultura antigua. "La Biblia," observa Rigoberta,

> tiene muchas relaciones como las relaciones que tenemos nosotros con nuestros antepasados ... Lo importante es que nosotros empezamos a integrar esa realidad como nuestra realidad. (156)

Lógicamente, entonces, empiezan a estudiar los textos bíblicos que están estrechamente vinculados a sus experiencias actuales, como por ejemplo

> la vida de Moisés que trató de sacar a su pueblo de la opresión.... Nosotros comparábamos al Moisés de aquellos tiempos como los "Moiseses" de ahora, que somos nosotros....
> Nosotros empezamos a buscar textos que representan a cada uno de nosotros. Como comparando un poco con nuestra cultura indígena. (156-157)

De modo que para los hombres hay Moisés; para las mujeres hay Judith ("que luchó tanto por su pueblo"); para los niños hay David ("un pequeño pastorcito... que pudo dominar el rey"). "Nosotros los acomodamos los antepasados de la Biblia como si fueran nuestros antepa-

I&L 4:1 Spring 1989

sados," explica Rigoberta, "siguiendo en nuestra misma cultura y nuestras mismas costumbres" (107).

A través de lo que dice Rigoberta sobre Cristo como el héroe Quiché Tecún Umán se puede ver cómo el catolicismo está plenamente integrado a la cultura Quiché. Como Cristo, Tecúm Umán "fue derrotado por los españoles, (y) fue perseguido". Así es, dice Rigoberta,

> como fuimos acomodándolo, aceptando lo que es la religión católica y el deber de un cristiano, como nuestra cultura. Es *otro medio*, como decía. *No es la única forma* establo para expresarnos sino que es *un medio para seguir expresándonos y no abandonar nuestro medio de expresar* lo de nuestros antepasados. (107; el énfasis es mío).

Lo importante es que se entiende este proceso, este arreglo, como algo plenamente conciente. "Es un doble trabajo para nosotros," dice Rigoberta con una claridad asombrosa al discutir las oraciones católicas:

> Como los curas... hacen las oraciones en español entonces la tarea de nosotros es memorizar las oraciones, memorizar los cantos. Pero no entendemos exactamente que quiere decir. Pero *es un medio que aceptamos como canal de nuestra expresión.* (107; el énfasis es mío).

Teológicamente lo que procede de tal concepción es una teología de liberación; prácticamente, se crea la "Iglesia popular" (270); existencialmente, conduce a Rigoberta y a sus compañeros hacia una autotranscendencia.

LA POLITICA DE AUTOTRANSCENDENCIA

Un ejemplo de autotranscedencia que se puede observar muy facilmente ocurre en la vida religiosa de Rigoberta. Al principio, ella empieza a ser catequista de la religión católica. Pero después, se concibe a sí misma como "catequista que sabe caminar sobre la tierra y no una cate-

I&L 4:1 Spring 1989

quista que piensa en el reino de Dios sólo para después de la muerte" (269).

Sin embargo, la autotranscedencia no está limitada al sector religioso, sino que toca eventualmente todos los sectores de la vida. Se rompen, por ejemplo, muchas de las barreras construidas originalmente por los aspectos más rígidos de la cultura. La ladinización es un peligro a un cierto nivel, pero Rigoberta empieza a sentirse vinculada a los ladinos pobres; o sea su nueva concepción de *clase* supera las fronteras rígidas entre las étnias aisladas y también entre los indígenas y los ladinos (191). Rigoberta logra comprender que "La separación de indios y ladinos es lo que ha contribuido... a la situación en que vivimos" (193), de modo que "Para hacer el cambio teníamos que unirnos, indios y ladinos" (194). Los cambios, además, no son fáciles. En un momento difícil, Rigoberta se da cuenta de que

> Aunque éramos pobres todos, no nos entendíamos. Así fue cómo empecé a ser más sensible a la situación. Yo comprendía que a pesar de mis duras experiencias, a pesar de mi amor hacia todos los compañeros, hacia el pueblo, muchas cosas me costaba aceptar. Y empecé a descubrir ciertas actitudes que yo tenía. (194)

Al mismo tiempo que Rigoberta declara en la página final del libro, "Todavía sigo ocultando mi identidad como indígena", ella agrega que "no soy dueña de mi vida" (270). Es decir que ella logra comprender que la vida tiene su propia dinámica, que es una dinámica de transformación continua, la cual requiere de cada persona un estado permanente de autotranscendencia. Por tanto, la lucha no puede tener como su objeto principal ni un retorno a una "época de oro" cultural ni una supresión de las estructuras más obviamente explotadoras, sino que hay que crear una política de autotranscedencia social y cultural.

El mejor ejemplo de esta necesidad ocurre en cuanto al machismo. Porque caracteriza a la cultura tradicional de los Quiché y la de los demás (otras étnias, los ladinos, los blancos), la naturaleza dialéctica de la política que se requiere se puede entender claramente a través del mito.

I&L 4:1 Spring 1989

La cultura Quiché es una cultura de algunas maneras machista. Los hombres y las mujeres socializan de maneras diferentes. La "pureza" de las niñas y muchachas tiene que ser protegida, así que ellas no pueden ni siquiera hablar con los muchachos en las calles (88, 89, 110). "La muchacha, más que todo,

> tiene que aprender las cositas de la casa, los detalles de la mamá. La mamá nunca se queda sentada en la casa sin hacer nada. La mamá siempre está en constante oficio ...(109)

Al contrario, los muchachos son "un poco más libres". En la cultura "muchas veces se estima al hombre como algo distinto," hasta hay que lavar separada su ropa (239). Cuando el padre está furioso, no contesta la madre (241); cuando hay problemas en la famillia, el padre puede escaparse y emborracharse, mientras que —observa Rigoberta— "mi mamá no se [da] el lujo de emborracharse" (244). Además cuando Rigoberta empieza a trabajar en el movimiento, enfrenta lo mismo. Porque es un jefe del movimiento, Rigoberta tiene que tratar de resolver la problemática: "Compañero," dice ella, "estas son tus tareas, campañero, éstos son tus defectos; ¿cómo vamos a hacer para solucionarlos?" (246). Aunque dijo temprano en el libro que "para nosotros no es tanto que el machismo no exista, pero es un elemento dificultoso en la comunidad ya que de hecho vamos a tomar en cuenta las costumbres" (35), alcanza la realización de que el machismo sí es parte de toda la sociedad (241) y al fin "una enfermedad común de todo el mundo" (247).

Superar el machismo requiere una política de auto-transcedencia, porque (como dijo ella) el machismo también es una "costumbre," una parte de la cultura. De hecho, parece que de alguna manera su conocimiento del machismo como una enfermidad universal sirve en la misma manera que sirvió su conocimiento anterior de los ladinos pobres: le muestra a ella que algunas barreras son arbitrarias y destructivas, que la comunidad de intereses y esperanzas es (en algunos momentos y de algunas maneras) algo más fundamental que la comunidad orgánica de la cultura.

Por tanto al final Rigoberta ha logrado una autotrascendencia compleja. Como al principio, ella se describe a sí misma como "mujer, cristiana, e indígena", pero han sucedido cambios fundamentales. Su mundo se ve como mucho más amplio, y ella está permanentemente e irrevocablemente dedicada a una lucha que concibe en términos globales. "Yo no soy dueña de mi vida," nos dice. "He decidido ofrecerla a una causa" (270). Sigue "ocultando" sus secretos y su identidad como indígena, pero tiene a la vez una nueva visión político–cultural en la cual la valorización de las fronteras marcadas (y las categorías definidas) por la tradición es modulada por un concepto de clase (es decir, por otro concepto de la comunidad). Su concepto (tomado prestado de sus antepasados) de la relación dialéctica entre el pasado y el futuro modera y enfoca su enojo y su compromiso con la revolución. Rigoberta es marxista y feminista, pero tiene siempre en cuenta de que ningún "ismo" hermético— tales como marxismo, feminismo, cristianismo, ni siquiera indigenismo— contiene toda la verdad, sino que tiene que ser informado y transformado por elementos de todos los otros.

La decisión que toma Rigoberta al final —la de no casarse ni tener hijos— es un acto profundo de autotrascendencia personal y cultural. Para meterse plenamente en la lucha, tiene que rechazar (al menos temporalmente) su papel tradicional de mujer, su vida en la comunidad de su nacimiento y su posición como un eslabón en la cadena que vincula a los antepasados al futuro. Pero como siempre, es un rechazo paradójico, porque la dialéctica funciona todavía: ella es una luchadora y como luchadora es fiel a la imagen más acariciada de los antepasados. Como ellos, ella nunca se siente cobarde; como ellos, ella lucha en un acto de amor para "todo de lo que existe". De tal manera, será madre de muchos.

NOTAS

[1] Voy a usar aquí el término "la cultura *tradicional*" en vez de "la cultura *indígena*", porque este último, aunque se usa con frecuencia en los textos latinoamericanos, conlleva la implicación de que la cultura ha sido desde siempre tal como es. Por esto, es un concepto demasiado rígido y limitado. Sin embargo el término "cultura tradicional" se refiere a la cultura que *existe* y que *se entiende* por los individuos de un grupo cultural como algo típico de ellos, como algo que les marca e identifica como un grupo único, sin referencia al hecho de que su cultura sea una mezcla de elementos "indígenas" y foráneos (aunque vengan de la cultura "moderna"). Hay que tener en cuenta, por ejemplo, que la cultura que Rigoberta Menchú describe como "indígena" incluye (funcionalmente si no concientemente) a la iglesia católica. Entonces "indígena" es una categoria ontológica, mientras que "tradicional" es una categoría operativa o funcional, de modo que este último término se refiere a la vez a la cultura misma y al concepto que los miembros de la comunidad tienen de su cultura.

En la preparación de este análisis he recibido sugerencias muy útiles de mis colegas John H. Sinnegen y Germán F. Westphal.

[2] Eduardo Galeano, *Las venas abiertas de América Latina* (México: Siglo Veintiuno Editores, 1971); Bernard W. Sheehan, *Savagism and Civility: Indians and Englishmen in Colonial Virginia* (London: Cambridge University Press, 1980).

[3] He explorado este tema extensamente en *Modernizing the Mountaineer: People, Power and Planning in Appalachia* (Boone, N.C.: Appalachian Consortium Press, 1980), especialmente en el último capítulo.

[4] Rigoberta Menchú, *Me llamo Rigoberta Menchú y así me nació la conciencia* (Mexico, D. F.: Siglo Veintiuno Editores, 1985), redactado por Elizabeth Burgos. Todas las referencias de página que siguen en paréntesis se refieren a esta edición.

[5] También hay otro ejemplo del mismo tipo en el libro, el que se muestra cuando los trabajadores de la finca son forzados a presentar un baile folklórico para los terratenientes (47). Este asunto se explora extensivamente en el contexto de las montañas del sur de los EE UU en David E. Whisnant, *All That Is Native and Fine: The Politics of Culture in an American Region* (Chapel Hill: University of North Carolina Press, 1983), y también para otras culturas y épocas en Eric Hobsbawn and Terence Ranger (eds.), *The Invention of Tradition* (London: Cambridge University Press, 1983). El primero de estos libros examina formas institucionales de intervención sistemática en la cultura tradicional en

I&L 4:1 Spring 1989

las montañas del sur, principalmente por parte de misioneros culturales de la clase alta en los años 1890-1940. Los ensayos en el segundo trazan la manipulación de la cultura indígena y la invención de "tradiciones" nuevas por los poderes coloniales durante el siglo XIX para que se manipule a la gente nativa (por ejemplo en la sierra de Escocia, el País de Gales, la India Victoriana, y el Africa), y se legitime asi la dominación colonial.

[6] Debo esta observación analítica a una sugerencia de mi colega John H. Sinnegen.

[7] Aunque no es "indígena", la iglesia se ha convertido en algo "tradicional" —es decir, en una parte de la cultura.

[8] Volveré más adelante a otro aspecto importante de esta vulnerabilidad, el machismo.

I&L 4:1 Spring 1989

Acknowledgments

Graña, María Cecilia. "Tradición e innovación en la imagen urbana de Ernesto Sábato: *Sobre héroes y tumbas*. La ciudad como cuerpo y como texto." *Revista de crítica literaria latinoamericana* 22: 43–44 (1996): 247–65. Reprinted with the permission of *Revista de crítica literaria latinoamericana*.

Pellón, Gustavo. "The Loss of Reason and the Sin *Contra Natura* in Lezama's *Paradiso*." *Revista de estudios hispánicos* 19, no.2 (1985): 21–35. Reprinted with the permission of *Revista de estudios hispánicos*.

Khan, Haider Ali. "Paz's Poetics: Textuality, Sexuality, Politics." *Denver Quarterly* 27 (1992): 92–111. Reprinted with the permission of the University of Denver, Department of English.

Volek, Emil. "Eros, Semiotics of Space, and Avant-Garde in Octavio Paz: Homage and Erosions." *Litteraria Pragensia* 2 (1991): 61–74. Reprinted with the permission of *Literaria Pregensia*.

Stanton, Anthony. "Poetics of Apocalypse, Spatial Form and Indetermination: The Prose of Octavio Paz in the 1960s." *Siglo XX/20th Century* 10 (1992): 125–42. Reprinted with the permissin of the Society of Spanish and Spanish/American Studies.

Barrenechea, Ana María. "Los doblos en el proceso de escritura de *Rayuela*." *Revista iberoamericana* 49: 125 (1983): 809–28. Reprinted with the permission of the International Institute of Ibero-American Literature.

Bennett, Maurice J. "A Dialogue of Gazes: Metamorphosis and Epiphany in Julio Cortázar's 'Axolotl.'" *Studies in Short Fiction* 23 (1986): 57–62. Reprinted with the permission of Newberry College.

Borgeson, Paul W., Jr. "The Turbulent Flow: Stream of Consciousness Techniques in the Short Stories of Juan Rulfo." *Revista de estudios hispánicos* 13 (1979): 227–52. Reprinted with the permission of *Revista de estudios hispánicos*.

Ludmer, Josefina. "Las vidas de los héroes de Roa Bastos." *Cuadernos hispanoamericanos* 493 (1991): 113–18. Reprinted with the permission of the Instituto de Cooperación Iberoamericana.

Rowe, William. "José Donoso: 'El obsceno pájaro de la noche' as Test Case for Psychoanalytic Interpretation." *Modern Language Review* 78 (1983): 588–96. Reprinted with the permission of the Modern Humanities Research Association.

Lindstrom, Naomi. "Women's Expression and Narrative Technique in Rosario
Castellanos's *In Darkness*." *Modern Language Studies* 13, no.3 (1983): 71–80.
Reprinted with the permission of *Modern Language Studies*.

Aponte, Barbara Bockus. "Estrategias dramáticas del feminismo en *El eterno femenino*
de Rosario Castellanos." *Latin American Theatre Review* 20 (1987): 49–58.
Reprinted with the permission of the University of Kansas, Center for Latin
American Studies.

Borinsky, Alicia. "Avatars of Intelligence: Figures of Reading in the Work of Gabriel
García Márquez." *University of Dayton Review* 18 (1986): 5–12. Reprinted
with the permission of the *University of Dayton Review*.

Castillo, Debra A. "The Storyteller and the Carnival Queen: 'Funerales de la Mamá
Grande.'" *Romance Quarterly* 35 (1988): 457–67. Reprinted with the
permission of the Helen Dwight Reid Educational Foundation. Published by
Heldref Publications, 1319 Eighteenth St., N.W., Washington, D.C. 20036–
1802. Copyright 1988.

Casteñeda, V. Émilio. "*The Death of Artemio Cruz*: The False Gods and the Death of
Mexico." *Centennial Review* 30 (1986): 139–47. Reprinted with the
permission of the *Centennial Review*.

Tittler, Jonathan. "Gringo viejo/The Old Gringo: 'The Rest Is Fiction.'" *Review of
Contemporary Fiction* 8 (1988): 241–48. Reprinted with the permission of
Review of Contemporary Fiction Inc.

Goytisolo, Juan. "A Cervantine Reading of *Three Trapped Tigers*." Translated by Norma
Helsper. *Review of Contemporary Fiction* 4, no.2 (1984): 20–34. Reprinted with
permission of *Disidencias* and Juan Goytisolo.

Kerr, Lucille. "The Fiction of Popular Design and Desire: Manuel Puig's *Boquitas
pintadas*." *Modern Language Notes* 97 (1982): 411–21. Reprinted with the
permission of Johns Hopkins University Press.

Steele, Cynthia. "Testimonio y autor/idad en *Hasta no verte Jesús mío*, de Elena
Poniatowska." *Revista de crítica literaria latinoamericana* 36 (1992): 155–80.
Reprinted with the permission of *Revista de crítica literaria latinoamericana*.

Franco, Jean. "Self-Destructing Heroines." *Minnesota Review* 22 (1984): 105–115.
Reprinted with the permission of the *Minnesota Review*.

Alonso, Carlos J. "*La guaracha del Macho Camacho*: The Novel as Dirge." *Modern
Language Notes* 100 (1985): 348–60. Reprinted with the permission of Johns
Hopkins University Press.

Prieto, René. "The Ambiviolent Fiction of Severo Sarduy." *Symposium* 39 (1985):
49–60. Reprinted with the permission of Heldref Publications.

Tompkins, Cynthia. "La posmodernidad de *Como en la guerra* de Luisa Valenzuela."
Nuevo texto crítico 4, no.7 (1991): 169–76. Reprinted with the permission of
Nuevo texto crítico.

Jaffe, Janice A. "Translation and Prostitution: Rosario Ferré's *Maldito amor* and *Sweet
Diamond Dust*." *Latin American Literary Review* 23: 46 (1995): 66–82.
Reprinted with the permission of the *Latin American Literary Review*.

Antoni, Robert. "Parody or Piracy: The Relationship of *The House of the Spirits* to *One
Hundred Years of Solitude*." *Latin American Literary Review* 16: 32 (1988):

16–28. Reprinted with the permission of the *Latin American Literary Review*.
Borinsky, Alicia. "Re-escribir y escribir: Arenas, Ménard, Borges, Cervantes, Fray Servando." *Revista iberoamericana* 41: 92–93 (1975): 605–16. Reprinted with the permission of the International Institute of Ibero-American Literature.
Whisnant, David E. "La vida nos ha enseñado: Rigoberta Menchú y la dialéctica de la cultura tradicional." *Ideologies and Literature* 4 (1989): 317–43. Reprinted with the permission of the Prisma Institute.